Taxing Profits in a Global Economy

Domestic and
International Issues

ORGANISATION FOR ECONOMIC CO-OPERATION AND DEVELOPMENT

Pursuant to Article 1 of the Convention signed in Paris on 14th December 1960, and which came into force on 30th September 1961, the Organisation for Economic Co-operation and Development (OECD) shall promote policies designed:

— to achieve the highest sustainable economic growth and employment and a rising standard of living in Member countries, while maintaining financial stability, and thus to contribute to the development of the world economy;
— to contribute to sound economic expansion in Member as well as non-member countries in the process of economic development; and
— to contribute to the expansion of world trade on a multilateral, non-discriminatory basis in accordance with international obligations.

The original Member countries of the OECD are Austria, Belgium, Canada, Denmark, France, Germany, Greece, Iceland, Ireland, Italy, Luxembourg, the Netherlands, Norway, Portugal, Spain, Sweden, Switzerland, Turkey, the United Kingdom and the United States. The following countries became Members subsequently through accession at the dates indicated hereafter: Japan (28th April 1964), Finland (28th January 1969), Australia (7th June 1971) and New Zealand (29th May 1973). The Commission of the European Communities takes part in the work of the OECD (Article 13 of the OECD Convention). Yugoslavia takes part in some of the work of the OECD (agreement of 28th October 1961).

Publié en français sous le titre :
L'IMPOSITION DES BÉNÉFICES
DANS UNE ÉCONOMIE GLOBALE :
questions nationales et internationales

Foreword

This report was prepared by Working Party No. 2 on Tax Analysis and Tax Statistics of the Committee on Fiscal Affairs. A major input to the report was made by Michael Devereux (presently at the University of Keele) and Mark Pearson of the Institute for Fiscal Studies in London. They undertook the calculations which appear in Chapters 4 and 5 and contributed to the development of the analytical approach used in the report. The conceptual framework set out in Chapter 2 was developed with the assistance of Peter Birch Sørensen of Copenhagen Business School. Chapter 3 and the country chapters were prepared with the assistance of Jacob Visser of the Netherlands.

The report was submitted to the Committee on Fiscal Affairs which recommended that the report be derestricted by the OECD Council. The Council subsequently agreed on its derestriction on the 14th November, 1991.

Table of Contents

List of Tables and Charts

Chapter 4:

Chapter 5:

Chapter 6:

Annex 1:

Annex 2:

Chapter 1

Introduction and Summary

A. Introduction

The reform of taxes on corporate profits has over recent years been a major preoccupation in many OECD countries. Corporate tax systems have been criticised on a number of grounds: their alleged adverse effects on domestic investment and saving; the fact that they may create distortions in the international allocation of capital; complexity; their lack of neutrality between corporate investment and the activities of unincorporated enterprises. Particular concerns have been expressed about the coexistence of different corporate tax regimes in a world where globalisation of business activities has increased and where most non-tax barriers to international flows of capital, services and technology have been removed. It is these concerns that led the Committee on Fiscal Affairs to undertake an examination of the different ways in which Member countries tax corporate profits and the potential implication of these differences for domestic and international investment flows.

This topic is approached from three different angles. First, a comprehensive description is provided of the tax treatment of profits. Second, an attempt is made to quantify the effects of the different domestic and international tax provisions by calculating effective tax burdens, not just on domestic investments, but also on cross-border investments. Finally, policy issues raised by the taxation of profits are examined.

The main objectives set for the report are:

— to contribute to the current debate on the most appropriate way to tax both domestic and foreign profits at the national level;

— to provide a conceptual and economic framework within which the effects of taxation of cross-border investments can be analysed;

— to provide an input into the examination currently being undertaken by the Committee on Fiscal Affairs of the existing international arrangements for sharing out the tax base and ensuring that cross-border profits are neither overtaxed nor undertaxed in relation to profits accruing from domestic investments.

The report should be seen as part of an ongoing review by the Committee of the ways in which existing arrangements to co-ordinate national tax policies can be improved, thereby enabling individual countries to reap the benefits of globalisation and liberalisation and yet maintain a certain freedom in setting their tax policies and in protecting their tax base. It does not set out recommendations to governments since this was not the aim set for this project although the report will be used as an imput into the Committee's on-going examination of international tax arrangements.

B. Scope and coverage

The report examines the main taxes which apply to corporate profits, whether retained in the corporation or distributed as dividends. The descriptions and analyses focus mainly on the normal tax regimes which apply to incorporated enterprises, little attention being paid to the provisions which apply to unincorporated enterprises.

Chapter 2 provides a conceptual framework within which the main domestic and international tax policy issues can be discussed. The descriptive information provided in Chapter 3 and the country chapters in Annex 4 provide an inventory of the corporate income taxes, personal income taxes, personal and corporate capital gains taxes and net wealth taxes, and other tax provisions which are of relevance to the determination of the tax treatment of corporate profits. This information covers taxes levied by central, state and local governments and refers to the situation as at 1st January 1991.

Chapters 4 and 5 use most, but by no means all, of this information to calculate effective tax rates on domestic and international direct investment in the manufacturing sector. The calculation of "effective tax rates" requires consideration not only of nominal or schedular rates of tax, but also of the treatment of the tax base (see appendix to this chapter). The calculations take into account those tax provisions which could affect the amount of tax paid on new investment by corporations. Systems of taxing profits are, however, far too complex to be encompassed fully in the methodology used in the study and many of the special features of individual tax systems have to be ignored. The methodology used in these chapters builds on that developed by King and Fullerton[1], which has become the most widely accepted approach to calculating effective tax rates. Whereas their study was limited to four countries (Germany, Sweden, United Kingdom and the United States), this study provides consistent results for 24 OECD countries and, in comparision to some recent studies which use this methodology[2], greater emphasis is placed upon the international dimension, though only investment flows between OECD countries are taken into account.

Chapter 6 uses the conceptual framework and the descriptive and quantitative information provided in the earlier chapters to analyse the policy choices open to countries in the taxation of corporate profits, with particular emphasis on two issues: the ways in which distributed profits are taxed at the corporate and shareholder level, and the options open to individual countries and groups of countries to improve the international allocation of capital.

Annexes to the report provide more details on country practices, on the methodology used in Chapters 4 and 5 and on the information required to calculate effective tax rates.

C. Background

Capital markets in OECD countries are increasingly integrated as Member countries have removed controls on international investment and foreign exchange regulations. At the same time, the proportion of international activities accounted for by large multinational enterprises (MNEs) has increased. One consequence of this gradual liberalisation and globalisation is that international capital flows may have become more sensitive to differences in the tax regimes as between countries. Differences in the taxation of corporate profits may now be one of the few remaining potential barriers to a better international allocation of capital. With the commitment of the European Communities (whose Member States now comprise one half of those of OECD) to establish a single market by 1993, removal of potential obstacles, including tax obstacles, has increased in importance.

Taxation is, however, only one and in many cases not the most important determinant of investment and financing decisions. Among the other determinants of investment behaviour are the short and medium-term economic outlook in different market areas and countries, the cost of capital in relation to that of other productive inputs, the profitability of investments, the availability of finance and government investment grants, the quality of public infrastructure and the existence of an economic infrastructure. The relative importance of these determinants varies between countries and over the business cycle. Nevertheless, the taxation of profits can and often does have an important impact on marginal investments and their financing, as well as on locational decisions both within a country and across frontiers. Other taxes, such as those on payroll and social security contributions, may also affect costs and thus location of investment, particularly in the short to medium term.

At the national level, OECD governments have a number of common concerns regarding the corporation tax which is the main focus of this report, even if other related taxes on business profits are also covered. Despite their very different reliance on corporate tax as a revenue source (see Chapter 3), governments have to ensure that these revenues are efficiently and equitably collected. They have to weigh-up the various advantages and disadvantages of tax neutrality towards locational and investment decisions and interventionist policies to influence investment patterns. Recently there has been a shift from interventionism to neutrality, in part reflecting a greater skepticism on the efficacy of governments in "picking the winners" and an increased awareness that the cost of incentives in terms of revenue forgone may exceed the extra investment generated by these subsidies. Nevertheless, governments continue to subsidize particular activities and sectors.

Some of the main domestic policy issues currently discussed are:

— Should the economic double taxation of dividends be maintained, reduced or eliminated;

— If reduced or eliminated, is this best done at company or shareholder level and what integration approach should be used;

— How should the tax base be defined and measured (e.g., depreciation practices, adjustment for inflation);

— If incentives are to be given for investment, what form should they take (tax holidays, rate reductions, accelerated depreciation, special write-offs);

— What should be the relationship between the corporate and personal income tax rates;

— What are the appropriate statutory rates to employ and should they be progressive or proportional.

At the international level, the policy issues which arise are more difficult to discuss since they involve not only the design of domestic tax systems, but also the need to take into account how different national systems interact. Each government has to address two broad sets of policy issues. The first is to protect the revenue yield from taxes on profit and to ensure that it gets its fair share of the tax base associated with international transactions. The second goal is to maintain a favourable tax climate for inward investment and to avoid encouraging an outflow of domestic capital which would otherwise not have taken place. For many years it has been realised that countries cannot successfully address these issues on a unilateral basis and that mechanisms for co-ordination are required. Consequently, over the last seventy years or so international allocation rules have been developed, first in the League of Nations, then in the OECD and the United Nations[3]. These organisations have established "international rules of the game" which help countries arrange their tax relationships with other countries. Rules have been developed, for example, concerning the allocation of taxing rights between source and residence countries and principles have been agreed to govern transfer prices for tax purposes when goods, services, technology and loans are exchanged between affiliates of a multinational enterprise. In the light of the recent events referred to in the first paragraph of this report, it is considered timely to see how far existing tax practices and tax treaty policies may require modification.

Some of the issues currently being discussed in the international sphere are:

— How can greater capital export and import neutrality be achieved for international capital flows?

— If there is a conflict between these goals, which should take priority and should this choice differ as between direct and portfolio investment?

— Do existing tax arrangements place an unfair tax burden on international as compared to domestic investment?

— What would constitute a fair division of the tax base for international transactions between source and residence countries?

— What is the appropriate method of international double taxation relief?

— What is the relevant relationship between statutory rates of tax in different countries which have very different structures (e.g., classical and imputation) and tax bases (e.g., in relation to depreciation and inflation)?

— Should countries use tax incentives to encourage inward investments? Are such measures effective? Should the resident countries recognise such tax incentives by means of tax sparing agreements?

— What is the impact of tax differentials on the location and financing decisions of MNEs?

— Is it necessary to accept a certain degree of economic inefficiency if this provides greater freedom to national tax administrations to determine the level and structure of taxation of profits?

— To what extent do the principles embodied in the OECD 1977 Model Convention and the 1979 Transfer Pricing Guidelines need to be reviewed in the light of the trend towards increased globalisation and liberalisation of capital flows?

Not all of these issues are discussed in depth, but the analysis is relevant to all of them. The report does not attempt to measure what is the impact of the tax differentials referred to in Chapter 5 on international investment flows since this is beyond the scope of this study and is, in practice, difficult to do.

D. Summary of main issues

As previously indicated, this report does not attempt to set out recommendations for changes in national tax practices or for modifications to existing international tax arrangements. It does, however, provide a conceptual framework and a quantitative background within which such recommendations could be considered. The purpose of this section is to set out some issues which may require further discussion. The Committee on Fiscal Affairs will, over the coming years, provide a forum where these issues, particularly those with an international dimension, will be discussed. The Committee also intends to use this report as an input into its current review of the 1977 Model Double Taxation Convention on Income and on Capital and as part of its continuing review of tax obstacles to a better international allocation of capital, services and technology.

One reason why international tax arrangements may need to be reviewed is because of the trend towards the globalisation of economies as barriers to trade and investment flows are gradually being removed. This liberalisation, which has gone furthest within the EC countries with their commitment to a single unified market, offers new opportunities for policymakers, but also implies new constraints. The importance of international considerations in the determination of national tax policies will increase, especially for small open economies. The broad issue which faces policymakers is how to reconcile these new constraints with the desire to adapt their own tax systems to the social, economic and institutional conditions within their country, whilst at the same time to enable all countries to reap the potential efficiency gains from liberalisation.

The increased openness of national economies has, in practice, made it more difficult to separate out domestic and international tax issues. When changes to national tax systems are made attention has increasingly to be paid to the international implications of any proposed modifications. This, in turn, may mean that the traditional criteria used to evaluate tax reforms have to be reconsidered. Policies which may have been appropriate in economies where exchange controls and other limitations on international transactions were prevalent may be neither feasible nor desirable once these non-tax barriers are removed. This report provides a framework within which these emerging issues can be discussed.

The elimination of economic double taxation

There is no consensus on the desirability of integrating the personal and corporate income tax or on what would be the best method to achieve such integration. Whilst most, but by no means all, public finance experts accept that economic double taxation (see the appendix to this chapter for a definition of this term) may be distorting the financing and investing decisions of enterprises, there is no agreement on the quantitative significance of these distortions. Also, the introduction of imputation systems may be costly in revenue terms and can complicate international fiscal arrangements.

The reduction of tax induced distortions in domestic investment patterns

Even after the recent wave of tax reform, tax systems continue to distort investment patterns. The analysis in this report which is limited to the manufacturing sector suggests that tax systems tend to favour investment in machinery in relation to buildings and, particularly, in relation to inventories. At the same time, work done in certain Member countries shows wide differences in the effective corporate tax burden on different sectors of the economy and different activities, in part reflecting the continued use of selective tax incentives and in part the often unintended interactions between different parts of the corporate tax system and economic conditions in different sectors. Incentive provisions may also favour capital intensive rather than labour intensive investment projects. The data show that inflation accentuates these distortions. All of this suggests that there may be a need to examine further the use of tax incentives for domestic investments.

Taxation and corporate finance

Tax systems are not neutral as between alternative sources of corporate finance. The data in Chapter 4 indicate that debt finance tends to be favoured over retained earnings and equity. How far governments should be concerned about these non-neutralities depends, inter alia, upon the view taken on the efficiency of capital markets in allocating funds and on risks attached to corporations placing a high reliance on debt financing.

The relative tax treatment of domestic and foreign investment

Issues of international taxation are more complex to deal with since they involve the interaction between national tax systems and tax treaties. The approach adopted in this report is to evaluate the tax treatment of cross-border investment flows against the criteria of capital import and capital export neutrality (see the appendix to this chapter for a definition of these terms). These concepts are used as benchmarks by which to judge the efficiency effects of international tax arrangements. Yet these neutrality benchmarks cannot capture all of the complexity of these arrangements. First, they do not allow for the many-sided nature of international investment decisions. Investors can change their place of residence and the form of their investment (whether their investment takes place in a subsidiary or by means of a branch). They have a wide-range of choices on how to finance an investment (e.g., finance could be provided by subsidiaries in a third country or locally). Each of these decisions cannot be encompassed in a simple conceptual framework. Secondly, capital export neutrality is particularly difficult to achieve where domestic systems in the source and residence countries provide for different tax treatments of different sectors and activities. Effective tax rates will then vary widely across assets, industries and sources of finance. Thirdly, even if neutrality were achieved under these circumstances, differences in nominal rates may nevertheless give rise to cross-border arbitrage. Fourthly, the analysis is unable to take account of the different possibilities to evade and to avoid tax that are open to domestic and international investors. Finally, these neutrality concepts provide only a starting point for the negotiation of tax treaties, the outcome of which reflects the balance of interest between the parties at a given moment. Nevertheless, the neutrality concepts set out in this report provide a convenient starting point to analyse international tax arrangements. The use of these concepts may also encourage policymakers to take a more global view of the benefits and costs of existing international tax arrangements and proposed changes thereto.

The data presented in this report, which are calculated under the normal tax regimes applied to corporations operating in the manufacturing sector, show that the potential tax burden is generally higher on direct investment flows from one country to another than on purely domestic investment, i.e., capital export neutrality is not achieved. Whilst this may in part be explained by the methods used to relieve international double taxation (i.e., the use of the exemption system, or credit with deferral and limitations on credit systems), it appears that the operation of withholding taxes on dividends and interest paid to non-resident corporations also tends to result in a less favourable treatment of foreign direct investment in comparison to domestic direct investment. A general removal or reduction of these taxes could help move countries towards greater capital export neutrality, to the extent that it can be done without opening up new avenues for tax evasion and avoidance. This may, however, imply a redistribution of the tax base between countries. It is also noteworthy that the existence of tax treaties reduces distortions in international investment flows.

The appropriate method of removing international juridical double taxation

Economists tend to favour the credit method over the exemption method because it is more likely to achieve capital export neutrality, to which they give more importance than capital import neutrality (the former is more relevant to locational neutrality whereas the latter is more relevant to neutrality in the international allocation of savings). However, although the analysis in Chapter 2 suggests that credit systems provide, on balance, a less distorting treatment of international investments, few countries operate pure credit systems. Thus, Chapter 6 suggests that in practice neither credit nor exemption systems achieve capital export neutrality. The question which then arises is whether the administrative advantages associated with exemption systems more than offset the potential efficiency gains associated with less than pure credit systems.

Extending the advantages of integration of the personal and corporate income taxes to non-residents

This is a complex area and one where the data provide no clear guidelines for policymakers. Chapter 6 identifies the conditions under which either the extension of imputation credits to non residents by source countries or the granting of imputaion credits to residents for foreign taxes paid by residence countries could remove distortions. In practice, either policy could lead to other economic distortions as companies seek to avoid tax, and problems arise as how to share revenue costs. The final section of Chapter 6 shows that there is no consensus on this issue, and countries follow divergent practices in this area.

Sharing out the international tax base

Although this is an issue which is only indirectly addressed in the report, the analysis provided does suggest that efficiency and revenue raising goals can conflict unless there is some co-ordination of national tax policies. Also, since different financing schemes result in different effective tax rates, it can be expected that tax arbitrage will take place, with a consequent shifting of the tax base between countries. This is an issue which encompasses a wide range of policy considerations, including, inter alia, Member countries' treaty practices, the approach to the determination of transfer prices, the need to counteract international tax evasion and avoidance.

Appendix
Terminology Used

This appendix defines only those terms and expressions which have been used in different and incompatible senses. The other technical terms used in the report are defined in the relevant chapters.

One difficulty is the traditional use of "economic double taxation" to refer to the fact that distributed profits may be subject first to corporate tax and secondly to income tax on the dividends of shareholders. Originally (e.g. in the 1963 OECD Draft Double Taxation Convention) "economic double taxation" was used as an expression to contrast with "juridical double taxation". In each case the reference is to international double taxation, but whereas juridical double taxation refers to the case where the income of the same taxpayer is taxed by two different tax jurisdictions, "economic double taxation" refers to the case where the same profits of economically related entities (usually parents and subsidiaries of multinational enterprises in the transfer pricing context - see Article 9 of the 1977 OECD model) are taxed by two tax jurisdictions. Apart from the fact that "economic double taxation" is used in this totally different sense unconnected with corporate tax systems, it is also not an altogether satisfactory expression, having been used in many other senses[4] and sometimes being employed because of its normative flavour[5]. However, it remains a convenient shorthand expression to refer to the fact that distributed profits are taxed first at the corporate level and then in the hands of the shareholder and in this report it is used exclusively in this sense. A synonym for "economic double taxation", in this sense, that has also been widely used is 'the double taxation of dividends' and this expression is also employed in the same sense.

"Integration" is another term that has been employed in many different ways[6]. In this report the most widespread usage is employed, which refers to any reduction or elimination of "economic double taxation", whether granted at company or shareholder level. "Full integration", on the contrary, which is also used in different senses[7], refers in this report to the meaning given in the Canadian Carter report to refer exclusively to the situation that would occur if full credit were given to shareholders not only in respect of corporate tax paid on distributed profits, but also for that paid on retained profits, so that in effect the corporation tax, as such, would become merely an advance payment of personal income tax. In practice, for the reasons described in Chapter 2, such a system is not used in any OECD country.

The expression "imputation system" has been used in two separate senses:

a) to cover systems where there is a direct link between the amount of corporation tax actually paid on distributed profits and the tax credit given to shareholders under the personal income tax;

b) to cover any system where resident shareholders get a tax credit for income from domestic equities, even though no corporate tax may have been paid or if it has been paid, there is no link between the amount paid and the amount of the shareholders' tax credit.

In this report the expression "imputation system" refers exclusively to the first of these two cases, a distinction being made between "full imputation" where corporation tax paid on distributed profits is totally credited against shareholders' income tax liability and "partial imputation" when the credit is only partial. Where there is no necessary connection between the amount of corporation tax paid on distributed profits and the amount of credit against the shareholders' income tax liability, the systems are referred to as "shareholder relief schemes" as an abbreviation for "partial tax relief on dividend income for resident shareholders investing in domestic equities".

The expression "classical system" is used to refer to systems where there is no relief or almost no relief from "economic double taxation". Such systems have been variously described as classic, classical, separate system and separate entity system. Against classic or classical it has been argued that there is nothing classic or classical about non-reduction. Against separate and separate entity that there could be confusion with the separate entity accounting systems. There is no compelling argument to prefer any terminology, but it is simpler if only one expression is used, and "classical" system has been chosen.

The expression "partial dividend deduction" is used to describe systems where a deduction for distributions is made from the corporate tax base. Such systems have also been referred to as primary dividend system, but the title chosen seems to describe them more clearly. There is an obvious analogy with split rate systems where a lower rate is accorded to distributions instead of a deduction from the base. If, as in a few countries, "economic double taxation" is totally abolished at company level, dividend deduction and split rate systems converge and such systems are described as zero rate systems.

Another expression which needs to be defined is "effective tax rates". An effective tax rate takes into account not only the statutory or schedule rate of tax but also other aspects of the tax system which determine the amount of tax paid. This sum is then expressed as a percentage of the pre-tax return on the investment.

Two other general expressions which have often been used in different ways are capital export neutrality (CEN) and capital import neutrality (CIN). CEN occurs where the tax system is neutral towards the export of capital since investors face the same marginal effective tax rate on income from similar investments, whether they invest in the domestic economy or abroad. CIN prevails when domestic and foreign suppliers of capital to any given national market obtain the same after-tax rate of return on similar investments in that market, taking account of the corporate and personal taxes paid in the country of source and of residence.

Notes and references

1. *The Taxation of Income from Capital*, University of Chicago Press, 1984.

2. See, for example, *International Comparissions of the Cost of Capital* ed. D. Jorgenson and M. King, 1992

3. See *Model Convention on Income and Capital*, OECD, 1977; *United Nations Model Double Taxation Convention between Developed and Developing Countries*, 1980; *Transfer Pricing and Multinational Enterprises*, OECD, 1979.

4. Some commentators have used economic double taxation to refer to the non-neutralities that arise either from the different tax treatments of retained earnings, new equity and debt or from the different treatment of profits of incorporated and unincorporated enterprises. Others have equated it with some of the causes of these non-neutralities, such as the tax treatment of capital gains or the non-alignment of personal and corporate statutory income tax rates.

5. "Economic double taxation" gives the impression that it is something inherently bad and should be reduced or eliminated.

6. Not only is "integration" frequently used as a synonym for "mitigation," but it has even been applied to describe the alignment of rates of corporation income tax with the top or standard rate of personal income tax. A stricter use which is also sometimes employed would restrict the term to cases where there is a link between corporate tax and income tax paid as under imputation system — hence the use of integration through the back door (McLure, 1979) to describe corporate tax relief for distributions.

7. "Full integration" is sometimes used in a looser sense to cover a) any system which fully eliminates "economic double taxation" in the sense used in this report; b) full imputation systems, but not zero rate tax on distributed profits.

Chapter 2
Conceptual Framework

A. The corporate income tax in an international setting

As economic integration in the OECD area proceeds, the economic, technological, and institutional barriers to cross-border investment continue to wane. The pattern of international investment in corporate assets is therefore likely to become increasingly sensitive to cross-country differences in corporate tax rules. In particular, tax differentials may come to exert an important impact on international portfolio investment in shares. Moreover, even though non-tax factors will probably remain the dominant determinants of foreign direct investment in most cases, the influence of tax differentials on the location decisions of multinational enterprises may also be expected to become stronger. The increasing international mobility of capital therefore may increase the need for international coordination of taxes on corporate-source income.

In general terms, corporate taxes should of course aim at promoting the basic goals of tax policy, including the goals of ensuring a fair distribution of the tax burden, a minimisation of tax-induced distortions of the allocation of resources, and simplicity and administrative feasibility of tax laws. In the area of corporate taxation, policymakers have been particularly concerned with the potential distortions and inequities caused by double taxation of corporate-source income at the domestic as well as the international level. At the same time, the possibilities for avoidance and evasion of taxes on cross-border corporate investments and the question how to ensure a fair international distribution of the revenue from such taxes have also been major policy concerns. These different possibilities, as well as the exchange of information policies of Member countries, are not taken into account in the calculations in Chapters 4 and 5 even though they can influence the achievement of the neutrality goals set for tax systems. Since issues of international tax avoidance and international tax evasion have been studied in previous OECD reports[1], the analysis below focuses mainly on problems of tax obstacles to international flows of capital, particularly in the form of foreign direct investment, spotlighting areas where the tax treatment may be less favourable than that accorded to domestic investment. Some remarks are also made on the tax regime applied to domestic investment, particularly in relation to its relative treatment of investment in equities and in bonds.

There are many important policy decisions to be taken in the area of corporate taxation, including the choice of tax base, the choice of capital cost allowances, depreciation systems, inflation adjustments etc. This chapter touches on some of these topics, but most of the discussion focuses on domestic and international double taxation issues.

Table 2.1 summarises the most important issues of domestic and international double taxation. In the domestic field, a basic question is whether there should be a separate corporate income tax at all, and if so, whether and to what extent the personal income tax liability of shareholders should take account of the fact that income tax is also levied at the corporate level. If policymakers decide in favour of some form of integration of corporate and personal taxes, they must then choose an appropriate method of integration and decide whether they wish to offer equal tax treatment of retained and distributed corporate profits and to what extent they wish to align the personal and corporate income tax rates. When the shareholder is a corporation, the issue is to what extent should its dividend income from other corporations be subject to the corporate income tax, despite the fact that the corporations distributing the dividends have already been subject to this tax?[2]

Table 2.1. Issues of double taxation at the domestic and international level

Type of Investor	Domestic Level	International Level
Households	- To what extent if any) should the personal and the corporate income tax be integrated? - What is the appropriate method of integration? - To what extent if any) should the tax treatment of distributed and retained corporate profits be harmonised? - To what extent if any) should personal and corporate income tax rates be aligned?	- What principles should guide the setting of withholding tax rates on distributions to foreign portfolio investors? - To what extent should any domestic integration measures be extended to foreign shareholders? - To what extent should international economic double taxation of foreign portfolio investment income be relieved? - What is the appropriate method of relief from international juridical double taxation?
Corporations	- How should intra-corporate dividend payments be treated for tax purposes?	- What principles should guide the setting of source country tax rates on income from foreign-controlled corporations? - To what extent should international double taxation of foreign direct investment income be relieved? - What is the appropriate method of international juridical double taxation relief?

In the international field the following issues arise. Should dividend payments to shareholders residing abroad be subject to withholding taxes, and if so, at what rates? Should any relief from the economic double taxation of corporate-source income be extended to foreign shareholders? If corporate-source income is taxed both by the country of source and by the shareholder's residence country, to what extent should such juridical international double taxation be alleviated, and what is the best method of double taxation relief?

The sections below offer a brief discussion of these issues, beginning with the domestic aspects and proceeding to international policy problems. The analysis has to take into account the following controversial issues: how do alternative corporate tax systems affect the domestic and international allocation of resources; who bears the burden of the corporate income tax; how can revenues from corporate taxes be maintained under conditions of international competition; how should the potential conflict between revenue raising goals and the neutrality objective be resolved; how should the revenue from the taxation of cross-border corporate investments be divided among countries? These matters have long been debated among tax economists and policymakers. This chapter seeks to identify the issues on which a reasonable degree of consensus has emerged and those which are still unresolved.

B. Domestic issues

1) The economic rationale for the corporate income tax

The economic justification for imposing a separate tax on corporate profits is that under ideal conditions it is a non-distorting source of revenue, at least insofar as the practical difficulties in identifying pure profits can be overcome. In an economic sense the "pure" profits of a corporation consist of net income in excess of the remuneration of all factors of production, including capital. In a competitive economy such pure profits in excess of the normal rate of return on capital is in the nature of an economic rent i.e. a surplus) accruing to fixed factors of production. A tax levied on the pure profit will then becomes a tax on factors in fixed supply and is therefore a neutral tax which does not distort the allocation of resources.

In practice, however, OECD countries do not allow a deduction for a "normal" rate of return on corporate equity from the corporate income tax base, despite the fact that interest payments on debt are generally deductible from taxable profits. The conventional corporate income tax is thus a tax on the return to corporate equity capital and is therefore potentially distortive[3]. The most fundamental problem in corporate tax policy is whether there should be such a separate tax on corporate equity at all?

The formal justification for the corporation income tax is that a corporation has the status of a legal person and, like physical persons, should therefore be liable to income tax. Sometimes the corporation tax is also seen as a payment for the legal privilege of limited liability or for cost-reducing public services to the corporate sector e.g. the provision of infrastructure facilities). These arguments are theoretically weak, since there is hardly any systematic relationship between the corporate income tax and the benefits stemming from limited liability or from public services provided to the corporation. Also, corporations as such cannot bear the burden of the corporation tax since a tax burden can be borne only by physical persons, in their capacity as wage and salary-earners, consumers and savers, including shareholders.

According to the traditional theory of taxation, the income tax should be levied on an individual's potential consumption, defined as the maximum amount which the taxpayer would be able to consume without eroding his real stock of net wealth. To realize this ideal of so-called comprehensive income taxation, all corporate profits, whether distributed or retained, should in principle be allocated to individual shareholders and taxed as personal income. In other words, corporate-source income should be subject to the same tax treatment as income from partnerships or other unincorporated enterprises. Under such a full integration system there would be no room for a separate corporate income tax except as a withholding tax to be fully credited by shareholders against the personal income tax due on their imputed share of corporate profits.

In practice, no country has attempted to implement a general system of full integration of corporate and personal taxation, because of the difficulties of taxing retained corporate profits at the personal level[4]. To mention but two of these difficulties, a personal tax on undistributed profits could impose serious liquidity problems on shareholders. Secondly, it would be administratively cumbersome to impute corporate profits to individual shareholders since shares frequently change hands within the fiscal year.

Instead of imputing corporate profits to shareholders, one could theoretically levy personal income tax on dividends plus full capital gains tax on shares, whether these gains have been realized or not. However, in practice it would often be very difficult to evaluate non-realized capital gains on shares in unquoted private corporations, and even if this valuation problem could be overcome, a tax on non-realized gains could still impose a liquidity problem on shareholders. If income tax is levied only on realized capital gains, however, shareholders will have an incentive to postpone the realization of their gains and this could reduce the efficiency and liquidity of the stock market.

Apart from its possible function as a withholding tax and thereby also as an anti-evasion device, the corporate income tax can thus be seen as a pragmatic method of taxing retained corporate profits, given the practical difficulties of imputing these profits to individual shareholders, and considering the obstacles to personal taxation of accrued capital gains on shares.

The corporate income tax is sometimes also seen as a tool of government stabilization policy and structural policy, since changes in corporate tax rules can be used to influence the level and pattern of investment in the corporate sector and its timing, although opinions differ on the desirability and efficiency of tax measures to influence investment patterns see Chapter 6.B).

In an international setting, the corporation income tax can be viewed as an instrument whereby source countries exercise their established right to tax all corporate income originating within their borders, including the income accruing to foreign-owned corporations operating in the country. This function of the corporation tax seems particularly important in cases where corporate profits contain an element of "economic rent" stemming, say, from low-cost extraction of easily accessible natural resources.

2) Double taxation issues

While the above considerations provide some justification for a separate tax on corporate profits, they do not offer a rationale for higher taxation of these profits compared to the tax on alternative sources of finance, for example, interest on bonds. A higher relative tax burden on corporate profits can be said to arise when the total effective tax rate on the return to equity-financed corporate investment exceeds the effective tax rate on the return to alternative investments. Such a situation may occur when corporate profits are subject to the corporate income tax and dividends and capital gains on shares are also taxed at the level of individual shareholders.

Though the double taxation in an economic sense does not necessarily occur just because corporate-source income is taxed at two levels, the combined corporate and personal tax burden on <u>distributed</u> corporate profits does in fact often exceed the marginal personal tax rate on interest income, sometimes even by a substantial margin. Indeed, under a classical corporate tax system dividends are fully taxed at the shareholder's marginal personal income tax rate even though the profits underlying the dividend have already been subject to full taxation at the standard corporate tax rate.

In some OECD countries the combination of the corporate income tax and the personal tax on capital gains on shares also implies a high relative taxation of <u>retained</u> corporate profits, compared to the taxation of the return to interest-bearing assets. However, since taxes on capital gains are typically postponed until the time of realization, and since capital gains tax rates are often low or even zero, high relative taxation of retained corporate profits is much less common than that of dividends. Further, since interest payments are normally fully deductible from the base of the corporate income tax, <u>debt-financed</u> corporate investment is not subject to economic double taxation at all.

The problem of double taxation of dividends has traditionally been one of the most controversial issues in corporate tax policy. Many observers believe that this double taxation discriminates against the corporate form of organisation, favours debt finance at the expense of equity finance, discriminates against finance by new share issues compared to finance by retained earnings and discourages corporate investment by raising the cost of corporate capital. The double taxation of dividends is thus held to distort the allocation of resources, and it is also seen by these observers to create horizontal inequities among taxpayers by levying an extra tax burden on corporate-source income, although this will in part depend upon how this tax burden is shifted throughout the economy.

Other commentators take a much less critical view of the double taxation of dividends and sometimes favour the classical system. This may be because they prefer to see the corporation as a separate entity distinct from its shareholders, believing that corporations should be taxed in their capacity as legal persons. They may claim in addition that the double taxation of dividends does not seriously discourage investment in the corporate sector because only a minor part of that investment is financed by new share issues. Under debt finance there is no problem of economic double taxation, and in the case of investment financed by retaining earnings the return to shareholders accrues in the form of lightly-taxed capital gains on shares. On this basis it is concluded that abolition of the double taxation of dividends would yield an arbitrary windfall gain to existing shareholders and cause a loss of government revenue without significantly reducing the required rate of return on corporate investment. Of relevance to the debate on whether or not economic double taxation should be removed or reduced are a number of other mainly administrative considerations discussed more fully in Chapter 6.B.

As already indicated, the allocation and distribution effects of the corporate tax system depend crucially on the way corporate investment is financed. The next section therefore discusses how taxes are likely to affect the financial policies of corporations.

3) Taxation and corporate financial policy

It is often considered desirable that the income tax system should not provide incentives for using one type of investment finance rather than another. One reason for this is that lack of tax neutrality may lead to tax arbitrage which could cause an unfair distribution of the tax burden and which could impart a revenue loss on the government, thereby forcing it to rely more heavily on other taxes e.g. payroll taxes) which could imply other distortions.

The tax system can be shown to be neutral towards corporate financing decisions if a given pre-tax flow of corporate profits produces the same after-tax income in the hands of the ultimate investors, whether the return to investors takes the form of interest payments, of dividends, or of capital gains on shares. This requires that the combined corporate and personal tax burden on a unit of distributed profits be equal to the combined tax burden on retained profits, and that the total burden on distributions or retentions in turn be equal to the effective tax rate on a unit of corporate interest payments.

One hypothetical set of tax rules which would satisfy these conditions for financial neutrality in a closed economy would be a system with identical flat rates of tax on all corporate profits and all interest income, and with no taxes on dividends or on capital gains on shares.

Actual income tax systems in the OECD area are much more complex than that and are generally not neutral towards corporate financing decisions, in part because it may be difficult to find one set of rules that achieves neutrality for both small and large firms in view of the different financing possibilities of these enterprises). Typically, the tax system tends to favour debt finance, because corporate interest payments are deductible from the corporate tax base, and because effective tax rates on interest income are often low. For instance, it has been estimated that in the United States in 1988 only about 5 per cent of corporate interest payments were received by domestic household investors subject to the ordinary personal income tax on interest receipts[5]. A substantial part of the interest on corporate debt is channelled through tax-exempt institutions or through financial intermediaries.

The tax incentive for debt finance has caused some concern that corporations may be tempted to rely excessively on debt. If this were the case, it could threaten the financial stability of the corporate sector and make corporations too vulnerable to downturns of the business cycle, thereby destabilising the national economy. In several countries the debt-equity ratio of the corporate sector does indeed seem to have increased during the 1980s, but at the same time there has been a development of new debt instruments which allow corporations, especially large firms, more flexibility in meeting their interest obligations. While it is therefore not quite clear whether the vulnerability of the corporate sector has in fact increased in recent years, it is unquestionable that if the tendency towards increased use of debt continues, there will be an erosion of the aggregate tax base in those countries where the average effective tax rate on interest income is relatively low.

As already noted a typical feature of many OECD tax systems is that the combined corporate and personal tax burden on distributed profits exceeds that on retained profits. One consequence is that corporations have an incentive to retain their earnings, thereby providing shareholders with a lightly taxed capital gain on their shares instead of paying out a more heavily taxed dividend. Like the tax incentive for debt finance, the tax preference for retentions over distributions has been the source of some concern. It has been claimed that a high retention ratio makes it more difficult to reallocate funds from mature, slow-growing companies to more innovative and fast-growing corporations which have to rely on external sources of finance. If the dividend-payout ratio were higher, funds would be more smoothly channeled to those firms and sectors where it can be invested most productively, especially where capital markets functioned efficiently.

Some policymakers have held that a tax policy encouraging corporate retentions will help to increase aggregate savings and capital accumulation in the private sector, since the marginal propensity to consume is higher out of dividend income than out of capital gains. Although the capital gains on shares produced by corporate retentions may stimulate household consumption, the evidence suggests that consumption usually does not increase by the full amount of an increase in retained corporate profits[6]. Hence higher

25

corporate retentions should in fact tend to increase aggregate private savings, and if this is an important policy goal, it may be found to justify some tax discrimination against corporate distributions.

Concern about the unequal tax treatment of different modes of corporate finance would obviously be somewhat misplaced if corporate financing decisions were not very sensitive to tax parameters. There are undoubtedly many other and potentially more important determinants of corporate financial policy. There are, however, indications that tax factors may indeed influence corporate financing decisions[7]. As an example, dividend pay-out ratios in the United States have increased sharply in recent years following the 1986 tax reform which subjected 100 per cent of realized nominal capital gains on shares to ordinary personal income tax, thereby discouraging corporate retentions[8].

The lack of a generally accepted theory of corporate finance and disagreement on the effects of taxation on corporate financial policy are often the basic reasons for the conflicting views on the corporate income tax expressed in professional and public debates on tax policy. It is possible to distinguish at least three views each of which is based on a specific assumption regarding the interaction of taxation and corporate financial policy. The following sections briefly describe these alternative viewpoints.

4) The "optimistic" view of the corporate income tax

The most optimistic view of the corporation tax assumes that corporations typically use debt as their marginal source of investment finance, because the tax system in almost all countries tends to favour this mode of finance. When interest payments are deductible, and depreciation for tax purposes coincides with the actual decline in asset values so-called "true economic depreciation"), it can be shown that it will be profitable for corporate as well as non-corporate firms to carry debt-financed investment to the point where the risk-adjusted) pre-tax rate of return on the marginal investment project is just equal to the rate of interest before tax.

Thus the "optimistic" view holds that the coexistence of a tax on corporate profits and a personal tax on dividends will not discourage corporate investment relative to investment in the unincorporated sector, because at the margin corporations use debt finance which is not subject to economic double taxation. Without distorting the pattern of investment, the corporation tax simply transfers part of the "pure" profits on the intramarginal corporate investment projects to the government, provided depreciation allowances accurately reflect true economic depreciation. In this way the corporate income tax appropriates part of the economic rent surplus profits) which would otherwise have accrued to shareholders, but since no corporation tax is collected from the marginal investment projects that are just barely profitable, the tax is not "shifted" onto other economic groups through reduced investment activity in the corporate sector[9].

When depreciation allowances deviate from true economic depreciation, it is recognized that the corporation tax will no longer be neutral with respect to corporate investment. The cost of corporate capital will then depend on the corporate income tax rate, even if debt is the marginal source of finance. However, if the tax system allows accelerated deductions for depreciation, as is frequently the case, it can be shown that a higher corporate tax rate will actually tend to <u>stimulate</u> debt-financed corporate investment, because it increases the value of the tax subsidy implicit in accelerated depreciation allowances. Moreover, it will still be the case that relief from the double taxation of dividends will not encourage corporate investment, as long as debt is the marginal source of finance.

To summarize, those who believe that corporations typically rely on debt finance at the margin would claim that the corporate income tax is approximately neutral or even beneficial to corporate investment.

There is considerable scepticism concerning this optimistic view of the corporation tax, however. Some critics observe that because the return to most corporate investment projects is uncertain, and because investors wish to avoid excessive risks of bankruptcy, corporations in practice often have to finance at least part of their marginal investments by equity. Others point out that in practice the interaction of accelerated depreciation allowances and limited loss offsets implies that corporations relying excessively on debt finance will often be unable to exploit all their deductions for depreciation and interest payments. Seeking to avoid such "tax-exhaustion", corporations will thus wish to use some equity finance at the margin, and the economic double taxation of equity-financed investment will therefore tend to raise the cost of capital to the corporate sector.

In short, most observers find it unrealistic to assume that corporations rely entirely on debt finance at the margin, and that the corporation tax is approximately neutral. However, these critics disagree on the relative importance of retained earnings and new share issues as marginal sources of finance, and they therefore have different views on the importance of the economic double taxation of dividends, as the next sections will seek to explain.

5) The "old" view of dividend taxation

According to the so-called "old" view, the double taxation of dividends significantly hampers corporate investment. For various reasons, shareholders are believed to value dividends higher than capital gains on their shares. Since double taxation discourages dividend payments and reduces the dividend pay-out ratio, it therefore raises the required total rate of return on shares, thereby increasing the cost of equity finance for corporations.

Apart from the transaction costs e.g. brokers' fees) of realising capital gains the reasons for the alleged shareholder preference for dividends over capital gains are not very clear. One hypothesis is that dividends are used as a "signal" to shareholders that the corporation is financially healthy and that its future earnings prospects are good. Sceptics object that the payment of dividends subject to economic double taxation seems a very costly means of conveying information to shareholders, and that there should be more efficient ways of sending credible "signals" to the stock market.

Another hypothesis is that shareholders and corporate managers sometimes have conflicting interests and that it is difficult for shareholders to monitor and control the performance of managers. Shareholders therefore favour the distribution of a substantial part of corporate profits, because this will restrict the opportunities of managers to spend retained earnings on projects which serve the interests of management and employees rather than the shareholder interest.

Whatever the basis for the benefits stemming from dividend payments, supporters of the old view hold that corporations will raise their dividend pay-out ratio to the point where the marginal benefit from extra dividends is just offset by the extra tax imposed on dividends relative to capital gains. A lower effective rate of tax on dividends will reduce the marginal tax cost of distributions and raise the optimal dividend pay-out ratio, and the ensuing increase in the benefits associated with dividends will lower the shareholders' required rate of return, thus stimulating corporate investment.

It is worth noting the implications of the old view for the incidence of the corporate tax system in a closed economy the open-economy case is treated in section C). By raising the cost of corporate capital, the double taxation of dividends implies a tendency for capital to flow from the corporate to the non-corporate sector until the after-tax rates of return in the two sectors are equalized. In that process the pre-tax rate of return in the corporate sector will rise while the non-corporate rate of return will fall, so the burden of the extra tax on corporate investment will tend to be shared among <u>all</u> owners of capital. Because of reduced supplies and higher relative prices of goods produced in the corporate sector, consumers with special preferences for such goods may also come to bear some of the burden of the corporation tax. Moreover, since the lower net return to capital is likely to discourage savings, the economy may end up with a lower total stock of capital. In the long run this will tend to raise the pre-tax rate of return to capital and to lower labour productivity and real wages, and in this way part of the burden of the corporation tax may be shifted onto wage earners although this shifting could be modified if the reallocation of capital from the corporate to the non-corporate sector involves a reallocation to more labour-intensive forms of production).

A preference among shareholders for a relatively high dividend pay-out ratio would seem to imply that corporations will often have to issue new shares to meet their need for equity. Hence it is often said that the old view assumes that new share issues are quite important as a marginal source of finance. In contrast, supporters of the so-called "new view" of dividend taxation believe that retained earnings are the most important marginal source of equity finance.

6) The "new" view of dividend taxation

Adherents of the "new view" are sceptical of the alleged benefits associated with dividend payments. Instead they stress that shareholders should prefer lightly taxed capital gains on shares to heavily taxed dividends, and that corporations should therefore retain all the earnings for which they can find a profitable investment outlet, paying out only the remaining amount as dividends.

The new view does not deny that the double taxation of dividends will raise the required pre-tax rate of return on corporate investment financed by new share issues. However, it points out that retained earnings account for the major part of equity-financed corporate investments and claims that dividend taxes do not distort such investments. A simple numerical example may serve to illustrate the new view: suppose a corporation considers paying out a dividend of 100 dollars to a shareholder facing a marginal tax rate of 50 per cent on dividends. Suppose further that the corporation may alternatively retain the 100 dollars and invest them in a one-year project yielding a 10 per cent rate of return after payment of corporate income tax. If the investment is undertaken, the shareholder will forego an after-tax dividend of 0.5x100 = 50 dollars in the first year, but in return receives an after-tax dividend of 0.5x110 = 55 dollars in the second year. The shareholder will thus earn a net return of 10 per cent on the income foregone in the first year, as would have been the case in the absence of the dividend tax.

In other words, the new view holds that dividend taxes do not affect the profitability of investment financed by retained earnings. Once equity capital has been injected into the corporation by the issue of shares, it is "trapped" in the sense that distributions from the company cannot escape the dividend tax, whether they are undertaken now or later. Provided the tax rate stays constant over time, the dividend tax therefore should not affect the incentive to retain earnings for investment now with the purpose of increasing distributions later[10].

In contrast, the corporate income tax and the personal tax on the rise in share prices produced by retentions will obviously reduce the profitability of investments financed by retained earnings. Hence, rather than focusing on the double taxation of dividends, the new view stresses the importance of the potential double taxation stemming from the coexistence of the corporate income tax and taxes on capital gains on shares. According to the new view, a lower capital gains tax rate will tend to stimulate corporate investment, whereas a reduction of the effective dividend tax rate will only produce windfall gains to existing share-holders without promoting investment. The reason for the latter phenomenon is that the double taxation of dividends is capitalised in lower share prices, since investors would not otherwise be willing to purchase shares rather than, say, bonds, and accordingly the new view is also sometimes referred to as the "capitalisation view" of dividend taxation. The implication is that a dividend tax induces a fall in stock prices and thereby works like a capital levy on holders of shares at the time of introduction of or increase in) the tax.

At least two other implications of the new view should be noted. The first one is that while an unexpected permanent change in the dividend tax rate will not affect corporate investment, anticipated temporary changes in the dividend tax will certainly influence capital formation. More specifically, corporations would tend to lower investment and increase distributions before a temporary dividend tax increase, while lowering distributions and increasing retentions-financed investments during the period of the higher dividend tax rate.

Second, the new view applies only to mature corporations where retained profits are sufficient to meet the need for equity finance. When a new corporation is set up, or when a corporation is growing so fast that its need for equity cannot be met by internal funds, new shares will have to be issued, and investment will then be discouraged by the double taxation of dividends.

28

7) *The new versus the old view*

The new view of dividend taxation is consistent with the observed fact that retained earnings typically account for a major share of corporate equity finance in OECD countries. The hypothesis that dividend taxes are capitalised in stock market prices also offers an explanation for the observation that the market value of corporations often appears to be systematically lower than the replacement cost of the real assets owned by these corporations. Finally, there is some empirical evidence to suggest that the required pre-tax rate of return on corporate investment financed by new share issues is significantly higher than the required rate of return on investment financed by retentions[11]. This also accords with the new view.

At the same time, another oft-quoted empirical study has found that the post-war British experience tends to favour the old rather than the new view of the economic effects of dividend taxation[12]. More generally, the old view according to which dividends yield certain special benefits to shareholders seems consistent with the fact that corporations often try to maintain a fairly steady stream of dividend payments, despite the volatility of corporate profits and investment expenditures.

In contrast, the new view holds that the dividend is a residual which is paid out when corporations have exhausted their opportunities for profitable investment financed by retained earnings. It has therefore been argued that the new view would imply widely fluctuating dividend payments, because of fluctuations in corporate profits and investment opportunities. This is not obvious, however. If investment opportunities are perceived to be good when current earnings are high, an increase in retentions-financed investment would tend to take place in periods of rising profits and therefore would not necessitate sharp reductions in dividend pay-outs.

Moreover, the old view stressing the benefits to shareholders from a high dividend pay-out ratio appears to be at odds with the observation that new shares are typically issued rather infrequently and normally account for only a minor share of total corporate equity finance.

In summary, the evidence does not unequivocally favour one view over the other, and it is likely that both views contain important elements of the truth. Further, one should not exaggerate the difference in the policy implications of the two views. It is true that adherents of the new view would certainly consider relief of the double taxation of dividends to be less important than those favouring the old view. However, the new view does admit that economic double taxation distorts the investment decisions of "immature" and rapidly expanding corporations where retained earnings are insufficient to cover the need for equity finance. Since these corporations are often the most dynamic and innovative ones, the benefits of relieving the double taxation of dividends would not necessarily be negligible, even if the new view provides a correct description of mature corporations.

Whatever the magnitude of the efficiency gains from double taxation relief, these gains must of course be weighed against the revenue cost and potential administrative complexity of such relief and against the potential distributional problem of the concomitant windfall gains to shareholders.

8) *The elusive goal of financial neutrality*

As mentioned in section B.3 above several observers have expressed concern that the tax incentive for debt finance embodied in most corporate tax systems may threaten the financial stability of the corporate sector by inducing corporations to rely too heavily on debt. It has also been noted that the additional tax burden on external relative to internal equity finance tends to imply an undesirable discrimination against young and expanding corporations.

For these and other reasons it is often argued that the tax system should not favour one source of finance over another. Section B.3 briefly described a simplified system of capital income taxation which would be neutral towards corporate financing decisions: if interest income and corporate profits were taxed at identical flat rates and dividends and capital gains on shares were tax-free at the shareholder level, all corporate-source income would be taxed exactly once and at the same rate, regardless of the way corporate investment is financed.

The problem with such a solution based on proportional capital income taxation is that it is incompatible with the traditional goal of progressive taxation of comprehensive income. Although a flat-rate income tax combined with a personal exemption would imply some degree of tax progressivity - because the personal exemption would weigh more heavily in the low income brackets - and although some OECD countries have recently moved in the direction of proportional flat-rate taxes on capital income, other countries still prefer to tax interest and dividends according to a progressive rate schedule, despite the practical obstacles to progressive personal taxation of retained corporate earnings[13].

With a progressive personal income tax, it is more difficult to achieve a neutral corporate tax system. If the double taxation of dividends is fully relieved by means of an imputation system and if dividends and interest are both subject to ordinary personal income tax, the tax system will be neutral between debt finance and finance by new share issues, because distributed profits will be taxed only at the level of the shareholder who will face the same marginal tax rate on dividends and on interest income. However, such a system would still tend to favour finance by retained earnings, if the corporate tax rate were lower than the marginal personal income tax rate of the representative shareholder, and if there were no tax on capital gains on shares. Conversely, in the presence of a substantial capital gains tax, the combined corporate and personal tax burden on retained earnings could exceed the burden on earnings paid out as interest and dividends when the double taxation of dividends is fully relieved).

Some tax theorists have claimed that market forces will automatically tend to produce financial neutrality, however. To illustrate their argument, suppose there is no double taxation of dividends and that the corporate tax rate is <u>higher</u> than the marginal personal tax rate of the "marginal"[14] shareholder. Corporations could then increase their market value by switching from finance by retained earnings to finance by debt and by new share issues. Such a financial restructuring of the corporate sector will raise the interest and dividend incomes of households, thereby increasing the income tax base and pushing taxpayers into higher tax brackets until the marginal personal tax rate of the marginal shareholder reaches the level of the corporate tax rate, and the tax incentive for finance by external sources is eliminated. Yet, while theoretically interesting, such a scenario seems rather implausible, because it would require an unrealistically high degree of progressivity in the personal income tax schedule, with steeply rising marginal tax rates.

In practice, a system of capital income taxation which does not distort the financing decisions of corporations is therefore very difficult to implement. The potential for non-neutralities is often exacerbated by the presence of <u>tax-exempt institutions</u> which often are not paying tax on their interest and dividend income[15]. Even if these institutions received a full refund for the corporate tax underlying their dividend income which is rarely the case), they would still face some tax discrimination against investment in shares as long as they are not compensated for their pro rata share of the corporate tax on retained profits.

9) *Other dimensions of tax neutrality*

One frequent objection to differential tax treatment of different financial instruments and different types of capital income is that such non-neutralities provide scope for tax arbitrage arrangements which tend to frustrate the equity goals of policymakers. Another reason for objections is that asymmetries in the taxation of capital income tend to distort the allocation of society's stock of capital.

To eliminate distortions in capital income taxation, it is not sufficient that the tax system be neutral towards corporate financing decisions. The tax system must also be neutral in the broader sense that tax rules do not prevent an equalization of the marginal pre-tax rate of return to capital across and within the different sectors of the economy. If there were differences in marginal pre-tax rates of return, it would be possible to raise national income by reallocating capital from assets and sectors with lower rates of return to assets and sectors with higher returns.

If the tax system imposes a particularly high low) tax burden on corporate equity capital, and if corporations rely to some extent on equity for their marginal source of finance, the required pre-tax rate of return on capital will be higher lower) in the corporate than in the non-corporate sector, and the goal of tax neutrality will be violated. However, removal of the additional tax on or the special tax subsidy to) corporate equity would not be sufficient to equalize the required rates of return across different types of investment. For such an equalization to take place, it is also necessary that the deduction for depreciation allowed by the tax code corresponds to the so-called "true economic depreciation", i.e. to the actual decline in the market value of the specific asset in question. Allowance for true economic depreciation -- no more and no less — is needed to guarantee that the tax base for each asset type is neither smaller nor greater than the actual economic profits earned by the asset.

In practice it is extremely difficult to obtain an exact estimate of the economic depreciation associated with each individual business asset. For administrative reasons the authorities often choose to group assets into a few broad categories, and they then apply the same rate of depreciation to all assets within a given category to arrive at taxable profits. For assets with relatively long lives this means that depreciation for tax purposes will tend to exceed the true economic depreciation, while depreciation allowances will tend to be insufficient for assets with relatively short lives. The tax system will thus tend to favour "long" investment projects at the expense of "short" projects, even if depreciation allowances are neither too generous nor too restrictive on average. In addition, the authorities often deliberately deviate from the norm of neutrality by allowing accelerated depreciation or other special deductions in order to stimulate investment in particular assets, regions or sectors.

The presence of inflation adds another potential impediment to tax neutrality. Ideally, capital income taxes should be levied only on the _real_ return to capital while the inflation premium in the nominal rate of return should go untaxed. In the field of corporate income taxation this means that tax should be imposed only on real economic profits. Thus depreciation allowances should be indexed to allow for inflation, and only capital gains in excess of inflation should be subject to tax. At the same time, corporations should be allowed to deduct only their real interest payments, while deduction for the inflation premium in nominal interest expenses should be denied.

At the moment no OECD country consistently taxes only the real income from capital, in part because the administrative difficulties of moving towards a real income tax base. In particular, it is customary to allow corporations full deductibility for all nominal interest expenses, despite the fact that inflation erodes the real value of corporate debt. Under such circumstances the corporate tax system provides an artificial stimulus to debt-financed corporate investment unless the government offsets the privilege of full interest deductibility by levying full tax on all accrued nominal capital gains, and by restricting deductions for depreciation to the decline in the _nominal_ value of business assets. Since the latter two conditions are rarely met, inflation thus tends to exacerbate the incentive for debt-financed investment embodied in existing corporate tax systems.

Another neutrality goal sometimes referred to by policymakers is that the tax system should ideally impose the same tax burden on corporate and non-corporate firms, i.e. the system should be neutral towards the decision of businessmen to incorporate their firms. Although apparently rather different, this goal is in fact closely related to the goal of financial neutrality. Assuming that the controlling shareholders are household investors, financial neutrality in the corporate sector prevails when the total corporate and personal tax burden on corporate equity income equals the personal tax rate on interest income. If all personal income — including interest income and income from self-employment — were taxed at the same proportional rate, financial neutrality would then imply that a self-employed businessman would neither raise nor lower his total tax liability by incorporating his firm. The total tax on the return to the equity of the incorporated firm would equal the personal tax on the business income from the unincorporated firm.

In practice, the personal tax on income from self-employed is usually progressive, and the marginal personal tax rate faced by self-employed businessmen is often higher than the total effective tax rate on retained corporate profits. For businessmen with a perceived need to accumulate profits within their firm, this provides an incentive to incorporate. The frequent double taxation of dividends may of course discourage incorporation, but owners of closely held corporations who also work as managers can sometimes escape this economic double taxation by paying themselves salaries rather than dividends, although this would be less attractive where payroll taxes are high.

Since generally the corporate income tax is a proportional tax whereas the personal income tax is a progressive tax, some amount of tax discrimination between the corporate and non-corporate forms of business organisation thus seems inevitable. One possible way out of this dilemma would be to retain progressive taxation of non-property income but to introduce a flat tax rate on all net capital income, including an imputed return to the physical assets of unincorporated business firms. By setting the flat capital income tax equal to the corporate tax rate, one could then ensure an equal tax treatment of corporations and self-employed businessmen, albeit in a rather rough manner[16].

10) The cash flow tax

Because of the inherent problems of measuring true economic profits under a conventional business income tax, many tax economists have argued that neutrality can be achieved only by levying the tax on the corporation's net cash flow rather than on estimated corporate profits. Under a cash flow tax the government would effectively participate as a "sleeping partner" in all corporate investment projects by allowing immediate expensing of all investment expenditure. In other words, via a tax reduction the government would finance a share of investment outlays corresponding to that share of the subsequent cash inflows which would be taxed away. The net rate of return on the private investor's net investment outlay would therefore be unaffected by the cash flow tax provided the tax rate stayed constant over time), and hence the tax would not distort the level and pattern of corporate investment.

The literature on the cash flow corporation tax usually distinguishes three variants of such a tax[17]: a so-called "R base" tax which would tax only the net cash flow from the corporation's real transactions; an "R + F base" tax which would also include financial transactions, and an "S base" tax which would be levied on the net distribution from corporations to shareholders.

Under an "R base" tax companies would be taxed on all inflows of cash from their real activities, i.e. their trading profits including the proceeds of any sales of real assets. Investment in real physical assets would attract a 100 per cent initial allowance, but no allowance would be made for financial costs, implying in particular that interest expenses would not be deductible, just as interest receipts would go untaxed.

While it should be a simple matter to calculate tax liability under an R base tax, such a tax might not ensure an adequate taxation of financial institutions where profits often arise as the difference between borrowing and lending rates of interest. This problem would not arise under a so-called real and financial base R + F base) tax where firms are taxed on the difference between all cash inflows and outflows, including financial transactions, except dealings in shares and issues of new equity and dividends. More precisely, the R + F base tax would allow deductions for interest plus repayment of debt, while subjecting the proceeds from new loans to tax.

A so-called S base cash flow tax would essentially achieve the same result as an R + F base tax. The S base tax would tax dividends plus net purchases of shares in other companies and give relief for new equity issued. The symmetry of the company's balance sheet means that changes in net outflows on the real and financial accounts must be matched by changes in the share account. Thus any excess of inflows over outflows must be used to pay a dividend or to buy shares in another company. Hence the S base tax would be equivalent to the R + F base tax, although the flow of funds taxed under the S base would be simpler to administer because so few transactions would need to be monitored.

Moreover, if a cash flow corporation tax is combined with a traditional personal income tax, it can be shown that the tax system would be neutral towards corporate financing decisions only if the marginal personal tax rates on interest, dividends, and accrued capital gains on shares were identical. Given the difficulties of ensuring uniform taxation of capital gains and other forms of capital income, it is therefore unlikely that the full neutrality gains from a tax on corporate cash flows can be reaped, as long as the personal income tax is maintained. If, however, the personal income tax were to be replaced by a personal expenditure tax — which can be seen as a form of cash-flow tax at the personal level — a tax on corporate cash flows could supplement an expenditure tax since they are both based on the same broad principles and have the same neutrality characteristics.

Because of their attractive neutrality properties, the various cash flow taxes have attracted a great deal of attention in the academic literature and have also been studied by government committees in a few OECD countries. However, so far no country has implemented a cash flow corporation tax. Apart from the transitional problems, governments are concerned that the introduction of a corporation tax differing markedly from the corporate income tax of other countries would cause problems in the international sphere. For instance, the Canadian McDonald Commission report expressed fears that a Canadian cash flow corporation tax paid by foreign-owned companies operating in Canada would not be eligible for the foreign tax credits of other countries and would therefore discourage Canadian capital imports.

11) Limits to the goal of tax neutrality

Even if the practical obstacles to tax neutrality in its various forms could be overcome, it should be mentioned that neutrality is obviously not the only legitimate goal of tax policy. For instance, it was noted above that a desire to "fine tune" depreciation allowances in order to approximate true economic depreciation would have to be traded off against the desire for administrative simplicity.

More generally, policymakers with an interventionist approach may deliberately wish to deviate from neutrality in order to encourage or discourage certain activities, and insofar as the activities in question render positive or negative side effects so-called "externalities") to society, such a "non-neutral" tax policy may indeed be justified even from the viewpoint of economic efficiency. A desire to redistribute income towards certain groups or sectors may also motivate deviations from tax neutrality.

On the other hand advocates of tax neutrality have pointed out that the various goals of social, regional and industrial policy etc. can often be furthered more effectively by other means than various types of tax incentives, e.g. by direct government transfers. A tax system characterized by a very large number of special provisions tends to become non-transparent and often offers unintended opportunities for tax avoidance. The trend in the past decade towards broader income tax bases in most OECD countries may reflect a recognition of this fact and can be seen as an attempt to move towards greater tax neutrality.

C. The incidence of the corporation tax in an open economy

In rounding off this discussion of major policy issues relating to the taxation of corporations and shareholders, it seems relevant to point out the implications of international capital mobility for the incidence of taxes on corporate-source income. The discussion also provides an introduction to the next section which deals with the international dimension of corporate tax policy.

As noted in Section B 6, it could well be that part of the burden of the corporate income tax is shifted to owners of capital in the non-corporate sector through an inflow of competing capital from the corporate sector; that another part of the tax is shifted to consumers through higher prices of corporate products; and finally that some part of the burden falls on wage earners in the form of lower wages.

In an open economy where corporate capital has the option of migrating to other countries, it is even more likely that a substantial part of the corporate income tax is shifted. Under the present tax regimes in the OECD area, the corporation tax works very much like a tax based on the source principle, because of the widespread use of the exemption method of international double tax relief, because of the limits on foreign tax credits, and because of the practice of credit countries to defer domestic taxation of profits retained abroad. Generally, this means that a higher domestic corporate tax burden can be fully or partly escaped by investing abroad rather than at home.

A domestic corporate tax increase will therefore tend to cause an outflow of corporate capital and in the long run, the resulting shortage of capital in the domestic economy will drive up the pre-tax rate of return to corporate investment, implying at least a partial shifting of the tax increase. The burden will be shifted to wage earners, because the lower capital intensity of domestic production will reduce labour productivity and real wage rates. Part of the burden may also fall on owners of immobile factors of production such as land and natural resources, because the outflow of capital may reduce the demand for land, resulting in falling land rents and land prices. In the extreme case of a small open economy faced with perfect international mobility of capital, a rise in the domestic corporation tax above the tax rates prevailing abroad would in fact tend to be fully shifted in the long-run, because no corporation would be willing to invest in the domestic economy unless it could obtain an after-tax rate of return equal to the net return obtainable on foreign investment.

In practice such full tax shifting will not occur, because physical business investment is not as mobile across borders as portfolio investment in securities. One reason for the imperfect mobility of business investment is that part of the earnings on such investment often relies on specific local factors such as high-quality infrastructure, labour with special skills, consumers with special tastes, or easy access to high-quality raw materials. Since the "excess" profits deriving from these local factors cannot be maintained if investment is shifted abroad, they can be partly taxed away via the domestic corporate income tax without causing capital flight from the country.

Nevertheless, since the corporate tax base is increasingly mobile across borders e.g. profits can be shifted by means of transfer pricing practices), the corporate income tax is probably not a very effective means of redistributing income from the owners of corporations to other groups in society, whereas the tax may influence the level of investment in the domestic economy.

While the corporate income tax can be seen as a tax on domestic <u>investment</u> because it tends to be based on the source principle), the personal income tax on the dividends distributed from corporations can be seen as a tax on a specific form of domestic <u>savings</u>. In an open economy with high capital mobility a change in the corporate income tax rate will therefore mainly affect the level of business investment in the corporate sector without influencing the level of domestic savings very much, whereas a change in the personal tax on dividends will mostly affect the <u>composition</u> of domestic savings and have little impact on domestic investment.

To analyse the effects of changes in personal dividend taxes more closely[18], it may again be instructive to consider the benchmark case of a small open economy which faces a given world interest rate and a given rate of return to corporate investment in the rest of the world. If the government in such an economy decides to introduce dividend tax relief to resident shareholders via the imputation method, and if relief is granted to all distributed corporate profits whether these profits stem from domestic or from foreign sources, there will be <u>no</u> effect on domestic investment undertaken by <u>mature</u> domestic corporations which do not rely on new share issues as a marginal source of finance. The reason is that profit-maximizing corporations will take domestic investment only to the point where its rate of return after corporation tax equals the given net-of-corporate-tax return obtainable on investment abroad. Since the latter's net return is not affected by the provision of domestic dividend tax relief, any additional domestic corporate investment would yield lower net profits than could be earned abroad and therefore would not be worthwhile. However, since finance by new share issues will become cheaper, the establishment and growth of <u>new</u> domestic corporations having to rely on this source of funds will indeed be encouraged.

As to the effects on the supply side of the capital market, the introduction of dividend tax relief in a small open economy will have a negligible impact on saving incentives. The explanation is that after-tax rates of interest are not affected by dividend tax relief when domestic interest rates are tied to the interest rates prevailing abroad. As a consequence, the net return to domestic saving will remain unchanged, since the risk-adjusted net return on shares must equal the given after-tax return on interest-bearing assets for the capital market to be in equilibrium. Thus the granting of dividend tax relief will only serve to raise the prices of shares in the domestic stock market until share investments are no longer more attractive than investment in interest-bearing assets. In short, in the present stylized scenario the introduction of dividend tax credit will provide a windfall gain to existing shareholders without stimulating aggregate domestic saving. Indeed, the shareholder capital gains may lead to a temporary boost in consumption and a concomitant temporary drop in savings, but the main effect will be to change the composition of total savings, since the weight of domestic shares in domestic investor portfolios will increase, and since the tax disincentive to use new share issues as a source of finance will diminish. More specifically, the major effect of dividend tax relief to resident shareholders may be to increase the degree of domestic ownership of shares in domestic corporations, since domestic shareholders will be willing to pay higher prices for domestic shares after the introduction of a dividend tax credit.

If the strong assumptions underlying the above scenario are relaxed, dividend tax relief could be expected to have more noticeable effects on real economic activity. For instance, even if the domestic economy is small relative to the world economy, domestically-owned corporations may possess substantial market power in the specific foreign markets in which they operate. Hence they may not face a given constant rate of return on their marginal investments neither abroad nor at home. When the introduction of dividend tax credits reduces shareholders' required rate of return on investment financed by new share issues, these corporations are therefore likely to undertake some additional investment in foreign as well as domestic markets, on the assumption that dividend tax relief is granted to all distributed profits, including those deriving from foreign sources.

If relief is given only to distributions of profits from domestic sources — as it is often the case in practice see chapter 6) — domestic corporate investment will become relatively more attractive and is therefore likely to be stimulated even in the extreme case where the corporation faces a given net rate of return on foreign investment. Moreover, if investors consider shares to be rather imperfect substitutes for bonds and other interest-bearing assets, the introduction of dividend tax relief will not be fully capitalized in higher share prices. The dividend tax credit will then yield a permanent stimulus to savings in shares and may consequently produce some increase in aggregate private savings.

In summary, international capital mobility will not completely neutralise the real economic effects of relief of the economic double taxation of dividends, but it will tend to reduce them[19].

D. International issues

1) The policy issues raised by cross-border investments

When corporations and individual shareholders are given the opportunity to invest abroad as well as at home, policymakers are faced with new problems.

First of all, new issues on distribution arise. For instance, how can policymakers ensure an equitable tax treatment of foreign compared to domestic investments and how can tax avoidance and tax evasion through exploitation of international investment opportunities be prevented? In addition to these problems of achieving equity among taxpayers there is the important issue of "inter-nation equity": how can a fair cross-country distribution of the revenue from taxes on cross-border investments be achieved?

Second, there is the problem of international resource allocation: how can the corporate tax system be designed so as to minimise distortions in the allocation of capital across countries?

Finally, there is the question of administrative feasibility and simplicity: given other legitimate goals of tax policy, how can policymakers minimise the additional administrative complexities which inevitably arise when different national tax systems interact in the international sphere?

In principle, most of the problems under discussion could be alleviated if all countries were to harmonize their corporate tax rules and tax rates. However, the premise of the discussion below is that national governments have different preferences regarding the design of their corporate tax systems and the level of tax rates on income from corporate capital. In this setting the challenge of international policy making is to suggest measures of international corporate tax coordination which will leave national governments with as much room of manoeuvre as possible, while at the same time conforming with accepted norms of equity and efficiency in the field of tax policy. This is often a formidable challenge.

The main emphasis in the exposition below is on issues of resource allocation, as seen from an international viewpoint. However, since policymakers are also concerned about the international division of tax bases and tax revenues, the initial sections focus on these topics.

2) *The source principle versus the residence principle*

In an open economy it is important to distinguish between two basic principles for delineating the national tax base: under the source principle - also designated the "territorial" principle - a government taxes all income originating within its jurisdiction, whether such income accrues to residents or to non-residents. Under a pure residence principle - sometimes referred to as taxation of "worldwide" income - tax is levied on all income accruing to domestic residents, whether that income derives from domestic or from foreign sources.

In practice most OECD Member states levy corporate income tax on all "permanent establishments" of corporations operating within their jurisdiction. Moreover, it is customary for source countries to levy withholding taxes on dividends paid from resident corporations to shareholders residing abroad. At the same time, countries impose corporation tax on the repatriated foreign-source income of their "resident" corporations and levy personal income tax on the foreign-source dividends received by resident individual shareholders. In other words, both the source principle and the residence principle are applied in the taxation of income from corporate investments in the OECD area.

To enforce the source principle, countries must define rules determining the amount of income which is considered to be derived within their jurisdiction. When the worldwide profits of a multinational corporation have to be allocated among source countries, the authorities have traditionally relied on separate accounts for each branch or subsidiary of the multinational group to determine where profits have been earned, and have required adherence to the so-called "arm's length" principle according to which transactions among the various parts of the firm should be priced in the same way as transactions with other unrelated firms.

Proper "arm's length" prices are often very hard to identify, because there may be no comparable open market prices for the transactions in question. Moreover, there is often no obviously correct way of allocating common overhead costs among the various units of the multinational enterprise. In the absence of countervailing measures, the separate accounting method may therefore leave corporations with considerable opportunities for profit-shifting from high-tax to low-tax jurisdictions by, for instance, over- or under-invoicing and by allocation of overheads and interest payments on debt to subsidiaries or branches in high-tax countries. When different jurisdictions apply different rules for the pricing of intra-company transactions, there is also a possibility that the various national tax bases will overlap or that part of the worldwide profits will go completely untaxed. In an effort to reduce these problems, the OECD has encouraged member states to adopt a set of common guidelines for the setting of arm's length prices on intra-group transactions[20].

To levy corporation tax according to the residence principle, the authorities must first be able to establish the residency of corporations. While countries may use different criteria for the determination of the residence of corporations, the "place of effective management" is the preferred criterion used in tax administrations to solve cases of double residence. The problem then becomes one of establishing where the "effective management" is located.

3) *The issue of inter-nation equity*

It is generally accepted that source countries are entitled to tax income originating within their borders, including income accruing to foreigners. One justification for this entitlement is that the foreign-owned factors of production usually benefit from the public services and the protection of property rights provided by the government of the host country. A source-based tax like the corporation tax may also serve to prevent foreign investors from capturing all of the "economic rent" which may arise when foreign capital moves in to exploit the host country's production opportunities, e.g. its natural resources.

When the source country has prior claim to tax the income deriving within its jurisdiction, the inter-country division of income generated by cross-border economic activity such as international corporate investment will be determined solely by the tax levied by the source country, whereas taxes subsequently imposed by the country of residence will determine the division of the residual income between the public and private sectors in that country. The division of the gains from international economic transactions thus depends on the tax rates set by source countries, and it is therefore important to study the principles guiding the setting of these tax rates.

In the field of corporate taxation, it has traditionally been suggested that foreign-owned and domestically-owned corporations operating in the country should be subject to the same corporate tax rate, as is indeed usually the case in practice. The philosophy underlying this policy is that foreign and domestic corporations should be allowed to compete on equal tax terms. Thus governments should not be able to "export" the tax burden by shifting a disproportionate part onto foreigners, nor should foreign companies enjoy a competitive advantage relative to domestic producers by virtue of not being subject to source country corporate tax. Considerations of equity as well as economic efficiency thus seem to have motivated this rule.

However, to achieve this goal it is not sufficient to apply the same corporate tax provisions and rates to foreign-owned and domestic corporations. If source countries' withholding taxes on dividends transferred to foreign shareholders are not fully credited by residence countries, these taxes will tend to put the foreign-controlled corporations at a competitive disadvantage in the host country. Moreover, if alleviation of the economic double taxation of dividends is granted only to resident but not to non-resident shareholders, foreign-owned corporations may likewise face a higher cost of capital than corporations owned by domestic shareholders, although this will also depend upon the residence country's treatment of foreign source income.

Further, even if dividend tax credits were extended to foreign shareholders, and even if withholding taxes on cross-border dividends were abolished, the combined corporate and personal tax burden on domestically-owned capital would still differ from the total tax burden on imported capital, due to cross-country differences in personal and/or corporate income tax rates. Thus it would require a very high degree of international harmonisation of capital income taxation to achieve identical tax treatment of domestic and foreign corporations within each source country. One feature giving rise to difficulties would be the payment of dividend tax credits to foreign shareholders resident in a country which has a classical system and which does not pay a tax credit either to its domestic or foreign shareholders.

This is one reason why some observers have been sceptical about the traditional goal of identical tax treatment. It has also been suggested that reciprocity in source-country tax rates would seem a more natural standard of "inter-nation equity" than identical tax treatment. In other words, it has been argued that a fair international division of tax revenue is obtained when all source countries impose the same effective tax rate on income accruing to foreigners.

Broadly speaking, the current practice in the OECD area is to adhere to the principle of identical treatment in the field of corporate income taxation and to apply the principle of reciprocity in bilateral negotiations over withholding tax rates. Critics have pointed out that this procedure does not guarantee "effective reciprocity", since it implies that source countries with relatively low corporate tax rates will also obtain a relatively low total revenue from taxes on the profits of foreign-owned corporations, compared to source countries with high corporate tax rates. These observers therefore suggest that source countries with relatively low corporate tax rates on distributed profits should be allowed to apply relatively high withholding tax rates, and vice versa, so that the total tax burden on profits distributed to foreign shareholders becomes roughly the same in all source countries[21].

So far an international consensus on the issue of identical treatment versus "effective reciprocity" has not yet materialised.

4) *International double taxation and methods of double taxation relief*

As already suggested, the existence of cross-border investment introduces added potential for double taxation of the return to corporate capital. While one can speak of <u>domestic</u> economic double taxation when corporate-source income is taxed twice by the same national jurisdiction, <u>international</u> juridical double taxation is said to occur when the same income is taxed by two different national jurisdictions.

The possibility of international juridical double taxation of income from corporate sources arises because such income is typically liable to tax both in the country of source and in the shareholder's country of residence. Realizing the distortions and inequities likely to result from such double taxation, OECD countries have taken a number of steps to alleviate it through domestic legislation and through an intricate web of bilateral tax treaties with other member states based on the 1977 Model Double Taxation Convention. Usually these treaties recognize the prior right of source countries to tax all income from the "permanent establishments" of firms operating within their borders. In accordance with the recommendations of the OECD Model, residence countries then typically relieve international double taxation either through the method of exemption or by granting a tax credit.

Under the method of <u>exemption</u> income from foreign sources is simply exempt from domestic tax. In practice this is normally achieved by calculating domestic tax on worldwide income and subsequently reducing the domestic tax liability by a fraction equal to the proportion of foreign-source income in total worldwide income. Through this method of "exemption with progression" income from foreign sources is allowed to influence the taxpayer's marginal tax rate on domestic income when taxes are calculated according to a progressive schedule.

The practical details of the tax <u>credit</u> method can be quite complicated, but the basic principle is simple: the residence country calculates domestic tax on worldwide income, and from this tax bill it subtracts the amount of taxes paid abroad to arrive at domestic net tax liability. Under a pure credit system the taxpayer's total tax bill on worldwide income will therefore always correspond to the domestic tax bill on this income[22]. However, in practice residence countries typically limit their tax credits to the amount of domestic tax on income from foreign sources, to prevent foreign high-tax countries from eroding the net revenue from taxes on domestic incomes. This means that the taxpayer will in effect pay the higher of the domestic and the foreign tax on his foreign-source income. The limitation on tax credits may apply to taxes paid in each individual foreign country (so-called "per-country limitation" - these limitations may also be combined with a limitation by type of income "separate baskets"), or the tax law may stipulate that the total tax credit cannot exceed the total domestic tax bill on income from all foreign sources ("worldwide or overall limitation"). It is also important to record that countries practicing worldwide income taxation with a foreign tax credit normally defer domestic corporate tax on income from foreign subsidiaries until the time this income is repatriated as a dividend to the domestic parent company. This practice of "deferral" means that profits of foreign subsidiaries which are retained abroad are taxed only by the source country (although parent company shareholders may also have to pay domestic capital gains tax on the gain in parent company share values resulting from the retention of profits abroad).

A third method of international double tax alleviation is the method of <u>deduction</u>. Under a deduction system taxes paid in the source country are deductible from the worldwide income liable to tax in the residence country. Clearly, this system only alleviates but does not eliminate international double taxation, since foreign-source income is first subject to tax abroad, while the remaining income is then subject to tax at home.

The tax codes of OECD member countries rarely prescribe explicit use of the deduction method of double tax relief. However, residence countries can be said implicitly to use the deduction method when they levy domestic taxes on dividends on foreign <u>portfolio</u> investment, since these dividends are paid out of profits which have already been subject to corporation tax in the source country, and only the actual amount of the dividends, i.e. the after-corporate tax profits, are taxed domestically - with no credit or exemption relief for the underlying corporation tax[23].

The deduction method has received some attention in the academic literature because it can be shown under certain circumstances to be optimal from the national viewpoint of a small open economy. However, because of its rather harsh tax treatment of international investment income, it is widely recognized that a general application of the deduction system would unduly restrict cross-border investments. Therefore, the deduction method is not examined further in this chapter.

Individual countries rarely use consistently one single method of international double taxation relief for all sources of income (see tables 3.5 and 3.6). As far as income from international portfolio investment in shares is concerned, relief for the underlying corporation tax is implicitly granted through the deduction method (as explained above), but relief for source country withholding taxes on dividends is typically granted through the credit method. In the case of foreign direct investment relief for withholding taxes and for the underlying foreign corporation tax is usually granted through the same method, which may be either credit or exemption, depending on the regulations of bilateral tax treaties and of domestic tax law.

As a consequence of their priority in taxing rights on corporate source income arising in their jurisdiction, source countries with an imputation system usually do not extend their dividend tax relief to shareholders residing abroad, and residence countries applying the imputation system do not allow dividend tax relief for corporate taxes paid abroad (see end of Chapter 6). Consequently, even if economic double taxation is reduced or eliminated in a domestic context such relief is frequently not extended to cross-frontier investment.

To clarify the basic issues involved in the choice among alternative methods of international double tax alleviation, the next two sections abstract from the problem of economic double taxation and assume that the same method of international double tax relief is applied to all types of foreign investment. The complications introduced by the presence of several types of investors with different tax status, and the problem of ensuring simultaneous relief from economic (domestic) as well as international double taxation are subsquently considered.

5) *Credit versus exemption and capital export neutrality versus capital import neutrality*

The choice between the methods of credit and exemption involves a choice between "capital export neutrality" (CEN) and "capital import neutrality"(CIN) as defined in the appendix to Chapter 1. Annex 3 and Chapter 6 are also relevent to the discussions.

Capital export neutrality is said to prevail when the tax system provides no incentive to invest at home rather than abroad, or vice versa[24]. More precisely, the tax system is neutral toward the export of capital when investors face the same marginal effective tax rate on income from capital, whether they invest in the domestic economy or in foreign countries. This is achieved when investors are taxed on accrued worldwide income and receive full credit against the domestic tax liability for all taxes paid abroad. In other words, a pure credit system[25] with no limitation on the foreign tax credit and no deferral of domestic taxes on profits retained abroad would ensure capital export neutrality. Under such a tax regime, the free mobility of capital would tend to equate the pre-tax rates of return to investment across countries, because each investor would then also obtain the same after-tax return on domestic and foreign investment. In so far as the pre-tax rate of return reflects the marginal productivity of capital, a cross-country equalization of the rates of return before tax implies that no output gain can be made by reallocating capital from one country to another. A regime of capital export neutrality therefore tends to ensure an efficient allocation of investment across countries.

Capital import neutrality prevails when domestic and foreign suppliers of capital to any given national market obtain the same after-tax rate of return on their investment in that market. Provided that source countries do not practise tax discrimination between domestic and foreign investors operating in their jurisdiction, capital import neutrality will thus be attained if residence countries exempt all income from foreign sources from domestic tax. In other words, non-discrimination in source countries combined with exemption in residence countries will ensure that imported and domestic capital in each jurisdiction will compete on equal tax terms. In this tax regime, capital mobility would tend to equalize the after-tax return received by savers in different countries, and this in turn would tend to guarantee an efficient international allocation of the world flow of savings[26].

If marginal effective tax rates on capital income were identical across countries, capital export neutrality (CEN) and capital import neutrality (CIN) could be achieved simultaneously, but it is obviously unrealistic to expect such far-reaching international tax harmonisation in the foreseeable future. In this situation, should policymakers give priority to CEN or to CIN and should this priority vary depending on the type of investment being considered?

When capital income tax rates differ across countries, achievement of CEN implies different net returns to saving in different countries and will therefore tend to distort the international allocation of savings. At the same time, as noted above, CEN would tend to equate the "cost of capital" (the required pre-tax rate of return) across countries. By contrast, achievement of CIN would guarantee roughly identical after-tax rates of return to savings for savers in different countries, but would distort the pattern of international investment by causing the cost of capital to deviate from one country to another. Consequently, if investment demand is very sensitive to the cost of capital, and savings are rather insensitive to variations in the after-tax rate of return, a regime of CIN is likely to cause more distortion in the international allocation of capital than a regime of CEN. Conversely, if the elasticity of savings with respect to the after-tax rate of return is high relative to the elasticity of investment with regard to the cost of capital, a tax system ensuring CIN will be less distortionary than a system characterized by CEN (see annex 3 for an illustration of these results).

If the elasticities of saving and investment are roughly similar among countries, the literature suggest that neither total CEN nor total CIN would minimise tax distortions. Instead, the "optimal" tax rate on international investment income will lie somewhere between the rates implied by full aderence to CEN or CIN[27]. However, implementing this optimal tax rule would probably be administratively cumbersome, because foreign investment in high-tax countries would have to be taxed at a rate exceeding the domestic tax rate, whereas foreign investment in low-tax countries should be taxed at a rate below the domestic rate. In any case, it would be very difficult to identify the "optimal" tax rates on international investment, given the uncertainty surrounding empirical estimates of savings and investment elasticities. Moreover, it would be difficult to communicate the philosophy of such a tax regime to taxpayers. For these reasons, the practical policy choice is probably still between CEN (as exemplified by the credit system) and CIN (as exemplified by the exemption system).

Traditionally, the academic literature has tended to assume that private savings are rather inelastic with respect to the net rate of return and that CEN is therefore preferable to CIN from the viewpoint of economic efficiency. It can also be argued that a cross-country equalization of after-tax rates of return (CIN) is not an obvious goal, as long as capital income taxation inevitably distorts consumer choices between present and future consumption by driving a wedge between the pre-tax and the after-tax rate of return to saving. Thus one could argue that if savings were elastic in some countries and inelastic in others, it might be worthwhile to violate the principle of capital import neutrality and have higher after-tax rates of return in the former group of countries and lower net rates of return in the latter, in order to reduce the overall tax distortion of savings decisions.

By contrast, it has been shown (under certain simplifying assumptions) that even if consumer decisions are distorted, it would still be desirable to equate the marginal productivity of capital across different uses (and hence across different countries) to maximize the volume of output obtainable from any given global stock of capital[28]. This provides some theoretical support for a regime of CEN, because CEN tends to ensure a cross-country equalization of the pre-tax rates of return which in turn tend to reflect the marginal productivities of capital.

Supporters of CEN also point out that this regime accords with the time-honoured norm of horizontal equity among taxpayers, in contrast to a regime of CIN. Thus, under a pure credit system two taxpayers resident in the same country with the same worldwide income would always pay the same amount of tax, regardless of the division of total income between domestic and foreign sources.

One further argument in favour of the credit system is that it enables a country to choose a higher capital income tax rate than that prevailing abroad without causing a large capital outflow, since domestic investors can escape the higher domestic tax only by changing their residence. By comparison, under a system of exemption a higher domestic tax rate could be avoided by investing abroad rather than at home. Indeed, with high international mobility of capital, the exemption system would give individual countries a strong incentive to reduce domestic capital income tax rates below the foreign rates in order to attract foreign capital. This could initiate a process of international tax competition whereby all countries might feel compelled to set their capital income tax rates at a lower level than they would have preferred in the absence of competition.

Finally, supporters of the credit system sometimes stress that a system of exemption leaves multinational enterprises with considerable scope for international tax avoidance through the manipulation of prices on intra-company cross-border transactions. While a consistent credit system (with no credit limits and no deferral) ensures that the total tax bill on worldwide income is determined solely by domestic tax rules, an exemption system implies that the total tax bill can be reduced by shifting profits from high-tax to low-tax jurisdictions through transfer-pricing. Also, because the income statements delivered to the authorities of the residence country include income from foreign branches, the method of exemption with progression sketched in section C enables multinationals to exploit deductions for losses in foreign branches twice: at first, the loss on foreign branch operations can be deducted from taxable profits on domestic operations in order to reduce domestic tax liability, and in subsequent years the loss can be carried forward abroad to reduce foreign taxes levied on the foreign branch.

There are, however, certain arguments in favour of the exemption system which should be recorded here. It is quite difficult to implement a pure and consistent credit system in practice, whereas an exemption system is undoubtedly simpler to administer. Also, the substantial compliance cost which may be associated with a credit system implies a loss of welfare which may on balance render an exemption system relatively more attractive.

At a more basic level, some observers have argued that exemption may in fact ensure the best approximation to both capital export neutrality and capital import neutrality, on the assumption that cross-country differences in tax rates on business investment tend to reflect differences in the value of cost-reducing public services which source countries offer to business. Essentially, business taxes are seen as so-called "benefit taxes", i.e. user charges for public services. Different tax rates on investment in different countries are therefore considered only to neutralise differences in investment incentives emanating from the expenditure side of public budgets, so a credit system implying identical tax rates on domestic and foreign investment would be distortionary, whereas the exemption system is nondistortionary because it implies that investors are only taxed by the source country offering the compensating public services.

While interesting, the hypothesis that source country taxes approximate benefit taxes is hardly realistic. The most important business tax levied by source countries is the corporate income tax which does not seem to bear any systematic relationship to the value of the public services offered to businesses. Besides, it may well be the case that international investment also benefits to some extent from the services supplied by the public sector of the residence country. This is another reason why a tax system based on a pure source principle (exemption) is unlikely to be fully neutral.

There is one special case in which exemption could ensure a type of neutrality unattainable under a credit system. This is the situation where there are no significant differences in the productivity of capital depending on the international location of investment, but where one company, say company A, is systematically more efficient than another company B in all the locations where the two companies operate and compete. Under an exemption system, the two companies would be faced with the same tax rate in each jurisdiction, so the cost advantage of company A would not be neutralized by tax factors. In contrast, under a credit system with a higher tax rate in the residence country of company A than in the home country of company B, company A could not fully exploit its competitive advantage vis-à-vis company B, because A would be taxed at a higher rate than B on all operations. The tax system would thus tend to reallocate resources from the more efficient to the less efficient company, and this would obviously be distortionary.

Hence, when the marginal productivity of capital depends on the company owning the capital but not on the location of investment, only the exemption system can guarantee tax neutrality[29]. The importance of such "capital ownership neutrality" relative to capital export neutrality depends on the difference in marginal products between different companies as opposed to between different locations. If great cost savings can be made by reallocating investment from one country to another, it is important that the tax system does not discourage such reallocation, i.e. it is important that CEN prevails. It seems likely that in practice costs vary more by location than by ownership, and that CEN is therefore the more relevant neutrality criterion.

Some observers have found it undesirable that a pure credit system aimed at ensuring CEN should neutralise the tax incentives which source countries sometimes offer to imported capital in order to attract foreign investment and promote economic development. If the tax incentives are in fact offered to types of investment which are likely to generate positive spillovers to the rest of the economy, they may represent desirable deviations from capital export neutrality which should not be offset by a higher tax liability in the residence country of the foreign investor.

On balance, while there is not universal agreement, most writers on the subject have found that the weight of the arguments implies a preference for capital export neutrality over capital import neutrality and hence for the credit system over the exemption system, at least when differences in capital income tax rates across countries are large. On the other hand, when these differences are fairly small, investment incentives will not be very much affected by the choice between credit and exemption, and administrative considerations may then tend to favour the exemption system.

Chapter 6 describes some of the practical obstacles to the achievement of capital export neutrality in international investment, distinguishing between direct investment undertaken by a parent corporation through a foreign branch or subsidiary, and international portfolio investment in minority shareholdings by households and institutional investors.

Notes and References

1. See, e.g., the report of the OECD Committee on Fiscal Affairs on "Transfer Pricing and Multinational Enterprises", OECD 1979, and the report on "International Tax Avoidance and Evasion", *Issues in International Taxation*, No. 1, OECD 1987, Thin Capitalisation, OECD 1987.

2. In fact, in the domestic setting intra-corporate dividends are almost always exempt from tax when the corporate shareholder controls more than a certain minimum fraction of the shares in the other corporation see chapter 3). Therefore this issue is not discussed further in the present chapter.

3. In fact a recent British report has suggested that - as an alternative to the present imputation system of double taxation relief - corporations should be given an equity allowance, i.e. that they should be allowed to make a deduction for a normal rate of interest on the accumulated equity put into the firm via new share issues and retained earnings see "Equity for Companies: A Corporation Tax for the 1990s", Report of the Capital Taxes Group, Institute for Fiscal Studies, Commentary No. 26, London 1991).

4. It has, however, been done in limited ways, namely in the case of small personal corporations e.g. "S" corporations in the United States, which are taxed as partnerships).

5. This estimate has been produced by M. Gertler and G. Hubbard, in *Tax Policy and the Economy,* National Bureau of Economic Research, No. 4, 1990.

6. See James M. Poterba: *Dividends, Capital Gains and the Corporate Veil: Evidence from Britain, Canada and the United States*, National Bureau of Economic Research, Working Paper No. 2975, 1989 and *Saving Trends and Behaviour in OECD Countries,* OECD Working Papers, No. 67, June 1989.

7. For example, several authors have found evidence that the additional tax on distributed relative to retained earnings reduces the pay-out ratio of profits. See, e.g., M. Davenport and J. Wiseman, *Theoretical and Empirical Aspects of Corporate Taxation,* OECD, Paris 1974, and C. McLure, *Must Corporate Income Be Taxed Twice?*, The Brookings Institution, Washington D.C., 1979. On the other hand, Davenport and Wiseman claim that no evidence was provided that the quality apart from the quantity of investment was adversely affected by internal financing.

8. See Krister Andersson: *Possible Implications of Integrating the Corporate and Individual Income Taxes in the United States*, IMF Working Paper, No. 66, 1990.

9. The analytical basis for this view of the corporation tax was developed in Joseph E. Stiglitz: "Taxation, Corporate Financial Policy, and the Cost of Capital", *Journal of Public Economics,* vol. 2, 1973, pp. 1-34.

10. Critics of this so-called "trapped equity view" point out that there may be other ways of distributing cash to shareholders than paying dividends, e.g. share repurchases and take-overs of other firms. However, if dividend taxes can be escaped in these ways, it will tend to <u>reinforce</u> the conclusion that these taxes do not seriously distort corporate investment decisions see Hans-Werner Sinn: "Taxation and the Cost of Capital: The 'Old' View, the 'New' View, and Another View", forthcoming in *Tax Policy and the Economy,* National Bureau of Economic Research, USA.

11. See Alan J. Auerbach: "Taxes, Firm Financial Policy, and the Cost of Capital: An Empirical Analysis". *Journal of Public Economics*, vol. 23, 1984, pp. 27-57.

12. The study referred to is James M. Poterba and Lawrence H. Summers: "The Economic Effects of Dividend Taxation", ch. 9 in: E. Altman and M. Subrahmanyam, eds., *Recent Advance in Corporate Finance*, Homewood, Illinois: Irwin, 1985.

13. According to the standard of comprehensive income taxation, only the <u>real</u> income from capital should be included in the tax base. One of the pragmatic arguments for moving towards proportional taxation of capital income has been that full progressive taxation of nominal capital income, without allowance for inflation-induced capital losses on nominal assets, often results in excessively high marginal effective tax rates on the real rate of return.

14. The "marginal" shareholder is the investor who is indifferent at the margin between investing in shares and investing in alternative assets such as bonds and whose behaviour is therefore in principle governing share prices.

15. In some cases, withholding taxes levied on interest and dividend payments cannot be reclaimed by tax-exempt institutions.

16. The tax rules sketched here are embodied in the recent Norwegian tax reform, and a variant of them was included in the Danish tax reform of 1987.

17. See "The Structure and Reform of Direct Taxation". Report of a Committee chaired by J.E. Meade, IFS, London, 1978.

18. The present analysis focuses on the effects of dividend tax relief on domestic and foreign direct investment by corporations owned by domestic residents. Note, however, that the main effect of changes in dividend taxation may in fact be to shift ownership of shares from one country to another.

19. For an extensive analysis of the effects of the corporate tax system in an open economy, see Robin Boadway and Neil Bruce: "Problems with Integrating Corporate and Personal Income Taxes in an Open Economy", paper presented at the international conference on "Taxation Issues in Open Economies", June 15-16, 1989, at CORE, Louvain-la-Neuve, Belgium.

20. Specific guidelines are suggested in the two OECD reports on "Transfer Pricing and Multinational Enterprises" from 1979 and 1984. Critics of this approach argue that such guidelines tend to make the tax code very complicated and non-transparent, that the rules cannot deal with all the different transactions occurring in practice, and that the economically "correct" arm's length prices are often impossible to identify anyway. These critics therefore propose that the international corporate tax base be apportioned among source countries

according to various formulae, based for instance on the division of sales, property and payroll or some conbination thereof across countries. Such a formula has long been used by many U.S. states to delineate the base for the state corporate income tax.

21. See, e.g. Richard M. Bird and Mitsuo Sato: "International Aspects of the Taxation of Corporations and Shareholders", *IMF Staff Papers*, vol. 22, 1975, pp. 384-455. These suggestions were discussed by the OECD Committee on Fiscal Affairs, and rejected.

22. Assuming that the credit is refundable if there is not sufficient domestic tax to fully offset it.

23. Some credit countries use the deduction method with respect to the amount of withholding taxes paid abroad that exceed their own rate of withholding taxes.

24. Sometimes capital export neutrality is also referred to as "locational neutrality". See Peggy B. Musgrave: "Interjurisdicitional Coordination of Taxes on Capital Income", in Sijbren Cnossen (ed.): *Tax Coordination in the European Community,* Series on International Taxation, No. 7, Kluwer Law and Taxation Publishers.

25. Which, by definition, would allow for the refund of unused credits.

26. This may be explained as follows: Households will tend to increase their savings until the real after-tax rate of return is just sufficient to compensate for the postponement of an additional unit of consumption. Thus, if the net rate of return in country A is 5 per cent per annum, savers in that country will be willing to give up one unit of present consumption in return for 1.05 units of additional consumption one year later. By analogy, if the after-tax rate of return in country B is 10 per cent, savers in B would be willing to give up 1.1 units of extra consumption next year in return for one extra unit of consumption this year. It follows that if one were to increase savings by one unit in country A and reduce it by one unit in country B this year, while transferring 1.1 units of consumption from B to A next year, consumers in B would be just as well off as before, and consumers in A would be better off by an amount of 0.05. Hence the international allocation of savings is inefficient, as long as after-tax rates of return to saving differ across countries.

27. See Thomas Horst: "A Note on the Optimal Taxation of International Investment Income", *Quarterly Journal of Economics*, vol. 94, 1980, pp. 793-798.

28. See Alan A. Auerbach: "The Theory of Excess Burden and Optimal Taxation", ch. 2 in Alan A. Auerbach and Martin S. Feldstein (eds.): *Handbook of Public Economics,* vol. I, North-Holland, Amsterdam, 1985.

29. For further elaboration of this point, see Michael Devereux: *Capital Export Neutrality, Capital Import Neutrality, Capital Ownership Neutrality and All That.* Institute for Fiscal Studies, June 1990.

Chapter 3
A Summary of Corporate and Other Relevant Tax Provisions

A. Introduction

This chapter provides an inventory of corporate and other tax provisions relevant for the calculations of effective tax rates on corporate income. The description relates to the systems in force at 1st January 1991[1]. The main focus is on those tax provisions which apply throughout the economy and to all sectors and activities though in the case of local taxes a "typical" locality has been chosen in some countries. More detailed information is provided in the country chapters (see Annex 4). Section B first provides an overview of the different corporate tax systems applied in different countries; second it examines countries' treatment of the corporate tax base (including depreciation practices, treatment of losses, treatment of inventories and special tax incentives), but in this subsection only the treatment of fixed assets and inventories are covered, intangible assets (such as goodwill) being outside the scope of the report; third section B provides details of schedule rates of tax and on corporate tax collection lags. Section C covers non-corporate taxes on business including net wealth taxes, various local business taxes only partially related to profits and taxes on immovable property and payroll. Section D presents information on personal tax provisions which are relevant for the taxing of profits and Section E provides data on the yield from the various taxes on enterprises.

Of the different taxes summarised in this chapter, only those taxes which are based on corporate profits and dividends are used in the calculations of effective tax rates presented in chapters 4 and 5. Besides the corporate profit tax there are a number of other taxes on enterprises (see Table 3.24). In deciding which of these taxes should be included in calculating the effective tax rates referred to in chapters 4 and 5, it was decided for pragmatic and methodological reasons to restrict these to taxes on profits. Accordingly, the profit element of certain local business taxes are taken into account, but net wealth taxes, immovable property and payroll taxes, financial transaction taxes, as well as those parts of business taxes unrelated to profits are not taken into account. It was also decided that those corporate tax provisions which are relevant to a few countries only (e.g., the treatment of reserves) would be excluded from the calculations. It should be noted, however, that some of these taxes (e.g., on the net wealth of corporations) are close substitutes for profit-related taxes. Of taxes on individuals, only those income and capital gains taxes which are levied on interest, dividends and capital gains on shares are included in the calculations of effective tax rates. At a more general level, the calculations do not take account of either differences across countries in tax collection lags or country differences in enforcement rules and tax compliance.

B. Corporate Tax Provisions
The tax treatment of dividends under corporate and personal income tax systems

Table 3.1 provides a classification of countries in relation to their tax treatment of dividends under the personal and corporate income tax (see Appendix to Chapter 1 for definitions of terminology used). The table indicates the systems applied by <u>central</u> governments of OECD countries as at 1st January 1991. However, corporate tax systems at subordinate levels of government do not always reduce or eliminate economic double taxation. Consequently, table 3.1 may overstate the overall reduction of economic double taxation in countries which have important local or state corporate income taxes, or which have analogous taxes at subordinate levels of government (e.g. the German Gewerbesteuer).

Attention is drawn also to a number of limitations or simplifications in table 3.1, some of which are indicated in the footnotes to the table:

— It does not give any information about the amount of mitigation (for this see Annex 2);

— It neglects targeted rather than general shareholder reliefs as exist, for example, in France and the United Kingdom and also relatively small reliefs as exist in Spain.

The classical system featured in the left hand column of Table 3.1 is one in which profits distributed to resident individual shareholders are fully or almost fully liable to both corporation tax and personal income tax. Luxembourg, the Netherlands, Switzerland and the United States have had a classical system for many years and in 1989 Belgium has also adopted this system as a general rule (see note 2 to table 3.1).

Systems reducing as distinct from eliminating the double taxation of dividends are divided into countries which provide the reduction at company level and those which provide it at shareholder level. At company level, the reduction may be made through a lower rate (split-rate system — column 2 of Table 3.1) or as deduction from the tax base (dividend deduction system — column 3 of Table 3.1). As at January 1991, only Germany uses the split-rate system but until recently it was also in operation in Austria, Japan and Portugal. As at January 1991, the dividend deduction system is in operation in Iceland, Spain and Sweden, but until recently it was also in operation in Finland.

There are also two methods of reducing economic double taxation at shareholder level: partial imputation systems (column 4 of Table 3.1) and partial shareholder relief schemes (column 5 of Table 3.1). Under partial imputation systems the tax credit given to the shareholder is added to the dividends that he has received, and his personal income tax is calculated on the basis of the grossed-up amount for which he receives a credit of a specified amount. The amount of credit granted to the shareholder is a function of the corporation tax actually paid by the company on its profits. As at January 1991, this system applies in France; in Ireland and the United Kingdom where the amount of credit is a function of the advanced corporation tax (ACT).

Under partial shareholder relief schemes a tax allowance of a fixed percentage of the dividend received by resident shareholders in domestic equities is given, irrespective of whether or not corporate tax has been paid by the company distributing the profits. Alternatively, in Denmark (since 1990) and Japan the relief may take the form of a lower rate of tax on dividend income compared to other kinds of income instead of a percentage credit on the dividend received. As of January 1991, this system operates in Austria, Canada, Denmark, Iceland (see footnote to table 3.1), Japan and Portugal and until recently operated in Belgium. A further difference between partial imputation systems and partial shareholder relief schemes is that under the former system, the taxpayer may receive a payment from the government where the tax credit exceeds personal income tax liabilities, whereas this is not possible under partial relief schemes.

Systems eliminating economic double taxation may also be given at either company level or shareholder level. At company level, this is done by not subjecting distributed profits to the corporate tax. As at 1st January 1991, this is done in Greece and in Norway (central government only). At shareholder level under full imputation systems, the entire tax paid by the company on its distributed profits is credited against the shareholder's personal income tax liability. As at 1st January 1991, this system operates in Australia, Finland, Germany, Italy and New Zealand. The practical difference between elimination of economic double taxation at company level and at shareholder level is that in the former case no tax is levied on distributions, whereas in the latter it is levied at company level and refunded at shareholder level.

Table 3.2 shows the following features of imputation systems:

— In all countries [i.e. Australia, Finland, France (with exceptions, see footnote), Germany, Ireland, Italy, New Zealand and the United Kingdom] a company is liable to tax in respect of distributed profits which are exempted from, or have no liability to, the "standard" corporation tax or which are taxed at a lower rate. In Italy, the distributing company withholds the amount of tax from the dividends paid out of profits which have been exempt or taxed at a lower rate;

— Ordering rules for profit distributions have to be established under imputation systems (see Column 2). The profits that are taxed at the highest rate (domestic profits that have actually been taxed at the standard rate) are usually assumed to be those that are distributed first (which tends to lessen the effects in respect of dividends tax, to the taxpayer's advantage);

— In five countries (France, Germany, Ireland, Italy and the United Kingdom), but not Australia or New Zealand, the credit can be paid to a resident shareholder (individual) to the extent that it exceeds his actual total tax liability (see Column 8). In New Zealand, however, it may be converted into a tax loss to be carried forward.

It should also be mentioned that under imputation systems, when a company collects dividends (from a "portfolio" investment) on which it is liable for corporation tax, it can, just like an individual shareholder, impute the tax credit to its tax liability on the dividends collected, and is entitled to a refund if the credit exceeds its actual tax liability. However, the situation is different if the dividends relate to direct investment. In most countries the dividends that a company pays to its parent company (or to a company that has a major stake in it) are exempted from corporation tax at the level of the parent company (under the so-called rule of "ties of affiliation"). When a company (and particularly a parent company) collects dividends (on which it has not paid corporation tax) which it then redistributes to its own shareholders (who can impute the tax credit against their own tax) under the above-mentioned rule, it must pay tax; however, in France, Ireland and the United Kingdom, a company that redistributes dividends received can impute the tax credits to which it is entitled to the tax it pays in respect of dividends. A major reform occurred in France concerning the equalisation tax. As of January 1st 1990, French holding companies with foreign participation whose exclusive purpose is the holding of shares have been exempt from equalisation tax, provided:

— two-thirds of their assets consist in a 10 per cent or more participation in foreign companies;

— two thirds of their income (other than capital gains) is derived from their foreign participation.

Since no equalisation tax is paid, the shareholder is not entitled to the imputation credit.

The pros and cons of the various systems, together with some government statements on why it was decided to change their system, are provided in Chapter 6, along with a list of changes in government attitudes towards economic double taxation over the last three decades.

Measuring the tax base

Taxable income is generally calculated in similar ways under the corporate tax systems of OECD Member countries. Income arising from all sources, including business or trading income, as well as non-business income, is normally included in the corporate tax base. Although the concept of income is usually not defined, taxable income is as a rule computed on the ordinary principles of "sound commercial accounting practice" and is generally based on the profits shown in the company accounts (see, however, chapter 6.B.4). In order to get to taxable profit used for tax purposes some adjustments are often required by statute.

The general rule is that all expenses wholly and exclusively incurred in earning taxable income and in maintaining the assets used in the company's activity are deductible.

Treatment of intercorporate dividends. Intercorporate dividends received from domestic subsidiaries are normally not subject to any additional taxes and either are exempt or give rise to "indirect" tax credits. Table 3.3 outlines the treatment of cash dividends received from domestic subsidiaries, which have not been subjected to any anti-avoidance measures under corporation income tax. It is assumed that the minimum holding period and other requirements for the preferential treatment are met. The rules applying to withholding taxes on international dividend payments are outlined in table 3.15.

Treatment of capital gains. The rules governing the taxation of corporate capital gains are summarised in Table 3.4. Most countries provide for taxation of corporate capital gains at the full corporate tax rate, though a number of countries exempt capital gains which are reinvested in the corporation.

Anti-avoidance measures. Several countries have measures for currently taxing (i.e. avoiding deferral) certain income of overseas subsidiaries, in the absence of declaration of any dividend (Australia, Canada, France, Germany, Japan, New Zealand, Sweden, United Kingdom, United States).

Treatment of investment grants and other general investment reliefs. There are different ways of providing such reliefs: allowances, where the whole or part of the investment cost is deductible from taxable income and credits, which are deducted from tax liability, and which may take the form either of a non-wasteable credit which is paid out to the company to the extent the credit exceeds the tax liability, or a wastable credit which is not. Incentive provisions can and often do take the form of cash grants. Most countries do not provide such reliefs but, as Table 3.5 indicates, there are exceptions. Allowances are available in Austria, Belgium, Finland, Greece, Iceland, Netherlands, Sweden and Turkey and credits are available in Luxembourg and Spain. General cash grants are not provided in any OECD country.[2]

Treatment of reserves. Some countries operate special corporate reserve schemes in which contributions to the reserves are deductible from taxable income. Because of their complexity and differences in objectives between countries (for example, reserves are used for pension purposes in Germany, for bad debts and retirement reserves in Japan) these reserve provisions are not taken into account in the remainder of this report.

Deferral. A number of countries operate special tax relief schemes in which tax payments are deferred, for example in relation to export earnings or income from special development areas (e.g. in Ireland in the case of special development areas, and in Italy).

Branch income and group taxation. Corporations generally include the results of overseas branches in their tax computation. Some countries exclude overseas branch profits if they are subject to tax locally. Others, such as Germany, exclude the profits of branches situated in tax-treaty countries. France is a country using the territorial principle under which overseas branch establishments, having a certain power of local decision even if located in tax havens, are outside the scope of the corporation income tax. Group taxation of corporations is available in a number of OECD countries.

Treatment of foreign source income. The main rules governing the treatment of foreign source income are outlined in Tables 3.6 (treaty countries) and 3.7 (non-treaty countries). It should be noted that almost all countries apply special provisions under special circumstances which diverge from the main rules shown in these tables (e.g. dividends received may be exempt if more than a specified proportion of shares or voting power is held). The tax treatment of foreign source income in the resident country can take a number of forms.

Under what is generally refered to as the exemption method, foreign income is exempt in the hands of the parent — so the tax in the source country, the withholding tax and any personal taxes due by the financiers of the parent company are the only taxes charged.

More commonly, a credit for foreign tax paid by the subsidiary may be given to the parent. Under the credit method, the total tax paid already (both the corporate tax in the source country and the withholding tax) is compared to the tax which would have been paid had the profits been generated domestically. If the foreign tax is higher than the domestic tax, no further tax is levied. If the foreign tax is lower, then the additional tax is levied by the resident country to leave the overall tax paid equal to the tax which would have been paid had the investment been entirely domestic. There are a number of broad variants of the credit method. One is to make comparisons on a country by country basis. Other limitations may be by reference to source or item of income, or by type of income (the so-called "basket approach"). Another method is to aggregate all foreign source income and foreign tax to make an overall comparision (the worldwide basis).

Clearly, the granting of credit on a worldwide basis is more generous than the granting of a credit on a country by country basis. If a company invested in both a low tax and a high tax country, then where the system was credit by source, the company would pay no extra tax on the profits from the high tax country, but would pay the excess tax on the profits from the low tax country. If the system were the worldwide credit, the "extra" tax paid in the high tax country could be used to offset the additional tax due on the profits from the low tax country.

Apart from exemption and credit methods, two other approaches to the taxation of foreign source income are occasionally used within the OECD. One is the use of a deduction system, under which tax is charged on the foreign source income, but in determining the tax base in the resident country the foreign tax paid is deducted. The other type of tax treatment of receipts by a parent from foreign subsidiaries is to exempt a proportion of the receipts, but to tax the remainder through the deduction system.

Table 3.6 summarises the tax treatment of foreign source income by OECD countries where the repatriation of profits is from a country with which the residence country of the parent has a tax treaty.

Where there is no treaty between the source and residence countries, the tax treatment of foreign source income is often less favourable. Table 3.7 gives the tax treatment of foreign source income where the treatment of non-treaty countries differs from that of treaty countries, together with a list of the non-treaty countries within the OECD area.

Deductions from the tax base

Treatment of losses. All countries allow a company to carry forward trading losses and eight OECD countries (Canada, France, Germany, Ireland, Japan, the Netherlands, United Kingdom, United States) allow a carry back of trading losses, varying from 1 to 3 years (see Table 3.8). The number of years over which trading losses can be carried forward ranges from five years to indefinitely.

Depreciation practices. An allowance for the depreciation of assets is available in all countries (see Tables 3.9 to 3.11). These tables refer to the treatment of assets in the manufacturing sector. The classification of countries' depreciation systems in a few groups as provided in the tables necessarily gives only a rough impression of the systems actually applied as a number of special provisions and exceptions have been omitted.[3] Table 3.9 provides a summary of actual depreciation systems as they are described in the country chapters. In a number of cases, the depreciation method is optional, and the rate varies over time for a given asset and between different types of assets. Tables 3.10 and 3.11, therefore, describe the information actually used in the calculations presented in Chapters 4 and 5.

A neutral depreciation system would provide depreciation for tax purposes corresponding as closely as possible to economic depreciation which takes into account the wearing out of assets, as well as obsolescence. If this objective is not achieved, effective tax rates will tend to vary between different assets — and for the same kind of asset over time. Accurate measurement of economic depreciation is technically and administratively very difficult and most countries therefore utilise some standardised depreciation rules (e.g. straight line or declining balance, see below). The yearly amount of depreciation on a given asset (and thereby the rate of depreciation) will be influenced by the choice of useful tax life of the asset. The useful tax life is generally determined for the main types of assets, although in some countries it may follow accepted accounting practices.

A variety of systems are used in different countries, the most frequently used method being straight-line depreciation (equal allowances over the length of the tax life of the asset) and declining balance (e.g. as a fixed percentage of depreciated book value); in the latter case the actual allowance will be larger in the initial year and gradually diminish in subsequent years.

It is apparent that, for example, 10 per cent straight line is more generous than 10 per cent declining balance. Consequently, declining balance depreciation is generally given at higher rates than straight line depreciation, and where countries give companies a choice about which method of depreciation to use, the declining balance rate is usually two or three times the straight line rate. Of relevance in this context is that some countries allow for periodical revaluations of assets which affect the base for depreciation.

A few countries give an extra first year allowance for new investments and this allowance does not reduce the depreciation base. These schemes are not the same as accelerated depreciation (see below). In Spain, for example, a company may deduct in the first year 3 per cent of the costs of a new building from their taxable profits (the normal depreciation) and 5 per cent in the form of the extra first year allowance, making a total of 8 per cent. However, the extra allowance does not reduce the original value of the asset to be depreciated (at the end of the first year 97 per cent).

Machinery is generally depreciated through the declining balance method except in Austria, Greece, Iceland and Italy which allow only the straight line method. For buildings the straight line method is the more common way of depreciation, although ten countries (Belgium, Canada, Finland, Italy, Japan, the

Netherlands, Norway, Spain, Switzerland, Turkey) allow also or only the declining balance method. If the tax authorities allow the declining balance method, in some cases a change to the straight line method is allowed or prescribed. The rate of depreciation for machinery varies between 8 per cent and 25 per cent on a straight line basis and between 15 per cent and around 60 per cent on a declining balance basis. The rate of depreciation for buildings varies between 1.5 per cent and 10 per cent on a straight line basis, and between 4 per cent and approximately 10 per cent on a declining balance basis.

Incentives granted in this field may take the form of <u>accelerated depreciation,</u> e.g. by allowing, in the early years of the useful life of the asset, depreciation at a higher rate than is justified on purely technical or economic grounds (this is sometimes known as initial allowance). The following countries operate accelerated depreciation systems: Germany (for small companies only), Ireland (though schemes are being phased out), Italy, Japan (for environmental and energy investment), Luxembourg (for environmental and energy investment), Portugal, Spain (only under certain conditions and in certain sectors) and Switzerland (for environmental and energy investment).

An attempt has been made in Table 3.12 to provide a quantitative illustration of the differences in depreciation systems applied in different countries. The table shows <u>net present values</u> of hypothetical streams of depreciation allowances generated within Member countries by an investment of 100 units of local currency in industrial buildings and machinery, using as discount rate a nominal interest rate (calculated as the actual inflation rate in each country[4] plus a common real interest rate of 3 per cent, see col. 1 and 4), the average nominal interest rate in OECD countries (col. 2 and 5) and a common real interest rate of 3 per cent [i.e. inflation is assumed to be nil in all countries (see col. 3 and 6)].

The calculations are based on the stream of depreciation allowances generated over the period that it takes for the asset to be fully depreciated. For the sake of simplicity, where countries use the declining balance method of depreciation, full depreciation has been taken to mean until 99 percent of the initial cost of the asset has been depreciated — except in the case of Japan where assets can only be depreciated up to 95 percent of their acquisition cost. The table is based on the information contained in Tables 3.9 to 3.11.

In order to isolate the impact of differences in depreciation systems as such, the calculations in columns 2 and 5 have been carried out using an OECD average rate of interest as discount rate. It could be held, however, that the rate of inflation in itself will influence the design of depreciation system. Consequently, results using rates which take into account actual inflation are also shown in the table (columns 1 and 4).

It appears that there are substantial differences across countries in the real value of depreciation allowances. However, the depreciation system is only one among many elements determining total effective tax rates on corporate investment.

<u>Treatment of inventories</u>. There are a variety of methods to value stock for tax purposes (e.g. actual cost, weighted average price, LIFO, FIFO, indexed FIFO, etc.) but basically these methods are variants of the LIFO/FIFO methods. Under the FIFO method the first items purchased are assumed to be disposed of first, whereas under the LIFO method the items last acquired are assumed to have been disposed first when the cost of sales from inventories is evaluated. The principal difference between the two systems is that where FIFO is used, increases in the value of inventories solely due to inflation are taxed, whereas with LIFO they are not. Inventories can be valued at the FIFO method in all countries with exception of Germany (see Table 3.13). The LIFO method is allowed in 13 countries (Austria, Belgium, Denmark, France, Germany, Greece, Italy, Japan, Luxembourg, the Netherlands, Portugal, Switzerland, United States) although five (Austria, Belgium, Denmark, Finland, France, Luxembourg) impose some restrictions on the use of this method. All OECD countries allow actual cost valuation where this method is feasible.

In the calculations of effective tax rates presented in chapters 4 and 5 the use of the most advantageous method is assumed, i.e. use of the FIFO method is assumed in all countries except Germany, Greece, Iceland, Italy, Japan, the Netherlands, Portugal, Switzerland and the United States, where it is assumed. Most inflationary gains are untaxed.

<u>Research and development</u>. Current expenditures on research and development are generally deductible in the year in which they are incurred, except in the Netherlands where in some cases (e.g. research or

patents which have been bought) costs must be spread over a number of years. Research assets qualify for accelerated depreciation or shorter agreed useful lives in a number of countries (e.g. in the United Kingdom.), whereas others (e.g. France) apply special tax credits, but mostly the general rules apply.

Corporate tax rates

Table 3.14 gives information on corporate tax rates. Where countries have additional national levies, these are included in the national tax rates. Some countries have different tax rates on retained profits and distributed profits. Half of OECD Member countries have intermediate or local government corporate taxes on corporate profits. The figures given in column three and four of table 3.14 have to be interpreted in the light of column five, which indicates whether the state and local taxes are deducted from the tax base when calculating the national tax to be paid. For example, the overall tax rate in Germany on retained earnings is $(1-0.50)0.13+0.50 = 0.565$. The final column in table 3.14 gives the imputation rate for countries with imputation systems defined as the credit as per cent of dividends plus the credit.

The overall tax rates shown in column six of table 3.14 have been used in the calculations of effective tax rates in chapters 4 and 5. For Switzerland, using a multiple rate system, the typical overall rate used in the calculations is 31.5 per cent. The overall corporate income tax rate levied on a company is between 30 per cent and 56.5 per cent, except for manufacturing profits in Ireland.

Rates of corporation tax at federal/central government level. All countries have corporation taxes at the central government level. The rates vary from 23 per cent to 50 per cent, except in Ireland (manufacturing only) and Switzerland where they are much lower. Lower rates are also provided for small businesses or firms making small profits in Belgium, Canada, Finland, Japan, Switzerland, the United Kingdom and the United States.

Rates of corporation tax at subordinate levels of government. Three OECD countries (Canada, Switzerland, United States) levy tax at the intermediate government level, while ten countries (Austria, Finland, Germany, Italy, Japan, Luxembourg, Norway, Portugal, Switzerland, United States) levy a tax at the local level. In some countries (Canada, Finland, Germany, Japan, Luxembourg, Switzerland, United States) the rates at the intermediate level and local level vary from region to region. For the purpose of this report, either a specific region or an average is chosen (see country chapters). In Austria, company profits are subject to a "Gewerbesteuer" levied at the federal level in addition to the corporate income tax, but almost half of the tax revenue is collected on behalf of local communities (see country chapter for details).

Withholding taxes on international interest and dividend payments. Tables 3.15 and 3.16 provide information on the treaty rates of taxes withheld on cross-border payments of dividends and interest, respectively. The tables give the withholding tax rates on flows from companies based in one country to those based in another, for dividends and interest payments respectively, taking into account double taxation treaties.

Withholding taxes are often levied at different rates according to the size of the participation by the resident company. Generally, the higher the proportion of a company owned by another company, the lower is the withholding tax rate. Tables 3.15 and 3.16 presuppose that the subsidiary is wholly owned by the parent company, and so the withholding tax rates are the lowest possible on direct investments from one country into another.[5] The withholding taxes in Tables 3.15 and 3.16 are the input parameters that are used to calculate the transnational effective tax rates in chapter 5.

Corporate tax collection lags

The effective tax burden on a corporation is determined by the way the tax base is calculated, by nominal tax rates and by the time lag between the income year and the tax actually paid to the tax authorities. As Table 3.17 illustrates, there are substantial differences across countries in the way tax payments are arranged. It should be noted that the instalment provisions applied in some countries may imply a tax refund after the end of the fiscal year.

C.   Non-corporate taxes on business

Net wealth taxes on corporations. Such taxes are levied in (see Table 3.18) Austria, Canada, Germany, Iceland, Luxembourg, Norway, Switzerland and Turkey. The statutory rates vary between 0.2 per cent and 1.5 per cent but the effective rate is generally lower due to the valuation rules for the base of the wealth tax as well as exemptions from the base.

Non-profit related or partially related taxes. A number of countries levy local taxes on business which are only partially or indirectly related to business profits. Such taxes are usually levied by lower levels of governments, and may constitute an important source of revenue for these levels of governments. The most important examples of such taxes are the German "Gewerbesteuer" and the French "Taxe professionelle." Others exist in Austria, Iceland and Luxembourg (for details, see country chapters) and the profit element in these schemes (if any) are also taken into account in the calculations presented in chapters 4 and 5.

Taxes on immovable property. These taxes exist in almost all OECD countries. The base of the tax is usually the capital value of the property although in a few countries (e.g. the United Kingdom) the annual rental value is used. Immovable property taxes on business are invariably local taxes (although in the United Kingdom the tax rate is set nationally and revenues are allocated to local governments). and are usually limited to buildings and land (with Japan and a few states in the United States including machinery and equipment). The tax rates, which may vary, are determined within certain limits by local governments. These taxes are invariably allowed as a deductible expense under the corporate income tax.

Taxes on payroll. In all countries except Australia, Denmark and New Zealand there are also very large employer "payroll taxes" used to finance social security benefits. In addition (or in the case of Australia alternatively) a number of countries apply taxes on payroll and/or work force paid by employers, employees or the self-employed either as a proportion of payroll or as a fixed amount per person, and which are not earmarked for social security expenditure. These taxes are, however, only of some revenue importance (measured as a percentage of total taxes in 1989) in Australia (5.7 per cent), Austria (6.0 per cent), Iceland (3.2 per cent) and Sweden (3.3 per cent). It should be added that apart from payroll taxes a number of other non-wage labour costs exist in all countries (e.g. fringe benefits, social security contributions, contributions to private pension schemes) and that these can form a significant part of the remuneration package.

D. Relevant taxes on individuals
Personal income taxes

The personal tax rates given in Table 3.19 reflect the highest statutory tax rate on dividends and interest receipts, and where data are available, the *average* marginal tax rate on dividends and interest payments are also given. Several countries have provisions whereby personal taxes on dividends are lower than the statutory rate. For example, Austria charges only half the statutory tax rate on dividends, so a top-rate taxpayer who would pay 50 per cent on earned income pays only 25 per cent on dividends.

Withholding tax on interest payments to individuals. A withholding tax on interest for resident individuals is levied in fourteen countries (Austria, Belgium, Finland, France, Greece, Ireland, Italy, Japan, New Zealand, Portugal, Spain, Sweden, Switzerland, Turkey) ranging between 10 per cent and 35 per cent (see table 3.20 column A). In Germany a 10 per cent withholding tax on interest was abolished as of July 1st 1989. In Belgium, France and Portugal, the receiver of interest can choose the withholding tax as the final tax paid.

Withholding tax on dividend payments to individuals. All countries except Australia, Canada, France, Iceland, Ireland, the United Kingdom and the United States levy a withholding tax on dividends paid to resident individuals ranging between 10 per cent and 50 per cent (see table 3.20, column B). In Belgium and Portugal the shareholder can choose the withholding tax as the final tax paid.

A number of countries (e.g. Denmark and the United States) require banks and other financial institutions to automatically provide the tax authorities with information on interest and dividend payments to individuals. These arrangements are seen as a substitute for or a supplement to withholding tax regimes.[6]

Capital gains taxes[7]

Capital gains tax rates are given in Table 3.21. The tax rates shown in the table apply to capital gains on quoted shares. A number of countries do not tax capital gains at all. Of those that do, Australia, Iceland, Ireland, Spain and the UK tax only real capital gains (and so ignore those nominal capital gains which occur because of inflation).

A complication is that several countries have different capital gains tax rates according to how long assets are held before any gains are realised. For example, Denmark taxes capital gains only if assets are sold within three years of their purchase. Even more generally, all countries who tax capital gains in practice only tax *realised* capital gains. Tax on the capital gains can therefore be deferred into the future. Generally, the rules described in the table apply to minority shareholders only, and only to corporations, quoted on the stock exchange.

Australia has a franked dividend system, which in effect means that companies have a choice as to how they give shareholders a capital gain in the value of the company. If they wish, companies may issue new equity to existing shareholders up to the value of the capital gain. These shares may be issued fully franked to shareholders which means that the tax treatment of new equity and of retention finance is the same as that of debt. As long as an Australian company makes full use of franked dividends for all of its capital gains (as is assumed here), all finance types are treated in the same way in the Australian tax system.

Net wealth taxes[7]

Table 3.21 shows that net wealth taxes on individuals are levied in Austria, Denmark, Finland, France, Germany, Iceland, Luxembourg, Netherlands, Norway, Spain, Sweden and Switzerland with rates ranging from 0.118 to 3 per cent.

Financial transaction taxes[7]

A number of countries operate financial transaction taxes on issues and purchases of shares. These taxes, which can be important in the financing decisions of corporations, are not included in the calculations in Chapters 4 and 5.

Tax compliance

There are differences across countries in tax compliance and in enforcement practices as well as in policies towards exchange of information which could modify the effective tax rates calculated in the following chapters[8].

Other non-tax related information relevant for the calculation of effective tax rates

Annex 5 provides supplementary information and other data necessary to calculate effective corporate tax rates. The data in question relate to the inflation rate, direct investment flows and weights on the structure of corporate assets, and on the structure of financing sources.

E.   Tax revenues from corporate profits

It is helpful in assessing the potential distortion on capital formation, to know what is the overall importance of taxes on corporations in different countries and how this tax burden has changed over time. Although the corporate income tax is in most countries the most important tax on corporate profits, its contribution to total government tax revenue is generally small, although far from insignificant. Chart 3.1 shows the unweighted average shares of different taxes in the total tax yield. In 1989 the corporate tax accounted for less than 10 per cent of total tax revenues, which is much lower than the relative share of the personal income tax, social security contributions and consumption taxes, although slightly higher than taxes on property.

The average figures conceal a wide degree of differences in country positions. Chart 3.2 shows that the yield from the corporate tax in 1989 ranged from a low of just under 3 per cent in Iceland to a high of 24 per cent in Japan. Australia, Luxembourg, Turkey and the United Kingdom have percentages above 10. The United Kingdom figures include revenue from petroleum revenue tax.

Over the last decade, the relative revenue contribution of the corporate tax has increased in seventeen countries, sometimes significantly so, with the OECD unweighted average raising from 7.5 to 7.8 per cent (see table 3.23).

In terms of the level of corporate tax burden as measured by the tax-to-GDP ratio, the corporate tax accounts, on average, for less than three per cent of GDP, with countries ranging from a low of 1.0 per cent in Iceland to 7.5 per cent in Japan and Luxembourg (see table 3.24).

The yield from the corporate income tax is not, however, an accurate guide to the total tax on corporate profits. Account also has to be taken of the personal income tax paid on distributed profits. Unfortunately data on these payments are not easily obtained. Although Chapters 4 and 5 of this report examine profit related taxes only, the reader should be aware that countries make varying use of the other taxes paid by enterprises, including corporations. Thus in all countries employers have to pay payroll taxes and in some countries taxes on business property also, including net wealth and property taxes. An indication of the relative importance of the taxes paid by enterprises is provided in table 3.25. This table entirely ignores the question of how these taxes are shifted and also does not take into account consumption taxes.

Notes and References

1.   Note, however, that as regards the rates of withholding taxes specified in tax treaties, the rates applied in this report refer, in Belgium and Ireland to the treaty rates as known at December 1990.

2.   A number of countries provide selective tax reliefs and/or cash grants to promote investment in specific sectors or for specific activities.

3.   See for example, *International Comparison of Tax Depreciation Practices,* OECD, Paris 1975.

4.   OECD estimates for the year 1991. It should be noted that using the inflation rate for just one year may substantially affect the results to the extent that these forecasts are not necessarily representative of long-run inflation rates.

5.   Withholding taxes on payments to individuals often differ from those to companies.

6.   For details, see *Taxpayers' Rights and Obligations: A Survey of the Legal Situation in OECD Countries,* OECD, Paris 1990.

7.   For more details on these taxes, see *Taxation of Net Wealth, Capital Transfers and Capital Gains of Individuals,* OECD, Paris 1988.

8.   For a survey of compliance powers, see *Taxpayers' Rights and Obligations: A Survey of the Legal Situation in OECD Countries,* OECD, Paris 1990.

Table 3.1 **Degree of Reduction of Economic Double Taxation (Central Government)**

None or very little reduction	Reduction of economic double taxation				Elimination of economic double taxation	
	Corporate level		Shareholder level		Corporate level	Shareholder level
1	2	3	4	5	6	7
Classical system(1)	Split rate system	Partial dividend deduction system	Partial imputation system	Partial shareholder relief schemes	Zero rate system	Full imputation system or full shareholder relief system
	Lower tax rate on distributed income	Partial deduction of dividends paid	Partial credit for corporate tax paid	Partial credit for domestic shareholders	Zero tax rate on distribted income	Full credit for corporate tax paid (imputation system)
Belgium (2)	Germany (3)	Iceland (4)	France (7)	Austria (8)	Greece	Australia
Luxembourg		Spain (5)	Ireland	Canada	Norway	Finland
Netherlands		Sweden (6)	United Kingdom	Denmark		Germany (3) (9)
Switzerland				Iceland(4)		Italy
United States				Japan		New Zealand
				Portugal		Turkey (10)
				Turkey (10)		

1. In most of these countries (and in those with reduction at the corporate level) some small degree of reduction is given to shareholders in the form of a relatively low exemption for dividends received.
2. Belgium has moved from a shareholder relief system to a classical system but continues to provide relief to shareholders who invest their dividends in their own professional activity (the use of a so-called mitigation technique to encourage retentions rather than distribution).
3. Systems in column nos. 2 and 7 are both operative in Germany.
4. The deductions for dividends paid may in some cases fully offset the corporate income tax and also the personal income tax, especially for dividends up to 15 per cent of capital value. Dividends exceeding this limit are fully taxed at both levels. Hence, Iceland is classified both under column 3 and 5.
5. Spain should strictly speaking be shown under column 5 as well as column 3 but as the credit to the shareholder is only 10 per cent (and much lower than other countries in column 5, it has been disregarded on *de minimus* grounds.
6. The deduction for dividends paid may in some cases result in elimination of the corporate tax (for dividends on newly issued shares, maximum 10% per year of the value of the issue with an overall maximum equal to the total value of the issue).
7. France is sometimes described as having approached elimination rather than mitigation of the economic double taxation, as shown in the table, because whilst the rate of corporation tax has been substantially reduced the amount of credit has not changed, but on the other hand since 1989 retained profits have become subject to a lower rate than distributed profits (currently 34 and 42 per cent respectively);
8. As from 1986 dividends paid to residents are taxed at half the normal rate in the hands of the shareholder. The split rate system (column 2) was abolished as from 1989.
9. Germany belongs to the extreme right of the table in over-compensating for the economic double taxation of dividends by giving both full imputation to the shareholder and subjecting distributed profits to a lower corporate rate than retained profits. On the other hand no credit to the shareholder is given for the payment of the local business tax.
10. No personal tax is charged on dividends distributed out of profits which have borne corporation tax which means in practice that the relief is sometimes partial, sometimes complete. This is why Turkey is shown in both columns 5 and 7.

Table 3.2 Description of imputation systems where resident shareholders are given full or partial credit for corporation tax paid
(1st January 1991) (1)

Country	Tax levied in respect of distributed profits not bearing "standard" corporation tax	Ordering rules for profit distribution	Tax credit for domestic corporate shareholders	
			Portfolio	Direct
Australia	Yes, at the shareholder level	Dividends required to be franked to the maximum extent possible	No, But rebate of tax for domestic dividends received by resident companies (rebate equal to the tax on this income) except for unfranked dividends recived by private companies	No
Finland	Yes	Highest-in-first-out	Yes	Yes
France	Yes(2), also on profits retained more than 5 years	Current profit; previous four years, profit (FIFO); profits subject to equalisation tax	Yes	No(2), but dividends from 95% + holding exempt. Tax credit deductible from equalisation tax on redistribution
Germany	Yes	Highest-in-first-out	Yes	Yes
Ireland	Yes. Profits of manufacturing companies taxed at the special rate of 10% carry a reduced credit	Proportional to corporate tax rates	No, dividends exempt. Tax credit deductible from equalisation tax upon redistribution.	Yes
Italy	Yes(3)	Not necessary	Yes	Yes
New Zealand	Yes	Not necessary	No, dividends exempt	No, dividends exempt
United Kingdom	Yes, through Advance Corporation Tax (ACT)	Not necessary	No, dividends not liable to corporation tax, tax credit franks ACT on redistribution. No ACT on intra-group dividends.	No, dividends exempt, Tax credit deductible from ACT on redistribution. No ACT on intra-group dividends.

C   Capital
VR Voting rights
1) This table refers to the countries indicated in Columns 4 and 7 of table 3.1(a).
2) As of January 1 1990, however there is an exemption of equalisation tax for holding companies under the following conditions:
   — the exclusive purpose of the companies is the holding of shares
   — 2/3 of their assets consist of a 10% or more participation in foreign companies -
   2/3 of their income is derived from their foreign participation. As a consequence the shareholder shall not receive the imputation credit, but the companies transfer their tax credits to the shareholders.
3) The equalization tax is withheld by the company from the dividends paid out of exempt profits or profits taxed at a lower rate.
4) But conversion of any excess imputation, credit into a tax loss to be carried forward.
5) A commentary on these columns is provided at the end of Chapter 6.

Table 3.2 (cont) **Description of imputation systems where resident shareholders are given full or partial credit for corporation tax paid**
(1st January 1991) (1)

| Country | Tax credit for foreign shareholders (under bilateral treaties)(5) | | | Refund to domestic shareholder if tax credit exceeds income tax | |
| | Individual | Corporate | | Individual | Exempt entity |
		Portfolio	Direct		
Australia	No	No	No	No	No
	However, no dividends withholdings tax is payable on fully franked dividends				
Finland	No	No	No	Yes	No
France	Yes: Australia Austria Belgium Finland Germany Japan Luxembourg Netherlands New Zealand Norway Spain Sweden Switzerland UK US. Refund of compensatory tax under all other treaties, and to all direct corporate share-holders under any treaty.	Yes: Austria<10%C, Finland<10%C Germany ,10%C Japan<15%VR Luxem.<25%C Netherlands<5%C N.Zealand<10%C Norway<10%C Spain<25%C Sweden<25%C Switz.<20%C UK<10%C US<15%VR		Yes	No
Germany	No	No	No	Yes	No
Ireland	Yes: Australia Austria New Zealand Sweden Switzerland UK	Yes: Australia<10%VR Austria<25%VR N.Zealand<10%VR Sweden<10%VR Switz.<25%VR UK<10%VR	No	Yes	Yes
Italy	No, except UK	No except UK<10%C	Half credit: UK	Yes	No
New Zealand	No	No	No	No(4)	No
United Kingdom	Yes: Australia Austria Belgium Canada Denmark Finland France Ireland Italy Japan Luxembourg Netherlands New Zealand Norway Spain Sweden Switzerland and US	<10%C Austria Belgium Canada Denmark Finland France Ireland Italy Japan Luxembourg Netherlands Norway Spain Sweden Switzerland US	Yes: Belgium Canada Denmark Finland Italy Luxembourg Netherlands Norway Sweden Switzerland US	Yes	Yes

C   Capital
VR   Voting rights
1)   This table refers to the countries indicated in Columns 4 and 7 of table 3.1(a).
2)   As of January 1 1990, however there is an exemption of equalisation tax for holding companies under the following conditions:
  -    the exclusive purpose of the companies is the holding of shares
  -    2/3 of their assets consist of a 10% or more participation in foreign companies -
       2/3 of their income is derived from their foreign participation. As a consequence the shareholder shall not receive the imputation credit, but the companies transfer their tax credits to the shareholders.
3)   The equalization tax is withheld by the company from the dividends paid out of exempt profits or profits taxed at a lower rate.
4)   But conversion of any excess imputation, credit into a tax loss to be carried forward.
5)   A commentary on these columns is provided at the end of Chapter 6.

Table 3.3. **The tax treatment of cash dividend received from domestic subsidiaries**

Australia	Exempt in effect (tax credit)
Austria	Exempt
Belgium	Net dividend (assumed 90% of gross - or 85% of gross for holding companies) exempt
Canada	Exempt
Denmark	Exempt (25% holding minimum)
Finland	Exempt in effect
France	Exempt (10% holding minimum) but add back to taxable income 5% of gross dividend equal to 7.5% of cash dividend (limited to actual expenses, if any)
Germany	Exempt in effect (excess credit refunded in cash)
Greece	Exempt
Iceland	Subject to central government income tax
Ireland	Exempt
Italy	Exempt
Japan	Exempt.
Luxembourg	Exempt (10% holding minimum or of LF50 million)
Netherlands	Exempt (minimum holding 5%)
New Zealand	Exempt
Norway	Only subject to national tax
Portugal	95% exempt if minimum holding of 25% of share capital
Spain	Exempt (25% holding minimum)[1]
Sweden	Exempt (25% holding minimum)
Switzerland	Relief (20% holding minimum)
Turkey	Exempt
United Kingdom	Exempt (but liable for ACT)
United States	70-80% of dividend exempt if minimum requirement is met. 100% if closely related.

1)   Strictly speaking not exempt, but parent company receives a 100 per cent credit on this type of dividend.

Table 3.4. **The treatment of corporate capital gains**

Country	Taxed at corporation rate	Tax at special rate	Inflation adjusted	Tax deferred if reinvested
Australia	Yes	—	Yes (holding period at least 12 month)	No
Austria	Yes	—	No	Yes(1)
Belgium	Yes (holding less than 5 years)	19.5% (more than 5 years)	No	Yes
Canada	75% of value	—	No	No
Denmark	Generally exempt	—	No	No
Finland	Yes (2)(3)	—	No	Yes
France	—	Less than 2 years 34% More than 2 years 19% or 25%(4)	No	No
Germany	Yes	—	No	Yes
Greece	Yes	20% partition of business 30% trademark, goodwill	No	No
Iceland	Yes	—	Yes	Yes
Ireland	—	Holding period Rate Less than 3 years 50% 3-6 years 35% More than 6 years 30%	Yes	Yes
Italy	Yes	—	No	No(5)
Japan	Yes (3)	—	No	No
Luxembourg	Yes	—	No(6)	Yes
Netherlands	Yes	—	No	Yes(7)
New Zealand	Exempt	—	—	—
Norway	Yes (8)	—	No	Yes
Portugal	Yes	—	Yes(9)	Yes(10)
Spain	Yes	—	No	Yes
Sweden	Yes(11)	—	No	No(11)
Switzerland	Yes(3)	—	No	No
Turkey	Yes	—	No	Yes
United Kingdom	Yes	—	Yes	Yes
United States	Yes	—	No	No

1. Under certain conditions (esp. 7 years minimum holding requirement, reinvestment in intangible assets).
2. Different rates for securities.
3. Special rates for real estate.
4. Must be reinvested, otherwise 34%
5. Except in special cases.
6. Capital gains on buildings, in case of liquidation of a company, are corrected for inflation.
7. Subject to a four years time limit.
8. For depreciable assets; other rules exist for other capital gains.
9. For depreciable assets and land.
10. Subject to a 2 years time limit.
11. With respect to the special reserve provision based on corporate equity (see table 3.4), the effective tax rate is 77% of the corporate tax rate.

Table 3.5. **General investment reliefs**[1]

Country	Under tax system		General cash grants available irrespective of sector or activity
	General investment allowance available	General investment credit available	
Australia	No	No	No
Austria	Yes, 20% of the cost of acquisition	No	No
Belgium	Yes, the rate depends on the development in the inflation index (minimum 3%, maximum 10%)	No	No
Canada	No	No	No
Denmark	No	No	No
Finland	Yes, investment reserve provisions	No	No
France	No	No	No
Germany	No	No	No
Greece	Yes, 40-70% of the investment cost	No	No
Iceland	Yes, investment reserve provisions	No	No
Ireland	No	No	No
Italy	No	No	No
Japan	No	No	No
Luxembourg	No	Yes, if investment exceeds average of last 5 years	No
Netherlands	Yes, between 2-18% of investment costs (with ceiling)	No	No
New Zealand	No	No	No
Norway	No	No	No
Portugal	No	No	No
Spain	No	Yes, new fixed assets	No
Sweden	Yes, (investment) reserve provisions[2]	No	No
Switzerland	No	No	No
Turkey	Yes, 30-100% of the investment cost	No	No
United Kingdom	No	No	No
United States	No	No	No

1. The tax treatment of reinvested capital gains is described in Table 3.3.
2. An amount of maximum 30% of equity according to closing balance sheets or maximum of 15% of payroll may be allocated to a special reserve.

Table 3.6 **Treatment of foreign source income from treaty countries**[1]

Resident Country	Treatment of foreign source dividend income from treaty countries	Treatment of foreign source interest income from treaty countries
Australia	exemption[2]	worldwide credit
Austria	exemption	credit by source
Belgium	exemption of 90% of gross dividend	worldwide credit[3]
Canada	exemption	credit by source
Denmark	exemption[4]	credit by source[5]
Finland	exemption	credit by source[6]
France	exemption of 95% of gross dividend	credit by source
Germany	exemption	credit by source
Greece	credit by source	credit by source
Iceland	worldwide credit	worldwide credit
Ireland	credit by source	credit by source
Italy	credit by source	credit by source
Japan	worldwide credit	worldwide credit
Luxembourg	exemption	credit by source
Netherlands	exemption	credit by source
New Zealand	credit by source	credit by source
Norway	credit by source	credit by source
Portugal	credit by source	credit by source
Spain	credit by source[7]	credit by source[8]
Sweden	exemption	credit by source
Switzerland	exemption[9]	credit by source
Turkey	credit by source	credit by source
United Kingdom	credit by source	credit by source
United States	worldwide credit[10]	worldwide credit

1. Based on a 100 per cent ownership of subsidiary.
2. Only for treaty countries designated as having corporate tax systems similar to Australia's.
3. Worldwide credit based on deemed withholding tax of 15%.
4. Dividend from a foreign subsidiary (minimum 25 per cent holding) in a country which has a corporate tax system similar to Denmark's. This also applies to non-treaty countries.
5. Denmark exempts interest payments from Portugal and Spain.
6. Finland exempts interest payments from Spain.
7. Spain exempts dividends from Switzerland.
8. Spain exempts interest payments from Portugal.
9. Strictly, Switzerland does not have an exemption system. However, total dividends recived from abroad are divided by total income, and this ratio is then used to reduce the Federal income tax. Similar reliefs are given in most cantons. Assuming that cantonal relief is precisely the same as Federal relief, the net effect is as if there were an exemption system.
10. In the United States the credit is separately calculated (on a world-wide basis) for several categories of income.

Table 3.7 **Treatment of foreign source income from non-treaty countries[1]**

Resident Country	Treatment of foreign source dividend income from non-treaty countries	Treatment of foreign source interest income from non-treaty countries	Non-treaty OECD countries
Australia[2]	worldwide credit	same as treaty	Greece, Iceland, Luxembourg, Portugal, Spain, Turkey
Austria	same as treaty	same as treaty[3]	Iceland
Belgium	same as treaty	same as treaty	Iceland, Turkey
Canada	worldwide credit	same as treaty	Greece, Iceland, Luxembourg, Portugal, Turkey
Denmark[4]	credit by source/exemption	same as treaty	Greece, Turkey
Finland	credit by source	same as treaty	
France	same as treaty	same as treaty	Iceland
Germany	credit by source	same as treaty	
Greece	same as treaty	same as treaty	Iceland, Portugal
Iceland	same as treaty	same as treaty[5]	
Ireland	deduction	deduction	Greece, Iceland, Portugal, Spain, Turkey
Italy	same as treaty[6]	same as treaty	Iceland, Turkey
Japan	same as treaty	same as treaty	Iceland, Portugal
Luxembourg	same as treaty	same as treaty	Australia, Greece, Iceland, Japan, New Zealand, Portugal, Switzerland, Turkey
Netherlands	same as treaty	deduction	Iceland, Portugal
New Zealand	same as treaty	same as treaty	Austria, Greece, Iceland, Luxembourg, Portugal, Spain, Turkey
Norway	deduction	deduction	Greece
Portugal	deduction	deduction	Australia, Canada, Greece, Ireland, Japan, Iceland, Luxembourg, Netherlands, New Zealand, Sweden, Turkey, USA
Spain	same as treaty	same as treaty	Iceland, Ireland, Greece
Sweden	credit by source	same as treaty	Belgium, Luxembourg, Portugal, Turkey
Switzerland	exemption[7]	deduction	Luxembourg, Turkey, Iceland
Turkey	same as treaty	same as treaty	Iceland, Portugal
United Kingdom	same as treaty	same as treaty	Iceland
United States	same as treaty	same as treaty	Portugal

1. Based on a 100 per cent ownership of subsidiary. "Same as treaty" refers to treatment described in table 3.5.
2. The treaty treatment of foreign source income is given to all countries which have a similar corporate tax system as Australia, including non-treaty countries.
3. If granted by the Ministry of Finance upon special application.
4. See note 4 to Table 3.5.
5. All OECD countries except for Denmark, Finland, Germany, Norway, Sweden and the United States.
6. Exemption of 60 per cent for parent companies.
7. Strictly, Switzerland does not have an exemption system. However, total dividends recived from abroad are divided by total income, and this ratio is then used to reduce the Federal income tax. Similar reliefs are given in most cantons. Assuming that cantonal relief is precisely the same as Federal relief, the net effect is as if there were an exemption system.

Table 3.8 **Treatment of trading losses**

	Carry forward (years)	Carry back (years)
Australia	Ind	—
Austria	7	—
Belgium	Ind	—
Canada	7	3
Denmark	5	—
Finland	5	—
France	5	3
Germany	Ind	2
Greece	5	—
Iceland	Ind	—
Ireland	Ind	1
Italy	5	—
Japan	5	1
Luxembourg	Ind	—
Netherlands	8	3
New Zealand	Ind	—
Norway	10	—
Portugal	5	—
Spain	5	—
Sweden	Ind	—
Switzerland	6[1]	—
Turkey	5	—
United Kingdom	Ind	1[2]
United States	15	3

1. Three computation periods. One computation period is the average of two years.
2. The Government has recently to increased the period to three years.

Ind: Indefinitely carrying forward of trading losses.
— : Not allowed.

Table 3.9 **Depreciation systems**

| | Depreciation | | Switch-over* | | Rate of depreciation in percent | | | |
| | Machinery | Buildings | Machinery | Buildings | Machinery | | Buildings | |
					SL	DB	SL	DB
Australia	SL/DB	SL	No	No	12%	1.5 x SL	2.5	—
Austria	SL	SL	na	na	10	—	4	—
Belgium	SL/DB	SL/DB	Yes	Yes	20	2 x SL	3-5	2 x SL
Canada	DB	DB	na	na	—	25	—	4
Denmark	DB	SL	na	na	—	30	6/2	—
Finland	DB	DB	na	na	—	30	—	9
France	SL/DB	SL	Yes	na	10-20	1.5/2.5 x SL	5	—
Germany	SL/DB	SL	Yes	na	10	3 x SL	2.5-10	—
Greece	SL	SL	na	na	10-20	—	8	—
Iceland	SL	SL	na	na	12-20	—	2	—
Ireland	DB	SL	na	na	—	10-25	4	—
Italy	SL	SL	na	na	10	—	5	—
Japan	SL/DB	SL/DB	Yes	Yes	10	3 x SL	2.2-4.3	3 x SL
Luxembourg	SL/DB	SL	Yes	na	10-20	3 x SL	2-4	—
Netherlands	SL/DB	SL/DB	Yes	Yes	10-15	2 x SL	3.3	2 x SL
New Zealand	SL/DB	SL	Yes	na	10	1.5 x SL	2	—
Norway	DB	DB	na	na	—	30	—	7
Portugal	SL/DB	SL	No	No	12.5-25	1.5/2.5 x SL	5	—
Spain	SL/DB	SL/DB	No	No	8	2.5 x SL	3	2.5 x SL
Sweden	SL/DB	SL	Yes	na	20	30	1.5-5	—
Switzerland	SL/DB	SL/DB	No	No	0.5 x DB	30-40	0.5 x DB	7-8
Turkey	SL/DB	SL/DB	Yes	Yes	20%	2 x SL	4	2 x SL
United Kingdom	DB	SL	na	na	—	25	4	—
United States	SL/DB	SL	Yes	na	14.3	2 x SL	3.2	—

*   Switch over from declining balance to straight line but not vice versa.

Symbols: SL = straight line;   DB = declining balance;   na = not applicable

Table 3.10 Typical capital allowances for machinery[1] used in the calculations

Country	First Period Straight Line or Declining Balance	First Period Allowance Rate Per Cent	First Period Length of First Period	Second Period Straight Line or Declining Balance	Second Period Allowance Rate Per Cent	Second Period Length of Second Period	First Year Allowance Per Cent
Australia	DB	18	ufd[2]				
Austria	SL	12.5	ufd				20.0
Belgium	DB	40	2[3]	SL	20	ufd	1 + inflation[4]
Canada	DB	25	ufd				
Denmark	DB	30	ufd				
Finland	DB	30	ufd				
France	DB	35.7	5[3]	SL	5.5	ufd	
Germany	DB	30	4[3]	SL	10	ufd	
Greece	SL	20	ufd				
Iceland	SL	12[5]	ufd				
Ireland	DB	50	1	DB	12.5	ufd	
Italy	SL	17.5	3	SL	10	ufd	
Japan	DB	30	3	SL	10	ufd[6]	
Luxembourg	DB	30	2	SL	20	ufd	
Netherlands	DB	25	3	SL	12.5	ufd	
New Zealand	DB	10	ufd				
Norway	DB	30	ufd				
Portugal	DB	31.25	ufd				
Spain	DB	20	ufd				5.0
Sweden	DB	30	ufd				
Switzerland	DB	30	ufd				
Turkey	DB	25	7	SL	13.3[7]	ufd	
UK	DB	25	ufd				
USA	DB	28.6	3	SL	9.1	ufd	

1. Where there is no statutory rate, or where statutory rates vary within the broad category of "machinery", a typical rate is shown and is used in the calculations in chapters 4 and 5.
2. Until fully depreciated.
3. Switchover at the optimal point is compulsory.
4. Between 3 and 10 per cent.
5. Indexed for inflation.
6. Until 95 per cent of the asset value is depreciated.
7. Turkey allows a switchover from declining balance to straight line depreciation at the optimum point. However, the remaining value of the asset is then depreciated at a constant rate over the rest of the asset's life.

Table 3.11 **Typical capital allowances for industrial buildings[1] used in the calculations**

Country	First Period			Second Period			Extra First Year Allowance Per Cent
	Straight Line or Declining Balance	Allowance Rate Per Cent	Length of First Period	Straight Line or Declining Balance	Allowance Rate Per Cent	Length of Second Period	
Australia	SL	2.5	ufd[2]				
Austria	SL	4.0	ufd				20.0
Belgium	DB	10.0	7[3]	SL	5.0	ufd	1+inflation[4]
Canada	DB	4.0	ufd				
Denmark	SL	6.0	10	SL	2.0	ufd	
Finland	DB	9.0	ufd				
France	SL	5.0	ufd				
Germany[5]	SL	10.0	4	SL	5.0	3	
Greece	SL	8.0	ufd				
Iceland	SL	2.06[6]	ufd				
Ireland	SL	50.0	1	SL	4.0	ufd	
Italy	DB	5.0	ufd				
Japan	DB	6.6	[3]	SL	2.2		
Luxembourg	SL	4.0	ufd				
Netherlands	DB	6.6	ufd				
New Zealand	SL	2.0	ufd				
Norway	DB	7.0	ufd				
Portugal	SL	5.0	ufd				
Spain	DB	7.5	ufd				5.0
Sweden	SL	3.3	ufd				
Switzerland	DB	8.0	ufd				
Turkey	DB	8.0	13[7]	SL	2.8	12	
UK	SL	4.0	ufd				
USA	SL	3.2	ufd				

1. Where there is no statutory rate, or where statutory rates vary within the broad category of "buildings", a typical rate is shown and is used in the calculations.
2. Until fully depreciated.
3. Switchover at the optimal point is compulsory.
4. Between 3 and 10 per cent
5. Germany allows for depreciation of assets at 10 percent for four years, 5 percent for a further three years and 3.5 per cent thereafter.
6. Indexed for inflation.
7. Turkey allows a switchover from declining balance to straight line depreciation at the optimum point. However, the remaining value of the asset is then depreciated at a constant rate over the rest of the asset's life.

Table 3.12 Net present values of depreciation allowances

Country	Industrial Buildings			Machinery		
	Actual nominal interest rate	Nominal interest OECD Average	Common real interest rate of 3 per cent	Actual nominal interest rates	Nominal interest OECD Average	Common real interest rate of 3 per cent
Australia	32.6	31.5	57.8	77.2	76.4	89.4
Austria	66.2	63.2	89.1	90.7	88.4	105.3
Belgium	65.1	60.7	80.4	88.1	86.1	94.0
Canada	29.4	32.9	55.2	62.3	65.1	76.6
Denmark	57.9	51.1	73.3	85.8	79.7	90.3
Finland	52.3	54.5	74.8	78.3	79.7	90.3
France	56.9	51.0	74.4	85.9	83.2	92.6
Germany	64.5	60.3	79.7	84.0	81.5	91.8
Greece	34.8	63.4	82.4	58.8	80.9	91.6
Iceland	21.7	25.9	51.5	46.6	48.6	55.0
Ireland	79.7	76.0	88.5	84.9	82.1	91.4
Italy	30.3	36.4	62.7	63.1	68.6	85.3
Japan	36.0	28.0	52.7	72.4	66.2	81.6
Luxembourg	49.2	44.6	69.7	85.6	83.4	92.8
Netherlands	47.1	39.1	65.1	78.6	73.2	87.7
New Zealand	27.6	25.9	51.5	58.8	57.1	76.7
Norway	56.2	53.7	74.9	81.2	79.7	90.3
Portugal	31.8	51.0	74.4	67.9	80.3	90.5
Spain	35.7	41.1	67.5	62.9	68.1	87.2
Sweden	25.7	39.1	65.1	70.4	79.7	90.3
Switzerland	50.6	51.6	72.6	79.1	79.7	90.3
Turkey	10.7	51.8	73.0	27.1	75.8	88.1
United Kingdom	39.3	44.6	69.7	73.3	76.7	88.7
United States	38.0	37.2	63.2	81.0	80.5	91.3

Note: The net present values are calculated on the basis of hypothetical streams of depreciation allowances in each country resulting from an investment of 100 units of local currency, using the information shown in tables 3.8 to 3.10. The nominal interest is calculated as predicted inflation in each country in 1991 (see table A.5.5) plus 3 percentage points real interest.

Table 3.13 **Inventories: Methods of evaluating cost**[1]

	FIFO	LIFO
Australia	Yes	No
Austria	Yes	Conditional
Belgium	Yes	Conditional
Canada	Yes	No
Denmark	Yes	Conditional
Finland	Yes	No
France	Yes	Conditional
Germany	No	Yes
Greece	Yes	Yes
Iceland	Yes	No[2]
Ireland	Yes	No
Italy	Yes	Yes
Japan	Yes	Yes
Luxembourg	Yes	Conditional
Netherlands	Yes	Yes
New Zealand	Yes	No
Norway	Yes	No
Portugal	Yes	Yes
Spain	Yes	No
Sweden	Yes	No
Switzerland	Yes	Yes
Turkey	Yes	No
United Kingdom	Yes	No
United States	Yes	Yes

1.   Other methods may also be allowed.
2.   Indexation of stocks is allowed.

Table 3.14 Corporation tax rates (in per cent)

Country	Central Government	Intermediate Government	Local Government	Local Tax Deductible	Overall Tax Rate	Imp. credit as prop. of gross div.[1] per cent
Australia	39	—	—		39	39
Austria	30	—	12.9	Yes	39	0
Belgium[2]	39	—	—		39	0
Canada[2]	28.84(23.84)[3]	12.9(11.9)	—	No	41.74(35.74)	20
Denmark	38	—	—		38	0
Finland[2]	23	—	17.2	No	40.2	40
France	34	—	—		34	
	42[4]	—	—		42[4]	33.3
Germany	50	—	13	Yes	56.5	
	36[4]	—	13	Yes	44.3[4]	36
Greece	46(40)	—	—		46(40)	0
Iceland	45	—	—		45	0
Ireland	43(10)[5]	—	—		43(10)[5]	28(5.3)
Italy	36	—	16.2	Yes[6]	47.83	36
Japan[2]	37.5	—	12 + 6.49	Yes	49.98	0
Luxembourg	33.33	—	9.09	Yes	39.39	0
Netherlands	35[7]	—	—		35	0
New Zealand	33	—	—		33	33
Norway	27.8	—	23	No	50.8	0
Portugal	36	—	3.6	No	39.6	0
Spain	35[8]	—	—[8]	Yes	35.34	0
Sweden	30	—	—		30	0
Switzerland	3.63-9.8[9]	4.32-12.96[9]	5.20-15.60[9]	Yes	13.15-38.36	0
Turkey	49.2	—	—		49.2	0
United Kingdom[2] [10]	34	—	—		34	25
United States[2] [11]	34	6.5[12]	—	Yes	38.3	0

1.   I.e. sum of dividend and tax credit.
2.   These countries apply lower rates to corporations with profits below a certain threshold or to small businesses.
3.   23.84 per cent for the manufacturing sector, otherwise 28.84 per cent.
4.   On distributed profits.
5.   10 per cent primarily for the manufacturing sector, otherwise 43 per cent. This rate will be reduced to 40 per cent as of 1 April 1991.
6.   Holds for 75 per cent of local tax.
7.   A higher rate of 40 per cent is applied on the first Gld. 250 000 of profits.
8.   In addition, a 1.5 per cent surtax levied by the Chamber of Commerce, see country chapter for details.
9.   Progressive rate schedule. A typical rate of 8 per cent for central government tax and 30.3 per cent for the overall rate have been chosen in the calculations presented in chapters 4 and 5.
10.   The corporate tax rate will fall to 33 per cent in 1991/92.
11.   Average rate for state and local taxes.
12.   Includes average tax rate for local governments.

Table 3.15 **Withholding taxes on dividends paid between member countries dividends**
(January 1 1991 for wholly owned subsidiary to parent company)

From: \ To:	Australia	Austria	Belgium	Canada	Denmark	Finland	France	Germany	Greece	Iceland	Ireland	Italy	Japan
Australia*	-	15	15	15	15	15	15	15	NT	0	15	15	15
Austria	15	-	15	15	10	10	15	25	25	NT	0	15	10
Belgium	15	15	-	15	15	10	10	15	15	NT	15	15	15
Canada	15	15	15	-	15	15	10	15	NT	NT	15	15	10
Denmark	15	10	15	15	-	0	0	10	NT	0	0	15	10
Finland	15	10	10	15	0	-	0	10	13	0	0	10	10
France	15	15	10	10	0	0	-	0	25	NT	0	15	10
Germany	15	25	15	15	15	10	0	-	25	5	10	10	15
Greece	NT	42	25	NT	NT	42	42	25	-	NT	15	10	15
Iceland	NT	NT	NT	NT	0	0	NT	5	NT	-	NT	25	NT
Ireland	0	0	0	0	0	0	0	0	NT	NT	NT	0	0
Italy	15	15	15	15	15	10	15	32.4	25	NT	15	-	10
Japan	15	10	15	10	10	10	10	10	NT	NT	10	10	-
Luxembourg	NT	5	0	5	0	5	0	0	0	NT	0	0	NT
Netherlands	15	5	5	10	0	0	5	10	5	NT	0	0	5
New Zeland	15	NT	15	15	15	15	15	15	NT	NT	15	15	15
Norway	15	15	15	15	0	15	5	0	NT	0	0	15	15
Portugal	NT	15	15	NT	15	10	10	15	NT	NT	NT	15	NT
Spain	NT	10	15	15	10	10	15	10	NT	NT	NT	10	10
Sweden	15	0	15	15	0	0	0	5	0	0	5	10	10
Switzerland	15	5	10	15	0	5	5	10	5	5	10	15	10
Turkey	NT	0	0	NT	NT	0	0	0	NT	NT	NT	NT	NT
United Kingdom²	0	0	0	0	0	0	0	0	0	0	0	0	0
United States	15	5	5	10	5	5	5	10	30	5	5	10	10

1.   Non-treaty rates.
2.   Details of abatement of tax credits are given in the United Kingdom country chapter.
*   No withholding on franked dividends, see country chapter.

Table 3.15 (cont) Withholding taxes on dividends paid between member countries dividends
(January 1 1991 for wholly owned subsidiary to parent company)

From:	To: Luxembourg	Netherlands	New Zealand	Norway	Portugal	Spain	Sweden	Switzerland	Turkey	UK	US	NT[1]
Australia*	NT	15	15	15	NT	NT	15	15	NT	15	15	30
Austria	5	5	NT	15	15	10	10	5	25	5	5	25
Belgium	10	5	15	15	15	15	15	10	NT	5	5	25
Canada	10	10	15	15	NT	15	15	15	NT	10	10	25
Denmark	5	0	15	0	10	10	0	0	NT	0	5	30
Finland	5	0	15	0	10	10	0	5	15	5	5	25
France	5	5	15	5	15	10	0	5	15	5	5	25
Germany	15	15	15	15	15	15	15	15	NT	15	10	25
Greece	NT	35	NT	NT	NT	NT	42	35	NT	42	42	42
Iceland	NT	NT	NT	0	NT	NT	0	5	NT	NT	5	20
Ireland	0	0	0	0	NT	NT	0	0	NT	0	0	0
Italy	15	0	15	15	15	15	10	15	NT	5	5	32.4
Japan	NT	10	15	10	NT	10	10	10	NT	10	10	20
Luxembourg	-	0	NT	5	0	0	5	NT	NT	0	5	15
Netherlands	2.5	-	15	10	NT	5	0	0	10	5	5	25
New Zealand	NT	15	-	15	NT	NT	15	15	NT	15	15	30
Norway	15	15	15	-	15	10	0	5	20	15	15	25
Portugal	NT	NT	NT	10	-	15	NT	10	NT	12	NT	25
Spain	10	10	NT	10	10	-	10	10	NT	10	10	20
Sweden	5	0	15	0	NT	10	-	5	NT	0	5	30
Switzerland	NT	0	15	5	10	10	5	-	NT	5	5	35
Turkey	NT	10	NT	0	NT	NT	0	NT	-	0	NT	0
United Kingdom[2]	0	0	0	0	0	0	0	0	0	0	0	0
United States	5	5	15	15	NT	10	5	5	NT	5	-	30

1. Non-treaty rates.
2. Details of abatement of tax credits are given in the United Kingdom country chapter.
* No withholding on franked dividends, see country chapter.

73

Table 3.16 **Withholding tax on interest paid on a loan from a parent company to a wholly owned subsidiary between member countries interest** (January 1 1991)

From: \ To:	Australia	Austria	Belgium	Canada	Denmark	Finland	France	Germany	Greece	Iceland	Ireland	Italy	Japan
Australia	-	10	10	10	10	10	10	10	NT	NT	10	10	10
Austria	0	-	0	0	0	0	0	0	0	NT	0	0	0
Belgium	10	10	-	10	10	10	10	10	10	NT	15	10	10
Canada	15	15	15	-	15	15	10	15	NT	NT	15	15	10
Denmark	0	0	0	0	-	0	0	0	NT	0	0	0	0
Finland	0	0	0	0	0	-	0	0	0	0	0	0	0
France	0	0	0	0	0	0	-	0	0	0	0	0	0
Germany	0	0	0	0	0	0	0	-	0	0	0	0	0
Greece	NT	10	15	NT	NT	10	10	10	-	NT	NT	10	NT
Iceland	NT	NT	NT	NT	0	0	NT	0	NT	-	NT	NT	NT
Ireland	10	0	15	30	0	0	0	0	NT	NT	-	10	10
Italy	10	10	15	15	15	15	15	0	10	NT	10	-	10
Japan	10	10	10	10	10	10	10	10	NT	NT	10	10	-
Luxemburg	NT	0	0	0	0	0	0	0	0	NT	0	0	NT
Netherlands	0	0	0	0	0	0	0	0	0	NT	0	0	0
New Zealand	10	NT	10	15	10	10	10	10	NT	NT	10	10	15
Norway	0	0	0	0	0	0	0	0	NT	0	0	0	0
Portugal	NT	10	15	NT	15	15	10	10	NT	NT	NT	15	NT
Spain	NT	5	15	15	10	10	10	10	NT	NT	NT	12	10
Sweden	0	0	0	0	0	0	0	0	0	0	0	0	0
Switzerland	0	0	0	0	0	0	0	0	0	0	0	0	0
Turkey	NT	10	NT	NT	NT	10	10	NT	NT	NT	NT	NT	NT
United Kingdom	10	0	15	10	0	0	0	0	0	NT	0	10	10
United States	10	0	15	15	0	0	0	0	0	0	0	15	10

1. Non-treaty rates.
Note: Whenever the non-treaty rate of withholding tax on interest paid for intercompany loans is nil or lower than the treaty rate (Austria, Denmark, Finland, France, Germany, Iceland, Luxembourg, Netherlands, Norway, Sweden, Switzerland, Turkey) then the non-treaty rate applies in practice.

74

Table 3.16 (cont) **Withholding tax on interest paid on a loan from a parent company to a wholly owned subsidiary between member countries interest** (January 1 1991)

From:	To: Luxemburg	Netherlands	N Zealand	Norway	Portugal	Spain	Sweden	Switerland	Turkey	UK	US	NT[1]
Australia	NT	10	10	10	NT	NT	10	10	NT	10	10	10
Austria	0	0	NT	0	0	0	0	0	0	0	0	0
Belgium	10	10	10	10	10	10	10	10	10	5	10	10
Canada	15	15	15	15	NT	15	15	15	NT	10	15	25
Denmark	0	0	0	0	0	0	0	0	0	0	0	0
Finland	0	0	0	0	0	0	0	0	0	0	0	0
France	0	0	0	0	0	0	0	0	0	0	0	0
Germany	0	0	0	0	0	0	0	0	NT	0	0	0
Greece	NT	10	NT	NT	NT	NT	10	10	NT	0	0	46
Iceland	NT	NT	NT	0	NT	NT	0	NT	NT	NT	0	0
Ireland	0	0	10	0	NT	NT	0	0	NT	0	0	30
Italy	10	10	15	15	15	12	15	12.5	NT	10	15	15
Japan	NT	10	20	10	NT	10	10	10	NT	10	10	20
Luxemburg	-	0	NT	0	NT	0	0	NT	NT	0	0	0
Netherlands	0	-	0	0	NT	0	0	0	0	0	0	0
New Zealand	NT	10	-	10	NT	NT	10	10	NT	10	10	15
Norway	0	0	0	-	0	0	0	0	0	0	0	0
Portugal	NT	NT	NT	15	-	15	NT	10	NT	10	NT	25
Spain	10	10	NT	10	15	-	15	10	NT	12	10	25
Sweden	0	0	0	0	NT	0	-	0	NT	0	0	0
Switzerland	NT	0	0	0	0	0	0	-	NT	0	0	0
Turkey	NT	10	NT	10	NT	NT	NT	NT	-	10	NT	10
United Kingdom	0	0	10	0	10	12	0	0	15	-	0	25
United States	0	0	10	0	NT	10	0	5	NT	0	-	30

1.   Non-treaty rates.

Note: Whenever the non-treaty rate of withholding tax on interest paid for intercompany loans is nil or lower than the treaty rate (Austria, Denmark, Finland, France, Germany, Iceland, Luxembourg, Netherlands, Norway, Sweden, Switzerland, Turkey) then the non-treaty rate applies in practice.

Table 3.17 Corporation tax collection lags

Country	Collection lag
Australia	85 per cent of the tax due must be paid within 28 days of the end of fiscal year. The remaining 15 per cent must be paid by the 15th day of the next month.
Austria	Taxes prepaid by quarterly instalment based on previous year's assessment.
Belgium	Tax is paid in quarterly instalments.
Canada	Monthly instalments. Balance of tax due two months after the end of the fiscal year.
Denmark	Lag will vary according to the company's own accounting period. Where the accounting period is the calendar year, the lag is 10 2/3 months.
Finland	Lag will vary according to the company's own accounting period. However, where the acounting period is the calendar year, the first instalment (December) is paid in advance and the remaining instalments (February and March) within three months of the end of the fiscal year.
France	Tax is paid in four instalments during the fiscal year totalling 38 per cent of the taxable income of the preceeding year. The balance must be paid no later than 3½ months after the end of the fiscal year.
Germany	Tax for the current year is paid in quarterly instalments. The final instalment is due when the final assessment is issued.
Greece	Tax is paid in seven equal instalments. The first instalment is due upon filing the tax return.
Iceland	Tax is paid in 10 monthly instalments in assessment year, the first five based on previous year's assessment, the last five on final assessment in July.
Ireland	Preliminary tax of not less than 90 per cent of the amount actually due is payable six months after the end of an accounting period. The balance becomes payable on submission of the tax return nine months after the end of an accounting period.
Italy	Tax is paid in two instalments: 39.2 per cent of the prior year's assessment is due when the prior year's return is filed and 58.8 per cent in the eleventh month of the company's financial year. The balance is due when the return for that year is submitted.
Japan	Tax must be paid at the same time the return is filed, usually three months after the end of the accounting period.
Luxembourg	Quarterly tax advances have to be paid. These are fixed by the tax authorities on the basis of the previous year's assessment.
Netherlands	Tax is paid in instalments during the year in which the income is earned on the basis of a provisional assessment. After the end of the accounting period, tax has to be paid within two months of the issue of a (provisional) assessment.
New Zealand	Tax is paid in instalments. Provisional tax on account of the current year's liability is payable in three instalments in the fourth, eighth and twelfth months of the taxpayer's income tax year. The balance is due in eleventh month of the year following the assessment.
Norway	Companies are required to make advance payments on tax on 15 February and 15 April in the year following the income year. The balance must be paid in two instalments within two months of the assessment being issued.
Portugal	Tax is paid in four instalments. The first three, each equivalent to 25 per cent of the previous year's assessment, are due in June, September and December of the year in which taxable income arises. The final instalment is due upon filing the annual return in April of the following year.
Spain	Three payments on account of the current year's tax equivalent to 20 per cent of the previous year's tax are required to be made on the 20th of April, October and December. The balance is payable at the time of filing the return.
Sweden	Tax is collected during the year in which the income is earned under a preliminary tax system. Tax is paid in six equal instalments starting in March of the tax year. The balance is paid in the year after the assessment is made.
Switzerland	Tax is usually paid in two or three instalments based on the previous year's assessment.
Turkey	Tax is paid in three equal instalments in April, July and October of the year of filing. 50 per cent of the tax assessed in the previous year must be paid as an advance tax.
United Kingdom	Nine months after the end of the accounting period.
United States	Tax must be paid in full either by the time of the filing of the return or by the 15th of the third month following the close of the fiscal year, whichever comes first.

Table 3.18 **Net wealth taxes on corporations**
(rates in per cent)[1]

Country	Rate
Australia	—
Austria	1+0.5 surtax
Belgium	—
Canada	0.2
Denmark	—
Finland	—
France	—
Germany	0.6
Greece	—
Iceland	1.45
Ireland	—
Italy	—
Japan	—
Luxembourg	0.5
Netherlands	—
New Zealand	—
Norway	0.3
Portugal	—
Spain	—
Sweden	—
Switzerland	0.439[2]
Turkey	0.3-0.6
United Kingdom	—
United States	—

1) The tax base may vary between countries: see *"Taxation of Net Wealth, Capital Transfer and Capital Gains of Individuals"*, OECD, 1988.

2) Rate for Zurich (federal, cantonal, municipal and church taxes).

Table 3.19 **Personal tax rates in per cent** (all levels of government)

Country	Tax Rate on Dividends[1]		Tax Rate on Interest	
	Top Rate	Average Marginal Rate	Top Rate	Average Marginal Rate
Australia	48.3	39	48.3	39
Austria[2]	25	19.8	50	39.7
Belgium[3]	25	25	10	10
Canada	49.1	44.6	49.1	39.5
Denmark	45	37.6	57.8	51.1
Finland[4]	60	45.2	10	10
France[5]	57.9	45	18.1[6]	5.6
Germany	53	39.1	53	39.1
Greece	50	n.a.	25	0
Iceland	39.8[7]	15.8	0	0
Ireland	53	50(27)[8]	53	38.4
Italy	50	39.4	30	12.5
Japan	35[9]	35	20	20
Luxembourg	51.25	24.6	51.25	24.6
Netherlands	60	49[10]	60	42[10]
New Zealand	33	28.6	33	25.9
Norway	19.5	n.a	40.5	n.a
Portugal	25[11]	25	25	25
Spain[12]	56	28.4	56	31.5
Sweden	30	30	30	30
Switzerland	43.8	30.8	43.8	30.8
Turkey	10	10	10	10
UK	40	32	40	24
USA	36	31	36	28

Notes: 1. Based on statutory rates prior to any gross-up and dividend tax credits.
2. The cost of newly issued shares is deductible from personal tax.
3. The 25% withholding tax on dividends and the 10% withholding tax on interest is the final tax paid.
4. Interest income from certain types of bonds is exempt from tax.
5. Including an additional tax of 1.1% introduced in 1991 (cotisation sociale généralisée).
6. Different withholding tax rates are applied to different sorts of interest income; the figure used reflects that in State bonds.
7. Iceland exempts dividends from personal tax up to 15% of total value of shares owned by the taxpayer. This exemption, however, is subject to an upper limit.
8. Figure in brackets is the average marginal rate on manufacturing dividends. This is lower than the overall average marginal rate on dividends because half of manufacturing dividend income is exempt from taxtation (subject to not more than Irish £7 000 being exempted in any tax year).
9. Japanese shareholders have a choice between a final withholding tax and personal tax. The above figures reflect the withholding tax.
10. The dividend and interest exemptions have not been taken into account.
11. A withholding tax of 25% is levied on 80% of the value of dividends from shares quoted on the Portuguese Stock Exchange. Individuals may elect withholding taxes as the final tax they pay on the dividends.
12. Spanish interest income is taxed as ordinary income, 10% of dividends received can be deducted from the personal income tax.

Table 3.20 **Domestic withholding tax on individuals** (per cent)

Country	A. Interest	B. Dividends
Australia	—	—
Austria	10	25
Belgium	10	25
Canada	—	—
Denmark	—	30
Finland	10	—
France	18.1	—
Germany	—	25
Greece	25	42-50
Iceland	—	—
Ireland	30	—
Italy	12.5-30	10
Japan	20	20
Luxembourg	—	15
Netherlands	—	25
New Zealand	24	33
Norway	—	25
Portugal	25	25
Spain	25	25
Sweden	30	30
Switzerland	35	35
Turkey	10	10
United Kingdom	—	—
United States	—	—

Table 3.21 Typical capital gains tax (CGT) rates on shares for individual investors
(minority shareholders in quoted companies)

Country	CGT rate in first period		Length of first period	CGT rate in second period		Indexation
	Top Rate	Average Marginal Rate		Top Rate	Average Marginal Rate	
Australia[1]	48.3	39.0	-	-	-	yes[2]
Austria	50	39.7	1	0	0	-
Belgium	0	0	-	-	-	-
Canada[3]	36.8	10.5	-	-	-	no
Denmark	57.8	51.1	3	0	0	no
Finland	60	55	5	30	2	no
France	18.1	0	-	-	-	no
Germany	0	0	-	-	-	-
Greece	0	0	-	-	-	-
Iceland	39.8	20.0	-	-	-	yes
Ireland[4]	50.0	50.0	3	35	35	yes
Italy	25	25[5]	-	-	-	-
Japan	20	20	-	-	-	-
Luxembourg	0	0	-	-	-	-
Netherlands	0	0	-	-	-	-
New Zealand	0	0	-	-	-	-
Norway	40.0	40.0	3	0	0	no
Portugal	10[6]	10[6]	2	0	0	no
Spain[7]	56.0	31.5	-	-	-	yes
Sweden	30	30	-	-	-	no
Switzerland	0	0	-	-	-	-
Turkey	50.0	27.0	-	-	-	no
UK	40.0	33.0	-	-	-	yes
USA	36.0	31.0	-	-	-	no

1. Franked dividend system .
2. Not indexed if sold within one year.
3. Canada has a large lifetime exemption limit (Can $ 100,000), and the average tax rate reflects this. This capital gains tax rate is three quarters of the statutory income tax rate.
4. Capital gains taxed at 50% if sold in the first three years, 35% if sold after holding for three to six years and 30% if sold after that.
5. Tax rates reduced to 15% under cetain conditions.
6. Capital gains are tax exempt in the case of bonds. Capital gains on shares are taxed at 10% if sold within 24 months and tax exempt if sold after that period.
7. Spain taxes capital gains on the basis of dividing the value of the gain by the number of years held (if the taxpayer does not know the holding period, then the period is taken to be five years), and including that figure into normal taxable income. The remainder is taxed at the average rate for general income tax.

Table 3.22 **Tax on net wealth of individuals**[1]

Country	Per Cent
Australia	-
Austria	1
Belgium	-
Canada	-
Denmark	1.0
Finland	0.9
France	0.5-1.5
Germany	0.5
Greece	-
Iceland	1.2-2.2
Ireland	-
Italy	-
Japan	-
Luxembourg	0.5
Netherlands	0.8
New Zealand	-
Norway	1 - 2.3
Portugal	-
Spain	0.2 - 2.0
Sweden	1.5 - 3
Switzerland[2]	0.118 - 0.711
Turkey	-
United Kingdom	-
United States	-

1) The tax base varies substantially across countries, see *"Taxation of Net Wealth, Capital Transfers and Capital Gains of Individuals"*, OECD, Paris 1988.

2) Rate for Zurich (federal, cantonal, municipal and church taxes).

Table 3.23 **Taxes on corporate income (1200) as percentage of total taxation**[1]

	1965	1970	1975	1980	1981	1982	1983	1984	1985	1986	1987	1988	1989
Australia	16.3	17.0	12.4	12.2	11.4	10.1	8.9	9.3	9.3	9.1	10.3	10.5	12.6
Austria	5.4	4.4	4.3	3.5	3.3	2.9	2.9	3.1	3.4	3.5	3.3	3.2	3.7
Belgium	6.2	6.8	7.2	5.7	5.3	6.0	5.8	6.2	6.4	6.5	6.5	6.8	6.7
Canada	15.1	11.3	13.6	11.6	9.7	7.5	7.5	8.7	8.2	8.2	8.2	8.4	8.5
Denmark	4.5	2.6	3.1	3.2	2.8	2.6	3.0	5.3	4.9	6.2	4.5	4.4	4.2
Finland	8.3	5.5	4.3	4.5	4.8	4.6	4.5	4.1	4.0	3.8	3.9	4.2	4.2
France	5.3	6.3	5.2	5.1	5.2	5.3	4.6	4.4	4.5	5.0	5.1	5.2	5.5
Germany	7.8	5.7	4.5	5.5	5.0	5.1	5.1	5.4	6.1	6.0	5.1	5.3	5.5
Greece	1.8	1.6	3.4	3.8	3.8	3.8	2.4	2.6	2.7	4.0	4.5	4.0	4.6
Iceland	1.8	2.0	2.6	2.5	1.8	2.6	2.7	2.6	3.1	3.0	2.2	2.7	3.0
Ireland	9.1	8.8	4.8	4.5	5.0	4.7	3.8	3.3	3.2	3.5	3.2	3.8	3.4
Italy	6.9	6.5	6.3	7.8	8.3	8.8	9.0	9.8	9.2	10.6	10.5	9.4	10.1
Japan	22.2	26.3	20.6	21.8	20.3	19.8	19.6	21.1	21.0	20.7	23.0	24.7	24.4
Luxembourg	11.0	19.3	15.7	16.5	15.4	15.2	17.0	15.5	18.2	16.7	17.1	17.1	17.7
Netherlands	8.1	6.7	7.7	6.6	7.0	6.8	6.1	5.7	7.0	7.3	7.7	7.3	7.7
New Zealand	20.7	17.8	11.8	7.8	7.1	7.8	6.2	8.7	8.3	6.6	8.9	7.9	9.0
Norway	3.8	3.3	2.8	13.3	16.0	16.4	14.5	16.5	17.0	13.3	6.6	5.6	5.3
Portugal													3.9
Spain	9.2	8.2	6.9	5.1	4.6	4.7	4.9	5.0	5.2	5.5	6.7	6.5	8.6
Sweden	6.1	4.4	4.3	2.5	2.9	3.3	3.4	3.7	3.5	4.7	4.1	5.2	3.8
Switzerland	7.1	7.6	7.7	5.8	5.9	6.2	6.0	5.8	6.0	6.3	6.3	6.7	6.5
Turkey	4.8	6.4	5.1	4.1	8.8	11.4	9.6	9.3	9.5	12.0	10.7	10.5	8.4
United Kingdom	7.1	9.1	6.7	8.3	9.5	9.9	10.9	11.8	12.6	10.5	10.5	10.8	12.3
United States	15.8	12.7	10.8	10.2	8.6	6.9	5.5	7.1	7.1	7.0	8.1	8.4	8.5
Unweighted average :													
OECD Total	8.9	8.7	7.5	7.5	7.5	7.5	7.1	7.6	7.9	7.8	7.7	7.8	7.8
OECD Europe	6.4	6.4	5.7	6.0	6.4	6.7	6.5	6.7	7.0	7.1	6.6	6.6	6.6
EEC	7.0	7.4	6.5	6.6	6.5	6.6	6.6	6.8	7.3	7.4	7.4	7.3	7.5

1.   The figures include all taxes on profits classified under OECD heading 1200. Thus, for example, the figures include the Noregian and the United Kingdom petroleum revenue taxes.

Source: *Revenue Statistics of OECD Member countries, 1991.*

Table 3.24 **Taxes on corporate income (1200) as percentage of GDP**

	1965	1970	1975	1980	1981	1982	1983	1984	1985	1986	1987	1988	1989
Australia	3.8	4.1	3.4	3.5	3.3	3.0	2.5	2.8	2.8	2.8	3.2	3.2	3.8
Austria	1.9	1.6	1.7	1.4	1.4	1.2	1.2	1.3	1.5	1.5	1.4	1.3	1.5
Belgium	1.9	2.4	3.0	2.5	2.4	2.8	2.7	2.9	3.1	3.1	3.1	3.2	3.0
Canada	3.9	3.5	4.4	3.7	3.3	2.5	2.5	2.9	2.7	2.7	2.8	2.9	3.0
Denmark	1.4	1.1	1.3	1.5	1.3	1.2	1.4	2.5	2.4	3.1	2.3	2.3	2.1
Finland	2.5	1.7	1.5	1.5	1.7	1.6	1.5	1.5	1.5	1.4	1.4	1.6	1.6
France	1.8	2.2	1.9	2.1	2.2	2.3	2.0	1.9	2.0	2.2	2.3	2.3	2.4
Germany	2.5	1.9	1.6	2.1	1.9	1.9	1.9	2.0	2.3	2.2	1.9	2.0	2.1
Greece	0.4	0.4	0.9	1.1	1.1	1.3	0.8	0.9	1.0	1.5	1.7	1.4	1.5
Iceland	0.5	0.6	0.8	0.8	0.6	0.8	0.8	0.8	0.9	0.9	0.6	0.8	1.0
Ireland	2.4	2.7	1.5	1.5	1.8	1.7	1.5	1.3	1.2	1.4	1.3	1.6	1.3
Italy	1.8	1.7	1.7	2.4	2.6	3.0	3.2	3.4	3.2	3.8	3.8	3.5	3.8
Japan	4.1	5.2	4.3	5.5	5.3	5.2	5.3	5.7	5.8	5.9	6.8	7.5	7.5
Luxembourg	3.4	5.8	6.2	6.8	6.3	6.2	7.6	6.7	8.0	7.1	7.3	7.2	7.5
Netherlands	2.7	2.5	3.4	3.0	3.1	3.1	2.8	2.6	3.1	3.4	3.7	3.5	3.5
New Zealand	5.1	4.9	3.7	2.6	2.4	2.7	2.0	2.9	2.8	2.3	3.4	2.9	3.6
Norway	1.3	1.3	1.3	6.2	7.8	7.9	6.8	7.6	8.1	6.7	3.2	2.7	2.4
Portugal													1.4
Spain	1.3	1.4	1.3	1.2	1.2	1.2	1.4	1.5	1.5	1.7	2.2	2.1	3.0
Sweden	2.2	1.8	1.9	1.2	1.5	1.7	1.7	1.8	1.7	2.5	2.3	2.9	2.1
Switzerland	1.5	1.8	2.3	1.8	1.8	1.9	1.9	1.9	1.9	2.0	2.0	2.2	2.1
Turkey	0.7	1.1	1.1	0.9	2.1	2.6	2.0	1.6	1.9	2.7	2.6	2.4	2.4
United Kingdom	2.2	3.3	2.4	2.9	3.5	3.9	4.1	4.5	4.8	3.9	3.9	4.0	4.5
United States	4.1	3.7	3.1	3.0	2.6	2.1	1.6	2.0	2.1	2.0	2.4	2.5	2.6
Unweighted average:													
OECD Total	2.3	2.5	2.4	2.6	2.6	2.7	2.6	2.7	2.9	2.9	2.9	2.9	2.9
OECD Europe	1.8	2.0	2.0	2.3	2.4	2.6	2.5	2.6	2.8	2.8	2.6	2.6	2.6
EEC	2.0	2.3	2.3	2.5	2.5	2.6	2.7	2.7	3.0	3.0	3.0	3.0	3.0

1. The figures include all taxes on profits classified under OECD heading 1200. Thus, for example, the figures include the Noregian and the United Kingdom petroleum revenue taxes.

Source: *Revenue Statistics of OECD Member countries, 1991.*

Table 3.25 **The main direct taxes related to business activities** *

	Corporate income tax (1200)	Social security contributions paid by employers (2200)	Taxes on payroll and workforce paid by enterprise (3000)	Taxes on property by other than households (4120)	Taxes on corporate net wealth (4220)	Other taxes paid solely by business (6100)
Australia	3.8	-	1.7		-	-
Austria	1.5	6.7	2.5	0.2	0.3	-
Belgium	3.0	9.3	-	0.01	-	-
Canada	3.0	3.0	-		0.3	0.3
Denmark	2.1	0.1	0.3	1.2	-	0.1
Finland	1.6	3.0	-	0.03	-	-
France	2.4	11.9	0.8	0.3	0.2	1.4
Germany	2.1	7.0	-	0.2	0.3	-
Greece	1.5	4.3	0.6	-	-	-
Iceland	1.0	0.9	1.1	0.7	0.3	1.2
Ireland	1.3	3.3	0.5		-	-
Italy	3.8	9.0	0.2		-	-
Japan	7.5	4.4	-			0.1
Luxembourg	7.5	6.0	-		1.7	-
Netherlands	3.5	7.5	-		-	0.1
New Zealand	3.6	-	0.7			-
Norway	2.4	7.9	-	-	0.2	0.1
Portugal	1.4	5.6	-	-	-	0.04
Spain	3.0	9.2	-	-	-	-
Sweden	2.1	13.9	1.8	0.3	0.01	-
Switzerland	2.1	3.3	-	-	0.5	-
Turkey	2.4	2.6	-			-
United Kingdom	4.5	3.5	-	2.2	-	-
United States	2.6	4.9	-	1.6	-	-
Unweighted average:						
OECD Total	2.9	5.3	0.4	0.5	0.2	0.1
OECD Europe	2.6	6.0	0.4	0.4	0.2	0.2
EEC	3.0	6.4	0.2	0.5	0.2	0.1

* This table entirely ignores the question of how taxes are shifted and also does not take into account consumption taxes. It is recalled that only the taxes in the 1200 heading are taken into account in the calculations presented in this report.

Source: *Revenue Statistics of OECD Member countries, 1991.*

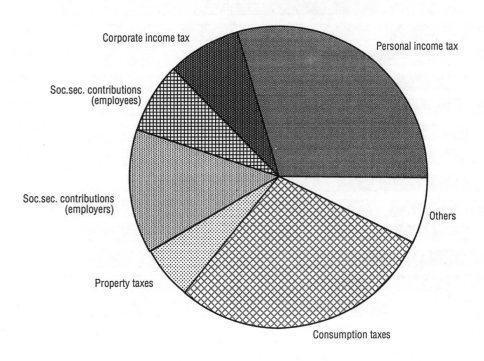

Chart 3.1 **Share of total tax revenue in 1989**
OECD unweighted average

Personal income tax

Corporate income tax

Soc.sec. contributions
(employees)

Soc.sec. contributions
(employers)

Property taxes

Consumption taxes

Others

Source : Revenue Statistics of OECD Member countries, 1991.

Chart 3.2 **Share of total tax revenues in 1989**

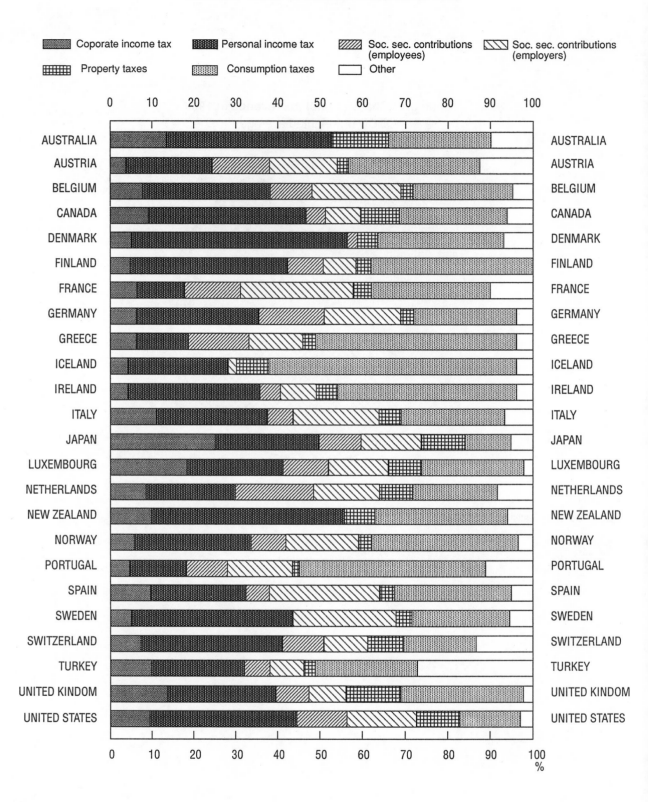

Chapter 4

Effective Tax Rates on Domestic Investment in OECD Countries

A. Introduction

Required rates of return

This chapter calculates effective tax rates on domestic marginal investments in the 24 OECD countries[1] taking the tax systems in operation as of the 1st January 1991 (transnational effective tax rates are discussed in the following chapter). It uses the information that is summarised in Chapter 3 and which is set out in more detail in the country chapters reproduced in Annex 4 and the methodology set out in Annex 1.

Effective tax rates are tax rates which take into account not only the statutory corporate tax rate, but also other aspects of the tax system which determine the amount of tax paid and profitability of investment, such as capital allowances and stock relief. Effective tax rates may also require a consideration of personal taxes, and the manner (if any) in which the corporate and personal tax systems are integrated (classical, split rate or imputation). Inflation will also alter effective tax rates in various ways, depending on how the tax system calculates taxable profits in the presence of inflation.

Marginal investments are projects which are expected to earn a rate of return on the initial outlay just sufficient to persuade investors that the project is worthwhile. All investments are expected to yield the supplier of capital with a rate of return at least as high as could have been achieved by putting the same amount of capital to an alternative use (buying government bonds, for example), as otherwise potential investors would choose the more lucrative alternative. Potential investors always have the option of getting the prevailing rate of interest from either banks or the government, so in the absence of corporate taxes and personal taxes, this would imply that the risk-adjusted return on the investment would have to be as high as the risk-adjusted market interest rate.

Taxes on corporate income generally raise the pre-tax rate of return required in order to yield the same (post-tax) return as in the absence of taxes. Hence the company has to earn a higher rate of return in order to be able to match the return which could be achieved by buying a government bond. Taxes on personal income from the corporate sector result in investors receiving less than the gross amount paid to them. The difference between the pre-corporate tax rate of return earned by companies and the post tax receipts an individual gets is a measure of the total distortion (total tax "wedge") caused by taxes.

Suppose, for example, it is possible to earn a real post-tax rate of return of 5 per cent by depositing money in an interest-bearing account in a bank. For a company to persuade an investor to finance an investment by buying shares in that company, it must expect to be able to provide dividends and/or capital gains of sufficient size so that after tax the investor would get a rate of return of at least 5 per cent.[2] To be able to give shareholders a return of 5 per cent the company may have to pay gross dividends of 7 per cent, the difference being paid to the authorities as personal tax. In order to be able to pay gross dividends of 7 per cent, the company may have to earn a pre-corporation tax return of 10 per cent, the difference being paid as corporation tax. Therefore tax has driven a wedge of five percentage points between the return to investors on the capital they originally invest in companies (5 per cent), and the return earned before tax by companies (10 per cent). This wedge can be calculated if the provisions of the tax code are known.[3]

There are three rates of return which it is useful to focus on when discussing the effects of the tax system on investment decisions — the real pre-corporate tax rate of return to companies ("p" in the terminology often used in studies such as this), the real interest rate, which is the return that can be earned on a Government bond or bank deposit before personal taxes are charged ("r") and the real post-personal tax rate of return received by the ultimate financiers of the investment ("s"). By fixing r at some level (usually 5 per cent, reflecting a typical real interest rate), then by applying the relevant parameters of a tax system the p (the pre-corporate tax rate of return) necessary to generate that r can be found,[4] as can s (the return to the providers of capital). The difference between p and s is the overall tax wedge and depends on both the corporate and personal tax systems.

The importance of this tax wedge is that it gives some indication of whether taxation creates a disincentive to new investment. For example, suppose that investors will only finance investment if they receive a 5 per cent return (after any tax). If the pre-corporate tax rate of return necessary to give potential investors a 5 per cent post-tax return is 10 per cent, then all those projects which earn a return of between 5 and 10 per cent and which would be viable in the absence of tax will not earn a sufficient return when income from capital is taxed, and such projects may therefore not be undertaken.[5]

Given the relationships specified between the pre-corporate tax return (p), the interest rate (r), and the post-personal tax return (s), various effective marginal tax rates or tax wedges can be calculated. The difference between p (the pre-tax rate of return to companies) and s (the post-tax rate of return to individuals) reflects the overall size of the distortion in the market caused by corporate and personal taxes. This means that there are three relevant measures of the effective tax rates on business. First is the p required to get a particular value of r; secondly is the tax wedge — the difference between p and s; and thirdly is the tax rate — the tax wedge divided by p. The tax rate is not always a useful figure, because the tax wedge may be similar in two different cases, but p may vary, giving substantial differences in the tax rate.[6] The tax wedge shows the full difference between the pre-corporate tax return and post-personal tax return. If attention is focused on the corporate tax system, then it is only necessary to look at p — the pre-corporate tax rate of return necessary to earn a given post-corporate tax rate of return, or the cost of capital.

Apart from the question of whether a project which is profitable in the absence of tax is still profitable when tax is applicable, there is the equally important issue of whether tax distorts the form of the investment. If tax is relatively generous to particular types of finance and assets, then resources may be diverted towards them rather than the sorts of investments which would take place were the tax system neutral. Comparisons of the required pre-tax rate of return or the tax wedge on similar investments financed in different ways (or in investments in different assets financed in the same way) give an indication of the extent to which the tax system achieves this "allocative" efficiency.

The King and Fullerton approach

The precise methodology used to calculate effective tax rates on marginal investments in this chapter is closely based on an approach developed by King and Fullerton (1984)[7]. The King-Fullerton methodology is highly versatile, and enables complicated provisions of tax codes to be modelled in a rigorous manner. It allows the effects of different types of tax treatments to be compared systematically, both within countries (on different types of investment, financed in different ways) and across countries. It is also the methodology which is most widely used to calculate both domestic and cross-border effective tax rates on corporate investment.

Despite these advantages, there are some limitations of the approach which are discussed in detail below, but which should be recognised at the outset. Because investments earn profits in the future, assumptions must be made about the future tax system. Different investments will have different effective tax rates; to make the results manageable, assumptions have to be made about which sorts of investment are important enough to consider, and this inevitably affects the results. The tax rates obtained using the King and Fullerton methodology should therefore not be treated as if they captured all relevant features of a corporate tax system, although they do capture most of them.

B. Methodology

This section is divided into three parts. The first section is intended to give a simple explanation of the King and Fullerton methodology - how the marginal investment is identified, and the required pre-tax rate of return derived from the tax code. The discount rate applied to future income and expenditure is affected by the tax treatment of different types of finance, and so is discussed in more detail. The middle section examines the ways in which provisions of the tax code in each country affect the results. In the final section some limitations of the King-Fullerton approach in general and with this particular study are discussed.

The intuition behind the theory

The easiest way of understanding the King-Fullerton methodology is to assume that a company, which is making some profit on its existing operations, considers obtaining funds in order to invest in a new project. The cost to the company of the project will be reduced by the current value of any capital allowances it receives on physical investment. Both these and the profits it expects to earn will be received in the future, so have to be discounted by some factor in order to obtain their present value. If the investment is a marginal one, then the return on the original investment must be just equal to the cost of the project. Hence given the value of capital allowances (as given by the tax code), the discount rate which is to be applied to a project (see the discussion below) and the tax rates, then the pre-tax rate of return necessary to give a present value equal to the cost of the project can be calculated, and this is the rate of return which is considered as "marginal".

Hence the underlying assumptions governing the calculation of effective tax rates are extremely simple, even if formalising them into equations relating to the actual provisions of national tax systems is quite intricate. This section outlines the way in which corporate and personal taxes enter the model, in order to explain the results given in the final section of this chapter. OECD tax systems are described in detail in the country chapters, and are summarised in Chapter 3, so this section merely provides a brief overview of how the different provisions of the tax systems enter the equations determining the marginal effective tax rates. Before describing the way in which each of the parts of the tax systems affect the calculations of effective tax rates, the issues of the required rate of return and the company's discount rate used in the King-Fullerton methodology is discussed.

The required rate of return

As noted above, there are three rates of return of interest: the real pre-corporate tax rate of return (p), the real post-tax return received by the providers of finance (s) and an intermediate return reflecting the real pre-personal tax rate of return paid by the company to the suppliers of finance (r). In order to calculate the difference between them and hence the impact of taxation it is necessary to choose a value of one of these rates of return and then calculate the implied values of the other two.

As implied above, the study adopts what is known as the 'Fixed-r' approach. That is, it assumes a value of r and calculates the implied values of p and s. In particular, it generally uses a value of r=5 per cent. This can be interpreted as a real interest rate in the case in which investors are risk-neutral or as a risk-adjusted interest rate. No attempt is made to use actual interest rates in different countries; rather the rate of 5 per cent is used throughout (the sensitivity of the results to this assumption is checked) so that attention is directed towards the impact of taxation.

The rationale governing the Fixed-r approach is that discussed above: investors require a return from the company at least as high as that which they could earn elsewhere; this will be the same irrespective of the form in which the investment in the company is made. This implies, as will be demonstrated later, that the pre-tax rate of return required depends on the source of finance used. An alternative, the Fixed-p case, would be to fix the pre-tax required rate of return to be the same for all investments, thus implying that investors receive different rates of return depending on the form in which their funds are invested. Neither approach is completely satisfactory, in that observed financial behaviour is not adequately explained.

It should be also noted that in principle in the closed economy case r is not really fixed: changing corporate and personal taxes will affect the equilibrium value of r, depending on the elasticity of the supply and demand of savings in the economy. For the purposes of this report this issue is ignored so that attention can be directed at the impact of taxation given r: the baseline taken is always that r is 5 per cent. In the open economy case, however, it may be more realistic to assume that r really is fixed because it can be assumed to be determined on world markets; if each country is relatively small its own savings and investment decisions will not affect the equilibrium world interest rate.

The discount rate

Derivation of the appropriate discount rate is not, as straightforward to explain as the rest of the methodology. In the King-Fullerton methodology the discount rate is determined by the manner in which the company raises funds for its investment. The discount rate of a company is seen as being determined from the point of view of a shareholder. By putting money in a bank, or buying a government bond, potential investors can earn some rate of return. They will put this money into a company only if the company can at least match this rate of return. In the absence of any taxes, the discount rate would be this rate of return — the interest rate, assuming risk-neutrality. This is the rate which is used to discount future income, irrespective of how the company raises finance (whether through debt, new equity or retentions) since it is the rate which investors take into account when deciding upon whether to give up funds now for higher income in the future, or borrow funds in return for less income in the future.

Tax complicates this description. It is often the case that at both the corporate and personal level, one rate of tax applies to interest payments, another to capital gains, and a third to profits paid out as dividends. If one form of finance is taxed at a lower rate than another, then a lower pre-tax rate of return need be paid to give the same after-tax rate of return. The King-Fullerton model therefore has a lower discount rate, and hence a lower cost of capital, for the projects financed in a tax minimising manner than under the alternative form of financing.

Debt

In all OECD countries, nominal interest payments are deductible from the corporate tax base. Obviously, the value of this interest deductibility will depend on the amount of tax which is saved due to the deductibility. If the corporate tax rate is 50 per cent, then the net cost to the investor of interest payments is only half that of the gross value of the payments, whereas if the tax rate were 10 per cent the net cost would be 90 per cent of the payments. In other words, the higher the corporate tax rate, the lower the discount rate a company needs to apply to a project. Thus for a marginal project, all the profits a company makes will be paid out in interest — the rate of return after corporation tax a company must earn to persuade an investor (in this case a bank) to give them the finance is simply the interest rate charged by the bank on that loan.

Personal taxes may also determine the size of the wedge between the interest rate and the post-personal tax return, although they do not affect the discount rate when companies borrow. This is because the discount rate which is applied in the King-Fullerton model is that of the shareholder on the assumption that firms act to maximize the wealth of their owners. Shareholders do not get any return directly from a marginal debt financed investment, because all the return is paid out in interest payments, so the personal tax treatment of the interest payments is irrelevant. This is not true of the other two main types of financing (nor would it be true if the debt-financed project earned more than a marginal return).

New equity

If a company raises money by issuing new equity, the tax treatment of a marginal investment may in some cases be the same as that of debt. For example, if a country imposes no corporation tax on dividends paid out to shareholders[8], then for a marginal investment this is the same as exempting interest payments. In this case, the only reason why the discount rate on projects financed by new equity might differ from projects financed by borrowing would be if the personal taxes charged on interest for debt differed from those charged on dividends. If dividends are taxed at a higher personal tax rate than interest, then companies will have to pay out a higher rate of return to equity investors in order to give them the same after tax rate of return as if they had invested in some interest-bearing asset. Hence the discount rate would be higher.

Full deduction of dividend payments under the corporate tax is uncommon. However, the identical result is achieved by full imputation systems. As long as the personal tax system does not discriminate between sources of investment income then the discount rate on a marginal investment is the same as for debt.

Where imputation of corporate taxes to shareholders is only partial, then the discount rate will be higher than in the full-imputation case. Some corporate tax is paid, as well as personal taxes. Similarly where there is a split rate system; even if the corporate tax rate on dividends is lower than the tax rate on retained profits[9] then as long as it is positive the discount rate will be higher than it is for debt, and there will be a larger tax wedge.

Retained earnings

If there is a classical tax system then at the corporate level the tax treatment of dividends and retained earnings are identical. If there is an imputation system, the situation is more complex; with retained earnings the imputation system is in effect irrelevant. In this case, the investment is financed by a reduction in dividend payments, and the return is paid to shareholders as a dividend. Since the tax rate on dividend payments is applied to both flows, it nets out of the analysis. However, personal taxes are usually more complicated when earnings are retained to finance investment. Where companies retain earnings in order to invest them, the value of the company will increase without any corresponding increase in the number of shares of that company. Hence all existing shares are worth more, an increase in value which may be subject to capital gains tax offsetting the reduction in taxation of dividends. The discount rate for retained earnings therefore reflects the relative size of this capital gains tax rate and the tax rate on interest (the alternative use of funds being lending). Since the personal tax treatment of capital gains is less onerous than the tax treatment of dividends or interest in many countries, the discount rate applicable to retained earnings is often lower when personal taxes are taken into account.

Personal tax rates

From the discussion of discount rates above, it is apparent that personal taxes have two effects in the calculation of effective tax rates on marginal investment. First, and most obviously, personal taxes determine the difference between the interest rate and the post-personal tax return. The larger are personal taxes, the larger this wedge will be. However, what is perhaps less obvious is that this wedge will not differ between debt, dividends and capital gains (i.e. retained earnings). The return which the shareholders must eventually expect to receive in order to induce them to agree to the project must be at least as good as the alternative use of their funds; in other words, regardless of how the project is actually financed, there is some rate of return which they must expect to receive. The assumption which is made in this study is that a typical alternative use of funds is either a bank deposit or some form of government bond. The difference between the interest rate and post-personal tax rate of return is due to the tax rate on this alternative use of funds. If the tax rate on dividends or capital gains differs from this rate, then the return the company will have to earn must alter. This is why personal tax rates enter the company discount rate in the King-Fullerton methodology, and this is the second way in which personal tax rates can alter the effective tax rate.

For example, in Iceland the personal tax rate on dividends is 39.8 per cent, but the tax rate on interest is 0 per cent. To induce financiers to take up new equity issues rather than debt, the company must pay a correspondingly higher pre-tax return than it would need to if it financed itself by borrowing. After tax, the return must be the same. Hence when looking at the return received by Icelandic investors, given a real interest rate of 5 per cent, they must receive 5 per cent. In terms of the tax wedge, the personal tax means a larger return is needed on equity financed investment before taxes than if debt were used; it does not mean that the final return on investment in different sorts of finance can be different.

Because the differential rates of tax on interest, dividends and capital gains will alter the discount rate which companies apply to investment projects, a change in the personal tax system may alter the difference between the interest rate and post-corporate tax rates of return. Consequently, it is not possible to make a clear distinction between that part of the tax wedge caused by corporate taxation, and that part attributable to the personal tax system.

Old view versus new view

The importance to be attached to the different tax treatment of new equity, retained earnings and debt, is strongly influenced by whether the old view or the new view of dividend taxation is preferred (see chapter 2). Under the old view, the taxation of income both at the corporate level and at the shareholder level, raises the rate of return required by companies and discourages finance for projects being provided in the form of equity, whereas under the new view, the overall tax rate on dividends is much less important, being capitalised in the share price. Under the old view, a much greater degree of importance is attached to the taxation of new equity issues than under the new view. Hence those who believe in the new view wish to give a much greater weight to the taxation of retained earnings than those who believe in the old view. In the results below, the tax wedges on projects financed by either sort of equity are reported, and generally retentions are included in calculations of the overall average tax wedge. However, the results for investments financed by just debt and new equity are also considered, and these might be interpreted as representing the old view.

C. The effects of different tax parameters

Corporate tax rates

The corporate tax rates given in table 3.14 in chapter 3 affect the marginal effective tax rates calculated in this chapter in several ways. Other things being equal, the higher the corporate tax rates the greater the value of nominal interest relief, so the lower the discount rates applied to an investment, and the smaller the tax wedges on a marginal investment financed by debt[10]. In contrast, profits made by marginal projects financed by new equity or retentions will be taxed, so the higher tax rate will generally tend to increase the tax wedge, although this depends in the new equity case on the degree of imputation (if any). For both debt and equity a complicating factor is the fact that capital allowances are given on new investment. These capital allowances reduce the tax base, and their value is therefore greater the higher is the tax rate. However, this factor will not offset the other factors unless the depreciation rate allowed for tax purposes is high.

Personal taxes on investment income

The average marginal tax rates may differ if those who receive dividends have different characteristics to those who get interest income (e.g have higher incomes). If this is the only reason for a difference in average marginal tax rates, then any particular individual person will face the same marginal tax rate on interest and dividends. This distinction is in fact an important one. As the King and Fullerton model is calculating the minimum rate of return which a company must earn in order to be able to match the rate of return on an alternative use of the financiers funds, it is the set of personal tax rates faced by a particular financier which matters, not the average marginal tax rates paid by all those who invest in dividends as opposed to the average marginal tax rates faced by those who invest in bonds issued by companies. Hence although the average marginal tax rate paid on interest in the United Kingdom is 24 per cent as compared to an average marginal tax rate on dividends of 32 per cent, no individual faces such a set of tax rates. In calculating the marginal effective tax rates on those paying the average marginal personal tax rates reported in the next section, the average marginal tax rates on dividends have been used.

There are a number of marginal tax rates in each country. In the context of the present study, two tax rates which are worth considering are those for the zero-rate personal taxpayers (usually investment intermediaries of some sort, such as pension funds or insurance companies) and top-rate taxpayers. Of course, the prevalence of each type of taxpayer will vary substantially from country to country, and for this reason some sort of average marginal tax rate is used. Table 3.19 in Chapter 3 gives some such rates. These average marginal tax rates may not actually apply to any investor but they are a useful synthetic number[11].

The tax rate on interest income has an impact on marginal effective tax rates which is different from that on dividend income. The higher the tax rate on interest income the lower will be the attractiveness of this as an alternative form of investment compared to investment in equities. Thus equity investment in the company is more attractive. This is reflected in a lower discount rate for retained earnings and new equity financed investments. As already noted, the tax rate on dividends is only relevant to investment financed by new equity, the return of which is paid as a dividend. The higher the tax rate on dividends the less attractive is a new equity investment. This is reflected in a higher discount rate for new equity finance. If the tax rates on interest and dividends are equal, these two effects on the discount rate for new equity finance exactly offset each other.

Personal taxes on capital gains

In several countries the capital gains tax rates vary according to how long the assets are held before any gains are realised. In Norway for example, capital gains are taxed only if assets are sold within three years of their purchase. All countries which tax capital gains tax only realised capital gains. Tax on the capital gain can therefore be deferred into the future. To take account of this practice, capital gains are treated on an accruals basis. The rationale for this is that it is assumed that in each year an individual sells (and therefore is taxed on) some proportion of the remaining value of his or her capital gain. Where tax rates fall over time, this means that those capital gains sold in the first few years will face a higher statutory tax rate than will have to be paid on those sold after the tax rate is reduced. The different tax rates are in effect being weighted by the length of time they last and how far they are into the future[12].

The personal capital gains tax rate is only relevant for investments financed by retained earnings. As noted above, reducing dividend payments to fund an investment saves the tax that would have been paid on the dividend, but introduces a potential tax on the increase in the share value of the company. The higher is this capital gains tax the less attractive will be retained earnings as the source of finance. Again, this is reflected in a higher discount rate applied to retained earnings.

Capital allowances

Capital allowances reduce the rate of return required from that asset in order to cover the initial outlay. The value of the allowance will be determined by the depreciation rate, but also by the corporate tax rate, as this determines the amount of tax which the allowance saves the company. The higher the capital allowance, the greater the value to the company as the effective cost of the investment is lowered, so reducing the rate of return they need earn. Therefore where companies are given a choice of depreciation rates, they are assumed to take the maximum rate. In some circumstances (for example, where companies are making a loss) this might not be the optimal strategy — a lower rate might sometimes be preferable. In this study, however, it is assumed that all companies are making profits, and that they always take the highest possible depreciation rate.

Tables 3.9-3.11 in Chapter 3 show that in some cases a "switchover" from declining balance to straight line depreciation is permitted. In these countries it is assumed that companies will make this "switch" as soon as the value of the straight line depreciation exceeds that of the declining balance[13]. In a few countries, the tax depreciation rate is based on the estimated lifetime of the asset. It clearly is in the interests of the businesses concerned to claim that this is shorter than it actually is, in order to get higher allowances. Where the depreciation rates for tax purposes are based on the estimated lifetime of the assets, an assumption is made that machinery lasts for eight years, and buildings for twenty-five, but these figures are lower than the estimates which are used for the true lifetime of the assets[14].

Inventories

Inventories are included in this study as one type of asset which a company can purchase. The return generated may not be as obvious as that for, say, machinery. But it does exist: consider the additional costs which the company would bear if it did not hold inventories - the saving of these costs represents a return to holding inventories. Under some accounting procedures (for example, first-in-first-out), inflation results in an increase in the book value of inventories which may then be taxed. Clearly, the higher the inflation rate and the higher the corporate tax rate, the greater will this tax be. For the purposes of the effective tax rate calculations, the precise accounting procedures need not be known. What is important is the degree to which inflation results in an increase in taxable profits due to the nominal appreciation in the value of inventories, with fully inflation-neutral systems (including last-in-first-out) being at one end of the scale, and unindexed systems (including first-in-first-out) at the other.

Weights

Annex 5 gives the proportion of investment in each type of asset and the proportion of company finance from each source of funds for those countries within the OECD where data were available. These are used to weight the relevant tax wedges for each of the nine asset/finance combinations to give an overall average tax wedge (see section E below). The weights which are used are those which reflect an equiproportional increase in the capital stock, financed in the same manner as the existing stock. This means that the average composition of the current capital stock and sources of finance is also the composition of the marginal investment.

This approach raises a number of conceptual difficulties. First, the asset and finance composition of the marginal investment may be different from the average of the asset composition and financing structure of stock of capital. Secondly, if the tax system distorts company choices either in terms of asset or financing structures, then that activity is given a higher weight in the overall average tax wedge. Supposing, for example, in the absence of tax, companies would finance investments equally by debt and new equity, but that the tax system encourages firms to use debt to provide 80 per cent of their finance. Using these actual weights to calculate the overall average would weight the average tax rate closer to that of debt. Whilst this set of weights is of some importance, it would also be of interest to know the set of weights which would be appropriate in the absence of tax distortion. The weights appropriate for marginal investments in the absence of tax are, however, unavailable.

Ideally, weights based on an equiproportionate increase in the capital stock and the way in which it is financed should be based on the market value of the stock and the types of finance. Unfortunately, the weights discussed in Annex 5 have been calculated in different ways. There is no "right" set of weights, but a problem arises when different methods of calculation are used — namely, two countries with identical tax systems and identical capital stocks and financing behaviour might be presented as having different tax rates because of differences in the calculation of weights. To avoid this the basic results given below reflect typical weights given by countries who valued their stock of assets at replacement cost and valued their debt:equity ratio at market value, with the split of equity into retentions and new equity made on the basis of recent experience. These come out as 50 per cent for machinery, 28 per cent for buildings and 22 per cent for inventories; and 35 per cent for debt, 10 per cent for new equity and 55 per cent for retentions.

Average effective tax rates using any weights provided by each country are reported in Section E. These averages will not be comparable across countries, but can be compared with the average tax rates for that country obtained using the average weights.

D. Limitations of the King-Fullerton approach

Before examining the results presented in the next section, it may be useful to gather together many of the limitations of the analysis which have already been outlined. Most of them reflect the fact that the King-Fullerton approach cannot accurately record the complexities of corporate tax systems; simplifications must be made in order to keep the number of results manageable.

Simplifications are required to reduce the number of possible calculations. First, this study considers only manufacturing industry. In some countries, different tax rates are applied to profits made in other sectors. Second, it considers three types of ultimate investor, who face different rates of personal tax: tax exempt institutions[15], individuals who face average marginal personal tax rates and individuals who face the highest marginal personal tax rates. Third, it is assumed that the company can raise finance in one of three ways — debt, new equity and retained earnings. More complex financial instruments, which generally blur the distinction between debt and equity, are not considered. Fourth, the investment is in one of three types of asset — industrial buildings, machinery, and inventories. Different machines and buildings depreciate at different rates, so limiting the type of investments to just three generic types in this way inevitably reduces the amount of variation in effective tax rates within each country's tax system. Furthermore, it is assumed that all companies are making a profit and will therefore generally take the maximum permissible capital allowances (i.e. there is no tax exhaustion). It is also necessary to make some assumptions as to the true economic depreciation rates of assets. The economic depreciation rates used in this study are summarised in the table 4.1, together with the main simplifications made. Inevitably, these simplifications affect the nature of the results obtained.

Variation in effective tax wedges is also reduced by the fact that only one parameter can be chosen as representative of what may be many different parameters relevant for different situations. For example, the USA has several different depreciation rates for various classes of asset, and many states have their own local corporate tax rates, but for the United States as a whole only a typical depreciation rate for machinery and industrial buildings can be chosen, and a typical local tax rate used. In addition, the actual real economic depreciation of any particular building or item of machinery may differ from the assumed real depreciation rates given in the table above. Taking only nine measures of the tax wedge in each country is a large simplification of the true situation.

The tax wedge will vary according to the type of asset (because of different capital allowance rates relative to the assumed true economic depreciation rates) and the type of finance (because the tax treatment of debt, dividends and retained earnings differs). This results in many different possible combinations of assets and finance. In order to facilitate an overall interpretation of the effective tax rates, an average of the different options is calculated using the proportion of the total capital stock in each country accounted for by each asset and the proportion of finance raised by the company accounted for by each type of finance. This average measure is seen as representing an equiproportional increase in the size of the corporate sector. Although this averaging provides a general assessment of the situation in any particular country, to some extent it does lead to an estimate of the average marginal tax wedge which may be lower than the "true" average marginal tax wedge. This is due to the fact that most investment may be done in a particular asset financed by a particular investment because it is the most tax efficient way to operate, so exaggerating the importance of that element of the investment/finance matrix in calculation of the average tax wedge.

Table 4.1. **Summary of restrictions and assumptions**

1. Restrictions		
Sector	Manufacturing	
Sources of Finance	Retained earnings, new equity, debt	
Types of asset	Machinery, buildings, inventories	
Shareholders	Tax exempt institutions, average personal tax rates, highest personal tax rates	

2. Assumptions		
	Machinery	Buildings
Economic depreciation rate[16]	12.3%	3.6%
Length of life for tax purposes where no other rate is specified	8 years	25 years
Inventories are assumed not to depreciate		

Some other fundamental limitations which relate to the King and Fullerton methodology are that current investment decisions are assumed to be made on the basis of the current tax system, and the current inflation rate. In fact, the "expected" profitability of investment depends on expected future returns and so on expected future inflation rates and tax parameters. Only if current inflation and tax rates are an unbiased guide to expected future inflation and tax rates will the King and Fullerton tax wedges be the appropriate parameters for simulating business decision-making. The general downward trend of tax rates within the OECD in recent years suggests that this condition may not be satisfied, in which case the relevant interpretation of the results generated by this model is that they are the basis on which firms would make decisions if they expected no further changes.

Secondly, it should be recognised that the King and Fullerton methodology is not the only possible way of generating estimates of the effects of different tax systems. Alternative assumptions will give different results[17]. However, the King and Fullerton methodology has the advantage of being internationally the most familiar of such models. The results produced by the model should be understood as summarising and quantifying the essential features of the tax system in a relatively straightforward manner; they calculate an estimate of the distortive effects of the tax system for typical investments. The actual effects of the tax system will, of course, vary according to the particular project which a company undertakes.

Besides these broad limitations on the study, there are a number of specific limitations which have, in most countries, a relatively minor influence on the tax wedge calculations. All wealth taxes are ignored, as are grants. Grants are often given to companies investing in particular regions or types of industry, or are given by government discretion. Including grants would require some judgement to be made about which are sufficiently general to warrant inclusion. Instead of making such arbitrary decisions, it is more satisfactory to exclude them altogether, especially because they are rarely generally available to all companies irrespective of their circumstances[18]. Finally, it is assumed that there are no differences in the timing of tax payments in different countries, which, as shown by Table 3.17, is certainly not the case.

Although this list of limitations is long, it remains the case that the estimates which are generated do reveal many of the potential distortions which are caused by taxing corporate profits -- namely, the bias against certain types of financing arrangements, the effects of inflation, and (with less precision) broadly the degree to which the tax system encourages or discourages investment in certain sectors or activities.

96

E. Results

Base case

The first case to be considered is one where all personal taxes are set to zero. Note that assuming that the personal tax rate is zero is not necessarily the same as saying that the personal taxpayer is exempt from tax[19]. There are three good reasons for taking this as a base case: first, it is the simplest case and permits the impact of the corporate tax on its own to be considered; second, in many countries tax-exempt institutions are a prominent source of company finance; third, in an open economy where the interest rate is primarily determined on the international capital market and where stocks are efficiently traded across borders, it is unclear, at least for mature companies, as to whom is the marginal shareholder — residents of the country in question, or non-residents. Consequently, it can be difficult to decide which personal taxes are relevant for the calculations. For this base case, inflation is set at the projected average OECD rate for 1991 — 4.5 per cent — so all the variation in effective tax rates between countries is purely due to differences in their corporate tax systems.

Because there are no personal taxes, the most appropriate measure of the effects of the tax system is the pre-corporate tax rate of return necessary to earn a given post-corporate tax return. This will also be the return to the financier — since there are no personal taxes. Throughout this chapter (and the following one), the given post-corporate tax real return is taken to be 5 per cent.[20] For this case, there are nine possible combinations of asset and finance for which tax rates can be calculated. Before looking at these results for all 24 countries an example of the calculations is discussed in more detail.

An example: Austria

Table 4.2 gives the appropriate required pre-tax rates of return for Austria.

Table 4.2. **Required pre-corporate tax rates of return with a 5 per cent real interest rate in Austria***

Finance	Asset			
	Buildings	Machinery	Inventories	Average
Retentions	7.2	5.7	11.0	7.3
New Equity	7.2	5.7	11.0	7.3
Debt	2.2	1.2	5.0	2.3
Average	5.4	4.1	8.9	5.5

* No personal taxes, inflation at the OECD average of 4.5 per cent.

This table should be interpreted as follows: for a typical investment in a new building, financed by retained profits, a pre-tax return of 7.2 per cent on the capital invested is required in order to generate a high enough post-tax return when real interest rates are 5 per cent. In this particular case, the return will be in the form of a capital gain. In the absence of tax, projects earning between 5 per cent and 7.2 per cent would be profitable; if tax had to be paid, they would be unprofitable. If the only possible finance is retained earnings, then tax would have discouraged economically profitable investment from taking place. For machinery, a return of 5.7 per cent is necessary, but for an investment in inventories a return of 11.0 per cent is required. If the company financed the same investment by issuing new shares, exactly the same pre-tax rates of return would be necessary in order to pay a 5 per cent return to the shareholders in the form of a dividend as was required when the company retained earnings. In contrast, for investments in inventories financed by borrowing, a return of exactly 5 per cent is required before tax to pay 5 per cent after tax, and for machinery the company only needs to earn 1.2 per cent to be able to give the debtholders a return of 5 per cent.

A worked example is given in Annex 1 which describes in some detail how these results are obtained, but some flavour of the reasons can be given here. The discount rate, for example, is relatively simple to understand in this case. Since there are no personal taxes, and Austria does not have an imputation system, the discount rate which shareholders will apply to investments financed by either new equity or retentions will be the real interest rate (5 per cent) plus the rate of inflation (4.5 per cent) plus the product of the two rates to get a discrete time nominal interest rate of 9.7 per cent. Any income or expenditure one year into the future therefore has to be divided by 1.097 in order to get its current value.

The overall corporate tax rate in Austria is 39.1 per cent. Nominal interest payments are tax deductible, so any additional interest payments reduce companies' tax bills. The discount rate for debt is therefore 60.9 per cent of 9.7 per cent — which is 5.9 per cent. Any allowances received in the future are therefore evaluated at a lower discount rate if the source of finance is debt than if it were equity. The current value of capital allowances given in Austria for machinery when evaluated at the equity discount rate is around 36.7 per cent of the original cost of the asset, for example, whereas when evaluated at the debt discount rate it is worth 40 per cent. Similarly, the returns on the investment can be discounted at a lower rate for debt. Hence for any particular asset in this base case, the difference between the debt calculation and the calculation for the two types of equity is due to the application of a different discount rate.

The reason why investments in machinery and buildings have different required pre-tax rates of return to obtain the same post-tax return is that capital allowances differ from the true economic depreciation rates in some unsystematic way. In this case, for example, the depreciation rate for buildings is relatively less generous (compared to true depreciation rates) than is the one for machinery. Hence the cost of the project is lower, so the required return is lower. For debt, the combination of nominal interest relief and capital allowances results in the government effectively subsidising marginal investments. A project earning less than 5 per cent before tax (and therefore earning insufficient profit to persuade a financier to undertake it in the absence of tax) earns 5 per cent after tax. For inventories, the nominal gain in their value is taxable (at 39.1 per cent), and this results in relatively large differences between the required pre-corporate tax return and the post-corporate tax return.

Using the weights outlined in section C (50 per cent machinery, 28 per cent buildings and 22 per cent inventories), the average required pre-tax return necessary to finance a project financed by new equity or retentions in Austria is 7.3 per cent, whereas for debt it is 2.3 per cent. Similarly, the weights for finance (35 per cent debt, 10 per cent new equity and 55 per cent retentions) result in average required pre-tax rates of return on investment in machinery, buildings and inventories of 5.4 per cent, 4.1 per cent and 8.9 per cent. Overall, across all nine asset and finance combinations, the average required rate of return is 5.5 per cent.

Therefore it is reasonable to say that regardless of the type of asset, the Austrian tax system favours debt finance, and regardless of the precise way in which a project is financed, stocks are treated relatively harshly compared to the other sorts of asset. It is more difficult to say anything conclusive about the relative taxation of machinery and buildings; the precise estimates of required pre-tax returns are sensitive to the assumptions made about real economic depreciation rates, which are not known with any degree of certainty. However, generally it is possible to assert that the Austrian tax system distorts investment patterns and financing decisions. As is shown below, Austria is not peculiar in this regard — all other OECD countries have similar distortions.

Table 4.3. The pre-corporate tax required rate of return necessary when the real interest rate is 5 per cent[1]

Country	Average for each source of finance			Average for each type of asset			Overall average	Standard deviation
	retained earning	new equity	debt	buildings	machinery	inventories		
Australia	9.0	9.0	3.6	7.0	6.4	8.9	7.1	2.8
Austria	7.3	7.3	2.3	5.4	4.1	8.9	5.5	3.0
Belgium	7.1	7.1	2.4	5.3	4.0	8.9	5.4	2.9
Canada	8.1	5.5	3.5	6.3	5.3	8.1	6.2	2.4
Denmark	7.5	7.5	2.8	6.0	5.3	7.0	5.9	2.3
Finland	8.0	2.8	2.8	5.3	4.9	7.7	5.6	2.8
France	7.3	3.1	3.2	5.4	4.5	7.6	5.4	2.4
Germany	9.5	1.6	0.6	5.9	5.1	6.2	5.6	4.5
Greece	7.3	2.2	2.2	4.9	4.8	5.5	5.0	2.6
Iceland	8.0	8.0	4.3	7.7	5.8	7.6	6.7	2.0
Ireland	5.5	5.0	4.5	4.8	5.0	5.6	5.1	0.5
Italy	9.1	1.9	1.9	6.5	5.5	5.7	5.9	3.6
Japan	9.0	9.0	1.6	7.0	5.9	6.7	6.4	3.6
Luxembourg	8.1	8.1	3.0	6.8	4.9	8.9	6.3	2.9
Netherlands	7.1	7.1	2.8	6.0	5.2	5.9	5.6	2.1
New Zealand	8.3	8.3	3.9	6.7	6.3	8.0	6.8	2.2
Norway	10.0	4.5	2.4	6.4	5.3	10.6	6.8	4.2
Portugal	7.5	7.5	2.3	6.1	5.2	6.1	5.7	2.5
Spain	7.8	7.8	3.2	5.7	5.5	8.4	6.2	2.5
Sweden	6.6	4.3	2.7	5.0	4.3	6.6	5.0	2.0
Switzerland	6.6	6.6	3.1	5.6	5.1	5.8	5.4	1.7
Turkey	9.8	9.8	2.5	6.5	6.0	10.9	7.2	4.0
United Kingdom	7.7	4.6	3.5	5.7	5.2	7.8	5.9	2.3
United States	7.6	7.6	2.6	6.6	5.2	6.1	5.8	2.5
Average	7.9	6.1	2.8	6.0	5.2	7.5	5.9	2.7

1.   No personal taxes, average inflation at 4.5 per cent, average weights

Table 4.4: **Corporate tax wedges**[1]

Country	Average for each source of finance			Average for each type of asset			Overall average	Standard deviation
	retained earnings	new equity	debt	buildings	machinery	inventories		
Australia	4.0	4.0	-1.4	2.0	1.4	3.9	2.1	2.8
Austria	2.3	2.3	-2.7	0.4	-0.9	3.9	0.5	3.0
Belgium	2.1	2.1	-2.6	0.3	-1.0	3.9	0.4	2.9
Canada	3.1	0.5	-1.5	1.3	0.3	3.1	1.2	2.4
Denmark	2.5	2.5	-2.2	1.0	0.3	2.0	0.9	2.3
Finland	3.0	-2.2	-2.2	0.3	-0.1	2.7	0.6	2.8
France	2.3	-1.9	-1.8	0.4	-0.5	2.6	0.4	2.4
Germany	4.5	-3.4	-4.4	0.9	0.1	1.2	0.6	4.5
Greece	2.3	-2.8	-2.8	-0.1	-0.2	0.5	0.0	2.6
Iceland	3.0	3.0	-0.7	2.7	0.8	2.6	1.7	2.0
Ireland	0.5	0.0	-0.5	-0.2	0.0	0.6	0.1	0.5
Italy	4.1	-3.1	-3.1	1.5	0.5	0.7	0.9	3.6
Japan	4.0	4.0	-3.4	2.0	0.9	1.7	1.4	3.6
Luxembourg	3.1	3.1	-2.0	1.8	-0.1	3.9	1.3	2.9
Netherlands	2.1	2.1	-2.2	1.0	0.2	0.9	0.6	2.1
New Zealand	3.3	3.3	-1.1	1.7	1.3	3.0	1.8	2.2
Norway	5.0	-0.5	-2.6	1.4	0.3	5.6	1.8	4.2
Portugal	2.5	2.5	-2.7	1.1	0.2	1.1	0.7	2.5
Spain	2.8	2.8	-1.8	0.7	0.5	3.4	1.2	2.5
Sweden	1.6	-0.7	-2.3	0.0	-0.7	1.6	0.0	2.0
Switzerland	1.6	1.6	-1.9	0.6	0.1	0.8	0.4	1.7
Turkey	4.8	4.8	-2.5	1.5	1.0	5.9	2.2	4.0
United Kingdom	2.7	-0.4	-1.5	0.7	0.2	2.8	0.9	2.3
United States	2.6	2.6	-2.4	1.6	0.2	1.1	0.8	2.5
Average	2.9	1.1	-2.2	1.0	0.2	2.5	0.9	2.7

1.   These wedges represent the difference between the pre-corporate tax rate of return necessary when interest rates are at 5 per cent and the post-personal tax rate of return. No personal taxes, inflation at 4.5 per cent, average weights.

Base Case - All Countries

The average pre-corporate tax rates of return necessary to earn a high enough post-corporate tax when the real interest rate is 5 per cent for all 24 OECD countries are given in table 4.3. In table 4.4 the tax wedges are given. In this particular case, the assumption that the marginal personal tax rate is zero means that the post-personal tax rate (s) is the same as the interest rate (r), so the tax wedge (p-s) is the same as the difference between the pre-corporate tax rate of return and the interest rate (p-r); with the latter fixed at 5 per cent, the tax wedges in table 4.4 are always the required pre-tax rates of return less five per cent.

In each table, the seven columns are the average required rates of return for each finance type, for each asset type, and the overall average. The calculation of these averages is as for the Austrian case; namely, the average required rate of return (or tax wedge, where relevant) for projects financed by retained earnings is the average of the required rates of return for investments in the three asset types, weighted in the appropriate proportions. This table brings out most clearly the tendency for tax systems to favour certain types of asset and finance, but compared to tables such as table 4.2 the information which is lost is some sense of the variation in effective tax rates. To resolve this problem, the final column of tables 4.3 and 4.4 provides the (weighted) standard deviation of the cost of capital for the nine possible combinations of assets and finance types. The OECD average consumption price deflator of 4.5 per cent is assumed to prevail in all countries and it is assumed that the marginal personal tax rate is zero.

Different forms of finance

Tables 4.3 and 4.4 clearly indicate several salient features of the corporate tax systems of many OECD countries. First, in almost every country, the finance type which is most tax efficient is debt. The deduction from tax of nominal interest payments significantly reduces the marginal tax rate on investments financed through debt. In those countries where tax rates are highest (e.g. Germany) the required pre-tax rate of return necessary when inflation is 4.5 per cent may even fall almost to zero, due to the high value of nominal interest deductibility.

Some countries have full imputation of corporate taxes to personal taxpayers. These countries (for example, Finland) give as generous a treatment to new equity finance as they do to debt[21]. The rationale is that no tax is charged on a debt financed project (as the project is marginal, all profits go on paying the interest payments) and similarly no corporation tax is charged on dividends — all the corporate tax is imputed to be pre-payment of personal tax, and if none is due, the personal taxpayers reclaim the tax they have "paid" (in the form of the corporate tax) from the government. A similar treatment is more explicitly given in Greece, where dividends as well as debt are deductible from the corporate tax base. In France, a reduction in the tax rate on dividends paid on new share issues results in a favourable treatment of new equity as compared to debt.

A second group of countries comprises those with no mitigation of the double taxation dividends when there are no personal taxes. Austria, Belgium, Denmark, Japan, Luxembourg, the Netherlands, Portugal, Spain, Switzerland, Turkey and the United Sates, (together with Australia and New Zealand for zero rate personal taxpayers) do not discriminate between use of retained earnings and new equity when personal taxes are ignored. (When personal taxes are included in the calculation of effective tax rates, only if the effective personal tax rate on capital gains is the same as that on other investment income in classical corporate tax systems is there no distortion between the two types of equity finance.) As with the full imputation group of countries, the intuition behind this result is that where projects are financed either by retentions or new equity any profits earned on the project are taxed at the same tax rate at the corporate level, and then regardless of whether shareholders take the profits in the form of dividends or capital gains, no further tax is due.

All other countries fall between these two groups, in that debt is the most favoured form of finance, and retentions the least tax-efficient, with new equity somewhere between the two. These countries have one of the four systems referred to in columns 2 to 5 of table 3.1.

Different types of asset

It is difficult to draw broad conclusions as to the relative taxation of buildings and machinery, as was already noted when discussing the specific Austrian case. Although tables 4.3 and 4.4 indicate that machinery is generally taxed at a lower rate than buildings, this may be because the true economic depreciation rates of the two types of assets are incorrectly specified. Though the estimates used have been derived in a rigorous manner (Hulten and Wykoff, 1981), they refer to the USA and may be inappropriate to other countries. However, there are clearly differences between countries. For example, in contrast to all other countries, under the assumptions about economic depreciation rates underlying this study, Ireland, favours buildings over machinery, and Greece and Spain are barely more generous to machinery than to buildings. The United States, Luxembourg and Iceland stand out as being relatively more generous to machinery over buildings than the rest of the countries[22].

A clear distinction can be drawn between those countries without any indexation of inventories and those countries which either use LIFO or have some other way of reducing taxation on the nominal gain in the value of inventories under conditions of inflation. The average required pre-tax rate of return on an investment in inventories in the thirteen countries which tax the nominal inflationary gain in value is 8.4 per cent; for the other eleven countries with some form of inflationary adjustment it is 6.4 per cent. In other words, at a common inflation rate of 4.5 per cent, indexation provisions are successful in keeping effective tax rates on marginal investments significantly lower than they otherwise would be.

Within the group of countries which use FIFO or related systems, particularly high rates of return are required where there are high tax rates. In several countries with such systems, the effective tax rate on inventories is substantially above that on other assets[23]. Use of LIFO means that investments in inventories are insulated from the effects of inflation, whereas the absence of indexation of capital allowances means that investments in other assets are not. In principle, this could provide a case against indexation of inventories if for some reason it is not considered practicable to index capital allowances, as otherwise investment may be diverted away from investment in machinery and buildings. In practice, this would not seem to be a problem in any OECD country since the effective tax rate on inventories is only rarely much below that on other assets[24].

Variation in effective tax rates

In several countries, the overall average required rate of return on new investments is fairly close to 5 per cent. It would obviously not be true to say that because the average rate of return tended to be around 5 per cent the tax systems in most OECD countries did not provide an incentive nor a disincentive to invest. This conclusion would be possible only if the existence of large equal and opposite distortions is deemed to be unimportant, which is an unreasonable assertion. The variance of required rates of return within each country for different asset and finance types indicates that the system discourages some types of investment relative to others. A simple measure of the extent of this distortion in the type of assets and forms of finance is to calculate the standard deviation of the effective tax rates on the nine possible combinations of asset and finance[25].

There is considerable variation in the standard deviation of required rates of return between different OECD countries, but some simple explanations can be made. Most of the variation arises from differences due to the form of finance. In addition, where there is no inflation adjustments of inventories there is often an additional difference in the treatment of buildings and machinery compared to inventories. Given that the marginal personal tax rates in tables 4.3 and 4.4 are zero, all the variation in effective tax rates due to different financing arrangements is due to the combination of the corporate tax rate and the type of tax system. The higher the tax rate, the more important is any difference in the tax treatment of different types of finance (and the more important is the absence of any indexation of depreciation allowances). Hence Ireland has the lowest deviation and Germany, Norway and Turkey are at the opposite extreme.

Why do effective tax rates differ?

So far, discussion has focused on differences in tax treatments of assets and forms of finance within each country. A second issue arising from tables 4.3 and 4.4 is whether comparisons can be made of the average effective tax rates in different countries. Overall, relative statements of the position across different countries are possible — although they are subject to the many provisos already mentioned: the assumed real economic depreciation rates may be inappropriate for a particular country, complex financing arrangements may not be captured by the simple King-Fullerton model, the weights used may put too great a weight on asset and finance types which are relatively highly taxed in that country. Subject to these caveats, Greece, Sweden, Ireland and Belgium had the most generous corporation tax systems (at the common OECD inflation rate) whereas Turkey, New Zealand, Australia and Norway have systems which put a high tax burden on marginal new investment.

Trying to find some common underlying cause for either high or low average effective marginal tax rates across countries is less easy than explaining the variation in required rates of return between different assets and finance types within a country. Table 4.5 below gives the key aspects of the corporate tax systems of the four countries with the highest required rates of return and the four with the lowest required rates of return.

Table 4.5 illustrates that there is no one aspect of the tax system which might be the key in determining whether effective tax rates are high or low. There is considerable heterogeneity even among those tax systems which result in tax rates at the extremes of the OECD scale. High effective tax rates might seem to be associated with the classical system (Australia and New Zealand have what is in effect a classical system for zero rated taxpayers), but this tentative conclusion must be heavily qualified. Belgium has a classical system but a low effective tax rate. Sweden has a tax system which is similar to a classical system (although it has the "Annell" deduction, which gives some mitigation of the tax rate on dividends). The United States and Switzerland both have classical systems, yet have low effective tax rates.

The relationship between statutory tax rates and effective tax rates is equally complex, with New Zealand (one of the lowest statutory tax rates in the OECD) in the same group as Turkey and Norway, both high rate countries. High statutory tax rates make the cost of raising capital by borrowing lower, as well as leading to a higher taxation of any profits which are made, so there is no particular reason why high nominal tax rates should result in large effective tax rates. One reason why those countries with high statutory tax rates do seem to have high effective tax rates is due to the assumption made about weights. Assuming the same proportions of finance throughout the OECD ignores the fact that the incentive to use debt in countries with high corporate tax rates is much greater than elsewhere. To see the advantage in using debt in these countries, compare the required rates of return and tax wedges when just using debt presented in table 4.3 and 4.4. Turkey and Norway both have effective tax rates below the OECD average. In other words, companies in countries with seemingly high average marginal effective tax rates, may be relatively unaffected as long as they do not face some credit constraint. The effect of using country-specific asset and finance weights (presumably endogenous to the tax systems) are examined in table 4.8 below.

What about differences in the tax base? Again, table 4.5 suggests that general conclusions about what causes high effective tax rates are not likely to be convincing. It is clear, for example, that the relatively high effective tax rate in New Zealand is due to the low depreciation rate applied to machinery. But Turkey has generous depreciation rates in comparison with the rest of the OECD. None of the four countries with the highest marginal effective tax rates in the OECD allow inventories to be valued in an inflation-resistant manner, but then nor do the four countries with low effective tax rates, which indicates that the tax treatment of inventories is of insufficient importance to ensure either a low or a high required rate of return.

In conclusion, the differences in the average effective tax rates for each country reported in tables 4.3 and 4.4 cannot be explained by any one feature of the corporate tax system. In individual cases, it is possible to say why the effective tax rate exceeds or falls short of the OECD average, but the particular features of the tax systems responsible for this vary from country to country.

Table 4.5. A comparison of the characteristics of countries with high and low effective tax rates[1]

Country	Integration of corporate and personal income taxes	Highest overall corporate tax rate (%)	Treatment of inventories	Depreciation rates a) Buildings b) Machinery
Highest average effective tax rates:				
Turkey	Shareholders relief	49.2	unindexed	a) 8% DB with switch; b) 25% DB with switch
New Zealand[2]	Full imputation	33	unindexed	a) 2% SL; b) 10% DB
Norway	Zero rate system	50.8	unindexed	a) 7% DB; b) 30% DB
Australia[2]	Full imputation/ Franked dividends	39	unindexed	a) 2.5% SL; b) 18% DB
Lowest average effective tax rates:				
Greece	Zero rate system	42-50	indexed	a) 8% SL; b) 20% SL
Ireland	Partial imputation	10	unindexed	a) First year allowance then 4% SL b) First year allowance then 12.5% DB
Sweden	Partial dividend deduction	30	unindexed	a) 3.3% SL; b) 30% DB
Belgium	Classical	39	unindexed	a) 10% DB with switch plus extra allowance b) 40% DB with switch plus extra allowance

1. Under common inflation conditions and weights.
2. New Zealand and Australia have an imputation system but do not give the tax credit to zero-rate taxpayers (see the country chapters).

Personal taxes

Tables 4.3 and 4.4 were based on a marginal personal tax rate of zero. In Table 4.6 top marginal personal taxes are also considered. Personal taxes have two effects in the King-Fullerton framework. First, they alter the discount rate which is applied to investment projects, thereby changing the required pre-tax rate of return on a marginal investment. Second, they drive a wedge between the post-corporate tax rate of return, and the interest rate. In a closed economy, the net effect of these two effects is to increase the total tax wedge.[26]

Personal taxes do more than simply increase the wedge driven between the initial return on the investment and the return finally received by the financier,[27] since they alter the whole structure of incentives to use one form of finance rather than another. It no longer is true, for example, to say that debt is always the form of finance which minimises the effective tax rate. In nine OECD countries, retaining earnings results in the lowest tax wedge. The reason for this is simply that capital gains are frequently either not taxed at the personal level, (whereas debt or dividends are) or else that capital gains are not taxed on accrual but only on realisation, whereas with dividends and debt any tax due cannot be postponed in this way.

The most extreme difference in tax wedges on different forms of finance is in Iceland, where a marginal investment financed by debt is effectively subsidised, whereas one in new equity faces a tax wedge of over ten per cent. Yet this example illustrates why care needs to be exercised in the interpretation of the wedges in table 4.6. Iceland exempts debt from tax, but also exempts a substantial amount of dividends from tax. In addition, a special tax allowance is granted to individuals investing in shares (see country chapter for details). The wedges in table 4.6 are the "worst" possible scenario from the point of view of the taxpayer, and are only faced by a very small fraction of taxpayers and, more importantly in this context, may account for only a very small amount of funds made available to companies. This is especially true for those countries (e.g. Denmark, Finland) where the capital gains tax rate falls after a period, so many taxpayers seek to reduce their tax bills by deferring realisation of the capital gain until the lower tax rate is applicable.

Actual inflation rates

All tables so far have abstracted from different inflation rates which can cause significant deviations in tax wedges between countries. Applying average inflation rates concentrates attention on differences between tax systems, but in reality companies face very different inflation rates. Table 4.7 therefore allows inflation rates[28] to be at the OECD forecasts for 1991.[29]

Inflation has a complex series of effects on the marginal effective tax wedges. First, it may result in the taxation of increases in the book value of inventories, even though their real value has not changed. Hence the effective tax rates on inventories in those countries without some form of inflationary adjustment to the value of inventories might be expected to increase as inflation increases. Secondly, where capital allowances are given on the purchase price of the asset (historic cost), rather than the replacement value, high inflation reduces the current value of the allowances received in future years in those countries where they are not indexed to inflation. A further slightly more subtle effect will also take place. Some countries spread the depreciation allowances evenly over the lifetime of the asset, whereas others "front-load" the allowances by giving more in the first few years and less thereafter (either through having a higher straight-line rate for some period, then a lower one, or else by having a declining balance system). Suppose that the current value of two different allowances were the same at zero inflation. As inflation increased, the current value of a "front-loaded" system would fall at a slower rate than an evenly-distributed system, because more of the value of the allowance is gained in the first few years, whereas the cumulative effects of inflation will substantially reduce the value of the higher allowances which the company with the evenly-distributed system gets in the last few years of the life of the asset.

Table 4.6. Corporate and personal income tax wedges combined[1]

Country	Average for each source of finance			Average for each type of asset			Overall average	Standard deviation
	retained earnings	new equity	debt	buildings	machinery	inventories		
Australia	0.6	0.6	3.1	1.1	1.1	2.7	1.5	1.4
Austria	0.9	2.7	1.9	1.3	0.4	4.0	1.4	1.6
Belgium	1.8	5.4	-1.7	0.8	-0.4	4.3	0.9	2.9
Canada	3.6	5.0	3.0	3.5	2.9	5.1	3.5	1.1
Denmark	1.4	5.0	3.2	2.3	2.1	3.2	2.4	1.3
Finland	7.2	8.5	-1.3	4.2	3.3	7.0	4.4	4.4
France	3.0	7.4	-0.1	2.3	1.4	4.6	2.3	2.5
Germany	1.0	1.5	0.5	1.2	1.2	-0.1	0.9	0.6
Greece	2.3	4.9	-2.8	0.7	0.5	1.5	0.8	2.8
Iceland	5.4	10.7	-0.7	5.0	2.7	4.8	3.8	3.8
Ireland	0.3	2.5	4.4	1.7	1.9	2.3	1.9	2.0
Italy	4.3	2.8	-0.3	3.2	2.3	2.3	2.6	2.2
Japan	4.5	9.3	-1.6	3.4	2.4	3.1	2.8	3.6
Luxembourg	1.3	7.9	2.8	2.6	1.6	4.4	2.5	2.2
Netherlands	0.3	7.7	3.4	2.4	2.1	1.8	2.1	2.3
New Zealand	2.0	2.0	2.0	1.9	1.6	3.1	2.0	0.6
Norway	3.6	0.8	1.1	2.0	1.4	5.5	2.5	2.1
Portugal	1.7	4.8	-0.3	1.6	1.1	1.5	1.3	1.5
Spain	0.9	3.2	3.5	1.5	1.6	3.5	2.0	1.5
Sweden	2.9	2.1	0.5	1.9	1.4	3.5	2.0	1.4
Switzerland	0.6	5.7	2.2	1.8	1.6	1.6	1.7	1.5
Turkey	9.8	4.2	-1.6	4.6	3.8	9.3	5.3	5.8
United Kingdom	2.1	1.4	2.2	1.7	1.5	3.6	2.0	0.8
United States	3.8	5.9	0.9	3.7	2.5	3.1	3.0	1.7
Average	2.7	4.7	1.0	2.3	1.8	3.6	2.3	2.2

1. The difference between the pre-corporate tax rate of return necessary when real interest rates are 5 per cent post tax and the post-personal tax rate of return. Top marginal rate of personal taxes, average OECD inflation 4.5 per cent, average weights.

Table 4.7: **Corporate and personal income tax wedges with country specific inflation rates[1]**

Country	Average for each source of finance			Average for each type of asset			Overall average	Standard deviation
	retained earnings	new equity	debt	buildings	machinery	inventories		
Australia	0.7	0.7	3.0	1.2	1.2	2.6	1.5	1.3
Austria	0.8	2.4	1.8	1.3	0.2	3.8	1.3	1.5
Belgium	1.6	4.9	-1.4	0.8	-0.3	3.8	0.9	2.5
Canada	3.8	5.6	3.3	3.6	3.1	5.7	3.8	1.2
Denmark	1.3	4.2	2.7	2.1	1.8	2.7	2.1	1.1
Finland	7.5	9.0	-1.4	4.3	3.5	7.3	4.5	4.7
France	2.7	6.4	-0.1	2.1	1.2	4.0	2.1	2.2
Germany	1.2	1.6	0.7	1.3	1.1	0.7	1.0	0.4
Greece	3.5	9.4	-7.8	0.1	0.6	-0.7	0.2	6.1
Iceland	5.1	11.6	-0.8	5.0	2.6	4.8	3.7	4.0
Ireland	0.5	2.5	3.8	1.7	1.8	2.2	1.9	1.5
Italy	4.5	2.9	-0.8	3.1	2.6	1.7	2.5	2.5
Japan	4.1	7.9	-0.8	3.3	2.2	3.6	2.8	3.0
Luxembourg	1.2	7.1	2.6	2.6	1.4	3.9	2.3	2.0
Netherlands	0.5	6.5	2.9	2.2	1.8	2.0	1.9	1.9
New Zealand	2.0	2.0	2.0	1.9	1.6	2.9	2.0	0.5
Norway	3.5	0.8	1.1	2.0	1.4	5.1	2.4	1.9
Portugal	1.9	7.0	-1.5	1.5	1.4	0.3	1.2	2.6
Spain	0.6	3.2	3.9	1.4	1.6	3.8	2.0	1.9
Sweden	3.6	3.5	0.6	2.1	1.7	5.1	2.6	2.0
Switzerland	0.6	5.9	2.2	1.8	1.6	1.6	1.7	1.6
Turkey	21.2	12.7	-16.1	-2.3	1.9	31.8	7.3	21.8
United Kingdom	1.9	1.3	2.4	1.6	1.5	3.8	2.0	1.0
United States	3.7	5.8	0.9	3.7	2.5	3.1	3.0	1.7
Average +	3.3	5.2	0.1	2.0	1.7	4.4	2.4	3.0
Average *	2.5	4.9	0.8	2.2	1.7	3.2	2.1	2.1

+ Averages including Turkey
* Averages excluding Turkey

1) The difference between the pre-corporate tax rate of return necessary when real interest rates are 5 per cent and the post-personal tax rate of return. Top marginal rate of personal taxes, country specific inflation, average weights.

Thirdly, it is often the case that individuals are taxed on the nominal increase in the value of their shares when they realise them, and not their real value (although in many countries a lower rate is applied if shares are held for a number of years, which acts as a form of inflationary adjustment). Inflation will in this case require companies to provide a higher capital gain to shareholders, and in the King-Fullerton methodology, this is modelled by increasing the discount rate applied to retention finance. Hence projects will need to earn a higher pre-tax return to be able to satisfy the ultimate financiers if capital gains are not indexed to inflation.

The inventory, capital allowance, and capital gains effects of inflation will raise the effective tax rate, but there is a way in which inflation will reduce it; namely, the value of nominal interest deductibility rises as inflation rises[30]. At zero inflation, a real interest rate of 5 per cent means that the company has a reduction in its tax base of 5 per cent of the stock of the company's outstanding debt. The value to the company of interest deductibility on a new project is therefore the corporate tax which would be paid on profits equal to 5 per cent of the cost of the new project, if it is financed by debt. At 10 per cent annual inflation, the nominal interest payments will be just over 15 per cent, so the value of nominal interest deductibility on the new project will have increased accordingly. Consequently any tendency to favour debt over equity at low inflation rates becomes all the more marked as inflation rises.

The impact of inflation on the tax system is therefore both pervasive and complex. The country where the tax wedges change most from table 4.6 to table 4.7 is Turkey. This is not surprising given the extremely high rate of inflation — in excess of 60 per cent. Indeed, Turkey is such an outlier, that its inclusion or otherwise when calculating the OECD average tax wedge has a significant impact. Other countries where the use of the actual inflation rates, rather than the OECD average inflation rate, makes a significant difference are Greece and Sweden. Interestingly, in both these countries actual inflation is significantly higher than OECD average inflation, but in Greece the overall average tax wedge falls whereas in Sweden it rises when actual rather than average inflation rates are used — underlining once again that the interaction between inflation and different tax systems is complex.

Less ambiguity surrounds the effects on the variation of tax wedges according to asset and finance type. As inflation increases, the variation in tax wedges increases. It may well be that the higher tax rate on inventories, for example, is offset on average by a lower tax wedge on debt-financed projects, but clearly in the one case the tax wedge has increased whereas it has fallen in the other. In all those cases where actual inflation exceeds the OECD average, the variation in wedges increases from table 4.6 to table 4.7. This inflation-induced increased variation matters since it indicates an increasing potential tax-based distortion in the type of investment taking place in the high inflation countries.

Actual weights

The final variation which can be introduced into calculation of effective tax rates is to vary the importance given to each asset/finance combination, in order to reflect local preferences and circumstances. Table 4.8 uses the weights given in annex 5. Where there are no available weights, no tax wedges are presented. Where there are only partial weights (e.g. the debt/equity ratio, but no split of equity into retentions and new share issues) whatever information which can be utilised is used, supplemented where necessary by the typical weights (for example, the average ratio of new equity to retentions is used to appropriately split the equity weight). Note that it is not appropriate to calculate averages across the countries in this case. The weights are calculated in different ways in different countries, and so the average wedges should not be compared across countries. The appropriate comparison is to see what happens within each country when different weights are used.

If companies are rational they should be responsive to tax differences so that if one particular type of finance or asset is favoured over others, they should invest more in that asset or use relatively more of that source of finance. Of course, there are non-tax reasons why certain financial sources may be preferred in one country to a greater extent than in another, and so it would be simplistic to claim that a relatively lower tax rate on a particular type of finance in one country should result in a greater use of that finance in that country compared to a country with a higher tax rate. Nevertheless, the average wedge using country specific weights is lower than the average wedge using average weights in 12 of the 19 countries for which there is some information. This suggests that companies do take advantage of tax differences, and that tax can affect and therefore distort investment decisions.

Table 4.8: Corporate and personal income tax wedges under country specific inflation rates and weights[1]

Country	Average for each source of finance			Average for each type of asset			Overall average	Standard deviation
	retained earnings	new equity	debt	buildings	machinery	inventories		
Australia	0.7	0.7	3.1	1.3	1.3	2.8	1.7	1.3
Austria	0.7	2.3	1.6	1.5	0.4	4.0	1.4	1.4
Belgium	2.3	5.7	-1.0	0.5	-0.5	3.4	1.2	3.2
Canada	3.8	5.6	3.3	3.6	3.1	5.7	3.8	1.2
Denmark	1.4	4.4	2.9	2.7	2.3	3.4	2.8	1.0
Finland	7.5	9.0	-1.5	2.8	2.2	5.6	3.0	4.7
France	2.6	6.3	-0.1	1.5	0.7	3.3	1.4	2.3
Germany	1.2	1.6	0.7	1.2	1.0	0.6	0.9	0.4
Iceland	6.0	12.8	-0.3	4.0	1.8	3.9	3.6	3.2
Ireland	0.5	2.4	3.8	1.7	1.8	2.2	1.8	1.5
Netherlands	0.5	6.4	2.9	2.0	1.7	1.8	1.8	1.7
New Zealand	2.0	2.0	2.0	1.9	1.6	2.9	2.0	0.5
Norway	3.2	0.6	0.9	1.0	0.6	3.9	1.2	1.3
Portugal	1.9	6.8	-1.3	0.6	0.6	-0.8	0.5	2.0
Sweden	3.8	3.7	0.9	2.0	1.6	5.1	2.8	2.1
Switzerland	0.6	6.0	2.2	1.7	1.5	1.5	1.6	0.9
Turkey	21.2	12.7	-16.1	-5.2	-0.5	28.6	4.6	22.2
United Kingdom	1.9	1.3	2.4	1.5	1.4	3.7	1.9	1.0
United States	3.7	5.8	0.9	3.2	2.2	2.7	2.6	1.5

1 The difference between the pre-corporate tax rate of return necessary when real interest rates are 5 per cent and the post-personal tax rate of return. Top marginal rate of personal taxes, country specific inflation, country specific weights. Only those countries with some information on weights are included.

This still leaves five countries where using local weights results in a higher wedge than when average weights are used (the other two average tax wedges are unchanged). The tax wedges are based on the situation as at the start of 1991, but the weights are generally constructed on the basis of the existing capital stock in some earlier year. If the tax system has changed, the capital stock may be in the process of adjusting to new circumstances. The five countries with average wedges based on local weights which are not lower than when typical weights are used are Australia, Austria, Belgium, Denmark and Sweden — all of whom have had to calculate weights on the basis of data collected either before or only shortly after a tax reform.

Average personal tax rates

In table 4.9 and 4.10, average personal tax rates are compared with zero and top marginal personal tax rates. Table 4.9 gives the post-tax return to investors who invest in marginal projects -- the "s" in King and Fullerton terminology, and Table 4.10 gives the full tax wedge — the difference between the pre-corporate tax rate of return and the post-personal tax return to financiers, for marginal investment projects.

The first column of table 4.9 confirms that by definition where there are no personal taxes, the real post-personal tax return on marginal investments is the same as the real interest rate, which by assumption is 5 per cent. The relation between the various tables can best be understood by noting that the overall average column of table 4.7 and the last column in table 4.10 are the same. If this tax wedge is added to the post-personal tax rate of return given in the last column of table 4.9, the required pre-corporate tax rate of return which must be earned by a company given the real interest rate can be found. Hence an average marginal investment in the USA financed by top rate marginal personal taxpayers when the real interest rate is 5 per cent is one which earns 4.7 per cent before corporation tax, and 1.7 per cent after personal tax.

In the second column of tables 4.9 and 4.10, the average marginal personal tax rates on interest, dividends and capital gains given in tables 3.18 and 3.20 of chapter 3 are applied. In every case except Greece and Iceland, the return received by the financiers of the project falls. Indeed, it is clear from Table 4.9 that post-tax real rates of return need not be positive — in two countries, the real return a financier facing the top marginal personal tax rate gets after all tax has been paid is negative. It might be thought that no potential financier would invest in a project if the expected real return were negative, but this is not in fact the case. A negative return may still be better than the alternative of not investing, where the effective real return is equal to the negative of the inflation rate, since the value of cash held will be eroded.

In Greece and Iceland, the tax rate on some interest income is zero. Regardless of the tax rate on capital gains or dividends, this means that owners of capital have the option of simply investing in the interest-bearing account and getting a tax-free return of the interest rate. The fact that the other forms of capital are taxed means that to be as equally attractive as buying the interest-bearing asset, companies must offer them a higher rate of return. In other words, the return received by financiers is decided not directly by the tax rate on that particular form of investment income (although this will determine the rate of return a company must pay out before personal taxes are charged), but by the taxation of the alternative use of funds[31].

As well as the post-tax return to financiers falling when there are positive personal taxes, the tax wedges increase in every case except that of Australia. For example, whereas in the zero-personal tax rate case, the average wedge driven between the pre-tax return and the post-tax return in Belgium was just 0.4 percentage points, including personal taxes at their average rate increases the wedge to around 0.9 percentage points — the return earned by companies before tax is 0.9 percentage points more than the return to financiers. Australia is seemingly different because the imputation credit is not given to zero-rated taxpayers, only to those with a positive personal tax liablity.

Applying the maximum statutory personal tax rates further reduces the return financiers receive and increases the wedges between pre- and post-tax returns for those countries with progressive tax rates on investment income.

Table 4.9 **Post-tax return to investors with different marginal personal tax rates**[1]

Country	Zero marginal personal tax rate	Average marginal personal tax rate	Top marginal personal tax rate
Australia	5.0	1.5	0.6
Austria	5.0	1.6	0.7
Belgium	5.0	4.2	4.2
Canada	5.0	0.3	-0.2
Denmark	5.0	1.1	0.5
Finland	5.0	4.0	4.0
France	5.0	4.6	3.6
Germany	5.0	1.8	0.7
Greece	5.0	5.0	5.0
Iceland	5.0	5.0	5.0
Ireland	5.0	2.0	0.8
Italy	5.0	3.6	1.7
Japan	5.0	3.5	3.5
Luxembourg	5.0	3.0	0.8
Netherlands	5.0	1.3	0.4
New Zealand	5.0	n.a.	2.1
Norway	5.0	n.a.	1.5
Portugal	5.0	1.1	1.1
Spain	5.0	1.6	-1.0
Sweden	5.0	0.9	0.9
Switzerland	5.0	2.1	0.8
Turkey	5.0	0.6	0.6
United Kingdom	5.0	1.6	0.7
United States	5.0	2.2	1.7

1.   Country specific inflation. Average weights.

Table 4.10 **Corporate and personal income tax wedges combined**[1]

Country	Zero marginal personal tax rate	Average marginal personal tax rate	Top marginal personal tax rate
Australia	2.1	1.2	1.5
Austria	0.4	1.1	1.3
Belgium	0.4	0.9	0.9
Canada	1.2	2.7	3.8
Denmark	0.8	1.9	2.1
Finland	0.8	2.6	4.5
France	0.4	1.0	2.1
Germany	0.8	0.9	1.0
Greece	-1.5	0.2	0.2
Iceland	1.7	2.4	3.7
Ireland	0.1	1.5	1.9
Italy	0.6	2.5	2.5
Japan	1.5	2.8	2.8
Luxembourg	1.3	1.7	2.3
Netherlands	0.7	1.7	1.9
New Zealand	1.7	n.a.	2.0
Norway	1.7	n.a.	2.4
Portugal	0.2	1.2	1.2
Spain	1.3	2.2	2.0
Sweden	-0.1	2.6	2.6
Switzerland	0.4	1.3	1.7
Turkey	3.2	5.0	7.3
United Kingdom	1.0	2.0	2.0
United States	0.8	2.7	3.0

1.   Country specific inflation. Average weights

The variation in average wedges between countries does not significantly alter when personal taxes are included compared to the case where the marginal personal tax rate is zero. Excluding Turkey, in the first column of table 4.10 wedges vary from -1.5 to 2.1 (in Greece and Australia, respectively). In the third column, the wedges vary from 0.2 to 4.5 (in Greece and Finland). As the change in the country having the highest tax wedges indicates, the ranking of the countries by the smallest to the largest tax wedge is substantially altered by the inclusion of personal taxes in the analysis.

Consequently, statements made on the basis of any one of these tables about the effects of the corporate tax system on the overall incentive to invest should be heavily qualified. A country which has a relatively high effective tax rate on investment financed by zero-rate investors may not be taxing business more heavily than a country with a lower effective tax rate. This depends on the availability of funding by zero-rate taxpayers as compared to higher rate personal taxpayers.

F. Sensitivity analysis

Various assumptions have been made to generate the results given so far. This section examines the effects of altering these assumptions, thereby illustrating the sensitivity of the results to the assumptions made.

Inflation rates

In the main body of this chapter, tax wedges under two different inflationary environments were analysed — when inflation was at the OECD average rate and when inflation was at the country specific 1991 level. As noted in the discussion on methodology, the theoretically appropriate inflation rate to use is that which is expected to prevail in the future. Neither of the two inflation rates so far presented may approximate to this rate. In this section, the effects of making different inflationary assumptions is examined.

Table 4.11 uses average asset and finance weights, and applies identical inflation rates across the different countries. Personal tax rates are taken to be zero. The tax wedges across countries under zero inflation prove to be positive in most cases, with only Iceland and Japan having a tax wedge above 1.5 and Austria below 0. Increasing the common inflation rate to the OECD average of 4.5 per cent results in the tax wedge falling to zero in Greece, and increasing the inflation rate further to 10 per cent results in the tax wedge becoming negative in Germany, Greece and Sweden. However, this fall in the size of tax wedges as inflation rises is not a general phenomenon throughout the OECD. In nine of the 24 OECD countries, the tax wedge falls steadily; in another ten it increases and in Belgium, Finland, France, Ireland and Sweden it remains roughly constant in size.

The diversity in the effects of inflation on tax wedges in the OECD is due to most tax systems defining values in nominal rather than real terms, with contradictory impacts on different parts of the tax system. As inflation rises, so the value of nominal interest payment deductibility becomes more important, and this effect may or may not dominate over the prevailing lack of indexation provisions for capital allowances, and the absence of stock relief in those countries without LIFO or equivalent methods of inventory valuation.

Other assumptions

Assumptions have been made about the typical values of real interest rates and real economic depreciation rates. It has been assumed that the marginal investment is one which must earn 5 per cent after corporation tax, and that the true economic depreciation rate for machinery is 12.25 per cent and that for industrial buildings is 3.6 per cent. The robustness of the results to these assumptions is tested below.

Table 4.11: **Average wedges with common inflation rates**[1]

Country	Zero inflation rate	Average OECD inflation rate (4.5%)	High inflation rate (10%)
Australia	1.5	2.1	2.5
Austria	-0.2	0.5	1.0
Belgium	0.3	0.4	0.4
Canada	0.9	1.2	1.3
Denmark	0.6	0.9	0.9
Finland	0.6	0.6	0.5
France	0.3	0.4	0.4
Germany	1.2	0.6	-0.4
Greece	0.4	0.0	-0.6
Iceland	1.9	1.7	1.5
Ireland	0.1	0.1	0.1
Italy	1.3	0.9	0.1
Japan	1.7	1.4	0.8
Luxembourg	1.0	1.3	1.6
Netherlands	0.8	0.6	0.3
New Zealand	1.2	1.8	2.1
Norway	1.2	1.8	2.0
Portugal	0.8	0.7	0.3
Spain	0.7	1.2	1.5
Sweden	0.0	0.0	-0.1
Switzerland	0.6	0.4	0.1
Turkey	1.4	2.2	2.8
United Kingdom	0.7	0.9	1.0
United States	1.0	0.8	0.4
Average	0.8	0.9	0.9
(Average Standard Deviation)	1.6	2.7	4.1

1. Average weights, no personal taxes.

The first column of table 4.12 reproduces the tax wedge under the standard assumptions of a 5 per cent real interest rate, with economic depreciation rates of 3.6 per cent and 12.25 per cent, for the case where there is no inflation and no personal taxes. Typical weights are applied when calculating the overall averages. In the second column of figures, the real interest rate is set to be 10 per cent. The tax wedges rise, usually to around 2-2.5 times the original wedge, but in some cases by rather more. However, the increase in the real interest rate does little to alter the relative burden of taxation within the OECD — the countries with the largest tax wedges at the lower interest rate have the largest wedges under the higher interest rate. The changes in the ranking of countries from the largest to the smallest tax wedges are very minor, no country moving by more than a few places.

In the next two columns, the economic depreciation rates are increased to 6 per cent for buildings, and 20 per cent for machinery (the real interest rate is assumed to be 5 per cent). The tax wedges rise compared to the base case given in the first column, but not by a large amount. As was the case with the change in the required rate of return, the ranking of the 24 countries from the largest tax wedge to the smallest tax wedge is insignificantly altered by the change in assumed real depreciation rates.

In the final two columns, the same underlying tax wedges for top-rate tax payers are given a different weight, in that instead of giving new equity a 10 per cent overall weighting (18 per cent of the total weighting given to equity finance), it is given a 55 per cent weight with retentions given a zero weight (so the finance weights are 35 per cent debt and 65 per cent new equity). This is sometimes held to be equivalent to assuming that the "old view" of equity taxation is true. Those countries which favour new equity over retentions (those with imputation or split rate systems or those with relatively high capital gains tax rates) consequently have lower wedges than under the typical weights. The reduction in the tax wedge is largest in the countries with full imputation or equivalent systems. This confirms that if the tax rate on investment financed by new equity is felt to be important and that on retentions irrelevant, having a full imputation system (or equivalent) can make a substantial difference to the effective tax rate, as can differences in personal tax rates. Whether such a view is justified cannot be determined by looking at the tax code.

In conclusion, changes in the assumptions about the required rates of return, or the true economic depreciation rates or the appropriate weight to give to different forms of financing do affect the size of tax wedges. Given the considerable uncertainty over what assumptions should be made about these two influences on company behaviour, statements of the form "on average country X has a larger tax wedge than Y" must be qualified with the provisos that the tax wedge depends on the rate of return on a marginal investment and the actual depreciation rates of the assets needed in the marginal investment. However, on balance, the overall impression gained from the main tables remains unchanged, regardless of the uncertainty surrounding the appropriate depreciation rates.

G. Summary

The aim of this chapter has been to assess the degree to which taxation affects the incentive to undertake domestic investment in each OECD country by trying to answer the following question: *"For a real interest rate of 5 per cent in each country, what is the pre-tax required rate of return (the cost of capital) on different types of investment financed from different sources, and what is the difference between the pre-tax return and the post-tax return earned by individual investors (the tax wedge)?"* Under a fully neutral tax system (such as a cash flow tax), the cost of capital would also be 5 per cent, the tax wedge would be zero and the tax system would not affect investment decisions.

The results presented here suggest that this neutrality is not achieved and systems in the OECD countries introduce at least some potential distortion to investment and savings incentives. In some circumstances, these effects can be very large. It should be emphasized, however, that the methodology used does not answer the question of to what extent these potential distortions are actual effects of savings and investment decisions.

Table 4.12 **Sensitivity analysis**[1]

Country	Standard assumptions	10% real interest rate	Economic depreciation rate for buildings of 6%	Economic depreciation rate for machinery of 20%	Standard assumptions - top personal tax rate	No weight given to retentions ("old view") - top personal tax rate
			Standard Assumptions with modifications:			
Australia	1.5	3.2	1.7	1.9	2.0	2.0
Austria	-0.2	0.9	-0.1	-0.3	0.3	0.8
Belgium	0.3	1.0	0.4	0.3	0.6	1.6
Canada	0.9	1.9	1.1	1.1	2.3	2.6
Denmark	0.6	1.5	0.8	0.8	1.4	2.5
Finland	0.6	1.4	0.7	0.8	2.9	3.0
France	0.3	0.9	0.4	0.5	1.4	2.7
Germany	1.2	2.9	1.4	1.5	1.4	1.5
Greece	0.4	1.1	0.5	0.6	0.8	1.6
Iceland	1.9	4.1	2.2	2.3	4.3	5.6
Ireland	0.1	0.2	0.1	0.1	1.8	2.6
Italy	1.3	2.8	1.5	1.6	2.3	1.7
Japan	1.7	3.4	1.9	2.1	2.6	3.9
Luxembourg	1.0	2.1	1.2	1.1	1.6	3.5
Netherlands	0.8	1.7	0.9	0.9	1.6	3.8
New Zealand	1.2	2.6	1.4	1.6	1.4	1.4
Norway	1.2	2.8	1.5	1.6	1.6	0.8
Portugal	0.8	2.0	1.0	1.0	1.2	2.1
Spain	0.7	1.8	0.8	0.9	2.1	3.0
Sweden	0.0	0.3	0.1	0.1	1.2	0.7
Switzerland	0.6	1.3	0.6	0.7	1.2	2.7
Turkey	1.4	3.3	1.6	1.8	3.7	1.4
United Kingdom	0.7	1.5	0.8	0.9	2.2	1.7
United States	1.0	2.2	1.1	1.2	2.3	2.8
Average	0.8	2.0	1.0	1.1	1.8	2.3

Average wedges with zero inflation rates, average weights and zero marginal personal tax rates under different assumptions.

1. Standard Assumptions: Real interest rate of 5 per cent, buildings depreciate at 3.6 per cent. Machinery depreciates at 12.25 per cent, and new equity issues have a weight of 10 per cent and retentions 55 per cent when working out the average wedge.

To give some idea of the magnitude involved of these potential distortions and ignoring personal taxes, the pre-tax return required by companies from an investment with a real interest rate of 5 per cent is, on average, about 6 per cent[32]. However, this figure hides considerable variation between different forms of investment, which ranges from close to zero to 11 per cent (in exceptional circumstances, such a variation may even be found within a single country). This variation in itself is a source of distortion: not only might the tax system reduce total investment by increasing the required rate of return, it might lead to a misallocation of resources from more profitable activities (before tax) to less profitable activities (before tax).

There is a remarkable similarity between countries in the way that different forms of investment are treated. Investments financed by debt are treated more favourably than those financed by equity. In the absence of personal taxes, investments financed by new equity are, on average, more favourably treated than those financed by retained earnings[33]. Similarly, investment in machinery tends to be treated more generously than investment in buildings[34]. However, investment in inventories is generally discriminated against, often because purely inflationary increases in the value of inventories are taxed.

When personal taxes are also taken into account the potential for distortion is even greater. The average tax wedge (the difference between the pre-tax return and the post-tax return) grows to 2.5 per cent. Once more, this hides considerable variation between different forms of investment which is even greater when personal taxes are allowed for. The forms of discrimination between the different types of investment remain, although it is now the case that, on average, investments financed by retained earnings are more favourably treated than investments financed by new equity.

Tax wedges generally increase as personal tax rates and inflation increase. However, this is not always the case, since some aspects of tax systems become more favoured under these circumstances. The sensitivity analysis carried out suggests, however, that the results are fairly robust to changes in the assumptions made in the calculations.

Notes and references

1. Whilst Spain has participated in this study, it should be noted that the Spanish data provided in Chapters 4 and 5 are subject to a number of additional qualifications other than those which are set out in the text. Much of the background data and the tax parameters are subject to a wide margin of error and it was difficult to model accurately the Spanish tax system. Consequently, the effective tax rate calculations for Spain should be used with some caution.

2. If it is assumed that companies are risk neutral.

3. Full details of the formulae involved, together with a worked example, are given in Annex 1.

4. Hence, this study focuses on the "Fixed-r" case — the pre-corporate tax return necessary to earn a given interest rate. In a closed economy, fixing the interest rate and looking at tax changes is misleading. In fact, the interest rate is likely to change by some (unknown) amount. However, as both p and s for the marginal investment will alter, one of the three has to be fixed in order to make calculations possible, it remains valid to talk about tax wedges for a fixed interest rate, even though this might in fact change. The reason for preferring the Fixed-r case to any other assumption is that in the next chapter the analysis is extended to look at transnational investment, where it is assumed that capital is internationally mobile and so the real interest rate is constant across countries. To be consistent, the Fixed-r case is also used here.

5. For marginal investments, the required pre-corporate tax rate of return (p) is often called "the cost of capital". The reason is that in order to raise capital for a project, the company must expect to earn at least that rate of return in order to be earning enough to be able to pay the providers of the capital with a sufficient return.

6. For example, in one case p might be 5.0 and s 3.0, and in another, p might be 2.0 and s 0.0. The tax wedge in each case is 2, but the marginal tax rates are 40 per cent and 100 per cent. Tax rates are only useful if p is held constant, and r allowed to vary, but in a world of free capital movements, it seems likely that the after corporate tax rate of return will be equalised across countries to some extent, making the Fixed-r case more realistic.

7. King, M.A. and Fullerton, D. (eds) (1984) *The Taxation of Income From Capital: A Comparative Study of the United States, the United Kingdom, Sweden and West Germany.* University of Chicago Press.

8. As happens in Greece.

9. In France, the split is in the opposite direction — a higher tax rate on dividends than on retentions.

10. The tax wedge may become negative in which case to give an investor a marginal return, a pre-tax return of less than that amount need be earned. The rationale for this result is that whilst a high corporate tax rate implies that the tax which would be paid on a company's

existing profits, would be high, the interest payments are tax deductible; so the value of this deduction in terms of a saving in tax is also high, at least if the company would have had a positive tax liability in the absence of this deduction

11.   As noted in the text, the average personal tax rates on dividends or capital gains are not important in themselves when calculating marginal effective tax rates; rather, what matters is the relative taxation of capital gains or dividends compared to other uses of funds by financiers. Hence a problem with calculating the average tax rate on each different sort of investment income separately is that the average may differ solely because different people invest in different forms of assets. Those people with dividend income tend to be richer and hence face higher marginal tax rates in progressive tax systems than those with interest income. The average marginal tax rates may be different, but in fact it may well be the case that no individual faces a different marginal tax rate on interest than on dividends (although note that the effective accrual tax rate on capital gains is likely to differ from either, even if all the statutory tax rates are the same). Where the average marginal personal tax rates on interest and dividends differ, the latter is used in the calculations.

12.   When calculating the effective tax rates and tax wedges below, it is assumed that 10 per cent of any remaining capital gain is sold each year. See Annex 1 for a more technical explanation of the accruals basis of treating capital gains taxes.

13.   For example, Belgium allows depreciation of machinery at 40 per cent declining balance or 20 per cent straight line. In the first year of depreciation of an asset worth BF100, BF40 could be written off if declining balance depreciation were used, as against BF20 in the straight line case, so the company will start depreciating on the declining balance basis. In the second year the firm may deduct 40 per cent of BF60 (BF24), but by the third period, 20 per cent of the original purchase price exceeds the BF14.4 which could be deducted if the firm persisted with declining balance depreciation, so it becomes optimal to switch to straight line depreciation at 20 per cent for the rest of the tax life of the asset. In other countries (e.g. France) the straight line rate is calculated by dividing the remaining undepreciated part of the asset by the number of remaining years of the asset's estimated life. Consequently the straight line alternative will become optimal much later in the asset's life. Several countries permit a switchover only in the depreciation of all the companies' assets, rather than allowing a change for individual assets. In these cases, this study does not allow a switch, as the criteria for switching are clearly rather different.

14.   As noted below, true economic depreciation rates are assumed to be 12.25 per cent and 3.6 per cent.

15.   This is a further reason for treating the results shown in tables 4.3 and 4.4 below with caution. Australia, for example, has very few tax-exempt institutions; pension funds pay 15 per cent on their income.

16.   These estimates are derived from Hulten, C.R. and Wykoff, F.C. (1981), *The measurement of economic depreciation* in C.R. Hulten (ed) Depreciation, Inflation and the Taxation of Income from Capital, Washington DC: Urban Institute.

17.   See, for example, R. Boadway, N. Bruce and J. Mintz *Taxation, inflation and the effective marginal tax rate of capital in Canada*, Canadian Journal of Economics, Vol. 17, 1984, pp. 62-79 and M. Devereux, M. Keen and F. Schiantarelli *Corporation tax asymmetries and investment: evidence from UK panel data*, Institute for Fiscal Studies, London, 1991.

18.   However, where extra depreciation allowances are made generally available (Belgium, for example, allows an additional depreciation of inflation plus 1 per cent) they are included.

19. The difference can have an important effect on the results depending on whether the value of a tax credit under an imputation system can be claimed by the shareholder. In France, for example, tax-exempt shareholders cannot claim the credit, but zero-rated shareholders can.

20. The effects of relaxing this assumption are given in the sensitivity analysis at the end of this chapter.

21. Germany almost falls into this group, in that its national corporation tax system is a full-imputation one, but the local corporate tax is not imputed to the shareholder.

22. This conclusion should be qualified; the United States gives a range of different depreciation allowances but the effective tax rate in table 4.3 reflects just a typical one for each type of asset.

23. For example, Austria, Belgium, Norway and Turkey.

24. Note that inflation increases the effective tax rates on inventories, but reduces the cost of debt finance. For an investment in inventories financed by debt, the two effects cancel out — the required pre-tax rate of return is constant at 5 per cent regardless of the inflation rate.

25. In fact, the *weighted* standard deviation is used to take account of the differences in the importance of the nine permutations.

26. The effect on the required pre-tax rate of return is more complex. When personal taxes are introduced in addition to corporate taxes, then in a closed economy the equilibrium real interest rate will generally rise, and the pre-corporate tax required rate of return will usually be higher than when there are only corporate taxes. However, by construction in this model, the real interest rate is held constant. Although the total tax wedge increases, there is no particular reason why the difference between the pre-corporate tax and the interest rate should rise — indeed, generally the opposite will be the case. Hence if the required pre-corporate tax rates of return *given a fixed real interest rate* were presented they would tend to be lower the higher were personal taxes. Each individual set of required rates of return (for a given set of personal tax rates) would be consistent, but they would not be comparable with each other if the personal tax rates of the financiers differed.

27. With zero marginal personal taxpayers, the average wedge in the OECD is 0.9 percentage points compared to 2.3 percentage points when personal taxes are at their highest statutory rate.

28. Strictly, the OECD estimates of the consumption prices deflator, for calendar year 1991.

29. In Sweden, the inflation rate in 1991 is higher than is usual, due to increases in indirect taxes. These increases may have added up to 3.2 per cent onto the inflation rate. In Canada, there has also been a one-off increase in the inflation rate due to the introduction of GST and associated changes in the tax system in 1991.

30. In this model this is done through application of the "Strict Fisher's Law", so the nominal interest rate is the sum of the real interest rate and inflation in continuous time, and in discrete time is $(1 + r)(1 + \pi)$ where r is the real interest rate and π is the inflation rate. See Bradford and Fullerton; "Pitfalls in the construction and use of effective tax rates" in C.R. Hulten (ed) *Depreciation, Inflation and the Taxation of Income from Capital* (1981), Urban Institute, Washington.

31. See the discussion of personal taxes in the Methodology section of this chapter and the worked example in Annex 1.

32. Based on the assumptions underlying table 4.3.

33. This is due to the practice in some countries of offering an imputation-type tax credit to shareholders zero-rated for personal tax.

34. Although this comparison depends crucially on assumptions made regarding the economic depreciation rate of each asset.

Chapter 5
Effective Tax Rates on International Investment in OECD Countries

A. Effective tax rates on transnational investment

This chapter describes how the framework used to analyse the domestic corporate tax systems of the OECD Member states can be extended to cover investments located in one country by companies resident in another. The conceptual approach is discussed in the first section, together with the simplifying assumptions which are made to prevent the analysis becoming too complex[1]. The second section discusses the additional data on withholding taxes and the treatment of foreign source income which are required in order to calculate transnational effective marginal tax rates. The calculations are presented in the following section. A final section examines the sensitivity of the results to different assumptions.

The tax treatment of transnational investment

Investment across frontiers results in a substantially more complex tax position than investment in one country. The tax treatment of purely domestic investment is determined by one tax system. Transnational investment involves not only dealing with two (or more) tax systems, but also dealing with the interaction of these systems.

A parent company which makes an investment in a foreign country through a subsidiary[2] could raise funds outside the country in which it is resident. However, to keep the study manageable, it is assumed that the relevant shareholder (at the margin) of the parent company resides in the same country. Consequently this study considers only transnational direct investment. Transnational portfolio investment may take place, but either personal taxes are irrelevant for investment decisions or they are assumed to be those faced by domestic shareholders (in which case they may be zero). It is generally assumed that the tax system of the residence country uses the same tax base as the source country. An exception to this assumption is made for the United States where taxable profits are adjusted to reflect differences in the tax base.

Under these assumptions, profit made by the subsidiary may be taxed at four levels. First, it is taxed in the country where the subsidiary is located (the source country) under the corporation tax of that country. Second, it may be taxed by the source country when the profits are repatriated to the parent company. Third, the country where the parent is resident (the residence country) may impose a further corporation tax on the foreign source income of the parent. Fourth, personal taxes may be paid by individual investors on their return.

The relevance of each level of taxation in determining the post-tax profitability of a new investment depends on how the investment is financed. Numerous financing arrangements exist. The parent company could provide funds to the subsidiary by an injection of new equity in the subsidiary, or by lending to the subsidiary and charging interest on the funds. In each case, the parent itself also needs to raise the funds, which it could do by issuing new equity, retaining earnings, or borrowing on its own account. Finance could also be provided by the parent foregoing the receipt of dividends from the subsidiary (ie. the subsidiary could retain its profits rather than repatriate them to the parent) in which case it is assumed that the parent also reduces its own dividend payments.

Each of these seven financing possibilities are examined in this study. The tax treatment of the profits made by the subsidiary will be different in each case. The form in which finance is raised by the parent affects the discount rate which must be applied to the return on the project, for the same reasons as when the project takes place entirely in one country.

Two other forms of financing might be considered, but are excluded on the grounds that they are already covered by domestic calculations. They are that the subsidiary is financed locally, either by issuing equity locally (giving a stake only in the subsidiary, not in the parent) or by borrowing locally. If the subsidiary raises finance locally by borrowing or issuing new equity, then the investors who require a particular rate of return are residents of the country in which the profits are made and the tax is paid. In these cases the investment can be treated as being no different from a purely domestic investment. The fact that the company is formally owned by a parent resident in another country has no impact on the tax situation since[3] all that matters is the return to those who provide finance for the investment.

The role of personal taxes under conditions of international capital mobility.

Individual investors have access to international capital markets. They therefore have a choice between earning the post-tax rate of return on domestic investment, or the post-tax rate of return which companies in another country are prepared to pay. If investments in different countries are perfect substitutes and if the domestic rate of return is below the international rate, all individuals will invest abroad. To prevent this the post-tax domestic rate of return must be at least as high as the post-tax international return. Since the same is true for all countries, the post-tax rate of return must be the same irrespective of the country in which the investment is undertaken. Furthermore, if no one country is large enough to affect this interest rate, then all countries must take it as given. Therefore, there is no reason for savings to equal investment in any particular country. If the international real interest rate results in a lower amount of savings than the companies in that country require to fund the amount of investment they are prepared to undertake at that interest rate, then companies can raise the rest of the funds they require from foreign savers.

The existence of international capital markets has a significant impact on the importance of personal taxes in determining company investment behaviour. A personal tax rate on all forms of interest income will result in a lower post-tax return to savers; consequently they will save less. But assuming that domestic saving is small relative to the world supply of savings, the world interest rate will be unaffected, and so the investment decisions of the domestic corporate sector will be unaffected. In contrast, taxes on corporate income generated in a particular country will affect corporate behaviour, regardless of how the project is financed.

This conclusion depends on there being internationally mobile portfolio capital. If companies can only raise money domestically, then changes in the personal tax treatment of investment income will alter company behaviour. However, if international portfolio investment does take place tax wedges for personal taxpayers will not affect the investment decisions of companies.

The compromise position adopted in this study is that transnational portfolio investment is not ruled out, and so it is generally assumed that personal taxes do not affect investment decisions. Nevertheless, the effective tax rates on transnational portfolio investments are not calculated and it is assumed that parent companies raise finance for marginal projects domestically[4]. Both of these assumptions reduce the complexity of the analysis.

Inflation and exchange rate regimes

In addition to the complexities of international taxation, a further problem is faced when analysing transnational investment. Investors provide companies with funds for investment in one currency. When companies use these funds to finance investments in a different country, they exchange the money for the local currency, and the return on those investments will be in the local currency. To provide the return to the original investors, the earnings of the subsidiary must be changed back into the domestic currency. However, if exchange rates have changed in the period between providing the finance and receiving the return, then the percentage return which the subsidiary appears to have earned on the funds will depend on the currency in which the return is valued.

The principal assumption in this study is that exchange rates reflect changes in purchasing power parity; that is, the value of a stream of earnings from the subsidiary to the parent when expressed in the parent's currency is unaffected by differences in the inflation rates in the two countries. In fact, for many of the tables below it is further assumed that inflation rates are common across countries[5], which implies that there are no movements in exchange rates. Although for the purposes of comparison the fixed exchange rate case is examined in the sensitivity analysis, this assumption can lead to absurdly high or low implied required rates of return[6].

Other limitations

All the limitations with the King and Fullerton methodology (see Chapter 4) are, of course, still present when the analysis becomes transnational, but there are in addition several others. The restriction that the parent raises finance only in the country in which it is resident is one; others are the neglect of thin capitalisation rules[7], the assumption that assets are transferred between members of the same group at their true economic values, the absence of any attempt to assess the effects of the taxation of exchange rate gains and losses, and the restriction of the analysis to the simplest form of group relations — parent:subsidiary — rather than looking at more complex group structures and possibilities for treaty shopping. Nevertheless, the estimates in this study give some indication of the potential distortion by the tax system of transnational investment. The fact that companies may use more complex financial arrangements and group structures in order to minimise tax burdens indicates that the potential distortions reported in this study can be sufficiently large to alter company financial behaviour from that which would otherwise prevail. It should also be recalled that there are costs associated with these complex financial arrangements and cases of failure to pay tax in any country may create new distortions.

B. International tax parameters

As noted above a direct transnational investment may be taxed at four levels. However, in two of these cases, the tax treatment of the transnational investment is identical to the tax treatment of domestic profits. The taxation of the profits of the subsidiary in the source country is generally the same as if the investment were entirely domestic. Similarly, the tax treatment of dividends, interest receipts, or capital gains received from the parent by investors in the parent's country of residence is not generally affected by the origin of the profits[8]. The relevant parameters of these aspects of the tax systems are found in Chapter 3, and their effects on effective tax rates are discussed in Chapter 4. In this section, withholding taxes on dividends and interest payments and the tax treatment of foreign source income are introduced into the calculation of effective tax rates on transnational investment.

Withholding taxes

Withholding taxes are often levied at different rates according to the size of the participation by the resident company in the subsidiary. Generally, the higher the proportion of a company owned by another company, the lower is the withholding tax rate[9]. For the purposes of calculating transnational effective tax rates, an assumption is made that the subsidiary is wholly owned by the parent company, so withholding tax rates are the lowest possible on direct investments from one country into another[10].

Tax treatment of foreign source income.

.   The tax treatment of foreign dividends and interest receipts from the subsidiary in the resident country can take many forms as described in Chapter 3 and analysed in Chapter 2. In the simplest case, foreign income is exempt in the hands of the parent company — so the tax in the source country, the withholding tax and any personal taxes due by those investing in the parent company are the only taxes charged.

Alternatively a credit for foreign tax paid by the subsidiary may be given to the parent[11]. From the point of view of the calculations presented in this chapter, it needs to be noted that in practice a parent from a country using the worldwide credit system is in one of two situations. First the total relevant tax which is paid abroad may be less than would be due under domestic tax, in which case additional investments abroad are subject to the credit system as if it operated on a case- by-case basis. Second, it may pay more tax abroad than it would pay were it investing domestically. In this case, either additional profits earned abroad are effectively exempt in the residence country (if additional foreign tax is less than the equivalent additional domestic tax), or total domestic tax is reduced (if additional foreign tax is greater than the equivalent additional domestic tax). For worldwide credit countries, the basic assumption which is made is that the first situation prevails.

Investment flow weights

The effective tax rate on a transnational investment will determine whether such an investment which would be profitable in the absence of tax remains so once tax is taken into account. However, it is also of interest to know how the average tax rate on transnational investments compares to domestic investments. For example, it is of interest to know whether the effective tax rate on foreign companies investing in a particular country is higher or lower than the tax rate on domestic companies undertaking the same investment.

Some sort of averaging of the effective tax rates on transnational investment involving the different pairs of countries is required, but it is far from obvious what the appropriate weights should be. As in the domestic case, there is a serious conceptual issue regarding the marginal investment that is considered here. The location of the marginal investment is unknown and may be unrelated to the location of infra-marginal investments. This complete lack of information suggests that a simple average may be no worse than a weighted average using, for example, investment flows as weights. Such an approach would be reasonable if, at the margin, the parent company could earn the same post-tax rate of return regardless of the source country. But this raises the problem that some investment flows may be relatively uncommon (e.g. the number of Turkish companies investing in Iceland may be rather small). Indeed, in these cases, governments may not have considered it worthwhile to negotiate a tax treaty, with the result that the effective tax rate is high, but is faced by few companies.

Consistency with the King-Fullerton approach would involve a consideration of an equi-proportional increase in the capital stock, with the implication that weights should be the market values of the capital stock in one country owned by a parent in another country. However, such data do not exist. An alternative would be to use investment flows from recent years, but reliable investment flow data for much of the OECD are also unavailable. Consequently, in most of the results below, simple averages across countries are used. However, averages using investment flow data for those countries where such data are available are reported, and later on in this chapter an approximation to investment flow data for all countries is made using trade flows.

C. Results

This section is divided into seven parts which deal with the following issues: the first sub-section presents the results of what may be called the "base case", i.e. calculation of effective transnational tax rates assuming a common inflation rate across countries, common asset weights, no personal taxes and simple averages of financing weights for the subsidiary. The results are summarised by calculations of simple averages of the effective tax rates on marginal transnational investment from any one country to all other OECD countries — there is no weighting according to the size of actual investment flows.

With this "base case" as the point of departure, each of the following sub-sections then deal with specific issues, by relaxing a number of the assumptions of the "base case". First, there is an analysis of the effects of tax treaties on the required rate of return on a transnational investment (i.e. the impact of the different treatment of foreign source income and withholding taxes between treaty and non-treaty countries).

Then the question of the impact of the level of inflation rates is taken up by applying actual inflation rates for each country, but leaving the other simplfying assumptions of the base case unchanged. The following sub-section takes into account personal income taxes, again, with the other assumptions of the "base case" left unchanged.

The next sub-section looks at the impact of using actual flows of investment between countries as a basis of calculating average effective tax rates, and this is followed by an analysis of the sensitivity of the results to "outliers" (i.e. extreme cases).

The next sub-section provides a sensitivity analysis of the importance of a number of the assumptions referred to above, including the impact of varying the level of inflation and the use of trade flows to weight the tax rates instead of simple averages.

i) Effective tax rates with common economic assumption.

The simplest scenario is to assume that the inflation rate is the same in all countries and that there are no movements in the exchange rate. With these assumptions, the effects of the tax system on transnational investment can be isolated from the effects of prevailing economic conditions.

Where the parent must raise finance which is either loaned to the subsidiary or else injected into the subsidiary in the form of new equity, the same proportions which were used in Chapter 4 are used, namely: 35 per cent debt, 55 per cent retained earnings and 10 per cent new equity. Initially, the marginal personal tax rate for the financier funding the marginal investment is taken to be zero, and as discussed above, this can be interpreted as being the case when there is perfect portfolio capital mobility.

Three fundamental matrices of transnational tax rates are given in tables 5.1, 5.2 and 5.3. These give the required pre-tax rates of return necessary when there is a 5 per cent real interest rate of return when investing from one country to another. The residence country (the country in which the parent is located) is given down the side of each matrix and the source country (the country in which the subsidiary undertaking the investment is located) is given along the top of the matrix. Table 5.1 gives the required pre-tax rates of return when the subsidiary is financed through retaining earnings in the subsidiary, table 5.2 when the finance is through new equity from the parent, and table 5.3 when the parent lends funds to the subsidiary. Table 5.4 presents an average of these matrices to give an overall average required rate of return when investing in one country from another. Note that table 5.1 differs from tables 5.2 and 5.3 in that in the latter two cases, the parent must raise funds. Tables 5.2 and 5.3 are therefore already averages: they show the transnational effective tax rates when finance is provided to the subsidiary in the form of equity and debt respectively in each case across the three forms of finance used by the parent. In all three cases, the reported figure represents the average of the three asset types — buildings, machinery and inventories. The weights used are those reported in Chapter 4: 28 per cent buildings, 50 per cent machinery and 22 per cent inventories.

Table 5.1. Required pre-tax rates of return when the subsidiary is financed by retained earnings[1]

Source:	Australia	Austria	Belgium	Canada	Denmark	Finland	France	Germany	Greece	Iceland	Ireland	Italy
Residence:												
Australia	9.0	7.3	7.1	8.1	7.5	8.0	7.3	9.5	7.3	8.0	5.5	9.1
Austria	9.0	7.3	7.1	8.1	7.5	8.0	7.3	9.5	7.3	8.0	5.5	9.1
Belgium	9.0	7.3	7.1	8.1	7.5	8.0	7.3	9.5	7.3	8.0	5.5	9.1
Canada	9.0	7.3	7.1	8.1	7.5	8.0	7.3	9.5	7.3	8.0	5.5	9.1
Denmark	8.3	6.8	7.1	7.5	7.5	7.7	6.8	8.7	7.3	7.5	5.2	8.4
Finland	9.0	7.3	7.1	8.1	7.5	8.0	7.3	9.5	7.3	8.0	5.5	9.1
France	9.0	7.3	7.1	8.1	7.5	8.0	7.3	9.5	7.3	8.0	5.5	9.1
Germany	9.0	7.3	7.1	8.1	7.5	8.0	7.3	9.5	7.3	8.0	5.5	9.1
Greece	9.0	7.3	7.1	8.1	7.5	8.0	7.3	9.5	7.3	8.0	5.5	9.1
Iceland	9.0	7.3	7.1	8.1	7.5	8.0	7.3	9.5	7.3	8.0	5.5	9.1
Ireland	9.0	7.3	7.1	8.1	7.5	8.0	7.3	9.5	7.3	8.0	5.5	9.1
Italy	9.0	7.3	7.1	8.1	7.5	8.0	7.3	9.5	7.3	8.0	5.5	9.1
Japan	9.0	7.3	7.1	8.1	7.5	8.0	7.3	9.5	7.3	8.0	5.5	9.1
Luxembourg	9.0	7.3	7.1	8.1	7.5	8.0	7.3	9.5	7.3	8.0	5.5	9.1
Netherlands	9.0	7.3	7.1	8.1	7.5	8.0	7.3	9.5	7.3	8.0	5.5	9.1
New Zealand	9.0	7.3	7.1	8.1	7.5	8.0	7.3	9.5	7.3	8.0	5.5	9.1
Norway	9.0	7.3	7.1	8.1	7.5	8.0	7.3	9.5	7.3	8.0	5.5	9.1
Portugal	9.0	7.3	7.1	8.1	7.5	8.0	7.3	9.5	7.3	8.0	5.5	9.1
Spain	9.0	7.3	7.1	8.1	7.5	8.0	7.3	9.5	7.3	8.0	5.5	9.1
Sweden	9.0	7.3	7.1	8.1	7.5	8.0	7.3	9.5	7.3	8.0	5.5	9.1
Switzerland	9.0	7.3	7.1	8.1	7.5	8.0	7.3	9.5	7.3	8.0	5.5	9.1
Turkey	9.0	7.3	7.1	8.1	7.5	8.0	7.3	9.5	7.3	8.0	5.5	9.1
United Kingdom	9.0	7.3	7.1	8.1	7.5	8.0	7.3	9.5	7.3	8.0	5.5	9.1
United States	9.0	7.3	7.1	8.1	7.5	8.0	7.3	9.5	7.3	8.0	5.5	9.1

1. Weighted average of investment in three different assets. Inflation of 4.5 per cent everywhere. No personal taxes.

Table 5.1. (Cont.) **Required pre-tax rates of return when the subsidiary is financed by retained earnings**[1]

Source:	Japan	Luxembourg	Netherlands	N. Zealand	Norway	Portugal	Spain	Sweden	Switzerland	Turkey	UK	US
Residence:												
Australia	9.0	8.1	7.1	9.1	10.0	7.5	7.8	6.1	6.6	9.8	7.7	7.6
Austria	9.0	8.1	7.1	9.1	10.0	7.5	7.8	6.1	6.6	9.8	7.7	7.6
Belgium	9.0	8.1	7.1	9.1	10.0	7.5	7.8	6.1	6.6	9.8	7.7	7.6
Canada	9.0	8.1	7.1	9.1	10.0	7.5	7.8	6.1	6.6	9.8	7.7	7.6
Denmark	8.3	7.5	6.7	7.6	9.1	7.0	7.3	6.1	6.3	8.9	7.2	7.3
Finland	9.0	8.1	7.1	9.1	10.0	7.5	7.8	6.1	6.6	9.8	7.7	7.6
France	9.0	8.1	7.1	9.1	10.0	7.5	7.8	6.1	6.6	9.8	7.7	7.6
Germany	9.0	8.1	7.1	9.1	10.0	7.5	7.8	6.1	6.6	9.8	7.7	7.6
Greece	9.0	8.1	7.1	9.1	10.0	7.5	7.8	6.1	6.6	9.8	7.7	7.6
Iceland	9.0	8.1	7.1	9.1	10.0	7.5	7.8	6.1	6.6	9.8	7.7	7.6
Ireland	9.0	8.1	7.1	9.1	10.0	7.5	7.8	6.1	6.6	9.8	7.7	7.6
Italy	9.0	8.1	7.1	9.1	10.0	7.5	7.8	6.1	6.6	9.8	7.7	7.6
Japan	9.0	8.1	7.1	9.1	10.0	7.5	7.8	6.1	6.6	9.8	7.7	7.6
Luxembourg	9.0	8.1	7.1	9.1	10.0	7.5	7.8	6.1	6.6	9.8	7.7	7.6
Netherlands	9.0	8.1	7.1	8.3	10.0	7.5	7.8	6.1	6.6	9.8	7.7	7.6
New Zealand	9.0	8.1	7.1	9.1	10.0	7.5	7.8	6.1	6.6	9.8	7.7	7.6
Norway	9.0	8.1	7.1	9.1	10.0	7.5	7.8	6.1	6.6	9.8	7.7	7.6
Portugal	9.0	8.1	7.1	9.1	10.0	7.5	7.8	6.1	6.6	9.8	7.7	7.6
Spain	9.0	8.1	7.1	9.1	10.0	7.5	7.8	6.1	6.6	9.8	7.7	7.6
Sweden	9.0	8.1	7.1	9.1	10.0	7.5	7.8	6.1	6.6	9.8	7.7	7.6
Switzerland	9.0	8.1	7.1	9.1	10.0	7.5	7.8	6.1	6.6	9.8	7.7	7.6
Turkey	9.0	8.1	7.1	9.1	10.0	7.5	7.8	6.1	6.6	9.8	7.7	7.6
United Kingdom	9.0	8.1	7.1	9.1	10.0	7.5	7.8	6.1	6.6	9.8	7.7	7.6
United States	9.0	8.1	7.1	9.1	10.0	7.5	7.8	6.1	6.6	9.8	7.7	7.6

1. Weighted average of investment in three different assets. Inflation of 4.5 per cent everywhere. No personal taxes.

Table 5.2. **Required pre-tax rates of return when the Subsidiary is financed by new equity from the parent[1]**

Source: Residence:	Australia	Austria	Belgium	Canada	Denmark	Finland	France	Germany	Greece	Iceland	Ireland	Italy
Australia	7.1	7.5	7.3	8.3	7.7	8.2	9.2	6.2	5.9	9.3	4.2	6.5
Austria	7.1	5.5	7.3	8.3	7.0	7.5	9.2	7.9	5.9	9.3	4.2	6.5
Belgium	7.6	8.0	5.4	8.8	8.2	8.0	9.0	6.7	3.7	10.0	4.5	7.0
Canada	6.1	6.8	6.7	6.2	7.1	7.5	8.0	5.0	8.4	8.7	3.5	5.4
Denmark	6.5	6.4	7.3	7.7	5.9	6.0	6.6	6.0	6.0	5.6	4.0	6.2
Finland	6.5	6.8	6.6	8.7	5.3	5.6	7.3	4.3	5.5	5.3	3.7	4.8
France	7.1	8.0	6.9	7.9	5.8	6.2	5.4	3.8	6.1	10.4	4.0	6.4
Germany	5.6	12.3	7.4	8.4	6.5	6.9	6.8	5.6	1.3	5.4	3.1	10.3
Greece	6.8	11.3	7.7	12.0	13.8	8.2	15.8	7.5	5.0	10.6	11.9	8.0
Iceland	8.1	8.9	8.6	9.7	6.9	6.9	10.7	4.6	6.3	6.7	9.2	9.3
Ireland	7.7	6.1	7.1	8.1	6.5	6.5	8.3	5.9	15.1	22.9	5.1	5.6
Italy	9.5	8.0	7.7	10.0	8.4	8.0	12.1	3.6	7.4	11.0	11.1	5.9
Japan	9.1	7.4	7.2	8.9	7.8	7.8	8.4	5.7	7.2	8.6	10.3	7.0
Luxembourg	7.1	6.1	6.6	7.5	6.4	6.8	7.7	6.2	5.9	9.3	4.1	6.5
Netherlands	7.3	6.3	6.2	7.7	6.0	6.4	7.9	6.4	4.8	9.6	4.3	4.8
New Zealand	7.4	9.6	7.6	8.6	8.0	8.5	9.6	6.5	6.2	9.7	7.4	6.8
Norway	10.2	8.4	7.1	10.4	8.9	8.7	7.6	4.7	27.9	6.9	3.4	6.9
Portugal	15.1	7.5	7.3	19.9	7.0	7.4	9.2	6.2	13.6	20.4	9.7	6.5
Spain	7.3	6.9	7.4	8.4	7.2	7.6	8.6	6.3	6.1	9.5	7.8	6.7
Sweden	7.5	7.2	7.7	8.7	6.2	6.6	7.5	6.6	6.3	6.4	4.5	6.2
Switzerland	7.5	6.5	7.0	8.7	6.2	7.2	8.2	6.6	5.0	7.1	4.5	6.9
Turkey	9.0	8.7	8.4	9.4	9.8	7.7	8.6	7.3	7.0	8.6	10.1	9.0
United Kingdom	7.0	6.1	6.0	7.7	5.7	6.8	8.2	5.9	5.9	10.1	8.2	4.8
United States	7.1	6.1	6.0	7.6	6.4	6.8	7.8	5.5	6.0	6.7	8.6	5.2

1. Parent raises finance by a weighted average of retentions, new equity and debt. Weighted average of investment in three different assets. Inflation of 4.5 per cent everywhere. No personal taxes.

Table 5.2. (cont.) Required pre-tax rates of return when the subsidiary is financed by new equity from the parent[1]

Source: Residence:	Japan	Luxembourg	Netherlands	N. Zealand	Norway	Portugal	Spain	Sweden	Switzerland	Turkey	UK	US
Australia	9.2	8.3	7.3	9.3	4.7	9.5	9.8	6.4	6.9	7.7	6.0	7.8
Austria	8.4	6.9	6.0	12.4	4.7	7.7	7.3	4.7	5.6	7.7	6.0	6.4
Belgium	9.9	6.8	6.5	9.9	5.1	8.2	8.6	6.8	6.6	8.3	5.3	6.9
Canada	7.5	6.1	5.9	8.6	3.6	9.2	7.4	5.8	6.2	8.0	4.6	6.3
Denmark	7.8	5.9	5.1	7.9	3.1	7.3	6.8	4.7	4.8	7.1	4.6	6.2
Finland	8.4	6.6	4.9	9.8	3.3	7.0	7.3	4.3	5.3	7.1	4.1	6.0
France	8.7	6.4	6.1	9.9	3.1	7.3	8.6	4.5	5.7	7.7	6.0	6.5
Germany	7.7	4.9	6.1	9.5	0.9	7.9	6.7	4.4	5.7	6.1	4.6	6.5
Greece	11.5	6.0	6.2	16.1	4.8	11.6	11.8	6.7	7.0	7.1	7.1	14.1
Iceland	9.8	8.0	8.7	12.0	6.3	9.1	9.4	7.0	7.5	7.4	7.9	6.9
Ireland	8.1	6.8	6.7	9.1	5.8	22.2	22.1	6.7	7.2	18.0	7.5	6.5
Italy	8.1	8.4	9.4	10.1	5.7	8.2	9.7	10.6	11.2	6.6	10.5	8.4
Japan	6.4	8.2	8.1	9.4	7.2	8.8	8.6	7.9	8.5	7.4	8.9	7.8
Luxembourg	10.2	6.3	5.8	12.4	4.7	9.5	7.3	5.2	10.6	7.7	4.9	6.4
Netherlands	8.6	6.5	5.6	9.6	4.8	9.7	7.5	4.8	5.2	7.9	5.1	6.6
New Zealand	9.6	8.7	7.7	6.8	4.9	9.9	10.1	6.6	7.1	8.0	6.3	8.1
Norway	7.7	9.1	9.7	10.7	6.8	6.4	10.1	3.9	10.9	7.1	4.4	7.6
Portugal	21.1	13.8	18.7	24.1	5.5	5.7	7.3	17.6	6.6	16.4	7.0	21.6
Spain	8.5	6.5	6.1	12.6	5.0	7.9	6.2	5.9	6.3	7.9	6.5	7.2
Sweden	8.9	7.4	5.8	9.8	3.5	10.0	7.8	5.0	6.0	8.2	5.3	6.8
Switzerland	8.9	8.8	5.8	9.8	4.0	8.2	7.7	5.5	5.4	8.2	5.3	6.8
Turkey	9.5	8.0	7.9	11.7	7.0	8.9	9.2	8.2	9.9	7.2	8.7	10.0
United Kingdom	8.6	6.2	6.0	9.8	4.1	7.5	7.5	5.3	5.7	7.6	5.9	6.4
United States	8.4	7.0	6.1	9.4	5.2	9.5	7.3	5.8	6.4	7.8	6.9	5.8

1. Parent raises finance by a weighted average of retentions, new equity and debt. Weighted average of investment in three different assets. Inflation of 4.5 per cent everywhere. No personal taxes.

Table 5.3. **Required pre-tax rates of return when the subsidiary is financed by a loan from the parent[1]**

Source:	Australia	Austria	Belgium	Canada	Denmark	Finland	France	Germany	Greece	Iceland	Ireland	Italy
Residence:												
Australia	7.1	6.1	6.0	7.3	6.5	6.6	7.3	4.2	6.5	9.2	7.0	5.6
Austria	7.1	5.5	6.0	7.3	6.3	6.4	7.3	4.7	5.5	9.2	7.0	5.6
Belgium	6.7	4.6	5.4	7.5	5.0	5.0	5.5	2.7	4.9	7.3	7.1	5.7
Canada	8.5	7.8	7.6	6.2	8.2	8.3	9.0	5.2	8.4	11.9	8.3	6.7
Denmark	7.0	5.8	5.9	7.2	5.9	6.0	6.6	4.1	6.5	8.1	6.9	5.5
Finland	6.7	5.7	5.7	7.6	5.6	5.6	6.9	2.5	5.2	8.7	7.8	4.4
France	6.1	5.2	4.9	6.3	5.1	5.1	5.4	2.3	4.6	8.8	6.8	4.3
Germany	9.4	13.1	9.6	11.5	9.4	9.5	10.3	5.6	5.7	12.9	10.2	10.3
Greece	6.8	7.2	6.0	8.7	8.5	6.4	10.1	3.2	5.0	10.8	11.9	5.2
Iceland	8.1	7.3	7.1	8.5	6.9	6.9	8.6	4.3	6.4	6.7	9.2	7.2
Ireland	7.7	6.1	6.3	7.7	6.5	6.5	7.5	4.4	15.7	14.6	5.1	5.6
Italy	7.9	7.9	7.6	10.0	8.4	8.0	11.1	3.2	7.4	14.0	14.6	5.9
Japan	9.1	7.4	7.2	8.9	7.8	7.8	8.4	5.3	7.2	10.6	10.3	7.0
Luxembourg	7.1	5.7	5.8	7.1	6.1	6.3	6.9	4.2	6.4	9.3	7.0	5.6
Netherlands	6.7	5.3	5.3	6.7	5.6	5.7	6.5	3.8	4.8	8.7	6.8	4.7
New Zealand	6.6	5.9	5.4	6.7	5.9	6.0	6.7	3.6	6.7	8.5	7.4	5.0
Norway	10.2	8.4	7.6	10.4	8.9	8.7	8.9	4.4	31.0	11.3	8.7	6.9
Portugal	11.0	6.2	6.0	15.2	6.3	6.5	7.4	4.3	14.2	12.6	11.7	5.6
Spain	6.8	5.6	5.7	7.0	6.0	6.1	6.8	3.9	6.6	8.8	7.8	5.3
Sweden	6.3	5.0	5.1	6.4	5.2	5.3	5.9	3.3	4.7	7.3	6.4	4.5
Switzerland	6.3	4.9	5.0	6.4	5.2	5.4	6.0	3.4	4.5	7.5	6.5	4.7
Turkey	9.0	7.8	7.6	9.0	8.5	7.7	8.4	5.8	7.0	10.5	10.1	7.7
United Kingdom	6.2	4.8	4.8	6.3	5.1	5.3	6.2	2.7	4.6	8.8	8.2	4.0
United States	7.0	5.6	5.5	7.0	6.0	6.2	6.8	3.9	5.5	8.4	8.2	5.1

1. Parent raises finance by a weighted average of retentions, new equity and debt. Weighted average of investment in three different assets. Inflation of 4.5 per cent everywhere. No personal taxes.

132

Table 5.3 (cont) **Required pre-tax rates of return when the subsidiary is financed by a loan from the parent[1]**

Source: Residence:	Japan	Luxembourg	Netherlands	N. Zealand	Norway	Portugal	Spain	Sweden	Switzerland	Turkey	UK	US
Australia	6.0	6.9	6.5	7.9	5.2	6.7	7.6	6.2	6.6	6.2	6.6	6.5
Austria	5.7	6.5	6.1	8.9	5.2	6.2	6.8	5.7	6.2	6.2	6.6	6.0
Belgium	5.5	5.0	4.8	7.5	4.1	6.4	7.2	4.9	5.1	5.8	6.4	6.2
Canada	7.2	7.8	7.8	9.8	5.9	8.9	8.8	7.8	8.3	8.0	7.7	7.8
Denmark	5.6	6.2	5.9	7.8	4.7	2.6	2.8	5.6	6.0	6.1	6.3	6.0
Finland	4.8	6.2	5.8	8.1	4.1	5.8	0.8	5.8	6.4	5.2	6.0	5.8
France	4.3	5.4	5.3	7.0	3.8	5.0	6.2	5.1	5.6	4.9	5.9	5.1
Germany	8.2	8.4	9.6	12.3	4.8	10.1	10.2	8.7	10.0	7.8	9.1	9.5
Greece	5.6	6.0	6.2	10.2	4.4	7.3	8.4	6.7	7.0	5.2	7.1	8.5
Iceland	7.0	7.5	7.7	9.7	6.3	7.4	8.2	7.0	7.5	6.8	7.9	6.9
Ireland	6.0	6.8	6.7	8.4	5.8	16.3	16.9	6.7	7.2	11.5	7.5	6.5
Italy	6.2	8.5	9.4	10.1	5.7	7.9	9.7	10.6	11.2	6.3	10.5	8.4
Japan	6.4	8.2	8.1	9.4	7.2	8.0	8.6	7.9	8.5	7.4	8.9	7.8
Luxembourg	6.3	6.3	6.1	8.9	5.2	6.8	6.9	5.8	7.7	6.2	6.4	6.1
Netherlands	5.3	6.0	5.6	7.5	4.9	9.1	6.5	5.4	5.8	5.8	6.0	5.7
New Zeland	5.3	6.3	5.9	6.8	4.7	6.1	6.9	5.7	6.1	5.6	6.2	5.9
Norway	6.8	9.1	9.7	10.7	6.8	7.4	10.1	6.9	10.9	7.1	7.5	8.3
Portugal	13.4	8.6	9.9	15.5	5.5	5.7	6.9	9.6	6.6	10.4	7.0	10.6
Spain	5.4	6.0	5.8	8.5	5.0	2.7	6.2	5.7	6.1	5.9	6.5	6.0
Sweden	4.7	5.7	5.2	7.0	4.2	5.7	6.0	5.0	5.5	5.3	5.7	5.2
Switzerland	4.8	6.0	5.2	7.0	4.3	5.3	6.0	5.2	5.4	6.4	5.7	5.3
Turkey	7.5	8.0	7.9	10.2	7.0	7.9	8.7	7.9	8.9	7.2	8.7	8.6
United Kingdom	4.4	5.4	5.4	7.1	4.1	5.2	6.1	5.3	5.7	4.9	5.9	5.2
United States	5.6	6.4	6.0	7.9	5.3	6.7	6.8	5.9	6.4	6.1	6.8	5.8

1) Parent raises finance by a weighted average of retentions, new equity and debt. Weighted average of investment in three different assets. Inflation of 4.5% everywhere. No personal taxes.

133

Table 5.4. **Required pre-tax rates of return when the subsidiary is financed by one third loans from the parent, one third equity from the parent and one third retentions by the subsidiary[1]**

Source:	Australia	Austria	Belgium	Cananda	Denmark	Finland	France	Germany	Greece	Iceland	Ireland	Italy
Residence:												
Australia	7.1	6.9	6.8	7.9	7.2	7.6	7.9	6.6	6.5	8.8	5.6	7.1
Austria	7.7	5.5	6.8	7.9	6.9	7.3	7.9	7.4	6.2	8.8	5.6	7.1
Belgium	7.8	6.6	5.4	8.1	6.9	7.0	7.3	6.3	5.3	8.4	5.7	7.3
Canada	7.9	7.3	7.1	6.2	7.6	7.9	8.1	6.6	8.0	9.5	5.8	7.1
Denmark	7.3	6.3	6.8	7.5	5.9	6.6	6.7	6.3	6.6	7.1	5.4	6.7
Finland	7.4	6.6	6.4	8.1	6.1	5.6	7.2	5.4	6.0	7.3	5.7	6.1
France	7.4	6.8	6.3	7.4	6.1	6.4	5.4	5.2	6.0	9.1	5.4	6.6
Germany	8.0	10.9	8.0	9.3	7.8	8.1	8.1	5.6	4.8	8.8	6.2	9.9
Greece	7.5	8.6	6.9	9.6	9.9	7.5	11.1	6.7	5.0	9.8	9.7	7.5
Iceland	8.4	7.8	7.6	8.7	7.1	7.3	8.9	6.1	6.6	6.7	8.0	8.5
Ireland	8.1	6.5	6.8	7.9	6.9	7.0	7.7	6.6	12.7	15.2	5.1	6.8
Italy	9.4	7.7	7.5	9.4	8.1	8.0	10.2	5.4	7.4	11.0	10.4	5.9
Japan	9.1	7.3	7.1	8.6	7.7	7.9	8.0	6.8	7.2	9.1	8.7	7.7
Luxembourg	7.8	6.4	6.5	7.6	6.7	7.0	7.3	6.6	6.5	8.9	5.6	7.1
Netherlands	7.7	6.3	6.2	7.5	6.4	6.7	7.2	6.6	5.7	8.8	5.5	6.2
New Zealand	7.7	7.6	6.7	7.8	7.1	7.5	7.8	6.5	6.7	8.7	6.7	7.0
Norway	9.8	8.0	7.3	9.6	8.5	8.4	7.9	6.2	22.1	8.8	5.9	7.7
Portugal	11.7	7.0	6.8	14.4	6.9	7.3	7.9	6.6	11.7	13.7	9.0	7.1
Spain	7.7	6.6	6.7	7.8	6.9	7.2	7.5	6.6	6.6	8.8	7.0	7.0
Sweden	7.6	6.5	6.6	7.7	6.3	6.6	6.9	6.5	6.1	7.3	5.5	6.6
Switzerland	7.6	6.2	6.4	7.7	6.3	6.9	7.2	6.5	5.6	7.6	5.5	6.9
Turkey	9.0	7.9	7.7	8.8	8.6	7.8	8.1	7.6	7.1	9.1	8.6	8.6
United Kingdom	7.4	6.1	6.0	7.4	6.1	6.7	7.2	6.0	5.9	9.0	7.3	6.0
United States	7.7	6.3	6.2	7.6	6.7	7.0	7.3	6.3	6.2	7.7	7.4	6.5

1. Parent raises finance by a weighted average of retentions, new equity and debt. Weighted average of investment in three different assets. Inflation of 4.5 per cent everywhere. No personal taxes.

Table 5.4 (cont) **Required pre-tax rates of return when the subsidiary is financed by one third loans from the parent, one third new equity from the parent and one third retentions by the subsidiary[1]**

Source:	Japan	Luxembourg	Netherlands	N. Zealand	Norway	Portugal	Spain	Sweden	Switzerland	Turkey	UK	US
Residence:												
Australia	8.0	7.8	7.0	8.8	6.6	7.9	8.4	6.2	6.7	7.9	6.8	7.3
Austria	7.7	7.2	6.4	10.1	6.6	7.1	7.3	5.5	6.2	7.9	6.8	6.7
Belgium	8.1	6.6	6.1	8.8	6.4	7.4	7.9	5.9	6.1	7.9	6.5	6.9
Canada	7.9	7.3	7.0	9.2	6.5	8.5	8.0	6.6	7.1	8.6	6.7	7.2
Denmark	7.2	6.6	5.9	7.8	5.6	5.6	5.6	5.5	5.7	7.4	6.0	6.5
Finland	7.4	7.0	5.9	9.0	5.8	6.8	5.3	5.4	6.1	7.4	5.9	6.5
France	7.3	6.6	6.2	8.7	5.6	6.6	7.5	5.2	6.0	7.5	6.5	6.4
Germany	8.3	7.1	7.6	10.3	5.2	8.5	8.2	6.4	7.4	7.9	7.1	7.8
Greece	8.7	6.7	6.5	11.8	6.4	8.8	9.3	6.5	6.9	7.4	7.3	10.1
Iceland	8.6	7.9	7.8	10.2	7.5	8.0	8.5	6.7	7.2	8.0	7.8	7.1
Ireland	7.7	7.3	6.9	8.8	7.2	15.3	15.6	6.5	7.0	13.1	7.6	6.8
Italy	7.8	8.3	8.7	9.8	7.1	7.9	9.1	9.1	9.7	7.5	9.6	8.1
Japan	6.4	8.1	7.8	9.3	8.1	8.1	8.3	7.3	7.9	8.2	8.5	7.7
Luxembourg	8.5	6.3	6.3	10.1	6.6	7.9	7.3	5.7	8.3	7.9	6.3	6.7
Netherlands	7.6	6.9	5.6	8.7	6.6	8.8	7.3	5.4	5.9	7.8	6.3	6.6
New Zealand	7.9	7.7	6.9	6.8	6.5	7.8	8.3	6.1	6.6	7.8	6.7	7.2
Norway	7.8	8.8	8.9	10.2	6.8	7.1	9.3	5.6	9.5	8.0	6.6	7.8
Portugal	14.5	10.2	11.9	16.2	7.0	5.7	7.3	11.1	6.6	12.2	7.2	13.2
Spain	7.6	6.9	6.4	10.1	6.7	6.0	6.2	5.9	6.4	7.9	6.9	6.9
Sweden	7.5	7.1	6.1	8.6	5.9	7.7	7.2	5.0	6.0	7.8	6.2	6.5
Switzerland	7.5	7.6	6.1	8.6	6.1	7.0	7.2	5.6	5.4	8.1	6.2	6.5
Turkey	8.7	8.0	7.7	10.3	8.0	8.1	8.6	7.4	8.5	7.2	8.4	8.7
United Kingdom	7.3	6.6	6.2	8.6	6.1	6.7	7.1	5.6	6.0	7.4	5.9	6.4
United States	7.7	7.2	6.4	8.8	6.8	7.9	7.9	6.0	6.5	7.9	7.1	5.8

1   Parent raises finance by a weighted average of retentions, new equity and debt. Weighted average of investment in three different assets. Inflation of 4.5 per cent everywhere. No personal taxes.

The results can be interpreted in the following ways. When a Belgian parent company decides to expand the operations of its Canadian subsidiary by retaining funds in the subsidiary, then on average it must earn a pre-tax rate of return in Canada of 8.1 per cent in order to be able to give its Belgian investors a post-tax return of 5 per cent (see table 5.1); whereas if the Canadian subsidiary were financed by an injection of new equity from the parent, which raises the finance in Belgium by using a mix of new equity, borrowing and retained earnings, the subsidiary would need to earn 8.8 per cent (table 5.2). If the subsidiary financed the expansion by borrowing from the parent (which again in turn issued new equity, debt financed, and retained earnings), it would need to earn just 7.5 per cent (table 5.3) to give the same return to the Belgian investors. If all these possibilities are given an equal weighting, an overall average rate of return in Canada of 8.1 per cent would be required to give the Belgian financiers their 5 per cent return (table 5.4).

The required rates of return when investing in a particular country are nearly always the same (see table 5.1), except when the parent company is based in Denmark (see below). Thus, the tax system is almost entirely based on the tax provisions of the source country. The reason for this is that the tax associated with the repatriation of profit from the subsidiary to the parent is netted out of the calculation: when repatriations are reduced to finance the investment the tax associated with the repatriation is also reduced; when repatriations are increased, tax increases in the same proportion. The only source of variation in the required rate of return that might depend on the tax situation in the residence country is that the discount rate applied to the investment is determined by the tax treatment of capital gains in the residence country. However, in table 5.1 it is assumed that the marginal personal tax rate is zero everywhere, so even the discount rate does not vary between residence countries (the required returns do vary down the column when personal tax rates are positive).

The exception to this source-based taxation is when the parent company is Danish. In the Danish case, a foreign tax allowance is given to Danish parents with income earned abroad in certain countries, and where this is applicable the return required on the investment is consequently rather lower than if the same investment were undertaken by a subsidiary owned by a parent from another country[12].

It is relatively easy to explain the variation in required rates of return shown in table 5.1. Insofar as the tax treatment of retentions differs between countries on purely domestic investment, so the tax treatment of transnational investment in each country varies accordingly. For tables 5.2 and 5.3 the situation is far more complex, and many more factors influence the required rates of return.

In some cases, the answer is obvious: investments in Austria by a Dutch subsidiary are subject to the Austrian tax rate with a 5 per cent withholding tax on repatriated dividends, whereas a New Zealand subsidiary pays the Austrian tax plus 25 per cent withholding tax. Consequently, it is not surprising to find that to pay 5 per cent to the ultimate financiers, the Dutch subsidiary needs to earn 6.3 per cent before tax and the New Zealand subsidiary 9.6 per cent (table 5.2). Thus a significant proportion of the variation in required rates of return for investments in a particular country (i.e. looking down the columns of tables 5.2 and 5.3) is explained by differences in withholding tax rates.[13]

Where the treatment of foreign source income varies according to the source of that income, there are substantial differences in the required rates of return facing the subsidiaries of a particular parent. For example, Portugal gives a credit for those countries with which it has a treaty, but has a deduction system for other foreign source income. Consequently Belgium or Denmark are more attractive locations for investments by a Portuguese parent company funding a subsidiary by new equity than is Canada.

However, it would be wrong to imply that all the variation in required rates of return can be reduced to differences in withholding taxes and the treatment of foreign source income. A large number of other tax factors play some part. For example, in Ireland there is a lower tax rate on manufacturing operations taking place within the country than on foreign source income received from abroad. With a few exceptions, countries with imputation systems do not give the tax credits on dividends flowing out of the country thereby effectively imposing a classical system for foreign investors. However, this is not true of split-rate systems.

In table 5.3 the required rate of return is generally relatively low where the statutory tax rate in the source country is relatively high (subject to the tax treatment of foreign source income by the residence country and the size of any withholding taxes). For example, looking down the German column, the required returns are lower than they are in the column for France. The reason for this is that where subsidiaries are financed by debt they can deduct interest payments from the tax base, and this deduction is more valuable where the tax rate is high (Germany) than where it is lower (France).

The difference between the figures in table 5.3 and in table 5.2 depends on many factors. What is perhaps not obvious is that the withholding tax on dividends paid abroad is relevant in calculating effective tax rates on investments financed by loans from the parent to the subsidiary. Nominal interest deductibility reduces the tax which would otherwise be paid on other profits of the subsidiary. The subsidiary can therefore pay higher post-tax profits back to the parent, and here it is assumed that they do so in the form of increased dividend payments.

Each of tables 5.1-5.4 give the 576 different possible combinations of source and residence countries within the OECD, and clearly it is these which are of relevance to a company considering undertaking an investment. It is difficult to draw any general conclusions from such a large quantity of data. A summary of table 5.1 is given in table 5.5. The first column of table 5.5 gives the purely domestic required pre-tax rates of return (the diagonal of table 5.1). The second column gives the average required rate of return faced when a company from that country invests in all other countries (the average — excluding the purely domestic case — of the rows in table 5.1, when the named country is the residence country). The third column gives the average [14] required rate of return when companies from all other countries invest in that country (in other words, the average — again excluding the purely domestic case -- of each of the columns in table 5.1, when the named country is the source country). Thus, the required rate of return for German companies investing domestically and financing the investment through retained earnings is 9.5 per cent, whereas if German companies invest abroad they need on average to earn 7.8 per cent; foreign-owned investments in Germany require on average around 9.5 per cent. Note that the overall OECD-wide average of the average required returns for each country as a source and each country as a residence are identical -- 7.9 per cent. In each case the overall average figure is the average of all the 552 required rates of return for all combinations of two countries given in table 5.1.

This is, however, just for the case where the investment abroad is financed by retained earnings. The situation is rather different when the subsidiary is financed by debt or by new equity from the parent. Tables 5.6 and 5.7 give similar summary statistics as in tables 5.2 and 5.3, and table 5.8 averages over the three tables (based on table 5.4 above). Table 5.8 shows that averaging across all the different possible financing arrangements, investors from Germany into the rest of the OECD require a return of 7.9 per cent before corporate tax in order to achieve a post-tax return of 5 per cent, whilst investors from the rest of the OECD in Germany require a pre-tax return of 6.4 per cent to gain a similar post tax return.

A comparission of the required returns when investing in a country with the required returns when investing from that country might give some indication of the effects of the tax system on investment flows. Many factors will, of course, determine investment flows, and tax may be only a minor influence. Insofar as tax is of any importance, then if the required rate of return when investing domestically is lower than that when investing abroad, companies will prefer domestic operations (assuming, of course, that there are equal investment possibilities in each country). Whether this results in a net inflow of capital depends on whether investment in that country is more attractive to foreign-owned companies than investment in their own domestic economies[15].

By computing the average required rate of return when investing in or from each country a lot of the information contained in the matrices is lost. In particular, the variation in required returns is lost. To compensate, the standard deviation of each column and each row of the matrices (tables 5.1 to 5.4) are given in the last two columns of tables 5.5 to 5.8. These figures give some indication of the degree to which the international tax system results in subsidiaries which operate in the same country face different effective tax rates according to the residence of their parent company, and the extent to which the location of a subsidiary for a parent company might affect the effective tax rate. A low figure in the last column, for example, suggests that there is only a small dispersion across countries in the effective tax rates faced by a company when considering in which country to undertake an investment.

Table 5.5 **Average required transnational pre-tax rates of return when the susbidiary is financed through retentions**[1]

Country	Average required rate of return			Standard deviations of required rates of return	
	Domestic Investment	Residence (investment from named country into all other countries)	Source (investment from all other countries into named country)	Residence	Source
Australia	9.0	7.9	9.0	1.1	0.2
Austria	7.3	7.9	7.2	1.1	0.1
Belgium	7.1	8.0	7.1	1.1	0.0
Canada	8.1	7.9	8.0	1.1	0.1
Denmark	7.5	7.4	7.5	0.9	0.0
Finland	8.0	7.9	8.0	1.1	0.1
France	7.3	7.9	7.3	1.1	0.1
Germany	9.5	7.8	9.5	1.1	0.2
Greece	7.3	7.9	7.3	1.1	0.0
Iceland	8.0	7.9	8.0	1.1	0.1
Ireland	5.5	8.0	5.5	1.0	0.1
Italy	9.1	7.9	9.1	1.1	0.1
Japan	9.0	7.9	8.9	1.1	0.1
Luxembourg	8.1	7.9	8.1	1.1	0.1
Netherlands	7.1	7.9	7.1	1.1	0.1
New Zealand	8.3	7.9	9.0	1.1	0.3
Norway	10.0	7.8	9.9	1.0	0.2
Portugal	7.5	7.9	7.5	1.1	0.1
Spain	7.8	7.9	7.8	1.1	0.1
Sweden	6.1	8.0	6.1	1.1	0.0
Switzerland	6.6	8.0	6.6	1.1	0.1
Turkey	9.8	7.8	9.7	1.1	0.2
United Kingdom	7.7	7.9	7.7	1.1	0.1
United States	7.6	7.9	7.5	1.1	0.1
Average (2)	7.9	7.9	7.9	1.1	0.1

1. Weighted average of investment in three assets. Inflation of 4.5% everywhere. No personal taxes. Domestic figures are based on use of retention finance by the parent to finance an investment.
2. Unweighted average of each column; the same definition is used in tables 5.6, 5.7 and 5.8.

Table 5.6 **Average required transnational pre-tax rates of return when the subsidiary is financed through new equity from parent[1]**

Country	Average required rate of return			Standard deviations of required rates of return	
	Domestic Investment	Residence (investment from named country into all other countries)	Source (investment from all other countries into named country)	Residence	Source
Australia	7.1	7.5	7.8	1.5	1.9
Austria	5.5	7.1	7.7	1.7	1.6
Belgium	5.4	7.4	7.2	1.6	0.6
Canada	6.2	6.6	9.2	1.5	2.5
Denmark	5.9	6.1	7.3	1.2	1.7
Finland	5.6	6.0	7.3	1.6	0.7
France	5.4	6.7	8.8	1.8	1.9
Germany	5.6	6.3	5.9	2.5	1.1
Greece	5.0	9.7	7.5	3.2	5.1
Iceland	6.7	8.2	9.6	1.6	4.1
Ireland	5.1	9.8	6.3	5.6	2.9
Italy	5.9	8.9	6.7	1.9	1.4
Japan	6.4	8.1	9.4	1.0	2.7
Luxembourg	6.3	7.2	7.5	2.0	1.8
Netherlands	5.6	6.7	7.3	1.6	2.8
New Zealand	6.8	7.9	11.0	1.4	3.3
Norway	6.8	8.6	4.6	4.6	1.4
Portugal	5.7	12.6	9.2	6.1	3.0
Spain	6.2	7.4	9.0	1.5	3.1
Sweden	5.0	7.0	6.5	1.5	2.8
Switzerland	5.4	7.0	7.1	1.5	1.8
Turkey	7.2	8.8	8.4	1.1	2.8
United Kingdom	5.9	6.8	6.2	1.5	1.6
United States	5.8	6.9	8.0	1.2	3.4
Average	5.9	7.7	7.7	2.1	2.3

1. Weighted average of three sources of finance by parent. Weighted average of investment in three assets. Inflation of 4.5% everywhere. No personal taxes.

Table 5.7 **Average required transnational pre-tax rates of return when the subsidiary is financed through debt from parent[1]**

Country	Average required rate of return			Standard deviations of required rates of return	
	Domestic Investment	Residence (investment from named country into all other countries)	Source (investment from all other countries into named country)	Residence	Source
Australia	7.1	6.6	7.7	1.0	1.4
Austria	5.5	6.5	6.5	1.0	1.8
Belgium	5.4	5.7	6.3	1.2	1.1
Canada	6.2	8.1	8.1	1.3	2.0
Denmark	5.9	5.9	6.7	1.3	1.4
Finland	5.6	5.7	6.6	1.7	1.2
France	5.4	5.3	7.6	1.2	1.5
Germany	5.6	9.6	3.9	1.9	0.9
Greece	5.0	7.3	7.8	2.1	3.6
Iceland	6.7	7.4	9.9	1.1	2.1
Ireland	5.1	8.5	8.5	3.6	2.0
Italy	5.9	9.0	5.7	2.5	1.4
Japan	6.4	8.1	6.2	1.1	1.8
Luxembourg	6.3	6.5	6.8	1.1	1.2
Netherlands	5.6	6.0	6.8	1.2	1.6
New Zealand	6.8	6.0	9.0	0.9	1.9
Norway	6.8	9.6	5.1	4.8	0.9
Portugal	5.7	9.2	7.0	3.3	2.6
Spain	6.2	6.1	7.5	1.3	2.9
Sweden	5.0	5.5	6.6	0.9	1.5
Switzerland	5.4	5.5	7.1	0.9	1.7
Turkey	7.2	8.3	6.6	1.1	1.6
United Kingdom	5.9	5.5	7.1	1.3	1.2
United States	5.8	6.3	6.9	1.0	1.5
Average	5.9	7.0	7.0	1.6	1.8

1. Weighted average of three sources of finance by parent. Weighted average of three assets. Inflation of 4.5% everywhere. No personal taxes.

140

Table 5.8: **Overall average required transnational pre-tax rates of return**[1]

Country	Average required rate of return			Standard deviations of required rates of return	
	Domestic Investment	Residence (investment from named country into all other countries)	Source (investment from all other countries into named country)	Residence	Source
Australia	7.1	7.3	8.2	0.8	1.0
Austria	5.5	7.2	7.1	1.0	1.0
Belgium	5.4	7.0	6.8	0.9	0.5
Canada	6.2	7.5	8.4	0.9	1.5
Denmark	5.9	6.5	7.2	0.7	0.9
Finland	5.6	6.6	7.3	0.9	0.5
France	5.4	6.6	7.9	1.0	1.0
Germany	5.6	7.9	6.4	1.4	0.5
Greece	5.0	8.3	7.5	1.6	3.6
Iceland	6.7	7.8	9.2	0.9	1.8
Ireland	5.1	8.8	6.8	3.1	1.5
Italy	5.9	8.6	7.2	1.2	0.9
Japan	6.4	8.0	8.1	0.6	1.4
Luxembourg	6.3	7.2	7.5	1.0	0.8
Netherlands	5.6	6.9	7.1	1.0	1.3
New Zealand	6.8	7.3	9.7	0.6	1.6
Norway	6.8	8.7	6.6	3.1	0.7
Portugal	5.7	9.9	7.9	3.1	1.8
Spain	6.2	7.1	8.1	0.9	1.9
Sweden	5.0	6.8	6.4	0.7	1.3
Switzerland	5.4	6.8	7.0	0.8	1.1
Turkey	7.2	8.3	8.2	0.7	1.4
United Kingdom	5.9	6.7	7.0	0.9	0.9
United States	5.8	7.1	7.5	0.7	1.5
Average	5.9	7.5	7.5	1.2	1.3

1. Subsidiary financed by one third loans from the parent, one third new equity from the parent, and third retentions by the subsidiary. Weighted average of three sources of finance by parent. Weighted average of three assets. Inflation of 4.5% everywhere. No personal taxes.

Capital export neutrality (CEN) exists if the required return for a company is independent of the location of their investment. In the tables, this would be reflected in the average required return for a company resident in a particular country when investing abroad being the same as the required return when investing domestically, and the standard deviation of required rates of return when investing abroad being zero. Similarly, capital import neutrality (CIN) exists when all companies operating in a particular country are treated equally for tax purposes. In the tables this would be the case where the domestic required rate of return is the same as the average required rate of return for all other countries when investing in that country, and the standard deviation in the required returns when that country is the source country is zero.

Table 5.5 indicates that when the subsidiary is financed by the retention of earnings, neither CEN nor CIN holds. An Australian company, for example, investing domestically must earn 9.0 per cent on the marginal investment, whereas if the subsidiaries of an Australian parent invested elsewhere the required return would be 7.9 per cent. Hence CEN does not hold. In addition, the standard deviation in the required returns abroad is 1.1 — there is some variation around the mean of 7.9 per cent, again indicating that CEN does not hold. Another example is Iceland: the average return required when investing abroad if Iceland is the residence country of the parent is almost the same as if an Icelandic company invested domestically, so satisfying the first of the two conditions for CEN. However, there is some variation around this average, so tax could still in principle influence the location of an investment by an Icelandic parent.

In the overall summary in table 5.8, the average required return on domestic investment is 5.9 per cent compared to an average required return on transnational investment of 7.5 per cent[16]. In other words, the additional components of the transnational tax system — withholding taxes and the tax treatment of foreign source income — add significantly to the marginal effective tax rates on investment. This also applies on a more disaggregated level. Whereas table 5.4 indicates that it is by no means necessarily true that domestic investment always receives the most generous tax treatment, table 5.8 shows that nowhere is the average required return faced by resident companies considering investing elsewhere in the OECD lower than the average required return on domestic investment. Similarly, the average required return faced by companies considering investing in a particular foreign country is always higher than the average required return which a domestic company from that country must earn.

It might be expected that the dispersion across companies investing in each country would be less than the dispersion across companies investing from each country, reflecting the fact that in a number of cases the tax liability is based most heavily on the source country tax system. For example, where the residence country has an exemption system for the taxation of foreign source income, or the subsidiary is financed by retained earnings when there are no personal taxes, the tax system in the residence country plays a relatively minor part in calculating the required rates of return[17]. However, table 5.8 shows that the overall average standard deviation of required returns for residence countries is almost the same as the average variation when each country is taken as a source. In fact, this seems to be principally due to a few outlying countries. This problem of outliers is discussed in greater detail below.

The effect of tax treaties

Tax treaties usually have the effect of reducing source country withholding taxes and the amount of tax charged on foreign source income. Two issues arise: first, do treaties significantly reduce the effective tax rates on marginal transnational investments; and second, to the extent that tax treaties result in more favourable tax treatment on some cross-border flows than on others, does the fact that the treaty network is incomplete mean that treaties result in a greater variation in tax rates across countries?

Table 5.9 **The effects on the overall average required return of bilateral tax treaties**[1]

Country	Domestic	Residence (investment from named country into other countries)			Source (investment from other countries into named country)		
		With treaties	No treaties	% Difference	With treaties	No treaties	% Difference
Australia	7.1	7.3	8.0	0.7	8.2	11.9	3.7
Austria	5.5	7.2	8.0	0.8	7.1	9.2	2.1
Belgium	5.4	7.0	8.1	1.1	6.8	9.0	2.2
Canada	6.2	7.5	9.1	1.6	8.4	10.6	2.2
Denmark	5.9	6.5	8.0	1.5	7.2	10.0	2.8
Finland	5.6	6.6	9.0	2.4	7.3	9.8	2.5
France	5.4	6.6	8.0	1.4	7.9	11.3	3.4
Germany	5.6	7.9	13.9	6.0	6.4	7.9	1.5
Greece	5.0	8.3	9.1	0.8	7.5	7.7	0.2
Iceland	6.7	7.8	8.2	0.4	9.2	10.5	1.3
Ireland	5.1	8.8	14.4	5.6	6.8	8.7	1.9
Italy	5.9	8.6	10.4	1.8	7.2	9.4	2.2
Japan	6.4	8.0	8.5	0.5	8.1	10.1	2.0
Luxembourg	6.3	7.2	8.0	0.8	7.5	9.1	1.6
Netherlands	5.6	6.9	8.4	1.5	7.1	9.3	2.2
New Zealand	6.8	7.3	7.9	0.6	9.7	12.2	2.5
Norway	6.8	8.7	23.6	14.9	6.6	7.6	1.0
Portugal	5.7	9.9	12.8	2.9	7.9	9.5	1.6
Spain	6.2	7.1	8.0	0.9	8.1	10.4	2.3
Sweden	5.0	6.8	8.0	1.2	6.4	9.0	2.6
Switzerland	5.4	6.8	8.3	1.5	7.0	10.4	3.4
Turkey	7.2	8.3	8.4	0.1	8.2	9.2	1.0
United Kingdom	5.9	6.7	8.2	1.5	7.0	9.0	2.0
United States	5.8	7.1	8.2	1.1	7.5	10.7	3.2
Average	5.9	7.5	9.7	2.2	7.5	9.7	2.2

1   Subsidiary financed by one third loans from the parent, one third new equity from the parent, and one third retentions by the subsidiary. Parent raises finance by a weighted average of retentions, new equity and debt. Investment in a weighted average of assets. Inflation of 4.5% everywhere. No personal taxes.

Table 5.9 looks at the average required returns with and without tax treaties. With regard to the first question the answer would seem to be that in the absence of treaties, the average tax wedge on transnational capital flows would on average be much higher. There is, however, a large variation in the amount by which the average required returns to and from each country fall. Three factors determine most of this variation. First, the extent of the treaty network. Where countries have only a few treaties (for example, Turkey and Iceland) then only the tax rates involving those few countries are affected, so the average change is likely to be small. Second, some countries (for example, New Zealand) do not tax income going to or from non-treaty countries in a substantially different way from income going to or from treaty countries, so once again the effects of tax treaties are small. Finally, where the residence country has a high tax rate and operates the credit system, the total tax paid is determined primarily by the tax system of the residence country. Increases in withholding tax rates have to be sufficiently large to result in the total tax already paid exceeding the domestic tax rate before they alter the overall required return (for example, in Japan).

The second issue of interest is whether the presence of gaps in the treaty network results in greater variation in required rates of return between countries than would be the case were there no treaties at all. The data do not support this hypothesis. The average overall standard deviation in required returns given the existing network of treaties is 1.2 for residence countries and 1.3 for source countries. In the absence of treaties, the average standard deviation of all countries as residence countries rises to 1.3, and of source countries trebles to 3.5. There are some individual exceptions to this general rule. The standard deviation in required returns faced by companies resident in Australia, Greece, Iceland, Ireland and Portugal, and for investments in Greece as a source country, would fall if treaties were abolished; in every other case, including all countries (except Greece), the standard deviation is lower when treaties are taken into account[18].

Why should treaties which do not apply generally and whose provisions vary bilaterally nevertheless reduce variation in required returns? The reason why the variation in required returns for each country as a source increases lies in the treatment of foreign source income. Treaties generally result in foreign source income being either exempted or given a credit. In the absence of treaties, many countries have a deduction system, or failing that, a credit system. In other words, the residence country is far more likely to impose some tax in the absence of treaties than in their presence. Hence it can be expected that for any given source of profits, the tax position varies more — residence country tax is more likely to be applied in addition to source country tax, and there is significant variation in residence country tax rates. This factor outweighs the fact that in the absence of treaties, all withholding tax rates on profits leaving the country are the same.

For residence countries, the cause of the increase in variation in required returns is more subtle. Where there is a credit system, the generally higher rates of withholding tax in the absence of treaties mean that the tax already paid is more likely to exceed the domestic tax. Hence there is an increase in variation. More generally, although the withholding taxes on income leaving a country will be the same regardless of the location of the residence country, there is a large variation in non-treaty withholding tax rates between each country (see tables 3.15 and 3.16 of withholding tax rates, chapter 3), so raising the variation in required returns between source countries.

Hence it is possible to be relatively positive about the effects of the current network of double tax treaties, at least for marginal investments, since they both lower the average required return and they reduce the variance in required returns between alternative locations.

Table 5.10 **Overall average required transnational pre-tax rates of return with actual inflation rates[1]**

Country	Average required rate of return (excluding Greece and Turkey)			Standard deviations of required rates of return (excluding Greece and Turkey)	
	Domestic Investment (source = residence)	Residence (investment from named country into all other countries)	Source (investment from all other countries into named country)	Residence	Source
Australia	7.1	7.5	7.9	1.2	0.7
Austria	5.4	7.4	6.6	1.1	1.1
Belgium	5.4	7.4	6.4	1.2	0.6
Canada	6.2	7.4	8.8	1.3	1.2
Denmark	5.8	6.7	6.4	0.8	0.6
Finland	5.6	6.5	7.4	1.0	0.7
France	5.4	7.0	7.0	1.3	0.7
Germany	5.8	8.3	6.1	1.6	0.6
Iceland	6.7	7.7	9.9	1.1	2.3
Ireland	5.1	9.4	6.2	5.0	1.1
Italy	5.6	8.4	7.3	1.7	1.2
Japan	6.5	8.6	7.2	1.1	0.6
Luxembourg	6.3	7.5	7.0	1.4	0.6
Netherlands	5.7	7.3	6.4	1.4	0.7
New Zealand	6.7	7.5	9.1	1.1	0.9
Norway	6.7	8.2	6.4	1.4	0.6
Portugal	5.2	7.6	10.5	2.5	3.6
Spain	6.3	6.9	8.7	0.9	2.5
Sweden	4.9	6.1	7.5	0.9	1.8
Switzerland	5.4	6.8	6.9	0.9	1.2
United Kingdom	6.0	6.5	7.2	1.0	1.0
United States	5.8	7.2	7.0	1.1	0.7
Average[2]	5.9	7.5	7.5	1.4	1.1

1. Purchasing Power Parity. No personal taxes. Weighted average of finance, investment in weighted average of assets — as in table 5.8
2. Excluding Greece and Turkey.

Different inflation rates and purchasing power parity

The above tables were calculated on the basis of common inflation rates across countries. Exchange rates can be assumed to be constant in such a scenario, and this assumption is consistent both with fixed exchange rates and exchange rates which reflect movements in purchasing power parities (PPP). Where inflation rates differ across countries the assumption of fixed exchange rates is not tenable, so it is assumed that PPP describes the movement in the exchange rate[19]. Table 5.10 gives the average real required pre-tax rates of return necessary to earn 5 per cent post-tax, with zero personal tax rates, using expected inflation rates for 1991. The rates used are the OECD estimates of consumer price deflators for the calendar year 1991 (given in Annex 5).

Where the exchange rate reflects movements in purchasing power parity, high inflation countries become attractive as a residence for companies investing abroad, but unattractive to foreign companies as a location for investments. The extreme examples are Turkey and Greece — so extreme that the average required rates of return involving these two countries are too far out of line with the rest of the OECD to be included in the averages.

Consider for example, Portugal, with an inflation rate of 11.7 per cent, well above the OECD average of 4.5 per cent. Using actual inflation rates as in table 5.10, compared with the average inflation rates in table 5.8, the position of Portuguese parents operating subsidiaries abroad improves, with required rates of return falling from 9.9 per cent to 7.6 per cent. By contrast, as a location for investments from other countries, however, this country becomes less attractive; the average return required of the Portugese subsidiaries of foreign parents increases from 7.9 per cent to 10.5 per cent respectively. Conversely, Japan and the Netherlands with inflation rates of 2.5 per cent and 2.7 per cent respectively become more attractive as locations for inward investment, but subsidiaries of parents located in these countries must earn a higher rate of return when actual inflation rates and PPP are assumed as opposed to a common OECD inflation rate and fixed exchange rates.

Letting exchange rates be determined by PPP introduces the inflation rate as an additional source of variation between countries but has relatively little impact on the variation in required returns. The average standard deviations of required rates of return are little different in table 5.10 than in table 5.8. Though those countries with low inflation rates will face an increase in variation in tax rates facing them as locations for parent companies, there will be a decrease in variation of such countries as a location for the foreign direct investment of others (and vice versa for high inflation countries).

Personal taxes

As with purely domestic calculations, tax wedges can be calculated (the difference between the pre-corporate tax rate of return to subsidiaries and the post-personal tax rate of return to individuals). As discussed above, if international portfolio capital is not perfectly mobile, then it is possible that these transnational tax rates affect the incentive to invest in a particular country. Table 5.11 gives the average tax wedges for top rate taxpayers when they invest in companies which invest abroad. Table 5.11 is equivalent to table 5.4 — it is the average of 7 matrices of transnational tax wedges, corresponding to all the different financing possibilities. It shows, for example, that an Australian top-rate personal taxpayer, when investing in an Australian company which owns a subsidiary in Belgium which in turn invests in a marginal investment, receives a return 1.6 percentage points lower than the return which the subsidiary earns before any tax. Table 5.12 averages along each row and column of table 5.11. Hence, for example, an Irish company investing abroad must earn on average a rate of return on a marginal investment 2.3 percentage points higher than its financiers actually receive, as compared with 1.9 percentage points if the company invested domestically.

Table 5.11 Overall average required tax wedge for top rate personal taxpayers[1]

Source:	Australia	Austria	Belgium	Canada	Denmark	Finland	France	Germany	Greece	Iceland	Ireland	Italy
Residence:												
Australia	1.7	1.5	1.6	2.4	2.0	2.1	2.5	0.6	1.5	2.4	1.7	1.3
Austria	2.5	1.3	1.7	2.5	1.9	2.1	2.4	1.4	1.3	2.1	1.6	1.6
Belgium	2.9	1.7	1.2	3.0	2.0	2.1	2.2	1.6	0.6	3.0	0.9	2.4
Canada	4.2	3.3	3.4	3.6	3.7	3.9	4.0	2.9	3.6	4.3	2.9	3.4
Denmark	2.6	1.7	2.1	2.6	2.1	2.1	2.2	1.3	1.9	1.7	1.9	1.8
Finland	6.5	5.3	5.0	6.6	4.9	5.3	5.6	5.4	4.8	6.4	3.4	5.6
France	3.9	2.9	2.6	3.6	2.7	3.0	2.6	2.4	2.5	4.5	1.6	3.4
Germany	2.3	1.7	1.6	2.3	1.8	1.9	1.9	0.9	0.7	1.5	1.6	1.9
Greece	3.0	2.7	1.9	3.6	3.4	2.6	3.6	2.7	1.3	3.8	2.2	3.0
Iceland	5.4	4.6	4.3	5.5	3.8	4.1	5.5	3.4	3.5	4.3	4.1	5.8
Ireland	2.5	1.3	1.6	2.3	1.7	1.8	2.1	0.9	4.0	3.6	1.4	1.3
Italy	4.6	3.1	3.0	4.2	3.5	3.5	4.1	2.2	2.9	4.7	3.6	3.1
Japan	4.9	3.2	3.1	4.4	3.6	3.8	3.8	3.1	3.2	4.6	3.9	3.8
Luxembourg	2.5	1.4	1.7	2.4	1.9	2.0	2.2	1.3	1.6	2.0	1.5	1.7
Netherlands	2.5	1.5	1.7	2.4	1.9	2.0	2.2	1.2	1.3	1.9	1.7	1.4
New Zealand	2.2	1.8	1.4	2.3	1.8	2.0	2.2	0.8	1.5	2.3	1.8	1.3
Norway	4.1	2.7	2.4	3.9	3.1	3.1	3.0	1.3	9.6	3.1	2.1	2.4
Portugal	5.2	1.8	1.8	6.7	2.0	2.3	2.7	1.6	5.1	5.7	3.4	2.0
Spain	2.1	1.1	1.4	2.1	1.6	1.7	1.9	0.6	1.3	1.5	1.9	1.2
Sweden	4.1	3.0	3.2	4.1	2.9	3.2	3.4	3.0	2.7	3.6	2.3	3.1
Switzerland	2.5	1.4	1.6	2.5	1.7	2.0	2.1	1.3	1.1	1.7	1.4	1.7
Turkey	8.4	7.8	7.3	8.8	9.0	6.9	7.9	6.6	6.3	9.4	10.7	8.3
United Kingdom	2.6	1.4	1.5	2.5	1.7	2.0	2.3	1.1	1.3	2.8	2.4	1.3
United States	4.5	3.2	3.1	4.3	3.5	3.8	4.0	3.1	3.1	4.1	4.0	3.3

1. Subsidiary financed by one third loans from the parent, one third new equity, and one third retentions by the subsidiary. Parent raises finance by a weighted average of retentions, new equity and debt. Investment in weighted average of assets. Common inflation of 4.5 per cent.

Table 5.11 (cont) **Overall average required tax wedge for top rate personal taxpayers[1]**

Source: Residence:	Japan	Luxembourg	Netherlands	N. Zealand	Norway	Portugal	Spain	Sweden	Switzerland	Turkey	UK	US
Australia	1.7	2.3	1.7	2.9	1.4	2.0	2.7	1.5	1.7	2.1	1.9	1.7
Austria	1.8	2.1	1.5	3.5	1.8	1.7	2.2	1.3	1.5	2.4	2.0	1.6
Belgium	3.0	1.9	1.3	3.7	1.8	2.3	2.8	1.0	1.3	3.1	1.7	1.9
Canada	3.7	3.8	3.3	4.9	3.4	3.9	4.0	3.1	3.3	4.5	3.4	3.4
Denmark	2.0	2.2	1.7	2.7	1.8	1.0	1.3	1.5	1.7	2.5	2.0	1.8
Finland	6.8	5.8	4.6	7.8	5.3	5.5	4.6	3.6	4.5	6.9	4.7	5.3
France	3.8	3.2	2.6	4.7	2.8	2.9	3.6	1.6	2.3	4.2	3.0	2.8
Germany	1.5	1.9	1.5	2.7	1.3	1.5	2.0	1.2	1.5	2.1	1.9	1.5
Greece	3.6	2.2	1.7	5.1	2.5	2.9	3.4	1.2	1.7	3.2	2.4	3.5
Iceland	5.8	4.7	4.5	7.2	4.7	4.8	5.2	3.1	3.8	5.2	4.6	3.9
Ireland	1.6	2.0	1.5	2.7	2.0	4.4	4.9	1.4	1.6	4.1	2.1	1.5
Italy	3.5	3.8	3.5	4.8	3.6	3.2	4.0	3.3	3.7	3.8	4.2	3.4
Japan	3.4	4.1	3.6	5.1	4.3	3.8	4.1	3.1	3.6	4.3	4.3	3.6
Luxembourg	2.3	2.1	1.5	3.5	2.0	2.0	2.2	1.3	2.3	2.5	1.9	1.6
Netherlands	1.9	2.1	1.5	2.9	2.0	2.6	2.2	1.4	1.5	2.5	1.9	1.7
New Zealand	1.9	2.1	1.5	2.0	1.4	1.9	2.5	1.2	1.4	2.1	1.6	1.6
Norway	2.5	3.4	3.2	4.3	2.9	2.2	3.7	1.6	3.6	3.0	2.3	2.6
Portugal	6.6	4.1	4.7	7.8	2.2	1.4	2.3	4.1	1.7	5.5	2.3	5.4
Spain	1.3	1.7	1.2	2.9	1.5	0.5	1.6	1.2	1.3	2.0	1.7	1.3
Sweden	3.8	3.6	2.7	4.9	2.7	4.0	3.7	2.1	2.7	4.2	2.9	3.1
Switzerland	2.0	2.4	1.4	3.0	1.7	1.7	2.2	1.2	1.3	2.8	1.8	1.6
Turkey	8.5	7.2	7.2	11.3	6.6	8.1	8.5	7.4	9.5	6.8	8.1	9.3
United Kingdom	2.0	2.0	1.6	3.2	1.7	1.8	2.3	1.4	1.5	2.5	2.0	1.7
United States	4.2	4.0	3.3	5.3	3.8	4.3	4.1	2.9	3.3	4.6	4.0	3.2

1. Subsidiary financed by one third loans from the parent, one third new equity, and one third retentions by the subsidiary. Parent raises finance by a weighted average of retentions, new equity and debt. Investment in weighted average of assets. Common inflation of 4.5 per cent.

Table 5.12 **Overall average tax wedge for top rate personal taxpayers**[1]

Country	Average rate of return			Standard deviations of required rates of return	
	Domestic Investment (source = residence)	Residence (investment from named country into all other countries)	Source (investment from all other countries into named country)	Residence	Source
Australia	1.5	1.9	3.7	0.5	1.6
Austria	1.4	1.9	2.6	0.5	1.5
Belgium	0.9	2.1	2.6	0.8	1.4
Canada	3.5	3.7	3.7	0.5	1.7
Denmark	2.4	1.9	2.9	0.4	1.6
Finland	4.4	5.4	2.8	1.0	1.2
France	2.3	3.1	3.2	0.8	1.5
Germany	0.9	1.7	2.2	0.4	1.5
Greece	0.8	2.9	2.8	0.8	2.1
Iceland	3.8	4.7	3.5	0.9	1.8
Ireland	1.9	2.3	2.7	1.1	1.9
Italy	2.6	3.7	2.7	0.6	1.7
Japan	2.8	3.9	3.3	0.6	1.9
Luxembourg	2.5	2.0	3.1	0.5	1.4
Netherlands	2.1	1.9	2.7	0.5	1.5
New Zealand	2.0	1.8	4.6	0.4	2.1
Norway	2.5	3.2	2.7	1.6	1.4
Portugal	1.3	3.8	3.0	1.9	1.7
Spain	2.0	1.5	3.4	0.5	1.5
Sweden	2.0	3.3	2.2	0.6	1.4
Switzerland	1.7	1.9	2.6	0.5	1.8
Turkey	5.3	8.2	3.5	1.3	1.3
United Kingdom	2.0	1.9	2.9	0.5	1.5
United States	3.0	3.8	2.9	0.6	1.8
Average	2.3	3.0	3.0	0.7	1.6

1 Subsidiary financed by one third loans from the parent, one third new equity, and third retentions by the subsidiary. Parent raises finance by a weighted average of retentions, new equity and debt. Investment in weighted average of assets. Inflation is 4.5 per cent.

The average standard deviation of the tax wedges when investing abroad (0.7) is lower than that facing investors looking to invest in a particular country (1.6). This is because introducing personal taxes (in the residence country) moves the system away from source-based taxation, for two reasons. First, discount rates are determined in part by the personal tax treatment of the ultimate financiers of the project. Where a zero rate of personal tax was assumed, discount rates did not vary very much; when the various different rates of personal taxes are considered, then there is much more variation for each source country. Secondly, personal taxes directly drive a wedge between the real interest rate (by assumption, 5 per cent) and the return to each financier of the parent, and this part of the tax wedge does not vary according to the original location of the investment.

Although the average tax wedge on transnational investments is higher than on domestic investments (3.0 percentage points, as opposed to 2.3) this is not true in all cases. In Spain, for example, the tax wedge is larger on domestic investments than it is (on average) if the company in which the personal taxpayer invests chooses to invest outside of Spain.

D. Sensitivity analysis

Inflation and exchange rates

Most of the analysis above was based on a common inflation rate of 4.5 per cent (the OECD average) with unchanging exchange rates. As in the domestic case, varying this common inflation rate (while preserving unchanging exchange rates) will alter the required pre-tax returns. Table 5.13 gives the average overall required rates of return when investing in and from each country, for different inflation rates which are nevertheless common to all countries. This table shows that, in general, as inflation increases, so does the overall average required rate of return, although in Germany as a source country the reverse is the case reflecting the interaction of a high nominal tax rate with rising inflation. Changing the common inflation rate assumption does alter the "ranking" of countries according to the size of the required rate of return, but not by so much as to make general conclusions made on the basis of one particular inflation rate misleading.

Although in the long term it is improbable that countries could preserve fixed exchange rates in the presence of different inflation rates, this is possible in the short term (and is, therefore, of special relevance for investment projects which have only a short life).

With fixed exchange rates those countries with relatively high inflation rates become attractive locations for inward investment because the nominal increase in the value of assets is equivalent to a real return in the residence country. Consequently, companies resident in those countries will required high rates of return when they invest abroad since they need to earn a high return abroad to compensate them for a high nominal required return at home. The results in table 5.14 generally confirm these predictions. Investors from Greece and Portugal (both of whom have double digit inflation) require on average a return of around 30 per cent and 20 per cent respectively when they invest abroad in order to earn a real return of 5 per cent post-tax. In contrast, foreign investors in these two countries require negative returns. Even more extreme results are found for Turkey with its inflation rate in excess of 60 per cent. Indeed, these three cases between them substantially alter the average required returns of the other 21 countries. As it is clearly unreasonable to assume that such inflation differentials can be sustained in the presence of fixed exchange rates, they are excluded when calculating the average required returns and standard deviations of the other countries.

Table 5.13 **Effects of inflation on the overall average transnational rates of return[1]**

Country	Residence (investment from named country into all other countries)			Source (investment from all other countries into named country)		
	Zero inflation	Average inflation (4.5 per cent)	High inflation (10 per cent)	Zero inflation	Average inflation (4.5 per cent)	High inflation (10 per cent)
Australia	6.6	7.3	8.0	7.1	8.2	9.1
Austria	6.5	7.2	7.7	5.7	7.1	8.5
Belgium	6.4	7.0	7.5	6.0	6.8	7.5
Canada	6.7	7.5	8.3	7.1	8.4	9.7
Denmark	6.1	6.5	6.7	6.3	7.2	7.9
Finland	6.2	6.6	6.8	6.5	7.3	8.0
France	6.2	6.6	6.9	6.6	7.9	9.2
Germany	6.9	7.9	8.9	6.7	6.4	5.9
Greece	7.1	8.3	9.5	6.8	7.5	8.3
Iceland	6.8	7.8	8.8	8.2	9.2	10.3
Ireland	7.4	8.8	10.2	6.0	6.8	7.6
Italy	7.2	8.6	9.9	7.0	7.2	7.1
Japan	6.9	8.0	9.1	7.6	8.1	8.5
Luxembourg	6.5	7.2	7.8	6.6	7.5	8.3
Netherlands	6.3	6.9	7.3	6.5	7.1	7.5
New Zealand	6.6	7.3	7.9	7.9	9.7	11.4
Norway	7.3	8.7	10.1	6.1	6.6	6.7
Portugal	8.0	9.9	11.9	7.0	7.9	8.7
Spain	6.5	7.1	7.7	6.7	8.1	9.4
Sweden	6.3	6.8	7.2	5.8	6.4	7.0
Switzerland	6.3	6.8	7.2	6.4	7.0	7.5
Turkey	7.1	8.3	9.5	7.0	8.2	9.4
United Kingdom	6.3	6.7	7.1	6.2	7.0	7.7
United States	6.4	7.1	7.6	6.8	7.5	7.9
Average	6.7	7.5	8.3	6.7	7.5	8.3

1. Subsidiary financed by one third loans from the parent, one third new equity from the parent, and one third retentions by the subsidiary. Parent raises finance by a weighted average of retentions, new equity and debt. Investment in weighted average of assets. No personal taxes.

Table 5.14 Overall pre-tax rates of return using fixed exchange rates but country-specific inflation rates[1]

Country	Average required rate of return			Standard deviations of required rates of return	
	Domestic investment (source = residence)	Residence (investment from named country into all other countries)[2]	Source (investment from all other countries into named country)[2]	Residence[2]	Source[2]
Australia	7.1	7.0	8.3	2.1	2.5
Austria	5.4	6.3	7.8	2.2	2.4
Belgium	5.4	5.5	8.3	2.0	2.3
Canada	6.2	9.4	6.5	2.2	2.4
Denmark	5.8	4.3	9.0	2.0	2.2
Finland	5.6	7.6	6.4	2.3	2.2
France	5.4	4.9	9.4	1.9	2.6
Germany	5.8	6.3	8.2	2.1	2.4
Iceland	6.7	10.4	6.5	2.3	2.7
Ireland	5.1	5.9	8.1	2.3	2.6
Italy	5.6	11.8	4.3	2.0	2.3
Japan	6.5	5.1	10.9	1.8	2.5
Luxembourg	6.3	5.7	8.7	2.1	2.4
Netherlands	5.7	4.5	9.2	2.0	2.4
New Zealand	6.7	6.6	9.9	2.1	2.7
Norway	6.7	7.2	7.4	2.4	2.2
Spain	6.3	9.5	6.0	2.3	2.6
Sweden	4.9	13.7	1.0	1.9	1.9
Switzerland	5.4	7.3	6.5	2.2	2.4
United Kingdom	6.0	8.9	5.1	2.2	2.3
United States	5.8	6.8	7.2	2.1	2.3
Average	5.9	7.4	7.4	2.1	2.4

1. Subsidiary financed by one third loans from the parent, one third new equity from the parent, and one third retentions by the subsidiary. Parent raises finance by a weighted average of retentions, new equity and debt. Investment in weighted average of assets. No personal taxes.
2. Average or standard deviation of the 20 countries excluding Greece, Portugal and Turkey.

Similar effects to those of Greece, Portugal and Turkey are found to some extent in Iceland, Italy, Sweden and the United Kingdom — they are unattractive as locations for parent companies with foreign subsidiaries, but become attractive as locations for foreign source investment. The opposite effects will be felt by companies in investing in and from countries with low inflation, examples being Germany, Japan and the Netherlands. Unsurprisingly, compared to the purchasing power parity (PPP) case reported in table 5.10 there is substantially more variation in required rates of return — the average standard deviation rises from 1.4 and 1.1 in the PPP case for countries as residences and sources of transnational investment to 2.1 and 2.4 respectively.

Weighting with real investment flows

The method of averaging required rates of return when investing in or from each country used in tables 5.5-5.8 is arguably not ideal. Following King-Fullerton, the appropriate weights would be those reflecting an equiproportional increase in the capital stock in each country. In other words, the appropriate weights would be given by the existing distribution of investments by the country of residence of the parent company. The marginal investment would be in the same proportion as the average stock of investments. Unfortunately, data regarding the actual stock of investment are rarely available, and even where they can be obtained, are unreliable. Contradictory data is common — the estimate by country A of capital in B owned by A is often very different to the estimate by country B of the same item, whereas they should, of course, be identical. More often investment flows are available, but even these raise problems; negative flows are common — reflecting net disinvestment from a country — and the tax consequences of such flows may be very different from the tax situation facing a subsidiary expanding its operations. Gross flows or stocks of foreign direct investment would avoid this problem, but are available for even fewer countries. It is not possible to construct a matrix of direct investment between all 24 OECD countries.

Given that the set of weights which it would be most easy to justify using are not available, an essentially arbitrary assumption must be made about the appropriate weights to use. Giving each country the same weight as was done for tables 5.5-5.8 may be justified on the grounds that the location of the marginal investment may be very different from the average location: in this case there is no reason to give one country a higher weight than any other. However, the required return on a marginal investment for the Icelandic or New Zealand subsidiary of a Portugese parent is considerably higher than the required return of the French or Spanish subsidiary of the same parent. It might reasonably be thought that France and Spain are more likely to be recipients of Portugese-financed investment than the other two countries, so when averaging the required return they should be given a larger weight. If this were done, the average required return when investing from Portugal would be substantially lower than if each country were given the same weight.

This is not an issue devoid of policy relevance; it was noted earlier that the average required return on all transnational investments was significantly higher than the average required return on purely domestic investment. If this is due at least in part to high required returns on investments which are unlikely to ever take place regardless of the tax situation, then quite different conclusions should be drawn about the nature of obstacles to investment set up by the international tax system than if the higher rates of return were general to all possible investment flows.

Table 5.15: **The effects of different methods of averaging returns for the G7 countries[1]**

Country	Domestic investment	Residence (investment from named country into the other G7 countries)		Source (investment from the other G7 countries into named country)	
		Simple average	Weighted average	Simple average	Weighted average
Canada	6.2	7.2	7.1	8.3	7.6
France	5.4	6.6	5.7	8.2	6.8
Germany	5.6	8.1	7.8	5.9	6.2
Italy	5.9	8.4	8.4	6.9	7.1
Japan	6.4	7.9	7.8	7.7	7.7
United Kingdom	5.9	6.9	6.5	7.6	7.0
United States	5.8	7.1	7.3	7.3	6.9
Overall average	5.9	7.4	7.2	7.4	7.0

1. Based on required pre-tax rates of return taken from table 5.4. Subsidiary financed by one third loans from the parent, one third new equity from the parent, and one third retentions by the subsidiary. Simple averages are the sum of transnational required returns on investments in or from the other G7 countries, divided by 6 (except for the bilateral combinations of Canada with France, Germany with Italy, and for Italy and Germany and the United Kingdom where there are no investment data. In these cases the averages are appropriately adjusted). Weighted average weights the required returns by the proportion of investment flows going to (or from) the country from (or to) each of the G7 countries for which there are data.

Although it is not possible to use data about investment flows for all countries, reasonable data are available for the outward investment of the G7 countries[20] (although there are gaps even in these data). Of course, all the G7 have tax treaties with one another, and so in practice there is little problem with extreme situations within this group; nevertheless, some indication of what might be expected to happen to the average required returns of the full matrix can be gleaned from looking at this sub-group (a note on the calculation of these investment flow weights is given in Annex 5.)

Table 5.15 takes the overall average rates of return from table 5.4 for the G7 countries, and then averages the required returns in different ways. For the second column of numbers, the simple average of required returns faced by the G7 subsidiaries of parent companies based in the named country is taken (in exactly the same way as in tables 5.5-5.8). In other words, the subsidiaries of an American parent based in Canada, Japan, Germany, France, Italy and the UK on average must earn 7.1 per cent. The following column averages the same required returns in a different way, giving a greater weight to the required returns of British and Canadian subsidiaries of the American parent, as in fact a far larger amount of money is invested by American countries in these two countries (see table in Annex 5). The final two columns look at investment in the USA by subsidiaries of parent companies based in the other six G7 countries; if each country is given equal weight then the average required return is 7.3 per cent whereas if a larger weight is given to Japan and the UK (which together account for 70 per cent of investment in the USA by G7 countries — see table A.5.3) the average falls to 6.9 per cent.

In every case, except for the United States, using actual investment flows to weight required returns on investment out of a country into the others results in a lower average required return than if a simple

154

average were calculated. When looking at investment into each country from all the others, the average when using investment flows as weights is higher for Germany and Italy, but lower in all other cases. Overall, the weighted average of required returns is lower than the simple average — 7.2 per cent as opposed to 7.4 per cent for residence countries, and 7.0 per cent as compared with 7.4 per cent for source countries. This difference is not a large one, but it has to be remembered that all these countries have treaties with one another, so it would be surprising if any bilateral flow were subject to particularly high effective tax rates. It is not possible to say whether governments ensure that effective tax rates on particularly important bilateral investment flows are low, or whether investment flows follow low effective tax rates; either way the result is that the average transnational effective tax rate on marginal investments which companies actually pay is lower than the simple average of all possible transnational effective tax rates. However, the average required return remains significantly higher than the average required return on purely domestic investment (5.9 per cent).

Weighting with trade flows

Another alternative to these procedures is that trade data could be used to weight the flows. These data also raise many problems. Two adjacent countries may trade a lot, but the amount of investment which takes place between the two countries may be much smaller — there is no need to set up a new production plant when the foreign market is so close. More generally, in theory exports and direct investment may be substitutes for one another. Despite this, it is worth looking at trade data as a source of weights for two reasons; both investment and exports into small countries will tend to reflect the small size of the domestic market, and internationally integrated markets (the European Community, for example) will tend to exhibit both much trade and a large amount of direct investment. Annex 5 gives one such set of trade flows, for the OECD countries.

Table 5.16 is based on the average required returns given in table 5.4 above, but now the export data of Annex 5 is used to weight the rows and columns, rather than taking a simple average. Using trade data reduces the overall average required rate of return (ie on average, trade and required returns are negatively correlated), but by only a fraction. Use of trade data to weight flows obviously results in a much greater weight being given to the big trading nations — in particular, the USA, Germany and Japan.

Trade weights make a large difference to the average required returns for Portugal and Norway, reflecting the fact that very high required returns are necessary on investments in countries with which these countries do little trade. The averages for Canada fall, reflecting the importance of the United States — with relatively low effective tax rates — as a trading partner.

Whether these weights are a suitable substitute for actual investment flows is of course difficult to determine. Compared to the actual weights for the G7 countries given in Annex 5 it seems that trade flows are a tolerably good approximation of investment flows for Canada, for example. However, they are very poor for the big EC countries; actual investment flows to and from the US and Europe are much greater (in proportionate terms) than flows of exports. In their favour, use of trade flows does at least give a much lower weight to required returns between small geographically distant countries, and common-sense suggests that such investment flows are comparatively rare. For the larger countries, use of export flows may be no better than taking the simple average.

Table 5.16 Comparison of trade flows and simple averages as ways of weighing required returns[1]

Country	Residence		Source	
	Simple Average[2]	Trade-Weighted Average[3]	Simple Average[2]	Trade-Weighted Average[3]
Australia	7.3	7.5	8.2	8.4
Austria	7.2	7.2	7.1	8.6
Belgium	7.0	6.7	6.8	6.8
Canada	7.5	7.2	8.4	7.7
Denmark	6.5	6.2	7.2	7.0
Finland	6.6	6.0	7.3	7.1
France	6.6	6.1	7.9	8.0
Germany	7.9	8.1	6.4	6.2
Greece	8.3	7.8	7.5	6.2
Iceland	7.8	7.3	9.2	8.1
Ireland	8.8	7.4	6.8	6.8
Italy	8.6	7.9	7.2	7.4
Japan	8.0	7.9	8.1	7.7
Luxembourg	7.2	6.8	7.5	7.1
Netherlands	6.9	6.6	7.1	6.9
New Zealand	7.3	7.5	9.7	9.0
Norway	8.7	7.1	6.6	6.1
Portugal	9.9	8.2	7.9	7.3
Spain	7.1	6.9	8.1	7.8
Sweden	6.8	6.6	6.4	6.0
Switzerland	6.8	6.7	7.0	7.0
Turkey	8.3	8.2	8.2	7.8
United Kingdom	6.7	6.5	7.0	7.0
United States	7.1	7.3	7.5	7.2
Average[1]	7.5	7.2	7.5	7.3

1. Overall average required transnational pre-tax rates of return: Subsidiary financed by one third loans from the parent, one third new equity, and third retentions by the subsidiary. Parent raises finance by a weighted average of retentions, new equity and debt. Investment in weighted average of assets. Inflation of 4.5 per cent everywhere. No personal taxes.
2. Simple averages of 23 countries.
3. Because of the economic union between Belgium and Luxembourg it is not possible to separately identify Belgium and Luxembourg. Both countries are therefore given the same weights.

Table 5.17 **The effects on the average required return of outliers.**

Country	Domestic	Residence		Source	
		(1)	(2)	(1)	(2)
Australia	7.1	7.3	7.0	8.2	7.7
Austria	5.5	7.2	6.8	7.1	6.7
Belgium	5.4	7.0	6.7	6.8	6.6
Canada	6.2	7.5	7.2	8.4	7.9
Denmark	5.9	6.5	6.2	7.2	6.8
Finland	5.6	6.6	6.2	7.3	7.1
France	5.4	6.6	6.3	7.9	7.5
Germany	5.6	7.9	7.4	6.4	6.3
Greece	5.0	8.3	7.7	7.5	6.2
Iceland	6.7	7.8	7.5	9.2	8.4
Ireland	5.1	8.8	7.2	6.8	6.1
Italy	5.9	8.6	8.1	7.2	6.8
Japan	6.4	8.0	7.8	8.1	7.7
Luxembourg	6.3	7.2	6.8	7.5	7.1
Netherlands	5.6	6.9	6.5	7.1	6.5
New Zealand	6.8	7.3	7.1	9.7	9.1
Norway	6.8	8.7	7.7	6.6	6.3
Portugal	5.7	9.9	8.6	7.9	7.3
Spain	6.2	7.1	6.8	8.1	7.5
Sweden	5.0	6.8	6.5	6.4	5.9
Switzerland	5.4	6.8	6.5	7.0	6.5
Turkey	7.2	8.3	8.1	8.2	7.7
United Kingdom	5.9	6.7	6.4	7.0	6.6
United States	5.8	7.1	6.8	7.5	6.9
Average	5.9	7.5	7.1	7.5	7.0

1.   Average of all 23 required rates of return.
2.   Average of the 18 lowest required pre-tax rates of return. Based on required pre-tax rates of return.

157

Impact of extreme rates of return

Table 5.4 indicates that there are several combinations of source and resident countries which have very high required returns. As an alternative method of analysing the sensitivity of the results based on simple averages in table 5.8, table 5.17 explores whether these few cases are responsible for the large differences between the required returns on domestic investment and the average required returns on transnational investment, by deleting the five highest required rates of return faced by each country.

The highest five effective tax rates increase the overall average required return by 0.4 percentage points. This is a large reduction, the average transnational tax wedge is 1.6 percentage points; removing the five highest required returns thus reduces this average wedge by 25 per cent. There is much variation between different countries. Portugal and Ireland, for example, have a few countries with which they have no treaty and as a result the deduction system is applied, leading to a few very high required returns on transnational investments by Portugese or Irish parents. Companies from some countries investing in the US have significantly higher than average required returns, principally because the credit system of treating foreign source income calls for higher returns than for those countries with an exemption system. In contrast, there is little effect on the average required return resulting from deleting the highest five required returns on investments abroad funded by Turkish or Japanese parents. This is because most foreign source income faces roughly the same tax rate. In both these countries, a credit system is applied. The statutory tax rates in both countries are high, and so additional tax is applied in each country to most foreign source income, ensuring that the total tax is at least as large as it would be were the investment wholly domestic. In sum, table 5.17 indicates that outliers do sometimes significantly raise the average required return. Nevertheless, it remains the case that even ignoring these few countries, the average required return on transnational investment is substantially higher than the average required return on purely domestic investment.

E. Summary

Chapter 4 examined the impact of taxation on the incentive to undertake domestic investment. This chapter used the same approach to consider the impact of taxation on the incentive to undertake transnational investment. The chapter concentrated on direct transnational investment by a parent company in one country investing through a wholly-owned subsidiary in another country. In addition, several ways in which the parent might finance its subsidiary were examined and the focus was on the international aspects of taxation; the treatment of foreign source income and rates of withholding taxes levied on payments of dividends and interest to foreign investors both become relevant.

The basic set of results of this analysis are shown in table 5.8, which presents a required rate of return which must be earned by the subsidiary, given a 5 per cent real interest rate, averaged across various different forms of financing by the parent, and no personal taxes. The most striking feature of this table is that the average required return for transnational investment is just under 7.5 per cent, whereas, on average, the required return for domestic investment is 5.9 per cent. Within the limitations of the methodology used, all countries appear to discourage outward investment compared to domestic investment by their resident companies. They also place a high effective tax rate on inward investment by foreign companies compared to domestic investment by resident companies. Further, this result holds irrespective of the means of financing the subsidiary chosen by the parent, unless the subsidiary merely retains its earnings.

This difference in tax burdens is lessened by the existence of tax treaties. If such treaties were not in place, the average required rate of return on transnational investment would rise from just 7.5 per cent to 9.7 per cent.

However, these figures do hide a large variation in the way that each country treats other countries. Thus, the return required by a subsidiary of a parent country in one country depends crucially on where that subsidiary is located. This suggests that there is considerable incentive for companies to choose tax-favoured locations for their investments which may not be the most favourable locations in the absence of tax. To the extent to which companies respond to such incentives, the tax system therefore creates a global misallocation of resources as activities may be undertaken in high cost locations because they are tax-favoured. Similarly, subsidiaries operating in a given country face different required rates of return depending on where their parent company is located. This study does not, however, provide any measures of the impact of these potential distortions on international investment patterns and ignores many of the complexities associated with international tax arrangements, as well as such factors as any differences in the compliance behaviour of domestic and international investors.

These results are again robust to changes in the assumptions used in the calculations. For example, using country-specific inflation rates rather than a common average inflation rate for all countries has little effect on the overall results. Nor does adjusting the common inflation rate used. Finally, averages were also constructed using weights corresponding to the relative importance of some countries as locations for inward or outward investments from other countries. As was to be expected, attempts to reflect real-world investment flows by using actual investment flows for the G7 countries or trade flows for all countries resulted in lower average required transnational returns. The tax burden on marginal transnational investment remains, however, substantially higher than on similar domestic investments.

Notes and References

1. The technical treatment of international investment and the modifications to the basic King and Fullerton model equations are given in annex 1.

2. Taxation when investment abroad is done through a branch is not discussed in this report since, in practice, most investment in the manufacturing sector is done by means of subsidiaries.

3. Except for changes in the exchange rate, which may affect the required rate of return.

4. There is a distinction between the case in which the marginal shareholder is domestic but faces a zero rate of tax, and the case in which the marginal shareholder is foreign with an unknown, but possibly zero, rate of tax; the former may receive tax credits on dividends which the latter may not.

5. This permits an examination of the effects solely of taxation.

6. For example, if inflation is 50 per cent in the source country and there are fixed exchange rates, even a zero return on the investment would nevertheless yield a substantial gain to the investor, simply because of the increase in the value of the asset.

7. Two possible justifications are that either debt takes a sufficiently small proportion of the total financial transfers to be unaffected by such rules or that the model is looking at marginal investments -- as long as it is assumed that the average financing of the subsidiary is within thin capitalisation limits, the parent can use whichever form of financing on a (small) new investment is most attractive without breaching the threshold. For a discussion of these issues see *Thin Capitalisation* OECD 1989.

8. Although in some circumstances (surplus ACT in the United Kingdom, for example) companies (and hence indirectly, shareholders) may be taxed at a higher rate on foreign source income than on domestic investment.

9. Withholding taxes on payments to individuals often differ from those to companies.

10. For a discussion of the impact of tax treaties, see paragraph 5.47 to 5.52.

11. Apart from the credit and exemption systems, two other treatments of foreign source income are occasionally practiced within OECD see (table 3.6). One is the use of a deduction system where tax is charged on the profit underlying the foreign source income, but in determining the tax base in the resident country the foreign tax paid is deducted. The other is where the tax treatment of receipts by a parent from foreign subsidiaries is to exempt a proportion of the receipts, but to tax the remainder through the deduction system.

12. A note of explanation is necessary for the domestic case. Investments in the home country of the parent are treated in a slightly different manner to investments abroad; an assumption is made that the parent undertakes the investment directly (so there is no need to take account of the tax treatment of income flows between companies in the same country). In Table 5.1, the domestic investment is taken to be financed solely by retained earnings in order to bring

out most clearly the fact that for zero-rate personal taxpayers, there is no tax discrimination on investments in a country according to the nationality of the parent company. For Tables 5.2, 5.3 and 5.4, in contrast it is assumed that finance is provided by a weighted average of debt, new equity and retentions.

13. This refers to withholding taxes which create final tax liabilities, and not to those which are merely payments on account.

14. The unweighted average required rates of return -- so that, for example, Luxembourg and the US are given equal weight in the calculations.

15. In fact, even this statement should be qualified; the required pre-tax rates of return on marginal investments may not always be good indicators of the effective tax rate on average investments. Investment flows may be influenced by the mobility and effective tax rates on a projects earning a whole range of pre-tax returns.

16. This overall average required return is the average of 11,592 possible required rates of return in the OECD -- three different types of asset, seven different forms of financing, and all the possible combinations of source and residence of the 24 OECD countries (excluding the purely domestic investments).

17. The tax system in the residence country determines the discount rate which should be applied to the earnings of the subsidiary, so does have some influence on the required rates of return although in the absence of personal taxes only the discount rate on debt finance is affected.

18. It is apparent that the combination of a relatively high tax rate and the deduction system in Norway results in a very high average required return. If Norway were excluded from the analysis, tax treaties would still reduce the required return by 1.7 percentage point, and the general conclusion about treaties reducing variation would still hold.

19. The sensitivity analysis at the end of this chapter looks at the required rates of return which would be necessary were exchange rates fixed but actual inflation rates were applied in each country.

20. The United States, Canada, Japan, Germany, France, Italy and the United Kingdom.

Chapter 6
The Main Policy Choices

A. Introduction

This chapter uses the descriptive and quantitative information provided in earlier chapters to discuss the main policy choices arising for governments in determining how they should tax profits from domestic and international investment.

Section B examines the domestic arguments for and against the various options in designing or changing a corporation tax, and tables 6.1 and 6.2 show recent changes respectively in the tax treatment of dividends and in the rates and the base of corporate taxes. Evidently these choices are influenced by what other countries do, so even in Section B an international dimension occurs. Section C deals with international issues and focuses on the central question of how tax distortions to international capital flows can be minimised in a world where corporation tax systems are unharmonised, and where some countries are predominantly capital-importing and others predominantly capital-exporting. The aim of this section is to enquire how far there is room for improvement in the international rules of the game which at present govern the tax treatment of international capital flows.

B. Domestic issues

1) The tax treatment of dividends under the corporate and personal income tax

Table 6.1 illustrates what OECD countries have actually done over three decades in changing their treatment of distributed profits. It calls for the following general observations:

— Countries do not lightly change their system. Such changes imply uncertainties for the business community and complicated transitional provisions affecting both taxpayers and tax administrators.

— Nevertheless, almost all OECD countries have changed their approach to economic double taxation at least once over the last three decades.

— After a one-way move in the early and mid-seventies towards a reduction of the double taxation of dividends, there was little change between 1975 and 1985 in country tax systems.

— Since 1985 (often in conjunction with other corporate tax reforms) around half of OECD countries have changed corporate tax systems, sometimes eliminating the double taxation of dividends (Australia, Finland and New Zealand), and others increasing it in a variety of different ways (Austria, Belgium, France).

Table 6.1 Changing approaches to economic double taxation 1962 to 1991

1962:   Belgium from classical to partial shareholder relief scheme;
1965:   United Kingdom from partial shareholder relief to classical system;
1965:   France from classical system to imputation system;
1968:   Austria from classical system to split rate system;
1968:   Sweden from classical system to partial dividend deduction (for new issues only);
1970:   Norway from classical system to split rate system;
1973:   United Kingdom from classical to partial imputation system;
1976:   Germany from split-rate to split-rate plus full imputation;
1983:   Italy from partial to full imputation;
1986:   Turkey introduces a zero personal tax rate on dividends;
1986:   Austria introduces partial shareholder relief scheme;
1987:   Australia from classical to full imputation;
1988:   New Zealand from classical to full imputation;
1989:   Austria abolishes split rate system;
1989:   Portugal from split rate to partial shareholder relief;
1989:   France introduces lower rate for retained profits;
1989:   Finland moves from partial dividend deduction to full imputation;
1990:   Belgium moves from partial shareholder relief scheme to classical system;
1990:   Japan abolishes split rate system.
1991:   Denmark abandons full imputation proposal in favour of a different variant of partial shareholder relief (separate lower rate tax on dividends).

Proposals from the Commission of the European Communities

1962:   Neumark Report recommends split rate system for European Communities;
1970:   Consultant report of the European Communities recommends classical system as their harmonized system;
1975:   EC Commission recommends adoption of partial imputation system;
1990:   EC Commission withdraws 1975 proposals, pending a further enquiry into the need and desirability of harmonizing its member countries' systems, rate and base.
1990:   EC Directives on parent/subsidiaries and on intercompany dividends.
1990:   Establishment of a Group of Independent Experts to examine corporate tax systems.

Table 6.2 **Corporate income tax changes and proposals since 1986
relating to base and rate schedule**[1]

Country	Base Broadening	Reduction of Rates	Other
Australia	1988 1991	1988	Removal of various incentives in 1988 and in 1991.
Austria	1989	1989	Removal of various incentives in 1989.
Belgium	1989/90	1989/90	
Canada	1988	1988	
Denmark	1990/91	1990/91	
Finland	1989 1990 1991	1990 1991	Limits to incentives in 1989-1991.
France		1989[2] 1990[2]	Introduction of new incentives relating to new firms in 1989 and to firms which reduce the working hours of their personnel in 1990.
Germany		1990	Limits to regional incentives in 1988.
Greece		1988	
Ireland	1988 to 1991	1988 1989 1991	Accelerated depreciation phased out. Tax rates reduced and rationalised. Export sales relief ended.
Iceland	1991	1991	Lowering of investment credits.
Italy		1989	
Japan		1988 1989 1990	
Luxembourg		1987 1988 1989 1990	
Netherlands	1988	1988	
New Zealand		1988	
Norway	1992	1992	
Portugal	1989	1989	Removal of various incentives in 1989.
Spain			Limits to investment credit in 1989.
Sweden	1991	1991	
Switzerland	-	-	Flat rate proposals (June 1991)
United Kingdom	1986	1986 1991 1992	Reduction in rate for small companies in 1987 and 1988.
United States	1987	1987	Removal of various incentives and introduction of the new branch tax in 1987.

1.   No major changes have been made or proposed in Turkey.
2.   Only for retained profits

165

This section provides a summary of the arguments for and against the various ways of dealing with economic double taxation. No conclusions are reached, because the differences in the economic situation of countries may prove the decisive factor, as suggested by the many different approaches actually in operation (Table 3.1) and the many changes in divergent directions (Table 6.1). The rest of this section examines in turn relevant criteria which govern these choices and the arguments for and against the various systems and methods. An appendix at the end of the chapter reproduces a number of OECD government statements on why they have made changes in this area.

2) *Relevant factors governing the choice of a system*

Economic efficiency and tax neutrality

This would appear to be the most important reason for government's choice of whether or not to eliminate or reduce economic double taxation and the relevant considerations have already been set out in detail in Chapter 2. It is appropriate here to recall two points. First, though the majority view tends to equate economic efficiency and tax neutrality, so that investment and localisation decisions should be influenced as little as possible by tax considerations, many countries continue to use the corporate tax system as an instrument to influence investment patterns. Second, tax non-neutralities take distinct forms and the economic double taxation of dividends would appear to accentuate three different kinds of non-neutralities: first, between the choice of equity and debt; second, between self-financing of corporations and the raising of equity capital through the market; third between enterprises' decision to incorporate or not. However, in each case economic double taxation is not the only, and perhaps not even the most important, cause of these tax non-neutralities. Among others may be mentioned tax deductibility of interest, capital gains regimes, tax depreciation and valuation rules, relative rates of personal and corporate income tax, thin capitalisation rules and the tax treatment of financial institutions.

International considerations

International considerations may not have much influence on the choice between classical and other systems, but they have had a considerable influence on the preference of most OECD countries for giving relief for distributed profits at shareholder rather than at company level (see below).

Administrative and transitional considerations

Administrative considerations are important in the choice of a corporate tax system. Simplicity and practicability provide an important argument in favour of classical systems since reduction or elimination of economic double taxation results in a number of practical problems summarized as follows by McLure:

— Should tax preferences be passed through or washed out on distributed income? And what are to be the presumptive ordering rules? Should tax preferences be stacked first (against dividends) or last (against retained earnings)? Or should preferences be attributed proportionately to distributed and retained earnings? What technique should be used to achieve the desired tax treatment of tax preferences? Should there be a time limit within which income must be distributed if it is not to be considered preference income subject to corporate taxation (précompte) again, as in the French system?

— Should excess credits be refunded to both individual and corporate portfolio shareholders?

— Should credits be refunded to tax-exempt organisations, or would the answer depend on the nature of various organisations? (An analogous question in the case of the split-rate and dividend deduction methods is whether integration should be joined with a tax on the

166

dividends or investment income of such organisations). [McLure, (1979), *Must Corporate Income be Taxed Twice?* p.p. 70-77]

Changes in corporate tax systems imply arbitrary gains and losses for particular taxpayers which may require complex transitional provisions. Because of the arbitrary windfall gains which would follow a move from a classical to a non-classical systems, it has been suggested by W. Andrews [inter alia in C. McLure (1979)] that any such relief should be confined to new shares, as was done in Sweden. Also of relevance is the business community's preference for stability and certainty since frequent changes increase compliance and administrative costs which imply a welfare loss for society. This is perhaps the major reason why, although most OECD countries have changed their system over the last three decades, only five have done so more than once (see table 6.1).

Budgetary constraints

Other things being equal, reducing or eliminating economic double taxation requires raising the rate of tax on retained profits to raise the same amount of revenue from the corporate tax. A high rate of tax on retained profits may, however, be considered to have drawbacks (e.g. reducing the availability of funds for self-financing and encouraging MNEs to shift their tax base from high to low tax jurisdictions). This is probably why a number of countries with imputation systems have preferred partial to full imputation and why in most countries with relief at company level some tax is charged on distributed profits. Thus, the United States Treasury report states: "Despite the advantages of full relief from double taxation of dividends, the Treasury Department proposal would provide a deduction of only one-half of dividends paid from income taxed to the corporation. This decision is based primarily on considerations of revenue loss, and can be reconsidered once the proposal is fully phased in." (US Treasury, 1984, p. 119, Vol. 1)

Equity

Equity arguments have been advanced in favour of maintaining or eliminating economic double taxation. The 1973 OECD report on company taxation notes (paragraph 26), however, that "the redistribution of income plays no important part in the choice of a company tax system as this can be done more effectively by other means". Nevertheless, as was pointed out in Chapter 2, the choice of whether or not to eliminate economic double taxation can have a significant impact on the distribution of the tax burden on profits. Also, as was pointed out in paragraph 6.8, a change of tax regimes can imply arbitrary windfall gains and losses for taxpayers.

Tax compliance

This factor has been used as an argument for adopting imputation systems, because taxpayers are provided with an incentive to declare their dividend income in order to obtain their tax credit. Whilst the same effect could be achieved under other systems by use of withholding taxes, there may be other difficulties (including especially double tax treaty negotiations) in imposing them. However, this is certainly not a decisive reason for adopting such a system.

3) The various choices within a corporate tax system

The choice between maintaining, reducing or eliminating economic double taxation

At this point, it is perhaps helpful to summarize the arguments that have been put forward in favour of maintaining or eliminating economic double taxation. A first point to mention is that the option of reducing rather than maintaining or eliminating economic double taxation can be seen as a pragmatic compromise taken on budgetary grounds.

The case for abolishing economic double taxation is argued above all on economic efficiency grounds. The double taxation of dividends increases at least three kinds of tax non-neutralities:

— The choice between debt and equity;

— The decision to retain or distribute profits;

— The decisions of enterprises to incorporate.

It is held that the likely effect of increasing these kinds of tax non-neutralities is to reduce productive investment and to penalise new dynamic enterprises in relation to mature enterprises — encouraging the survival of the fattest rather than the fittest, as it has been expressed.

Some of the arguments for maintaining economic double taxation have already been summarised in Chapter 2. It has been suggested that there is little hard evidence that the double taxation of dividends has had the adverse effects claimed by those who want to get rid of it — especially if the new view of dividends is taken — and that other tax factors, such as the favourable treatment of interest and capital gains, may be more important. Elimination of economic double taxation will also require a higher rate of tax on retained profits if revenues are to be maintained. Some commentators have argued that it may be preferable to encourage enterprises to retain profits and engage in self-financing rather than to encourage distributions which may increase consumption at the expense of productive investment and such a policy may also have the advantage of increasing the level of private saving. The other main argument in favour of the classical system is that it is simpler to operate within one country and that at the international level fewer complications and distortions occur in investment flows when countries have classical systems.

The choice between relief of economic double taxation at company and shareholder level

Once a policy decision has been taken to reduce or eliminate economic double taxation the question then arises whether this best be done at company or shareholder level or both. To simplify the discussion this last choice — currently taken only in Germany — is not discussed.

Although numerous examples have been provided in the literature to indicate that formal equivalence can be provided for relief at company and shareholder level[1], the following arguments have been advanced in favour of relief at the shareholder level rather than at the company level:

— Capital import neutrality may be easier to achieve under a split rate system which gives the benefit of the lower rate to all shareholders, than under an imputation systems which may, and in practice often does, apply only to resident shareholders. But a State with a split rate system has no bargaining power in negotiating double taxation conventions. In the days when German tax rate on retained profits (51 per cent) was much higher than on distributed profits (15 per cent), Germany was unable to persuade its partners, and especially the United States, to let Germany levy a compensatory withholding tax at source on dividends distributed by the German companies to foreign shareholders. This prompted Germany eventually to amend its system to introduce full imputation in addition to its split rate. And it was especially to avoid the same kinds of difficulty that France and the United Kingdom preferred to choose a partial imputation system, though on other grounds the United Kingdom had earlier opted for a split rate system;

— The United States Treasury Department recommended, in its 1984 tax reform proposals, that the corporate tax system should include a partial deduction of distributed profits (dividend deduction system). A proposal for a dividend deduction system was approved by the House of Representatives in 1986 but was subsequently abandoned partly because it would have led to the transfer of untaxed profits (or profits paying only the 15 per cent withholding tax) to non-resident shareholders. The Treasury Department's suggestion of a "compensatory" levy could have conflicted with double taxation agreements;

— Under split-rate systems, the problem arises as to what is the appropriate rate to apply to the profits distributed by branches to their parents abroad;

— From the point of view of tax evasion and avoidance the credit under imputation systems, if available to non-residents, can be claimed only if the income is declared, which means that from the point of view of tax enforcement there is no need for a withholding tax. Whilst it is theoretically possible to achieve similar results by a higher withholding tax under split-rate systems, tax treaty negotiations may preclude such a solution (see above reference to the Germany-United States case).

On the other hand, Sweden recently chose to maintain a dividend deduction system (for dividends on new issues) for residents liable to tax on dividend income and for dividends paid to non-residents liable to a withholding tax. Apart from budgetary reasons, such a system was seen as achieving a better balance for resident shareholders between the corporate and personal tax burden on investments financed by new issues and investments financed by retained earnings, taking into account the relatively lower tax burden on capital gains due to deferral. The reform thereby contributed to reducing the 'locking-in-effect'.

But for the international dimension, relief at company level would probably have been preferred by France, Germany, United Kingdom and United States to imputation systems because of its greater simplicity and transparency. It is true that if relief is given at company level administrative complications arise when the dividends are distributed from a subsidiary to a parent company and the latter does not redistribute them immediately to its own shareholders. This means that as the subsidiary has benefited unfairly from a reduced rate of corporation tax, the difference has to be "recouped" from the parent company in the form of a compensatory tax. But in other situations relief at the company level would appear to be administratively simpler than imputation systems.

Some commentators have argued that because of the conflicting interests of company directors and shareholders, equivalent relief at company level and shareholder level in some forms could result in different behavioural responses with regard to pay-out ratios and investment and savings decisions of enterprises and shareholders. For example:

— Relief at the company level may be effective in achieving the neutrality of the tax system in respect of the two main types of corporate funding (equity and loan finance), and will also reduce the motivation to indulge in thin capitalisation;

— The amount of company tax relief can be varied according to the size of the firm; for example, it can be restricted to small and medium-sized firms to allow them to raise capital more easily;

— The greater the tax credit for shareholders, the more households may be prompted to purchase shares rather than bonds, even if such behaviour is based on a "money illusion" since, if capital markets work effectively, overall risk-adjusted rates of return on loans and equities should be equalised.

There appears to be a conflict between what is regarded as the advantages of company level relief at the domestic level and its disadvantages at the international level. In opting in 1984 for company tax relief, the 1984 United States Treasury report took the view (vol. 2 pages 142-3) that "because dividend deduction and imputation systems are economically equivalent, it would be unwarranted to adopt an imputation system, rather than a dividend deduction system, merely to avoid technical treaty violations. Moreover, in the context of the United States economy and tax system, an imputation approach to dividend relief would be extremely cumbersome. A dividend deduction system, therefore, has been proposed". The contrary view has been taken in Australia, New Zealand and most West European countries.

The choice between the different methods of reducing or eliminating economic double taxation
At the company level: split rate versus dividend deduction

Relief at the company level can be given either by reducing the rate of tax for distributed profits (split rate system) or by reducing the base on which the rate is applied (dividend deduction system). As noted in table 6.1 some countries have chosen the first and others the second option. Although arguments have been advanced for or against the relative merits of these two systems (e.g. Van den Tempel (1970) much preferred the split rate system whereas the United States Treasury (1984) preferred the dividend deduction method), there would seem little to choose between them on policy grounds, for in principle it would seem that special problems (e.g. separating qualifying distributions from those to which governments consider that relief should not be given) arise under either system. It could be that the choice between the two systems is taken on grounds of how the system can be most conveniently adapted to a country's legal and administrative system.

At the shareholder level: imputation systems versus shareholder relief schemes

Basic differences between these two methods have already been described in Chapters 1 and 3. The following paragraphs elaborate on further differences:

— Under the imputation system, all corporate profits, in respect of which relief is granted will have been subject to corporate income tax levied at statutory rates; part or all of the corporate income tax paid on the distributed profits is set off against the shareholder's tax liability (the imputation credit is usually expressed as a percentage of the cash dividend but its rate is determined in relation to the statutory rate of corporate tax) on the dividends received or refunded to him if the corporate income tax thus paid exceeds his own income tax liability. In collecting the corporate tax, the tax authorities are collecting tax for which otherwise the shareholder would be liable according to his personal circumstances (total income, number of dependents, etc.). The imputation credit for corporate tax may thus be seen as equivalent to a of refund of advance taxation of dividends in the hands of the shareholder;

— In contrast, under shareholder relief schemes, the tax credit does not depend on any amount of corporate tax that may have been paid by the company. The tax credit, usually expressed as a percentage of the amount of the dividend, is seen merely as a form of tax incentive designed to encourage resident individuals to invest in resident companies or alternatively as a way of reducing the tax disadvantages of investing in equities instead of, say, bonds or real estate.

There remains disagreement among commentators whether the similarities or differences between imputation systems and shareholder relief schemes are the more important. What may be most relevant for the shareholder under both methods is the amount of relief on dividend income. The relation or non-relation to corporation tax deemed to have been paid, however, is not only of academic interest since it could influence the shareholder's decision on whether to invest at home or abroad. For governments and for international double taxation treaties the distinction also is of practical importance in that under imputation systems sometimes, but under shareholder relief schemes never, is the credit granted to non-residents. Nevertheless, under shareholder relief schemes the credit can and in Canada is granted to domestic shareholders of domestic corporations for foreign dividends received by these corporations.

Tax credits under shareholder relief schemes bear no direct relationship to the amount of tax collected from the company. But one practical aspect of imputation systems is that several countries design their systems to ensure that the corporate tax collected is sufficient to cover tax credits paid, where appropriate, to shareholders. In the United Kingdom, this is one of the functions of advance corporation tax. In France, the *précompte* is payable only when dividends are payable out of profits which have not suffered French corporation tax or which relate to a tax year which has been closed for more than five years. Countries tend to be concerned over paying tax credits to domestic shareholders when no tax has been received and, in the absence of reciprocal arrangements, about paying tax credits to foreign shareholders. In some cases (e.g., holding companies in the imputation country with both subsidiaries and shareholder in a classical system country where profits are being earned), the taxes reduce risks of substantial tax losses to the imputation country and distortions to the location of holding companies. But the effect of some forms of imputation may be to discriminate against distributions and to encourage domestic investment by the parent which it would not otherwise have taken and so discriminate against overseas investment.

The shareholder relief schemes may be judged by the simpler criterion of whether the incentive for domestic investment is worth the revenue forgone, or at what rate of credit is the ideal balance achieved? There is an obvious trade-off between on the one hand a possible increase in economic efficiency through greater investment in domestic equities, and on the other a loss of revenue and international neutrality. At the domestic level, the advantage of shareholder relief schemes over imputation systems is their greater simplicity, their disadvantage in their greater randomness in taking no account of whether firms which distribute dividends have ever paid corporation tax.

The special advance tax described above is not a necessary feature of imputation systems, however, and it does not apply in Australia where dividends distributed by resident companies qualify for full imputation credits provided they are paid out of company income which has borne the full rate of company tax, so that these qualifying dividends are effectively relieved of any further income tax in the hands of the shareholder. Any credits in excess of that required to relieve dividends from income tax are available to offset income tax on other income of the shareholder, but no tax refunds or carry forward of imputation credits are allowed. Qualifying dividends are exempt from dividend withholding tax when paid to non-residents; however dividends paid to non-residents out of company income which has not borne company tax are liable for the existing 15 per cent dividends withholding tax for dividends paid to treaty countries. Dividends received by companies from other resident companies continue to be freed of company tax in the hands of the receiving company. Where dividends are paid out of company income which has borne company tax, they are relieved of further tax by imputation credits. Dividends paid out of such taxed company income are referred to as qualifying dividends (or "franked" dividends). To establish whether dividends are qualifying dividends to which imputation credits are attached, companies are required to establish and maintain a qualifying dividends account.

4) *Tax base and rate issues*

The other main policy issues in designing a corporate tax system are defining the tax base and setting the rate schedule. One difficulty in commenting upon these issues is that there is little information available on why countries have made the choices that they have. This in part reflects the fact that current corporate tax structures have developed over a number of years and in part that changes to the systems are influenced by the specific economic, conjunctural and political circumstances in each country. Thus there is no unique set of guidelines which apply to all countries.

Recent trends

The schedule rates of tax have fallen in almost all countries over the last five years[2]. At the same time, the corporate tax base has been widened by eliminating or reducing tax incentives, by bringing tax depreciation nearer to economic depreciation and by eliminating inflation adjustments schemes for inventories. The main explanation for these changes are:

— Removing tax incentives. It is increasingly accepted that tax incentives are a costly (in terms of revenue foregone) and an inefficient means of influencing investment patterns. Governments are placing more emphasis on providing a neutral tax structure under which investment patterns are primarily determined by non-tax factors. Nevertheless, as can be seen from table 3.4 in Chapter 3, there remain significant incentive provisions in most tax systems. Two approaches can be identified. First, some governments favour the provision of across-the-board investment incentives which apply to most sectors and types of activities. Here the objective is to increase the overall level of investment, but to leave the market to determine its allocation. A second approach, which is more prevalent, is to provide incentives for particular sectors or activities. The rationale behind this approach is that the government rather than the market is better placed to "pick the winners", or that positive externalities may be associated with certain activities. It should be recalled, however, that incentives in the Member states of the EC must conform to guidelines set down by the Commission.

—   Maintaining the revenue base. Tax incentives require higher schedule rates to maintain the same corporate revenue yield. Many governments have now decided to eliminate these incentives and thereby finance cuts in schedule rates.

—   International competition. A major influence on the trend towards lower schedule rates of tax is the need to ensure that a country's tax rate does not get too much out of line with that of its major trading partners. Schedular rates are important because (i) they may influence taxpayers' perceptions of the effective tax rate, which is not always easy to measure and (ii) because they can influence how the worldwide tax base of a MNE is allocated between countries (by transfer pricing policies, for example). Thus, once the United Kingdom and the United States reduced substantially their rates in the 1980s, many other countries were under pressure to reduce their rates.

Tax base issues

A number of issues arise in defining and measuring the corporate tax base. The first is whether tax rules should follow commercial accounting practices. Countries adopt one of three broad approaches. In the first, accountancy practices are largely influenced by tax regulations. The second approach is where the tax rules follow for the most part accountancy standards and the third is where accounting and tax standards are for the most part independent. Under the first two approaches (followed, for example, by France, Germany, Italy and Norway) the tax authorities accept as taxable income the profits shown in the company's account, usually with some minor modifications. Under the third approach (used in Denmark, the Netherlands, the United Kingdom and the United States, for example), a number of adjustments are made to determine taxable profits. A description of these different approaches is provided in *The Relationship between Taxation and Financial Reporting: Income Tax Accounting*, OECD 1987 and such differences can have important economic effects[3]. It is also relevant to recall that under the Fourth Directive of the EC, company accounts have to show a true and fair view of the performance of the enterprise.

Secondly, there is the issue of how to define and calculate tax depreciation. A few countries (e.g. the United States) have attempted to keep tax depreciation as close as possible to economic depreciation. Others (e.g. France) have intentionally provided tax depreciation rules which are more generous than economic depreciation. There is also the question of the choice of the depreciation method. Table 3.8 in Chapter 3 shows that there are two main approaches: the declining balance method and the straight line depreciation. The choice between these methods is usually made on grounds of administrative simplicity and reduction in compliance costs both for the tax authorities and taxpayers (which usually favour the declining balance method) and whether or not a country wishes to "front-load" the allowances (which is easier to achieve under a declining balance method). Expectations on the rate of inflation may also influence this choice.

Thirdly there is the issue how the tax base should be corrected for inflation. All income tax systems provide for some measures which aim at taxing real economic income by correcting for inflation (though some of these corrections are so favorable that they tend to be investment subsidies). Inflation adjustments are primarily aimed at preventing effective tax rates on investment income from depending on the rate of inflation in ways that vary across asset types and industries so that investment decisions are motivated solely by economic realities rather than by tax considerations. This concern is confirmed by the results shown in Chapter 4, which clearly illustrate that tax wedges are very sensitive to the rate of inflation.

Correcting for inflation may be relevant at least for the following three aspects of the measurement of the tax base: the depreciation system; capital gains taxation; treatment of stocks. In practice, however, the objective of taxing real income is in most countries achieved in an ad hoc way, e.g. a percentage of capital gains is exempt but taxation is at the same time based on nominal gains; depreciation rules and rates may be favorable (e.g. accelerated depreciation), but depreciation allowances are at the same time based on historical cost. As regards the treatment of stocks, the use of the LIFO method provides some adjustment for the impact of inflation on the replacement of inventories. The use of LIFO, however, can sometimes produce very large tax liabilities as companies reduce stocks during a severe downturn. Also to the extent that stocks are financed by debt, and in addition relief is given for interest, adjustments for inflation may over-compensate the corporation for inflation.

It should in this context be noted that interest income taxation is generally based on nominal and not real interest, as are interest expenditure deductions. This may tend to discourage saving and to encourage borrowing.

General investment reliefs should in some cases be seen in the context of real income taxation since some of these reliefs were introduced during periods of rapid inflation to stimulate investment by preventing capital consumption allowances based on historical costs from being eroded by inflation.

Correcting for inflation entails, however, also a very great amount of complexity with respect, for example, to the design of indexing procedures, to the definition of a real interest rate, the handling of financial assets and liabilities within an international group of companies, etc. This complexity is probably one of the main reasons why actual systems copmromise between real and nominal income as the tax base.

It is also of relevance that indexation or real income taxation does not always result in lower tax: for example, it would probably raise taxes for those firms that make debt-financed investments in relatively longer-lived assets (e.g. real estate). In addition accurate inflation adjustments do require much more record keeping. In that context it has been held that if it is important to make necessary inflation adjustments for tax purposes, then it is equally important to make them for financial reporting purposes. It has, however, not so far been possible to develop a generally acceptable inflation adjusted accounting standard.

Finally, it may be noted that the potential distortions implied by divergences between the actual tax base and real economic income will be smaller — ceteris paribus — the lower the inflation rate and the lower the tax rates. The large number of corporate tax reforms implemented in recent years in which a common objective has been to cut tax rates and sometimes to broaden the tax base have thus contributed to reduce the distortions created by less-than-perfect real income taxation.

The use of tax incentives

The use of tax incentives raises a number of complex issues. First, there is the question of whether the incentives have any impact on the level and pattern of domestic investment. Here the evidence is ambiguous. Although recent OECD studies suggest that these incentives do not greatly influence the level of investment or decisions on where to locate such investment, the timing of the project, however, and its financing, may be affected[4]. A closely related question is that even if additional investment were generated, how does the cost of such incentives, in terms of revenue foregone, compare to the amount of new investment. Studies in Canada and elsewhere suggest that in many cases the value of new investment is less than the revenue loss[5]. A third question relates to the productivity of the investment undertaken. Work undertaken in the United Kingdom suggests that in the long run tax induced investment may have a lower productivity than other investment, in part because it may be difficult to target such subsidies[4]. Another argument that has been advanced against the use of tax incentives is that they tend to alter the composition of investment, favouring capital intensive activities.

A related issue is the effect of these incentives on tax administration and budgetary control. On the first issue, it is widely accepted that tax incentives increase the complexity of the tax system for both the taxpayer and tax administration. Incentives also open up new avenues for tax evasion and avoidance. It is also generally accepted that the provision of incentives by means of the tax system is a less transparent way of providing subsidies compared to cash grants and thereby makes it more difficult to control the cost of these investment programmes.

If, however, a government decides that it wishes to provide a subsidy to a particular sector or activity, the tax system may, depending on the structure of the subsidies, provide an administratively convenient way of implementing the programme, thus avoiding the creation of new administrative mechanisms. Governments may also wish to use tax incentives as part of their conjunctural policy, especially if they believe that such incentives influence the timing of investment.

Insofar as these tax incentives are provided to foreign corporations, their effectiveness will depend upon the methods used to relieve international double taxation in the residence country. Where a country uses a tax credit system and does not provide tax sparing credits, it is the treasury of the residence country rather than the foreign enterprise that benefits from the incentive provision.

Tax rate issues

There are three main issues that governments have discussed in relation to the corporate rate schedule:

— First, there is the question of what should be the level of the tax rate(s). There are, as noted above, no unique guidelines in setting the corporate tax rate, but some of the factors which influence governments are the following: the need for revenue; the desire to minimise the difference between the corporate tax rate and the personal tax rate (usually the top marginal rate) that would apply to profits made in unincorporated enterprises, thereby reducing any tax bias in favour of unincorporated businesses; the recognition that if the rate is set at too high a level, there is a risk that inward international investment will be discouraged and MNEs will be encouraged to shift their tax base to lower tax jurisdictions;

— Second, should the rate schedule be progressive or a single rate. Most OECD countries opt for a single rate of tax in part because they are concerned that a progressive schedule would encourage enterprises to splinter their activities thereby reducing their overall tax liability and in part because a single rate system is easier to administer. There are, however, a few countries (e.g. Switzerland) which use progressive rate schedules and one country (the Netherlands) uses a regressive rate schedule. In the former group of countries a lower rate of tax is applied to profits below a certain level. The main arguments put forward in favour of this approach are that it may provide an incentive for the development of small to medium size enterprises; it may compensate these enterprises for their relatively higher compliance costs and it may reduce any tax disincentives to carry out a business in an unincorporated form.[6] These are issues which are currently being examined by the Committee on Fiscal Affairs;

— A third issue, which has been of particular concern in Austria and the Nordic countries, is that savers should pay the same tax rate whether they invest directly in corporations or do so by financial intermediaries. This is part of the broader concern that all capital income should be taxed at the same rate.

5) Country practices

Although there are a number of limitations on the domestic effective tax rate calculations provided in Chapter 4, they do enable a number of tentative conclusions to be drawn.

First, tax systems are generally not neutral in their treatment of different assets. Table 4.3 shows that in all countries (except Ireland, Italy and Spain) the tax system favours investment in machinery rather than in buildings and that in all countries (except Iceland, Italy, Japan, the Netherlands and United States) investment in inventories bear the highest tax burden[7]. Chapter 4 provides an explanation for these differences. Although this study does not attempt to quantify the impact of these differences on the pattern of investment, it would be surprising if they did not encourage investment in machinery, at the expense of investment in buildings and stocks. These results ignore, however, the fact that the relative tax treatment of similar assets may differ substantially as between sectors; that the categories machinery and building encompass a wide range of types of assets, each of which may be subject to a different tax treatment and that this treatment may also depend upon the maturity of the assets.

Secondly, the results in Chapter 4 also show that tax systems are not neutral towards alternative financing sources. The current corporate and personal income tax systems provide a strong incentive for corporations to finance new investment by means of debt. In some countries, projects which would otherwise have a negative rate of return become profitable if financed by means of debt. It is more difficult to generalise about the tax treatment of retained earnings and new equity, although in fourteen countries (see table 4.3) the tax system is neutral as between these two sources of finance. Once again, Chapter 4 provides an explanation for these differences, but no attempt has been made to quantify their impact on corporate financing decisions. In practice, the main concern of governments is that the favourable tax treatment of debt financing encourages companies to become highly geared (i.e. a high level of debt finance relative to equity finance) and that this could expose them to financial bankruptcy in case of a serious economic downturn.

One area which is not examined in Chapter 4, but which has been discussed by governments, is the relative tax treatment of different sectors and types of activities[8]. Work carried out in a number of countries[9] shows that the effective tax rates on new investment in different segments of the economy vary substantially. Recent tax reforms have tried to reduce these variations by providing a more even treatment of different types of investment.

A recent OECD survey of Norway[10] noted that there are large differences in the effective tax rates "between types of investment, as to where the investment is located, whether the asset is reinvested or not" (page 51). Recent reform proposals attempt to address this issue by providing a more neutral tax treatment of different sectors and activities. Thus tax reliefs which discriminate between regions, ownership structures and different kinds of investment will be eliminated, and tax depreciation brought closer into line with economic depreciation. An earlier survey of Canada[11] noted that the "average rates of corporate tax by sector varied from 14.5 per cent to 24.5 per cent of financial statements' income" (page 69). Reforms carried out in 1988 were specifically aimed at reducing the effect of taxation on the allocation and financing of investment. The reforms narrowed these differences, but they remained large (15.5 to 22.6 per cent), with mining, agriculture, forestry and fishing sectors continuing to have below average corporate tax rates.

A similar situation exists in Portugal, where effective tax rates vary considerably as between sectors and by type of asset[12]. Recent reforms have not reduced the dispersion of rates. Belgium has a similar experience with effective tax rates varying substantially as between sectors, ranging from 1.2 per cent of profits from producers of electricity, gas and water to 30.7 per cent for chemical companies[13]. Studies carried out in many other countries[14] confirm that there is a wide dispersion in the effective tax rates on different sectors of the economy and for different types of activities and financing structures.

Many of the recent tax reforms have tried to eliminate or at least reduce the differences in the tax treatment of different sectors and activities. These changes have been presented as a move to provide a "more level playing field" by producing a tax system which is more neutral towards different types of investment. A recent report prepared for a Committee on Fiscal Affairs seminar on tax reform[15] showed that many countries have made changes to the special reliefs available for particular types of investment; in some cases general investment incentives have been removed. Also a number of countries (e.g the United Kingdom and the United States) have tried to move tax depreciation nearer to economic depreciation and have reviewed the methods used to calculate corporate income.

It is still too early to evaluate the impact of these reforms, although the results presented in Chapter 4 do suggest that taxation continues to influence the asset structure of corporations as well as their financing decisions. The next section examines how these domestic distortions interact with international tax arrangements and the extent to which this interaction causes deviations from capital export and capital import neutrality.

C. International issues

1) Introduction

The removal of non-tax barriers (e.g. capital controls, exchange controls) to international capital flows and the globalisation of financial markets, has focused attention on the effect of taxation on foreign direct investment. Governments and others are concerned about how taxation may influence inward and outward direct investment flows and the ways in which these investments are financed. They are also concerned with the ways in which revenues from international transactions are shared between countries and the new avenues opened up by globalisation for the avoidance of tax. These factors suggest that governments may need to re-evaluate the traditional criteria used to assess domestic tax policies. An examination of these issues requires an analysis of not only the domestic tax regimes but also how these regimes interact in the context of existing international tax arrangements. This section analyses these issues, focusing mainly on the efficiency aspects and ignoring many of the complexities that arise in practice. The analysis draws upon the conceptual framework developed in Chapter 2 and the quantitative results presented in Chapter 5.

It is impossible to isolate the effects of particular features of a country's tax system on international capital flows. The tax wedge calculations provided in Chapter 5 do, however, provide some indication of the degree to which the taxation of international capital income flows departs from the concepts of neutrality and taxpayer equity discussed in Chapter 2. Departures from these standards and those of inter-nation equity and simplicity can influence the allocation of capital between countries, which, in turn, has implications for global efficiency and the division of tax revenue between countries.

Departures occur because of deliberate policy decisions made by governments to influence international capital flows, the consequences of the interaction of source and residence countries' tax systems and the practical difficulties of implementing and administering legislative measures designed to secure these standards. The extent of these distortions varies depending on the location of the investment, the residence of investors, whether capital income flows through third countries, the sector the investment is made in (for example, manufacturing, construction etc) and whether the project is financed by debt, new equity or retained earnings.

The following two subsections examine the implications for capital flows and global efficiency of selected policies dealing with the taxation of international capital income implemented by countries in their role as either country of source or country of residence.

2) *Tax policies, international capital flows and economic welfare*

To achieve an economically neutral tax treatment of international capital income flows on the basis of the source principle requires that source countries agree on certain rules to determine the proportion of a multinational enterprise's profits derived within their jurisdictions[16]. Similarly, neutral taxation of international capital income flows on the basis of the residence principle requires the establishment of mutually agreed jurisdictional rules to determine residency. Jurisdictional rules are needed for both individuals (for example, domicile or physical presence for a fixed period of time) and companies (for example, place of incorporation or place of effective management). If countries are unable to agree upon these issues taxation is likely to distort the pattern of international capital flows. The role of tax treaties in determining common source and residence rules was referred to in Chapter 2.

Tax policies can cause departures from tax neutrality, and can make it more difficult to achieve equity between taxpayers and the goals of inter-nation equity and simplicity. These policies can be assessed from the perspective of either a source or residence country. In reality, of course, most countries are both exporters and importers of capital and therefore their taxation of international capital income flows will reflect their dual role as both a source country and a residence country. A country's position as either a net exporter or net importer of capital at a particular time will influence the relative weight it places on either source or residence country rights in relation to the taxation of international capital income flows. The following sub-sections first examine how countries could achieve capital export and import neutrality, then discuss the question of inter-nation equity and lastly examine a number of specific issues[17].

3) Achieving capital export neutrality
For international direct investment

This sub-section discusses how far source and resident countries acting alone can achieve capital export neutrality. Generally, the source country is unable by is own policies to achieve capital export neutrality since the achievement of this goal depends, in part, upon the policies followed by residence country. Chapter 2 illustrated that if the residence country uses the exemption method, capital export neutrality will generally not be achieved. Therefore a move from exemption to a pure credit method would be desirable if capital export neutrality was the main policy goal. However, no country uses a pure credit method. This sub-section examines the changes required to existing credit systems if capital export neutrality were to be achieved.

The discussions in Chapters 2 and 5 suggest some modification of existing credit methods if governments wish to achieve full capital export neutrality for foreign direct investment. First, the residence countries of parent companies would have to introduce current taxation of the retained profits of subsidiaries. This is important, although very difficult to achieve, since the present practice of deferring residence country tax until the time of repatriation of profits implies that existing credit methods will work like an exemption method when foreign direct investment is financed by the retained earnings of subsidiaries, and when shareholders have no special preference for distributed over retained profits.

To illustrate this, suppose a subsidiary operates in a host country with a corporate tax rate of 30 per cent, while the home country of the parent company has a 40 per cent corporate tax rate. When the subsidiary remits a unit of dividends, the home country applying the credit system will "gross up" the dividend by the corporate tax rate paid abroad and subject the resulting pre-tax income of $1/(1-.3)$ to tax at the 40 per cent domestic rate, finally deducting the tax already paid abroad from the domestic tax liability. This procedure will leave an after-tax income of $(1-.4)/(1-.3)$ in the hands of the parent company, so this is the net income foregone by the parent if the subsidiary retains an extra unit of profits for investment abroad. If the pre-tax rate of return on the subsidiary's investment is R, and the return of $R(1-.3)$ after payment of foreign corporation tax is subsequently repatriated, the net income accruing to the parent will be $R(1-.3)(1.4)/(1-.3)$. Dividing this net income by the after-tax income of $(1-.4)/(1-.3)$ foregone during the previous year, one finds that the parent ends up with a net rate of return of $R(1-.3)$ which is seen to be independent of the domestic corporate tax rate of 40% and to depend only on the foreign corporation tax of 30 per cent, just as would have been the case under an exemption system where no domestic tax is levied on foreign investment[18].

If parent company shareholders have a preference for dividends over retained profits, as claimed by supporters of the old view of dividend taxation (see Chapter 2), the example above would have to be modified, since retention of profits abroad would then tend to raise the rate of return required by domestic shareholders. However, even the old view can be shown to imply that deferral will lead to some reduction of the cost of capital in foreign direct investment, as long as the corporate tax rate in the foreign host country is lower than the domestic corporate tax rate.

In short, the practice of deferral provides an incentive for multinational corporations to undertake foreign direct investment by retaining profits in subsidiaries operating in low-tax countries, in clear violation of capital export neutrality.

Unfortunately, however, the abolition of deferral would involve a number of technical difficulties. For instance, proper ways of accounting for foreign exchange gains and losses on foreign operations would have to be found, and there would be the general problem that the tax authorities of residence countries would have to rely on accounts submitted by foreign subsidiaries without being able to check this information through field audits, although exchange of information agreements may be able to overcome this problem. Indeed the need for the country of residence of the parent company to tax the profits retained abroad by a company incorporated and managed abroad raises wider issues of extra-territoriality. Moreover, capital export neutrality would require that investment incentives offered by the home country, such as accelerated depreciation, investment tax credits, etc., should also apply to foreign investment and not just to domestic capital formation, as it is usually the practice today. For these and other reasons, residence countries have so far been unwilling to abandon the practice of deferral, except in cases where certain types of foreign direct investment is undertaken in certain tax haven countries[19]. Thus some countries have introduced legislation (e.g. sub-part F legislation in the United States) designed to tax without deferral certain income realised through foreign controlled corporations established in low-tax jurisdictions.

Another controversial change required to achieve capital export neutrality would be the abolition of limits on foreign tax credits. As noted in Chapter 2, residence countries generally grant credit for foreign taxes only up to a limit given by the amount of domestic tax on foreign-source income. When the foreign tax rate exceeds the domestic rate of tax, investors thus effectively end up paying the higher foreign rate, implying a tax preference for domestic over foreign investment.

One argument for the limitation on the foreign tax credit is that unlimited credits may give source countries an incentive to impose excessively high tax rates on foreign investors. Source countries could do this without deterring foreign investment, because foreign investors would receive a full refund from their home country for taxes paid abroad. In this way, source countries could extract revenues from the fisc of residence countries.

This problem might be partly alleviated by strict adherence to the principle of non-discrimination, which requires that source countries impose the same rates of corporate tax on foreign-owned and domestically owned corporations, as is already the case in most countries. However, as source countries have the right to impose withholding taxes on dividends, there is still a potential for governments to collect additional revenue from foreign investors without simultaneously raising the burden on domestic investors. But this potential is somewhat limited by the fact that the 1977 OECD Model Convention recommends a maximum withholding tax of 5 per cent in the context of corporate direct investment, a recommendation adopted by many countries.

The achievement of capital export neutrality is further complicated by the fact that multinational corporations have access to a multitude of alternative financing possibilities, as illustrated in table 6.3. If a multinational enterprise does not wish to rely on funds supplied by the parent, the subsidiary can finance its investment by borrowing or issuing shares in the capital market, or by retaining its own profits. Further, finance from the parent company may be obtained in the form of loans or in the form of injections of equity via new share issues, and the parent in turn may raise its funds by borrowing, by issuing shares, or by retaining its profits. In total, this leaves nine different financing opportunities for the multinational, assuming for the sake of simplicity a clear dividing line between debt finance and equity finance, which, in practice, may not always be the case. Since the tax code may discriminate between debt and equity finance and between the two sources of equity, and since retained and repatriated foreign profits may be given different tax treatment, the required rate of return on foreign direct investment will typically vary according to the particular financing pattern chosen by the multinational. Whether the tax system provides an effective incentive or a disincentive to foreign as opposed to domestic investment may thus depend on the financial policy of the multinational enterprise.

If residence countries were to relieve international double taxation through a system of full credit without deferral, subsidiaries and parent companies would effectively be taxed as one unit, and income from foreign sources would be given ordinary domestic tax treatment. This would imply equal tax treatment of foreign and domestic debt-financed investment, and equal treatment of equity-financed investment at home and abroad. In this narrow sense (i.e., disregarding other types of non-neutralities), capital export neutrality would thus be attained. However, as long as tax discrimination between debt and equity and between the two forms of equity finance is maintained, the required rate of return on foreign and domestic investments would still differ, if for some reason the two forms of investment were to be financed in different ways. Also, if depreciation allowances deviate from true economic depreciation, the cost of capital will typically vary across different assets. Hence the required rates of return at home and abroad would also differ, if foreign investment goes into other types of assets than domestic investment.

**Table 6.3 Alternative sources of finance of investment undertaken by a
foreign subsidiary of a multinational corporation**

A. External funds raised by the subsidiary

1. Borrowing in the host country or in the global capital market.

2. Issues of new shares to minority shareholders in the host country or in third countries.

B. Internal funds raised by the subsidiary

3. Retention of profits in the subsidiary

C. Funds raised from the parent company

4. Borrowing by parent and lending to the subsidiary.

5. Borrowing by parent and issuing of new shares from subsidiary.

6. New share issues by parent and lending to the subsidiary.

7. New share issues by parent and purchase of shares from subsidiary.

8. Retention of profits by parent and lending to the subsidiary.

9. Retention of profits by parent and issuing of new shares from subsidiary.

Note: The alternative financing possibilities and the impact of taxation on the financial policies of multinational enterprises are analysed in Julian A. Alworth: *The Finance, Investment and Taxation Decisions of Multinationals*, Basil Blackwell, Oxford 1988.

These observations illustrate the importance of approximating to tax neutrality in the domestic sphere if it is desired to achieve tax neutrality in the international sphere. It would be somewhat inconsistent to insist on full capital export neutrality if the tax system were still highly non-neutral towards the different types of domestic investment.

Finally, it is worth mentioning one more difficulty associated with a system of pure credit without deferral. Under such a tax regime, multinational corporations in high-tax countries would have an incentive to shift their legal residence to low-tax countries in order to minimise tax on their worldwide income. Through incorporation of parent companies in low-tax jurisdictions, multinationals would only have to pay the low residence country tax rate on their operations in other jurisdictions, and the transactions costs involved in changing the place of legal residence would probably often be low compared to the potential tax savings. The net result of a concentration of corporate headquarters in tax havens would obviously result in a loss of global corporate tax revenue. This revenue loss would be felt both by the low-tax countries which would have to grant refunds to resident parent corporations for the higher taxes paid abroad (assuming they operated a pure credit system), and by the high-tax countries faced with a flight of parent companies earning income from foreign sources. To counteract the revenue loss, low-tax jurisdictions would have an incentive to raise their corporate tax rates while high-tax countries would be tempted to reduce their rates, so a gradual convergence of corporate tax rates would be likely to emerge. Tax factors are, however, only one factor that influences the location of the parent company and in many cases tax-haven countries are unable to offer the facilities required by the headquarters of a multinational.

As this stylized scenario suggests, the scope for cross-country tax rate differentials offered by a pure credit system should not be overestimated. Much like a system of exemption, the credit system might not leave individual governments with very much freedom to choose a corporate tax rate widely different from the rates prevailing abroad. However, while tax competition under an exemption system will tend to harmonize corporate tax rates at the level of the lowest common denominator, it appears that the pressures for tax harmonisation would be more evenly felt by low-tax and high-tax countries under a pure credit system.

For international portfolio investment

The practical obstacles in achieving full capital export neutrality in international portfolio investment are of the same order of difficulty in achieving neutrality in international direct investment.

The requirements for capital export neutrality in corporate portfolio investment are essentially the same as the tax rules necessary for neutrality in corporate direct investment. Corporate portfolio investors would have to be subject to current taxation of their pro rata share of the profits of the foreign corporation in which they have invested, and they should be given full credit for foreign corporation and withholding taxes. Further, at the subsequent distribution of foreign-source income, the ultimate shareholders should receive full domestic dividend tax credit, without any offsetting domestic tax being levied at the corporate level.

As far as foreign portfolio investment by households is concerned, full capital export neutrality would in principle require an adjustment of each investor's personal income tax to eliminate the differential between the foreign and the domestic corporation tax. More precisely, it would be necessary to impute to each investor his or her pro rata share of foreign corporate profits, and to impose a surtax or to grant a refund equal to the difference between the domestic and the foreign corporation tax on these profits. Further, the foreign withholding tax on dividends would have to be fully credited against domestic personal income tax. Finally, in so far as relief of the economic double taxation of dividends is granted in the domestic sphere, a similar relief for the adjusted corporation tax would have to be granted when dividends are received from abroad.

To achieve full capital export neutrality vis à vis tax-exempt institutional investors which do not receive refunds for the corporate taxes underlying their tax-free dividends, special arrangements would also be necessary.

It goes without saying that the tax rules sketched above would be very difficult and costly to administer and therefore probably impossible to implement in practice. In particular, the integration of foreign corporation tax and domestic personal tax outlined here would surely be too cumbersome. It might, however, be possible for imputation countries to grant dividend tax credits to domestic shareholders for underlying corporate taxes paid abroad and such a measure could, depending on the circumstances of each country, move the international tax system somewhat closer to the ideal of CEN[20] but this raises a number of policy and administrative problems which are discussed in subsection 6) below.

4) Achieving capital import neutrality (CIN)

Although CEN is perhaps the most relevant neutrality concept in the context of foreign direct investment, CIN cannot be neglected for although most public finance experts tend to emphasise CEN, businessmen attach equal importance to CIN, in part because of the emphasis they place on non-discrimination at the corporate level. CIN requires, as noted in Chapter 2, that foreign and domestically owned corporations have the same combined effective corporate and personal tax rates on similar investment. This concept requires examining the corporate taxes, the withholding taxes and the relevant personal taxes in both the source and residence countries. CIN goes far beyond the principle of non-discrimination set out in Article 24 of the 1977 Model. Except in the limited circumstances of the taxation of branches of foreign enterprises or with respect to the deductibility of some payments, this Article does not generally prevent discrimination based on whether a taxpayer is resident or non-resident. For instance, Paragraph 6 of the Article, which forbids a contracting State to give less favourable treatment to an enterprise the capital of which is owned or controlled, wholly or partly, directly or indirectly, by one or more residents of the other contracting State, relates to the taxation only of subsidiaries resident in the source country and not of the persons owning or controlling their capital. Its object therefore is to ensure equal treatment for taxpayers residing in the same State, and it does not purport to subject foreign capital, in the hands of the shareholders, to identical treatment to that applied to domestic capital. It is therefore clear that CIN is broader than the non-discrimination treatment provided for in the Model.

To achieve CIN would require a very high degree of convergence in the tax treatment of profits as between countries, and in the taxation of cross-border investments. As with CEN, the source country acting alone could not generally achieve CIN, although it could achieve non-discrimination as described above. For the sake of simplicity, the next two paragraphs assume that both the source and residence country operate a classical system. The problems that can arise when either the source or residence country introduces some form of integration of corporate and personal income taxes are discussed later in this chapter.

For international direct investment

Provided all source countries apply the same tax treatment to foreign and domestically owned companies and do not impose withholding taxes on dividends, residence countries can achieve capital import neutrality at the corporate level by exempting from tax foreign source corporate income. Consequently, it is easier for residence countries to achieve capital import neutrality for international direct investment than it is for them to achieve capital export neutrality when the source country does not discriminate between domestic and foreign owned corporations and does not impose withholding taxes on dividends.

The imposition by source countries of withholding taxes on dividends does not breach the non-discrimination provisions of Article 24. Nevertheless, such taxes represent an additional layer of source country taxation. Consequently, the residence country would need to provide a full credit to companies for foreign withholding tax paid in order to achieve capital import neutrality at the corporate level for international direct investment.

For international portfolio investment

In the case of corporate portfolio investment, capital import neutrality at the corporate level requires that residence countries exempt from tax income derived from such investments abroad and provide a full credit for withholding taxes on dividends paid in the source country. This is the same condition required to achieve capital import neutrality in corporate direct investment.

In contrast to the relative ease with which it can be secured for corporate investment (direct or portfolio), the achievement of capital import neutrality for portfolio investment by households would, in practice, be very difficult for any country to implement. It would require that each investor's personal income tax liability for each item of foreign source capital income be adjusted to equal the personal income tax liability in respect of that income, if it was received by a resident of the source country in which the income was derived. The resident country would need to ensure that resident household investors paid tax at the same time as they would if they were residents of the source country. The resident country would also need to provide full foreign tax credits. Implementation of either of these policies would be no less difficult than in the case discussed above relating to capital export neutrality. In addition, the resident country would have to face the practical problem of determining the appropriate source country resident with which to align the investor's personal income tax liability, which would entail prohibitive compliance and administrative costs. These costs would escalate if either the source or residence country operated a corporate tax system that provided some form of relief of economic double taxation.

5) *Country practices*

This sub-section uses the conceptual framework outlined in Chapter 2, the descriptive information provided in Chapter 3 and the quantitative results provided in Chapter 5 to see how far the policy goals described above are achieved in practice. All of the assumptions and limitations on the methodology used to calculate results referred to in Chapter 5 should be kept in mind when examining the summary tables in this section. It should also be recalled that the effective tax rates shown in these tables do not take into account the different tax evasion and avoidance possibilities associated with domestic and international investment within a country and differences in tax compliance as between countries and also ignore many of the complexities of international tax arrangements.

The methods used by countries to provide relief from international double taxation are described in Chapter 3. Table 6.4 compares, for OECD countries, the difference between average required pre-tax rates of return where a company finances a new investment in a wholly owned foreign subsidiary through new equity and those where it invests domestically. Countries are grouped according to the method they use to tax foreign source dividends received by corporate shareholders (exemption, credit by source, worldwide credit and exemption/deduction mixed).

The difference between the average required pre-tax rate of return for investments in other OECD countries (residence) and that for domestic investments (domestic), when considered along with the average standard deviation provides an indication of the extent to which capital export neutrality is achieved in each Member country in respect of international direct investment. The difference between the domestic and residence required returns, which is shown in the third column of table 6.4, of course, depends on factors other than the methods used by OECD countries to tax foreign source dividends. For example, the tax treatment of capital income from domestic investments, the imposition of non-resident withholding taxes by source countries and the assumed rate of inflation will affect the required pre-tax rates of return. The average figures for each group of countries is also influenced by extreme values, found in certain countries (e.g. Greece and Portugal in Table 6.4), and in some cases assigning countries to one or other of the categories of countries identified in the Table is not easy. Ireland, Norway and Portugal have credit systems, but for non-treaty countries a deduction system is used. Where the deduction method is used, average required returns and (especially) standard deviations are substantially increased, and so it would be misleading to categorise them as a credit countries. Therefore, the results in Table 6.4 should be interpreted with care. Nevertheless, some interesting conclusions can be drawn from the data.

The figures in Table 6.4 show that those Member countries that exempt from corporate tax foreign source dividend income from treaty countries are far from achieving capital export neutrality. On average, companies resident in these countries directly investing in other OECD countries require a pre-tax rate of return 1.0 percentage points higher than if they were to invest domestically, and the variation is high (an average standard deviation of 1.7). For there to be no tax incentive for a company to invest in one country rather than another, both measures of distortion would have to be zero. These figures should be compared with the average required return and standard deviation in those countries with credit systems — 1.9 and 1.6 percentage points respectively. Table 6.4 therefore suggests that OECD countries with credit systems are on average closer to equal treatment of countries once a decision to invest abroad has been made, but at the cost of a greater average tax wedge on foreign investment than OECD countries with an exemption system for new investments wholly financed by equity and ignoring personal income taxes. This result is what would be expected, given the way the credit system works.

Table 6.4 Average required transnational pre-tax rates of return: subsidiary financed through new equity from parent[1]

Country	Average required rate of return			
	Domestic investment	Residence (investment from named country into all other countries)	Residence less domestic	Standard Deviation
Exemption:				
Australia	7.1	7.5	0.4	1.5
Austria	5.5	7.1	1.6	1.7
Belgium	5.4	7.4	2.0	1.6
Canada	6.2	6.6	0.4	1.5
Denmark	5.9	6.1	0.2	1.2
Finland	5.6	6.0	0.4	1.6
France	5.4	6.7	1.3	1.8
Germany	5.6	6.3	0.7	2.5
Luxembourg	6.3	7.2	0.9	2.0
Netherlands	5.6	6.7	1.1	1.6
Sweden	5.0	7.0	2.0	1.5
Average	5.8	6.8	1.0	1.7
Credit by source:				
Greece	5.0	9.7	4.7	3.2
Italy	5.9	8.9	3.0	1.9
New Zealand	6.8	7.9	1.1	1.4
Spain	6.2	7.4	1.2	1.5
Switzerland	5.4	7.0	1.6	1.5
Turkey	7.2	8.8	1.6	1.1
United Kingdom	5.9	6.8	0.9	1.5
Worldwide credit				
Iceland	6.7	8.2	1.5	1.6
Japan	6.4	8.1	1.7	1.0
United States	5.8	6.9	1.1	1.2
Average	6.1	8.0	1.9	1.6
Other:				
Ireland	5.1	9.8	4.7	5.6
Portugal	5.7	12.6	6.9	6.1
Norway	6.8	8.6	1.8	4.6
Average	5.9	10.3	4.4	5.4
OECD average	5.9	7.7	1.8	2.1

1. Weighted average of three sources of finance by parent. Weighted average of investment three assets. Inflation of 4.5% everywhere. No personal taxes.

The exemption method of relieving international double taxation is often criticised on the ground that it encourages residents of countries that operate this system to move capital to countries whose effective tax rates are lower than domestic rates[21]. However, among OECD countries it seems to discourage companies resident in countries that operate this system from directly investing in other OECD countries. (Compare columns 1 and 2 of Table 6.4.)

This result is partly explained by the fact that Member countries impose fairly similar rates of source country corporate tax as shown in Chapter 3. Consequently the non-resident dividend withholding taxes levied by Member countries in their role as source country will deter such investment where Member countries in their role as residence country operate exemption systems (or credit systems where these taxes generate excess credits that cannot be set off against residence country taxation of other foreign source income). For example, non-resident dividend withholding taxes will be less likely to deter investment abroad if excess credits can be used to set off either low-taxed income from the same source (in the case of a credit by source system) or low-taxed income from any foreign source (in the case of a worldwide credit system). No country operating either a credit by source system or a worldwide credit system allows excess credits to be refunded or set off against domestic source income.

Without data on the proportion of income coming from different countries, it is not possible to distinguish between the situation faced by those companies resident in countries where the foreign tax credit available to taxpayers is calculated on the basis of a per country limitation (credit by source) and by companies resident in Iceland, Japan and the United States where the maximum foreign tax credit available to taxpayers is calculated on the basis of an overall limitation (worldwide credit). For the purposes of table 6.4 it has been assumed that both systems are identical, as discussed in Chapter 5.

In principle the overall limitation method of allowing excess credits in high-tax countries to be set off against domestic taxes due on income from low-tax countries is likely to come closer to achieving capital export neutrality than the per country method. The per country method in particular discourages investment in high-tax countries and therefore a global welfare loss arises because too little capital is located in these countries, whereas if there are unused credits from low tax countries, a worldwide credit system enables these to be offset against high tax, so reducing the barriers to investments. These results depend, of course, on the assumption that resident taxpayers are not able to defer their domestic tax liabilities which, at least in the short-term, is probably not the case.

The tax disincentive for companies resident in OECD countries to invest directly in other Member countries would seem most likely to be caused by either source country dividend withholding taxes or residence country treatment of foreign source income.

Table 6.4 shows that where a subsidiary is financed through new equity from its parent, this tax disincentive remains significant no matter what method Member countries use to tax foreign source income. For example, although the difference between the required pre-tax rate of return for investments in other OECD countries less that for domestic investments in the exemption countries (1.0 percentage points) is smaller than that in the credit countries (1.9 percentage points) the difference is still large. The lower average required return for residence countries with exemption systems is unsurprising — the credit system only adds to the tax faced by companies, it never reduces the overall tax. Therefore, withholding taxes on dividends represent one important reason why CEN is not achieved.

Moreover, the calculations shown in Table 6.4 are likely to overstate the importance of the method Member countries use to tax dividend payments received from abroad because they do not take account of deferral. Nine Member countries — the United States, Japan, Germany, the United Kingdom, France, Canada, Australia, Sweden and New Zealand — have introduced measures designed to attribute to resident shareholders, without deferral, certain income earned by foreign corporations 'controlled' by their residents.

The controlled foreign corporation measures of most of these countries are designed basically to prevent tax avoidance and evasion involving the relocation of passive income rather than to secure capital export neutrality. With the exception of New Zealand, deferral is generally eliminated only in respect of various types of investment income derived from passive investments sourced in low-tax countries.

Therefore the taxation of business income retains a strong bias in favour of capital import neutrality and investment abroad in low-tax countries.

Overall, it seems that in relations between countries that impose similar effective rates of source country corporate tax or allow deferral, the effect of the credit system on the allocation of capital between these countries may be slightly superior to that of the exemption system. Of course, the generally higher compliance and administrative costs of credit systems means that there is some trade off between the superior allocative efficiency of the credit system and the practical advantages of the exemption system. The balance will favour the credit system where a source country has a much lower effective tax rate than the residence country.

In addition, the extent to which any method of providing relief from international double taxation is able to secure capital export neutrality will be determined by the degree to which the residence country's corporate and personal income taxes are integrated. Although the effects of integration were discussed above, it is worth noting at this stage that capital export neutrality is more likely to be secured if foreign tax credits are passed on by the residence country to the ultimate investor.

Table 6.5 compares, for each Member country, the difference between average required pre-tax rates of return where a company finances a new investment in a wholly-owned foreign subsidiary through debt (in the absence of thin capitalisation rules) and those where it invests domestically. OECD countries use either the credit by source method or the worldwide credit method to tax foreign source interest income from treaty countries received by corporate shareholders. As in table 6.4, the third and fourth columns of table 6.5 gives an indication of the extent to which capital export neutrality is achieved in each Member country.

The average required pre-tax rate of return calculations show that domestic investment is favoured over investment in other OECD countries no matter which one of the two methods Member countries use to tax foreign source interest income. On average, companies resident in OECD countries that use the "credit by source" method require a pre-tax rate of return for direct investments in other OECD countries 1.2 percentage points higher than for equivalent domestic investments. The corresponding average figure for companies resident in OECD countries that use the worldwide credit method is 0.5 percentage points.

A more interesting result shown by table 6.5 is that the average figure for companies resident in all OECD countries in respect of direct foreign investments financed through debt is 1.1 percentage points. This figure is significantly lower than the corresponding figure of 1.8 percentage points shown in table 6.4 where a subsidiary is financed through new equity from its parent. These figures suggest that capital export neutrality comes closer to being achieved where transnational investments between OECD countries are financed by debt rather than equity.

Part of the explanation for this result is that, on average, OECD source countries impose lower withholding taxes on interest payments from a wholly-owned subsidiary to its parent than they impose on dividend payments.

Another explanatory factor is that withholding taxes are the only form of source country taxation applied to interest income paid to non-residents in most OECD countries. Moreover, such payments are generally deductible in OECD source countries. Therefore, parent companies are more likely to receive a credit for interest withholding taxes paid in other OECD countries because all OECD countries use some form of the credit method to tax foreign source interest income and because these taxes are unlikely to exceed the credit limit. A further point is that the taxation of interest payments is not affected by the use of different systems of corporate taxation — in particular classical and imputation systems.

As a result, residence country taxation accounts for the greater part of the total tax burden on these capital income flows. A much greater proportion of the total tax burden on transnational dividend payments (including withholding taxes), however, is accounted for by source country taxation. Consequently it is not surprising that generally in OECD countries the difference between the overall level of taxation of income from direct investments in other OECD countries and that from domestic investments is lower where debt financing is used rather than equity financing.

Table 6.5 Average required transnational pre-tax rates of return: subsidiary financed through debt from parent[1]

| Country | Average required rate of return | | | |
	Domestic investment	Residence (investment from named country into all other countries)	Residence less domestic	Standard Deviation
Credit by source:				
Austria	5.5	6.5	1.0	1.0
Canada	6.2	8.1	1.9	1.3
Denmark	5.9	5.9	0.0	1.3
Finland	5.6	5.7	0.1	1.7
France	5.4	5.3	-0.1	1.2
Germany	5.6	9.6	4.0	1.9
Greece	5.0	7.3	2.3	2.1
Ireland	5.1	8.5	3.4	3.6
Italy	5.9	9.0	3.1	2.5
Luxembourg	6.3	6.5	0.2	1.1
Netherlands	5.6	6.0	0.4	1.2
New Zealand	6.8	6.0	-0.8	0.9
Norway	6.8	9.6	2.8	4.8
Portugal	5.7	9.2	3.5	3.3
Spain	6.2	6.1	-0.1	1.3
Sweden	5.0	5.5	0.5	0.9
Switzerland	5.4	5.5	0.1	0.9
Turkey	7.2	8.3	1.1	1.1
United Kingdom	5.9	5.5	-0.4	1.3
Average	5.8	7.1	1.2	1.8
Worldwide credit:				
Australia	7.1	6.6	-0.5	1.0
Belgium	5.4	5.7	0.3	1.2
Iceland	6.7	7.4	0.7	1.1
Japan	6.4	8.1	1.7	1.1
United States	5.8	6.3	0.5	1.0
Average	6.3	6.8	0.5	1.1
OECD average	5.9	7.0	1.1	1.6

1. Weighted average of three sources of finance by parent. Weighted average of three assets. Inflation of 4.5% everywhere. No personal taxes.

Table 6.6 compares, for each Member country, the difference between average required pre-tax rates of return where a company finances a new investment in a wholly owned foreign subsidiary through retentions and those where it invests domestically. The third column of Table 6.6 shows that, on average, companies resident in OECD countries require a pre-tax rate of return for direct investments in other OECD countries financed through retentions roughly equal to that for equivalent domestic investments. Thus comparison with tables 6.4 and 6.5 suggests that withholding taxes tend in practice to discriminate against new as opposed to mature firms.

The tax burden on capital income flows from transnational direct investments financed through retentions, like that on those financed through new equity, is largely composed of source country taxation. This result is dependent, in part, on both the assumption embodied in the calculations that the marginal personal tax rate in each country is zero and the fact that capital gains tax at this level largely accounts for residence country taxation of income from investments financed through retentions.

Whereas countries can influence the degree of capital export neutrality through their choice of credit or exemption methods of taxing foreign source income, they have some control over capital import neutrality through their use of withholding taxes. Regardless of the tax treatment of foreign source income in the residence country, if the source country has very high withholding tax rates the result is likely to be that the effective tax rate on inward investment into that country will be higher than investment by domestic companies in the same country. In addition, application of different withholding tax rates according to whether or not a treaty is in operation, for example, may well lead to variation in effective tax rates on inward investment. High and variable withholding tax rates will be likely to move a country away from CIN.

Table 6.7 gives the average required return and the variation in required returns on investment in each of the OECD countries. Even in the absence of withholding taxes, there is a substantial difference between the average required pre-tax rate of return on domestic investment (5.9 per cent) and on transnational investment (6.9 per cent). In addition, the average standard deviation in required returns is 0.9, indicating a significant variation in these required returns according to the residence of the parent company. Thus CIN is not achieved even if the effects of withholding taxes are ignored. The reason for this (at first sight, perhaps rather surprising) conclusion is that differences in the costs of raising finance in the residence country and the effects of credit and deduction systems used by the residence country have a marked impact on required returns.

However, inclusion of withholding taxes results in a large increase in the average required return on transnational investment. Indeed, it is possible to say that between a third and a half of the extra burden on companies investing transnationally as opposed to domestically is due to withholding taxes. Switching from a common withholding tax rate (of zero per cent) to actual withholding tax rates increases the dispersion in required returns.

If personal taxes are also considered relevant, then table 6.8 shows that the conclusions drawn from table 6.7 are still broadly applicable. The tax wedge on transnational investment is larger than on domestic investment even if withholding taxes are ignored, and the variation in tax wedges is substantial (the average standard deviation is 1.4), so abolition of withholding taxes would not result in all companies investing in a particular country facing the same effective tax rate — there would be no CIN in the OECD. However, withholding taxes add to the average transnational tax wedge, and the average variation in tax wedges remains high.

Table 6.6 Average required transnational pre-tax rates of return: subsidiary financed through retentions[1]

Country	Average required rate of return			
	Domestic investment	Residence (investment from named country into all other countries)	Residence less domestic	Standard Deviation
Australia	9.0	7.9	-1.1	1.1
Austria	7.3	7.9	0.6	1.1
Belgium	7.1	8.0	0.9	1.1
Canada	8.1	7.9	-0.2	1.1
Denmark	7.5	7.4	-0.1	0.9
Finland	8.0	7.9	-0.1	1.1
France	7.3	7.9	0.6	1.1
Germany	9.5	7.8	-1.7	1.1
Greece	7.3	7.9	0.6	1.1
Iceland	8.0	7.9	-0.1	1.1
Ireland	5.5	8.0	2.5	1.0
Italy	9.1	7.9	-1.2	1.1
Japan	9.0	7.9	-1.1	1.1
Luxembourg	8.1	7.9	-0.2	1.1
Netherlands	7.1	7.9	0.8	1.1
New Zealand	8.3	7.9	-0.4	1.1
Norway	10.0	7.8	-2.2	1.0
Portugal	7.5	7.9	0.4	1.1
Spain	7.8	7.9	0.1	1.1
Sweden	6.1	8.0	1.9	1.1
Switzerland	6.6	8.0	1.4	1.1
Turkey	9.8	7.8	-2.0	1.1
United Kingdom	7.7	7.9	0.2	1.1
United States	7.6	7.9	0.3	1.1
Average	7.9	7.9	0.0	1.1

1. Unweighted average of each column. Weighted average of three assets. Inflation of 4.5 per cent everywhere. No personal taxes.

Table 6.7 **Average required returns: the importance of withholding taxes in determining the size and variation of required returns for each source country[1]**

Country	Domestic Investment	Source (investment from other countries into named country)		Standard deviations of required returns	
		No withholding taxes	Withholding taxes	No withholding taxes	Withholding taxes
Australia	7.1	8.1	8.2	0.9	1.0
Austria	5.5	6.3	7.1	0.6	1.0
Belgium	5.4	6.1	6.8	0.5	0.5
Canada	6.2	7.5	8.4	1.0	1.5
Denmark	5.9	6.7	7.2	0.6	0.9
Finland	5.6	6.9	7.3	0.5	0.5
France	5.4	7.3	7.9	0.5	1.0
Germany	5.6	5.6	6.4	0.4	0.5
Greece	5.0	5.5	7.5	1.4	3.6
Iceland	6.7	8.0	9.2	1.3	1.8
Ireland	5.1	6.7	6.8	1.5	1.5
Italy	5.9	6.3	7.2	0.6	0.9
Japan	6.4	7.1	8.1	0.8	1.4
Luxembourg	6.3	7.3	7.5	0.9	0.8
Netherlands	5.6	6.7	7.1	1.0	1.3
New Zealand	6.8	8.3	9.7	1.0	1.6
Norway	6.8	6.3	6.6	0.8	0.7
Portugal	5.7	6.5	7.9	1.2	1.8
Spain	6.2	7.1	8.1	1.3	1.9
Sweden	5.0	6.1	6.4	1.0	1.3
Switzerland	5.4	6.6	7.0	1.1	1.1
Turkey	7.2	8.2	8.2	1.3	1.4
United Kingdom	5.9	7.0	7.0	0.7	0.9
United States	5.8	6.7	7.5	0.6	1.5
Average	5.9	6.9	7.5	0.9	1.3

1.   Subsidiary financed by average of different types of finance

6) Some specific issues

Tax incentives

Source country provisions

Tax incentives produce a global efficiency loss to the extent that firms divert capital to locations where lower taxes outweigh higher production costs. Even if location decisions are unaffected, such incentives may adversely affect global efficiency because they may require the source country to increase its reliance on other distortionary taxes. Also, the quality of the investment induced by incentives may be questionable. There may, however, be favourable long-run effects where incentives generate positive externalities in countries using incentive provisions and, in fact, this is generally the argument put forward in favour of residence countries recognising the tax incentives given in the source country.

All governments that exercise source country taxing rights have an interest in attracting foreign capital in order to increase tax revenue. However, the willingness of these governments to offer tax incentives in order to attract foreign investment depends on their assessment of the overall effect on national welfare of certain investment projects. Therefore, the provision of tax incentives is influenced by the extent to which governments believe that there are particular benefits associated with the promotion of industrial development in sectors such as manufacturing and headquarter companies of their economies and that these benefits outweigh the costs in terms of revenue forgone.

Developing countries and some developed countries provide tax incentives to attract foreign investment. This is often done by way of a tax exemption for a specified number of years (a tax holiday) or by additional deductions, e.g. by accelerated depreciation.

Source countries are more likely to provide tax incentives to attract foreign direct investment if the productivity of industry-specific capital likely to be located within their jurisdiction would be relatively unaffected if it were located in another country. For example, a multinational firm planning to establish a textile manufacturing plant is able to choose from a wide variety of locations where manufacturing costs are similar. In this situation, source countries might compete for the project by offering tax incentives.

Source countries may be less inclined to offer tax incentives to attract foreign investment if the productivity of industry-specific, mobile capital is largely determined by its location. Foreign investment in mining or other resource-based projects, for example, is highly locational-specific. Indeed, source countries commonly impose additional taxes on income derived from these types of foreign investments in order to appropriate economic rents.

Source countries' policymakers may be prepared to give up all tax on foreign capital income and even provide subsidies to foreign investment if they believe that certain capital inflows will yield benefits in excess of the tax revenue forgone. Indeed, this type of policy will be justified if these projects are judged to be associated with positive externalities (whereby the social rate of return of a project exceeds the private rate of return), such as the provision of training and the building of infrastructure. Countries may also feel that a large inflow of foreign capital will promote in the long-run an expansion in the taxable capacity of the economy.

A recent tendency is for countries to reduce tax incentives for foreign direct investment, especially in the manufacturing sector. Some countries may think that the productivity of the foreign capital located within their jurisdictions is highly dependent on its location and multinational firms would have invested with or without tax incentives. Therefore the tax incentives provided by these countries would simply represent a windfall gain for either multinational enterprises investing in their jurisdictions or for foreign treasuries. Other countries may believe that the most substantial benefit to be gained by source countries from some types of foreign investment is tax revenue and that the supply response to incentives is insufficient to maintain that revenue. Another argument against the use of incentives is that the "quality" of the investment attracted may be low and that a widespread use of incentives by governments may make them gradually ineffective.

190

Table 6.8 Average tax wedge: the importance of withholding taxes in determining the size and variation of tax wedges for top-rate personal taxpayers for each source country[1]

Country	Domestic Investment	Source (investment from other countries into named country)		Standard deviations of tax wedges	
		No withholding taxes	Withholding taxes	No withholding taxes	Withholding taxes
Australia	1.5	3.7	3.7	1.6	1.6
Austria	1.4	2.2	2.6	1.3	1.5
Belgium	0.9	2.2	2.6	1.2	1.4
Canada	3.5	3.2	3.7	1.5	1.7
Denmark	2.4	2.6	2.9	1.3	1.6
Finland	4.4	2.6	2.8	1.2	1.2
France	2.3	2.9	3.2	1.4	1.5
Germany	0.9	1.6	2.2	1.3	1.5
Greece	0.8	1.7	2.8	1.5	2.1
Iceland	3.8	2.9	3.5	1.6	1.8
Ireland	1.9	2.7	2.7	1.9	1.9
Italy	2.6	2.2	2.7	1.4	1.7
Japan	2.8	2.6	3.3	1.4	1.9
Luxembourg	2.5	3.0	3.1	1.4	1.4
Netherlands	2.1	2.5	2.7	1.4	1.5
New Zealand	2.0	3.8	4.6	1.6	2.1
Norway	2.5	2.6	2.7	1.4	1.4
Portugal	1.3	2.2	3.0	1.5	1.7
Spain	2.0	2.9	3.4	1.4	1.5
Sweden	2.0	2.0	2.2	1.3	1.4
Switzerland	1.7	2.4	2.6	1.5	1.8
Turkey	5.3	3.4	3.5	1.3	1.3
United Kingdom	2.0	2.9	2.9	1.5	1.5
United States	3.0	2.4	2.9	1.4	1.8
Average	2.3	2.6	3.0	1.4	1.6

1.   (Subsidiary financed by average of different types of finance)

Residence country provisions

The tax systems of countries that exempt the foreign source income of companies resident in their jurisdictions automatically preserve the benefit to these companies' non-resident investors of tax incentives provided by source countries. Residence countries that use the credit method to tax this income must decide whether or not to pass on the benefits of the incentives to their taxpayers. This can be done by means of tax-sparing arrangements although this will result in a loss of tax revenue in the residence country and in reduction in global welfare insofar as foreign direct investment is directed towards projects where higher costs may be incurred but are outweighed by lower taxes. It is possible, however, that this policy could maximize global efficiency if there were significant positive externalities associated with certain investment projects.

It has been argued that a failure to provide tax sparing relief creates an obstacle to international capital flows and inhibits welfare-enhancing foreign investment. In the absence of tax-sparing, however, the incentives are still effective, to the extent that either a deferral advantage is gained or residence countries exempt foreign source income from tax.

Most developed countries that operate credit systems have tax sparing arrangements with developing countries in an effort to promote development in these countries. However, developed countries generally restrict tax sparing relief to projects in industries that satisfy certain conditions. These conditions cover such matters as economic development promotion, close links with the local economy and not providing opportunities for tax avoidance and evasion. Also most countries place a time limit on these arrangements.

Withholding taxes

Before discussing the effect of withholding taxes on the allocation of capital, it is appropriate to point out that from the point of view of the investor most withholding taxes are seen as only a collection technique and represent an advance payment of tax which can be credited against the taxpayer's final tax liability (except where dividend income is exempt in the country of residence). Insofar as they are a prepayment they do not (ignoring the impact on cash flow) affect the substantive tax liability of the taxpayer. Withholding taxes on cross-border payments will, however, influence the division of the tax base between the source and residence countries. Withholding taxes also have an important anti-avoidance role where funds could be routed through a tax haven or where the taxpayer does not declare his foreign source income to the tax authorities of his country of residence. In these circumstances the withholding tax becomes the final payment and ensures that at least some tax is paid. In these circumstances, withholding taxes may assist rather than hinder the attainment of CIN[22].

Withholding taxes imposed by source countries on the transfer of dividends earned on shares in foreign corporations will not normally distort international portfolio investment by households, because these taxes can usually be fully credited against the domestic personal income tax.

However, withholding taxes may discourage international portfolio investment by tax-exempt institutions and international direct investment by corporations. For tax-exempt institutions the problem is that they have no domestic tax liability against which the foreign withholding tax can be credited. For foreign direct investors a withholding tax implies an extra tax burden in so far as the tax cannot be fully credited due to limitations on the foreign tax credit, or in so far as international double taxation is relieved by means of the exemption method.

If the new view of dividend taxation is correct (see Chapter 2), the investment distortions stemming from withholding taxes on border-crossing dividends may not be very large. Once equity capital has been injected into a foreign corporation, the withholding tax cannot be escaped whether distributions from the foreign company are made now or later. The new view would therefore imply that the tax does <u>not</u> affect the incentive to finance foreign investment by retention of earnings abroad. In this respect withholding taxes in the international sphere work exactly like a personal income tax on dividends in the domestic sphere, although they also have additional anti-avoidance functions.

However, since parent companies expose themselves to a subsequent withholding tax when they inject new equity into a foreign subsidiary, supporters of the new view do not deny that the tax will in fact raise the tax cost of foreign investment when this investment is financed by new share issues from the subsidiary to the parent. Because they discourage finance by new equity, withholding taxes will thus tend to reduce the initial injection of equity by the parent corporation when new foreign subsidiaries are established. This reduced initial capital means that the new subsidiaries will have to go through a longer period of accumulation of retained earnings before they reach the stage of maturity in which they are able to transfer dividends to the parent and in which the "new view" of the effects of dividend taxation becomes relevant[23].

Moreover, if the old view that shareholders have a preference for dividends over retained earnings is correct, the distortions caused by withholding taxes will be even more serious than the above modification of the new view suggests. According to the old view dividend taxes discourage distributions and will thereby tend to raise the pre-tax rates of return required by parent company shareholders.

At any rate, it should be noted that investment distortions stemming from withholding taxes are in practice reduced to the extent that these taxes can be circumvented by channeling dividends through conduit companies located in countries which have negotiated a reduction or elimination of withholding taxes with their tax treaty partners. Still, it must be recognised that the establishment of such a conduit company involves a certain waste of resources from society's point of view and represents an improper use of tax treaties, which in a number of cases the tax authorities concerned have tried to prevent by approperate provisions in bilateral tax treaties.

It is also worth pointing out that a high withholding tax rate will not discourage inward foreign investment if it only serves to make up for a relatively low corporate income tax rate. Indeed, if one accepts the criterion of effective reciprocity explained in Chapter 2 under inter-nation equity, countries with relatively low corporate tax rates should be allowed to levy relatively high withholding tax rates, and vice versa, although this view is not generally accepted by tax authorities.

Moreover, source countries sometimes argue that the imposition of withholding taxes in addition to corporate taxes can be justified on the grounds of certain inter-nation equity criteria that encourage these countries to impose heavier tax burdens on non-resident investors than resident investors. Income derived from foreign investment projects in cases where the income includes a significant component of economic rent may justify the source countries imposing a high effective rate of tax on capital income. The mining of scarce mineral resources is an example of such a project. However, it could be argued that it would be better for a source country to impose a resource rent tax that appropriated all economic rents generated by such projects rather than impose a high withholding tax, at least insofar as they are creditable under treaty provisions.

Indeed, a strategy followed in certain circumstances by developing countries is to combine low corporate taxes with high withholding taxes. This strategy encourages subsidiaries to reinvest their profits in source countries. Consequently, source countries can take advantage of the residence country's foreign tax credit, which generally allows them to impose total taxes up to the level of the residence country's rate without discouraging foreign investment. In addition, foreign investors can benefit from deferral. Although this type of strategy may be in the interests of the country employing it, it would most likely reduce global welfare by disturbing investment patterns.

In addition, it should be recorded that withholding taxes may sometimes serve to prevent complete international tax evasion in cases where residence countries are not able to monitor dividend income from foreign sources. This monitoring problem may be particularly relevant in the case of international portfolio investment in source countries with strict bank secrecy laws. Whilst, apart from their reliance on withholding taxes, national tax authorities can counter international tax evasion through exchange of information, there are limits in practice to the efficacy of exchanges of information.

Table 6.9 **The effects of withholding taxes on the required pre-tax rates of return**[1]

Country		With Withholding Taxes				Without Withholding Taxes			
		Average Rate of Return		Standard Deviation		Average Rate of Return		Standard Deviation	
	Domestic	Residence	Source	Residence	Source	Residence	Source	Residence	Source
Australia	7.1	7.3	8.2	0.8	1.0	6.5	8.1	0.7	0.9
Austria	5.5	7.2	7.1	1.0	1.0	6.5	6.3	0.8	0.6
Belgium	5.4	7.0	6.8	0.9	0.5	6.2	6.1	0.8	0.5
Canada	6.2	7.5	8.4	0.9	1.5	6.9	7.5	1.0	1.0
Denmark	5.9	6.5	7.2	0.7	0.9	6.1	6.7	0.7	0.6
Finland	5.6	6.6	7.3	0.9	0.5	6.0	6.9	1.0	0.5
France	5.4	6.6	7.9	1.0	1.0	6.1	7.3	0.8	0.5
Germany	5.6	7.9	6.4	1.4	0.5	6.7	5.6	1.0	0.4
Greece	5.0	8.3	7.5	1.6	3.6	6.7	5.5	0.9	1.4
Iceland	6.7	7.8	9.2	0.9	1.8	7.3	8.0	0.6	1.3
Ireland	5.1	8.8	6.8	3.1	1.5	7.8	6.7	1.8	1.5
Italy	5.9	8.6	7.2	1.2	0.9	8.3	6.3	1.2	0.6
Japan	6.4	8.0	8.1	0.6	1.4	7.9	7.1	0.6	0.8
Luxembourg	6.3	7.2	7.5	1.0	0.8	6.5	7.3	0.8	0.9
Netherlands	5.6	6.9	7.1	1.0	1.3	6.4	6.7	0.8	1.0
New Zealand	6.8	7.3	9.7	0.6	1.6	6.5	8.3	0.6	1.0
Norway	6.8	8.7	6.6	3.1	0.7	7.8	6.3	1.4	0.8
Portugal	5.7	9.9	7.9	3.1	1.8	8.3	6.5	2.0	1.2
Spain	6.2	7.1	8.1	0.9	1.9	6.6	7.1	0.7	1.3
Sweden	5.0	6.8	6.4	0.7	1.3	6.4	6.1	0.8	1.0
Switzerland	5.4	6.8	7.0	0.8	1.1	6.4	6.6	0.8	1.1
Turkey	7.2	8.3	8.2	0.7	1.4	7.8	8.2	0.6	1.3
United Kingdom	5.9	6.7	7.0	0.9	0.9	6.3	7.0	0.7	0.9
United States	5.8	7.1	7.5	0.7	1.5	6.8	6.7	0.6	0.8
Average	5.9	7.5	7.5	1.2	1.3	6.9	6.9	0.9	0.9

1.   No personal taxes, inflation of 4.5 per cent, weighted average of all different types of financing and assets

Table 6.9 provides some illustration of the impact of withholding taxes on the required rate of return assuming no personal taxes, a common inflation rate and a weighted average of all different types of financing and assets. These simplified calculations show that abolition of withholding taxes, with a few exceptions, lead to a lower required pre-tax rate of return, in some countries with quite a substantial difference. It also shows that — on average — withholding taxes account for approximately half of the actual difference in the required rate of return between domestic and cross-border investment measured on a residence as well as on a source basis. Withholding taxes are also found to increase the average variation in required returns when investing from each country into the other — the average standard deviation of required returns for residence countries rises from 0.9 to 1.3 per cent. It should be recalled, however, that these results are based on simple averages and that extreme cases may unduly bias the results.

In summary, the discussion above suggests that a group of closely integrated countries with fairly similar corporate tax rates could probably reap some efficiency gain from an abolition of withholding taxes on cross-border dividends, although the magnitude of the gain is rather uncertain. The conceptual framework set out in Chapter 2 suggests that insofar as countries accept the concept of effective reciprocity then countries with low corporate tax rates may wish to impose relatively high withholding taxes. As mentioned in Chapter 2, this would imply a change in current practice in the OECD area where bilateral tax treaties often require reciprocity of withholding tax rates, without regard to differences in corporate tax rates between the two countries concerned. It would also imply a certain amount of arbitrariness in that effective rates differ as between sectors and types of activities.

The interaction of corporate and personal income taxes in the international sphere

Minimisation of departures from capital import and export neutrality, achieving taxpayer equity, international equity and simplicity, are easier to accomplish if both the source and residence countries apply similar rates of corporate tax to comparable real tax bases. In particular, minimisation of departures from these standards is most easily achieved if both the source and residence countries operate a classical system of corporate income taxation. It can be very difficult to accomplish if either the source or residence country introduces some form of integration of corporate and personal income taxes. Thus, outside of the domestic sphere, classical systems may enable countries to move nearer to achieving neutrality, equity and simplicity objectives.

One of the more important effects of the integration of corporate and personal income taxes that has occurred in several Member countries has been a reduction in the tax bias against domestic equity relative to debt that can exist under a classical system. A reduction in the relative taxation of distributed company profits in a particular country will reduce that country's domestic tax wedge for locally financed equity investment. If this reduction does not apply either to domestic source capital income received by non-residents (in the case of source countries) nor to foreign source capital income received by residents (in the case of residence countries), integration may create a tax bias against foreign investment and investment abroad. This bias may discourage international capital flows and consequently reduce global welfare.

In general, section B of this chapter shows that Member countries that have introduced some form of integration have done so primarily for domestic reasons. However, over recent years, as international capital flows have grown, the decision about what form integration should take has increasingly had to take account of international implications.

Integration of source country corporate and personal income taxes

Countries that introduce some form of integration of corporate and personal income taxes come under pressure to extend relief to non-residents. Non-resident investors argue that if this is not done then they will be discriminated against vis-a-vis resident shareholders. This debate centers upon whether source or residence principles should predominate and on how the revenue from international activities should be shared between source and residence countries.

Countries that have reduced the relative taxation of distributed company profits by providing relief at the corporate level, such as occurs under a split rate system, have consequently found it difficult, particularly during tax treaty negotiations, to impose a compensatory high-rate withholding tax on profits distributed to non-residents. These countries, depending on both the degree to which they provide relief and the rate of withholding tax they levy, may therefore receive little or no tax revenue in respect of income derived within their jurisdictions that is distributed to non-residents. Such a division of tax revenue generally conflicts with the principle of inter-nation equity, no matter by what criteria the principle is determined.

A significant attraction of forms of integration, such as imputation systems, that provide relief at the shareholder level rather than at the corporate level, is that these forms preserve source country taxing rights. The provision of relief at the shareholder level ensures that the source country can subject all the profits of foreign subsidiaries, both retained and distributed, to domestic corporate taxation.

Nevertheless, it is still argued by some that countries which operate imputation systems should provide imputation credits to non-resident shareholders. This may conflict with the inter-nation equity and could mean that source countries would determine the relative taxation of retained and distributed profits received by non-resident companies if the country of residence operated an exemption system for taxing foreign source corporate income.

In general, the question of whether the granting of imputation credits (or other equivalent benefits) to non-residents by source countries is effective in neutrality terms depends on how residence countries treat those benefits. For example, where residence countries that exempt from tax foreign source corporate income reduce the relative taxation of distributed company profits from domestic investments but not foreign ones, the provision of equivalent relief by source countries will help secure capital export neutrality.

In the case where residence countries do not reduce the relative taxation of distributed company profits (as occurs under a classical system of corporate taxation) and source countries provide relief, the achievement of capital export neutrality will depend on residence countries' treatment of foreign source income. For example, the total corporate tax paid on distributed profits received by companies resident in countries that provide a credit for foreign taxes paid and operate a classical system of corporate taxation will be unaffected by the provision of imputation credits by source countries.

This would occur because a country operating a classical system would not grant imputation credits to its residents in respect of dividends received from foreign corporations. To do so would reduce the total corporate tax burden on distributed company profits that are foreign sourced below that on those that are domestically sourced and would consequently violate capital export neutrality. Therefore, the imputation credits granted by a source country would simply represent a transfer of tax revenue to the treasury of the country of residence and would not be passed on to the non-resident investors[24].

It is possible, however, that the total tax liability of companies resident in countries that both provide a credit for foreign taxes paid and reduce the relative taxation of distributed company profits could be affected by the provision of imputation credits by source countries. The likelihood of this occurring would depend on the extent to which the imputation credits provided by a source country were passed on to investors by the country of residence.

For the same reason that a residence country operating a classical system would not wish to grant any source-country imputation credits to its residents, a residence country only partly reducing the relative taxation of distributed company profits from domestic investments would also not wish to grant such credits to its residents. Otherwise the tax burden on distributed company profits that are foreign sourced would be reduced below that on those that are domestically sourced. Again, the imputation credits not fully passed on to investors by the country of residence would simply represent a transfer of tax revenue to its treasury at the expense of the source country's treasury.

Although it might conflict with inter-nation equity, granting investors of source-country imputation credits by the residence country may help to secure capital export neutrality in the latter, if the relative taxation of distributed company profits that are foreign sourced were reduced to the same level as that of those that are sourced domestically.

Integration of residence country corporate and personal income taxes

Countries that introduce some form of integration of corporate and personal income taxes also have to face the issue of whether to reduce the relative taxation of distributed company profits derived from investments abroad to approximately the same degree as it is reduced for such profits derived from domestic investments. To the extent that this is not done, capital export neutrality and horizontal taxpayer equity at an international level will be more difficult to achieve and investment abroad vis-a-vis domestic investment will be discouraged. Source countries will be the main losers if this is not done because they will not only lose tax revenue, but will also share in the global welfare loss that results if, in consequence, capital is allocated inefficiently.

The method by which residence countries might attempt to secure a more neutral tax treatment with respect to the export of capital and help ensure horizontal taxpayer equity depends on how they tax corporate income. Residence countries operating imputation systems would need to grant imputation credits to resident shareholders for foreign taxes paid to the same extent as they would for domestic taxes paid. That would ensure that the relative taxation of retained and distributed company profits derived from domestic investments was the same as it was for such profits derived from investments abroad. Residence countries operating split-rate systems would need to ensure that distributed foreign source income was subject to approximately the same reduced effective rate of corporate tax as distributed domestic source income in order to achieve the same result.

In practice, countries generally do not provide imputation credits for taxes paid in another country because to do so would involve a significant cost to revenue and could also lead to greater rather than less distortions. While it is true that the introduction of any form of integration (in the absence of an increase in the rate on retained profits) involves a loss of tax revenue, the provision of imputation credits for foreign taxes paid would involve a residence country's forgoing revenue where an equivalent amount had not been collected by it at the corporate level.

It is sometimes argued that residence countries would be prepared to provide imputation credits for taxes paid in source countries if the latter countries agreed to share the revenue cost of doing so. For example, residence countries would be more likely to provide relief to resident taxpayers investing abroad if source countries operating imputation systems provided imputation credits to non-residents because the latter countries would largely bear the revenue cost. Similarly, residence countries would bear little of the cost of reducing the relative taxation of foreign source distributed company profits if source countries operating split-rate systems did not impose a compensatory withholding tax.

Two countries that operate imputation systems and impose similar effective rates of source country corporate taxation would be most likely to swap imputation credits if capital income flows between them were approximately equal. However, a country considering entering into such an agreement with another country would probably wish to be able to review the arrangement if capital income flows between the two countries became unbalanced. In addition, such a country would need to consider its position vis-a-vis all other countries with which it had direct investment relationships. Otherwise, such an agreement with one country could set a precedent for negotiations with other countries, with which such an agreement might be to its disadvantage. At the present time, no OECD countries have such arrangements.

7) Tax treaty practices in countries with an imputation system

Although it is beyond the scope of this report to go into the details of bilateral treaties, the present section provides a brief commentary on the way tax treaties have tried to resolve such problems. This is a complex issue since an extension of a full imputation credit to non-residents implicitly assumes that all repatriated dividends are further distributed, whereas some profits may be retained. In these circumstances, extending the credit to non-residents may create a bias against domestic investors. The only treaties to deal with this problem are certain treaties signed by the United Kingdom which grant to direct investors a credit equal to one-half of the tax credit available to an individual resident (less an abatement agreed with the treaty partner) and to individual and corporate portfolio investors the full credit (again less an abatement).

So far only three countries with an imputation system have agreed to extend the imputation credit to non resident investors on a unilateral basis (France, Ireland and the United Kingdom):

— France extends the imputation credit to non resident individuals and portfolio investors in about two thirds of its treaties with OECD countries. The definition of portfolio investment ranges between less than 5 per cent to 25 per cent ownership. In the new treaty with Italy half the imputation credit is granted to direct non-resident investors. When the imputation credit is not extended to direct non-resident investors they are entitled to the refund of the equalisation tax if they are resident of a tax treaty partner. There is also a possibility to be exempt from equalisation tax for French international holding companies (i.e. with foreign shares representing over two-thirds of their assets) provided certain conditions are met. The holding company is entitled to transfer to its shareholders the tax credits attached to the dividends but no imputation tax credit is granted;

— Ireland extends its domestic imputation credit to non-resident individual and corporate portfolio investors in six treaties with OECD countries. The definition of a corporate portfolio investor ranges between less than 10 per cent to 25 per cent ownership.

— The United Kingdom extends part of the imputation credit to individual portfolio investors in 18 treaties, to corporate portfolio investors in 16 treaties with OECD countries and to direct corporate investors as referred to above in eleven treaties with OECD countries.

Concerning other countries with an imputation system a new trend has emerged in the Italian international tax policy. Although Italy abandoned in 1977 the classical system for an imputation system for corporate profits, it is only recently that tax treaty negotiations have shown a concern with the tax treatment of cross-border dividends. The treaties with France and the United Kingdom now grant an extension of the imputation credit (see below). There is also a provision in the new treaties with France, Germany, the Netherlands, but not the United Kingdom, for the refund of the equalisation tax if the imputation credit is not granted. Only the treaty with the United Kingdom is in force. Under the treaties Italy has just signed with France and the United Kingdom, a shareholder of an Italian company resident of France or the United Kingdom is entitled to the imputation tax credit in full if he is an individual or a corporate portfolio shareholder. A corporate shareholder owning 10 per cent or more of the capital of the Italian company gets half the amount of the credit. The treaty with France also provides for the refund of the equalisation tax if no imputation credit is allowed. The treaty with France gives a choice to the direct shareholder between the half credit and the refund of the equalisation tax. The new Italy/Dutch and Italy/German treaties do not provide for an extension of the imputation tax credit but for a refund of the equalisation tax. It is available to both individual and corporate Dutch shareholders irrespective of their participation in the Italian company. Under the Italy/German treaty it is only available to corporate shareholders resident of Germany and owning at least 25 per cent of the capital of the Italian distributing company.

Finland, which introduced an imputation system in 1990, has indicated that it is prepared to negotiate on a reciprocal basis extending its imputation credit to non residents. In its treaties with France and the United Kingdom, there are unilateral provisions which extend the imputation credit to Finnish residents as regards individual and corporate portfolio investors and even direct investors in the treaty with the United Kingdom, but the credit is reduced by half.

Australia, which introduced its imputation system in 1987, has indicated that its policy is to not extend imputation credits to non-residents. However, Australia does not impose withholding taxes on fully "franked" dividends paid to non-residents. Also, as Australia uses an account-based system instead of an equalization tax, the issue of the refund of the equalization tax to non-residents does not arise.

It could be argued that Australia's practice of reducing withholding taxes applicable to qualifying dividends paid to non-residents provides an alternative method of extending the benefits of imputation to non-residents. However, since the amount of withholding taxes on a given dividend will usually be substantially lower than the amount of imputation credit to which a resident shareholder would be entitled with respect to the same dividend, this alternative method can only provide partial relief. Also, this method is likely to be ineffective for non-resident individual shareholders who are typically subject to the credit system of international double tax alleviation and who do not get relief for the corporation's underlying tax, as the benefit of reduced withholding taxes is then taxed back in their country of residence. This last difficulty could be overcome if the residence country were to agree to treat the reduction of the withholding tax in the same way as an imputation credit (i.e. as an extra dividend), a solution for which there is a precedent in double taxation conventions.

New Zealand, which introduced an imputation system in 1988, is currently reviewing its tax treaty policies.

Appendix

Government statements on why they have changed their practices with respect to economic double taxation

Introduction

At various times over the last twenty years a number of government statements have been made on why company tax systems had been changed or were under considerations for change. The first sub-section is confined to input provided to the 1973 OECD report on *Company Tax Systems in OECD Member Countries*, from which quotations are made, and the second sub-section reproduces government statements over the last few years on recent reforms undertaken or under consideration, including a statement from Canada on reasons for changes in the early seventies.

Views expressed in the early 1970s

United Kingdom

The 1965 change to the separate system with no set-off for the individual shareholder, was designed to encourage re-investment of profits at the expense of distribution of dividends so as to accelerate the growth of investment by the corporate sector. The government's decision to reverse this policy as from 1973 was taken "so as to remove the present discrimination against distributed profits" and followed from the view that systematic favouring of re-investment of profits by firms which earn them does not necessarily correspond to using capital in the most efficient manner, in particular because the qualitative aspects of investment are lost sight of.

Germany

In 1953, Germany was aiming at encouraging the distribution of dividends so as to re-activate the capital market and reduce reliance upon financing out of ploughed-back profits. The 1971 proposal for full imputation carried this process a step further as it was considered that the split rate system still encourages the controlling shareholders, who are in a position to influence the distribution policy of companies, to leave profits in the firm where they attract less tax than would be the case if they were taxed as part of shareholders' incomes.

France

The 1965 system of the "avoir fiscal" was also seen as a means of improving the yield of company shares; but as it was expected that the benefit of the new scheme would be split between the company and its shareholders it was rather a measure to improve, at one and the same time, the yield on shares and the self-financing possibilities of companies.

Views expressed in the late eighties

Canada

When Canada modified its partial dividend deduction in 1971, and later increased the amount of credit from 20 per cent to 33 1/3 per cent, the aim was not primarily to eliminate the double taxation of dividends but rather to encourage investment by Canadian residents in Canadian companies. It has been noted recently by Canada that the current system of dividend gross-up and tax credit at the personal tax level achieves three basic objectives:

— Full integration of the corporate and personal tax systems for small corporations taxed at the small business rate. This ensures neutrality with respect to the choice between unincorporated and incorporated business;

— Partial relief in the case of large corporations taxed at the regular corporate income tax rate, to provide an incentive for Canadians to invest in the equity of Canadian corporations. The current system is not considered to create a significant bias in the decision to retain or distribute profits, or in the decision to finance through debt or equity;

— Simplicity of compliance and administration.

It is these last two objectives that account for Canada's preference for reduction rather than elimination of economic double taxation, for operating the reduction at shareholder rather than company level and in the form of a shareholder relief scheme rather than an imputation system.

Australia

Australia shifted from a classical to a full imputation system of taxing company income on 1st July 1987. Changes to the taxation of superannuation funds in 1988 extended the imputation system and eliminated the disincentive for funds to invest in equities. Australia's move to imputation was directed towards neutral tax treatment of the rewards of different corporate financing strategies, i.e. addressing the bias against equity in the classical system. As a result of the imputation system and the capital gains tax, the impact of taxation considerations on whether to gear an investment or obtain equity finance, to purchase assets yielding capital gains or invest in income earning ventures, or to retain or distribute corporate income has been substantially reduced.

Austria

A first step was taken in 1968 by cutting the formal rate of the tax on distributed profits from 55 per cent to 27.5 per cent, but the real incidence was about 38 per cent because of what has been called the 'shadow effect' (i.e. the effect that a company which wished to distribute all of its profits had to retain so much of it as was necessary to settle its corporation tax liability; companies therefore could not avoid a 55 per cent tax on that portion of their profits). In 1986 formal elimination of the double taxation of dividends was achieved by adding half-rate taxation of the shareholder to half rate taxation of the distributed profits of the company, but the shadow effect remained so that in practice economic double taxation continued to be mitigated rather than eliminated. In 1989 the shadow effect was eliminated by the introduction of a single rate of 30 per cent for both distributed and retained profits, so that Austria is now formally as well as in practice, a country which reduces rather than eliminates economic double taxation. However, at the same time, Austria aligned personal and corporate rates of tax with a view to being tax neutral to the decision of shareholders to invest via corporations or directly and to the decisions of firms to incorporate.

Belgium

The recent move in the opposite direction by Belgium in abolishing tax relief for shareholders occurred because it was felt to be a less efficient way of promoting private investment in equities than lowering rates of personal and corporate income tax and that budgetary constraints could not accommodate both solutions.

Sweden

In Sweden the corporation tax rate was reduced to 30 per cent in 1991. This in combination with an introduction of a separate, flat-rate tax of 30 per cent on capital income (including dividends and nominal capital gains) was found to have reduced the need for mitigation of economic double taxation. However, in order to achieve a better balance between financing by new issues and retained earnings — taking into account the deferral effect in capital gains taxation on the shareholder level — and thereby reduce "locking-in-effects", a partial deductibility for dividends on newly issued shares was maintained.

Finland and Denmark

In Finland the choice of a full imputation system in place of the former dividend deduction system was mainly based on the view that only the full imputation system in practice is effective in ensuring the economic single taxation of dividends. In 1989 Denmark expressed similar views to Finland but in fact did not adopt full imputation. The actual changes adopted include a different form of shareholder relief scheme, under which dividend income is subject to a progressive schedular tax at lower rates than that applying to other kinds of income.

Notes and references

1. See, for example, Emil M. Sunley's article published in 1979 in the Bulletin of the International Bureau of Fiscal Documentation which compares a possible dividend deduction system with a possible partial imputation system:

    "Compared to the pre-integration regime, if the corporation maintains the same level of distribution under the dividend deduction system, the entire increase in cash flow will accrue to the corporation. If it maintains the same cash dividend under a shareholder imputation system, the shareholder will receive the full benefit of integration. As shown by the following two examples, the two basic approaches to partial integration can be made identical with respect to their impact on corporate and shareholder cash flow as well as on foreign shareholders.

Example 1 Dividend deduction system

Corporation		Shareholder		
			Tax rate	
			20%	60%
Income	$100	Cash dividend	$40	$40
Dividend	40	Tax	8	24
Dividend deduction (50%)	20	After-tax cash flow	32	16
Taxable income	80	Total, corporate plus shareholder, tax	48	64
Tax (50%)	40			
After-tax income	60			
Retained Earnings	20			
Dividend	40			

In this example, the corporation is entitled to a $20 dividend deduction, one-half of the actual dividend, pays $40 in tax, and is left with $20 in retained earnings. Shareholders are taxed at their individual rates on the dividend. A shareholder in the 20 per cent bracket would be left with after-tax cash flow of $32 and a 60 per cent shareholder with after-tax cash flow of $16.

Example 2 (b) **Shareholder imputation system**

Corporation		Shareholder	Tax rates 20%	Tax rates 60%
Income	$100	Cash dividend	$30	$30
Corporate tax	50	Gross-up (1/3)	10	10
After-tax income	50	Gross dividend	40	40
Retained earnings	20			
Dividend	30	Tax	8	24
		Tax credit	10	10
		After-tax cash flow	32	16
		Total, corporate plus shareholder, tax	48	64

In this example, the corporation pays $50 in tax, distributes a dividend of $30, and is left with $20 in retained earnings. This imputation system provides for a shareholder gross-up and credit equal to one-third the cash dividend or $10. In effect, the corporation distributes a cash dividend of $30 and a shareholder credit of $10. A 20 per cent shareholder is left with $32 in cash, a 60 per cent shareholder with $16.

Examples 1 and 2 illustrate that the dividend deduction and shareholder imputation systems can be made identical with respect to corporate and shareholder cash flow as well as total taxes paid. The two systems differ in terms of the amount of dividends declared and the amount of corporate after-tax profits. The corporation's cash dividend is lower under the imputation system, but this is because it also is distributing the right to a shareholding credit. The corporation's after-tax profits (but not the corporation's retained earnings) are higher under the dividend deduction system".

2. See *Taxation and International Capital Flows*, OECD 1990.

3. In Sweden, for example, where with a few exceptions tax is levied on accounting income, the payment of dividends out of taxable profits can give raise to a higher burden on distributed profits than on retained profits and, in some cases, produces a "locking-in" effect. This was especially the case before the recent tax reform where normally reserve options could not be exhausted. In combination with a relatively lower tax burden on capital gains and shares than on dividends, this contributed to "locking-in-effects" whereby realisation of equity capital was hindered. The recent tax reform — with cut in the statutory tax rate, abolition of most reserve options and with an increase in the relative tax burden on capital gains — has resolved this problem.

4. See, for example, *OECD Country Survey, United Kingdom* 1988.

5. See *The Role of Tax Reform in Central and Eastern European Economies in Transition*, OECD, 1991.

6. This issue goes beyond corporate income tax and governments have to examine personal income taxes, payroll taxes and consumption taxes to identify their potential impact on these enterprises.

7. Sometimes the view is expressed that buildings and stocks can carry more debt than machinery. Accordingly, effective tax rate calculations that assume the same financing shares across assets overestimate the tax bias in favour of machinery (see, for example, the note by Gordon, Hines and Summers in Feldstein (ed.), National Bureau of Economic Research, 19..).

8. It is recalled that this report looks at investment in the manufacturing sector only.

9. See, for example, *Blueprints for Basic Tax Reform*, US 1984.

10. *OECD Economic Survey - Norway* 1991.

11. *OECD Economic Survey - Canada* 1990.

12. See page 80 of *OECD Economic Survey - Portugal* 1991.

13. See Conseil Supérieur des Finances : *Rapport sur certains aspects d'une réforme de l'impôt des sociétés*. Annexe II. Taux d'imposition effectif par secteur d'activité. Exercice 1989.

14. See for example for France: *9ème Rapport au président de la Republique*, Conseil des Impôts 1987.

15. See, *The role of tax reform in Central and Eastern European Economies in Transition 1991*, OECD 1991.

16. This term is used to refer to any enterprises operating in more than one country.

17. It is also worthwhile to note that a cash flow corporate tax would enable CIN and CEN to be achieved at the corporate level, although as long as personal taxes on income and capital gains taxes differ it would not achieve complete CIN or CEN.

18. This view of the effects of deferral is further elaborated in David G. Hartman: *Tax Policy and Foreign Direct Investment*, Journal of Public Economics, vol. 26, 1985, pp. 107-121.

19. The technical problems involved in the abolition of deferral are further discussed by Leif Mutén: "Some Topical Issues Concerning International Double Taxation", in: Sijbren Cnossen (ed.): *Essays in Honour of Richard Goode*, North-Holland, Amsterdam, 1983.

20. Under certain circumstances the granting of imputation credits to domestic shareholders for underlying corporate taxes paid abroad could prevent CEN being achieved.

21. See Chapter 2 for the arguments for and against the credit and the exemption methods.

22. For a discussion on the use of conduit companies see: *International Tax Avoidance and Evasion: Four Related Studies*, OECD 1987.

23. For a dynamic analysis of the effects of dividend taxes on the development of foreign subsidiaries, see Hans-Werner Sinn: *Taxation and the Birth of Foreign Subsidiaries*, Working Paper, University of Munich, November 1990.

24. In practice, the payment of tax credits abroad by an imputation country may enable a multinational group to enjoy a lower effective rate of tax on distributed profits than its competitors in the source country. This could provide an incentive for "round tripping", maximising dividends from the source country to the country of residence, even where it is the intention subsequently to re-invest profits in the source country.

Computing the cost of capital for domestic and transnational direct investment: methodology, parameters and a worked example

Introduction

This Annex sets out the methodology used in Chapters 4 and 5, for the calculation of the cost of capital and hence marginal effective tax rates on direct investment, both domestic and transnational. It then describes the values of the tax parameters used in the calculations for each country, and concludes with a worked example.

1. Methodology

The methodology in this report closely follows the commonly used approach of King and Fullerton (1984). The basic aim of the approach is to derive the difference between the real rate of return required from an investment project pre-tax and post-tax. In the absence of tax these will, of course, be equal to each other and also equal, by assumption, to the prevailing real interest rate (r). However, corporation taxes may cause the pre-tax required real rate of return, also termed the cost of capital, (p), to diverge from the interest rate. In addition, personal taxes may reduce the post-tax real return to the individual investor (s) below the interest rate.

Chapters 4 and 5 of this report present estimates of both the cost of capital (p) and the effective tax wedge (p-s). The latter is especially relevant for the level of investment in a closed economy. In such an economy the interest rate adjusts to equate savings and investment and therefore depends on the tax system. However, for the purposes of comparison between countries a common real interest rate has been used.[1] By contrast, in an open economy funds may flow both into and out of the economy and so domestic savings need not equal domestic investment (see the discussion in Annex 3). In this case, the cost of capital is the more relevant measure in considering the impact of taxation on investment. It might also be noted that, even in a closed economy, if individual investors do not pay personal taxes then the post-tax real return equals the real interest rate (s=r). In this case, since there is a given level of r, the cost of capital is again an appropriate measure of the effects of taxation on investment incentives.

The relationship between the real interest rate, r, and the post-tax real return, s, can be simply stated:

$$S = \frac{1 + i\,(1 - m^i)}{1 + \pi} - 1 \qquad (1)$$

where π is the rate of inflation, i is the nominal interest rate, equal to $(1+r)(1+\pi)-1$, and m^i is the personal tax rate on interest income. Defining the real required pre-tax rate of return (cost of capital) is less straightforward and forms the rest of this section.

The King and Fullerton methodology was applied only to domestic investment and taxation and so has had to be extended to allow for transnational investment and taxation. The approach used here is closest to that of Keen (1990), which, in turn, extends the contribution of Alworth (1988). However, Keen's methodology differs from that of King and Fullerton (1984) and does not yield the same expressions for the cost of capital in the domestic case. The approach here therefore draws on the results of Sorensen (1990) to adapt Keen's approach to transnational investment to make it consistent with the approach of King and Fullerton. Consequently the expressions here for the cost of capital in the domestic case are identical to those of King and Fullerton.[2]

The methodology used and calculations shown in this report allow for all the main features of the taxation of corporate profits for both domestic and transnational investments. For domestic investments, these include the corporate tax rate, depreciation allowances and investment tax credits, the valuation of inventories, the way in which the corporate tax interacts with the personal tax, and personal tax rates on dividend income, interest income and capital gains. In addition, for transnational investments, withholding taxes on dividends and interest and the tax treatment of foreign source income are incorporated (under the simplifying assumption that the tax base of the source country[3] is accepted as the appropriate tax base by the residence country).[4] However, certain elements of tax systems have been ignored. This is true, for example, of wealth taxes faced by the company or faced by the individual investor, and taxes on foreign exchange gains and losses.

Three forms of financing the company in the domestic case are considered: retained earnings, borrowing and new equity. For transnational investments it is assumed that the activity is undertaken by a wholly-owned subsidiary of the parent. The subsidiary finances the investment in one of three ways: retained earnings (of the subsidiary) and debt or new equity from the parent. Where the finance comes directly from the parent, the parent in turn raises the funds in one of the three ways already noted. Taking account of the form of finance used by the parent, there are therefore seven ways in which the subsidiary may be financed. The exchange rate is an explicit parameter of the model (and various forms of exchange rate determination can therefore be incorporated).

The first part of this section provides a parameterisation of the main forms of taxation encountered in transnational investment. It defines three general tax parameters which vary with the form of the taxation of foreign source income. These parameters are then used in the second part of this section in a model of firm behaviour which finally is used in to derive expressions for the cost of capital.

Tax parameters

Two companies may be considered, a parent company operating in the "residence" country and a wholly-owned subsidiary of the parent operating in the "source" country. The parent company finances the operations of the subsidiary through purchasing new equity and by lending, although the latter can finance operations through retained earnings. The parent company also operates on its own behalf, independently of the subsidiary. The total tax liability of the two companies can be written:

$$T_t = T_t^h + E. \underline{T}_t^a + T_t^{ha} \tag{2}$$

where T_t^h is tax due on profits generated and distributed in the residence country, $E.\underline{T}_t^a$ is the tax due in the source country on profits and distributions of the subsidiary, and T_t^{ha} is the tax due in the residence country on profits and distributions of the subsidiary. The underscore on $\underline{T}_t^a$ signifies that it is denominated in the currency of the source country; E is the exchange rate which converts it to the currency of the residence country at the end of period t (the exchange rate at the beginning of period t is set to unity)[5].

Examining these components separately, the first two can be written as follows:

$$T_t^h = \tau^{hr}(\phi_t^h - G_t^h) + \tau^{hd} G_t^h + \omega^h D_t^h - c^h D_t^h \tag{3a}$$

and

$$\underline{T_t^a} = \tau^{ar}(\underline{\phi_t^a} - \underline{G_t^a}) + \tau^{ad}\underline{G_t^a} + \omega^a \underline{D_t^a} - c^a\underline{D_t^a} + \omega^r i^a \underline{B_t^a} \tag{4a}$$

where:

ϕ_t^h and $\underline{\phi_t^a}$ are taxable profits of the parent and subsidary respectively;

τ_t^{hr} and τ_t^{ar} are the statutory tax rates on retained earnings in the residence and source countries respectively;

τ_t^{hd} and τ_t^{ad} are the statutory tax rates on dividends in the residence and source countries respectively;

D_t^h and $\underline{D_t^a}$ are dividend payments by the parent and subsidary respectively gross of any imputation credit;

G_t^h and $\underline{G_t^a}$ are dividend payments by the parent and subsidary respectively, grossed up at the corporation tax rate on dividends;

ω_t^h and ω_t^a are the withholding tax rates on dividend payments of the parent and subsidiary respectively;

c_t^h and c_t^a are the imputation system credits available on dividend payments of the parent and subsidiary respectively; and

ω^r is the withholding tax rate charged on the interest paid by the subsidiary to the parent (interest at rate i^a on outstanding debt of $\underline{B_t^a}$).

These two expressions can be written as follows:

$$T_t^h = \tau^{hr}\phi_t^h + (\tau^{*hd} - \tau^{*hr} + \sigma^h)D_t^h \tag{3b}$$

and

$$\underline{T_t^a} = \tau^{ar}\underline{\phi_t^a} + (\tau^{*ad} - \tau^{*ar} + \sigma^a)\underline{D_t^a} + \omega^r i^a\underline{B_t^a} \tag{4b}$$

where τ^{*hd}, τ^{*hr}, τ^{*ad} and τ^{*ar} are "effective" corporation tax rates which apply to the dividend gross of the imputation credit, defined as:

$$\tau^{*ij} = \tau^{ij}\frac{(1 - c^i)}{(1 - \tau^{id})} \; , \; i = h, a \text{ and } j = d, r \tag{5a}$$

and σ^h and σ^a are "effective" withholding tax rates on dividend payments in the residence and source country respectively, defined as:

$$\sigma^i = \omega^i - c^i \; , \; i = h, a \tag{5b}$$

In the absence of withholding taxes and imputation credits, $\sigma = 0$. A withholding tax on dividend payments not reclaimable by the shareholders would, in the absence of imputation credits, yield $\sigma = \omega$, where ω is the rate of withholding tax. An imputation system without a withholding tax effectively reduces the total tax paid by the company (since the imputation credit is simply a prepayment of shareholders' income tax), in which case $\sigma = -c$. Since these two features of tax systems act in identical (though opposite) ways, they are incorporated into the same parameter, σ.

The third component of (2) depends on the treatment of foreign source income in the residence country. This income can come in two forms: dividends and interest. We therefore define

$$T_t^{ha} = T_t^{hd} + T_t^{hi} \tag{6}$$

where T_t^{hd} is the tax in the residence country on receipt of dividends from the subsidiary and T_t^{hi} is the tax in the residence country on receipt of interest from the subsidiary. For each of these cases three possible forms of taxation are considered (which between them account for all the systems described in Chapter 3).

(a) Exemption:

$$T_t^{hd} = 0, \quad T_t^{hi} = 0 \tag{7a}$$

(b) Partial credit with deferral:

$$T_t^{hd} = \max \left\{ \frac{(\tau^{hr} - \tau^{ad}) ED_{\underline{t}}^a}{(1 - \tau^g)} - \sigma^a ED_{\underline{t}}^a, 0 \right\}, \tag{7b}$$

$$T_t^{hi} = \max \left\{ (\tau^{hr} - \omega') Ei^a B_{\underline{t}}^a, 0 \right\}$$

(c) Deduction with deferral:

$$T_t^{hd} = \tau^{hr} (1 - \sigma^a) ED_{\underline{t}}^a, \quad T_t^{hi} = \tau^{hr}(1 - \omega') Ei^a B_{\underline{t}}^a \tag{7c}$$

In (7b), τ^g is the rate at which dividends received by the parent are grossed up in order to determine the tax base for residence country taxation. Essentially this is a question of whether the residence country accepts the source country tax base: if it does then $\tau^g = \tau^{ad}$. Generally, it is assumed that this is the case. However, the United States explicitly adjusts foreign source income when assessing domestic tax liablity to take account of differences in the tax base, and a different assumption is made in order to calculate effective tax rates when the United States is the residence country, giving a better approximation to the regulations of that country.[6]

These three forms of taxing foreign source income can be captured in the following general formulation of the total tax charge:

$$T_t = \tau^{hr}\phi_t^h + (\tau^{*hd} - \tau^{*hr} + \sigma^h)\,D_t^h + \tau^{ar}E\underline{\phi}_t^a + \sigma^*E\underline{D}_t^a + \omega^*i^aE\underline{B}_t^a \tag{8}$$

Thus, σ^* is the total tax arising from repatriation of profits as a dividend and ω^* is the total tax arising from repatriation of interest. It is also useful to define

$$\tau_d^* = \tau^{ar} + \sigma^*(1 - \tau^{ad}) \tag{9}$$

to be the effective tax rate on distributed profits of the subsidiary. The values of σ^* and ω^* for each of the three regimes for the taxation of foreign source income are as follows:

$$\text{Exemption } \sigma^*:\quad \sigma^a + \tau^{*ad} - \tau^{*ar}$$
$$\omega^*:\quad \omega^r$$

$$\text{Partial credit with deferral } \sigma^*:\quad \max\left\{\frac{\tau^{hr} - \tau^{ad}}{1 - \tau^{ad}},\ \sigma^a\right\} + \tau^{*ad} - \tau^{*ar}$$
$$\omega^*:\quad \max\{\tau^{hr},\ \omega^r\}$$

$$\text{Deduction with deferral } \sigma^*:\quad \tau^{hr}(1 - \sigma^a) + \sigma^a + \tau^{*ad} - \tau^{*ar}$$
$$\omega^*:\quad \tau^{hr}(1 - \omega^r) + \omega^r$$

A model of firm behaviour

The model developed in this section is in many respects a straightforward extension of the simple model of the firm in the tradition of King (1974); perfect certainty is assumed and firms aim to maximise the wealth of the shareholders, equivalent to maximising the present value of the firm's equity. The extension is to allow for a subsidiary based in a foreign country. This does not change the basic approach, but considerably complicates the analysis. It is assumed that the shareholders of the parent live in, and are taxed in, the residence country, i.e. there is no transnational portfolio investment.

We begin with a condition for capital market equilibrium in the residence country:

$$(1 - m^i)\,i^h V_t = (1 - m^d)\,D_t^h + (1 - z)(V_{t+1} - V_t - N_t^h) + \eta z\pi V_t \tag{10}$$

where V_t is the market value of the parent firm's equity at the beginning of period t, N_t^h is new equity issued by the parent during period t, π is the inflation rate and m^i, m^d and z are the marginal personal tax rates of the shareholders of the parent on interest income, dividend income and capital gains. The last term represents the value of indexation of capital gains for tax purposes ($\eta=1$ if indexation is allowed and zero otherwise). The value of this allowance is $z\pi V_t$ (see below). Condition (10) simply requires the post-tax

211

return from equity (the right hand side) to be equal to the post-tax return on debt (the left hand side). It is assumed that the firm aims to maximise V_t.

The capital gains tax rate, z, is the accrual equivalent rate applied to the nominal capital gain. To calculate this rate, it is necessary to make some assumption regarding the time at which the shareholder sells his shares, realises the gain and hence faces a tax liability. The approach of King (1977) is followed in assuming that the shareholder sells a constant proportion a, of his stock of assets in each period. In this case, the accrual equivalent rate is simply the present value of taxes due on a capital gain of one in period t, that is

$$z = \alpha z^R \left\{ 1 + \frac{1 - \alpha}{1 + j} + \frac{(1 - \alpha)^2}{(1 + j)^2} + \frac{(1 - \alpha)^3}{(1 - j)^3} + ... \right\} = \frac{\alpha z^R (1 + j)}{\alpha + j} \qquad (11)$$

where z^R is the statutory capital gains tax rate on realisations and $j=i(1-m^i)$ is the shareholder's discount rate. In the calculations in Chapters 4 and 5, a is normally taken to be 10 per cent. Note that it is possible to incorporate more complex forms of capital gains taxation into this approach. For example, it is straightforward to allow z^R to vary depending on the length of time the asset is held.[7]

To use condition (10) it is necessary to specify the value of D. This can be done by stating the equality of sources and uses of funds for both the parent and the subsidiary[8]:

Parent:

$$D_t^h + EN_t^a + EB_{t+j}^a + T_t^h + T_t^{ha} + (1 + i^h) B_t^h + q_t^h I_t^h$$

$$= (1 - \sigma^a) ED_t^a + p_t^h R^h (K_t^h) + B_{t+1}^h + N_t^h + EB_t^a [1 + i^a (1 - \omega^a)] \qquad (12)$$

Subsidiary:

$$(1 - \sigma^a) D_t^a + B_t^a [1 + i^a (1 - \omega^a)] + T_t^a + q_t^a I_t^a = p_t^a R^a (K_t^a) + B_{t+1}^a + N_t^a \qquad (13)$$

where:

D_t^h	is gross dividends paid by the parent during period t
D_t^a	is gross dividends paid by the subsidiary to the parent during period t
N_t^a	is new equity of the subsidiary purchased by the parent in period t,
B_{t+1}^a	is the stock of one period debt lent by the parent to the subsidiary during period t, which is repaid one period later together with interest at nominal interest rate i^a,
B_{t+1}^h	is the stock of one period debt borrowed by the parent during period t, which is repaid one period later together with interest at rate i^h,
I_t^h	is the stock of new capital goods purchased by the parent during period t, at price q_t^h,
I_t^a	is the stock of new capital goods purchased by the subsidiary during period t, at price q_t^a,
$R^h(K_t^h)$	is output, net of variable inputs, of the parent, which depends only on activities in the parent, valued at an output price p_t^h,
$R^a(K_t^a)$	is output, net of variable inputs, of the subsidiary, which depends only on activities in the subsidiary, valued at an output price p_t^a,
E	is the exchange rate at the end of period t (the rate at the beginning of period t is set to one): note that it is assumed that all flows take place at the end of the period.

The tax variables were defined in the previous section. However, it is also necessary to define taxable profits for both the parent and the subsidiary, ϕ_t^h and $\underline{\phi}_t^a$:

Parent:

$$\phi_t^h = p_t^h R^h(K_t^h) - i^h B_t^h - \beta^h q_t^h I_t^h - \delta^{Th} K_t^{Th} \tag{14}$$

Subsidiary:

$$\underline{\phi}_t^a = \underline{p}_t^a R^a(K_t^a) - i^a \underline{B}_t^a - \beta^a \underline{q}_t^a I_t^a - \delta^{Ta} \underline{K}_t^{Ta} \tag{15}$$

where:

K_{t+1}^{Th} is the net value of the parent's capital stock for tax purposes at the end of period t,

β^h is the proportion of the cost of investment in the residence country that can be claimed against tax in the year in which it is incurred,

δ^{Th} is the rate at which subsequent depreciation allowances can be claimed in the residence country,

$\underline{K}_{t+i}^{Ta}$ is the net value of the subsidiary's capital stock for tax purposes at the end of period t,

β^a is the proportion of the cost of investment in the source country that can be claimed against tax in the year in which it is incurred, and

δ^{Ta} is the rate at which subsequent depreciation allowances can be claimed in the source country.

The value of the capital stock for tax purposes therefore follows the following paths, for declining balance (16a) and straight line (16b) depreciation rules[9]:

$$K_t^{Ti} = (1 - \delta^{Ti}) K_{t-1}^{Ti} + (1 - \beta^i) q_t^i i_t^i, \qquad i = h, a \tag{16a}$$

$$K_t^{Ti} = \sum_{s=1}^{N^i} q_{t-s}^i I_{t-s}^i (1 - \beta^i - [s-1] \delta^{Ti}), \qquad i = h, a \tag{16b}$$

where N is the number of years for which depreciation can be claimed (if $\beta^i = \delta^{Ti}$ then $N = 1/\delta^{Ti}$)[10]. The equation of motion for the capital stock is

$$K_t^i = (1 - \delta^i) K_{t-1}^i + I_t^i, \qquad i = h, a \tag{17}$$

Finally, it is necessary to impose some constraints on the financial policy of the firm. This is common practice for this type of model, which is not well suited to the investigation of optimal financial policy. The constraints on the parent company are chosen in such a way as to be able to derive the King Fullerton expression for the cost of capital for domestic investment; the constraints on the subsidiary follow the same approach. Essentially, a constant debt equity ratio is assumed for each of the parent and the subsidiary (b^h and b^a, respectively). Further, new share issues by each company are assumed to be a constant proportion (a^h for the parent and a^a for the subsidiary) of the increase in the value of the equity of the company, $V_{t+1} - V_t$: this implies that retained earnings and new issues are always proportional. In order to make these assumptions operational, one further assumption is made: that the value of the subsidiary is a constant proportion (d) of the value of the parent (although in practice this proportion can be set to zero or one, to study investment by the parent or by the subsidiary). The constraints are therefore as follows:

Parent:

$$N_t^h = a^h(V_{t+1} - V_t);$$
$$B\text{-}t^h = b^h V_t;$$

(18a, b)

Subsidiary:

$$\underline{V_t^a} + \underline{B_t^a} = d(V_t + B_t^h);$$
$$E(\underline{V_{t+1}^a} + \underline{B_{t+1}^a}) = d(V_{t+1} + B_{t+1}^h)$$

(18c)

$$\underline{N_t^a} = a^a(\underline{V_{t+1}^a} - \underline{V_t^a})$$
$$= \frac{a^a d(1 + b^h)}{(1 + b^a)} \left[\frac{V_{t+1}}{E} - V_t \right]$$

(18d)

$$\underline{B_t^a} = b^a \underline{V_t^a} = \frac{b^a d(1 + b^h) V_t}{(1 + b^a)}$$

(18e)

where $\underline{V_t^a}$ is the value of the equity of the subsidiary at the beginning of period t.

To solve the model for the value of the firm, V_t, the constraints in (18) can be substituted, together with the definitions (14), (15) and (16) and the equation of motion (17), into the sources and uses of funds equalities (12) and (13), which in turn can be used to derive an expression for D_t^h in terms of the real variables, V_t, V_{t+1}, tax variables and the parameters from the constraints. Substituting this expression into the capital market equilibrium condition (10) yields the following expression for the maximand, V_t:

$$V_t = \sum_{s=t}^{\infty} \frac{\gamma' D_t^{h'}}{(1 + \rho')^{s+1-t}}$$

(19)

where γ', $D_t^{h'}$, and ρ' are defined in the Appendix to this Annex. Expression (19) simply says that the value of the parent's equity is equal to the discounted present value of taxed real, as opposed to financial, flows.

The nominal discount rate, ρ', is a complex combination of interest rates, tax variables, the exchange rate and the parameters from the financial constraints. Since ρ' plays an important role in the cost of capital expressions derived below, it is worth exploring in more detail now.

Four different cases can be considered. They are as follows:

214

Case A: only domestic investment. (d=0)

Case B: only transnational investment financed only by retained earnings in the subsidiary. $(d=1, a^a=b^a=0)$

Case C: only transnational investment financed only by new equity provided by the parent. $(d=1, a^a=1, b^a=0)$

Case D: only transnational investment financed only by debt provided by the parent. $(d=1, a^a=0, b^a \rightarrow \infty)$

For cases A, C and D, however, there is also the possibility of the parent company financing the investment in one of three ways:

Case i: Retained earnings. $(a^h=b^h=0)$

Case ii: New equity. $(a^h=1, b^h=0)$

Case iii: Debt. $(a^h=0, b^h \rightarrow \infty)$

The values of ρ' for these 10 different cases are shown in Table A.1.1.

In Table A.1.1, $\rho=[(1-m^i)i^h-z\pi] / (1-z)$ and $\gamma=[(1-m^d)(1-z^{hd})] / [(1-z)(1+\sigma^h)(1-z^{hr})]$. γ is sometimes known as the "tax discrimination variable" indicating discrimination between retained earnings and new equity finance in the parent company, and $\omega_d^*=\omega^*-\tau_d^*$ is the effective total tax charge on interest paid by the subsidiary to the parent, equal to the tax payable in the residence country plus the withholding tax, less interest relief gained in the source country so,

$$\sigma^{*'} = \frac{\sigma^{*'}(1-z^{ad})}{1-z^{ar}}$$

Several points may be noted from the table. First, Case A is identical to the expressions for the company discount rate given by King and Fullerton. Second, under the assumptions made here, Case B is identical to the domestic case when retained earnings are the marginal source of finance. This mirrors the result of Hartmann (1985). The discount rate is higher in Case C; this reflects the withholding tax charged by the source country on repatriations to the parent (this is obviously avoided in the domestic case, and in Case B is also avoided since the subsidiary retains earnings). In Case D, the basic discount rate is the same as in Case C: however, in this case, there is also an additional term reflecting the difference in the tax relief in the source country on interest paid to the parent and the tax due on that interest (both withholding tax and residence country tax). It is noted that the exchange rate is relevant only if the subsidiary is financed by debt or new equity from the parent.

Table A.1.1: Company discount rate under alternative financial regimes

Source of finance of parent

Case A:

Retained earnings	ρ
New equity	ρ/γ
Debt	$i^h(1-\tau^{hr})$

Case B:

Retained earnings	ρ
New equity	—
Debt	—

Case C:

Retained earnings
$$\frac{\rho + (1 - E)\gamma\,\sigma^{*'}}{1 - \gamma\,\sigma^{*'}}$$

New equity
$$\frac{\rho + (1 - E)\gamma\,\sigma^{*'}}{\gamma(1 - \sigma^{*'})}$$

Debt
$$\frac{i^h(1 - \tau^{hr}) + (1 - E)\gamma\,\sigma^{*'}}{1 - \sigma^{*'}}$$

Case D:

Retained earnings
$$\frac{\rho + (1 - E)\gamma\,\sigma^{*'} + Ei^a\gamma\,\omega_d^*}{1 - \gamma\,\sigma^{*'}}$$

New equity
$$\frac{\rho + (1 - E)\gamma\,\sigma^{*'} + Ei^a\gamma\,\omega_d^*}{\gamma(1 - \sigma^{*'})}$$

Debt
$$\frac{i^h(1 - \tau^{hr}) + (1 - E)\sigma^{*'} + Ei^a\omega_d^*}{1 - \sigma^{*'}}$$

The cost of capital

The domestic price of investment goods, q_t^h, rises each period at a rate π^h, and that the price of investment goods in the source country, $\underline{q}_t^a$, rises each period at a rate π^a. The exchange rate at the beginning of period t and the prices of investment and output goods in period t in both countries are all set to unity. Following the King and Fullerton notation, the present value of depreciation allowances on a unit of capital in the residence country is denoted A^h, and is given in (20a) for declining balance and (20b) for straight line depreciation schedules:[11]

$$A_D^h = \frac{\delta^{Th} \tau^{hr}(1 + \rho')}{\rho' + \delta^{Th}} \qquad (20a)$$

$$A_S^h = \frac{\delta^{Th} \tau^{hr}(1 + \rho')}{\rho'} \left[1 - \frac{1}{(1 + \rho')^N}\right] \qquad (20b)$$

where N is the number of years for which a depreciation allowance can be claimed (defined in (16b) and the following).

In some countries it is possible to switch from using the declining balance system to the straight line system. If the declining balance system has a rate of δ_1^{Th} and is used for M years and the straight line system for a further N years, the present value of allowances is[12]:

$$A_B^h = A_D^h \left[1 - \frac{(1 - \delta_1^{Th})^M}{(1 + \rho')^M}\right] + \frac{A_S^h}{(1 + \rho')^M} \qquad (20c)$$

The corresponding expressions for the source country are[13]:

$$A^a = \frac{E \delta^{Ta} \tau^{ar}(1 + \rho')}{(1 + \rho') - E(1 - \delta^{Th})} \qquad (21a)$$

$$A^a = \frac{E \delta^{Ta} \tau^{ar}(1 + \rho')}{(1 + \rho' - E)} \left[1 - \frac{E^N}{(1 + \rho')^N}\right] \qquad (21b)$$

The cost of capital can be found by maximising the value of the firm V_t subject to the equations of motion (16) and (17) and the financial constraints (18). At the margin the cost of capital is equal to the marginal product of capital. Using the definitions in (20) and (21) enables the cost of capital (p in King Fullerton terminology) for domestic investment (p^h) and for transnational investment (p^a) to be written as:

and

217

$$p^h = \frac{(1 - A^h)}{(1 - \tau^{h\prime})(1 + \pi^h)} \{\rho^{\prime} - \pi^h + \delta(1 + \pi^h)\} - \delta \qquad (22)$$

$$p^a = \frac{(1 - A^a)}{(1 - \tau^{a\prime}) E (1 + \pi^a)} \{(1 + \rho^{\prime}) - (1 - \delta) E (1 + \pi^a)\} - \delta \qquad (23a)$$

If purchasing power parity is assumed, so that $E = (1+\pi^h)/(1+\pi^a)$, then (23a) can also be written as:

$$p^a = \frac{(1 - A^a)}{(1 - \tau^{a\prime})(1 + \pi^h)} \{\rho^{\prime} - \pi^h + \delta(1 + \pi^h)\} - \delta \qquad (23b)$$

The expression in (22) is the discrete time equivalent of the commonly used King Fullerton expression[14]. The appropriate value of $\rho^{\prime}$ from Table A.1.1 for alternative forms of finance must be substituted into (22). The expressions in (23a) and (23b) are therefore the equivalent calculation for transnational investment. Once again, the appropriate value of $\rho^{\prime}$ must be used, and in addition, the appropriate values of the tax variables σ^*, ω^* and τ_d^* from the first Section must be used.

An additional term must be added for investment in inventories when inventories are valued by the FIFO method. This is because any increase in the value of inventories due to inflation is taxed. This does not occur if the LIFO method is used. If v represents the proportion of inventories valued by the FIFO method, then (22) and (23a) become:

$$p^h = \frac{(1 - A^h)}{(1 - \tau^{h\prime})(1 + \pi^h)} \{\rho^{\prime} - \pi^h + \delta(1 + \pi^h)\} + \frac{v\tau^{hr}\pi^h}{(1 - \tau^{h\prime})(1 + \pi^h)} - \delta \qquad (22b)$$

and

$$p^a = \frac{(1 - A^a)}{(1 - \tau^{a\prime}) E (1 + \pi^a)} \{(1 + \rho^{\prime}) - (1 - \delta) E (1 + \pi^a)\}$$
$$+ \frac{E v \tau^{ar} \pi^a}{(1 - \tau^{a\prime}) E (1 + \pi^a)} - \delta \qquad (23c)$$

218

Appendix

This Appendix gives the definitions of γ', ρ' and $D_t^{h'}$ from (19).

$$\gamma' = \frac{\gamma}{1 - a^a(1 - \gamma) + b^h\gamma - (a^a + b^q)\gamma\sigma^{*'}d(1 + b^h)/(1 + b^q)}$$

$$\rho' = \frac{\rho + b^h\gamma i^h(1 - \tau^h) + \left[b^a E\gamma i^a(\omega^* - \tau_d^*] + (a^a + b^q)\gamma(1 - E)\sigma^{*'}\right] d(1 + b^h)/(1 + b^q)}{1 - a^a(1 - \gamma) + b^h\gamma - (a^a + b^q)\gamma\sigma^*d(1 + b^h)/(1 + b^q)}$$

$$D_t^{h'} = p_t^h R^h(K_t^h)(1 - \tau^h) + E\underline{p_t^a} R^a(K_t^a)(1 - \tau_d^*)$$

$$- q_t^h I_t^h(1 - \beta^h\tau^{hr}) + \delta^{Th}K^{Th}\tau^{hr} - E(1 - \sigma^*)\left[\underline{q_t^a} I_t^a(1 - \beta^a\tau^{ar}) - \delta^{Ta}K^{Ta}\tau^{ar}\right]$$

2. Parameters used in the calculations

The tables in this section give the parameters used to calculate the results reported in Chapters 4 and 5. The parameters used in the calculations are based on an interpretation of the tax systems outlined in the country chapters. Generally, the tax systems fit into the algebraic model described in the previous section, but in some cases this is not so. The notes to the tables explain how the various provisions of tax codes which do not fit easily into the basic King and Fullerton model are treated. In the equations given with these tables, the following definitions apply:

τ The overall corporate tax rate
ρ The overall discount rate
δ The economic depreciation rate of assets
d   The tax depreciation rate of assets
π The inflation rate
a   The value of reductions in the cost of a project.

In order to keep the equations as simple as possible, changes in the exchange rate are ignored.

Table A.1.2: **Corporation tax rates used in the calculations.**

Country	National tax rate on distributed profits	National tax rate on retained profits	Local tax rate	Local tax deductible?	Imputation rate as a proportion of the gross dividend
Australia	39	39	0		39[1]
Austria	30	30	12.9	yes	0
Belgium	39	39	0		0
Canada	23.8[2,3]	23.8	11.9	no	20
Denmark	38	38	0		
Finland	23	23	17.2	no	40.2
France[4]	42	34	0		33.3
Germany	36	50	13	yes	36
Greece	0	40[3]	0		0
Iceland[5]	45	45	0		
Ireland	10[3,6]	10	0		5.3
Italy	47.8	47.8	0[7]		36
Japan	50	50	0[7]		0
Luxembourg	33	33.33	9.1	yes	0
Netherlands	35	35	0		0
New Zealand	33[11]	33[11]	0		33[1]
Norway	0	27.8	23	no	0
Portugal	36	36	3.6	no	0
Spain	35	35[8]	0	yes	0
Sweden[9]	30	30	0		0
Switzerland[10]	8	8	22.3	yes	0
Turkey	49.2	49.2	0		0
United Kingdom	34	34	0		25
United States	34	34	6.5	yes	0

Notes:
1. The imputation system does not permit a cash refund where the imputation credit exceeds the personal tax due.
2. Canadian Federal tax rate on foreign source income is 41.7%.
3. Tax rate on manufacturing companies
4. France has a system which permits a reduction in the tax due on dividends paid out for the first six years after a new share issue. In effect, the discount rate changes after six years. For new equity the discount rate for the first six years is amended so that the γ in Table A.1.1 in part one of this annex is γ where:

$$\gamma = \gamma \left(1 + \frac{0.534 \, \tau^R (1 - \tau^D)}{1 - \tau^r} \right)$$

5.   Iceland gives interest relief only for the real interest rate. However, it also gives an "inflationary allowance" of 45 per cent of the value of assets. Hence the cost of projects is reduced by $0.45\tau\pi$.

6.   Irish tax rate on foreign source income is 43 per cent.

7.   Local taxes included in overall national tax rates.

8.   Spain does not have a local tax, but there is a levy by local chambers of commerce of around 1.5 per cent.

9.   Sweden has the "Annell" deduction for new share issues. New shares qualify for a maximum deduction of 10 per cent of the paid-in capital. In addition firms may allocate funds to a tax equalisation reserve (SURV). These are modelled as reductions in the cost of the project. Hence the cost of the project is reduced by "ann" and "s" as follows:

$$ann = \left(\frac{\tau 0.1 \left(1 - e^{\frac{\rho}{0.1}} \right)}{\rho - \pi + \delta} \right) \left(1 - \frac{(\rho - \pi + \delta)}{\rho} \right) \left(\frac{a - \tau(\delta - \pi)}{\rho - \pi + \delta} \right)$$

$$s = 0.3\tau(1 - a)(1 + \tau) + \frac{0.3\rho\tau(1 - \tau)}{\rho + \delta - \pi}$$

10.   Switzerland has a Federal tax regime which is progressive according to the rate of return on assets, not proportional as in other countries. Similarly, most cantonal and local taxes are progressive. The figures shown in the table are based on companies earning the average rate of return, estimated to be around 13 per cent.

11.   On foreign-owned companies, 38 per cent.

Table A.1.3: **Personal tax rates used in the calculations**

Country	Tax rate on dividends		Tax rate on interest (where different from those of dividends)	
	Top rate	Average marginal rate	Top rate	Average marginal rate
Australia	48.3	39.0	48.3	39.0
Austria	25.0	19.8	50.0	39.7
Belgium[1]	25.0	25.0	10.0	10.0
Canada	49.1	44.6		
Denmark	45.0	37.6	57.8	51.1
Finland	60.0	45.2	10.0	10.0
France	57.9	45.0	18.1[2]	5.6
Germany	53.0	39.1		
Greece	50.0	n.a.	0.0	0.0
Iceland	39.8[3]	15.8	0.0	0.0
Ireland	53.0[4]	27.0	53.0	38.4
Italy	50.0	39.4	30.0	12.5
Japan	35.0[5]	35.0	20.0	20.0
Luxembourg	51.3	24.6		
Netherlands	60.0	49.0		
New Zealand	33.0	28.6		
Norway	19.5	n.a.	40.5	
Portugal[6]	25.0	25.0		
Spain[7]	56.0	28.4	56.0	31.5
Sweden	30.0	30.0		
Switzerland	43.8	30.8		
Turkey	10.0	10.0		
United Kingdom	40.0	32.0		
United States	36.0	31.0		

Notes:
1. The 25 per cent withholding tax on interest and dividends is the final tax paid.
2. Different withholding tax rates are applied to different sorts of interest income; the figure used reflects that in State bonds.
3. Iceland exempts dividends from personal tax provided less than 15 per cent of the company is owned by the taxpayer, subject to an upper limit.
4. Half of manufacturing dividend income is exempt from taxation (subject to not more than IR£7 000 being exempted in any tax year).
5. Japanese shareholders have a choice between a final withholding tax and personal tax. The above figures reflect the withholding tax.
6. Portuguese shareholders can choose the withholding tax as the final tax paid
7. Spanish interest income is taxed as ordinary income, 10 per cent of dividends received can be deducted from the personal income tax.

Table A.1.4: **Capital gains tax rates on individual investors used in the calculations[1]**

Country	CGT rate in first period		Length of first period	CGT rate in second period		Indexation
	Top rate	Average rate		Top rate	Average rate	
Australia[2]	48.3	39.0	—	—	—	yes[3]
Austria	50.0	39.7	1	0	0	—
Belgium	0	0	—	—	—	—
Canada[4]	36.8	10.5	—	—	—	no
Denmark[5]	57.8	51.1	2	0	0	no
Finland	60	55	5	30	2	no
France	18.1	0	—	—	—	no
Germany	0	0	—	—	—	—
Greece	0	0	—	—	—	—
Iceland	39.8	20				yes
Ireland[6]	50.0	50.0	3	35.0	35.0	yes
Italy	25.0	25.0	—	—	—	no
Japan	20.0	20.0	—	—	—	no
Luxembourg	0	0	—	—	—	—
Netherlands	0	0	—	—	—	—
New Zealand	0	0	—	—	—	—
Norway	40.0	40.0	3	0	0	no
Portugal	10.0	10.0	2	0	0	no
Spain[7]	56.0	31.5	—	—	—	yes
Sweden	30.0	30.0	—	—	—	no
Switzerland	0	0	—	—	—	—
Turkey	50.0	27.0	—	—	—	no
United Kingdom	40.0	33	—	—	—	yes
United States	36.0	31.0	—	—	—	no

Notes:
1. Many countries which have a zero capital gains tax rate do tax capital gains if a large stake in a company is sold, or if the value of the gain is large. Those with a capital gains tax often have exemptions and allowances. Details can be found in the country chapters. This table is not an exhaustive summary of capital gains tax provisions, it gives the figures used in the calculations.
2. Franked dividend system. Under certain circumstances, firms have the option of "paying out" a capital gain in the form of new shares. It is assumed for the purposes of the calculations that firms make full use of franked dividends. This implies that foreign source income is a sufficiently low proportion of total income that any bonus shares issued can be claimed to have come from domestic (i.e. franked) income.
3. Not indexed if sold within one year
4. Canada has a large lifetime exemption limit (Can $ 100 000), and the average tax rate reflects this. The capital gains tax rate is three quarters of the statutory income tax rate.

5. In Denmark there is a presumption that shares are sold in the order in which they where brought. This means a greater proportion of capital gains are in fact exempt from tax than is implied by the accruals equivalent tax rate methodology.

6. Capital gains taxed at 50 per cent if sold in the first three years, 35 per cent if sold after holding for 3 to 6 years and 30% if sold after that. The capital gain is only indexed if sold after one or more years.

7. Spain taxes capital gains on the basis of dividing the value of the gain by the number of years held (if the taxpayer does not know the holding period, then the period is taken to be five years), and including that figure into normal taxable income. The remainder is taxed at the average rate for general income tax. This leads to the accruals equivalent CGT rate being:

$$z^\wedge = z^s\lambda + \sum_{n=1}^{\infty} \left(\frac{\lambda z^s}{n}\right)\left(\frac{(1-\lambda)}{1+(1-m^i r)}\right)^{n-1}$$

where λ is the proportion of the remaining gain sold each year (in the results, this is set at 0.1); z^s is the statutory capital gains tax rate and m^i is average income tax rate.

Table A.1.5: **Capital allowances for industrial buildings used in the calculations[1]**

Country	first period			Second period			Extra first year allowance
	Straight line or declining balance	Allowance rate	Length of first period	Straight line or declining balance	Allowance rate	length of second period	
Australia	SL	2.5	ufd[2]				
Austria	SL	4.0	ufd				20.0
Belgium	DB	10.0	7[3]	SL	5.0	ufd	1% + inflation
Canada	DB	4.0	ufd				
Denmark	SL	6.0	10	SL	2.0	ufd	
Finland	DB	9.0	ufd				
France	SL	5.0	ufd				
Germany[5]	SL	10.0	4	SL	5.0	3	
Greece	SL	8.0	ufd				
Iceland	SL	2.0	ufd				
Ireland	SL	50.0	1	SL	4.0	ufd	
Italy	DB	5.0	ufd				
Japan	DB	6.6	18	SL	2.2	11[6]	
Luxembourg	SL	4.0	ufd				
Netherlands	DB	6.6	ufd				
New Zealand	SL	2.0	ufd				
Norway	DB	7.0	ufd				
Portugal	SL	5.0	ufd				
Spain	DB	7.5	ufd				
Sweden	SL	3.3	ufd				
Switzerland	DB	8.0	ufd				
Turkey	DB	8.0	13[7]	SL	2.8	ufd	
United Kingdom	SL	4.0	ufd				
United States	SL	3.2	ufd				

Notes:
1. Where there is no statutory rate, or where statutory rates vary within the broad category of "buildings", a typical rate is shown and is used in the calculations
2. Until fully depreciated
3. Switchover at the optimal point is compulsory.
4. The Belgian additional depreciation is set at 1 per cent plus the rate of inflation, within the limits of 3 per cent and 10 per cent.
5. Germany allows for depreciation of assets at 10 percent for four years, 5 per cent for a further three years and 3.5 per cent thereafter.
6. Japan allows only 95 per cent of the value of the asset to be depreciated.
7. Turkey allows a switchover from declining balance to straight line depreciation at the optimum point. However, the remaining value of the asset is then depreciated at a constant rate over the rest of the asset's life.

Table A.1.6: **Capital allowances for machinery used in the calculations**[1]

Country	First period			Second period			Extra first year allowance
	Straight line or declining balance	Allowance rate	Length of first period	Straight line or declining balance	Allowance rate	length of second period	
Australia	DB	18	ufd[2]				
Austria	SL	12.5	ufd				20.0
Belgium	DB	40	2[3]	SL	20.0	ufd	1% + inflation
Canada	DB	25	ufd				
Denmark	DB	30	ufd				
Finland	DB	30	ufd				
France	DB	35.7	5	SL	5.5	ufd	
Germany	DB	30	4	SL	10	ufd	
Greece	SL	20	ufd				
Iceland	SL	12	ufd				
Ireland	DB	50	1	DB	12.5	ufd	
Italy	SL	17.5	3	SL	10	ufd	
Japan	DB	30	4	SL	10	2[5]	
Luxembourg	DB	30	ufd				
Netherlands	SL	12.5	ufd				
New Zealand	DB	10	ufd				
Norway	DB	30	ufd				
Portugal	DB	31.25	ufd				
Spain	DB	20	ufd				5.0
Sweden	DB	30	ufd				
Switzerland	DB	30	ufd				
Turkey	DB	25	7	SL	13.3[6]	ufd	
United Kingdom	DB	25	ufd				
United States	DB	28.6	3	SL	9.1	ufd	

Note:
1. Where there is no statutory rate, or where statutory rates vary within the broad category of "machinery", a typical rate is shown and is used in the calculations
2. Until fully depreciated.
3. Switchover at the optimal point is compulsory.
4. The Belgian additional depreciation is set at 1 per cent plus the rate of inflation, within the limits of 3 per cent and 10 per cent.
5. Japan allows only 95 per cent of the value of the asset to be depreciated.
6. Turkey allows a switchover from declining balance to straight line depreciation at the optimum point. However, the remaining value of the asset is then depreciated at a constant rate over the rest of the asset's life.

Table A.1.7: **Tax treatment of inventories.**

Tax treatment of nominal gains in the value of inventories	Countries
untaxed (e.g. LIFO)	Germany, Greece, Iceland, Italy, Japan, Netherlands, Portugal, Switzerland, United States,
taxed (e.g. FIFO)	Australia, Austria, Belgium, Canada, Denmark[1], Finland[2], France, Ireland, Luxembourg, New Zealand, Norway, Spain, Sweden, Turkey, United Kingdom.

Notes:
1. 30 per cent of the value of stocks can be deducted each year but is added back into taxable income in the following year. This is modelled as setting $v=0.7$.
2. 25 per cent of the values of the stocks can be undervalued.

Table A.1.8: **Treatment of foreign source income.**

Resident country	Treatment of foreign source dividend income from treaty countries	Treatment of foreign source interest income from treaty countries
Australia	exemption	worldwide credit
Austria	exemption	credit by source
Belgium	exemption of 90%, deduction on rest[1]	worldwide credit[2]
Canada	exemption	credit by source
Denmark[3]	exemption	credit by source[4]
Finland	exemption	credit by source[5]
France	exemption of 95%, deduction on rest[1,6]	credit by source
Germany	exemption	credit by source
Iceland	worldwide credit	worldwide credit
Ireland	credit by source	credit by source
Italy	credit by source	credit by source
Japan	worldwide credit	worldwide credit
Luxembourg	exemption	credit by source
Netherlands	exemption	credit by source
New Zealand	credit by source	credit by source
Norway	credit by source	credit by source[7]
Portugal	credit by source	credit by source
Spain[8]	credit by source	credit by source
Sweden	exemption	credit by source
Switzerland	exemption[9]	credit by source
Turkey	credit by source	credit by source
United Kingdom	credit by source	credit by source
United States	worldwide credit	worldwide credit

Notes:
1. For Belgium, France and Italy, a weighted average of those for exemption and deduction has been applied.
2. Belgian interest income from abroad is grossed up by a rate of 15/85, but the tax due on the interest is then reduced by 15 per cent. This results in a tax payment on interest income of 24/85 on the net income received.
3. Denmark has a foreign tax allowance of half of the tax on foreign source income, calculated before treaty or non-treaty reliefs, if the income is from a branch or else from a 100 per cent owned subsidiary where an option to be taxed jointly is taken. In the calculations, this allowance is modelled as involving a reduction in the foreign statutory corporate tax rate of 4.75 per cent providing the project is equity financed. The exceptions are Belgium, Greece and Sweden which get no allowance, and Finland and the US which are modelled as receiving a half allowance.
4. Denmark exempts interest payments from Portugal and Spain.
5. Finland exempts interest payments from Spain.
6. France exempts all dividends from Ireland and Sweden.
7. Norway exempts interest from Belgium, France, Germany, Ireland, Portugal, Sweden, the UK and the US.
8. Spain exempts dividends from Switzerland and interest payments from Portugal.
9. Strictly, Switzerland does not have an exemption system. However, total dividends received from abroad are divided by total income, and this ratio is then used to reduce the Federal income tax. Similar reliefs are given in most cantons. Assuming that cantonal relief is precisely the same as Federal relief, the net effect is as if there were an exemption system.

Table A.1.9: **Treatment of foreign source income from non-treaty countries.**

Resident country	Treatment of foreign source dividend income from non-treaty countries	Treatment of foreign source interest income from non-treaty countries	Non-treaty countries[1]
Australia[2]	worldwide credit	same as treaty	Greece, Iceland, Luxembourg, Portugal, Spain, Turkey
Austria	same as treaty	same as treaty	
Belgium	same as treaty	same as treaty	
Canada	worldwide credit	same as treaty	Greece, Iceland, Portugal, Turkey
Denmark	credit by source	same as treaty	Greece, Turkey
Finland	credit by source	same as treaty	Turkey
France	same as treaty	same as treaty	
Germany	same as treaty	same as treaty	
Greece	same as treaty	same as treaty	
Iceland	same as treaty	same as treaty	
Ireland	deduction	deduction	Greece, Iceland, Portugal, Spain, Turkey
Italy	same as treaty	same as treaty	Iceland, Turkey
Japan	same as treaty	same as treaty	
Luxembourg	same as treaty	same as treaty	Australia, Greece, Iceland, Japan, New Zealand, Portugal, Switzerland, Turkey
Netherlands	same as treaty	deduction	Iceland, Portugal
New Zealand	same as treaty	same as treaty	
Norway	deduction	deduction	Greece
Portugal	deduction	deduction	Australia, Canada, Greece, Iceland, Ireland, Japan, Luxembourg, Netherlands, New Zealand, Sweden , Turkey, US
Spain	same as treaty	same as treaty	
Sweden	same as treaty	same as treaty	Belgium, Luxembourg, Portugal, Turkey
Switzerland	same as treaty	deduction	Luxembourg, Turkey
Turkey	same as treaty	same as treaty	
United Kingdom	same as treaty	same as treaty	
United States	same as treaty	same as treaty	

Note:
1. Only listed if the tax treatment of non-treaty countries is different from that of treaty countries.
2. Australia has a list system; in fact, all the OECD countries with which Australia does not have a treaty are treated as in Table 7.

Table A.1.10 **Withholding taxes on dividends paid between member countries dividends**
(January 1 1991 for wholly owned subsidiary to parent company)

From:	To: Australia	Austria	Belgium	Canada	Denmark	Finland	France	Germany	Greece	Iceland	Ireland	Italy	Japan
Australia*	-	15	15	15	15	15	15	15	NT	0	15	15	15
Austria	15	-	15	15	10	10	15	25	25	NT	0	15	10
Belgium	15	15	-	15	15	10	10	15	15	NT	15	15	15
Canada	15	15	15	-	15	15	10	15	NT	NT	15	15	10
Denmark	15	10	15	15	-	0	0	10	NT	0	0	15	10
Finland	15	10	10	15	0	-	0	10	13	0	0	10	10
France	15	15	10	10	0	0	-	0	25	NT	10	15	10
Germany	15	25	15	15	10	10	0	-	25	5	15	10	15
Greece	NT	42	25	NT	NT	42	42	25	-	NT	NT	25	NT
Iceland	NT	NT	NT	NT	0	0	NT	5	NT	-	NT	NT	NT
Ireland	0	0	0	0	0	0	0	0	NT	NT	NT	0	0
Italy	15	15	15	15	15	10	15	32.4	25	NT	15	-	10
Japan	15	10	15	10	10	10	10	10	NT	NT	10	10	-
Luxembourg	NT	5	0	5	0	5	0	0	0	NT	0	0	NT
Netherlands	15	5	5	10	0	0	5	10	5	NT	0	0	5
New Zealand	15	NT	15	15	15	15	15	15	NT	NT	15	15	15
Norway	15	15	15	15	0	15	5	0	NT	0	0	15	15
Portugal	NT	15	15	NT	15	10	10	15	NT	NT	NT	15	NT
Spain	NT	10	15	15	10	10	15	10	NT	NT	NT	10	10
Sweden	15	0	15	15	0	0	0	5	0	0	5	10	10
Switzerland	15	5	10	15	0	5	5	10	5	5	10	15	10
Turkey	NT	0	0	NT	NT	0	0	0	NT	NT	NT	0	NT
United Kingdom²	0	0	0	0	0	0	0	0	0	0	0	0	0
United States	15	5	5	10	5	5	5	10	30	5	5	10	10

1. Non-treaty rates.
2. Details of abatement of tax credits are given in the United Kingdom country chapter.
*   No withholding on franked dividends, see country chapter.

230

Table A.1.10 (cont) **Withholding taxes on dividends paid between member countries dividends**
(January 1 1991 for wholly owned subsidiary to parent company)

From: \ To:	Luxembourg	Netherlands	New Zealand	Norway	Portugal	Spain	Sweden	Switzerland	Turkey	UK	US	NT[1]
Australia*	NT	15	15	15	NT	NT	15	15	NT	15	15	30
Austria	5	5	NT	15	15	10	10	5	25	5	5	25
Belgium	10	5	15	15	15	15	15	10	NT	5	5	25
Canada	10	10	15	15	NT	15	15	15	NT	10	10	25
Denmark	5	0	15	0	10	10	0	0	NT	0	5	30
Finland	5	0	15	0	10	10	0	5	15	5	5	25
France	5	5	15	5	15	10	0	5	15	5	5	25
Germany	15	15	15	15	15	15	15	15	NT	15	10	25
Greece	NT	35	NT	NT	NT	NT	42	35	NT	42	42	42
Iceland	NT	NT	NT	0	NT	NT	0	5	NT	NT	5	20
Ireland	0	0	0	0	NT	NT	0	0	NT	0	0	0
Italy	15	0	15	15	15	15	10	15	NT	5	5	32.4
Japan	NT	10	15	10	NT	10	10	10	NT	10	10	20
Luxembourg	-	0	NT	5	0	0	5	NT	NT	0	5	15
Netherlands	2.5	-	15	10	NT	5	0	0	10	5	5	25
New Zealand	NT	15	-	15	NT	NT	15	15	NT	15	15	30
Norway	15	15	15	-	15	10	0	5	20	15	15	25
Portugal	NT	NT	NT	10	-	15	NT	10	NT	12	NT	25
Spain	10	10	NT	10	10	-	10	10	NT	10	10	20
Sweden	5	0	15	0	10	5	-	5	NT	0	5	30
Switzerland	NT	0	NT	5	10	10	5	-	NT	5	5	35
Turkey	NT	10	NT	0	0	NT	0	NT	-	0	NT	0
United Kingdom[2]	0	0	0	0	0	0	0	0	0	0	0	0
United States	5	5	15	15	NT	10	5	5	NT	5	-	30

1. Non-treaty rates.
2. Details of abatement of tax credits are given in the United Kingdom country chapter.
* No withholding on franked dividends, see country chapter.

Table A.1.11 Withholding tax on interest paid on a loan from a parent company to a wholly owned subsidiary between member countries interest (January 1 1991)

To:	Australia	Austria	Belgium	Canada	Denmark	Finland	France	Germany	Greece	Iceland	Ireland	Italy	Japan
From:													
Australia	-	10	10	10	10	10	10	10	NT	NT	10	10	10
Austria	0	-	0	0	0	0	0	0	0	NT	0	0	0
Belgium	10	10	-	10	10	10	10	10	10	NT	15	10	10
Canada	15	15	15	-	15	15	10	15	NT	NT	15	15	10
Denmark	0	0	0	0	-	0	0	0	NT	0	0	0	0
Finland	0	0	0	0	0	-	0	0	0	0	0	0	0
France	0	0	0	0	0	0	-	0	0	0	0	0	0
Germany	0	0	0	0	0	0	0	-	0	0	0	0	0
Greece	NT	10	15	NT	NT	10	10	10	-	NT	NT	10	NT
Iceland	NT	NT	NT	NT	0	0	NT	0	NT	-	NT	NT	NT
Ireland	10	0	15	30	0	0	0	0	NT	NT	-	10	10
Italy	10	10	15	15	15	15	15	0	10	NT	10	-	10
Japan	10	10	10	10	10	10	10	10	NT	NT	10	10	-
Luxemburg	NT	0	0	0	0	0	0	0	0	NT	0	0	NT
Netherlands	0	0	0	0	0	0	0	0	0	NT	0	0	0
New Zealand	10	NT	10	15	10	10	10	10	NT	NT	10	10	15
Norway	0	0	0	0	0	0	0	0	NT	0	0	0	0
Portugal	NT	10	15	NT	15	15	10	10	NT	NT	NT	15	NT
Spain	NT	5	15	15	10	10	10	10	NT	NT	NT	12	10
Sweden	0	0	0	0	0	0	0	0	0	0	0	0	0
Switzerland	0	0	0	0	0	0	0	0	0	0	0	0	0
Turkey	NT	10	NT	NT	NT	10	10	NT	NT	NT	NT	NT	NT
United Kingdom	10	0	15	10	0	0	0	0	0	NT	0	10	10
United States	10	0	15	15	0	0	0	0	0	0	0	15	10

1.   Non-treaty rates.
Note: Whenever the non-treaty rate of withholding tax on interest paid for intercompany loans is nil or lower than the treaty rate (Austria, Denmark, Finland, France, Germany, Iceland, Luxembourg, Netherlands, Norway, Sweden, Switzerland, Turkey) then the non-treaty rate applies in practice.

Table A.1.11 (cont) Withholding tax on interest paid on a loan from a parent company to a wholly owned subsidiary between member countries interest (January 1 1991)

From: / To:	Luxemburg	Netherlands	N Zealand	Norway	Portugal	Spain	Sweden	Switerland	Turkey	UK	US	NT[1]
Australia	NT	10	10	10	NT	NT	10	10	NT	10	10	10
Austria	0	0	NT	0	0	0	0	0	0	0	0	0
Belgium	10	10	10	10	10	10	10	10	10	5	10	10
Canada	15	15	15	15	NT	15	15	15	NT	10	15	25
Denmark	0	0	0	0	0	0	0	0	0	0	0	0
Finland	0	0	0	0	0	0	0	0	0	0	0	0
France	0	0	0	0	0	0	0	0	0	0	0	0
Germany	0	0	0	0	0	0	0	0	NT	0	0	0
Greece	NT	10	NT	NT	NT	NT	10	10	NT	0	0	46
Iceland	NT	NT	NT	0	NT	NT	0	NT	NT	NT	0	0
Ireland	0	0	10	0	NT	NT	0	0	NT	0	0	30
Italy	10	10	15	15	15	12	15	12.5	NT	10	15	15
Japan	NT	10	20	10	NT	10	10	10	NT	10	10	20
Luxemburg	-	0	NT	0	NT	0	0	NT	NT	0	0	0
Netherlands	0	-	0	0	NT	0	0	0	0	0	0	0
New Zealand	NT	10	-	10	NT	NT	10	10	NT	10	10	15
Norway	0	0	0	-	0	0	0	0	0	0	0	0
Portugal	NT	NT	NT	15	-	15	NT	10	NT	10	NT	25
Spain	10	10	NT	10	15	-	15	10	NT	12	10	25
Sweden	0	0	0	0	NT	0	-	0	NT	0	0	0
Switzerland	NT	0	0	0	0	0	0	-	NT	0	0	0
Turkey	NT	10	NT	10	NT	NT	NT	NT	-	10	NT	10
United Kingdom	0	0	10	0	10	12	0	0	15	-	0	25
United States	0	0	10	0	NT	10	0	5	NT	0	-	30

1. Non-treaty rates.

Note: Whenever the non-treaty rate of withholding tax on interest paid for intercompany loans is nil or lower than the treaty rate (Austria, Denmark, Finland, France, Germany, Iceland, Luxembourg, Netherlands, Norway, Sweden, Switzerland, Turkey) then the non-treaty rate applies in practice.

3. A worked example: the United Kingdom

This Section illustrates how the results in Chapters 4 and 5 are calculated using the methodology of Section 1 and the parameters shown in Section 2. The illustration here is for the United Kingdom.

The first part of this Section illustrates the computation underlying the results for the real required pre-tax return in the absence of personal taxes shown in Table 4.3. The second part introduces personal taxes, and illustrates the computation of the effective marginal tax wedges shown in Table 4.6. All of the other results in Chapters 4 and 5 are derived in a very similar way to these. The transnational computations for example, use a different definition for the company's discount rate (given in Section 1 of this Annex), but the methodology used is identical to that shown here.

(i) Base Case: Pre-tax real required return with no personal taxes

The starting point is Table 4.3 in the text, which gives the real required pre-tax rate of return, or cost of capital, in the absence of personal taxes. This table shows an average cost of capital for each of retained earnings, debt and new equity. Each is an average of investments in machinery, buildings and inventories. In addition, the table shows an average cost of capital for each type of asset, now averaged across the three types of finance. Finally, it also gives an overall average.

There are a number of steps in reproducing the results in Table 4.3 for the United Kingdom. They are as follows:

Step 1: find the nominal rate of interest (i^h).

This is given, in discrete time, by the formula $i=(1+r)(1+\pi) - 1$, where r is the real interest rate of 5 per cent (i.e. 0.05) and π is the inflation rate of 4.5 per cent (i.e. 0.045). This yields a nominal interest rate, i, of 9.725 per cent (i.e. 0.09725).

Step 2: find the company discount rate for each type of finance (ρ').

For the domestic case, the discount rates, labelled in Section 1 of this Annex, are given in the top row of Table A 1.1 of this Annex. Recall that all personal tax rates are set to zero in Table 4.3 i.e. $m^i=m^d=z=0$. We need to take each source of finance in turn.

Retained earnings: $\rho'=\rho= (1-m^i)i^h/(1-z)$. In this case, since $m^i=z=0$, $\rho'= i^h$
= 0.09725.

New Equity: $\rho'= \rho/\gamma= (1-m^i)(1+\sigma^h)i^h/(1-m^d)$. In this case, $m^i=m^d=0$ and σ^h is minus the imputation rate, which in the UK is 25 per cent (i.e. $\sigma^h=-0.25$). Thus, $\rho' = (1+\sigma^h)i^h = 0.75 \times 0.09725 = 0.0729$.

Debt: $\rho'= (1-\tau^h)i^h$. The UK statutory corporation tax rate, τ^h = 34 per cent (i.e. 0.34), and so $\rho'= (1-\tau^h)i^h = 0.66 \times 0.09725$ = 0.0642.

Step 3: find the present value of depreciation allowances (A^h).

The formulae for the calculation of the present value of depreciation allowances for the domestic case, A^h, are given in expressions (20a) and (20b) of Section 1 of this Annex, for declining balance and straight line schedules, respectively. This must be calculated for each of machinery and buildings (inventories do not receive any allowance). In each case, the present value depends on the company's discount rate, which, as we have seen in Step 2, in turn depends on the source of finance.

Machinery: in the UK, machinery receives a 25 per cent rate depreciation allowance on a declining balance basis. Hence, from the expression in (20a), $\delta Th = 0.25$. As noted above, $\tau^h = 0.34$. There are three possible values of the discount rate, ρ', corresponding to the values given above. We take each in turn:

Retained earnings: $A^h = 0.25 \times 0.34 + (0.75 \times 0.25 \times 0.34)/(0.09725 + 0.25) = 0.2686$.

New Equity: $A^h = 0.25 \times 0.34 + (0.75 \times 0.25 \times 0.34)/(0.0729 + 0.25) = 0.2824$.

Debt: $A^h = 0.25 \times 0.34 + (0.75 \times 0.25 \times 0.34)/(0.0642 + 0.25) = 0.2879$.

Buildings: in the UK, industrial buildings receives a 4 per cent rate depreciation allowance on a straight line basis. Hence, from the expression in (20b), $\beta^h = \delta^{Th} = 0.04$. This implies that buildings are depreciated over 25 years, so that N=25. Using (20b) we again need to take each of the sources of finance in turn.

Retained earnings: $A^h = 0.04 \times 0.34 + (0.04 \times 0.34/0.09725)(1 - 1/1.0972524)$}
                               $= 0.1384$.

New Equity: $A^h = 0.04 \times 0.34 + (0.04 \times 0.34/0.0729)(1 - 1/1.0729^{24}) = 0.1657$.

Debt: $A^h = 0.04 \times 0.34 + (0.04 \times 0.34/0.0642)(1 - 1/1.064224) = 0.1779$.

Thus, in each case the present value of depreciation allowances rises as the discount rate falls, since future allowances are not discounted so heavily.

Step 4: find the real required pre-tax rate of return (p^h).

The formula for the domestic case is given in expression (22) of Section 1 of this Annex. This requires four additional parameters not already used: the economic depreciation rate, δ for machinery, for buildings and for inventories, which are assumed to be 12.25 per cent (i.e. 0.1225) and 3.61 per cent (i.e. 0.0361) and zero, respectively, and the proportion of inventories which are valued using the FIFO method, v, which in the UK is 100 per cent (i.e. 1.0).

There are nine different rate of return which need to be calculated, corresponding to an investment in the three assets each funded from each of the three sources of finance. Again, they are taken in turn.

Machinery:

Retained earnings: $p^h = [(1 - 0.2686) / (0.66 \times 1.045)] \{0.09725 - 0.045$
                        $+ 0.1225(1+0.045)\} - 0.1225 = 0.0687$, or 6.87%.

New Equity: $p^h = [(1 - 0.2824) / (0.66 \times 1.045)] \{0.0729 - 0.045$
                        $+ 0.1225(1+0.045)\} - 0.1225 = 0.0397$, or 3.97%.

Debt: $p^h = [(1 - 0.2879) / (0.66 \times 1.045)] \{0.0642 - 0.045$
                        $+ 0.1225(1+0.045)\} - 0.1225 = 0.0295$, or 2.95%.

Buildings:

Retained earnings: $p^h = [(1 - 0.1384) / (0.66 \times 1.045)] \{0.09725 - 0.045$
                        $+ 0.0361(1+0.045)\} - 0.0361 = 0.0763$, or 7.63%.

New Equity: $p^h = [(1 - 0.1657) / (0.66 \times 1.045)] \{0.0729 - 0.045 + 0.0361(1+0.045)\} - 0.0361 = 0.0433$, or 4.33%.

Debt: $p^h = [(1 - 0.1779) / (0.66 \times 1.045)] \{0.0642 - 0.045 + 0.0361(1+0.045)\} - 0.0361 = 0.0318$, or 3.18%.

Inventories: expression (22b) in Section 1 of this Annex shows the calculation for the cost of capital when the inflationary increase in the value of inventories is taxed. With v=1, the calculations are therefore as follows:

Retained earnings: $p^h = [1/(0.66 \times 1.045)]\{0.09725 - 0.045\} + (0.34 \times 0.045)/[0.66(1+0.045)] = 0.0979$, or 9.79%.

New Equity: $p^h = [1/(0.66 \times 1.045)]\{0.0729 - 0.045\} + (0.34 \times 0.045)/[0.66(1+0.045)] = 0.0626$, or 6.26%.

Debt: $p^h = [1/(0.66 \times 1.045)]\{0.0642 - 0.045\} + (0.34 \times 0.045)/[0.66(1+0.045)] = 0.0500$, or 5.00%.

Step 5: find the weighted average real required pre-tax rates of return (p^h).

Step 4 yielded nine different costs of capital. These are combined into the weighted averages shown in Table 4.3 of Chapter 4 using, weights for asset type of 50 per cent for machinery, 28 per cent for buildings and 22 per cent for inventories, and weights for source of finance of 55 per cent for retained earnings, 10 per cent for new equity and 35 per cent for debt. These weights yield the following table, which correspond to Table 4.3 in Chapter 4.

Worked Example for the UK: domestic real pre-tax required rates of return; no personal taxes; inflation of 4.5 per cent

	Retained earnings	New equity	Debt	Weighted average
Machinery	6.87	3.97	2.95	5.21
Buildings	7.63	4.33	3.18	5.74
Inventories	9.79	6.26	5.00	7.76
Weighted average	7.73	4.57	3.47	5.92

(ii) Effective tax wedge with top rate personal taxes

To calculate the effective tax wedge shown in Table 4.6 in the text (still using an inflation rate of 4.5 per cent) requires two additional elements to those already outlined: the first is to compute the post-tax return to investors(s) and the second is to compute the revised cost of capital. As before, this is done in a number of steps. This example reflects top rate taxpayers in the United Kingdom.

Step 1: Find the post-tax return to investors (s).

This is straightforward, and given by expression (1) of Section 1 of this Annex. It is assumed that nominal interest receipts are taxed in the hands of investors, so that, on interest of i, they pay personal tax of im^i. A top rate taxpayer in the United Kingdom faces a tax rate of 40 per cent on interest income. Thus, for a nominal interest receipt of 9.725 per cent, the investor keeps 5.835 per cent. However, this must be adjusted for inflation to find the real post-tax return, and using expression (1) this is given by:

$$s = (1 + 0.05835) / (1 + 0.045) - 1 = 0.0128 \text{ or } 1.28\%$$

Thus taxing nominal interest receipts reduces the real post-tax return almost to zero: it is clearly possible that the real post-tax return may be negative.

Step 2: Find the revised company's discount rate (ρ').

Adding personal taxes changes the company's discount rate. This is because the return required by the company's shareholders depends on the post-tax return which they can earn elsewhere, and hence on their personal tax rates. A top rate taxpayer in the United Kingdom faces a marginal personal income tax rate on both dividends as well as interest of 40 per cent (i.e. $m^i=m^d=0.4$). She also faces a statutory tax rate on capital gains of 40 per cent. However, capital gains are indexed and not taxed until realisation. The effective accrual equivalent capital gain tax rate for a top rate taxpayer in the United Kingdom is calculated from expression (11a):

$$z = \alpha z^R(1+\rho)/(\alpha+\rho)$$

Setting the proportion of gains realised in each year, α to 10 per cent and taking the shareholders discount rate, ρ to be $(1-m^i)i = 0.6 \times 0.09725 = 0.0584$, yields an effective accrual equivalent capital gains tax rate of 26.73 per cent. The value of $z^i\pi$, the effective rate of indexation allowance for capital gains is the accruals equivalent tax rate multiplied by the inflation rate and so is 1.203 per cent.

These personal tax rates can now be used in the formulae for the company's discount rate given in Table A.1.1 of this Annex. Given the following parameter values: $m^i=m^d=0.4$, $z=0.2673$, $zi\pi=0.0120$, $\sigma^h=-0.25$ and $\tau^h=0.34$, the discount rate for each source of finance is as follows:

Retained earnings:	$\rho' = \rho = [(1-m^i)i^h-z\pi] /(1-z) = [(1-0.4)\times0.09725-0.01203]/(1-.2674) = 0.0632$.
New Equity:	$\rho' = (1+\sigma^h)[(1-m^i)i^h-z\pi]/(1-m^d) = (1-0.25)[(1-0.4)\times0.09725 -0.01203]/(1-0.4) = 0.0579$.
Debt:	$\rho' = (1-\tau^h)i^h = 0.66\times0.09725 = 0.0642$.

It is clear from these calculations that the discount rate for debt is unchanged from the zero personal tax rate case.

Step 3: Find the present value of depreciation allowances (A^h).

The formulae used here are exactly the same as those used above. The only difference is that the revised company discount rates must be used. Since only the retained earnings and new equity cases have changed, the debt formulae is as before.

Machinery:

Retained earnings:	$A^h = 0.25\times0.34 + (0.75\times0.25\times0.34)/(0.0632+0.25) = 0.2885$.
New Equity:	$A^h = 0.25\times0.34 + (0.75\times0.25\times0.34)/(0.0579+0.25) = 0.2920$.

Buildings:

Retained earnings:	$A^h = 0.04\times0.34 + [0.04\times0.34/0.0632][1 - 1/1.0632^{24}] = 0.1793$.
New Equity:	$A^h = 0.04\times0.34 + [0.04\times0.34/0.0579][1 - 1/1.0579^{24}] = 0.1876$.

Step 4: Find the real required pre-tax rate of return (p^h).

Again, the formula is identical to the case described above, and changes here only for retained earnings. The new costs of capital are as follows:

Retained earning:

Machinery: $p^h =$ [(1 - 0.2885) / (0.66 x 1.045)] {0.0632 - 0.045 + 0.1225(1+0.045)} - 0.1225 = 0.0283, or 2.83%.

Buildings: $p^h =$ [(1 - 0.1793) / (0.66 x 1.045)] {0.0632 - 0.045 + 0.0361(1+0.045)} - 0.0361 = 0.0304, or 3.04%.

Inventories: $p^h =$ [1/(0.66 x 1.045)]{0.0632 - 0.045} + (0.34x0.045)/[0.66(1+0.045)] = 0.0486, or 4.86%.

New Equity:

Machinery: $p^h =$ [(1 - 0.2920) / (0.66 x 1.045)] {0.0579 - 0.045 + 0.1225(1+0.045)} - 0.1225 = 0.0221, or 2.21%.

Buildings: $p^h =$ [(1 - 0.1876) / (0.66 x 1.045)] {0.0579 - 0.045 + 0.0361(1+0.045)} - 0.0361 = 0.0235, or 2.35%.

Inventories: $p^h =$ [1/(0.66 x 1.045)]{0.0579 - 0.045} + (0.34x0.045)/[0.66(1+0.045)] = 0.0409, or 4.09%.

Step 5: Find the weighted average real required pre-tax rates of return (p^h).

Once again, weighted average costs of capital can be computed, using the new values for retained earnings. These are as follows:

Worked example for the United Kingdom: domestic real pre-tax required rates of return; top personal tax rates; inflation of 4.5%

	Retained earnings	New equity	Debt	Weighted average
Machinery	2.83	2.21	2.95	2.81
Buildings	3.04	2.35	3.18	3.02
Inventories	4.86	4.09	5.00	4.83
Weighted average	3.34	2.66	3.47	3.32

Step 6: Find the weighted average effective marginal tax wedge (p^h-s).

This is simply the difference between the pre-tax real required rate of return (the cost of capital, p^h) and the post-tax return to the investor (s). the former is given from Step 5 and the latter from Step 1. The difference are given in the table below, the averages from which are the same as given in Table 4.6 in the Chapter 4.

Worked example for the United Kingdom: effective marginal tax wedges; top personal tax rates; inflation of 4.5%

	Retained earnings	New equity	Debt	Weighted average
Machinery	1.55	0.93	1.67	1.53
Buildings	1.76	1.07	1.90	1.74
Inventories	3.58	2.81	3.72	3.55
Weighted average	2.06	1.38	2.19	2.04

Notes

1. The *fixed-r*, case in King Fullerton terminology.

2. Although note that the expressions are derived here in discrete time and therefore differ slightly from the continuous time version of King and Fullerton.

3. Where the investment takes place.

4. Where the parent company is located.

5. All flows are assumed to occur at the end of the period. Thus tax due on profits earned in period t are converted at the exchange rate at the end of period t, labelled E. Setting the exchange rate to unity at the beginning of period t implies no loss of generality.

6. The precise procedure followed is to calculate the effective tax rate $(p-r)/p$ on a domestic investment, financed by new-equity by a zero-rate personal taxpayer who recives no imputation credit, adding withholding tax on dividends to the us to the domestic corporate rate. This effective tax rate can then be compared with the US tax rate to determine the US tax liability.

7. If, for example, a rate z_1^R applies for M years and a rate z_2^R applies for subsequent years, (11a) is modified to:

$$z = \alpha z_1^R \left\{ 1 + \frac{1-\alpha}{1+j} + \frac{(1-\alpha)^2}{(1+j)^2} + \dots + \frac{(1-\alpha)^{M-1}}{(1+j)^{M-1}} \right\}$$

$$+ \frac{\alpha z_2^R (1-\alpha)^M}{(1+j)^M} \left\{ 1 + \frac{1-\alpha}{1+j} + \frac{(1-\alpha)^2}{(1+j)^2} + \dots \right\}$$

$$= \frac{\alpha z_1^R (1+j)}{j+\alpha} \left\{ 1 - \frac{(1-\alpha)^M}{(1+j)^M} \right\} + \frac{\alpha z_2^R (1+j)(1-\alpha)^M}{(j+\alpha)(1+j)^M}$$

More generally, if for any rate z_n^R we label $z_n = \alpha z_n^R (1+j) / (j+\alpha)$, then if there are several changes of statutory rates, with the nth rate used being z_n^R and the length of time from the first year to the year in which each rate is used being M_n, (so that for example, $M_3 > M_2 > M_1$), then z is:

8. Note that the subsidiary does not raise finance from any source other than the parent.

240

$$z = z_1 \left\{ 1 - \frac{(1-\alpha)^{M_1}}{(1+j)^{M_1}} \right\} + z_2 \left\{ \frac{(1-\alpha)^{M_1}}{(1+j)^{M_1}} - \frac{(1-\alpha)^{M_2}}{(1+j)^{M_2}} \right\}$$

$$+ z_3 \left\{ \frac{1-\alpha)^{M_2}}{(1+j)^{M_2}} - \frac{(1-\alpha)^{M_3}}{(1+j)^{M_3}} \right\} + \dots$$

9.   Note that many countries have combinations of straight line and declining balance rules. These can normally be modelled as straightforward extensions of the expressions shown in (16a) and (16b).

10.   More generally, δ^{Ti} can be claimed up to the point at which the remaing proportion of the investment not yet claimed is less than δ^{Ti}. At this point the remainder can be claimed.

11.   The expression shown is for the case in which β^h is equal to δ^{Th}. Intuitively, these can be understood as follows. Under a declining balance system, the company can claim an allowance worth δ^{Th} in period 1, and in succeeding periods δ^{Th} multiplied by the remaining value of the asset: $1-\delta^{Th}$ in period 2, $(1-\delta^{Th})^2$ in period 3, and so on. These allowances must be multiplied by the tax rate, τ^{hr}, and discounted at the company's discount rate, ρ'. Thus:

$$A_D^h = \delta^{Th}\tau^{hr} \left\{ 1 + \frac{(1-\delta^{Th})}{(1+\rho')} + \frac{(1-\delta^{Th})^2}{(1+\rho')^2} + \frac{(1-\delta^{Th})^3}{(1-\rho')^3} + \dots \right\}$$

$$= \frac{\delta^{Th}\tau^{hr}(1+\rho')}{\rho' + \delta^{Th}}$$

Under a straight line system, the company can claim the same allowance, δ^{Th}, in each year until the asset is fully depreciated. In the last year, if the proportion of the asset not yet depreciated, rem, is less than δ^{Th}, then only rem can be claimed. The number of years for which the full allowance can be calculated is N, where $N\delta^{Th} = 1-$ rem. Thus, for example, if $\delta^{Th} = 6\%$, then N = 16 and rem = 4%. This means that an allowance of 6 per cent of the original cost of the asset can be claimed for 16 years and the remaining 4 per cent in the 17th year. Again multiplying by the tax rate, τ^{hr}, and discounting at the company's discount rate, ρ', we have:

The last term, incorporating rem is ignored in the simplified version in (20b).

$$A_S^h = \delta^{Th}\tau^{hr} \left\{ 1 + \frac{1}{(1+\rho')} + \frac{1}{1+\rho')^2} + \dots + \frac{1}{(1+\rho')^{N-1}} \right\} + \frac{\tau^{hr}\text{rem}}{(1+\rho')^N}$$

$$= \frac{\delta^{Th}\tau^{hr}(1+\rho')}{\rho'} \left[1 - \frac{1}{(1+\rho')^N} \right] + \frac{\tau^{hr}\text{rem}}{(1+\rho')^N}$$

12.   This can again be seen as follows. The declining balance system is in operation for M years, yeilding the first part of the allowances, A_1^h, defined from:

$$A_1^h = \delta^{Th}\tau^{hr}\left\{1 + \frac{(1-\delta_1^{Th})}{(1+\rho')} + \frac{(1-\delta_1^{Th})^2}{(1+\rho')^2} + \ldots + \frac{(1-\delta_1^{Th})^{M-1}}{(1+\rho')^{M-1}}\right\}$$

$$= \frac{\delta^{Th}\tau^{hr}(1+\rho')}{\rho'+\delta^{Th}}\left\{1 - \frac{(1-\delta^{Th})^M}{(1+\rho')^M}\right\}$$

The straight line system works as before, with the rate δ_2^{Th} appiled to the original cost of the asset. However, since this system does not begin until year M+1, it is discounted by a factor of $1/(1+\rho')^M$.

13. The expression shown is for the case in which β^h is equal to δ^{Th}.

14. The King Fullerton analysis is set up in continuous time. The difference has no significant impact on the results.

References

Alworth J.S. (1988) *The Finance, Investment and Taxation Decisions of Multinationals*, Basil Blackwell: Oxford.

Hartmann D.G. (1985) "Tax policy and foreign direct investment", Journal of Public Economics.

King M.A. (1974) "Taxation and the cost of capital," *Rewiew of Economic Studies* 41

King M.A. (1977) *Public policy and the corporation*, Chapman and Hall, London.

King M.A. and D. Fullerton (1984) *The Taxation of Income from Capital: a Comparative Study of the US, UK, Sweden and West Germany*, Chicago University Press: Chicago.

Keen M.J. (1990) *Corporation tax, foreign direct investment and the single market*, mimeo, University of Essex.

Sorensen P.B. (1990) *Taxation and the cost of capital in foreign direct investment*, mimeo, Insititute of Economics, University of Copenhagen.

References

Annex 2

Financial non-neutralities in OECD corporate tax systems and the measurement of the degree of mitigation of economic double taxation of dividends

Part 1. Financial non-neutralities

The combined corporate and personal tax burden on the return to corporate investment usually varies depending on the source of corporate finance. In part B of chapter 2 it was mentioned that this tax discrimination may have certain undesirable effects on corporate financing and payout decisions, and that it may also distort the allocation of real investment activity in the economy.

Against this background, the present annex suggests a simple method for quantifying the financial non-neutralities embodied in the corporate tax system and offers some estimates of these non-neutralities in OECD Member countries. The methodology assumes that the controlling shareholder is a household investor who would be subject to ordinary personal income tax on the return to alternative assets if he were to invest in, say, interest-bearing assets rather than shares. To the extent that this assumption is not met, for instance because the controlling shareholder is a tax-exempt institution, the suggested estimates of tax differentials may give a misleading picture of actual distortions of corporate financing decisions.

1. Measuring financial non-neutralities

Under a comprehensive income tax, corporate profits should in principle be taxed at the marginal personal income tax rate of the individual shareholders. In countries where personal income from capital is taxed at a different rate than personal income from other sources, tax neutrality in the capital market would require that corporate profits be taxed at the personal tax rate on capital income.

In the OECD area these neutrality requirements are typically not met. The combined corporate and personal tax burden on distributed corporate profits is usually higher than the tax on income from other sources, while the total tax burden on retained corporate profits is some times higher and sometimes lower than the tax on other types of income, particularly distributed profits. To describe the non-neutralities embodied in the corporate tax system one therefore needs at least two measures: a measure of the differential between the total tax rate on distributed corporate profits and the marginal personal income tax rate (or the marginal personal tax rate on capital income), and a measure of the differential between the total tax rate on retained corporate profits and the marginal personal tax rate (on capital income). These two differentials will characterize the tax discrimination between corporate-source income and other types of income, and the difference between the two differentials will measure the degree of discrimination between distributed and retained corporate profits.

The sections below suggest how the tax differentials mentioned above can be measured. For this purpose the following notation will be used:

T_d = Combined corporate and personal tax on a unit of distributed corporate profits
T_r = Combined corporate and personal tax on a unit of retained corporate profits

td	=	Corporate tax rate on distributed profits
tr	=	Corporate tax rate on retained profits
m	=	Marginal personal income tax rate (on capital income)
c	=	Proportion of dividends allowed as a tax credit against personal tax liability
z	=	Effective marginal personal tax rate on accrued capital gains on shares

2. The "d/i differential"

As already indicated, tax neutrality would require that distributed corporate profits be taxed at the marginal personal tax rate on interest income (m in the notation above). If the total corporate and personal tax on a unit of distributed profits is higher than this, the difference could be termed the "d/i differential" ("i" for "interest") and could be specified as follows:

$$d/i \text{ differential} = (Td - m)/m$$

The d/i differential thus measures the percentage excess of the total tax burden on dividends over the tax burden on interest income. The formula for the differential would be as follows under the different corporate tax systems:

Classical system or split rate system

Td	=	$td + m(1 - td)$
d/i differential	=	$[td + m(1 - td) - m]/m = td(1 - m)/m$

Full imputation

Td	=	$td + (m - td) = m$
d/i differential	=	$(m - m)/m = 0$

Partial imputation

Td	=	$td + m[(1 - td) + c(1 - td)] - c(1 - td)$
d/i differential	=	$\{td + m[(1 - td) + c(1 - td)] - c(1 - td) - m\}/m$
	=	$(1 - m)[td - c(1 - td)]/m$

Dividend deduction

td	=	$0 ==> Td = m$
d/i differential	=	0

Note that the formulas for the full imputation system can also be derived from the formulas for the partial imputation system by setting $c = td/(1 - td)$, since this is the magnitude of the dividend tax credit (c) which will be granted under an imputation system offering full credit for the corporation tax underlying the dividend. Similarly, the dividend deduction system may be seen as a special case of the split rate system where $td = 0$.

To calculate the d/i differential under the special shareholder relief schemes applied in some OECD member countries, the formula for Td would have to be adjusted. For example, in Austria where dividend are taxed at half the progressive personal income tax rate, one has:

Td	=	$td + 0.5(1 - td)m$.

To some readers an alternative interpretation of the d/i differential might be clearer. Under "full integration" of the corporate and the personal tax system, distributed corporate profits would be taxed at the personal tax rate m. An alternative definition — which is equivalent to the one given above — could therefore be:

$$\text{d/i differential} = (Ad - F)/F$$

where

Ad   =   actual corporate and personal tax on distributed corporate profits

F   =   tax on distributed profits under full integration

3. The "r/i differential"

Retained corporate profits are taxed at the rate tr at the corporate level (with tr often being equal to td), but in addition the capital gains on shares stemming from retentions may be subject to personal capital gains tax at shareholder level. Assuming that retentions are reflected in higher share values, the total tax bill produced by a unit of retained earnings is therefore equal to:

$$Tr = tr + z(1 - tr)$$

because one dollar of profits before tax will enable the company to retain 1 - tr dollars after payment of corporate tax, resulting in a personal capital gains tax liability of z(1 — tr).

The assumption that one unit of retained after-tax profits causes an equivalent rise in share values is consistent with the so called "old view" of dividend taxation. By contrast, the so called "new view" implies that share values will typically go up by less than the amount of retained earnings (see section B of chapter 2). In principle firms will invest until shareholders are indifferent at the margin between receiving additional dividend payments and reinvesting money within the firm. When the firm pays a dollar of dividend, the shareholder receives (1 — m) after personal income tax (assuming for simplicity a classical corporate tax system). If the firm retains the dollar for further investment, and the value of the firm's shares appreciates by an amount A, the shareholder will receive an after-tax capital gain of (1 - z)A. According to the new view shareholders have no special preference for net dividends over net capital gains. The firm will thus retain earnings until (1 - m) = (1 - z)A, implying that retention of one additional dollar will cause share values to rise by the amount A = (1 - m)/(1 - z) which is typically less than one, because the effective tax rate on accrued capital gains z is normally lower than the marginal personal tax rate m.

However, the fact that higher retained profits are not fully reflected in higher share values does not reduce the burden of capital gains from the viewpoint of the individual investor. If it is supposed, for instance, that one dollar of corporate investment translates into an increase in the company's stock market value of only 80 cents, an investment of one dollar in the company's shares will then provide the shareholder with a claim on 1/0.8 = 1.25 units of corporate assets. Assuming that one unit of corporate capital earns a profit of 10 cents per year after payment of corporation tax, the shareholder thus has a claim on an after-tax profit of 0.1 x 1.25 = 0.125 dollars. If this profit is retained for investment in the company, the shareholder's stock will appreciate by 0.8 x 0.125= 0.1 dollars, and his net income after capital gains tax will be (1 — z) x 0.1 dollars. Alternatively, if a dollar of corporate investment led to a capital gain on shares of exactly one dollar, the shareholder would have to spend one dollar to purchase a claim on one unit of corporate capital, and if the 10 per cent return on this capital were reinvested in the corporation, the shareholder would again earn a net return of (1 — z) x 0.1.

As this example demonstrates, the disincentive effect of capital gains taxes is not reduced even though retained earnings may not translate into capital gains on a one-to-one basis. For this reason, the above specification of the total tax burden on retained corporate profits (Tr) is not misleading, even if the "new view" might be more correct than the "old view".

By analogy to the "d/i differential", one may use the term "r/i differential" ("r" for "retained profits") to describe the tax discrimination between retained corporate profits and interest income. More precisely, one can define:

$$\text{r/i differential} = (Tr - m)/m = [tr + z(1 - tr) - m]/m$$

The r/i differential thus measures the percentage deviation of the tax burden on retained corporate profits from the tax burden on personal capital income. Note that while the d/i differential will almost always be non-negative, the r/i differential will probably be negative in many continental European countries where the corporate tax rate is typically lower than the top marginal personal income tax rate, and where personal capital gains taxes are very mild.

To calculate the r/i differential, one needs estimates of the effective tax rate on accrued capital gains on shares (z). Such estimates have been produced for the purpose of calculating the marginal tax wedges on corporate investment presented in chapters 4 and 5 of this report, and generally the same estimates of z will be used in the calculations later in this annex[1]. It should be noted that the estimated values of z are sensitive to the rate of inflation chosen.

4. A definition of financial neutrality

Using the two tax differentials defined above, it is possible to give a brief and precise statement of the conditions for neutrality of the corporate tax system towards corporate financing and dividend policies. It has been shown in the literature that the tax system will provide no incentive to use one source of finance rather than another if the total corporate and personal tax burdens on investment financed by debt, retentions and new equity are exactly the same. Since interest on debt is taxed only at the personal level (being deductible at the corporate level), the tax system will thus be neutral towards corporate financing and payout decisions if the d/i differential and the r/i differential are both equal to zero. In that case there will be no tax discrimination between debt and equity and between the two sources of equity.

5. The "d/r differential"

The d/i differential and the r/i differential provide all the information necessary to evaluate the degree of tax discrimination between debt-financed and equity-financed corporate investment as well as the degree of discrimination between new equity and retained earnings. If one wishes to focus particularly on the differential tax treatment of distributed and retained profits, one can explicitly calculate the difference between the d/i differential and the r/i differential. One thereby obtains a measure of the additional tax burden on distributed relative to retained corporate profits. This tax differential may be termed the "d/r differential."

6. The meaning of "economic double tax relief"

Relief of the so-called economic double taxation of dividends implies a reduction of the total tax burden on distributed corporate profits (Td), in one way or another. Such dividend tax relief will be reflected in a reduction of the d/i differential as well as the d/r differential, as these terms have been defined above.

Governments rarely make clear whether the purpose of dividend tax relief is to reduce the tax discrimination between debt and new equity, or whether the purpose is to reduce the discrimination between new equity and retentions. In most cases policy makers probably wish to reduce both types of discrimination. However, it is important to note that dividend tax relief will generally not imply the elimination of both the d/i differential and the d/r differential. For instance, under a full imputation system the d/i differential would be zero, but the d/r differential would be non-zero, unless the total tax burden on retained profits happened to equal the marginal personal income tax rate.

7. *Tax differentials in OECD corporate tax systems*

Table A.2.1 presents the data input used in the calculations whereas table A.2.2 summarises the results of the calculations, using statutory tax rates on capital gains and estimated accrued tax rates, respectively. Country specific information is provided in the notes to the table. Table A.2.2 shows clearly that whatever measure of rates of tax on capital gains are used, financial neutrality between debt and the two sources of equity is rarely achieved.

Table A.2.1 Measuring financial non-neutralities — data input, percentages

| | Corporate tax rates | | | | | Personal tax rates | | | |
| | Central Government | State/regional | Local | Overall tax rate | On Retained Profits | Central Government | State/local | Overall tax on dividends | Overall tax on interest |
	(1)	(2)	(3)	(4)	(5)	(6)	(7)	(8)	(9)
Classical									
Belgium (a)	39.0	-	-	39.0	39.0	25.0	-	25.0	10.0
Luxembourg	33.3	-	9.1	39.4	39.4	51.3	-	51.3	51.3
Netherlands (b)	35.0	-	-	35.0	35.0	60.0	-	60.0	60.0
Switzerland	9.8	12.0	12.0	38.4	38.4	13.0	13.0	43.8	43.8
United States	34.0	6.5	-	38.3	38.3	31.0	7.1	36.0	36.0
Full imputation									
Australia	39.0	-	-	39.0	39.0	48.3	-	48.3	48.3
Finland (c)	23.0	-	17.2	40.2	40.2	39.0	21.0	60.0	10.0
Germany	36.0	-	13.0	44.3	56.5	53.0	-	53.0	53.0
Italy	36.0	-	16.2	47.8	47.8	50.0	-	50.0	30.0
New Zealand	33.0	-	-	33.0	33.0	33.0	-	33.0	33.0
Full dividend deduction									
Greece	40.0	-	-	40.0	40.0	50.0	-	50.0	50.0
Norway (d)	27.8	-	23.0	50.8	50.8	14.0	5.5	19.5	40.5
Other									
Austria (e)	30.0	-	12.9	39.0	39.0	25.0	-	25.0	50.0
Canada	23.8	11.9	-	35.7	35.7	31.9	17.2	49.1	49.1
Denmark (f)	38.0	-	-	38.0	38.0	45.0	-	45.0	57.8
France (g)	42.0	-	-	42.0	34.0	57.9	-	57.9	18.1
Iceland (h)	45.0	-	-	45.0	45.0	32.8	7.0	39.8	0.0
Ireland (i)	10.0	-	-	10.0	10.0	53.0	-	53.0	53.0
Japan (j)	37.5	-	18.5	50.0	50.0	35.0	-	35.0	20.0
Portugal (k)	36.0	-	3.6	39.6	39.6	25.0	-	25.0	25.0
Spain	35.0	-	-	35.0	35.0	56.0	-	56.0	56.0
Sweden (l)	30.0	-	-	30.0	30.0	30.0	-	30.0	30.0
Turkey (m)	46.0	-	-	49.2	49.2	0.0	-	0.0	10.0
United Kingdom	34.0	-	-	34.0	34.0	40.0	-	40.0	40.0

Table A.2.1 (cont) **Measuring financial non-neutralities — data input, percentages**

	Statutory capital gains top rate	Effective tax rate on accrued capital gains	Actual total tax burden on dividends	Retained earnings	
				Actual total tax burden using statutory rates (col (10))	Actual total tax burden using accrued rates (col (11))
	(10)	(11)	(12)	(13)	(14)
Classical					
Belgium (a)	0.0	0.00	54.3	39.0	39.0
Luxembourg	0.0	0.00	70.5	39.4	39.4
Netherlands (b)	0.0	0.00	74.0	35.0	35.0
Switzerland	0.0	0.00	65.4	38.4	38.4
United States	36.0	23.51	60.5	60.5	52.8
Full imputation					
Australia	48.3	17.36	48.3	68.3	49.6
Finland (c)	60.0	27.18	60.0	76.1	56.5
Germany	0.0	0.00	56.9	56.5	56.5
Italy	25.0	15.90	52.6	60.9	56.1
New Zealand	0.0	0.00	33.0	33.0	33.0
Full dividend deduction					
Greece	0.0	0.00	50.0	40.0	40.0
Norway (d)	40.0	10.30	45.2	70.5	55.9
Other					
Austria (e)	50.0	5.00	54.3	69.5	42.1
Canada	36.8	25.83	57.9	59.4	52.3
Denmark (f)	57.8	10.78	65.9	73.8	44.7
France (g)	18.1	10.88	63.4	45.9	41.2
Iceland (h)	39.8	11.33	45.0	66.9	51.3
Ireland (i)	50.0	13.7	30.2	55.0	22.4
Japan (j)	20.0	12.12	62.5	60.0	56.1
Portugal (k)	10.0	1.84	51.7	45.6	40.7
Spain	56.0	14.73	64.9	71.4	44.6
Sweden (l)	30.0	19.06	40.5	46.1	37.7
Turkey (m)	50.0	29.00	49.2	74.6	63.9
United Kingdom	40.0	13.75	47.2	60.4	43.1

Table A.2.2 **Measuring financial non-neutralities — results (per cent)**

	Statutory rates			Accrued rates		
	Dividend/interest	Retained earnings/ interest	Dividend/ retained earnings	Dividend/ interest	Retained earnings/ interest	Dividend/ retained earnings
	(1)	(2)	(3)	(4)	(5)	(6)
Classical						
Belgium (a)	443.0	290.0	153.0	443.0	290.0	153.0
Luxembourg	37.4	-23.2	60.6	37.4	-23.2	60.6
Netherlands (b)	23.3	-41.7	65.0	23.3	-41.7	65.0
Switzerland	49.3	-12.3	61.6	49.3	-12.3	61.6
United States	68.1	68.1	0.0	68.1	46.7	21.3
Full imputation						
Australia	0.0	41.7	-41.4	0.0	2.7	-2.7
Finland (c)	500.0	661.0	-161.0	500.0	465.0	35.0
Germany	7.4	6.6	0.8	7.4	6.6	0.8
Italy	75.3	103.0	-27.7	75.3	87.0	-11.7
New Zealand	0.0	0.0	0.0	0.0	0.0	0.0
Full dividend deduction						
Greece	0.0	-20.0	20.0	0.0	-20.0	20.0
Norway (d)	11.6	74.1	-62.5	11.6	38.0	-26.4
Other						
Austria (e)	8.6	39.0	-30.4	8.6	-15.8	24.4
Canada	17.7	20.9	-3.1	17.7	6.5	11.2
Denmark (f)	14.0	27.7	-13.7	14.0	-22.7	36.7
France (g)	250.1	153.8	96.3	250.1	127.5	122.6
Iceland (h)	-	-	-	-	-	-
Ireland (i)	-43.0	3.8	-46.8	-43.0	57.7	14.7
Japan (j)	212.5	200.0	28.5	212.5	180.5	48.0
Portugal (k)	106.8	82.4	24.4	106.8	62.8	44.0
Spain	15.9	27.5	-11.6	15.9	-20.4	36.3
Sweden (l)	35.0	53.7	-18.7	35.0	25.7	9.3
Turkey (d)	392.0	646.0	-254.0	329.0	539.0	147.0
United Kingdom	18.0	51.0	-33.0	18.0	7.8	10.3

Notes to tables A.2.1 and A.2.2

(a) Belgium: WHT is final tax paid.
(b) Netherlands: Exemption for first Fl1000 (Fl2000 for couples) of interest income has not been taken into account.
(c) Finland: Rate of interest on unregulated deposits. Interest on regulated deposits and bonds are exempt
(d) Norway: Ignores exemption of first NOK 3000 (NOK 6000 for couples)on interest income.
(e) Austria: Individuals are exempt from tax on interest up to the extent that the par value of bonds does not exceed a certain amount and subject to certain conditions.
(f) Denmark: The effective tax rate on accrued capital gains will be zero if the shares are held for more than 3 years.
(g) France: Taxpayers can elect that the WHT be the final tax paid. It is assumed that such an election has been made.
(h) Iceland: Interest is exempt from tax.
(i) Ireland: WHT on interest is deducted at a rate of 30 per cent. Individuals subject to tax at higher rates are taxed at the difference between this rate and the appropriate higher rate, i.e interest is effectively taxed as ordinary income if the individual's marginal rate is 30 per cent or greater. Calculations include for 10 per cent "half-exemption" distributions.
(j) Japan: WHT is normally the final tax paid. The WHT rate on interest is 20 per cent.
(k) Portugal: WHT is normally the final tax paid. The WHT rate is 25 per cent on bonds and shares not quoted on the Portuguese stock exchange.
(l) Sweden: Interest income is taxed at a flat rate of 30 per cent. Corporate retained earnings are taxed at 33 per cent at the corporate level although the statutory tax rate is 30 per cent (effect of allocation to tax equalisation reserve on corporate equity).
(m) Turkey: See country chapter for details of system.
(n) United Kingdom: The corporate tax rate will fall to 33 per cent in 1991/92.

Part 2. Measurement of the degree of mitigation

I. Introduction

The purpose of this part is to define a measure of the degree of mitigation in corporate tax systems and to apply this measure to the various tax systems operating within Member countries. Calculation of the degree of mitigation is based on the following simplifying assumptions:

(i) Corporation tax is fully borne by profits, i.e. a rise in corporation tax would reduce profits by the same amount;

(ii) The dividend pay-out ratio of after-tax profits is 100 per cent. For split rate systems this implies that all profits are taxed at the distributed profits rate;

(iii) Dividends are received by resident individuals;

(iv) In determining what the "no mitigation" situation would be in each country, it is assumed that statutory rates of both personal and corporate tax would remain unchanged;

(v) The amount of pre-tax corporate income available for distribution remains the same, regardless of the level of tax rates or the degree of mitigation.

Relaxing the 100 per cent dividend payout assumption does not affect the degree of mitigation except in the case of imputation systems where the credit available exceeds the personal income tax liability and where such credits are non-refundable (i.e potentially for Australia, Italy and New Zealand). In addition to the above assumptions, the degree of mitigation has been calculated under the following three different scenarios:

Scenario 1: Taxpayers, both corporate and individual, face only the central government income tax;

Scenario 2: Individual taxpayers face the **maximum** marginal income tax rate, inclusive of state, regional and local taxes while corporations face the income tax of both central and lower levels of government;

Scenario 3: Individual taxpayers face the **average** marginal tax rate on dividends while corporations face the income tax of both central and lower levels of government.

2. Methodology

The degree of mitigation of the total income tax (corporate plus personal) on one unit of corporate profit under each different scenario is calculated as the percentage reduction actually provided in a given corporate tax system in the differential between total tax under no mitigation and total tax under full mitigation[2] i.e.

$$\text{Degree of mitigation} = \frac{\text{Tax under no mitigation} - \text{Actual total tax burden}}{\text{Tax under no mitigation} - \text{Tax under full mitigation}}$$

Tax under no mitigation (expressed in terms of scenario 2 for simplicity of presentation — as has been done throughout the annex) is the total income tax liability under a classical system:

$$\text{Tax under no mitigation} = TY + [(1-T)Y] M$$

Where;

Y   =   taxable profits
T   =   total corporate tax rate -- inclusive of state, regional and local taxes i.e:
T   =   tn + tl
tn   =   central government corporate tax rate
tl   =   combined state, regional and local government corporate tax rate
M   =   total maximum marginal personal tax — inclusive of state, regional and local taxes[3]
          , i.e. M = mc + ml
mc   =   central government maximum personal income tax rate
ml   =   combined state, regional and local government personal tax rate

Full mitigation occurs when corporate income is taxed at the taxpayer's marginal rate i.e.

Tax under full mitigation   =   MY

Here there is no corporate tax paid, the corporate tax being an advance payment of the personal income tax.

Actual total tax burdens vary according to the tax system in operation as follows:

(i) Classical systems

For countries operating classical tax systems total income tax liability (L) is equal to:

$$L = TY + [(1-T)Y]M$$

where TY represents tax at the corporate level and $[(1-T)Y]M$, personal tax on dividend income. Countries operating classical systems include Belgium, Luxembourg, Netherlands, Switzerland, and the United States.

(ii) Full imputation

Under full imputation systems the total income tax liability is given by:

$$L = TY + \{[(1-T)Y + TY]M — TY\}$$

tax at
corporate   — personal tax —-
level

Full imputation systems operate in Australia, Finland, Germany, Italy and New Zealand.

In addition, Turkey operates a system with a net effect similar to full imputation systems. However, dividends paid out of profits bearing corporate tax are excluded from taxable income. Thus, total income tax for Turkey is given by:

$$L = TY + 0$$

tax at
corporate   personal tax
level

(iii) Partial imputation

The total income tax liability under partial imputation systems is calculated in a similar manner to total income tax under full imputation except that the imputation credit is related to dividends received rather than tax paid at the corporate level. If the proportion of dividends allowed as a tax credit is defined as "c", total tax becomes:

$$L \quad = \quad \underset{\substack{\text{tax at} \\ \text{corporate} \\ \text{level}}}{TY} \quad + \quad \underset{\text{personal tax}}{\{[(1\text{-}T)Y + c(1\text{-}tn)Y]M - c(1\text{-}tn)Y\}}$$

Partial imputation systems operate in France, Ireland and the United Kingdom.

(iv) Full dividend deduction

Under full dividend deduction schemes distributed profits are not subject to central government tax at the corporate level. At the personal level the tax treatment varies.

(a) Greece

In Greece dividends are subject to withholding tax. The taxpayer can elect to include dividends from registerd shares in taxable income. In this case such income is taxed at ordinary rates and a credit for the withholding tax is allowed against income tax. The withholding tax rate for registered shares is 42 per cent. Assuming such an election is made the total tax liability is given by:

$$L \quad = \quad \{[(1 - 0.42)Y]M - 0.42Y\}$$

(b) Norway

In Norway dividends are deductible from the central government tax only and thus distributed profits are subject to municipal tax at the corporate level. At the personal level, domestic dividends are exempt from the municipal income tax but not the tax to the equalization fund, thus the total income tax liability becomes:

$$L \quad = \quad \underset{\substack{\textbf{tax at} \\ \textbf{corporate} \\ \textbf{level}}}{\frac{tl + te}{1 - tn} \cdot Y} \quad + \quad \underset{\textbf{personal tax}}{\left[1 - \frac{tl + te}{1 - tn}\right] \cdot Y \cdot (mc + me)}$$

Where;

te = corporate income tax to the tax equalisation fund; and
me = personal income tax to the tax equalisation fund.

(v) Partial dividend deduction

For Swedish corporations, dividends on <u>new issues</u> are deductible as far as the receiver of the dividends is liable to tax. The annual deduction is limited to 10 per cent of the amount of issue and the total deduction is limited to the amount of issue. The special nature of the deduction makes the calculation of the total income tax liability (as well as the other components in the measure of the degree of mitigation) rather complex and there is a need for some additional assumptions regarding among other things the interest rate and the growth of dividends. Furthermore, the effect of the tax equalisation reserve, which allows the corporation to allocate 30 per cent of equity capital to the reserve, must also be taken into account. Total income tax liability is given by:

$$L \quad = \quad \underbrace{(T-d)Y}_{\substack{\text{tax at} \\ \text{corporate} \\ \text{level}}} + \quad \underbrace{[1-(T-d)Y]M}_{\text{personal tax}}$$

Where;

$d =$ the effective deduction from corporate income tax for dividends on new issues.

(vi) Partial shareholder relief

Total income tax liabilities under partial shareholder relief schemes vary from country to country depending on the type of scheme used.

(a) Austria

In Austria corporate income is fully taxed while distributed profits are taxed at half the progressive personal income tax rate. Thus total income tax becomes:

$$L \quad = \quad \underbrace{TY}_{\substack{\text{tax at} \\ \text{corporate} \\ \text{level}}} + \quad \underbrace{0.5[(1-T)Y]M}_{\text{personal tax}}$$

(b) Canada

Dividends from Canadian corporations are grossed up by 25 per cent for inclusion in taxable income. A credit may then be claimed for 16.67 per cent of dividends received. An additional provincial credit is also available. The provincial credit is proportional to the province's tax rate and so the combined federal-provincial dividend tax credit will vary from province to province. For the purpose of this exercise, a weighted average provincial tax rate of 62 per cent (prior to surtaxes, flat taxes and provincial credits) has been used, giving a provincial credit of 10.33 per cent (62 per cent of 16.67) and a combined credit of 27 per cent. This gives a total tax liability under scenarios 2 and 3 equal to:

$$L \quad = \quad \underbrace{TY}_{\substack{\text{tax at} \\ \text{corporate} \\ \text{level}}} + \quad \underbrace{\{[(1-T)1.25Y]M - 0.27[(1-T)Y]\}}_{\text{personal tax}}$$

Under scenario one the dividend tax credit is 16.67 per cent

(c) Denmark

Danish dividends are taxed by a dividend withholding tax, at a rate of 30 per cent for dividends less than Dkr 30 000 per year and 45 per cent for dividends which exceed Dkr 30 000 per year. This latter rate is the rate used for both scenarios 1 and 2. The total tax liability under the Danish system under scenarios 1 and 2 is thus given by:

$$L \quad = \quad TY \quad + \quad 0.45(1\text{-}T)$$

$$\underset{\substack{\text{tax at} \\ \text{corporate} \\ \text{level}}}{} \qquad \underset{\text{personal tax}}{}$$

Under scenario 3 the average tax rate on dividends is substituted for the 45 per cent rate.

(d) Iceland

Provided certain conditions are met, Iceland can be classified as operating both partial dividend deduction and partial shareholder relief schemes, with the possibility of a degree of mitigation in excess of 100 per cent. For the purposes of this annex, however, it is assumed that dividends received are less than 15 per cent of the total amount of shares owned by the individual and, therefore, that dividends are exempt from personal income tax. Under this assumption the total income tax liability is given by:

$$L \quad = \quad (T \text{-} d)Y$$

where d equals the effective deduction of dividends from corpoorate income tax or 15 per cent of total value.

(e) Japan

Japan effectively operates a classical system with the exception that taxpayers can deduct 7.8 per cent (5 per cent for national tax, 2.8 per cent for local tax) of dividends received from their income tax. Under scenarios 2 and 3, total income tax is thus equal to:

$$L \quad = \quad TY \quad + \quad \{[(1\text{-}T)Y]M - 0.078(1\text{-}T)Y\}$$

$$\underset{\substack{\text{tax at} \\ \text{corporate} \\ \text{level}}}{} \qquad \underset{\text{personal tax}}{\underline{\qquad}}$$

Under scenario one, the 7.8 per cent income tax deduction becomes a 5 per cent deduction, i.e. the local deduction is excluded.

(f) Portugal

In Portugal a withholding tax of 25 per cent is the final tax paid unless the shareholder elects otherwise. If an election is made a tax credit of 35 per cent of the underlying corporate income tax is included in taxable income and deducted from the tax liability. Assuming that such an election is made, total income tax becomes:

$$L \quad = \quad TY \quad + \quad \{[(1\text{-}T)Y + 0.35tnY]M - 0.35tnY\}$$

$$\underset{\substack{\text{tax at} \\ \text{corporate} \\ \text{level}}}{} \qquad \underset{\text{personal tax}}{\underline{\qquad}}$$

(g) Spain

Spain operates a system wherby at the corporate level distributed profits are taxed as ordinary income and at the personal level taxpayers can deduct 10 per cent of dividends received from their income tax. Total income tax is thus equal to:

$$L = TY + \{[(1-T)Y]M - 0.1(1-T)Y\}$$

tax at corporate level ——— personal tax ———

3. Results

Table A.2.3 shows the degree of mitigation under various Member country tax systems in 1991 under the assumption that taxpayers face only central government taxes, Table A.2.4 shows the degree of mitigation under the assumption that taxpayers face the maximum personal marginal income tax rate including all levels of government, while Table A.2.5 shows the degree of mitigation under the assumption that taxpayers face the average rate of tax on dividends. The various assumptions made in compiling these rates, other than those outlined above, are summarised in the footnotes to the tables.

Key conclusions to emerge from the tables are:

— In the case of countries operating classical systems (Belgium, Luxembourg, Netherlands, Switzerland and the United States) there is, as expected no mitigation of corporate tax. This result is true irrespective of the existence of intermediate and local taxes and of the level of the personal income tax rate.

— Full imputation countries (i.e Australia, Finland, Germany, Italy, New Zealand), also as expected, ensure full mitigation of corporate income tax at the central government level. Once intermediate and local taxes are taken into account, however, corporate income tax becomes less than fully mitigated (for Germany). In the case of Italy, although local taxes exist, these are not levied on dividend income and thus the degree of mitigation is unaffected by their existence.

— At the central government level, full mitigation of the corporate income tax is ensured under full dividend deduction schemes (Greece, Norway).

— In other countries, there is substantial variation in the degree of mitigation across countries and even within countries classified in the same group. For example, the degree of mitigation in countries operating partial imputation systems (France, Ireland and the United Kingdom) ranges from 65 per cent in the case of United Kingdom to 50 per cent in the case of Ireland.

— The choice of personal income tax rate affects the degree of mitigation for Austria, Denmark, Iceland, Japan, Spain and Turkey.

— A final point to note is the link between the total tax burden (i.e combined corporate and personal income tax burden, see table A.2.4) and the choice of corporate tax system. For countries operating classical systems the average nominal total income tax burden is 65 per cent. This compares with only 50 per cent in the case of full imputation countries. Thus, it would appear that, on average, full imputation countries have chosen lower combined tax rates on distributed profits than classical countries.

Table A.2.3: Scenario 1 — **Degree of mitigation assuming taxpayers face central government tax only, 1991.** (per cent)

	Corporate tax	Personal tax	Tax under full mitigation	Tax under no mitigation	Actual total tax burden	Degree of mitigation
	(1)	(2)	(3)	(4)	(5)	(6)
Classical						
Belgium (a)	39.0	25.0	25.0	54.3	54.3	0.0
Luxembourg (b)	33.3	51.3	51.3	70.5	70.5	0.0
Netherlands (c)	35.0	60.0	60.0	74.0	74.0	0.0
Switzerland (d)	9.8	13.0	13.0	21.5	21.5	0.0
United States (a)	34.0	31.0	31.0	54.5	54.5	0.0
Full imputation						
Australia	39.0	48.3	48.3	68.5	48.3	100.0
Finland (e)	23.0	39.0	39.0	53.0	39.0	100.0
Germany (f)	36.0	53.0	53.0	69.9	53.0	100.0
Italy (g)	36.0	50.0	50.0	68.0	50.0	100.0
New Zealand	33.0	33.0	33.0	55.1	33.0	100.0
Full dividend deduction						
Greece	40.0	50.0	50.0	70.0	50.0	0.0
Norway (a)	27.8	14.0	14.0	37.9	14.0	100.0
Other						
Austria (h)	30.0	25.0	25.0	47.5	38.8	38.9
Canada (i)	23.8	31.9	31.9	48.1	39.5	53.2
Denmark (a)	38.0	45.0	28.0	55.4	65.9	-38.3
France	42.0	57.9	57.9	75.6	63.4	69.0
Iceland (j)	45.0	32.8	32.8	63.0	45.0	59.7
Ireland (k)	10.0	53.0	53.0	57.7	55.4	50.0
Japan	37.5	35.0	35.0	59.4	53.1	25.8
Portugal	36.0	25.0	25.0	52.0	48.8	11.9
Spain	35.0	56.0	56.0	71.4	64.9	42.2
Sweden (l)	33.0	30.0	30.0	51.1	40.5	34.8
Turkey (m)	49.2	0.0	0.0	49.2	49.2	0.0
United Kingdom	34.0	40.0	40.0	60.4	47.2	64.7

Table A.2.4: Scenario 2 — Degree of mitigation assuming individuals face maximum marginal personal income tax rates on dividends, 1991. (Per cent)

	Corporate tax			Overall tax(l),(m)	Personal tax		Overall tax(m),(n)	Tax under full mitigation	Tax under no mitigation	Actual total tax burden	Degree of mitigation
	Central Govt	State/local	Local		Central Govt	State/local					
	(1)	(2)	(3)	(4)	(5)	(6)	(7)	(8)	(9)	(10)	(11)
Classical											
Belgium (a)	39.0	-	-	39.0	25.0	-	25.0	25.0	54.3	54.3	0.0
Luxembourg (b)	33.3	-	9.1	39.4	51.3	-	51.3	51.3	70.5	70.5	0.0
Netherlands(c)	35.0	-	-	35.0	60.0	-	60.0	60.0	74.0	74.0	0.0
Switzerland (d)	9.8	12.0	12.0	38.7	13.0	13.0	43.8	43.8	65.4	65.4	0.0
United states (a)	34.0	6.5	-	38.3	31.0	7.1	36.0	36.0	60.5	60.5	0.0
Full imputation											
Australia	39.0	-	-	39.0	48.3	-	48.3	48.3	68.5	48.3	100.0
Finland (e)	23.0	-	17.2	40.2	39.0	21.0	60.0	60.0	76.1	60.0	100.0
Germany (f)	36.0	-	13.0	44.3	53.0	-	53.0	53.0	73.8	56.9	81.2
Italy (g)	36.0	-	16.2	47.8	50.0	-	50.0	50.0	73.9	50.0	100.0
New Zealand	33.0	-	-	33.0	33.0	-	33.0	33.0	55.1	33.0	100.0
Full dividend deduction											
Greece	40.0	-	-	40.0	50.0	-	50.0	50.0	70.0	50.0	100.0
Norway (a)	27.8	-	23.0	50.8	14.0	5.5	19.5	40.5	70.7	45.2	84.8
Other											
Austria (h)	30.0	-	12.9	39.0	25.0	-	25.0	25.0	54.3	54.3	0.0
Canada (i)	23.8	11.9	-	35.7	31.9	17.2	49.1	49.1	67.3	57.9	52.0
Denmark (a)	38.0	-	-	38.0	45.0	-	45.0	57.8	73.8	65.9	49.4
France	42.0	-	-	42.0	57.9	-	57.9	57.9	75.6	63.4	69.0
Iceland (j)	45.0	-	-	45.0	32.8	7.0	39.8	39.8	66.9	45.0	81.0
Ireland (k)	10.0	-	-	10.0	53.0	-	53.0	53.0	57.7	55.4	50.0
Japan	37.5	-	18.5	50.0	35.0	-	35.0	35.0	67.5	62.5	15.4
Portugal	36.0	-	3.6	39.6	25.0	-	25.0	25.0	54.7	51.7	10.0
Spain	35.0	-	-	35.0	56.0	-	56.0	56.0	71.4	64.9	42.2
Sweden (l)	30.0	-	-	30.0	30.0	-	30.0	30.0	51.0	40.5	50.0
Turkey (m)	46.0	-	-	49.2	0.0	-	0.0	0.0	49.2	49.2	0.0
United Kingdom	34.0	-	-	34.0	40.0	-	40.0	40.0	60.4	47.2	64.7

261

Table A.2.5 Scenario 3 — Degree of mitigation assuming individuals face the average marginal tax rate on dividends, 1991 (per cent)

| | Corporate tax | | | Overall tax(l),(m) | Average tax rate on dividends | Tax under full mitigation | Tax under no mitigation | Actual total tax burden | Degree of mitigation |
	Central Govt	State/local	Local						
	(1)	(2)	(3)	(4)	(5)	(6)	(7)	(8)	(9)
Classical									
Belgium (a)	39.0	-	-	39.0	25.0	25.0	54.3	54.3	0.0
Luxembourg (b)	33.3	-	9.1	39.4	24.6	24.6	54.3	54.3	0.0
Netherlands (c)	35.0	-	-	35.0	49.0	49.0	66.9	66.9	0.0
Switzerland (d)	9.8	12.0	12.0	38.4	30.8	30.8	57.3	57.3	0.0
United States (a)	34.0	6.5	-	38.3	31.0	31.0	57.4	57.4	0.0
Full imputation									
Australia	39.0	-	-	39.0	39.0	39.0	62.8	39.0	100.0
Finland (e)	23.0	-	17.2	40.2	45.2	45.2	67.2	45.2	100.0
Germany (f)	36.0	-	13.0	44.3	39.1	39.1	66.1	44.2	81.2
Italy (f)	36.0	-	16.2	47.8	39.4	39.4	68.4	43.9	84.5
New Zealand	33.0	-	-	33.0	28.6	28.6	52.2	28.6	100.0
Full dividend deduction									
Greece	40.0	-	-	40.0	n.a.	n.a.	n.a.	n.a.	n.a.
Norway (a)	27.8	-	23.0	50.8	n.a.	n.a.	n.a.	n.a.	n.a.
Other									
Austria (h)	30.0	-	12.9	39.0	19.8	19.8	51.1	51.1	0.0
Canada (i)	23.8	11.9	-	35.7	44.6	44.6	64.4	54.2	51.4
Denmark (a)	38.0	-	-	38.0	37.6	51.1	69.7	61.3	45.2
France	42.0	-	-	42.0	45.0	45.0	68.1	52.2	69.0
Iceland (j)	45.0	-	-	45.0	15.8	15.8	53.7	45.0	23.0
Ireland (k)	10.0	-	-	10.0	27.0	27.0	34.3	30.7	50.0
Japan	37.5	-	18.5	50.0	35.0	35.0	67.5	63.6	12.0
Portugal	36.0	-	3.6	39.6	25.0	25.0	54.7	51.7	10.0
Spain	35.0	-	-	35.0	28.4	28.4	53.5	47.0	25.9
Sweden (l)	30.0	-	-	30.0	30.0	30.0	46.1	40.5	34.8
Turkey (m)	46.0	-	-	49.2	0.0	0.0	49.2	49.2	0.0
United Kingdom	34.0	-	-	34.0	32.0	32.0	55.1	40.2	64.7

Notes to tables A.2.3 to A.2.5

(a)   Belgium, United States, Norway, Denmark: The state/local personal tax rates used are an overall average throughout the country. In addition, the rate shown for Norway is the combined total for local and regional taxes.

(b)   Luxembourg: Overall corporate tax rate based on rates for Luxembourg city. In addition, it includes the 1 per cent surcharge on corporate tax. The surtax is 2.5 per cent on personal income. This surtax is used for an unemployment fund.

(c)   The Netherlands have a divided exemption system of 1 000 Guilders per shareholder which has not been taken into account in the calculations.

(d)   Switzerland: The overall tax on corporate income in Switzerland ranges from 13.15 per cent to 38.36 per cent. For the purposes of this exercise maximum rates have been used. The rates shown are for Zurich. Overall rates are arrived at using the appropriate cantonal multipliers.

(e)   Finland: Overall average tax rates.

(f)   Germany: Overall personal income tax rate includes 9 per cent church tax.

(g)   Italy: No local tax is levied on dividend income.

(h)   Austria: Dividends are taxed at one-half of the statutory income tax rates.

(i)   Canada: Weighted average provincial rates applicable, inclusive of surtaxes and flat taxes. The corporate tax rate is the rate applicable to manufacturing profits.

(j)   Iceland: Calculation assumes that dividend payments in question are in excess of the 15 per cent of the total value of shares and, therefore, are not deductible from the corporate tax base. Relaxing this assumption could result in greater than full mitigation.

(k)   Ireland: This calculation ignores the "half-exemption" for 10 per cent distributions.

(l)   Sweden: The nominal corporation tax rate of 30 per cent and the tax equalization reserve gives an effective tax rate at the corporate level of 23 per cent in the no mitigation case, and 15 per cent in the actual total tax case.

(m)   Turkey: Overall corporate tax rate includes supplement levies to a total of 7 per cent; see also note d. to tables A.2.1. and A.2.2.

(n)   Overall corporate tax calculations based on Country Chapter overall tax calculations (refer DAFFE/WP2/90.1/REV). Rates shown apply to distributed profits.

(o)   Deductibility of state and/or local taxes has been taken into account in the overall tax calculations where applicable.

(p)   Excluding social security contributions.

Notes and references

1.   In fact, the figures are not identical for those countries which index capital gains, where the value of the indexation enters as a seperate variable for the purposes of the calculations in chapters 4 and 5.

2.   An alternative methodology for measuring the degree of mitigation is expressed in terms of the proportionate change in net income received rather than in terms of tax liabilities. This alternative measure (M2) can be defined as follows:

$$\text{Degree of Mitigation} = \frac{\text{Actual net income}}{\text{Net income under full mitigation}}$$

The two measures are, of course, related and the relationship between the two can be expressed as follows, using the partial imputation system as an example:

$$\text{Measure 1} = c\frac{(1 - T)}{T}$$
$$\text{Alternative measure M2} = (1 - T)(1 + c)$$
$$\text{i.e. M2} = T\frac{(1 + c)}{c} \times \text{measure 1}$$

3.   For the degree of mitigation under the assumption that taxpayers face the average rate of tax on dividends, M becomes the average rate of tax on dividends.

Annex 3

Taxation and the international allocation of capital: Some theoretical observations

As a supplement to the discussion in part D of Chapter 2, this annex explains in more detail some effects of the tax system on the international allocation of capital. The first section illustrates the impact of various types of capital income taxes on net capital imports in an open economy. This is followed by a section offering a simplified illustration of the potential conflict between source and residence countries and of the potential gains from international tax coordination. The final section illustrates the welfare losses stemming from the absence of capital export neutrality and capital import neutrality in an integrated world economy and illuminates some factors which determine the size of these losses.

1. Tax wedges and capital flows in an open economy

One of the main motivations for the attempt in Chapters 4 and 5 of this report to quantify capital income tax wedges in the OECD area is that these wedges may have important effects on savings and investment in individual countries and on capital flows among countries.

In closed as well as in open economies the total tax wedge between the pre-tax marginal rate of return on business investment and the post-tax marginal rate of return received by savers is an important indicator of the tax-induced distortion of capital markets and the potential impediment to economic growth caused by capital income taxation. If capital markets work smoothly, implying among other things that investors are not subject to severe liquidity constraints, it does not matter very much in a closed economy whether taxes are levied at the business level, say in the form of a corporate income tax, or at the level of the individual investor in the form of personal income and wealth taxes. The reason is that planned savings must equal planned investment for the capital market of a closed economy to be in equilibrium. Hence capital income taxes will discourage both savings and investment, whether they take the form of taxes on household savings or whether they appear to be taxes on the return to business investment.

In short, what matters in a closed economy — or in an economy having no links with the international capital market — is the total corporate and personal tax wedge between the pre-tax return to investment and the after-tax return to savings, as illustrated in chart A.3.1. The II-curve indicates the pre-tax rate of return to investment. The curve is downward-sloping, reflecting the diminishing marginal productivity of capital as investment is increased and the more profitable investment oppurtunities are exhausted. The SS curve indicates the response of private savings to the marginal net rate of return on saving. It is seen that a higher after-tax rate of return is assumed to call forth a higher level of savings. In the absence of taxation, the capital market would clear at point A where desired savings equal desired investment. However, corporate and personal income taxes drive a wedge between the pre-tax rate of return on investment and the after-tax return received by savers. As a result, the equilibrium levels of saving and investment are seen to be reduced relative to the hypothetical no-tax situation. It is also seen from chart A.3.1 that some of the burden of capital income taxes is shifted on to other groups in society, since part of the tax wedge is reflected in a higher pre-tax rate of return.

In an open economy with access to the international capital market it is no longer necessary for total domestic savings to equal total domestic investment, since any difference between the two magnitudes can be cleared through capital imports or capital exports. In this situation it turns out that the composition of the total capital income tax wedge becomes crucial for the effects of the tax system on savings, investment, and net capital imports.

This is illustrated in chart A.3.2 which depicts the capital market of a small open economy facing a given international rate of interest "r". Since interest income is taxed according to the residence principle, investors will obtain the same after-tax return on foreign and domestic interest-bearing assets when the foreign and domestic pre-tax rates of interest are the same. Given perfect capital mobility, the domestic rate of interest before tax will therefore equal the international interest rate "r" in chart A.3.2. The personal tax on capital income (and the personal wealth tax if such a tax is applied) reduces the net return to private savers below the international interest rate. This is indicated as the "savings tax wedge" in chart A.3.2. In addition, the double taxation of corporate-source income may drive a wedge between the interest rate and the required pre-tax rate of return on corporate investment. This is shown as the "investment tax wedge" in chart A.3.2.

If marginal investments are at least partly financed by equity, an isolated rise in the corporate income tax rate will increase the investment tax wedge, thereby reducing domestic investment and net capital imports. At the same time, the higher corporate income tax rate will not affect the savings tax wedge[1]. By contrast, a higher personal tax on capital income will raise the savings tax wedge, and it will also increase the relative profitability of corporate investment financed by retained earnings, thereby reducing the investment tax wedge (see the formal analysis below). Consequently, the higher personal capital income tax will induce higher capital imports.

Thus the two capital income tax wedges have very different effects on savings and investment and directly opposite effects on international capital flows. It is also worth noting that when the pre-tax rate of interest is given from abroad, none of the burden of a higher investment tax wedge will be borne by the owners of capital in the long run, since the pre-tax rate of return to investment will rise by the full amount of the increase in the investment tax wedge. The burden of a higher savings tax wedge, however, will be fully borne by wealth owners when the pre-tax rate of interest is given.

For these reasons it is very important to distinguish between the two tax wedges indicated in chart A.3.2. In the figure the investment tax wedge is assumed to be positive, but in some cases it may in fact be negative. Below some important determinants of the investment tax wedge are investigated. The analysis is simplified and does not attempt to capture all details of the tax system. For ease of exposition, the analysis also abstracts from foreign direct investment, assuming that corporations operating in the domestic economy are controlled by domestic household investors[2]. The notation will be as follows:

p = pre-tax marginal rate of return on corporate investment
    (net of economic depreciation)

r = pre-tax market rate of interest

τ = corporate income tax rate

m = marginal personal tax rate on capital income
    (tax rate on interest and dividends)

z = effective personal tax rate on accrued capital gains on shares

θ = dividend received by shareholder per unit of distributed profits

266

The parameter θ indicates the shareholder's dividend including a possible dividend tax credit. Under a classical corporate tax system no such credit is granted, and θ is simply unity, but under an imputation system θ will exceed unity. It should be noted that θ measures the dividend plus the tax credit before payment of personal tax on this income.

The derivation of the investment tax wedge when marginal corporate investment expenditure is financed by debt is first considered. Assuming for simplicity that depreciation for tax purposes corresponds to the true economic depreciation, the taxable net profit on an extra unit of investment will be (p-r), since interest payments are deductible. Hence the corporate tax bill (T) on income from a unit of additional debt-financed investment is equal to:

$$T = \tau(p-r) \tag{1}$$

As long as net profits on additional investment are positive, it will pay the corporation and its owners to increase investment expenditure. Hence the corporation will carry out debt-financed investment to the point where net profits on the marginal investment project are zero:

$$p - r - T = 0 \tag{2}$$

Insertion of (1) into (2) and rearrangement gives the simple expression for the investment tax wedge (p-r) under debt finance:

$$p-r = 0 \tag{3}$$

It is seen from (3) that when depreciation allowed for tax purposes coincides with true economic depreciation, the investment tax wedge will be zero and the corporate tax system will have no distortionary effect on investment. In practice many countries allow accelerated depreciation, and in that case the investment tax wedge will be <u>negative</u> because of the tax subsidy implied by the generous depreciation allowances.

In general, a higher rate of depreciation allowance will always reduce the investment tax wedge, regardless of the mode of investment finance. However, to simplify the exposition we shall continue to assume that depreciation for tax purposes coincides with true economic depreciation.

It is now supposed that the marginal investment is financed by new issues of shares. For shareholders to be willing to inject additional equity into the firm, the subsequent increase in net dividends after payment of corporate and personal taxes must be at least as high as the after-tax interest income which shareholders might alternatively have earned by investing their funds in interest-bearing assets. The required rate of return on the marginal corporate investment may therefore be found from the following arbitrage condition[3]

$$(1-m)\theta p(1-\tau) = r(1-m) \tag{4}$$

where the left-hand side represents the after-tax dividends on the extra share investment, allowing for a possible dividend tax credit, while the right-hand side reflects the after-tax income forgone by investing in shares rather than, say, bonds. Rearranging (4), one finds the investment tax wedge under finance by new share issues:

$$p-r = \frac{r[1-\theta(1-\tau)]}{\theta(1-\tau)} \qquad (5)$$

It can be shown from (5) that a higher corporate tax rate τ will increase the investment tax wedge whereas a higher degree of corporate-personal tax integration (a higher value of θ) will reduce the wedge. Under a classical corporate tax system with no alleviation of the double taxation of dividends, the parameter θ is simply unity, and (5) simplifies to

$$p-r = \frac{\tau r}{(1-\tau)} \qquad (6)$$

By contrast, under a system of full imputation with complete relief of the corporate tax underlying the dividend, we have $\theta=1/(1-\tau)$, and it then follows from (5) that the investment tax wedge will vanish.

Finally if the case where corporate investment is financed by retained profits is considered, at the margin, where such investment is just barely worthwhile for the shareholder, the after-tax dividend forgone through retentions plus the capital gains tax payable on the resulting increase in share values will just be offset by the capital gain on shares[4]. Hence, if the retention of "I" additional units of net corporate profits induces a capital gain of one unit, this gain will equal the net dividend of $I\theta(1-m)$ forgone by the shareholder plus his additional capital gains liability "z", implying

$$I\theta(1-m)+z = 1 \qquad (7)$$

In addition, the shareholder will require that the after-tax dividend of $(1-m)\theta pI(1-\tau)$ earned on the extra corporate investment is at least equal to the net return on interest-bearing assets:

$$(1-m)\theta pI(1-\tau) = r(1-m) \qquad (8)$$

Solving (7) for I, substituting into (8) and reorganizing, obtains the investment tax wedge when financed by retained profits:

$$p-r = \frac{r[\tau+z(1-\tau)-m]}{(1-z)(1-\tau)} \qquad (9)$$

The term $\tau+z(1-\tau)$ in the square bracket in (9) is the sum of the corporate tax bill and the personal capital gains tax liability resulting from an extra unit of corporate profits which is retained in the corporation. When this combined tax bill exceeds the tax liablility "m" on a unit of interest income, it is seen from (9) that the investment tax wedge on retentions-financed corporate investment is positive.

When a classical corporate income tax is combined with a comprehensive personal income tax where the effective capital gains tax rate equals the marginal personal income tax rate ($z=m$), it is easy to verify that (9) reduces to (6), implying that the investment tax wedge becomes the same whether equity finance is raised through retentions or through new share issues. A more realistic situation in most countries is that the effective tax rate on accrued capital gains is virtually nil ($z=0$), in which case (9) simplifies to

$$p-r = \frac{r(\tau-m)}{(1-m)} \qquad\qquad (10)$$

A zero capital gains tax thus implies that the investment tax wedge will be positive or negative, depending on whether the corporate tax rate is higher or lower than the marginal personal tax rate on capital income.

Based on the analysis above, table A.3.1 summarizes the effects of some important tax instruments on the savings tax wedge, the investment tax wedge and on international capital flows in a small open economy. It is seen that in some cases the effects may depend crucially on the marginal source of corporate finance. As argued in Chapter 2, it is probably most realistic to assume that marginal investment expenditures are financed by a mixture of debt and equity, with retained earnings being normally the dominant source of equity finance.

Chapters 4 and 5 in this report present estimates of required pre-tax real rates of return on corporate investment in the OECD area, assuming a common real interest rate before tax of 5 per cent. The difference between these required rates of return (corresponding to "p" in the above notation) and the 5 per cent real interest rate provide an estimate of the investment tax wedge illustrated in chart A.3.2.

In order to isolate the effects of the corporate income tax and to compare these effects across countries, some of the estimates of tax wedges in chapters 4 and 5 abstract from personal taxes. In that case the savings tax wedge depicted in chart A.3.2 obviously becomes zero, and the total tax wedge becomes identical to the investment tax wedge which will then be determined solely by corporate tax parameters such as the corporate income tax rate, the rates of depreciation allowance etc. For this reason the investment tax wedge might also be termed "the corporate tax wedge" when personal tax rates are zero. It should be noted that these estimated corporate tax wedges will in fact correspond to the actual total tax wedge when the investor supplying corporate finance is a tax-exempt institution.

As indicated earlier, the importance of the distinction between the savings tax wedge and the investment tax wedge stems from the fact that interest income is usually taxed according to the residence principle in the OECD area. Under free capital mobility this implies a tendency for the pre-tax rates of interest to be equalised across countries and hence the rate of interest before tax will tend to be given from abroad in an open economy which is small relative to the world economy.

If interest income were instead taxed according to a pure source principle, that is if residence countries levied no tax on interest income from abroad, capital mobility would instead tend to equate the <u>after-tax</u> rates of interest across countries. In a small economy this would mean that the after-tax rather than the pre-tax rate of interest would be given from abroad. Consequently, in chart A.3.2 the <u>net</u> return to saving would be fixed, and a higher savings tax wedge would simply translate into a higher pre-tax domestic interest rate (i.e. the "r"-line in chart A.3.2 would shift upwards). Thus a higher savings tax wedge as well as a higher investment tax wedge would tend to reduce domestic investment and net capital imports under the source principle of interest income taxation, and the distinction between the two tax wedges would be less relevant.

The simple analysis in chart A.3.2 focuses on an open economy which is too small to have a significant influence on world interest rates. This situation is relevant to most of the OECD countries, but the capital markets of some large economies such as the United States do in fact have a noticeable impact on the international level of interest rates. In such cases it can be shown that a higher savings tax wedge will still tend to increase capital imports and that a higher investment tax wedge will still discourage capital imports, provided the residence principle of interest income taxation is applied effectively. However, compared to the case of a small open economy, the response of savings, investment, and net capital flows to changes in tax wedges will be dampened, due to induced changes in the world level of interest rates.

2. The potential gains from a reduction of surtaxes on international investment

While the previous section explored the impact of some important tax instruments on international capital flows, this section attempts to illustrate how international tax co-ordination can help countries to take greater advantage of these flows. At the same time, the discussion also illuminates the conflicting interests which may sometimes make it difficult for national governments to agree on such co-ordination.

To simplify the graphical exposition, the analysis focuses on the problem of ensuring an efficient allocation of a given world capital stock. Thus it relates mainly to the short and medium term where additions to total capital supply through savings flows are small relative to the existing stock of capital so that the assumption of a fixed aggregate capital stock is not a bad approximation. However, if savings are inelastic with respect to the after-tax rate of return on capital, the conclusions drawn below on the welfare effects of taxation will be just as valid in a long term perspective.

Another aspect of the analysis in this section is that countries are assumed to be able to influence the rate of return on international investment by varying their level of capital exports or capital imports. This assumption is clearly valid in large countries, and it can also be relevant for a group of co-operating countries such as the members of the European Communities. Even for small individual countries the subsequent analysis may have some relevance, because a multinational corporation may be large relative to the specific market in which it operates even if it is based in a small country.

As a starting point for the analysis, chart A.3.3. illustrates the welfare gains from international investment in a hypothetical situation of zero taxes on capital income. For simplicity, the world economy is divided into a "domestic economy" and a "foreign economy". The total world capital stock is given by the width of the diagram (the horizontal distance "OO"). The part of this capital which is owned by domestic investors is given by the distance OK_d, while the remaining distance $O*K_d$ represents the capital owned by foreign investors. The capital invested in the domestic economy is thus measured from left to right, and the marginal productivity of this investment is indicated by the curve II which is falling, reflecting diminishing marginal productivity of capital as production becomes more and more capital-intensive. Since a point on the II-curve measures the addition to national output resulting from the input of an extra unit of capital, the total area below the curve indicates the total output of the domestic economy.

Similarly, the capital invested in the foreign economy is measured from right to left on the horizontal axis; the marginal productivity of this investment is given by the I*I*-curve, and the area under this curve represents the total output of the foreign economy.

In the absence of international capital flows total investment in the domestic economy would equal OK_d, and total investment in the foreign economy would be $O*K_d$. Under competitive conditions the rate of return on investment would tend to reflect the marginal productivity of capital, so domestic investors would earn a return equal to the vertical distance K_dC, while foreign investors would earn a return of K_dB.

When free international capital flows are allowed, capital will tend to flow from the foreign economy to the domestic economy where it can earn a higher rate of return. In principle this process will continue until rates of return have been equalized. Thus the international capital market will settle in the equilibrium given by point A in chart A.3.3 where the common rate of return to investment in the two countries equals r^e and where the domestic economy has imported an amount of capital K_dK_o from the foreign economy.

As a result of this capital import total output in the domestic economy is increased by the area K_dCAK_o, whereas transfers of profits to foreign investors only amount to the area K_dJAK_o. Hence the domestic economy makes a net gain equal to the triangle ACJ from capital imports. This gain will take the form of higher real wages and higher land rents in the domestic economy, since the higher capital intensity of domestic production increases the productivity of domestic labour and land.

By analogy, the foreign economy loses an amount of output equal to the area K_dBAK_o, but on the other hand it earns foreign investment income amounting to K_dJAK_o, thereby making a net gain given by the area ABJ. Thus both countries gain from international investment, and the total gain to the world economy equals

270

the triangle ABC which reflects the increase in world output resulting from the reallocation of the world capital stock towards a country with a higher marginal productivity of capital.

However, while the domestic economy has gained from the inflow of foreign investment, it can make an even higher national gain by imposing a tax at an appropriate rate on the return to imported capital. This is illustrated in chart A.3.4 where the vertical distance between the curves II and I'I' measures the tax rate. From the viewpoint of the investors of the foreign capital-exporting economy the imposition of such a tax means that the return to capital exports is now given by the I'I'-curve[5]. The new international capital market equilibrium is therefore located in point G where foreign investors obtain the same net return on investment at home and abroad. In this equilibrium the gain to the foreign economy from capital exports has been reduced to the area BHG, whereas in the previous no-tax equilibrium A the gain equalled the triangle AJB. Hence the imposition of the tax has inflicted a loss amounting to area AJHG on the capital-exporting economy.

For the domestic economy the introduction of the tax implies a loss equal to area ADE due to reduced capital imports, and a gain equal to the rectangle DJHG due to a fall in the net return paid to foreign investors on the remaining capital imports. It is seen from chart A.3.4 that the capital-importing economy has chosen the tax rate so as to ensure a positive net national gain.

For the world economy as a whole, the introduction of the tax implies a net loss equal to area AEG which is the difference between the loss to the capital-exporting country and the gain to the capital-importing country. This global net loss represents the fall in aggregate world output as foreign investors repatriate part of their international investments despite the fact that the marginal pre-tax rate of return obtainable abroad exceeds the pre-tax rate of return which can be earned at home.

Proceeding along similar lines, it can be shown that the capital-exporting country could make a national gain by imposing a special tax on the return to foreign investment, while the world as a whole would suffer a loss. By causing a repatriation of part of the capital invested abroad, the tax on capital exports would induce a rise in the pre-tax rate of return earned on the remaining foreign investment. If the tax rate were chosen appropriately, the result would be an increase in the capital-exporting country's total earnings on foreign investment, even though the amount of capital invested abroad would go down, causing a misallocation of the world capital stock.

A practical example of the special tax on capital imports illustrated in chart A.3.4 could be the withholding taxes imposed by source countries on dividends and interest paid to foreign residents. As for the special tax on capital exports referred to in the previous paragraph, this could take the form of incomplete international double tax relief. The frequent failure of residence countries with an imputation system to grant dividend tax relief to distributions of profits from foreign sources is another example of an implicit surtax on capital exports.

The analysis in this section indicates that from a national perspective countries may have good reasons to impose such surtaxes on international investment. However, the analysis also suggests that the international community could make a net welfare gain if source and residence countries could agree on a co-ordinated reduction of these additional tax burdens on border-crossing investments.

3. Capital export neutrality versus capital import neutrality

Apart from the problem of the special (explicit or implicit) surtaxes on international investment, policy makers are also faced with the problem of choosing an appropriate method of international double tax relief to ensure that the competing tax claims of source and residence countries do not seriously hamper border-crossing investments.

In chapter 2 it was mentioned that the exemption method of international double tax relief would guarantee so-called "capital import neutrality", provided the source country adheres to the principle of non-discrimination in the taxation of foreign-owned capital operating in the country. It was also mentioned that a tax regime of capital import neutrality would tend to equate the after-tax rates of return to saving across countries in a world of free capital mobility and would hence tend to eliminate distortions in the international allocation of world savings.

On the other hand, if international double tax relief is granted by means of a pure credit system (with no deferral and no limits on foreign tax credits), it was noted in chapter 2 that this would apply a regime of "capital export neutrality" where capital mobility would tend to equate the pre-tax rates of return to investment across countries and to eliminate distortions in the allocation of world investment.

A pure credit system would thus have the same effect on the international allocation of capital as a system of capital income taxation based on a strict residence principle, because the investor's final tax liability would always be determined by the effective capital income tax rate of his/her residence country. By contrast, under the exemption method of international double tax relief capital income is effectively taxed according to the source principle.

In general, neither the source principle (the exemption method) nor the residence principle (the credit method) can prevent inefficiencies in international capital allocation. This final section offers a simple graphical illustration of the welfare losses emerging under the two alternative tax regimes. To focus sharply on the choice between capital export neutrality and capital import neutrality, the analysis abstracts from other complications such as tax discrimination across modes of investment finance. Thus it is assumed that each country imposes a uniform tax on all types of capital income and that depreciation for tax purposes coincides with true economic depreciation. These assumptions imply that the required pre-tax rate of return to business investment will always equal the market rate of interest before tax. It is also assumed that capital income tax rates differ across countries, since the conflict between capital export neutrality and capital import neutrality does not arise in the case of identical tax rates.

Chart A.3.5 illustrates an international capital market equilibrium under a system of residence-based capital income taxation (or under a pure credit system of international double tax relief). Once again the world is divided into a capital-exporting and a capital-importing country. The levels of saving and investment are measured along the horizontal axis, and the rates of return to these flows are shown on the vertical axis. The curves II and I*I* indicate the response of investment to changes in the rate of interest before tax, while the SS and S*S* curves show the response of savings to the rate of interest after tax.

Savers will reallocate their savings from one country to the other until they obtain the same after-tax rate of return on domestic and foreign securities. Under the residence principle this capital market equilibrium will be realised when the pre-tax rates of interest have been equalised across countries, since the individual saver faces the same tax rate on domestic and foreign investment. In chart A.3.5 the common world rate of interest before tax is given by point "a". The capital income tax rate in the capital-exporting country is equal to the distance "ab" on the vertical axis, while the tax rate in the capital-importing country equals the distance "ac". It is seen that at the equilibrium pre-tax rate of interest "a" the savings surplus (capital exports) of the first country is just matched by the savings deficit (capital imports) of the second country.

The common pre-tax rate of interest ensures an equalisation of the marginal productivity of capital in the two countries, implying an efficient allocation of world investment. However, the world allocation of savings is distorted because the after-tax return to saving differs between the two countries. To identify the resulting loss of welfare to the international community, it is necessary to discuss the interpretation of the savings curves in chart A.3.5 in some detail.

A tax on the return to saving affects the saver in two ways: First of all, it reduces his current and expected future income. This so-called income effect does not represent a loss to society, however, since it is matched by a revenue to the government. Second, the capital income tax reduces the net reward to saving, thereby inducing the saver to substitute present for future consumption at any given level of net income. This substitution effect of the tax does cause a loss of social welfare, for even if the government were (hypothetically) to return the tax revenue as a lump sum transfer to the saver, thus restoring his net income, the lower net reward to saving would still force the taxpayer into a pattern of saving which he would not have chosen in the absence of the tax[6].

If the savings curves in chart A.3.5 are to provide information on the welfare effects of capital income taxes, they must therefore reflect mainly the substitution effects of changes in the net return to saving[7]. This will indeed tend to be the case if governments have a fixed revenue requirement so that changes in capital income tax rates are roughly offset by changes in other taxes or transfers.

Given this interpretation of the savings curves in chart A.3.5, the global welfare loss from the cross-country difference in the net return to saving can now be illustrated. Each point on the savings curve shows the increase in future consumption which savers require in order to be willing to give up an extra unit of present consumption. Thus the total area under the curve measures the total compensation necessary to call forth a certain total amount of saving. Hence, if capital income tax rates were equalised across countries so that an amount of saving $S_e*S_h*=S_hS_e$ would be reallocated from the capital-exporting to the capital-importing country, savers in the latter country would need an increase in their future consumption equal to the area in the interval S_eS_h under the SS-curve in order to be just as well off as before.

On the other hand, savers in the capital-exporting country would be willing to give up an amount of future consumption equal to the area in the interval S_e*S_h* under the $S*S*$-curve in return for the increase in their level of present consumption. As the reader will see, the difference between these two areas under the savings curves equals the sum of the areas of the two black triangles in chart A.3.5. This sum measures the global welfare loss from the absence of capital import neutrality, because it represents the amount of future consumption which savers in the world economy as a whole would in principle be willing to forgo if the world moved to a system of harmonized capital income tax rates with identical net rewards to saving. Thus, if the future consumption given by the two black areas were split between savers in the two countries, both parties could be made better off than they were before the reallocation of world savings[8].

If the savings curves had been steeper in the initial equilibrium point, indicating a lower elasticity of savings with respect to the net rate of return, the reallocation of world savings induced by an equalisation of after-tax rates of return would have been smaller, and so would the areas of the black triangles in chart A.3.5. In other words, the lower the elasticity of savings with respect to the after-tax rate of return, the smaller the welfare loss caused by the absence of capital import neutrality, as mentioned in section D.5 of chapter 2.

Chart A.3.6 illustrates a world capital market equilibrium under a pure source-based system of capital income taxation (or under an exemption system). Under this tax regime, free capital mobility will enforce a common after-tax return to saving, given by point "c" in the figure. Hence capital import neutrality will prevail. However, with a capital income tax wedge equal to the distance "bc" in the capital-exporting country and a different tax wedge "ac" in the capital-importing country, the required pre-tax rate of return on investment will differ across countries, and hence capital export neutrality will be violated.

Suppose now that capital income tax rates are harmonized across countries so that an amount of investment $I_e*I_h*=I_hI_e$ is reallocated from the capital-exporting to the capital-importing country. Since a point on the investment curve indicates the marginal productivity of an extra unit of investment, the total area under the curve measures the addition to total output resulting from a certain amount of total investment. Hence the result of the reallocation of world investment would be a loss of output in the capital-exporting country equal to the area under the $I*I*$-curve in the interval I_e*I_h*, whereas output in the capital-importing country would go up by an amount given by the area under the II-curve in the interval I_hI_e. The difference between the two areas, which equals the sum of the black triangles in chart A.3.6, represents the net increase in world output caused by the reallocation of investment from a country with a lower marginal productivity of capital to a country with a higher marginal productivity. Thus the sum of the black triangles measures the welfare loss due to the absence of capital export neutrality in the initial equilibrium.

If investment had been less elastic with respect to the interest rate, the investment curves in chart A.3.6 would have been steeper. The reallocation of investment and the concomitant gain in global output from a harmonization of capital income tax rates would then have been smaller. This illustrates the point made in section D.5 of chapter 2 that the welfare loss stemming from the absence of capital export neutrality is less serious, the smaller the elasticity of investment with respect to the cost of capital.

Chart A.3. 1. **The effect of the capital income tax wedge in a closed economy**

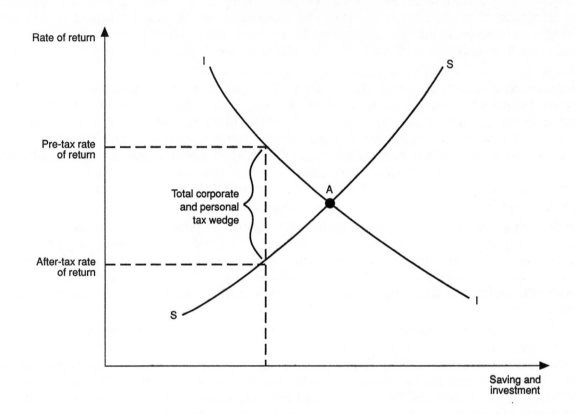

Chart A. 3. 2. **Tax wedges and capital flows in an open economy**

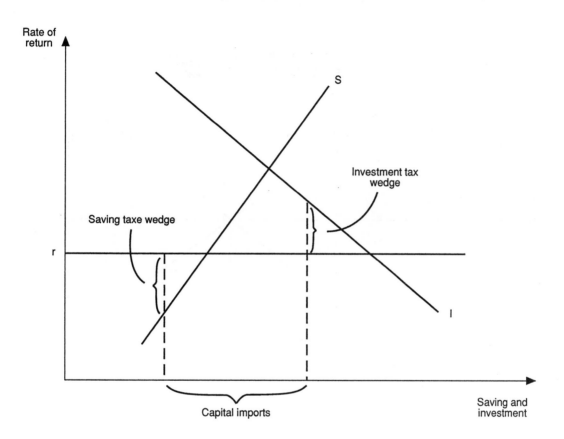

Note : The saving tax wedge reflects the personal tax on capital income. The investment tax wedge is mainly due to the corporate income tax. See the text for further explanations.

Chart A. 3. 3. **The welfare gains from international investment**

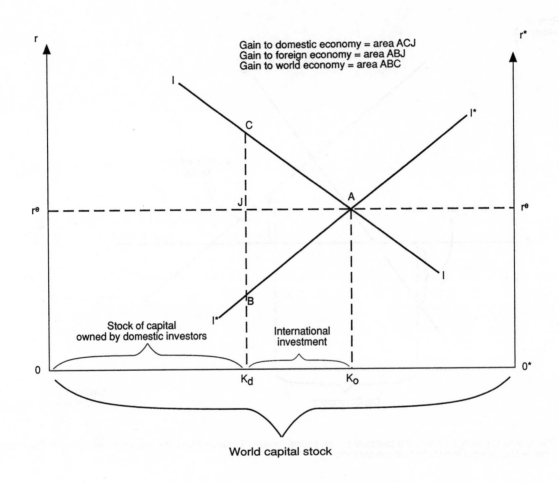

Gain to domestic economy = area ACJ
Gain to foreign economy = area ABJ
Gain to world economy = area ABC

Table A.3.1 **Effects of alternative tax instruments on tax wedges and international capital flows**

Rise in:	Effect on:		
	Savings tax wedge	Investment tax wedge	Net capital imports
Personal tax rate on capital income	+	$0 (-)^1$	+
Rate of dividend tax credit	0	$- (0)^2$	$+ (0)^2$
Personal tax rate on capital gains on shares	0	$+ (0)^3$	$- (0)^3$
Corporate income tax rate	0	$+ (-^1)^4$	$- (+^1)^4$
Rate of depreciation allowance or investment tax credit	0	-	+

1. The effect is negative if retained earnings are the marginal source of finance.
2. The effect is zero if new share issues are not used as a marginal source of finance.
3. The effect is zero if retained earnings are not used as a marginal source of finance.
4. This effect prevails if debt is the marginal source of finance and the tax code allows accelerated depreciation.

Chart A. 3. 4. **Welfare effects of a source-country tax on capital imports**

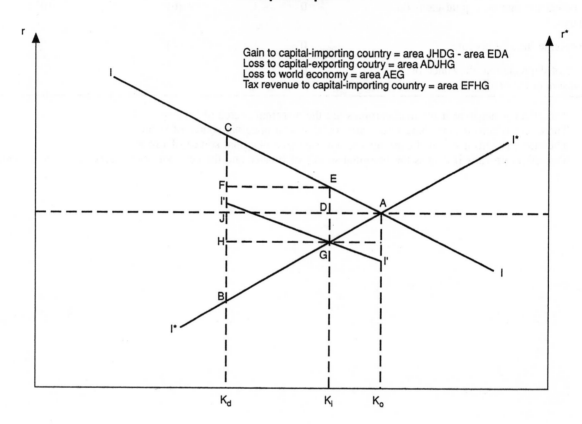

Gain to capital-importing country = area JHDG - area EDA
Loss to capital-exporting coutry = area ADJHG
Loss to world economy = area AEG
Tax revenue to capital-importing country = area EFHG

Chart A. 3. 5. **The welfare loss due to the absence of capital import neutrality under residence-based capital income taxation**

Sum of black areas = welfare loss due to inefficient allocation of world saving

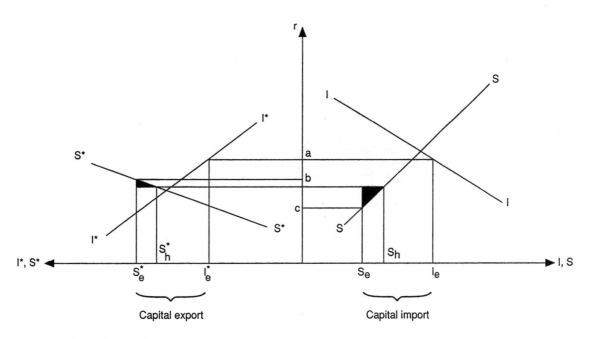

Capital export   Capital import

Notes : a = world rate of interest before tax.
b = after-tax rate of interest in capital-exporting country.
c = after-tax rate of interest in capital-importing country.

$S_e^* - I_e^* = I_e - S_e$ = International capital flow.

$S_e^* - S_h^* = S_e - S_h$ = (hypothetical) welfare improving reallocation of world savings

Figure A. 3. 6. The welfare lose due to the absence of capital export neutrality under source-based capital income taxation

Sum of black areas = welfare lose due to inefficient allocation of world investment

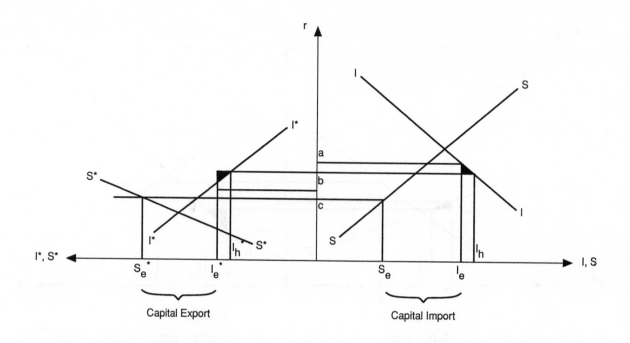

Notes : a = pre-tax rate of interest in capital-importing country.
b = pre-tax rate of interest in capital-exporting country .
c = world rate of interest after tax.

$S_e^* - I_e^* = I_e - S_e$ = international capital flow.

$I_e^* - I_h^* = I_h - I_e$ = (hypothetical) welfare-Improving reallocation of world investment.

Notes and references

1. A change in the corporate tax rate might nevertheless have an indirect effect on domestic savings by influencing private income and wealth and the distribution of income across different generations. In chart A.3.2 such indirect effects would be reflected in a <u>shift</u> in the S-curve and would tend to blur the present sharp distinction between taxes on investment and taxes on savings, although the distinction would certainly still be relevant.

2. The analysis below is simplified and does not attempt to capture all details of the tax system. For ease of exposition, the analysis also abstracts from foreign direct investment. A more rigorous mathematical analysis of tax wedges in open economies can be found in chapter 7 of Hans-Werner Sinn: *Capital Income Taxation and Resource Allocation*, North-Holland, 1987.

3. For simplicity we abstract from the possible risk premium required on investment in shares.

4. It is assumed for simplicity that shareholders have no special preference for dividends over capital gains, in accordance with the so-called new view of dividend taxation (see section B.6 of the main text of chapter 2).

5. It is assumed that foreign investors do not receive a credit for the source-country tax from their home government.

6. Assuming that the saver had optimized his saving before the tax was introduced, it is clear that the new tax-induced savings pattern must imply lower welfare for the saver even if his net income is left unaffected (otherwise he would have chosen the post-tax savings pattern right from the start).

7. In the jargon of economists, the slope of the curves must reflect the so-called <u>compensated</u> interest elasticity of savings.

8. It should be stressed that in order for the global welfare gain to be reflected in a gain to all individual consumers in the world, the move towards harmonized capital income tax rates would have to be accompanied by appropriate changes in the tax\transfer system in each country. Generally, an international transfer <u>between</u> the two

Annex 4
Country Chapters

Table of country chapters

Structure of country chapters

I. Corporation taxes

    1.1   Relations with the personal income tax
    1.2   Definition of income subject to tax
    1.3   Rate structure
            1.3.1 Central government
            1.3.2 Intermediate government
            1.3.3 Local government
            1.3.4 Overall tax rate
    1.4   Treatment of intercorporate dividends
    1.5   Provisions applying to interest receipts and payments
            1.5.1 Receipts
            1.5.2 Payments
    1.6   Treatment of trading losses
    1.7   Capital gains and losses
            1.7.1 Gains
            1.7.2 Losses
    1.8   Depreciation
            1.8.1 Machinery
            1.8.2 Buildings
            1.8.3 Switch-over
    1.9   Investment tax credits
    1.10 Inventories
    1.11 Treatment of reserves
    1.12 Treatment of other business expenses
    1.13 Tax period
            1.13.1   Individuals
            1.13.2   Corporations
    1.14 Life insurance/pension funds

II. Taxes on property and wealth

    2.1   Taxes on net wealth
            2.1.1 Individuals
            2.1.2 Corporations
    2.2   Taxes on immovable property

III. Domestic withholding tax

    3.1   Withholding taxes on interest
    3.2   Withholding taxes on dividends

IV. Personal income taxes

    4.1   Rate schedule
    4.2   Tax treatment of dividends
    4.3   Tax treatment of interest
    4.4   Weighted average marginal rates of personal income tax on dividends, interest and capital gains
    4.5   Taxes on capital gains

V. Investment grants generally available to the manufacturing sector

VI. International aspects

    6.1   International withholding taxes
          6.1.1 Direct investment
          6.1.2 Portfolio investment
    6.2   Treatment of foreign source income
          6.2.1 Non-treaty countries
          6.2.2Treaty countries

VII. Major changes

Australia

I. Corporation taxes

1.1 Relations with the personal income tax

A full dividend imputation system operates such that income tax paid at the corporate level is imputed (credited) to resident individual shareholders. Imputed tax credits may not be carried forward or refunded (see also tables 3.1 and 3.2).

1.2 Definition of income subject to tax

Central Government: the income for tax purposes for a resident company is the worldwide profit.

1.3 Rate structure

1.3.1 Central government

The corporate tax rate is 39 per cent.

1.3.2 Intermediate government

None.

1.3.3 Local government

None.

1.3.4 Overall tax rate

The overall tax rate is 39 per cent.

1.4 Treatment of intercorporate dividends

Dividend income from other resident companies is included as corporate taxable income. However, a rebate of tax on dividend income is generally allowed with the result that no tax is paid. Imputation credits may be passed from one company to another when a dividend is paid.

1.5 Provisions applying to interest receipts and payments

1.5.1 Receipts

Interest receipts are treated as ordinary income.

1.5.2 Payments

Interest payments are generally deductible.

1.6 Treatment of trading losses

Prior to 1 July 1989, domestic trading losses could only be carried forward seven years, although losses of primary producers could be carried forward indefinitely. However, this restriction will be removed in respect of all taxation losses incurred in the 1989-90 income year and subsequent income years. Unlimited carry-forward will apply. Trading losses can not be carried backwards.

1.7 Capital gains and losses

1.7.1 Gains

Capital gains on assets purchased after 19 September 1985 fall under a general gains system. Capital gains on assets held for 12 months or more are calculated after allowing for inflation, however, capital gains on assets held for less than 12 months or capital losses are not indexed. The net capital gain is included in the taxpayer's taxable income and taxed at the normal income tax rates.

1.7.2 Losses

Capital losses can be offset against current or future capital gains.

1.8 Depreciation

1.8.1 Machinery

Machinery acquired or constructed on or after 26 May 1988:

Method of depreciation: effective life plus a 20 per cent loading based on original cost on a prime cost or diminishing balance basis, i.e. an asset with an effective life of 10 years would be depreciated at 12 per cent per annum on a prime cost basis (18 per cent diminishing balance) until written off.

Rate of depreciation: based on estimated lives of assets (laid down by the tax authorities) Straight line: The prime cost method will provide an equal stream of deductions over the life of the asset.

Declining balance: Under the declining balance method the rate is 150 per cent of the prime cost rate (recalculated each year upon the remaining depreciated value of the asset).

Plant purchased after 19 July 1982 and on or before 25 May 1988: Method of depreciation: usually three or five years straight line.

1.8.2 Buildings

Income producing non residential buildings

Where construction commenced on or after 20 July 1982, and on or before 21 August 1984: 2.5 per cent a year.

For construction commenced on or after 22 August 1984 and on or before 5 September 1987: 4 per cent a year

For construction commenced after 15 September 1987: 2.5 per cent a year.

The above deductions do not apply to residential buildings where construction commenced before 18 July 1985. In respect of property the construction of which commenced on or after 18 July 1985 a deduction at the rates shown above is allowed regardless of whether the income producing building is residential, non-residential or short term traveller accommodation. Traveller accommodation buildings were allowed a deduction from 22 August 1979 to 21 August 1984 of 2.5 per cent a year. From 22 August 1984 to 15 September 1987 a deduction of 4 per cent a year was allowed.

Method of depreciation: straight line. Buildings used in agriculture, mining, scientific research or eligible research and development are granted a special write off.

1.8.3 Switch-over

For post 25 May 1988 plant the diminishing value method applies unless a taxpayer elects to have the prime cost method apply. An election for the prime cost method will apply in respect of all units of property that first become depreciable in the year of income to which the election relates and which qualify as post 25 May 1988 plant.

The taxpayer cannot revert to the diminishing value method on these assets.

1.9 Investment tax credits

None.

1.10 Inventories

Trading stock is valued at cost price (purchase price), selling value or replacement value.

Cost price can be determined by:

— The FIFO method; the first items purchased are assumed to have been disposed of first and the cost of trading stock on hand at the end of the accounting period is considered to be the cost of the items most recently acquired.

— The average cost method: the cost of each item of a particular type on hand at the end of the accounting period is taken to be the weighted average of those of all such items which were on hand at the beginning of the period and those acquired during the period.

— The standard cost method: a predetermined standard cost unit is used. The method is acceptable provided that standards are reviewed regularly to reflect current prices.

— The retail inventory method: goods in stock are marked at their sales price, the market prices are added together in the course of stock taking and the figure thus obtained is reduced by the percentage mark-up to arrive at the cost of goods at hand. This method is acceptable as long as old stock is not marked down as it falls in value or some adjustment is made to account for fall in value.

The following methods are not acceptable.

— The LIFO-method: the items last acquired are assumed to have been disposed of first and the cost of the items on hand at the end of an accounting period is considered to be the cost of the same number of items first acquired.

— The base stock method: this method assumes the necessity for a minimum or basic amount of stock for the operation or business. The base stock is valued at cost as at the date of the manufacturing process to which it relates and quantities in excess of the base stock are valued by some other method.

The LIFO method is not permitted unless it approximates actual physical flows.

1.11 Treatment of reserves

No investment or inventory reserve.

1.12 Treatment of other business expenses

For expenditures on research and development (basic research, applied research, and experimental development) of over A$ 50 000 a tax deduction of 150 per cent is available. This concession will be reduced to 125 per cent from 1 July 1993 until 30 June 1995. Thereafter the deduction will be reduced to 100 per cent. For expenditures between A$ 20 000 and A$ 50 000 a tax deduction on a sliding scale applies.

Plant and machinery used for this purpose is eligible for 150 per cent tax deduction over a three year period.

Write-off may take place over three years where the building was constructed prior to 20 November 1987. Buildings constructed after that time may be written off over 40 years at 2.5 per cent per annum.

1.13 Tax period

1.13.1 Individuals

Generally the fiscal year ends at 30 June. The tax authorities may allow in limited circumstances an alternative date.

1.13.2 Corporations

See 1.13.1.

A company will pay its tax by an instalment on the 28th day of the month after the year of income of 85 per cent of the estimated tax liability for the year. The balance of the tax is due by the 15th of the next month.

1.14 Life assurance/pension funds

Generally speaking, the taxable income of a life insurance company is computed in the same way as that of other companies. They are currently taxed at a rate of 39 per cent. Certain concessions are granted:

— Amounts received as bonuses by policyholders on policies held for ten or more years are exempt from tax;   while

— Amounts received in the tenth year are assessable as to one-third;   and

— Amounts received in the ninth year are assessable as to two-thirds.

From 1 July 1988, the income (including tax deductible contributions and realized capital gains) of pension funds was taxed at a rate of 15 per cent.

Lump sum benefits paid by superannuation funds are concessionally taxed. 5 per cent of benefits relating to service before July 1983 is included in assessable income. Benefits received by superannuants aged 55 or older (excluding a person's own undeducted post-June 1983 contributions), which are referable to post-June 1983 service are taxable at a rate of 6 per cent (plus Medicare levy which is currently 1.25 per cent) in 1990-91, up to an indexed threshold of A$ 68 628 and at a rate of 21 per cent (plus Medicare levy) thereafter.   These rates of lump sum tax will be progressively reduced to zero and 15 per cent (plus Medicare levy) as of 1 July 1992. Benefits received by superannuants aged less than 55 (excluding a person's own undeducted post-June 1983 contributions), which relate to post-June 1983 service are taxable at a rate of 24 per cent (plus Medicare levy) in 1990-91. This rate will be progressively reduced to 20 per cent (plus Medicare levy) as of 1 July 1992.

Pensions and annuities financed from superannuation savings are fully assessable in the hands of the recipient as ordinary income, with a deduction for the return of a person's own undeducted contributions. From 1 July 1988, a rebate of 15 per cent (phased in over five years) of the post-June 1983 taxable component of a superannuation pension or roll over annuity has been available to compensate for the effect of the tax on employer and deductible member contributions.

Deductible member contributions and contributions by employers made after 1 July 1988 are taxed at a rate of 15 per cent.

From 1 July 1990, the maximum deduction for personal superannuation contributions for persons not covered by employer-sponsored schemes was increased to A$ 3 000 plus 75 per cent of the excess over A$ 3 000. Persons who receive only employer superannuation support under an award wage based industry arrangement are eligible for a tax deduction for personal superannuation contributions up to a maximum of A$ 3 000 per annum. Persons with employer superannuation support (not including that which may be provided under an award wage arrangement) may receive a tax rebate for up to A$ 3 000 of personal superannuation contributions, with the maximum rebate of A$ 750 falling by A$ 0.50 for every dollar increase in assessable income above A$ 25 000.

II. Taxes on property and wealth

2.1 Taxes on net wealth

There are no annual net wealth taxes or wealth transfer taxes in Australia.

2.1.1 Individuals

None.

2.1.2 Corporations

None.

2.2 Taxes on immovable property

Land tax is levied by all State and Territory governments on the unimproved capital value of land, with exemptions for owner-occupied residential land and land used for primary production. In some cases exemptions are also provided for land used by charitable, religious or educational institutions. In addition, local governments levy rates on the basis of land values. The rate of tax and methods of valuation vary.

III. Domestic withholding taxes

3.1 Withholding taxes on interest

None.

3.2 Withholding taxes on dividends

See 4.2 (below).

IV. Personal income taxes

4.1 Rate schedule

Income range ($)		Marginal tax rate (cents per dollar)
0-	5 100	0
5 100-	5 400	0
5 401-	17 650	20
17 651 -	20 600	20
20 601-	35 000	38
35 001-	36 000	38
36 001-	50 000	46
over	50 000	47

For taxable income greater than $5 400 a medicare levy of 1.25 percentage points is applied in addition to the rates shown.

4.2 Tax treatment of dividends

Full imputation system. Dividends received by Australian resident individual shareholders from Australian resident companies are grossed up by the amount of Australian corporation income tax already paid. The grossed up dividend is taxable income to the shareholder who is allowed a tax credit equal to the corporation tax component.

The rate of corporation tax payable in 1990-91 income is 39 per cent and 39 per cent is the reference rate for grossing up dividends paid during 1990-91. That is, for every $61 of dividends paid out of profits taxed at 39 per cent a tax credit of $39 is attached.

4.3 Tax treatment of interest

Taxed as ordinary income.

4.4 Weighted average marginal rates of personal income tax on dividends, interest and capital gains

The weighted average rates of personal income tax for 1989-90 are not yet available. The rates for 1987-88 are as follows:
— on dividends   : 42 per cent
— on interest   : 27 per cent
— on capital gains : 35 per cent

The weighted average rates on dividends and interest are the average rates of income tax of persons with dividend and interest income weighted by the amounts of dividend and interest income respectively.

In the case of dividends, dividend income is the grossed-up amount and the average rate of tax is calculated based on dividend recipients' tax liabilities before deduction of imputation credits.

Net capital gains of persons are taxed at the rate applicable to 20 per cent of the net capital gain added to the person's other income. Thus the weighted average rate for capital gains is the weighted average of the marginal rates of tax of persons with net capital gains.

Although there were personal income tax rates scale changes from 1988-89 to 1989-90, it is expected that the weighted average rates for 1989-90 will be little different from those for 1988-89.

4.5 Taxes on capital gains

See 1.7.1.

V. Investment grants generally available to the manufacturing sector

None.

VI. International aspects.
6.1 International withholding taxes
6.1.1 Direct investment

The Australian tax treatment of dividends payable to non-residents depends on whether the dividend is franked (i.e., is paid out of profits taxed at the company tax rate) or not. Franked dividends are not subject to any Australian tax; unfranked dividends are subject to a final withholding tax of 15 per cent (generally) if paid to treaty countries or 30 per cent if paid to non-treaty countries (Greece, Luxembourg, Portugal, Spain and Turkey). As a general rule, this treatment does not differ between direct and portfolio investments.

6.1.2 Portfolio investment

Interest payable by an Australian resident to a non-resident is normally subject to a final withholding tax of 10 per cent, irrespective of the country of residence of the non-resident. Some exemptions apply.

6.2 Treatment of foreign source income
6.2.1 Unlisted countries

Income from all foreign sources is added together and the total tax on the total foreign income is calculated. A tax credit for the total sum of foreign taxes paid is then granted against the domestic tax.

6.2.2 Listed countries

Same as under 6.2.1.

However, dividends received by an Australian corporate shareholder from companies resident in comparable-tax jurisdictions are tax exempt provided the shareholder has a 10 per cent or greater interest in the company paying the dividend.

VII. Major changes

Under the Retirement Income Measures announced in the 1989-90 Budget, the Australian Government is to introduce a better integrated system of social security and tax administration for age and service (veteran) pensioners. Under existing arrangements, by means of a pensioner rebate that is progressively withdrawn above a threshold level of income, full-rate pensioners are removed from income tax liability and the liabilities of part-rate pensioners are deduced. From 1995, this rebate will be increased for age and service pensioners so that part-rate pensioners in these categories will be removed from income tax liability and subject only to the 50 per cent withdrawal rate on their income-tested pensions, with the rebate being withdrawn beyond the pension cut-out income level.

Austria

I. Corporation taxes

1.1 Relations with the personal income tax

Personal and corporation income tax are not fully integrated. However distributed profits are taxed at half the progressive personal income tax rate (see also table 3.1).

1.2 Definition of income subject to tax

Central government: the income for tax purposes for a resident company is the worldwide profit.

1.3 Rate structure

1.3.1 Central government

The corporate tax rate is 30 per cent.

1.3.2 Intermediate government

None.

1.3.3 Local government

Trade tax varies, but is about 15 per cent. The Austrian business tax rate (Gewerbesteuer) is based on:

—   Business income (Gewerbeertrag) at the basic federal rate of 4.5 per cent which is applied to an adjusted tax basis (adjusted by application of the multiplier referred to below;
—   A tax on payroll at 0.2 per cent.

The local authorities of the Federal Tax Administration apply a municipal multiplier (Hebesatz).

The multiplier for this tax consists of:

—   A multiplier for the local governments (e.g. 150 per cent);
—   A multiplier for the federal government (150 per cent);
—   A multiplier for the federal economic chamber (e.g. 5 per cent for 1991);
—   A multiplier for the provincial economic chamber (e.g. 14 — 36 per cent for 1991).

The multiplier for the business income tax may therefore vary from 319 per cent to 341 per cent.

The multiplier for the payroll tax may not exceed 100 per cent.

The base for the Austrian business tax is the federal tax base after various adjustments such as:

—   Plus: interest paid on long-term debt in so far the payment exceeds Sch 100 000;
—   Plus: half the rental fee for movable property unless subject to the business tax in the hands of the lessee;

— Minus: 3 per cent of the assessed value (Einheitwerte) of real estate.

1.3.4 Overall tax rate

The business tax is deductible from its own tax base and from that of the national corporation tax. The rate is (under the assumption of a multiplier of 329, see 1.3.3) 329 x 4.5 per cent = 14.81 per cent. On a tax inclusive basis the tax rate becomes 12.9 per cent.

The overall tax rate 12.9 per cent x (1-0.30) + 30 per cent = 39 per cent.

pretax profit	1 000 000
business tax	129 000
	871 000
corporation tax	261 300
post-tax profit	609 700

1.4 Treatment of intercorporate dividends

Intercorporate dividends and other profit distributions received by resident companies from other resident or non-resident companies are exempt from tax (the participation exemption).

Only for participation in non-resident companies it is required that the recipient owns 25 per cent or more of the share capital of the distributor during a period of at least 12 months.

1.5 Provisions applying to interest receipts and payments

1.5.1 Receipts

Interest receipts are treated as ordinary income.

1.5.2 Payments

Interest on loans economically connected with any type of taxable income or used for the purchase of business assets is deductible. Long-term debt is not deductible for the computation of the tax base for the business tax (see 1.2).

1.6 Treatment of trading losses

Normal domestic trading losses may be carried forward for seven years. Trading losses can not be carried backwards.

1.7 Capital gains and losses

1.7.1 Gains

Capital gains are included into taxable income. Under certain conditions the gain on fixed assets can be charged against the sale of new assets in the same or in the next three years, but the assets should be held for at least seven years.

1.7.2 Losses

Capital losses are deductible in so far as they are taxed.

1.8 Depreciation

Assets with a value of AUS 5 000 or less can be deducted in the year of purchase.

The straight-line method is allowed. Depreciation is mandatory including during loss-making years.

1.8.1 Machinery

Method of depreciation: straight line.

Rate of depreciation: estimated lifetime of asset. In cases of doubt the rate for intangible fixed assets of 10 per cent is generally accepted.

1.8.2 Buildings

Method of depreciation: straight line

Rate of depreciation: estimated lifetime of asset. The depreciation rate prescribed by law for industrial buildings is 4 per cent, for office buildings 2 per cent.

1.8.3 Switch-over

Not applicable.

1.9 Investment tax credits

An investment deduction (or allowance) of 20 per cent is available on depreciable assets. This allows 120 per cent of the purchase price to be depreciated. The eligible transport equipment rate is 10 per cent (in the case of noise protected trucks: 20 per cent).

If an asset is sold within 4 years after the acquisition, the amount of the investment allowance must be added back to taxable profits.

The investment allowance does not reduce the taxable income if it has to be charged against an investment reserve set up in previous accounting periods.

1.10 Inventories

Trading stock is valued at cost price or going concern whichever is lower. Cost price can be determined by FIFO. The LIFO method is not permitted unless it approximates actual physical flows.

1.11 Treatment of reserves

A special tax-free investment reserve of 10 per cent of taxable profits less the investment deduction may be set up. Within 4 years this reserve must be used to purchase assets which qualify for the investment deduction. After 4 years the unused reserves plus 20 per cent must be included in taxable profits. For each year the reserve is dissolved earlier the 20 per cent surcharge is lowered by 5 percentage points.

1.12 Treatment of other business expenses

Royalty fees are deductible. Expenditures for patents can be depreciated over the useful life. Assets with a cost of no more than AUS 5 000 can be depreciated in the year they are acquired.

1.13 Tax period
1.13.1 Individuals

The fiscal year is the same as the calendar year if the enterprise is enrolled in the Austrian Trade Register. Other accounting periods may be chosen.

1.13.2 Corporations

The fiscal year is the same as the calendar year, but they may opt for other accounting periods. Taxes are paid by quarterly prepayment of tax, based on the assessment of the preceding year. The prepayments are adjusted in case of substantial changes.

1.14 Life assurance/pension funds

Approved pension funds are tax-exempt.

II. Taxes on property and wealth
2.1 Taxes on net wealth
2.1.1 Individuals

Individuals are subject to a tax on their net wealth of 1 per cent a year. An exemption of Sch 150 000 for the taxpayer and each dependent is available.

2.1.2 Companies

Companies are liable for the net wealth tax of 1 per cent plus a surtax of 0.5 per cent on the net value. This tax is deductible for the purpose of the corporate income tax since 1989. The tax base is worldwide net wealth. They are valued according to the Valuation Act (Bewertungsgesetz). As of 1 January 1984 the taxable base is fixed at 90 per cent of the nominal assessed value (Einheitswert). Shares in domestic companies are exempt from tax. The minimum tax base in case of a joint-stock cooperation (AG) is AS 1 million and in case of a limited liability company (GmbH) Sch 500 000. The surtax is levied on the proportion of the value of shares of the corporation held by foreigners and non-individuals.

2.2 Taxes on immovable property

The tax on immovable property varies throughout the country.

III. Domestic withholding taxes

3.1 Withholding taxes on interest

A withholding tax of 10 per cent on interest received on saving deposits with Austrian banks and on securities deposited in Austrian banks is due by the payer of interest. Many types of interest are exempt from the tax on interest.

3.2 Withholding taxes on dividends

Rate: 25 per cent.

IV. Personal income taxes

4.1 Rate schedule

Schilling			Rate (%)
0	-	50 000	10
50 188	-	150 000	22
130 100	-	300 000	32
300 000	-	700 000	42
Over		700 000	50

4.2 Tax treatment of dividends

Dividends are treated as income from capital and they are taxed at one-half of the statutory income tax rates. The cost of the acquisition of newly issued shares in certain companies (mainly companies in the productive sector) as well as the cost of certificates issued by the so-called Participation Fund Companies (Beteiligungsgesellschaften) are deductible for the purposes of the individual income tax as special expenses (Sonderausgaben) up to a certain amount and under certain conditions.

4.3 Tax treatment of interest

Interest above Sch 300 is taxable at ordinary rates; if tax has been withheld, this tax is credited against the assessed income tax.

4.4 Weighted average marginal rates of personal income tax on dividends, interest and capital gains

4.5 Taxes on capital gains

Non-business capital gains are normally not taxed if derived after the expiring of the "speculative period" (one year for movable assets, in general ten years for immovable property). Capital gains derived from the sale of shares are taxable regardless of the speculative period if the interest in the company exceeds 10 per cent.

V. Investment grants generally available to the manufacturing sector.

None.

VI. International aspects.

6.1 International withholding taxes

6.1.1 Direct Investment

The withholding tax rate on dividends for countries that have a tax treaty with Austria varies between 5 per cent and 25 per cent. For non-treaty countries the tax rate is 25 per cent.

6.1.2 Portfolio Investment

The withholding tax rate for portfolio investment ranges also between 5 per cent and 25 per cent. For the non-treaty country New Zealand the tax rate of 25 per cent also applies.

6.2 Treatment of foreign source income

6.2.1 Non-treaty countries

Double taxation relief may be granted by the Ministry of Finance.

6.2.2 Treaty countries

Income from foreign sources is segregated and the tax credit for foreign taxes paid is only granted for a particular activity or investment in a particular country against the domestic tax due on that particular investment.

Dividends received from foreign sources is tax exempt for the domestic tax if an interest of more than 25 per cent is held in a foreign company and the holding period is at least 12 months prior to the end of the financial year.

VII. Major changes

No major changes in the legislation are presently in discussion for 1991 or subsequent years.

Belgium

I. Corporation taxes

1.1 Relations with the personal income tax

Personal and corporate income tax are not integrated. However the withholding tax on dividends is the final tax paid unless the taxpayer elects otherwise (see also table 3.1).

1.2 Definition of income subject to tax

Central Government: the income for tax purposes for a resident company is the worldwide profit.

1.3 Rate structure

1.3.1 Central government

The national tax rate is 39 per cent.

Small business rates:

Taxable income			Rate
0	-	1 000 000	28 per cent
1 000 000	-	3 600 000	BF 280 000 plus 36 per cent of the difference between the taxable income and BF 1 000 000
3 600 000	-	13 000 000	BF 1 216 000 plus 41 per cent of the difference between the taxable income and BF 3 600 000

These reductions are not granted when at least 50 per cent of the shares are held by another company or other companies, Belgian or foreign, or in case of "financial companies", or when the company distributes a dividend exceeding 13 per cent of its share capital.

1.3.2 Intermediate government

None.

1.3.3 Local government

None.

1.3.4 Overall tax rate

The overall tax rate is 39 per cent.

1.4 Treatment of intercorporate dividends

Dividends received by a Belgium company are taxable, but 90 per cent (85 per cent for financial companies) of the dividends is excluded from tax if the holding period is at least one year. If the holding period is less than one year, the tax credit is equal to 50 per cent of the company's income tax computed at the ordinary tax rate.

The dividends are subject to the withholding tax of 25 per cent. The net dividends received must be increased by 1/3 in order to include the withholding tax. The tax is creditable against taxable income and only the withholding tax is refundable.

1.5 Provisions applying to interest receipts and payment

1.5.1 Receipts

Interest receipts are treated as ordinary income.

1.5.2 Payments

Interest payments are deductible if they are not excessive. An interest rate is considered to be excessive if the interest rate is three points higher than the interest rate of the Belgian National Bank. Limitation does not apply to interest paid by and to financial institutions and publicly issued bonds.

1.6 Treatment of trading losses

Normal domestic trading losses may be carried forward without time limitation. Trading losses cannot be carried backwards.

1.7 Capital gains and losses

1.7.1 Gains

A. Buildings, machinery, vehicles

Capital gains realized within five years of the acquisition date are taxed as ordinary income.

Capital gains on assets held over a period of more than five years are subject to "spread taxation", if the revenue of the sale is reinvested. In case of spread taxation, the amount of capital gains realized is spread over the depreciation period according to the depreciation rate of the asset purchased, and taxation of each net annuity occurs at the ordinary tax rate.

B. Shares

Capital gains realized within five years of the acquisition date are taxable as ordinary income. Capital gains on shares held over a period of more than five years are taxed at a flat rate equal to half the ordinary tax rate (19.5 per cent in 1991) unless the revenue of the sale is reinvested in shares.

1.7.2 Losses

For a company, capital losses can be offset against trading income.

1.8 Depreciation

1.8.1 Machinery

Suggested rates are:

Office buildings	3 per cent
Industrial buildings	5 per cent
Furniture	20 per cent
Machinery and equipment	10 per cent or 20 per cent.
Vehicles	20 per cent or 25 per cent

Method of depreciation:	straight line. declining balance
Straight line: Rate of depreciation	estimated lifetime of asset.
Declining balance: Rate of depreciation	twice the straight line rate
Double straight line:	only in certain regions.

1.8.2 Buildings

Method of depreciation:	straight line. declining balance.
Rate of depreciation:	estimated lifetime of asset (see above for assets).

1.8.3 Switch-over

Switch-over from declining balance to straight line is mandatory at the optimum point.

1.9 Investment allowance

An investment allowance under certain conditions is allowed in addition to normal depreciation. The investment allowance can be taken in the year of investment or spread over the depreciation period. The base for the investment allowance depends on the inflation in the preceding year increased with 1 per cent. However the total basic deduction can be no less than 3 per cent and no more than 10 per cent.

The basic deduction plus the inflation rate is increased to 10.5 points for scientific research and development, and energy saving.

Increased allowances are applicable to; small to medium business, new companies, and to investments generating new jobs (working time reduction with compensatory occupation).

Investment tax allowances are not permitted if an investment is financed through a coordination centre. However, specific incentives are available for these investment.

1.10 Inventories

Trading stock is valued at cost price or replacement value, whichever is lower. The LIFO method is not permitted unless it approximates actual physical flows. The valuation methods as initial stock or base stock are not permitted. There is a special allowance for products which fluctuate in price on the world markets.

1.11 Treatment of reserves

Tax free reserves: a reserve for probable losses can be built under certain conditions (clear description of losses). This reserve can amount to 5 per cent of the profits of the relevant year and may not exceed 7.5 per cent of the highest profit made in 1 of the 5 precious years.

Reserve for probable charges: there is no limit for this reserve, however the likelihood of the charges must be proven.

1.12 Treatment of other allowances

An incentive of BF 103 000 is granted for each additional person employed in qualifying research work above the average number of researchers on the same project the previous year.

1.13 Tax period
1.13.1 Individuals

The accounting year is the same as the civil year.

1.13.2 Corporations

The fiscal year is the same as the accounting period. Corporate income tax is payable in quarterly instalments. If they are not paid or if they are insufficient, an additional tax (penalty) equals to 22.5 per cent of the corporate income tax is due.

1.14 Life assurance/pension funds

Life assurance companies are subject to the corporation income tax. Pension funds are tax exempt for the corporation income tax; however, they do not receive a rebate on the withholding tax for dividends or interest.

II. Taxes on property and wealth
2.1 Taxes on net wealth
2.1.1 Individuals

None.

2.1.2 Corporations

None

2.2 Taxes on immovable property

The tax on immovable property varies throughout the country.

III. Domestic withholding taxes
3.1 Withholding taxes on interest

The withholding tax is 10 per cent on interest.

3.2 Withholding taxes on dividends

The withholding tax is 25 per cent on dividends.

IV. Personal income taxes
4.1 Rate schedule

The ordinary personal income tax rates do not apply to interest and dividends (See 4.2 and 4.3).

4.2 Tax treatment of dividends

The withholding tax is the final tax on investment income if income from such sources is not included into taxable income, and such income is not deriving from professional activities.

The taxpayer may however elect to incorporate his dividends received into his taxable income. The withholding tax is included into taxable income and a tax credit is granted for the withholding tax.

The withholding tax is deductible form the computed tax or refunded in cash if no tax is due.

4.3 Tax treatment of interest

The withholding tax is the final tax paid, if not deriving from a professional activity.

4.4 Weighted average marginal rates of personal income tax on dividends, interest and capital gains

See 4.2, 4.3 and 4.5.

4.5 Taxes on capital gains

Capital gains of private property are not taxable except when speculative intention is proved. Capital gains deriving from professional activities are taxable. Capital gains realized within five years of the acquisition date are taxed as ordinary income.

Capital gains on assets held over a period of more than five years are taxed at a flat rate of 16.5 per cent.

V. Investment grants generally available to the manufacturing sector.

None.

VI. International aspects.

6.1 International withholding taxes

6.1.1 Direct investment

The withholding tax rate on dividends for countries that have a tax treaty with Belgium is 15 per cent. For the non-treaty country Turkey a tax rate of 25 per cent applies.

6.1.2 Portfolio investment

The withholding tax rate for countries that have a tax treaty with Belgium is 15 per cent.

6.2 Treatment of foreign source income

6.2.1 Non-treaty countries

Same as treaty countries. (See 6.2.2).

6.2.2 Treaty Countries

Interest payments received from abroad are fully taxable. A tax credit equal to 15 per cent of the "border income" is added to the taxable income and credited against the corporation income tax. The tax credit is not refundable (15 per cent is the general rule).

Dividend payments received from abroad, where the shares are held the entire accounting period of 12 month, are for 90 per cent exempt from the Belgium tax. In all other cases the same rule as for interest applies.

VII. Major changes

None.

Canada

I. Corporation taxes

1.1 Relation with the personal income tax

Personal and corporation income tax are not fully integrated. However, distributed profits carry a tax credit to mitigate the double taxation (see also table 3.1).

1.2 Definition of income subject to tax

Central government: the income for tax purposes for a resident company is the worldwide profit.

1.3 Rate structure

1.3.1 Central government

Rates in per cent	1/1 1988	1/7 1988	1/7 1989	1/7 1990	1/7 1991
Basic Rate	46	38	38	38	38
Federal rate (1)	35	28	28	28	28
Manufacturing corporations (1)	28	26	25	24	23
Small business corporations (1) (2)	14	12	12	12	12

1. These rates are after the 10 points reduction for income earned in a province. They are the rates effectively applicable to the federal tax base if the income is earned in a Canadian province.
2. The small business rate applies only to the first Can $ 200 000 of business profits of qualifying firms. A 3 per cent surtax is applicable on tax otherwise payable.

1.3.2 Intermediate government

The statutory federal tax rate is reduced by a 10 point abatement when income is earned in a Canadian province. The last three rows of the above table are net of this abatement.

Provincial tax rates are as follows:

	General rates %		Small business tax rate %	
Alberta	15	(9.0)	5	(0.0)
British Columbia	14		9	
Manitoba	17		10	
New Brunswick	16		9	
Newfoundland	17		10	
Northwest Territories	10		10	
Nova Scotia	15		10	
Ontario	15.5	(14.5)	10	
Prince Edward Island	15		10	
Quebec	5.5		3	
Saskatchewan	15		10	
Yukon	10	(2.5)	5	(2.5)

Note: Numbers in parentheses are the rates applicable for manufacturing corporations on income earned in the province from manufacturing and processing activities. In Ontario, this rate is extended to income from mining, farming, logging and fishing.

1.3.3 Local government

None.

1.3.4 Overall tax rate

The average federal-provincial tax rate applicable to the income of small and large manufacturing corporations as from 1 July 1991 is determined as follows:

	Large corp. (%)	Small corp. (%)
Federal rate (1)	23.84	12.84
Provincial rate (2)	11.9	7.4
Combined Federal-Provincial rate (1)	35.74	20.24

1.   Includes the 3 per cent federal surtax computed on the basic 28 per cent rate.

2.   Weighted average statutory rate for all provinces.

1.4 Treatment of intercorporate dividends

Dividend income from other resident companies is included in the corporate net income. However, such dividends are fully deductible in the computation of taxable income, so that they are effectively received free of additional tax.

1.5 Provisions applying to interest receipts and payments

1.5.1 Receipts

Interest receipts are treated as ordinary income.

1.5.2 Payments

Interest payments are deductible.

1.6 Treatment of trading losses

Normal domestic trading losses may be carried forward for seven years. Trading losses can be carried backwards three years.

1.7 Capital gains and losses

1.7.1 Gains

Rate of inclusion of realized capital gains in taxable income:

Before 1 July 1988	: 50 per cent
After 30 June 1988, but	
before 1 January 1990	: 66 2/3 per cent
After 31 December 1989	: 75 per cent

1.7.2 Losses

Capital losses (to the extent that they are taxed, see above) can be offset against future capital gains. The capital losses that can not be offset against capital gains can be carried forward indefinitely and carried backwards three years.

1.8 Depreciation

1.8.1 Machinery

Method of depreciation	: declining balance.
Rate of depreciation	: laid down by the tax authorities.

1.8.2 Buildings

Method of depreciation	: declining balance.
Rate of depreciation	: laid down by the tax authorities.

Class	Asset	Annual rate on undepreciated balance
3	Buildings or structures	4%
7	Vessels (other than certified Canadian vessels)	15%
7	Certified Canadian vessels	3 year straight-line
7	Drillships and offshore platforms	25%
8	Machinery, equipment, etc.	20%
9	Aircraft	25%
10	Automotive equipment	30%
41	Resource extraction assets	25%
39	Canadian manufacturing and processing machinery and equipment:	
	1 Jan. 1988	40%
	1 Jan. 1989	35%
	1 Jan. 1990	30%
	1 Jan. 1991	25%

A half-year convention applies on all the above classes in the year the asset is acquired, which means that a corporation can only claim 50 per cent of the deduction otherwise computed in that year.

1.8.3 Switch-over

Not applicable.

1.9 Investment tax credits

ITC-Rates after Tax Reform. The general investment tax credit (ITC) rates are phased-out under Tax Reform. Only regional ITCs and credits for R&D-expenditures are retained, at reduced rates. The phase-out schedule, and remaining ITC rates are set out in the table below:

	1988 (%)	1989 and subsequent years (%)
7 per cent general rate	3	0
10 per cent general rate	3	0
Special regional rate for manufacturing in designated areas (1)	40	30
Research and development (2) depending on location and size of firm	20, 30, 35	20, 30, 35
Atlantic region (3) Cap Breton (4)	20	15

1. Available in prescribed areas of Canada for prescribed buildings, machinery and equipment used in manufacturing and processing.

2. Available for expenditures in respect of scientific research and experimental development.

3. Available for qualifying property used in manufacturing, mining, oil and gas, agriculture, forestry and fishing in Atlantic Canada.

4. Available for assets accquired before 1993 to be used on Cap Breton (in a project approved by the Minister of Regional Industrial Extensions before 1 July 1988)

Yearly limitation on claim: effective on 1 January 1988, the amount of investment tax credit that can be used to reduce federal tax payable will be limited. In general, only 75 per cent of the taxpayer's federal tax otherwise payable can be offset by available (i.e. carried forward plus earned in the year) ITC. However, Canadian-controlled private corporations (CCPCs) will be given a full offset of federal tax on their business income eligible for the small-business deduction. Thus, the limit for a CCPC in a year will be 12 per cent of its income eligible for the small business deduction (for a maximum of Can $24 000), plus 75 per cent of federal corporate taxes payable on other income.

CCA Grind: effective on 1 January 1988, the capital cost of a depreciable property is reduced by the amount of ITC claimed in preceding taxation years. Before 1988, current-year ITC claims reduced the capital cost.

ITC Carry-Forward: the unclaimed portion of investment tax credits earned after 19 April 1983 is eligible for a ten year carry-forward and a three year carry-back.

ITC Refund: investment tax credits that are unused in the year in which they are earned can be partially refunded. The rate of refund is 40 per cent of unused ITC, and is eligible only to Canadian-controlled private corporations. In addition, small R&D corporations can be refunded in full the unused portion of the 35 per cent ITC earned on up to Can $ 2 000 000 of research and development expenditures each year.

1.10 Inventories

Trading stock is valued at cost price, selling price or replacement value. Cost price can be determined by FIFO and the average cost method. The LIFO method is not permitted.

1.11 Treatment of reserves

Inventory reserve: None.

1.12 Treatment of other business expenses

Expenses other than capital in nature (machinery, equipment and building, whose cost must be capitalised and depreciated according to statutory depreciation rates) can be written off in the year they are incurred.

1.13 Tax period

1.13.1 Individuals

The fiscal year is the same as the calendar year.

1.13.2 Corporations

Corporations use their fiscal period (not exceeding 53 weeks) as their fiscal year. The tax authorities must approve of a change in the fiscal period.

Corporate tax instalments are due on the last day of the month. The balance is due on the last day of the second month following the end of the tax year.

1.14 Life assurance/pension funds

In most countries these institutions are tax exempt.

II. Taxes on property and wealth

2.1 Taxes on net wealth

The federal government levies a tax on the net wealth of the capital of deposit-taking institutions (banks, trusts, mortgage loans companies) and life assurance companies. The graduated rate of tax is:

Value of capital	Tax rate (%)
0 - C$ 200 million	0
C$ 200 - C$ 300 million	1
In excess of C$ 300 million	1.25

This tax is creditable against the regular federal corporate income tax. The federal government also levies a Large Corporation Tax, which applies on the capital of all corporations. Effective on January 1 1991, the basic rate is 0.2 per cent, applicable on the value of the capital in excess of C$ 10 million. This tax is creditable against the federal corporate surtax.

2.2 Taxes on immovable property

The tax on immovable property varies throughout the country.

III. Domestic withholding tax

3.1 Withholding taxes on interest

None.

3.2 Withholding taxes on dividends

None.

IV. Personal income taxes

4.1 Rate schedule

Federal
As of January 1, 1991:

Taxable income Can $		Marginal tax rate (%)
0 -	28 784	17
28 784 -	57 568	26
In excess of	57 568	29

Effective 1 January 1991, the surtax is 5 per cent, and an additional surtax of 5 per cent applies on basic federal tax in excess of C$ 12 500.

Provincial: Provincial personal tax rates, with the exception of Quebec, are expressed as a percentage of basic federal tax. The following are the statutory rates as of January 1, 1991:

	Basic rate (%)		High income surtax (%)		Flat tax rate (%)	
Alberta	46.5		8.0	(8)	0.5	(9)
British Columbia	51.5		—		—	
Manitoba	52.0		2.0	(4)	2.0	(5)
New Brunswick	60.0		—		—	
Newfoundland	61.0		—		—	
Northwest Territories	43.0		—		—	
Nova Scotia	56.5		—		—	
Ontario	53.0		10.0	(3)	—	
Prince Edward Island	57.0		10.0	(1)	—	
Quebec	N/A	(2)	—		—	
Saskatchewan	50.0		12.0	(6)	2.0	(7)
Yukon	45.0		—		—	

1. Applicable on provincial tax payable in excess of C$ 12 500.
2. Quebec uses its own income definitions and rate structure.
3. Applicable on provincial tax payable in excess of C$ 10 000.
4. Applicable on net income in excess of C$ 30 000.
5. Applicable on net income.
6. Applicable on provincial tax payable in excess of C$ 4 000.
7. Applicable on net income.
8. Applicable on provincial tax payable in excess of C$ 3 500.
9. Applicable on taxable income.

4.2 Tax treatment of dividends

Grossed-up dividends are subject to a dividend tax credit. As of 1 January 1988, the rates of gross-up and credit are as follows:

	Federal tax only (%)	Combined Federal-Provincial taxes (%)
Rate of gross-up applied on dividends received	25	25
Rate of tax credit as a percentage of dividends received	16.67	about 25

The provincial credit is proportional to the province's tax rate, and so the combined federal-provincial dividend tax credit will vary from province to province. For example, if the provincial tax rate is 50 per cent of basis federal tax, the provincial credit is 8,33 per cent, for a combined federal-provincial credit of 25 per cent.

4.3 Tax treatment of interest

Taxed as ordinary income.

4.4 Weighted average marginal rates of personal income tax on dividends, interest and capital gains

The federal effective marginal tax rates on investment income for 1991 (including all surtaxes) are provided below.

	Weighted average (%)	Highest marginal rate (%)
Interest income	25.3	31.9
Dividends	28.7	31.9
Capital gains	6.8	23.9

The above weighted average rate for capital gains is the rate applicable to realised capital gains, and includes the impact of the lifetime capital gains exemption. To compute a joint federal-provincial effective marginal tax rate for any given province, one applies the statutory provincial tax rate provided in the table of section 4.1 on the federal effective rate shown above.

The provincial effective marginal tax rate so obtained is then added to the federal rate to obtain a joint federal-provincial rate.

The joint federal-provincial marginal tax rates averaged over all provinces are provided below. They reflect the use of an average provincial effective marginal tax rate (inclusive of surtaxes and flat taxes) of 59.4 per cent:

	Weighted average (%)	Highest marginal rate (%)
Interest income	39.5	49.1
Dividends	44.6	49.1
Capital gains	10.5	36.8

Again, the above rate for capital gains is for realized capital gains, and includes the impact of the lifetime capital gains exemption.

4.5 Taxes on capital gains

Individuals are allowed a lifetime exemption of capital gains up to a total value of C$ 100 000 (C$ 500 000 for small business shares and farms). The inclusion rates of realized capital gains in taxable income is the same as those provided for corporations, i.e. 66 two-thirds per cent as of 1 January 1988, and 75 per cent after 1989.

V. Investment grants generally available to the manufacturing sector

None.

VI. International aspects

6.1 International withholding taxes

6.1.1 Direct investment

The withholding tax rate on dividends for countries that have a tax treaty with Canada is 15 per cent (with the exception of France, Japan, the Netherlands, the United Kingdom and the United States in which case the base rate is 10 per cent). For the non-treaty countries Greece, Portugal and Turkey a tax rate of 25 per cent applies.

6.1.2 Portfolio investment

The withholding tax rate for countries that have a tax treaty with Canada is 15 per cent. For the non-treaty countries Greece, Portugal and Turkey a tax rate of 25 per cent applies.

6.2 Treatment of foreign source income

6.2.1 Non-treaty countries

Portfolio dividends: dividends received are included in income, and a credit for foreign withholding taxes paid is provided.

Direct investment (ownership of 10 per cent or more of the share capital): dividends received are included in income, and a credit for foreign withholding taxes paid and underlying foreign corporate income taxes paid is provided.

6.2.2 Treaty Countries

Portfolio dividends: same as 6.2.1

Direct investment (ownership of 10 per cent or more of the share capital): dividends received are included in income, but are fully deductible in computing taxable income. In effect, dividends are exempt from Canadian corporate income tax.

VII Major changes

None.

Denmark

I. Corporation taxes

1.1 Relations with the personal income tax

Personal and corporation income tax are not fully integrated. However distributed profits are subject to a special tax treatment under which dividend income is subject to a schedular tax at a lower rate than other kinds of income. The rates are adjusted so that the sum of corporate and personal tax is approximately the same as the taxation of capital income for small investors and similar to the taxation of earned income for large investors (see also table 3.1).

1.2 Definition of income subject to tax

Central government: the income for tax purposes for a resident company is the worldwide profit.

1.3 Rate structure

1.3.1 Central government

The tax rate is 38 per cent.

1.3.2 Intermediate government

None.

1.3.3 Local government

None.

1.3.4 Overall tax rate

The overall tax rate is 38 per cent.

1.4 Treatment of intercorporate dividends

Danish companies owning at least 25 per cent of the stock of another company are not subject to tax on dividends they recive from another Danish company. This also applies to dividends recived from subsidiaries in most OECD-countries.

316

1.5 Provisions applying to interest receipts and payments

1.5.1 Receipts

Interest receipts are treated as ordinary income.

1.5.2 Payments

Interest payments are deductible.

1.6 Treatment of trading losses

Normal domestic trading losses may be carried forward for five years. Trading losses can not be carried backwards.

1.7 Capital gains and losses

1.7.1 Gains

Capital gains are included in taxable income in so far as they are taxed. Capital gains on bonds and security assets are taxed at the corporate rate if the bonds are issued with an interest rate below a certain minimum. The minimum rate is adjusted according to the matched rate of interest on bonds. Capital gains on bonds in foreign currency are taxed at the corporate rate. Capital gains on shares are exempt if held more then three years. Capital gains on real estate are exempt after seven years. From three to seven years the gains are taxed at a lower rate.

1.7.2 Losses

Capital losses (as far as they are taxed) can be offset against capital gains. However, the capital loss incurred on the disposal of buildings and its features is not deductible.

Capital losses incurred on the disposal of intellectual property are fully deductible.

1.8 Depreciation

Assets with a useful life of less than three years or a value less than DK 5 000 are deductible in the year of acquisition. Inventory can be depreciated by 30 per cent annually. As regards stock-taking please see 1.10.

1.8.1 Machinery

Method of depreciation: declining balance. Each year a maximum deduction of 30 per cent of the balance value may be taken.

The taxpayer has each year the option to take:
— no depreciation
— a lower rate of depreciation.

1.8.2 Buildings

Method of depreciation: straight line.

Rate of depreciation: the taxpayer chooses the depreciation percentage each year, up to a maximum, which is 4 per cent (hotels, cinemas, etc), 6 per cent (industrial buildings) and 8 per cent, respectively, for different categories of buildings and facilities. The taxpayer may continue to apply the initial (maximum) percentages until the accumulated depreciation amounts to 40 per cent, 60 per cent or 80 per cent, respectively. For subsequent years, 1 per cent, 2 per cent and 4 per cent, respectively, are the maximums.

No depreciation on buildings used only as offices or dwelling houses.

1.8.3 Switch-over

Not applicable.

1.9 Investment tax credits

None.

1.10 Inventories

Trading stock is valued at cost price (market value at the accounting date purchase price or cost of manufacturing. Cost price can be determined by FIFO. However, it should be noted that none of these theoretical rules are authorized by Danish law. The actual practice is, however, to recognize the FIFO-principle, and it may be assumed that also an average principle is acceptable. The LIFO method is not permitted unless it approximates actual physical flows.

1.11 Treatment of reserves

No investment or inventory reserve.

1.12 Treatment of other business expenses

Time-limited rights (patents, royalties, leases, etc.) are deductible in equal annual parts. Non-limited rights can be deducted within 10 years.

1.13 Tax period
1.13.1 Individual

Generally the fiscal year is the same as the calendar year. The tax authorities may allow in limited circumstances an alternative period.

1.13.2 Corporations

See 1.13.1. The total amount of corporate tax due is charged on 1 November in the same calendar year that the tax return is filed. Tax must be paid no later than 20 November. Advance payments of corporation tax are generally not made in Denmark.

1.14 Life assurance/pension funds

Pension funds subject to supervision in accordance with the Act on supervision of pension funds or the Act on assurance activities are non-taxable. Life assurance companies are taxable.

II. Taxes on property and wealth

2.1 Taxes on net wealth

2.1.1 Individuals

Individuals are subject to a tax on net wealth of 1 per cent after a deduction of Dkr. 1 452 700.

Business assets are stated at their depreciable value and a reduction of 40 per cent. Securities are stated at the marked value. Private furniture and other movable assets (such as pieces of art) are not included.

2.1.2 Corporations

Corporations are not subject to a tax on net wealth.

2.2 Taxes on immovable property

The tax on immovable property varies throughout the country.

III. Domestic withholding taxes

3.1 Withholding taxes on interest

None.

3.2 Withholding taxes on dividends

There is a withholding tax of 30 per cent on dividends and 30 per cent on royalties.

IV. Personal income taxes

4.1 Rate schedule

4.2 Tax treatment of dividends

Dividend income is taxed by a "dividend withholding tax" at a rate of 30 per cent for dividends less than DKR 30 000 per year and 45 per cent for dividends which exceeds DKR 30 000.

4.3 Tax treatment of interest

Taxed as ordinary income.

4.4 Weighted average marginal rates of personal income tax on dividends interest and capital gains

Weighted average marginal rates on interest: 51.1 per cent
Weighted average marginal rates on dividends: 37.6 per cent

4.5 Taxes on capital gains

Individuals

Some capital gains are taxed according to the Special Income Tax Act, with a rate of 50 per cent.

Captial gains realised on the sale of shares:

— Owned less than three years included in taxable income and taxed at the normal income tax rates.

— If shares are owned for more than three years and the total value of the share is not more than 25 per cent of the total share capital of the company they are exempted from tax.

— The gains on the sale of shares are calculated share per share. If the shares in the same company have been quired at different times the shares held for the longest period are considered having been sold first.

Profits from the alienation or redemption of bonds, mortgage deeds, debt instruments, and other money claims must be included in ordinary taxable income if the claim is returning a yield which is less than the officially fixed minimum rate of interest at the time of contracting. The minimum rate was 9 per cent throughout the year 1990.

V. Investment grants generally available to the manufacturing sector

None.

VI. International aspects

6.1 International withholding taxes

6.1.1 Direct investment

The withholding tax rate on dividends for countries that have a tax treaty with Denmark varies between 0 per cent and 15 per cent. For the non-treaty countries Greece and Turkey a tax rate of 30 per cent applies.

6.1.2 Portfolio Investment

The withholding tax rate for interest is 0 per cent. The withholding tax rate for dividend varies between 0 and 15 per cent . For the non treaty countries Greece and Turkey a tax rate of 30 per cent applies.

6.2 Treatment of foreign source income

6.2.1 Non-treaty countries

Income from foreign sources is segregated and the tax credit for taxes paid abroad is granted for the domestic tax due on that particular income.

6.2.2 Treaty countries

Same as under 6.2.1. Dividends are fully exempt from the domestic tax if an interest of at least 25 per cent in the share capital is held during the entire financial year and the income has been taxed abroad in accordance with tax legislation which does not differ significantly from the Danish income tax system.

6.2.3. Additional tax credit for foreign business-income.

In addition to the treaty and non-treaty reliefs mentioned in 6.2.1 and 6.2.2. Danish companies are entitled to an additional tax-credit of half of the Danish tax on foreign business-income (calculated before the treaty or non-treaty reliefs). This applies to income from a foreign branch or from a 100 per cent owned subsidiary if the subsidiary is included in joint taxation with the Danish parent company.

VII. Major changes

None.

Finland

I. Corporation taxes

1.1 Relation with the personal income tax

Personal and corporation income tax are integrated by means of a full imputation system. As a result distributed corporate income will be taxed according to the marginal tax rate of the individual shareholder.

A company distributing dividends must pay a minimum amount of tax corresponding to the corporation tax calculated on the amount of the distribution and applying a rate of 40 per cent. If the tax payable on the basis of taxable income is less than the minimum amount, the company has to pay a compensatory tax that covers the difference. If the tax based on taxable income exceeds the minimum tax, a carry forward of the excess is allowed (see tables 3.1 and 3.2).

In principle a company or an individual resident in a foreign country is not entitled to any imputation credit. A double taxation treaty may extend the credit to foreign shareholders.

1.2 Definition of income subject to tax

Central government: the income for tax purposes for a resident company is the worldwide profit.

1.3 Rate structure

1.3.1 Central government

The national tax rate is 23 per cent.

A lower tax rate is applied to companies with profits less than Mk 100 000. The lower tax rate is calculated as follows:

Suppose a taxable profit of Mk 50 000. The tax rate is 50 000/100 000 = 50 per cent of 23 per cent = 11.5 per cent.

1.3.2 Intermediate government

None.

1.3.3 Local government

Municipalities levy a tax with the rates varying from 14 per cent to 18.5 per cent. The average rate for the country as a whole is 16 per cent. Church tax is levied at rates which vary between 1 and 2 per cent. The average church tax rate actually paid by companies is 1.2 per cent. For Helsinki, as an example, the municipal tax rate is 15 per cent and the church tax rate is 1 per cent.

1.3.4 Overall tax rate

The average overall tax rate for a company is 23 per cent + 16 per cent + 1.2 per cent = 40.2 per cent. The overall tax rate in Helsinki is 39 per cent.

1.4 Treatment of intercorporate dividends

Dividend income from other resident companies is included into the corporate taxable income. However, since the recipient company is entitled to the imputation credit, no double taxation will result.

1.5 Provisions applying to interest receipts and payments

1.5.1 Receipts

Interest receipts are treated as ordinary income.

1.5.2 Payments

Interest payments are deductible.

1.6 Treatment of trading losses

Normal domestic trading losses may be carried forward for five years. Losses in the first five years of a business can be carried forward to the tenth year of business. Trading losses can not be carried backwards.

1.7 Capital gains and losses

1.7.1 Gains

Capital gains are taxed as ordinary income. Capital gains on real estate and security are taxed differently.

If security owned for less than 5 years and real estate owned for less than 10 years, the difference between 60 per cent of the sale proceeds of such assets and the book value is added into taxable income and taxed at the normal income tax rates.

1.7.2 Losses

Capital losses are treated in the same way as other trading losses.

1.8 Depreciation

1.8.1 Machinery

Machinery and equipment with an useful life of less than three years can be depreciated in the year they are purchased.

| Method of depreciation: | declining balance. |
| Rate of depreciation: | 30 per cent of the total book value (entire stock of machinery and equipment). |

The taxpayer may use lower rates.

1.8.2 Buildings

Method of depreciation	: declining balance.
Rate of depreciation	: 5 per cent — 20 per cent
Industrial buildings (wood)	: 10 per cent
Industrial buildings (stone)	: 9 per cent
Office building (wood)	: 6 per cent
Office buildings (stone)	: 5 per cent
Buildings exclusively used for research and development	: 20 per cent
In certain regions up to	: 100 per cent

1.8.3 Switch-over

Not applicable.

1.9 Investment tax credits

None.

1.10 Inventories

Trading stock is valued at acquisition price, cost price or net selling price. Cost price can be determined by FIFO. The LIFO method is not permitted unless it approximates actual physical flows.

See 1.11 for inventory reserve.

1.11 Treatment of reserves

Finnish companies are entitled to several reserves, the most important are:

Operating Reserve:	The maximum cumalative appropriation that may be made to the operating reserve is 30 per cent of wage and salary payment during the previous 12 months.
Reserve for future investments:	Corporations are permitted to allocate to this reserve 20 per cent of their profits. Minimum amount of the reserve is Mk 30.000. 50 per cent of the appropriation must be deposited in an interest bearing restricted account with the Bank of Finland. The interest is paid when money is withdrawn from the account.
	The reserve may be used for such purposes as the construction of buildings used in the business, acquisition of machinery, or equipment, product development, training, and promotion of export. Assets acquired with funds from this reserve are not depreciable.
Inventory Reserve:	The maximum inventory reserve that may be deducted is 25 per cent of year-end inventory, after excluding all obsolete or unsalable goods.

1.12 Treatment of other business expenses

Patents and other rights with a limited life may be written off over a period of ten years on a straight line basis.   Accelerated depreciation is allowed if their economic life is shorter.

1.13 Tax Period

1.13.1 Individuals

The fiscal year is the same as the calendar year.

1.13.2 Corporations

The fiscal year is the accounting period. The corporate income tax is payable in three instalments in December, February (the next year) and March. If the tax paid in advance exceeds the final tax, the excess is refunded in December. No interest is paid or levied.

1.14 Life assurance/pension funds

Pension funds are tax exempt. Life assurance companies are fully taxed.

II. Taxes on property and wealth

2.1 Taxes on net wealth

2.1.1 Individuals

Amount of property	Tax on lower amount	Percentage of excess
1 000 000	500	0.9%

2.1.2 Corporations

Non-resident companies, including branches of foreign companies, are liable to an annual tax of 1 per cent on all property in Finland. Resident corporations whose shareholders are subject to net wealth tax with respect to their shares in the corporation are not subject to the national net wealth tax. Other legal entities are normally subject to net wealth tax.

2.2 Taxes on immovable property

None

III. Domestic withholding taxes

3.1 Withholding taxes on interest

The final withholding tax on interest is 10 per cent (see 4.3)

3.2 Withholding taxes on dividends

None.

IV. Personal income taxes

4.1 Rate schedule

Taxable income Mk	Basic Tax	Marginal tax rate %
40 000 - 56 000	50	7
56 000 - 70 000	1 700	17
70 000 - 98 000	3 550	21
98 000 - 154 000	9 430	27
154 000 - 275 000	24 550	33
275 000 and more	64 480	39

4.2 Tax treatment of dividends

Dividend income, grossed up by the imputation credit, is included in the taxable income. A resident shareholder receives an imputation credit equal to the corporation tax. For the purpose of the imputation credit the corporation income tax is always deemed to be 40 per cent.

4.3 Tax treatment of interest

Interest on unregulated deposits and bonds received by a Finnish resident is subject to a final withholding tax of 10 per cent. Interest on regulated bank deposits (low interest rate) and regulated bonds issued by State or a mortgage bank (low interest rate) is tax exempt.

4.4 Weighted average marginal rates of personal income tax on dividends interest and capital gains

The effective tax rates are:

	Weighted average marginal rate %
Dividends	45.2
Interest income	10.0
Capital gains	5.0

In the case of dividends, dividend income is the grossed-up amount. The tax rate is calculated based on dividend recipient's tax liabilities before deduction of imputation credits.

4.5 Taxes on capital gains

Individuals

Gains from the sale of immovable property held for a period of less than 10 years and from the sale of other property held for less than 5 years are taxed as ordinary income according to the following proportions:

Holding period	Taxable part of the gains %
less than 4 years	100
at least 4 but less than 6 years	80
at least 6 but less than 8 years	60
at least 8 years	50

If in any year the taxpayer's aggregated gain from the sale of any kind of property, held for respectively 10 or 5 years or longer, exceeds Mk 220 000, then 50 per cent of the excess is subject to tax as ordinary income. When calculating the amount of capital gain, the purchase price or 50 per cent of the sales price is deducted from the sales price of each asset sold. Thus, if the total annual sales price of assets held for over 10 or 5 years, respectively, does not exceed Mk 440 000 for the calendar year, no tax on capital gains is applied.

Capital gains from alienatation of the taxpayer's own dwelling are tax-free if he occupied it for at least two years before the sale.

V. Investment grants generally available to the manufacturing sector

None.

VI. International aspects

6.1 International withholding taxes

6.1.1 Direct investment

Unless lower tax rates are provided in a tax treaty, the withholding tax rate on dividends is 25 per cent. The treaty rates vary between 0 per cent and 15 per cent.

6.1.2 Portfolio investment

The non-treaty rate is 25 per cent. The treaty rates vary between 0 per cent and 15 per cent.

6.2 Treatment of Foreign Source Income

6.2.1 Non-Treaty Countries

Income from foreign sources is included as taxable income and a credit for foreign state income tax paid is granted on a per country basis up to the amount of Finnish state income tax payable on that income. Foreign local taxes do not qualify for tax credit.

6.2.2 Treaty Countries

Same as under 6.2.1.

However, where the terms of a tax treaty so provides, credit for foreign tax may also be given against Finnish municipal income tax (and also for foreign local income tax). As a general rule, foreign dividends are exempt from Finnish tax on income if the receiving company controls directly at least 10 per cent of the voting power in the company paying the dividends.

VII. Major changes

None.

France

I. Corporation taxes

1.1 Relations with the personal income tax

Personal and corporation income tax are not fully integrated. However distributed profits carry a tax credit to avoid double taxation (see also tables 3.1 and 3.2).

1.2 Definition of income subject to tax

Central government: the income for tax purposes for a resident company is the profit earned through business operating on French territoriality, according to the territory principle.

1.3 Rate structure

1.3.1 Central government

The tax rate is 34 per cent for retained profits and 42 per cent for distributed profits. Following a capital increase in cash (share issuing), companies can deduct from their taxable income, for a period of six years, 53.4 per cent of the dividends coming from these shares.

Annual lump sum tax: companies subject to the corporation tax are liable to an annual lump sum tax even if no profit is realised. The lump sum tax is dependable on the corporations turnover.

Turnover		Tax
Less than FF	1 000 000	FF 5 000
1 000 000	- 2 000 000	7 500
2 000 000	- 5 000 000	10 500
5 000 000	- 10 000 000	14 500
in excess of	10 000 000	21 000

If the corporation is profitable, this tax is deductible from the corporation tax in the tax year and the two subsequent years. Newly created companies are exempt from this tax during their first three years provided that cash contributions represent at least 50 per cent of their capital.

1.3.2 Intermediate government

None.

1.3.3 Local government

The tax "professionnelle" is based on the rental value of the corporate fixed assets and on a fraction of salaries.

1.3.4 Overall tax rate

The overall tax rate is 34 per cent on retained profits and 42 per cent on distributed profits.

1.4 Treatment of intercorporate dividends

Companies holding less than 10 per cent of the stock of the distributing company are entitled to the "avoir fiscal" for the dividends received. They are taxed on the net dividend received plus the "avoir fiscal". The avoir fiscal is creditable against the corporate tax liability. If the avoir fiscal is higher than the corporation tax liability for the year during which the dividends were received, the excess cannot be carried forward, nor is it refundable.

If a company holds at least 10 per cent of the capital of the distributing company, it may qualify as a "parent company", the received dividends are deducted from the taxable profit after the definition for a share representing the running cost of the participation. This share is fixed at 5 per cent of the gross dividends (dividend plus "avoir fiscal"). The avoir fiscal cannot be offset against the tax payments but on the equalization tax. If dividends are distributed, the company is liable for the equalization tax. However under certain conditions holdings of foreign companies are exempt from the equalization tax but no "avoir fiscal" is granted to the shareholders.

1.5 Provisions applying to interest receipts and payments

1.5.1 Income

Interest income is treated as ordinary income.

1.5.2 Payments

Interest payments are fully deductible.

1.6 Treatment of operating losses

Domestic operating losses may be carried forward for five years. Operating losses resulting from differed or deemed differed depreciation in loss years can be carried forward indefinitely.

Operating losses may be carried back three years if they are offset against undistributed net profits (after corporation tax) of three preceding years. The tax credit may be offset against corporate income tax of the following five years and thereafter any excess may be reimbursed in cash. It may also be discounted with a bank.

1.7 Capital gains and losses

1.7.1 Gains

Short term: realized within two years of the acquisition date. They are taxed at 34 per cent with the option to spread the payment of tax over three years.

Long term: realized after two years of the acquisition date. These capital gains are taxed at the rate of 19 per cent if their net amount (81 per cent) is booked in the special reserve for investment. If they are distributed a supplement of 23 per cent of tax to reach an effective rate of taxation of 42 per cent is due.

The rate is 25 per cent for gains from the sale of bonds, warrants for bonds and mutual investment funds and for gains on building sites.

1.7.2 Losses

Short term capital losses can be offset against short term capital gains. The balance is added to the taxable base and taxed at the normal corporate income tax rate (34 per cent). Long term capital losses can be offset against long term capital gains, during the present tax year or the next ten years.

1.8 Depreciation

1.8.1 Machinery

Method of depreciation: — straight line.

— optional declining balance applicable to new assets with an useful life of at least three years.

Rate of depreciation: — estimated lifetime of asset according to the rules in force for that business sector (rates are indicative)

Asset	Straight line rate (%)
Commercial buildings	2 - 5
Industrial buildings	5
Machinery	10 - 20
Plant (tools and office equipment)	10 - 15
Automobiles	20 - 25
Patents	20

Rate for declining balance:

Normal useful life	Declining balance rate
3 - 4 years	1.5 x straight line rate
5 - 6 years	2 x straight line rate
over 6 years	2.5 x straight line rate

For energy or raw materials saving machinery the above rates 1.5, 2, 2.5 are increased to 2, 2.5, 3.

1.8.2 Buildings

The declining balance is allowed neither for buildings with the exception of hotel buildings and certain light construction buildings with a useful life of less than 15 years nor for assets which life is less than three years. See 1.8.1.

1.8.3 Switch-over

Switch-over is allowed for equipment at the optimum point from declining balance to straight line, but not vice versa.

1.9 Investment tax credits

Special regional incentives are available.

1.10 Inventories

Inventory is valued at cost price (purchase price). If the market value is lower, a deduction can be taken. Cost price can be determined by FIFO. The LIFO method is not permitted unless it approximates actual physical flows. (See 1.11 for commodity market fluctuation reserve)

1.11 Treatment of reserves

Reserve for investment abroad: since 1988 companies have been entitled to set up a tax free reserve for investment in commercial establishments abroad. The investment must be in the form of the creation or acquisition of subsidiaries whose principal activities are the marketing of products made in France by the enterprise. No special government approval is necessary if certain conditions are met. Banks and other enterprises participating in foreign commercial or industrial ventures in support of a French company investing abroad are also entitled to this reserve. The reserve must be added back to taxable income in annual instalments as of the sixth year.

Reserve for commodity market fluctuations: a special allowance (provision pour fluctuation des cours) is available for a French business whose main business is the processing of listed raw materials.

1.12 Treatment of other business expenses

All R&D-expenses other than depreciable assets are deductible in the year they occur. Buildings may be depreciated in the first year up to 50 per cent.

A tax credit for research expenses is available. The credit corresponds to the difference between the amount of research expenses for the year in question and those incurred in the preceding year, and is limited to FF 40 000 000 annually, as of 1991.

1.13 Tax period

1.13.1 Individuals

The fiscal year is the same as the calendar year.

1.13.2 Corporations

The fiscal year is defined in the articles of the company. If the financial year exceeds 12 months, the company must issue a provisional financial statement as of 31st December.

The corporate income tax must be paid in four instalment during the fiscal year totalling 40.5 per cent of the taxable income of the preceding year. The balance, if any, must be paid no later than three and one-half months after the year-end.

1.14 Life assurance/pension funds

As in most countries these institutions are tax exempt.

II. Taxes on property and wealth

2.1 Taxes on net wealth

2.1.1 Individuals

The net wealth tax is levied on wealth other than business assets exceeding FF 4 260 000 according to the following schedule:

Value in FF		Rate
0	- 4 260 000	0
4 260 000	- 6 920 000	0.5
6 920 000	- 13 740 000	0.7
13 740 000	- 21 320 000	0.9
21 320 000	- 41 280 000	1.2
More than	41 280 000	1.5

2.1.2 Corporations

None.

2.2 Taxes on immovable property

The taxes on immovable property varies throughout the country.

III. Domestic withholding taxes

3.1 Withholding taxes on interest

For certain types of security taxpayers resident in France may opt for the "prélevèment libératoire" of 16 per cent (withholding tax on interest) and no further income tax on this interest is due. Additional taxes of 2.1 per cent social security contributions including the 1.1 per cent C.S.G (Generalised Social Contribution) are also due. The total tax rate is therefore 18.1 per cent.

3.2 Withholding taxes on dividends

None.

IV. Personal income taxes

4.1 Rate schedule applicable to 1990 income

Portion of taxable income for two shares ("parts")

			Rate (%)
0	-	36 280FF	0
36 280	-	37 290	5
37 920	-	44 940	9.6
44 940	-	71 040	14.4
71 040	-	91 320	19.2
91 320	-	114 640	24
114 640	-	138 740	28.8
138 740	-	160 060	33.6
160 060	-	266 680	38.4
266 680	-	366 800	43.2
366 800	-	433 880	49
433 880	-	493 540	53.9
Over	-	493 540	56.8

Tax reductions:

Tax resulting from the application of the schedule:

Amount of tax:	Reduction of tax
0 <tax< 25 480	11 per cent
25 481 <tax< 31 830	the difference between 6 370 and 14% of the tax
31 831 <tax< 38 200	6 per cent
38 201 <tax< 44 910	14 per cent
Over and provided the 44 910 taxable income does not exceed a certain amount	3% if the taxable income per share "part" does not exceed 322 670 C.S.G.

Income is also subject to the C.S.G at the rate of 1.1 per cent.

4.2 Tax treatment of dividends

Dividends paid by French companies carry a tax credit (avoir fiscal) to the benefit of the French shareholders.

The tax credit is 50 per cent of the dividends received. The tax credit is included into the taxable dividends received. The credit is deductible form the computed tax or refunded in cash if no tax is due.

Dividends are also subject at a uniform rate of 1.1. per cent (Generalised Social Contribution) and 1 per cent complementary contribution.

Investment income is exempt from tax up to FF 8 000 for single persons and FF 16 000 for married couples.

4.3 Tax treatment of interest

For certain types of securities taxpayers residents of France can elect to have their tax on interest income withheld as the final tax. The election for the prélèvement (withholding tax) can be made for interest from:

— Bonds approved by the Ministry of Finance and not indexed;

— "Bank notes" issued by certain French banks;

— Other loans, where nethier the capital nor the interest are indexed when the debtor is resident or has a permanent establishment in France.

In addition, the Finance Ministry is authorized to make taxation by a final withholding (prélèvement) obligatory for certain loans. These include certain Treasury bonds and bonds issued by the Caisse Nationale du Crédit Agricole. The rate of the "prélèvement" on interest is normally 18.1 per cent (including the two social surtaxes of 1 per cent and the C.S.G. of 1.1 per cent), but different rates may apply in certain cases (social surtaxes included) 38.1 per cent on interest from treasury bonds and 53.1 if the recepient remains anonymous.

4.4 Weighted average marginal rates of personal income tax on dividends, interest and capital gains

The average marginal tax rate on dividends is 45 per cent.
The average marginal tax rate on interest is 5.6 per cent.

4.5 Taxes on capital gains

Capital gains on bonds are taxed at 16 per cent (plus 2.1 per cent of social surtaxes, total 18.1 per cent) if the total value of the sale is more than FF 307 600.

If an individual alone or together with related persons holds more than 25 per cent of the unquoted shares of a company, at any time during the past 5 years the capital gains realised upon dispostion of the shares are taxed at 18.1 per cent. If such an individual holds less than 25 per cent, the capital gains are only taxed if the total value of the proceeds exceeds FF 307 600 for 1991.

V. Investment grants generally available to the manufacturing sector

None.

VI. International aspects

6.1 International withholding taxes

6.1.1 Direct investment

The withholding tax rate on dividends for countries that have a tax treaty with France varies between 0 and 25 per cent.

6.1.2 Portfolio investment

The withholding tax rate for portfolio investment varies between 0 per cent and 15 per cent and certain tax treaties extend the benefit of the "avoir fiscal" (tax credit) to portfolio investors resident of the other contracting state.

6.2 Treatment of foreign source income

6.2.1 Non-treaty countries

Deduction of the tax withheld abroad.

6.2.2 Treaty countries

Dividends: dividends from foreign sources are tax exempt for 95 per cent of their amount tax if the holding is more than 10 per cent of the share capital or the cost of the acquisition was at least FF 150 million. The remaining 5 per cent is subject to the domestic tax on the gross dividend (include the foreign tax paid) the foreign tax credit may be transferred to the shareholders. If the interest is less than 10 per cent of the share capital, the dividend is taxed and a credit is given for foreign tax paid.

Interest: interest from foreign sources is segregated and the tax credit for foreign taxes paid is the only granted for a particular activity or investment in a particular country against the domestic tax due on that particular investment.

In some cases different rules apply for dividend payments:

Australia: The French shareholders receiving Australian dividends are entitled to the avoir fiscal on the full dividend, that is including the credit granted for Australian taxes paid.

Ireland: All dividends received from Ireland are tax exempt.

Spain: All dividends subject to the Spanish tax on petroleum are deemed to have born a withholding tax of 25 per cent.

Sweden: All dividends received from Sweden are tax exempt.

VI. Major changes

None.

Germany

I. Corporation taxes

1.1 Relations with the personal income tax

Personal and corporation income tax are fully integrated. The tax rate on distributed profits is lower and the taxpayer can credit it against his personal income tax (see also tables 3.1 and 3.2).

1.2 Definition of income subject to tax

Central government: the income for tax purposes for a resident company is the worldwide profit.

1.3 Rate structure

1.3.1 Central government

The corporate tax rate is 50 per cent.

1.3.2 Intermediate government

None.

1.3.3 Local government

Municipalities impose a business tax on income and capital (i.e. Guesbsteuer). The federal base rate (Messzahl) for the municipal income tax is 5 per cent and for the business capital tax 0.2 per cent.

The local tax authorities multiply the federal rate with a multiplier (Hebesaetze) of 240 per cent — 480 per cent.

The base for the business income tax is the federal tax base:

— Plus: 50 per cent of interest on long-term debt;

— Plus: half the rental charges on movable business property (unless taxed in the hands of the lessee);

The base for the business capital tax is the last assessed value (Einheitswert) of total new assets (Betriebsvermoegen):

— Plus: 50 per cent of long-term liabilities minus DM 50 000;

— Plus: rented movable property (unless taxed in the hands of the lessee);

— Minus: value of real estate (owned);

— Minus: an amount of DM 120 000.

The municipal tax authorities, therefore, impose a trade tax on income (Gewerbeertragsteuer) which will vary between 10.7 per cent and 19.4 per cent (15 per cent = average rate) and a capital tax (Gewerbekapitalsteuer) which will vary from 0.5 per cent to 0.96 per cent

The business tax is deductible from the base for itself and from the central corporate income tax.

1.3.4 Overall tax rate

The overall effective tax rate is 13 per cent x (1 — 0.5) + 50 per cent = 56.5 per cent.

1.4 Treatment of intercorporate dividends

Dividend income from other resident companies is included in the corporate taxable income. The withholding tax on dividends and the corporation income tax of the company which pays the dividends are deductible from the corporation income tax liability of the company which receives the dividends.

Dividends paid by a domestic corporation to another domestic corporation are subject to corporation income tax in the hands of the receiving corporation. Even if the receiving corporation owns a substantial participation of the dividend paying corporation, dividends are not tax exempt.

1.5 Provisions applying to interest receipts and payments

1.5.1 Receipts

Interest receipts are treated as ordinary income.

1.5.2 Payments

Interest payments are deductible as business expenses.

1.6 Treatment of trading losses

Trading losses which cannot be offset against other positive receipts in the year they occur are first carried back for two preceding years. This is, however, only allowed up to a total amount of DM 10 million. As far as losses are not offset by this procedure they are carried forward to the five years following the year of occurrence.

Losses that occurred in 1985 or later can be carried forward without time limitation.

With regard to carrying losses backward or forward it is irrelevant whether they are locally registered or not.

1.7 Capital gains and losses

1.7.1 Gains

Gains from the sale of "substantial interest" are taxed at the normal tax rates.

Capital gains are taxed at the corporation income tax rates. Under certain conditions the profit on the sale of land, buildings, fixed assets with a long useful life, ships, and shares in corporations can fully or partly be offset against the purchase price of the new asset.

1.7.2 Losses

Capital losses are, in principle, treated in the same way as other trading losses (see 1.6). There is, however, one exception for corporations being not obligated to keep accounts if the time period between purchasing and selling of an asset is short (for real estate less than two years, less than six months for other assets). In these cases capital losses can only be offset against capital gains received by the corporation in the same year. Carrying capital losses backward or forward is ruled out to this extent.

1.8 Depreciation

The tax authorities have published tables for the "economic useful life" and AFA (depreciation for wear and tear allowed by tax regulations) for several assets.

1.8.1 Machinery

Method of depreciation: — straight line

— declining balance (if justified on the economic performance),
— accelerated depreciation.

Rate of depreciation : based on estimated lives of assets.
Straight line:

Assets	Straight line rate (%)
Machinery	10
Office equipment	20
Cars	20 - 25

Declining balance: up to three times straight line with a maximum of 30 per cent.

Accelerated depreciation: accelerated depreciation is allowed for small and medium companies with a taxable value of less than DM 240 000 and stock in trade of no more than DM 500 000. The accelerated depreciation is up to 20 per cent on the cost of acquisition on manufacturing of new movable assets during five years in addition to normal depreciation.

1.8.2 Buildings

Method of depreciation : straight line.

Depreciation for non residential buildings: buildings completed before 1 January 1925: the annual rate for depreciation is 2.5 per cent of the purchase price or construction costs.

Buildings completed after 31 December 1924, and before 31 March 1985. The annual rate for depreciation is 2 per cent of the purchase price or construction costs.

The taxpayer has the option to:
— Depreciate 5 per cent during the first eight years.
— Depreciate 2.5 per cent during the next six years.
— Depreciate 1.25 per cent during the last 36 years.

For construction permits applied for after 31 March 1985:

Method of depreciation : straight line. The annual rate for depreciation is 4 per cent of the purchase price.

The taxpayer has the option to:
— Depreciate 10 per cent during the first four years.
— Depreciate 5 per cent during the next three years.
— Depreciate 2.5 per cent during the last 18 years.

1.8.3 Switch-over

Is allowed from declining balance to straight line but not vice versa.

1.9 Investment tax credits

There are several investment incentives available for regional areas, Berlin and border areas.

1.10 Inventories

Trading stock is valued at cost price or market value, whichever is lower. The LIFO method of stock valuation is also admitted.

1.11 Treatment of reserves

No investment or inventory reserve provisions.

1.12 Treatment of other business expenses

Patents are deductible in the year they occur.

1.13 Tax period
1.13.1 Individuals

The fiscal year is the same as the calendar year.

1.13.2 Corporations

The fiscal year is the same as the calendar year or the accounting period but this may never exceed more than 12 months.

The corporate tax is due in quarterly instalments during the year, usually based on the last assessment. The last instalment is due when the final assessment is issued.

1.14 Life assurance/pension funds

Pension funds are exempt from the corporation income tax under certain conditions. Other life assurance companies are, however, subject to the corporation income tax.

II. Taxes on property and wealth

2.1. Taxes on net wealth

2.1.1 Individuals

The base for this tax is the market value for movable and immovable property. The base for land is a so-called unit value. This value is less than one half of the market value. At present the tax is based on a sum equivalent to 140 per cent of this unit. Rate: 0.5 per cent.

2.1.2 Corporations

The base for this tax is world wide net wealth valued according to the provisions of the Valuation Act (Bewertungsgesetz). The value of a "substantial interest" (10 per cent) is exempt from net wealth tax.

The first DM 125 000 is exempt from tax. Any value over DM 125 000 is valued at 75 per cent. Rate: 0.6 per cent.

2.2 Taxes on immovable property

The tax on immovable property varies throughout the country.

III. Domestic withholding taxes

3.1 Withholding taxes on interest

There is no withholding tax on interest.

3.2 Withholding taxes on dividends

The withholding tax on dividends is 25 per cent.

IV. Personal income taxes

4.1 Rate schedule

X = Taxable income.

$X \leq 5\ 616$	: Tax=0
$5\ 617 \leq X \Rightarrow 8\ 153$	: Tax= $0.19 * X - 1\ 067$
$8\ 154 \leq X \Rightarrow 120\ 041$	: Tax= $(151.94 * Y + 1\ 900) * Y + 472$
	$\quad Y= (X - 8\ 100)/(10\ 000)$
$120\ 042 \leq X$	: Tax = $0.53 * X - 22\ 842$

4.2 Tax treatment of dividends

The corporate tax rate for distributed profits is reduced to 36 per cent. The tax can be credited against the personal income tax. If profits or reserves which were taxed at 50 per cent are distributed, the difference between the two taxes (i.e. 14/50 of the net distribution) is refunded.

4.3 Tax treatment of interest

Taxed as ordinary income.

4.4 Weighted average marginal rates of personal income tax on dividends, interest and capital gains

The average marginal tax rate on interest and dividends in 1990 is 39.1 per cent. Due to the lack of actual data, the computation of this rate had to be based on the income distribution of 1986.

4.5 Taxes on capital gains

Capital gains are exempt from tax. There are a few exceptions: gains on the sale of land owned less than two years and other assets less than six months are taxed at the normal income tax rates.

V. Investment grants generally available to the manufacturing sector

None.

VI. International aspects

6.1 International withholding taxes

6.1.1 Direct investment

The withholding tax rate on dividends for countries that have a tax treaty with Germany varies between 5 per cent and 25 per cent.

6.1.2 Portfolio investment

The withholding tax rate for portfolio investment varies between 0 per cent and 25 per cent.

6.2 Treatment of foreign source income

6.2.1 Non-treaty countries

Income from foreign sources is segregated and the tax credit for foreign taxes paid is then only granted for a particular activity or investment in a particular country against the domestic tax due on that particular investment (credit by source)

6.2.2 Treaty countries

As under 6.2.1. Dividends are fully exempt from the domestic tax if more than 10 per cent of the voting power is held and Germany has a tax treaty with that particular country.

In some cases different rules apply for dividend payments:

Australia: In case of "passive" profits from an Australian company no exception is given for the German tax, instead the credit by source will be given.

Belgium: Dividends from a Belgium company that incorporate more than 20 per cent of dividends from countries that have no tax treaty with Germany do not profit from the exemption rule but are taxed according to the rules set out above.

Ireland: If the exemption rule does not apply, a relief of 18 per cent of the net dividend is given for foreign tax paid.

In some cases different rules apply for interest payments:

Portugal: The credit for the withholding tax is 15 per cent.

342

VII.   Major changes

None.

Greece

1. Corporation taxes

1.1 Relations with the personal income tax

Personal and corporate income tax are fully integrated. Dividends are fully deductible (see also table 3.1).

1.2 Definition of income subject to tax

Central government: the income for tax purposes for a resident company is the worldwide profit.

1.3 Rate structure

1.3.1 Central government

The tax rate on undistributed profits is 46 per cent.

Lower rates apply for:

— Manufacturing, handicraft, mining and quarrying 40 per cent;

— If the above are quoted on the Athens Stock Exchange or have made investments since 1 January 1987 up to 50 million. Drs which are entitled to state grants system (Law 1262/82) or had made investments until 31 December 1987 irrespective or their amount these investments were entitled to state grants system, 35 per cent;

— For the other corporations referred to in Art. 2 of Law 1262/82 i.e. hotel enterprises agriculture enterprises etc. which make or made investments are entitled to the state grants system, 40 per cent.

1.3.2 Intermediate government

None.

1.3.3 Local government

None.

1.3.4 Overall tax rate

See 1.3.1.

1.4 Treatment of intercorporate dividends

Dividend income from other resident companies is taxable at source at 47 per cent for registered shares and 50 per cent for bearer shares or unquoted shares; 42 per cent and 45 per cent correspondingly for quoted shares. Dividends from resident corporations are included in taxable income if earned from quoted or registered shares.

1.5 Provisions applying to interest receipts and payments

1.5.1 Receipts

Interest receipts are treated as ordinary income.

1.5.2 Payments

Interest payments are deductible.

1.6 Treatment of trading losses

Normal domestic trading losses may be carried forward for five years as well as losses of manufacturing, hotel and mining companies. Trading losses can not be carried backwards.

1.7 Capital gains and losses

1.7.1 Gains

Gains deriving from the alienation of any participation in a partnership or from the sale of an enterprise as a whole are taxed at 20 per cent and those deriving from the sale of any right pertaining to the enterprise such as the firm's name, trademark or goodwill etc. at 30 per cent rate.

Capital gains from the sale of business assets are taxed as ordinary income. Capital gains from immovable property or ships is tax exempt if such immovable property or ships were or are used by the enterprise itself. Capital gains resulting from the sale of machinery is tax exempt under the condition that it will be used for additional depreciation of new machinery bought within the next two years from the date the capital gains occured. Capital gains resulting from the sale of securities (bonds and shares) are exempt from income tax. In case of businesses keeping double entry books of account, such gains are credited to a special reserve fund available to offset possible losses of future sale of other securities.

1.7.2 Losses

Capital losses can only be offset against profit income of the same year.

1.8 Depreciation

1.8.1 Machinery

Method of depreciation: straight line. Accelerated depreciation up to 150 per cent of the ordinary depreciation rates in some regions is possible.

Rate of depreciation : laid down in the presidential decree 88/1973.

The basic rates in the law are:

Description of asset	Annual depreciation rate (%)
Industrial buildings	8
Other buildings	5
Machinery	10 - 20
Computers	20
Furniture and similar items	20
Office equipment	15
Trucks	20
Other vehicles	12

1.8.2 Buildings

Method of depreciation: straight line. Rate of depreciation: laid down in the decree 88/1973 (see above).

1.8.3 Switch-over

Not applicable.

1.9 Investment tax credits

There are several investment incentives for regional development in Greece amounting to 100 per cent of the investments' values.

Mergers in the manufacturing, handicraft, mining and quarrying enterprises, whose legal form is other than a limited company, are entitled to a partial tax exemption. 10 per cent of the total net profits shown in the balance sheet of the new formed S.A. are exempt from tax. The tax exemption is given for the first five years, provided that the paid-in share capital is at the time of the merger is not less than 100 000 000 Drs. During the period of five years, 75 per cent of the new formed S.A.'s shares are not transferable and must be registered.

1.10 Inventories

Trading stock is valued at cost price or fair market value, whichever is lower. Each item is valued separately, but group valuation of the same items is possible if they have the same price and are of the same kind. Cost price can be determined by FIFO. The LIFO method is permitted.

1.11 Treatment of reserves

Tax allowances are avaliable ranging from 25 per cent to 30 per cent of the taxable profits, which must be entered into a "special reserve" account that must be used for productive investments. However, if the investments are of an advanced technical nature, the tax-exempt profits are 40 per cent or 50 per cent of the total taxable profits.

1.12 Treatment of other business expenses

Deductible in the year they occur.

1.13 Tax period

1.13.1 Individuals

The fiscal year is the same as the calendar year.

1.13.2 Corporations

The fiscal year is the same as the calendar year. However companies with proper accounting records may choose 30 June or 31 December as the end of their fiscal year. Branches and subsidiaries of foreign companies may choose their parent's end of year.

The corporate income tax must be paid in seven equal instalments. The first instalment is due upon filing the tax return. If the total tax due is paid with the first instalment a discount of 10 per cent is granted.

1.14 Life assurance/pension funds

Life assurance enterprises are taxed. Pension funds are taxed on their income derived from hiring immovable property as well as from securities (dividends, interest, bonds etc.).

II. Taxes on property and wealth

2.1. Taxes on net wealth

2.1.1 Individuals

None.

2.1.2 Corporations

None.

2.2 Taxes on immovable property

Individuals and legal entities are subject to a property tax on immovable property situated in Greece. The base for this tax is the aggregated value of immovable property over 50 000 000 Drs. for legal entities and 55 000 000 Drs. for individuals minus mortgages granted by credit institutions.

Rate: — 1.5 per cent for legal entities

     — Progressive rate schedule for individuals.

Exemptions: (under certain conditions)

     — Agricultural property;

     — Property used for mining or manufacturing purposes.

III. Domestic withholding taxes

3.1 Withholding taxes on interest

25 per cent for residents and 46 per cent for non-residents without a permanent establishment in Greece (final taxation).

These rates are applied in cases where the recipient is a legal entity. An individual recipient is subject to progressive rates.

3.2 Withholding taxes on dividends

Quoted on the stock exchange:

— 42 per cent on the dividend of registered shares;

— 45 per cent on the dividend of bearer shares.

Not quoted on the stock exchange:

— 47 per cent on the dividend of registered shares;

— 50 per cent on the dividend of bearer shares.

IV. Personal income taxes

4.1 Rate schedule

Rate schedule 1991

Bracket	Rate (%)	Tax	Total Income	Total Tax
390 000	18	70 200	390 000	70 200
520 000	21	109 200	910 00	179 400
520 000	24	124 800	1 430 000	304 200
520 000	28	145 600	1 950 000	449 800
650 000	33	214 500	2 600 000	664 300
650 000	38	247 000	3 250 000	911 300
1 170 000	43	503 100	4 420 000	1 414 400
1 689 000	49	827 610	6 109 000	2 242 010
excess	50			

4.2 Tax treatment of dividends

Dividend from companies quoted on the Athens Stock Exchange are exempt from income tax up to 50 000 Drs. from each company with a total maximum of 200 000 Drs. for all dividends received by a taxpayer. However, a withholding tax is levied (see section III).

A taxpayer who receives dividends from registered or quoted shares on the Athens Stock Exchange has the option to include the dividends received into his taxable income, in which case it is taxed according to the income tax rates. In that case the withholding tax is credited against the income tax paid and refunded in cash if the credit can not be offset against the income tax liability. The taxation of 50 per cent on the dividends from bearer shares is final.

Companies must distribute dividends equal to 6 per cent of their share capital or 35 per cent of net profits, whichever is higher.

4.3 Tax treatment of interest

Resident individuals include interest received in their taxable income. The withholding tax (see 3.1) is credited against their personal income tax due and the excess is refunded. The interest received from government bonds and bank deposits is exempt from income tax (see 3.1 too).

4.4 Weighted average marginal rates of personal income tax on dividends, interest and capital gains
4.5 Taxes on capital gains

Capital gains resulting from the sale of securities are tax exempt.

V. Investment grants generally available to the manufacturing sector

None.

VI. International aspects.
6.1 International withholding taxes
6.1.1 Direct investment

The withholding tax rate on dividends for countries that have a tax treaty with Greece varies between 25 per cent and 47 per cent.   For the non-treaty countries Australia, Canada, Denmark, Ireland, Japan, Luxembourg, New Zealand, Norway, Portugal, Spain and Turkey, a tax rate of 42 per cent - 50 per cent applies (domestic legislation).

6.1.2 Portfolio investment

The withholding tax rate for portfolio investment varies between 10 per cent and 15 per cent. For the non-treaty countries Australia, Canada, Denmark, Ireland, Japan, Luxembourg, New Zealand, Norway, Portugal, Spain and Turkey a tax rate of 46 per cent applies.

6.2 Treatment of foreign source income
6.2.1 Non-treaty countries

Gross foreign source income is included in taxable income. A credit against income tax due is allowed for foreign taxes paid, but only up to the amount of Greek tax which would have been payable, had the income been derived from Greek sources.

6.2.2 Treaty Countries

Same as under 6.2.1. In some cases different rules apply for interest payments.

VII. Major changes.

None.

Iceland

I. Corporation taxes

1.1 Relations with the personal income tax

Personal and corporation income tax are not fully integrated. According to Icelandic tax laws, distributed profits carry a tax allowance, both on the personal and corporate level to avoid double taxation.

First, dividend received from corporations is exempt from personal income tax, if it is less than or equal to 15 per cent of the total amount of shares owned by the individual. Second, dividend payments of corporations up to 15 per cent of total value of shares are deductible from the corporate income tax base. This means, in fact, that dividend payments up to 15 per cent of total value of shares, is fully exempt from taxation (see also table 3.1).

1.2 Definition of income subject to tax

Central government: the tax base is defined as net profit; i.e. gross earnings less operating cost.

1.3 Rate structure

1.3.1 Central government

The tax rate is 45 per cent.

1.3.2 Intermediate government

None.

1.3.3 Local government

There is no corporate income tax at this level. However, there is a local turnover tax levied on corporations and unincorporated firms. The tax base is defined as total turnover cost of companies and the average tax rate is approximately 1 per cent. The marginal rate is different between branches, the maximum being 1.3 per cent. The turnover tax is deductible from the tax base of the central government income tax.

1.3.4 Overall tax rate

The overall income tax rate is 45 per cent.

1.4 Treatment of intercorporate dividends

Dividend income from other resident companies is generally included in the corporate taxable income and taxed as such.

1.5 Provisions applying to interest receipts and payments

1.5.1 Receipts

Interest receipts are treated as ordinary income.

1.5.2 Payments

Interest payments are deductible.

According to Icelandic tax laws companies are required to correct their balance sheet for inflation. The net amount of this correction is treated accordingly as a taxable income or trading cost. Of the taxable income stemming from this correction, however, 45 per cent may be used as an additional depreciation. Under certain conditions this percentage can be higher. The aim is to seek an estimate of the real interest payments of the company.

1.6 Treatment of trading losses

Trading losses indexed for inflation may be carried forward indefinitely. Trading losses cannot be carried backwards.

1.7 Capital gains and losses

1.7.1 Gains

Capital gains on assets fall under the corporate income tax system, regardless of the year of acquisition. Accordingly, net capital gains on assets allowing for inflation is included in the taxable income and taxed at the income tax rate, i.e. 45 per cent. Under certain conditions the capital gains in depreciable assets can be offset by additional depreciation of other assets or charged against new investment within two years of the realization of the gain.

1.7.2 Losses

Capital losses on assets other than equities or other rights of ownership in companies can be offset against taxable income in the same year.

1.8 Depreciation

1.8.1 Machinery

Method of depreciation: straight line.

Rate of depreciation: estimated lifetime of an asset with a 10 per cent residual value.

Asset	Straight line rate (%)
Industrial equipment and machinery	12
Office equipment	20
Vehicles	15
Buildings	2
Automobiles	8

Assets with a value less than 109 500 ISK are fully deductible in the year of acquisition.

1.8.2 Buildings

See 1.8.1.

1.8.3 Switch-over

Not applicable.

1.9 Investment tax credits

None.

1.10 Inventories

Trading stock is valued at cost price allowing for inflation (market value, cost of manufacturing or purchase price). The actual practice is in fact a recognition of the FIFO-principle without being specially authorized under the Icelandic law.

1.11 Treatment of reserves

Investment funds: companies can allocate 10 per cent of their net profits to an investment fund on the condition that 50 per cent of the amount will be deposited in a special bank account within five months from the end of the accounting year. The bank deposit must be held for a minimum period of six months to a maximum of six years.

The investment fund allocations are price-indexed (building cost index). On the date of withdrawal from the investment fund, a comparable amount is accounted for as taxable income of the company. This amount may be used against trading losses or as an accelerated depreciation of a new investment.

1.12 Treatment of other business expenses

Expenditure on rights (patents, royalties, lessons) and research is fully deductible in the year of acquisition.

1.13 Tax period

1.13.1 Individuals

The fiscal year is the same as the calendar year.

1.13.2 Corporations

The fiscal year is generally the same as the calendar year. Occasionally, tax authorities allow companies to use the accounting period but it may never exceed more than 12 months.

1.14 Life assurance/pension funds

Pension funds are exempt from corporate income taxation. Life assurance companies are, however, subject to corporation income tax.

II. Taxes on property and wealth

2.1 Taxes on net wealth

2.1.1 Individuals

Individuals are subject to a 1.2 per cent tax on their net wealth after allowing for a tax-free amount of approximately 3 million ISK. In addition 0.75 per cent surtax is levied on net wealth exceeding 9 million ISK. The surtax depends, however, on the taxpayer's taxable income. If it exceeds 1.8 million ISK yearly, the surtax is levied without reduction. If the taxable income is only half that amount 0.9 million ISK, no surtax is levied. Between these limits the surtax is levied proportionally.

Individuals are also subject to a special 0.25 per cent tax on their net wealth exceeding 4.8 million ISK, individuals older than 67 years and disabled being excluded.

2.1.2 Corporations

Corporations are subject to a 1.45 per cent tax on their net wealth.

2.2 Taxes on immovable property

Local governments levy real estate tax on individuals and corporations. The tax base is an estimated capital value of the individual's or corporation's real estate. The tax rate varies throughout the country.

The central government levies a special 1.5 per cent tax on real estate used for offices, wholesale and retail business. The tax base is identical to the real estate tax base.

III. Domestic withholding taxes

3.1 Withholding taxes on interest

None.

3.2 Withholding taxes on dividends

None.

IV. Personal income taxes

4.1 Rate schedule

The Iceland personal income tax system has only one tax rate, i.e. the total marginal tax rate is 39.8 per cent, made up of a 32.8 per cent central government tax rate and a 7.0 per cent local government tax rate. The average tax rate is, however, much lower or close to 13 per cent as a result of extensive use of tax credits.

4.2 Tax treatment of dividends

Dividends received from corporations are exempt from personal income tax if they are less or equal to 15 per cent of price-regulated value of the company's shares owned by the individual. Still, the total amount of dividends may not exceed 126 000 ISK for each individual or 252 000 ISK for married couples. If dividends exceed these amounts they are fully taxable.

354

To induce investment in shares, a special tax allowance is granted in the form of a deduction from the personal income tax base to a maximum of 126 000 ISK for each individual or 252 000 ISK for married couples.

4.3 Tax treatment of interest

Exempt from taxation.

4.4 Weighted average marginal rates of personal income tax on dividends, interest and capital gains

Dividends: approximately two thirds of the total dividend income of households in 1990 were tax exempt as result of extensive use of tax allowances as explained in 4.2. The rest is liable to taxation at 39.8 per cent marginal rate less personal tax credit if not fully used against other forms of taxable income. On the whole, the average marginal tax rate of dividends is estimated to be around 15.8 per cent.

Interest income: interest income of individuals is fully tax exempt.

Capital gains: capital gains from the sale of a residence are generally exempt from taxation as a result of various deferral rules. Price-regulated capital gains from sales of other assets are on the other hand fully taxed at 39.8 per cent marginal rate. The average tax rate is lower stemming from the use of the personal tax credit (approximately 20 per cent).

4.5 Taxes on capital gains

Capital gains from sale of a residence held for a period of less than five years are fully taxable. However, the taxation can be deferred for a period of two calendar years, if the individual declares his intention to buy another property within this time limit. Otherwise the gains are fully taxable.

Capital gains from sale of other assets, securities, and shares included, are subject to full taxation regardless of the period of ownership.

V. Investment grants generally available to the manufacturing sector

None.

VI. International aspects

6.1 International withholding taxes

6.1.1 Direct investment

The withholding tax rate on dividends for countries that have a tax treaty with Iceland varies between 0 per cent to 15 per cent. For non-treaty countries the tax rate applied is between 20 per cent to 26.7 per cent.

6.1.2 Portfolio investment

The withholding tax rate for portfolio investment is 15 per cent.

6.2 Treatment of foreign source income

6.2.1 Non-treaty countries

Income from all foreign sources (salaries, dividends, interest, etc.) is added together and the total tax on foreign income is calculated. A tax credit for the total sum of foreign taxes paid is then granted against the domestic tax.

6.2.2 Treaty countries

Same treatment as under 6.2.1 except in special cases.

VII. Major changes

Changes enacted as of 1st January 1991:

a. The central government tax rate was lowered from 50 per cent to 45 per cent

b. The allocation of profits to an investment fund was lowered from 15 per cent to 10 per cent.

Ireland

I. Corporation taxes

1.1 Relations with the personal income tax

Personal and corporation income tax are partly integrated (see also tables 3.1 and 3.2).

1.2 Definition of income subject to tax

Central government: corporation tax is charged on the "profits" for tax purposes of a resident company. "Profits" are worldwide income and worldwide capital gains. Royalties from patents developed in Ireland are tax exempt.

1.3 Rate structure

1.3.1 Central government

The company tax rate is 43 per cent as on and from 1 April, 1989 and will be reduced to 40 per cent as from 1 April, 1991.

The company tax rate for the manufacturing sector as well as for qualifying service activities is 10 per cent until December 31, 2010.

1.3.2 Intermediate government

None.

1.3.3 Local government

None.

1.3.4 Overall tax rate

See 1.3.1.

1.4 Treatment of intercorporate dividends

Dividends between Irish companies are in general treated as having been fully taxed.

1.5 Provisions applying to interest receipts and payments

1.5.1 Receipts

Interest receipts are treated as investment income except where they are received in the course of a banking or similar trade.

1.5.2 Payments

Interest payments incurred for the purpose of a trade are normally deductible in computing trading income. Other interest payments are deductible from a company's entire profits (including capital gains).

1.6 Treatment of trading losses

Trading losses may be carried forward indefinitely against trading income of the same trade.

Trading losses can also be offset against the company's entire profits (including capital gains) of the same year or the immediately preceding year.

1.7 Capital gains and losses

1.7.1 Gains

Companies are liable to corporate tax in respect of their capital gains. The amount of the gains charged is adjusted so that the effective rates of charge to corporation tax are the same as the following capital gains tax rates (which vary with the period of ownership of the asset):

Holding period	Rate (%)
Less than three years	50
Three to six years	35
More than six years	30

Tax on specified business assets (plant and machinery, land and buildings, and goodwill) can be deferred if the disposal proceeds are reinvested in such assets.

Relief for inflation is granted where the holding period is more than one year. The purchase price is multiplied by the increase in the consumer price index since the year in which the expenditure was incurred.

Expenditure incurred in	Inflation multiplier
1974/75	5.221
1975/76	4.217
1976/77	3.633
1977/78	3.114
1978/79	2.877
1979/80	2.596
1980/81	2.247
1981/82	1.857
1982/83	1.563
1983/84	1.390
1984/85	1.260
1985/86	1.188
1986/87	1.136
1987/88	1.098
1988/89	1.077
1989/90	1.043

Special rules apply to development land and to shares quoted on the Smaller Companies Market.

In the absence of advance clearance by the tax authorities, purchasers must withhold tax of 15 per cent of the consideration when acquiring Irish assets costing in excess of IR£ 50 000 (IR£ 100 000 for disposal on or after 24 May 1989).

1.7.2 Losses

A loss arising on a transaction is regarded as an allowable capital loss if, had it been a gain, it would have been regarded as a chargeable capital gain rather than trading income.

Capital losses can only be offset against capital gains of the same or subsequent accounting periods.

1.8 Depreciation

1.8.1 Machinery

Method of depreciation: declining balance.

Rate of depreciation: there are three basic rates available: 10 per cent, 12.5 per cent and 25 per cent for different assets.

For motor vehicles the rate of depreciation is 20 per cent subject to a capital ceiling of £ 7 000.

The taxpayer may speed up the depreciation allowances to 50 per cent (25 per cent on or after 1 April 1991 and nil on or after 1 April 1992) in the first year. However the taxpayer need not claim the relevant basic rate. But the allowable expenditure is reduced by the basic rate of allowance whether or not it is claimed.

Capital expenditure does not qualify for depreciation allowances to the extent that it is funded by state grants.

Total depreciation can not exceed the initial cost of the asset.

1.8.2 Buildings

Method of depreciation : straight line. Depreciation is only allowed on industrial and certain other buildings.

The basic rate is 4 per cent. Hotels and buildings for agriculture use qualify for a depreciation of 10 per cent annually.

Depreciation of up to 50 per cent on construction expenditure on industrial buildings may be claimed in any one year (25 per cent on or after 1 April, 1991 to 31 March, 1992 and nil thereafter).

1.8.3 Switch-over

Not applicable.

1.9 Investment tax credits

No investment tax credits available.

1.10 Inventories

Trading stock is valued at cost price or market value whichever is lower. Cost price can be determined by FIFO. The LIFO method is not permitted.

1.11 Treatment of reserves

None.

1.12 Treatment of other business expenses

Deductible as they occur.

1.13 Tax period

1.13.1 Individuals

The fiscal year is from 6 April to 5 April.

1.13.2 Corporation

The fiscal year is essentially the same as the period for which accounts are made up and may not exceed 12 months.

1.14 Life assurance/pension funds

Life assurance companies are charged with corporation tax. The investment income and chargeable gains of pension funds are exempt.

II. Taxes on property and wealth

2.1 Taxes on net wealth

2.1.1 Individuals

None.

2.1.2 Corporations

None.

2.2 Taxes on immovable property

The tax on immovable property varies throughout the country.

III. Domestic withholding taxes

3.1 Withholding taxes on interest

Withholding tax on interest : 30 per cent.

3.2 Withholding taxes on dividends

None.

IV. Personal income taxes

4.1 Rate schedule

For the income tax year 1990/1991 the rates were:

Rate (%)	Band of taxable income, IR£	
	Single	Married
30	6 500	13 000
48	3 100	6 200
53	Balance	Balance

4.2 Tax treatment of dividends

Under normal conditions the payment of dividends and other distributions will lead to the payment of Advance Corporation Tax (ACT). This tax can be offset against normal corporation tax of the period in which the dividend is paid. Any remaining balance of ACT can be carried back for one year only or forward without time limitation until it has been fully set off. The ACT for most companies is 28/72 (25/75 from 1 April, 1991), but for companies liable for the corporate tax rate of 10 per cent the ACT is 1/18.

The Irish taxpayer is liable for income tax on the sum of the dividend plus a tax credit equal to the ACT. The tax credit can be offset against his income tax payment.

Dividends from a company qualifying for the 10 per cent company tax rate are 50 per cent exempt from income tax, subject to a maximum of IR£ 7 000. This amount is increased to IR£ 9 000 for dividends under an approved profit sharing scheme for a company's employees.

4.3 Tax treatment of interest

A retention tax, at the standard rate of 30 per cent, must be deducted at source by deposit takers (e.g. banks, building societies, Post Office Savings Bank, etc.) from interest paid or credited on deposits of Irish residents. The retention tax does not apply to:

— Interest on deposits beneficially owned by non-residents;

— Deposits of persons who are entitled to charitable exemption from tax;

— Deposits denominated in foreign currencies.

Deposit takers are not required to make returns to the Revenue Commissioners of payments of interest subject to deduction of retention tax. Companies may offset the tax retained against their liability to corporation tax.

Individuals liable to income tax at the higher rates are taxed on their gross interest at the difference between the standard rate of 30 per cent and the appropriate higher rate.

No refunds of retention tax are payable except to:

— Companies within the charge to corporation tax in respect of the relevant interest;

— Charities;

— Individuals who are:

(a) aged 65 years or over or,

(b) permanently incapacitated, who would not otherwise (because of personal reliefs, age exemption etc.) be liable to income tax on the relevant interest.

4.4 Weighted average marginal rates of personal income tax on dividends, interest and capital gains

In 1990/91 the weighted average marginal rate of income tax on all income was 38.41 per cent. No reliable rates are available specifically for dividend or interest income. However, it is believed that the average marginal rate on interest income is the same as the overall average.

The rate on dividend income is estimated at 50 per cent overall before allowing for any tax credits. Because of the special treatment of dividend income from companies qualifying for the 10 per cent rate of corporation tax, the average marginal rate on manufacturing dividends is lower. A tentative estimate puts this figure at 27 per cent.

Due to data deficiencies it is not possible to reliably estimate the average marginal rate of capital gains tax. It is believed that the rate may be of the order of 40 per cent.

4.5 Taxes on capital gains

See 1.7.1.

V. Investment grants generally available to the manufacturing sector

Several investment incentives are available from the Industrial Development Authority. The level of assistance is not a fixed rate per cent of the capital expenditure. It is influenced by:

— The calibre of the client company;

— The quality of its business plan;

— The extent to which it incorporates a requirement for skilled people, an R&D function and other complete business functions;

— The level of competition from other countries for the investment;

— The location of the project;

— The speed of start-up and new job creation.

Within this overall guiding principle, there are limits on the amount of capital grant which IDA will pay. For a company which is expanding its existing plant in Ireland, the maximum capital grant is 25 per cent of the cost of eligible fixed assets. If the project is new, then the upper limit is 45 per cent (60 per cent in designated areas) of the cost of eligible fixed assets.

In addition to capital grants, IDA also gives rent subsidies and grants for feasibility studies, product development, technology acquisition and training.

VI. International aspects

6.1 International withholding taxes

6.1.1 Direct investment

The withholding tax rate on dividends is 0 per cent.

6.1.2 Portfolio investment

The withholding tax rate for portfolio investment is 0 per cent. Certain recent tax treaties allow a tax credit (less a withholding tax of up to 15 per cent on the aggregate of the dividend and the tax credit) to non-resident portfolio investors.

6.2 Treatment of foreign source income

6.2.1 Non-treaty countries

Foreign tax paid can be allowed as a deduction from the income.

6.2.2 Treaty countries

Income from foreign sources is segregated and the tax credit for foreign taxes paid is granted only for a particular activity or investment in a particular country against the domestic tax due on that particular investment.

In the case of foreign dividends, the Irish resident investors receive credit in certain circumstances for the underlying foreign tax on the profits out of which these dividends were paid.

VII. Major changes

Personal income taxes

The following rate schedule has been introduced for the 1991/92 tax year:

Rate (%)	Band of taxable income	
	Single	Married
29	£6 700	£13 400
48	£3 100	£6 200
52	Balance	Balance

Italy

I. Corporation taxes

1.1 Relations with the personal income tax

Italy has a full imputation system. The rate of imputation is equal to the corporate tax rate (see also tables 3.1 and 3.2).

1.2 Definition of income subject to tax

Central government: the income for tax purposes for a resident company is the worldwide profit.

1.3 Rate structure

1.3.1 Central government

The corporate tax rate is 36 per cent (IRPEG).

1.3.2 Intermediate government

None.

1.3.3 Local government

Companies established after 29 March 1986 in the south and part of the centre of Italy are 100 per cent exempted from IRPEG and ILOR (local) tax for the first ten years.

In certain regions in central and north of Italy, newly established companies are exempt from ILOR for ten years. Companies who invest part of their profits in the South are not taxed for IRPEG on such profits.

The local tax rate is 16,2 per cent (ILOR) and is for 75 per cent deductible from the corporate tax rate (IRPEG) (as of the fiscal year 1991).

1.3.4 Overall tax rate

The overall tax rate is 36 x (1 - 0.75 x 0.162) + 16.2 = 47.83 per cent.

1.4 Treatment of intercorporate dividends

Dividend income from other resident companies is included in the corporate taxable income. However, a tax credit on dividends is generally received so that no tax is paid.

1.5 Provisions applying to interest receipts and payments

1.5.1 Receipts

Interest receipts are treated as ordinary income.

1.5.2 Payments

Interest payments are deductible only when related to the activity of the company.

1.6 Treatment of trading losses

Normal domestic trading losses may be carried forward for five years and can be offset against IRPEG or IRPEF. The ILOR is always levied on profits. Trading losses can not be carried backwards.

1.7 Capital gains and losses

1.7.1 Gains

Capital gains are taxed at the corporation income tax rates (IRPEG and ILOR).

1.7.2 Losses

Capital losses can be offset against capital gains if they are taxed.

1.8 Depreciation

1.8.1 Machinery

Method of normal depreciation: straight line.

Rate of depreciation : the Ministry of Finance has established maximum rates of depreciation for various assets.

For manufacturing industries (metallergic and mechanical) the rates are:

—	General plant and machinery	: 17.5 per cent
—	Tools and laboratory equipment	: 25 per cent
—	Motor vehicles	: 25 per cent
—	Office equipment	: 12 per cent

Accelerated depreciation is available for:

— Assets which are intensively used;
— For new assets during their first three years. The depreciation rate can be as much as twice the normal depreciation rate.

1.8.2 Buildings

Method of depreciation : Straight line.
Rate of depreciation : The Ministry of Finance has established maximum rates of depreciation for various assets.

The rates are:
— Light buildings : 10 per cent
— Industrial buildings : 5 per cent

1.8.3 Switch-over

Not applicable.

1.9 Investment tax credits

None.

1.10 Inventories

Trading stock is valued at cost price (purchase or cost of production excluding interest and overhead) or market value whichever is lower. Cost price can be determined by FIFO or LIFO, and any other system is permitted that is conform to the principles described in the aliena above.

1.11 Treatment of reserves

No investment or inventory reserve provisions.

1.12 Treatment of other business expenses

The expenditures for patents are depreciable over its useful life.

1.13 Tax period
1.13.1 Individuals

The fiscal year is the same as the calendar year.

1.13.2 Corporations

The fiscal year is the same as the accounting period. Corporate income tax must be paid in two instalments. The first instalment of 39.2 per cent when the prior tax return is filed and 58.8 per cent in the eleventh month of the company's financial year. The balance is due when the annual tax return is submitted.

1.14 Life assurance/pension funds

These institutions are tax exempt.

II. Taxes on property and wealth
2.1 Taxes on net wealth
2.1.1 Individuals

None.

2.1.2 Corporations

None.

2.2 Taxes on immovable property

The tax on immovable property is based on the cadastral values.

III. Domestic withholding taxes

3.1 Withholding taxes on interest

The withholding tax on interest is generally (e.g. bonds) 12.5 per cent. The withholding tax rate on interest from bank deposits is 30 per cent. For non-residents the withholding tax rate is generally the same as that for residents, but in this case it is the final tax paid.

3.2 Withholding taxes on dividends

The withholding tax on dividends is 10 per cent as an advanced payment.

IV. Personal income taxes

4.1 Rate schedule

1991 Taxable income		Rates (%)
L 6 800 000		10
L 6 800 000 -	L 13 500 000	22
L 13 500 000 -	L 33 700 000	26
L 33 700 000 -	L 67 600 000	33
L 67 600 000 -	L 168 800 000	40
L 168 800 000 -	L 337 700 000	45
Over	L 337 700 000	50

4.2 Tax treatment of dividends

Dividends are subject to IRPEF (income tax) or IRPEG (corporate tax); no ILOR is levied on dividends. The taxpayer receives a credit equal to IRPEG paid. The credit must be added to the taxable income of the taxpayer but can be deducted from the tax liability of the taxpayer.

If a company distributes more than 64 per cent of its taxable profits, the excess is taxed at 56.25 per cent.

A tax rate of 56.25 per cent also applies if the dividends are paid from reserves consisting of premiums received on the issue of shares or other tax-free reserves which are not liable for the corporate tax.

4.3 Tax treatment of interest

Interest received is subject to the income tax except in the following cases where the withholding tax is the final tax:

— Interest on bonds is subject to a final withholding tax of currently 21.6 per cent, but a rate of currently 10.8 per cent applies to interest on bonds issued between 1 October 1982 and 31 December 1983; and a rate of currently 12.5 per cent applies to interest on bonds issued on or after 1 January 1984;

— Interest paid on bonds issued by qualifying credit institutions providing medium and long-term credit is subject to a final withholding tax of currently 10.8 per cent; a 12.5 per cent rate applies to interest on bonds issued on or after 1 January 1984;

— Interest paid on convertible bonds is subject to a final withholding tax of currently 10.8 per cent for a period not exceeding five years from the date of issue; a 12.5 per cent rate applies to interest on bonds issued on or after 1 January 1984;

— Interest on deposits and current accounts placed at credit institutions and the Post Office is subject to a final withholding tax of currently 30 per cent;

— Interest on public bonds issued between 20 September 1986 and 30 September 1987 is subject to a final withholding tax of 6.25 per cent;

— Interest on public bonds issued on or after 1 October 1987 will be subject to a final withholding tax of 12.5 per cent.

4.4 Weighted average marginal rates of personal income tax on dividends, interest and capital gains

Dividends: 39.4 per cent
Interest: 12.5 per cent
Capital gains: 25.0 per cent

4.5 Taxes on capital gains

A tax rate of 25 per cent is levied on capital gains deriving from the sale of shares; the tax is payable when the tax return is filed. This system is compulsory for the transfers of qualified shareholdings not received by inheritance.

If the sale is carried out by means of a notary or if banks, stock-brokers or broking companies take part in the operation as intermediaries or purchasers, an option is available — on certain conditions — for a 15 per cent tax on capital gains; in this case the payment of the tax chargeable to the transferer is performed by the intermediary.

V. Investment grants generally available to the manufacturing sector

Grants up to 40 per cent are available for investments in the south.

VI. International aspects

6.1 International withholding taxes

6.1.1 Direct investment

The withholding tax rate on dividends for countries that have a tax treaty with Italy varies between 15 per cent and 32.4 per cent. For the non-treaty countries Iceland and Turkey, a tax rate of 32.4 per cent applies.

6.1.2 Portfolio investment

The withholding tax rate for portfolio investment varies between 12.5 per cent and 30 per cent. For the non-treaty countries Iceland and Turkey, the tax rate varies also between 12.5 per cent and 30 per cent.

6.2 Treatment of foreign source income

6.2.1 Non-treaty countries

Income from foreign sources is segregated and the tax credit for foreign taxes paid is only granted for a particular activity or investment in a particular country against the domestic tax due on that particular investment.

6.2.2 Treaty countries

Same as under 6.2.1.

If 10 per cent (5 per cent for a quoted company) of the shares are held, 60 per cent of the receiving dividend is tax exempt.

VII. Major changes.

None.

Japan

I. Corporation taxes

1.1 Relations with the personal income tax

Personal and corporation income tax are not fully integrated. A shareholder is allowed to deduct 10 per cent of his dividends from the personal income tax. If the ordinary taxable income for personal income tax purposes including dividends exceeds 10 million yen, however, a tax credit of only 5 per cent is applicable to the ordinary taxable income minus 10 million yen, and that of 10 per cent is applicable to remaining dividend income (see also table 3.1).

1.2 Definition of income subject to tax

Central government: the income for tax purposes for a resident company is the worldwide profit.

1.3 Rate structure

1.3.1 Central government

The national corporate tax rate is 37.5 per cent.

Small business rate: for companies with a total capital of Yen 100 million or less, the corporate tax rate for the first Yen 8 million of income is 28 per cent.

1.3.2 Intermediate government

None.

1.3.3 Local government

Enterprise tax: the enterprise tax is computed on a tax-exclusive basis and deductible from the total corporate income tax for the purpose of corporate income tax.

The standard tax rates applicable to ordinary corporations for ordinary taxable income are as follows:

- Over first Yen 3,5 million   6 per cent
- Over second Yen 3,5 million   9 per cent
- In all other cases   12 per cent

The Corporate Inhabitants Tax; the Inhabitants tax is payable to prefectures and municipal where the company operates.

Standard Inhabitants tax rate:

- Prefectures   5 per cent
- Municipal   12.3 per cent

The tax rate is a percentage of the national tax rate. The effective Inhabitants tax on normal income for prefectures and municipal becomes therefore:

5 per cent + 12.3 per cent = 17.3 per cent x 0.375 = 6.49 per cent

In addition, Inhabitants tax per capita (equalization) are payable regardless of net income or national tax liabilities. The total tax for prefectures and municipal in Tokyo ranges from Yen 50 000 to Yen 3,750 000 depending on the size of the corporation.

1.3.4 Overall tax rate

Corporate national tax	37.5 %
Corporate enterprise tax	12.0 %
Corporate inhabitants tax	6.49 %
	55.99 %
Less deductibility of enterprise tax	6.01 %
Overall effective tax rate:	49.98%

The enterprise tax is calculated on a tax-exclusive base and becomes therefore: 10.7 per cent. (Enterprise tax = 12 -12 x Enterprise tax).

The enterprise tax is also deductible from the corporate income for the purpose of corporate income tax 10.71 x 0.5599 = 6.01.

1.4 Treatment of intercorporate dividends

Dividends paid between Japanese companies are normally excluded from gross income. However if a domestic corporation owns less than 25 per cent of the shares of another domestic corporation which pays dividends, only 80 per cent of those dividends received, less the interest chargeable to the shares on which those dividends were paid, is excluded from gross income.

1.5 Provisions applying to interest receipts and payments

1.5.1 Receipts

Interest receipts are treated as ordinary income.

1.5.2 Payments

Interest payments are deductible in general.

1.6 Treatment of trading losses

Corporation qualifying to file "blue returns" may elect to:

— carry forward normal trading losses for five years.
— carry backwards normal trading losses for one year.

372

1.7 Capital gains and losses

1.7.1 Gains

Capital gains are taxed at the corporation income tax rates. However, there is a special capital gains tax on land and land rights if held for less than:

Two years: additional national tax rate 30 per cent
additional inhabitants' tax rate 5.19 per cent

Five years: additional national tax rate 20 per cent
additional inhabitants' tax rate 3.46 per cent

1.7.2 Losses

Capital losses can be offset against ordinary income including capital gains.

1.8 Depreciation

Assets with a value of less than Yen 200 000 can be depreciated in the year of purchase. All assets can be depreciated up to 95 per cent of the acquisition costs.

The rates are prescribed by the tax law.

Some of the tax lives are:

Asset	Tax life (years)
Cars, trucks	3 - 6
Machinery (automobile industry)	10
Buildings (wood) for office	26
Buildings (wood) for factory	9 - 16
Buildings (reinforced concrete) for office	65
Buildings (reinforced concrete) for factory	23 - 45

On approval of the tax authorities accelerated depreciation is available. A first year depreciation is available ranging from 8 per cent up to 30 per cent in general depending on the area where the investment takes place, on the type of assets or on the type of business.

Some examples are:

Asset	First year additional depreciation (%)
Investment for environment protection	20
Investment for energy saving	30

For some assets the accelerated depreciation can be taken over a period of five years.

Some examples are:

Asset	Additional depreciation over five years (%)
Newly constructed rental housing	24 - 40
Warehouse	22

1.8.1 Machinery

Method of depreciation : straight line.
                                      declining balance.
Rate of depreciation
    straight line : based on the statutory useful lives.
    declining balance : statutory rate.

1.8.2 Buildings

Method of depreciation : straight line.
                                        declining balance.
Rate of depreciation
    straight line : based on the statutory useful lives.
    declining balance : statutory rate.

1.8.3 Switch-over

The taxpayer is allowed to switch over from the declining balance rate to the straight line method but not vice versa.

1.9 Investment tax credits

None.

1.10 Inventories

Trading stock is valued at cost price, selling value or replacement value. Several methods are acceptable for the purpose of inventory evaluation such as FIFO, LIFO and average cost method. Without prior approval of the tax authorities the chosen method of inventory valuation can not be changed.

1.11 Treatment of reserves

Some examples are reserve for bad debts, reserve for bonus, and reserve for retirement allowances.

1.12 Treatment of other business expenses

The excess of the largest R&D expenses since 1967 can be credited against national corporate income tax for 20 per cent with a maximum of 10 per cent of that tax until 31 March 1993.

Approved depreciable assets for R&D can be credited against the corporate national tax the lower of — 20 per cent of the increment in R&D plus 7 per cent of the acquisition costs — 15 per cent of the corporate national income tax.

A small company (share capital less than Yen 100 million) can deduct from national corporate tax 6 per cent of R&D instead of the 20 per cent increment in R&D as computed above.

1.13 Tax period

1.13.1 Individuals

The fiscal year is the same as the calendar year.

1.13.2 Corporations

The fiscal year is the same as the accounting period.

Corporate income tax must be paid at the same time the tax return is filled (usually three month after the ending of the accounting period). In case an extension is granted the tax must be paid on or before that date. A interest rate of 7.3 per cent per annum is added.

Provisional tax payment are required if the fiscal period is longer than six month. Provisional tax is usually one half of the tax liabilities of the previous year, it can be reduced by filing an interim tax return.

1.14 Life assurance/pension funds

Life assurance: normal corporate tax rate on surplus retained after dividend distribution to policy holders which mainly consists of loading surplus and mortality surplus.

Pension funds: In principle, they are tax exempt. However, in case of private retirement pension funds, corporation tax at the rate of 1 per cent per year is imposed on the balance of the funds. This tax is considered as interest on income tax during the period of tax deferrals from the time when a company makes a payment to the funds until the retirement pension becomes payable to the employees.

II. Taxes on property and net wealth

2.1 Taxes on net wealth

2.1.1 Individuals

None.

2.1.2 Corporations

None.

2.2 Taxes on immovable property

Land, houses and depreciable fixed assets are taxed at 1.4 per cent of their taxable value. There is an acquisition tax on land or houses of 3 per cent or 4 per cent on the taxable value.

III. Domestic withholding taxes

3.1 Withholding taxes on interest

Interest : 20 per cent (including inhabitants tax of 5 per cent).

3.2 Withholding taxes on dividends

The withholding tax on dividends : national tax 20 per cent.

An individual recipient of dividends, other than distribution of income from security investment trusts, may elect to have tax withheld at a rate of 35 per cent, with no assessment income tax being levied on those dividends, provided that certain conditions are met.

Corporations which are liable for the withholding tax can credit the withholding tax against their income tax. For the period between April 1, 1985 and March 31, 1990, any balance that can not be offset against income tax is not refunded in cash but can be carried forward for three years. If in the fourth year there is still a balance this is refunded in cash.

IV. Personal income taxes

4.1 Rate schedule

4.2 Tax treatment of dividends

Dividend payments to resident shareholders are normally subject to the withholding tax with no assessment income tax being levied on those dividends (see 3.2).

4.3 Tax treatment of interest

Interest payments are normally subject to the withholding tax as the final tax paid. (See 3.1).

4.4 Weighted average marginal rates of personal income tax on dividends, interest and capital gains

Dividends: 35 per cent
Interest: 20 per cent

4.5 Taxes on capital gains

The capital gains are generally taxed at normal income tax rates after a deduction of Yen 500 000. If held for more than five years 50 per cent of their gains are taxed.

Capital gains from the sale of certain stocks: income tax: separate taxation at 20 per cent through the filing of final return; or, at taxpayer's choice, separate taxation withheld at source at 20 per cent of the deemed gain of 5 per cent of the proceeds from the sales of listed stocks or stocks so called "Tentou-Touroku meigara". Individual Inhabitants tax: separate taxation at 6 per cent except where separate taxation at source is chosen for the Income tax.

Capital gains on the sale of real estate of more than 30 million yen:

— Less than five years (short term gains) 40 per cent of such gains;

— More than five years (long term gains) 20 per cent for gains up to Yen 40 000 000 and 25 per cent for that part of the gains over this amount;

— Short term and long term capital gains are taxed by the prefecture and municipal at 12 per cent and 6 per cent or 7.5 per cent. When the capital gains on real estate are until the alienation of the reinvested property reinvested in other real estate, there are cases where all taxes on capital gains are deferred.

V. Investment grants generally available to the manufacturing sector

None.

VI. International aspects

6.1 International withholding taxes

6.1.1 Direct investment

The withholding tax rate on dividends paid by subsidiaries for countries that have a tax treaty with Japan is 10 per cent, and a rate of 15 per cent for Australia and New Zealand. For the non-treaty countries Greece, Luxembourg, Portugal and Turkey, a tax rate of 20 per cent applies.

6.1.2 Portfolio investment

The withholding tax rate for countries that have a tax treaty with Japan is 10 per cent, and a rate of 15 per cent for Belgium and New Zealand. For the non-treaty countries Greece, Luxembourg, Portugal and Turkey a tax rate of 15 per cent applies.

6.2 Treatment of foreign source income

6.2.1 Non-treaty countries

Income from all foreign sources is added together and the total tax on the total foreign income is calculated. A tax credit for the total sum of foreign taxes paid is then granted against the domestic tax. The credit is only available if the receiving company owns at least 25 per cent of the shares or 25 per cent of the voting power (28 per cent for small companies). In other cases a deduction is granted for foreign taxes paid.

6.2.2 Treaty countries

Same as under 6.2.1.

In some cases different rules apply for dividend payments:

Australia:	The credit is available for companies that own at least 10 per cent of the voting power.
United States:	The credit is available for companies that own at least 10 per cent of the voting power.

VII. Major changes

None.

Luxembourg

I Corporation taxes

1.1 Relations with the personal income tax

Personal and corporation income tax are not integrated (see also table 3.1).

1.2 Definition of income subject to tax

Central government: the income for tax purposes for a resident company is the worldwide profit.

1.3 Rate structure

1.3.1 Central government

The national corporate tax rate 33 per cent. Other rates apply for lower profits:

Taxable income		Tax on lower amount		Percentage on excess
0 -	400 000			20
400 000 -	600 000	80 000	plus	50[1]
600 000 -	1 000 000	180 000	plus	30[2]
1 000 000 -	1 313 000	300 000	plus	42.6[3]
1 313 000				33

1. of excess over 400 000
2. of excess over 600 000
3. of excess over 1 000 000

A surtax of 1 per cent on national corporate tax is levied as a contribution to the unemployment insurance fund. The national effective rate is therefore 33.33 per cent.

Partial tax holiday: new industrial enterprises contributing to the country's economic development and not competing with existing activities may be exempted (with the authorities' approval) from corporate tax on 25 per cent of profits realized during the first eight years.

1.3.2 Intermediate government

None.

378

1.3.3 Local government

Municipalities levy a business tax on enterprises' profits and net worth. The standard rate of municipal tax on business profits is 4 per cent while the standard rate for that on net worth is 0.20 per cent. The local tax authorities apply a multiplier of 180-300 per cent to this standard rate.

The tax base for the municipal business profits tax is the same as for income tax

— with an abatement of LF 700 000.

The tax base for the tax on net worth is equal to the assessed value (Einheitswert) of all assets; plus:

— the value of leased movable assets (unless the lessor is taxed thereon; minus the value of real estate (owned by the enterprise);

— an abatement of LF 800 000.

The municipal authorities thus levy a tax on business profits (Gewerbeertragsteuer) at a rate of between 7.2 and 12 per cent (average 10 per cent) and a tax on net worth (Gewerbekapitalsteuer) at a rate of between 0.36 and 0.6 per cent.

The municipal tax is deductible from the tax base on which it is calculated as well as from the state corporation tax.

1.3.4 Overall tax rate

The overall corporate tax rate is therefore 39.39 per cent. (with lower rates for lower profits see 1.3.1)

1.4 Treatment of intercorporate dividends

Dividends received from a fully taxable company are exempt from tax if the recipient company owns at least 10 per cent of the share-capital or has an interest of at least LF 50 million in the distributing company.

1.5 Provisions applying to interest receipts and payments

1.5.1 Receipts

Interest receipts are treated as ordinary income.

1.5.2 Payments

Interest payments on exempt income derived from an interest in another company are deductible as trading costs.

1.6 Treatment of trading losses

Domestic trading losses arising in Luxembourg may be carried forward indefinitely. Trading losses cannot be carried backwards.

1.7 Capital gains and losses

1.7.1 Gains

Capital gains on the sale of an interest of not less than 25 per cent or LF 250 million are tax exempt.

Capital gains are taxed at the standard corporation tax rate. Profits on the sale of land, buildings, durable assets and shares may be partly or wholly set against the cost of buying new assets.

1.7.2 Losses

Capital losses are in principle treated in the same way as trading losses.

1.8 Depreciation

1.8.1 Machinery

Method of depreciation: — straight line
                                    — declining balance

Assets of more than LF 35 000 in value must be depreciated according to the rules set out below. Assets below that amount must be depreciated in the year they are acquired.

Rate of depreciation: based on the estimated life of the asset.

Straight line depreciation:

The straight line rates of depreciation commonly used are:

Asset	Rate (%)
Office buildings	2
Industrial buildings	4
Equipment and machinery	10-20
Vehicles	20-25
Office furniture (and fittings)	10-25

The tax authorities can approve other depreciation rates when circumstances so warrant.

Declining balance depreciation:

The declining balance rate is three times the straight line rate with a maximum of 30 per cent (except for buildings where the straight line rate applies).

For assets used for scientific and technical research purposes the declining balance rate is four times the straight line rate with a maximum of 40 per cent. Assets whose role is to contribute to environmental protection or energy saving, acquired in the years 1984 to 1992, may qualify for additional accelerated depreciation of:

— 50 per cent of cost in the case of movable property;
— 30 per cent of cost in the case of real property.

Accelerated depreciation can be applied in the first year or in any of the following four years or may be spread over the first five years.

1.8.2 Buildings

See 1.8.1.

1.8.3 Switch-over

The taxpayer has the option to switch over from declining balance to the straight line method of depreciation but not vice versa.

1.9 Investment tax credits

A tax credit of 12 per cent is accorded for additional investment in tangible depreciable assets other than buildings. The tax credit is calculated on the amount by which such investment exceeds the previous five years' average. The difference must be at least LF 75 000 to qualify.

An additional tax credit of between 2 to 6 per cent is accorded on the purchase price of qualifying assets (tangible depreciable assets other than buildings) acquired over the year.

The credit is not granted for:

— Assets with a useful life of less than four years;
— Second-hand goods;
— Assets with a value of less than LF 35 000;
— Vehicles used for transport except those for in-company use.

1.10 Inventories

Trading stock is valued at cost price or selling value, whichever is lower.

Cost price can be determined by the FIFO method.

The LIFO method is not permitted unless it approximates actual physical flows.

1.11 Treatment of reserves

No investment or inventory reserve.

1.12 Treatment of other business expenses
1.13 Tax period
1.13.1 Individuals

The tax year is the same as the calendar year.

1.13.2 Corporations

The tax year is the same as the calendar year. Another period corresponding to the accounting period may be adopted if the tax authorities agree to the change.

Corporation tax is paid in quarterly instalments, the amount of which is decided by the tax authorities on the basis of the previous year's assessment if this is available.

1.14 Life assurance/pension funds

Insurance companies and employers sponsored premium funds are generally tax exempt.

II. Taxes on property and wealth

2.1 Taxes on net wealth

2.1.1 Individuals

A wealth tax of 0.5 per cent is levied on net the value of the taxpayer. Real property is valued at the official value. The taxpayer is entitled to full deduction of liabilities and a deduction of LF 100 000 for himself, for his spouse and generally for the children. The total value of money, shares and other securities is reduced with an allowance of LF1 400 000. This amount is doubled for couples with joint taxation.

2.1.2 Corporations

National wealth tax. A wealth tax of 0.5 per cent is levied on net value of companies in Luxembourg. The net value of companies is determined by the official value of real property situated in Luxembourg and marked values of securities. Interest of at least 10 per cent or at least LF50 millions are exempt.

A registration duty of 1 per cent is levied on the paid-up share capital.

There is also a capital tax on the estimated value of issued capital:

—	Holding companies	0.20 per cent	minimum charge LF 2 000
—	S.A.R.L.	0.18 per cent	minimum charge LF 1 000
—	Investment funds	0.06 per cent	minimum charge LF 1 000
—	Others	0.36 per cent	minimum charge LF 1 000

III Domestic withholding taxes

3.1 Withholding taxes on interest

None, except on arrears and on interest on bonds with variable returns (giving right to an interest in profits) similar to dividends.

3.2 Withholding taxes on dividends

The withholding tax on dividends to shareholders is 15 per cent. No withholding tax is levied on inter-corporate dividends if the interest is more than 10 per cent or the value more than LF 50 million.

IV Personal income taxes

4.1 Rate schedule

4.2 Tax treatment of dividends

Dividends are taxed as normal income. Newly issued shares between 1984 and up to 1992 in fully taxable resident companies are deductible from income tax up to LF 27 000 (LF 54 000 for married couples). Dividends from such shares are exempt from income tax up to LF 60 000 in the following five years after the year of introduction. The LF60 000 are doubled in cases where couples are taxed jointly.

4.3 Tax treatment of interest

Taxed as ordinary income (allowance of 60 000 francs for a taxpayer; 120 000 for a taxable couple).

4.4 Weighted average marginal taxes of personal income tax on dividends, interest and capital gains

24 per cent marginal tax rate.

4.5 Taxes on capital gains

Capital gains are only taxed at the normal income tax rates if:

— Real estate is sold within two years;
— Gains on other property sold within six months.

If a shareholder sells more than 25 per cent of his interest in a company he is liable for half the income tax rates. The same rate applies to real estate sold after two years. There are however several deductions before this tax is due.

V. Investment grants generally available to the manufacturing sector

None.

VI. International aspects

6.1 International withholding taxes

6.1.1 Direct investment

The withholding tax rate on dividends paid to residents of countries that have a tax treaty with Luxembourg is between 2.5 and 15 per cent. The tax rate applying to non-treaty countries (Australia, Greece, Iceland, Japan, New Zealand, Portugal and Switzerland) is 15 per cent. Since 1 January 91 Luxembourg has applied the EC Directive on the common system of taxation applicable in the case of parent companies and subsidiaries of different Member States [90/435/EEC].

6.1.2 Portfolio investment

The withholding tax rate for portfolio investment varies between 0 and 15 per cent.

6.2 Treatment of foreign source income

6.2.1 Non-treaty countries

Income from foreign sources is segregated; the tax credit for foreign taxes paid is accorded only in respect of a specific activity or investment in a given country and is set against the domestic tax due on that investment.

6.2.2 Treaty countries

Dividends: same treatment as 6.2.1.

Dividends from foreign sources that are taxed abroad are exempt from domestic tax if the recipient holds at least 10 per cent of the share capital of the fully taxable distributing company (or an interest of at least LF 50 million) and if the shares have been held for at least 12 months at the end of the tax year. In all other cases where a treaty exists, a credit by source is granted (an explanation is given below under "Interest"). Luxembourg companies may opt for "worldwide" credit treatment instead of credit-by-source treatment if the foreign taxes paid do not exceed 25 per cent and if the amount of the tax credit is not more than 20 per cent of the tax due in Luxembourg.

Interest:

In cases where a tax treaty exists, interest from foreign sources is segregated and a tax credit for foreign taxes paid is accorded only against tax due in Luxembourg in respect of such interest. In all other cases a deduction is accorded for foreign tax paid.

Special rules apply in some cases in respect of dividend income.

Germany: Tax exemption on dividends is accorded to Luxembourg companies together holding a 25 per cent stake in a German company, provided the Luxembourg companies are each more than 50 per cent owned by the same Luxembourg parent company.

Ireland: If the holding in an Irish firm is less than 25 per cent, tax payable in Luxembourg on net dividends is reduced by 15 per cent in respect of the withholding tax charged. If the holding is over 25 per cent dividend income is exempt (10 per cent if the company is fully taxable).

VII. Major changes

None.

Netherlands

I. Corporation taxes

1.1 Relations with the personal income tax

Personal and corporation income tax are not integrated (see also table 3.1).

1.2 Definition of income subject to tax

Central government: the income for tax purposes for a resident company is the worldwide profit.

1.3 Rate structure

1.3.1 Central government

The national corporate tax rate is 40 per cent for the first FL 250 000 and 35 per cent for the profits exceeding FL 250 000.

1.3.2 Intermediate government

None.

1.3.3 Local government

None.

1.3.4 Overall tax rate

Income taxes are levied only at the central government level. The overall tax rate therefore is 35 per cent (40 per cent for the first FL 250 000 of profits).

1.4 Treatment of intercorporate dividends

Dividends received from a company in which the receiving company owns more than 5 per cent of the paid-in capital are exempt.

1.5 Provisions applying to interest receipts and payments

1.5.1 Receipts

Interest receipts are treated as ordinary income.

1.5.2 Payments

Interest payments are deductible.

1.6 Treatment of trading losses

Normal trading losses may be carried forward for eight years. Trading losses can be carried backwards for three years starting at the oldest year. The carry back of losses can be different in the case of a change of ownership.

1.7 Capital gains and losses

1.7.1 Gains

Capital gains are taxed at the corporation income tax rates. Profits on the sale of fixed tangible assets can be deferred if replacement is intended.

1.7.2 Losses

Capital losses can be offset against profits.

1.8 Depreciation

1.8.1 Machinery

Method of depreciation: straight line, declining balance.

Rate of depreciation: based on estimated life of assets.

Under normal conditions machinery may be depreciated in six to ten years using the straight line method. A tax life of eight years is not uncommon.

Declining balance: The rate of declining balance is twice the rate for the straight line depreciation.

1.8.2 Buildings

Method of depreciation: straight line, declining balance

Rate of depreciation: based on estimated lives of assets.

Under normal conditions buildings may be depreciated in 20 to 30 years using the straight line method. A tax life of 30 years is not uncommon.

Declining balance: The rate of declining balance is twice the rate for the straight line depreciation.

1.8.3 Switch-over

Switch over from declining balance to straight line and vice versa is allowed unless the only purpose of the switch over is obtaining a temporary fiscal benefit.

1.9 Investment tax credits

There is no investment tax credit. However, for certain small scale investments, a percentage of the investment is deductible. The percentage varies from 2 to 18 per cent depending on the amount of the investment. The investment sum must amount to at least FL 3,100 and at most FL 457 000.

1.10 Inventories

Trading stock is valued at cost price or any "sound business practice". Cost price can be determined by FIFO, LIFO or base stock method.

1.11 Treatment of reserves

No investment or inventory reserve provisions.

1.12 Treatment of other business expenses

Depreciation is based on the useful life.

1.13 Tax period
1.13.1 Individuals

The fiscal year is the same as the calendar year.

1.13.2 Corporations

The fiscal year is the same as the calender year. Under certain conditions a fiscal accounting period that departs from the calendar year is allowed.

Tax is collected during the year in which the income is earned under a system of provisional assessments and can be paid in instalments. The number of instalments depends on the date of the provisional assessment. Tax according to a (provisional) assessment dated after the end of the accounting period has to be paid within two month, of the assessment being issued.

1.14 Life assurance/pension funds

Life assurance companies are subject to corporation tax. Under certain conditions pension funds are exempt.

II. Taxes on property and wealth
2.1 Taxes on net wealth
2.1.1 Individuals

A wealth tax of 0,8 per cent is levied on the net wealth of individuals.

Exemptions:

Fl 58 000	for single taxpayer under 27 years of age
Fl 92 000	for single taxpayer over 27 years of age

FL 117 000	for married couples
Fl 7 000	for each dependent child up to 18 years of age
Fl 37 000	for each dependent child between 18 and 27 years, undergoing education.

For business capital of self employed there is an extra exemption: For business capital up to FL 122 000 the exemption is 100 per cent. For business capital between FL 122 000 and 1,180 000 the exemption is FL 122 000 plus 40 per cent of the excess over FL 122 000 and for business capital over FL 1,180 000 the exemption is FL 545 000.

There are additional exemptions available for people without pension plans and people in special lower income groups

2.1.2 Corporations

None.

III. Domestic withholding taxes

3.1 Withholding taxes on interest

None.

3.2 Withholding taxes on dividends

The withholding tax on dividends is 25 per cent.

IV. Personal income taxes

4.1 Rate schedule

Taxable income after deduction of basic standard reliefs	Marginal tax rate (%)
0 - 42 966	13
42 966 - 85 930	50
over 85 930	60

4.2 Tax treatment of dividends

Dividends received are taxed as normal income. The first FL 1 000 of dividends from resident corporations is exempt, for married couples the exemption is FL 2 000.

4.3 Tax treatment of interest

Interest received is taxed as normal income. The first FL 1 000 is exempted, for married couples the exemption is FL 2 000. In calculating the amount of the exemption paid interest, other than mortgage interest, is imputed.

4.4 Weighted average marginal taxes of personal income tax on dividends, interest and capital gains

Dividends:	49 per cent
Interest:	42 per cent

4.5 Taxes on capital gains

Capital gains are normally not taxed.

V. Investment grants generally available to the manufacturing industry

None.

VI. International aspects

6.1 International withholding taxes

6.1.1 Direct investment

The withholding tax rate on dividends is 25 per cent. Under the majority of double taxation treaties the rate is reduced to 15 per cent; the rate is further reduced to 5 per cent or 0 per cent in case the shareholder holds at least 25 per cent of the shares of the subsidiary.

6.1.2 Portfolio investment

The Netherlands do not levy a withholding tax on interest.

6.2 Treatment of foreign source income

6.2.1 Non-treaty countries

For developing countries a worldwide credit is granted. For other non-treaty countries a deduction is given.

6.2.2 Treaty countries

Dividends: dividends which a company receives from qualifying foreign participation are exempt from Netherlands taxation. For these dividends there is no relief available for foreign withholding tax. Other dividends are taxed as normal income but a tax credit is granted for foreign taxes suffered by the recipient of the dividends. This credit cannot exceed, however, the amount of Dutch tax that is attributable to the foreign income.

Interest: received interest is taxed as normal income but a tax credit is available for the foreign tax suffered by the recipient. This credit cannot exceed, however, the amount of Dutch tax that is attributable to the foreign income.

VII. Major changes

None.

New Zealand

I. Corporation taxes

1.1 Relations with the personal income tax

Personal and corporation income tax are fully integrated. The government introduced a full imputation system in the tax year 1988/89 with the result that the effective corporate tax rate on distributed profits is equal in most cases to the marginal tax rate of that individual taxpayer (see also table 3.1 and 3.2).

1.2 Definition of income subject to tax

Central government: the income for tax purpose for a resident company is worldwide profit.

1.3 Rate structure

1.3.1 Central government

Resident mining corporations

— Petroleum	33 per cent
— Other specified minerals	33 per cent

Non-resident mining corporations

— Petroleum	38 per cent
— Other specified minerals	38 per cent

All other resident corporations	33 per cent
All other non-resident corporations	38 per cent

1.3.2 Intermediate government

None.

1.3.3 Local government

None.

1.3.4 Overall tax rate

See 1.3.1.

1.4 Treatment of intercorporate dividends

Dividends received by another resident company are exempt from tax.

1.5 Provisions applying to interest receipts and payments

1.5.1 Receipts

Interest receipts are treated as ordinary income.

1.5.2 Payments

Interest payments are deductible.

1.6 Treatment of trading losses

Normal domestic trading losses may be carried forward indefinitely, however, there must be continuity of ownership of at least 40 per cent of shares. Trading losses cannot be carried backwards.

1.7 Capital gains and losses

1.7.1 Gains

Capital gains are not taxed with the exception of real estate property which under certain conditions can be taxed at the normal (corporation) income tax rate.

1.7.2 Losses

No relief for capital losses.

1.8 Depreciation

1.8.1 Machinery

Method of depreciation: straight line, diminishing value.

Rate of depreciation: based on estimated lives of assets.

The rates are fixed by the tax authorities.

Straight line rate: the rate of depreciation for machinery: 10 per cent.

For plant used in agricultural business and farming a first year high depreciation allowance was available until 31 March 1988.

Declining balance: the declining balance rate is 1.5 x the straight line rates.

1.8.2 Buildings

Method of depreciation: straight line.

Rate of depreciation: based on estimated lives of assets.

The rates are fixed by the tax authorities.

Straight line method:

Reinforced concrete, with steel	1 per cent
Brick, stone	2 per cent
Wood, frame	2.5 per cent

For certain buildings a first year high depreciation allowance was available until 31 March 1988.

1.8.3 Switch-over

The taxpayer is allowed to switch from declining balance to straight line but not vice versa.

1.9 Investment tax credits

None.

1.10 Inventories

Trading stock is valued at cost price, selling value or replacement value. Cost price can be determined by FIFO, average cost, standard cost, retail inventory. The LIFO, base stock method are not permitted (see for explanation 1.10 Australia).

1.11 Treatment of reserves

No investment or inventory reserve provisions.

1.12 Treatment of other business expenses

The cost for R&D can be depreciated in the year they occur. Plant and buildings must be depreciated according to the lines set out in 1.8. Depreciation based on estimated useful life of a patent.

1.13 Tax period

1.13.1 Individuals

The fiscal year ends 31 March. The tax authorities may approve of a different date.

1.13.2 Corporations

See 1.13.1.

Corporate tax is paid in three instalments, in the fourth, eighth and twelfth month of the taxpayer's income year. The final amount must be paid in the eleventh month of the income year following the year of the assessment. If the provisional tax is less than the terminal tax an interest rate of 10 per cent is charged and in cases where too much is paid an interest rate of 10 per cent per annum is paid to the taxpayer.

1.14 Life assurance/pension funds

Life assurance companies and superannuation schemes are subject to income tax at the corporate rate.

II. Taxes on property and wealth

2.1 Taxes on net wealth

2.1.1 Individuals

None.

2.1.2 Corporations

None.

2.2 Taxes on immovable property

Land tax on commercial land applies at a rate of 5 cents for every dollar of land value. Residential land is exempt from land tax. However, local government rates are payable on all land holdings unless specifically exempted.

III. Domestic withholding taxes

3.1 Withholding taxes on interest

Interest: 24 per cent

Withholding tax to be deducted from all interest paid to a recipient at a flat rate of 24 per cent, effective from 1 October 1989.

3.2 Withholding taxes on dividends

Dividends: 33 per cent
Royalties: Nil

Withholding tax to be deducted from all dividends paid to a recipient at a flat rate of 33 per cent, effective from 1 October 1989.

IV. Personal income taxes

4.1 Rate schedule

Taxable income	Tax rate
NZ$0 - NZ$30 875	24c/NZ$
NZ$30 875	33c/NZ$

4.2 Tax treatment of dividends

The imputation system came into effect on 1 April 1988. Imputation means that shareholders are able to be credited with the amount of tax paid by the company. The tax paid by the company is imputed to the shareholders in the form of credits which are attached to their dividends and deducted from their personal income tax.

Example:

Company level:

1. Company taxable income	1 000	
2. Tax liability at 33 per cent	330	
3. After-tax income [1-2]	670	

Shareholder level:

Shareholder marginal tax rate (%)		0	24	33
4.	Dividends or bonus issue (equal to 2)	670	670	670
5.	Imputation credit (equal to 2)	330	330	330
6.	Taxable income (4+5)	1 000	1 000	1 000
7.	Tax liability (6xMTR)	—	240	330
8.	Tax credit (equal to 5)	—	330	330
9.	Net tax liability (7-8)	—	(90)	0
10.	Total company and shareholder tax (2+9)	330	240	330

4.3 Tax treatment of interest

Taxed as ordinary income.

4.4 Weighted average marginal taxes of personal income tax on dividends, interest and capital gains

Dividends:	28.6 per cent
Interest:	25.9 per cent

4.5 Taxes on capital gains

See 1.7.1.

V. Investment grants generally available to the manufacturing industry

None.

394

VI. International aspects

6.1 International withholding taxes

6.1.1 Direct and portfolio investments

The withholding tax rate on dividends for countries that have a tax treaty with New Zealand is 15 per cent. For the non-treaty countries Austria, Greece, Iceland, Luxembourg, Portugal, Spain and Turkey a tax rate of 30 per cent applies.

6.1.2 Debt investment

The withholding tax rate for interest from debt investment is 10 per cent for treaty countries with the exception of Canada and Japan. The withholding tax rate in that case is 15 per cent. For the non-treaty countries Austria, Greece, Iceland, Luxembourg, Portugal, Spain and Turkey the tax rate is 15 per cent.

6.2 Treatment of foreign source income

6.2.1 Non-treaty countries

Income from foreign sources is segregated and the tax credit for foreign taxes paid is then only granted for a particular activity or investment in a particular country against the domestic tax due on that particular investment.

6.2.2 Treaty countries

Same as under 6.2.1.

VII. Major changes

7.1 Indirect tax

7.1.1 Goods and Services Tax

From 1 October 1986 a new form of indirect taxation was introduced, called Goods and Services Tax (GST). This coincided with a lowering of the personal tax rates, and applied to most supplies of goods and services that were consumed in New Zealand. GST was imposed at each level of the production cycle, and was finally borne by the ultimate consumer. Each of the intermediate consumers could claim a credit of the GST paid in relation to the intermediate production process. There were very limited exemptions to the imposition of GST, most notably, provision of financial services, domestic rental accommodation, salary and wages. The basic level of GST is now 12.5 per cent. Before October 1986 there was a limited form of indirect taxation in the form of 129 of selective sales taxes.

Norway

I. Corporation taxes

1.1 Relations with the personal income tax

Personal and corporation income tax are fully integrated, except for the tax equalization fund when the shareholders are personal taxpayers (see also table 3.1).

1.2 Definition of income subject to tax

Central government: the income for tax purposes for a resident company is the worldwide profit.

1.3 Rate structure

1.3.1 Central government

The national corporate income tax is 27.8 per cent.

1.3.2 Intermediate government

The tax rate imposed by the county districts varies between 6 and 7.5 per cent. The normal rate is 7.5 per cent. The tax is not deductible from the national corporate income tax.

1.3.3 Local government

The municipal corporate tax rate varies between 12 and 13.5 per cent. The normal rate is 13.5 per cent. The municipal tax rate is not deductible from the national corporate tax.

Tax equalization fund: the rate for this tax is 2 per cent and the base is equal to the base for the national corporate tax rate.

1.3.4 Overall tax rate

The overall nominal corporate rate is therefore:

27.8 per cent + 7.5 per cent + 13.5 per cent + 2 per cent = 50.8 per cent.

1.4 Treatment of intercorporate dividends

Dividends received from another resident company are subject to the national income tax only.

1.5 Provisions applying to interest receipts and payments

1.5.1 Receipts

Interest receipts are treated as ordinary income.

1.5.2 Payments

Interest payments are deductible except when loans are used to acquire a substantial participation (25 per cent or more) in another company.

1.6 Treatment of trading losses

Normal domestic trading losses may be carried forward for ten years. For the exploitation of oil operations the period over which losses can be carried forward is 15 years. In case of a merger or if more than 45 per cent of the shares are sold or if a buyer acquires more than 30 per cent of the shares and with that also the majority vote in the Annual Meeting the capital losses can no longer be carried forward.

Trading losses can be carried backwards for only two years in case the company goes into liquidation.

1.7 Capital gains and losses

1.7.1 Gains

Capital gains fall into three categories for tax purposes:

Taxable as ordinary income:

— Gains from the sale of depreciable or non-depreciable business assets;
— Gains from the sale of real property used for business purposes;
— Gains from the sale of securities and shares, used for business purposes;
— Gains from the sale of intangibles;

Taxable as capital gains at reduced rates:

— Gains from the sale of real property used for non- business purposes;
— Gains from the sale of shares used for non-business purposes and held for less than 3 years, or held for more than three years, if the "selling group" rule applies;

Not taxable:

— Gains from the sale of real property for public use;
— Gains from the sale of shares used for non-business purposes and held for more than 3 years;
— Gains from the sale of other securities held for non-business purposes.

Capital gains are taxed at the corporation income tax rates. Depreciable assets are excepted. The capital gains on depreciable assets can be taken to the relevant asset group. Assets with a value of over NOK 1,3 million (ships, aeroplanes, etc. also against buildings, which have lower depreciation rates) can be taken to a separate group. A negative balance can be carried forward and offset against new acquisitions or credited against the positive balance (capital gains) of asset with the same depreciation charges or assets with higher depreciation charges.

A positive balance must be used within four years (ships, aeroplanes, etc. eight years) otherwise it is taxed as ordinary income. Fifty percent of the positive balance must be deposited or guaranteed by a bank or Norwegian assurance company.

Non-depreciable assets: non depreciable assets used in a business can be credited against new acquisitions.

Sale of shares: see individuals (4.5.1).

1.7.2 Losses

Capital losses can be offset against capital gains, much in the same way as they are taxed (see capital gains on depreciable assets (1.7.1)).

1.8 Depreciation

1.8.1 Machinery

Method of depreciation: declining balance.
Rate of depreciation: partly based on estimated lives of assets.

For oil extraction and pipe laying activities there are special straight line depreciation rates.

Declining balance rates:

Assets	Rate (%)
Machinery, furniture, and other working movables	30
Private cars	20
Ships, fishing vessels, drilling platforms and movable platforms	25
Aeroplanes	15
Buildings and plant	7
Buildings and plant with a remaining useful life of less than 20 years	11
Hotels etc.	6
Hotels , etc. with a useful remaining useful life of less than 20 years	10
Ordinary commercial buildings	2
Commercial buildings in special areas	4

1.8.2 Buildings

Method of depreciation : declining balance.
For depreciation rates, see above.

1.8.3 Switch-over

Not applicable.

1.9 Investment tax credits

Special incentives are given in certain regions of Norway and for certain types of investments, such as environment improving assets. However, they will be abolished during 1991, as part of the tax reform planned for 1992.

1.10 Inventories

Trading stock is valued at cost price, selling value or replacement value, not exceeding the lesser of cost or market value. Cost price can be determined by FIFO. The LIFO method is not permitted. Deductions are permitted for risk of price fall and for dead stock.

1.11 Treatment of reserves

Consolidation reserve: resident companies can allocate 23 per cent of net profits as calculated for the local income tax purposes to a consolidation reserve (Konsolideringsfond). The allocation is deductible from taxable profits. Any amount withdrawn must be added back to profits. The reserve is not earmarked for any particular purpose.

Other reserves: tax free reserves may be created by mining enterprises, enterprises recently engaging in a business, and for investment in northern Norway and investments in unemployment areas.

1.12 Treatment of other business expenses

The patents are depreciated over their useful life.

1.13 Tax period
1.13.1 Individuals

The fiscal year is the same as the calendar year.

1.13.2 Corporations

The fiscal year is the same as the calendar year, although special reasons can justify a different period. Corporations' tax liabilities are calculated the year after the accounting year.

The corporate tax is paid in four instalments. Two instalments must be paid on the 15 February and 15 April in the year following the income year and should at least be 50 per cent of the expected total tax. The balance of 50 per cent must be paid in two instalments within two month after the assessments have been issued.

1.14 Life assurance/pension funds

These institutions are tax exempt with few but not important exceptions.

II. Taxes on property and net wealth
2.1 Taxes on net wealth
2.1.1 Individuals

Municipalities levy a net wealth tax of 1 per cent on capital exceeding NKr 60 000. The national net wealth tax on individuals is progressive, with a maximum tax rate of 1.3 per cent on capital exceeding NKr 825 000 in tax group 1 and NKr 855 000 in tax group 2.

2.1.2 Corporations

The national capital tax is 0.3 per cent on net wealth excluding capital in ships and domestic shares (see also 2.1.1.).

2.2 Taxes on immovable property

There is no national or county tax on immovable property. The municipalities can levy a tax on immovable property. If they do, the tax rate has to be between 0.2 and 0.7 per cent. For farms and immovable property in forestry, the maximum tax rate is 0.4 per cent. In 1988, 188 of the 448 municipalities were levying a tax on immovable property.

III. Domestic withholding taxes

3.1 Withholding taxes on interest

None.

3.2 Withholding taxes on dividends

The withholding tax is 25 per cent on dividends.

Investment tax: this tax of 7 per cent is levied on certain durable items of equipment for use in a business which are liable for VAT.

IV. Personal income taxes

4.1 Rate schedule

Central government: the national income tax has the following rate structure in the two tax groups:

Tax group 1 *		Tax group 2 **	
Net income	Tax rate (%)	Net income	Tax rate (%)
0 - 130 000	0.0	0 - 162 000	0.0
130 000 - 164 000	7.5	162 000 - 189 000	7.5
164 000	14.0	189 000	14.0

*   no dependents
**   with dependents

Intermediate and local government: the normal tax rate is 21.0 per cent on net income (7.5 per cent to the county, 13.5 per cent to the municipality). The tax free amounts are NKr 20 700 and NKr 41 400 in tax group 1 and 2, respectively.

Tax Equalisation Fund (Common tax): the rate for this tax is 5.5 per cent. The tax free amounts are the same as for the local taxes.

Taxes on gross income:

—   Social security tax
—   Top tax

400

The tax rate is 7.8 per cent on "pension earning" income (gross income) outside own business and in the primary industries. For other business income the tax rate is 12.7 per cent. For pension income the tax rate is 1.6 per cent. If the pension earning income is less than NKr 17 000, no social security tax is paid.

Top tax: the base for the top tax is almost the same as for the social security tax. The top tax rate is 9.5 per cent, and the tax free amounts are NKr 207 000 and NKr 249 000.

4.2 Tax treatment of dividends

Dividends are deductible from the national corporate tax. Dividends are taxed in the shareholders' hands, but exempt from the municipal and county tax. As a result of the above system double taxation is almost fully avoided. The exception is that the "common tax" for the tax equalization fund is paid twice when the shareholder is a physical person.

Investment income and interest income is exempt from income tax up to NKr 3 000 (NKr 6 000 for married couples).

4.3 Tax treatment of interest

Taxed as ordinary income. Investment income and interest income is exempt from income tax up to NKr 3 000 (NKr 6 000 for married couples). Interest income is not liable for the social security tax and the top tax.

4.4 Weighted average marginal taxes of personal income tax on dividends, interest and capital gains
4.5 Taxes on capital gains

(See 1.7.1.)

Capital gains are included in taxable income except for the gain on shares, which are taxed as follows:

— A 30 per cent tax rate is applicable if:

- More than 45 per cent of the shares of a limited liability company are sold.
- More than 30 per cent of the shares of a limited liability company are sold and buyer acquires the majority in the votes of the Annual Meeting.

— A 40 per cent tax rate is applicable in all other cases if the sale takes place within three years and exceeds NKr 4 000 (no dependents) or NKr 8 000 (dependents).

V. Investment grants generally available to the manufacturing sector

None.

VI. International aspects

6.1 International withholding taxes

6.1.1 Direct investment

The withholding tax rate on dividends for countries that have a tax treaty with Norway is 15 per cent, with the exception of Turkey in which case it is 25 per cent. For the non-treaty country Greece a tax rate of 25 per cent applies.

6.1.2 Portfolio investment

The withholding tax rate for portfolio investment is 0 per cent.

6.2 Treatment of foreign source income

6.2.1 Non-treaty countries

Deduction is the general rule in case there is no tax treaty.

6.2.2 Treaty countries

Income from foreign sources is segregated and the tax credit for foreign taxes paid is only granted for a particular activity or investment in a particular country against the domestic tax due on that particular investment. This credit system is only used in case of a tax treaty or by consent of the Ministry of Finance.

In some cases different rules apply for dividend payments:

Belgium: dividends are exempt from municipal and local taxes as if both companies were resident in Norway.

France, Germany, Ireland, Portugal, Sweden: dividends are exempt form municipal and local taxes in case of a 25 per cent or more shareholding as if both companies were resident in Norway.

United Kingdom and United States: dividends are exempt from municipal and local taxes in case of a 10 per cent or more shareholding as if both companies were resident in Norway.

VII. Major changes

None.

Portugal

I Corporation taxes

1.1 Relations with the personal income tax

Personal and corporate income taxes are not integrated. However, distributed profits carry a tax credit to avoid double taxation (see also table 3.1).

1.2 Definition of income subject to tax

Central government: the income for tax purposes for a resident company is the worldwide profit. A company is resident if the head office or effective management is in Portugal. Non resident companies are taxable on their income derived within the Portuguese territory.

1.3 Rate structure

1.3.1 Central government

Rate structure:
— Resident company and permanent establishment of a non resident company: 36 per cent
— Non resident companies and not attributable to a permanent establishment in Portugal: 25 per cent

Except for income below, to which the following rates apply:
— Income from any intellectual or industrial property, information concerning industrial, commercial or scientific experience as well as technical assistance: 15 per cent
— Income from the use or the right to use any agricultural, industrial, commercial or scientific equipment: 15 per cent
— Income from dividends and interest: 25 per cent
— Other income from movable capital not referred to above: 20 per cent

1.3.2 Intermediate government

None.

1.3.3 Local government

The tax rate is set by the municipal authorities, but can be no higher than 3.6 per cent (10 per cent of central government corporate tax) The tax is levied on the income derived by a resident company or a permanent establishment of a non resident company.

1.3.4 Overall tax rate

The overall tax rate for a resident company or a permanent establishment of a non resident company is 36 per cent + 3.6 per cent = 39.6 per cent (maximum rate, see 1.3.3).

1.4 Treatment of intercorporate dividends

Dividends received from another resident company liable for tax are taxed. However, 95 per cent of such dividends are excluded from tax provided that the company held at least 25 per cent of the capital stock of the company distributing the dividends and the holding period is not less than two continuous years or as from the constitution of the controlled company if such participation is held for at least two years.

The 95 per cent rule is also applied regardless of holding period of and holding percentage in the following cases:

— Venture capital companies (sociedades de capital de risco)
— Area development companies (sociedades de desenvoluimento regional)
— Business encouragement companies (sociedades de fomento empresarial)
— Investment banks (bancos de investimento)
— Investment companies (sociedades de investimento)
— Brokerage financing companies (sociedades financeinas de corretagem)
— Assurance companies (sociedades de seguros)
— Holding companies (sociedades de participacoes sociais)

If the participation in the capital stock of the company distributing the dividends is less than 25 per cent or is held for less than two years, a tax credit of 35 per cent of tax on dividends distributed is given. In this case a withholding tax is levied (see 3.2).

For tax purposes, dividends from shares registered in the Portuguese Stock Exchange are taken into consideration up to 80 per cent of their amount. Dividends from capital stock which has been acquired in connection with a privatisation process are taxed at 60 per cent for tax purposes during the five financial years subsequent to the acquisition. The controlling company is taxable on the dividend received including the tax credit.

Both the tax credit and the tax withheld at source are creditable against the tax payable by the controlling company. In case the tax credit is higher than the tax payable by this company, the excess is not refunded nor carried forward to subsequent years. The tax withheld at source may be refunded.

As far as concerns non resident companies without a permanent establishment in Portugal to which income is attributable, the tax withheld at source is the final tax paid.

Resident financial institutions are not liable for the withholding tax.

1.5 Provisions applying to interest receipts and payments

1.5.1 Receipts

Interest receipts are treated as ordinary income.

1.5.2 Payments

Interest payments are deductible.

1.6 Treatment of trading losses

Normal domestic trading losses may be carried forward for five years. Trading losses cannot be carried backwards.

1.7 Capital gains and losses

1.7.1 Gains

Capital gains are included in the taxable income. However, capital gains from the alienation of immovable assets subject to depreciation and from financial assets held for at least 12 months are excluded from tax if the realization value is reinvested in the acquisition of new assets, tangible assets or capital stock of resident companies and government bonds, during the next two years. If a reinvestment is made in financial assets, such assets must be held for at least two financial years following the acquisition of shares, participation or government bonds.

Capital gains on marketable securities realized by non resident companies without a permanent establishment to which such gains are attributable are exempted from tax.

1.7.2 Losses

Capital losses can be offset against capital gains.

1.8 Depreciation

Straight line method:

Assets	Rates (%)
Commercial buildings	2
Industrial buildings	5
Plant and machinery	12.5 up to 25
Office equipment	12.5
Heavy goods lorry	20
Passenger vehicles	25
Computers	25

The taxpayer is allowed to use lower depreciation rates (up to half the straight line rates).
Accelerated depreciation may be applied to equipment subject to intensive use.

Declining balance method:

Normal useful life	Rate
Up to 5 years	1.5 x straight line rate
5 to 6 years	2 x straight line rate
Over 6 years	2.5 x straight line rate

1.8.1 Machinery

Method of depreciation: straight line, declining balance (not applicable to used assets, buildings, passenger cars, furniture and social equipment)

Rate of depreciation: estimated lifetime as laid down by the tax authorities.

The rate of depreciation may vary between the rate laid down by the Government or 50 per cent of that rate. For equipment used in more than one shift the depreciation rates can be increased by 50 per cent.

1.8.2 Buildings

Method of depreciation: straight line.

Rate of depreciation: estimated lifetime as laid down by the tax authorities (see 1.8.1).

1.8.3 Switch-over

A switch-over from declining balance to straight line or vice versa is not allowed.

1.9 Investment tax credits

None.

1.10 Inventories

Trading stock is valued at cost price (market value at the acquisition date or cost of production). Cost price can be determined by the specific cost method, weighted average cost, FIFO or LIFO.

1.11 Treatment of reserves

No investment or inventory reserve provisions.

1.12 Treatment of other business expenses

Research and development expenditures may be allowed as costs in the year they are incurred. Assets with a unit cost of no more than Esc. 20 000 can be fully depreciated in the year they are acquired. Rights in connection with an exclusive use (patents, royalties, etc.) can be depreciated over their useful life.

1.13 Tax period

1.13.1 Individuals

The fiscal year is the same as the calendar year.

1.13.2 Corporations

Generally the fiscal year is the same as the calendar year. The tax authorities may allow in limited circumstances an alternative date for resident companies. Non-resident companies having a permanent establishment within the Portuguese territory may adopt an alternative tax period.

The corporate tax is paid in four instalments. The first three are paid in June, September and December and each of them should be 25 per cent of last years assessment. The fourth is paid on filing the annual return in April the following year. If the tax year ends on a date other than 31 December interim taxpayments are taking place on the sixth, ninth and twelfth month following the close of the tax year. Payments on account are not required if the previous year's corporate tax is less then Esc 40 000 and may be suspended upon declaring that no further tax is due. However, an interest of 5 per cent over the bank of Portugal's rate is due if more than 20 per cent of the tax otherwise paid is postponed.

1.14 Life assurance/pension funds

Assurance companies are liable for the corporate income tax. Pension funds are tax-exempt.

II. Taxes on property and wealth

2.1 Taxes on net wealth

2.1.1 Individuals

None.

2.1.2 Corporations

None.

2.2 Taxes on immovable property

Companies that own immovable property in Portugal are liable to a local property tax (Contribuicao autarquica). The tax rate varies according to the different municipalities from 1.1 per cent to 1.3 per cent.

The tax base is the capital value of the immovable property.

There is a tax levied on the transfer of immovable property (SISA), the base for this tax is usually the sales price. The Transfer Tax rate (SISA) is 10 per cent on the transfer of buildings or building land and 8 per cent in all other cases.

III. Domestic withholding taxes

3.1 Withholding taxes on interest

Interest on bank deposits	20 per cent
Government bonds	20 per cent
Other bonds	25 per cent

3.2 Withholding taxes on dividends

The withholding tax on dividends from registered and unregistered shares is 25 per cent.

The withholding tax on dividends from shares quoted at the Portuguese stock exchange applies to 80 per cent of respective amount.

For shares acquired as a result of privatisation the withholding tax applies to 60 per cent of the amount in the first five financial years following the acquisition date.

The withholding tax for other corporate rights:

— Dividends received by a resident company, a permanent establishment of non resident company: 15 per cent;

— Dividends received by a non resident company: 25 per cent (in this case the withholding tax is the final tax).

IV. Personal income taxes

4.1 Rate schedule

As of 1st January 1991.

Taxable income (Escudos)	Marginal rate (%)	Deduction (Escudos)
0 - 750 000	25	—
750 000 - 1 750 000	25	75 000
1 750 000 - 4 500 000	35	250 000
Over 4 500 000	40	475 000

4.2 Tax treatment of dividends

The withholding tax is the final tax paid unless the shareholder elects otherwise. In that case the tax withheld at source is credited against the tax payable by the taxpayer and any excess is refunded. The dividends carry a tax credit of 35 per cent of the central government corporate tax to the benefit of the shareholder. The tax credit is included into the taxable dividends received and deducted from the tax liability. Any excess is not refunded (see 3.2.).

4.3 Tax treatment of interest

The withholding tax is the final tax paid unless the interest recipient elects otherwise. In that case the withholding tax is deductible (see 3.1).

4.4 Weighted average marginal taxes of personal income tax on dividends, interest and capital gains

If the beneficial owner elects the withholding tax as the final tax:

The tax rate on interest from government bonds is	20 per cent
The tax rate on interest from bonds is	25 per cent
The tax rate on dividends is	25 per cent
The tax rate on capital gains (marketable securities) is	10 per cent[1]

1) without withholding tax at source

4.5 Taxes on capital gains

Capital gains are tax exempt in the following cases:

— Bonds;
— Certificates issued by investment funds;
— Shares held by the respective owner for at least 24 months.
— Capital gains from the sale of shares owned for less than 12 months are tax exempt until 1992.

Capital gains, after deduction for capital losses, which are not derived from the alienation of marketable securities are taxed as ordinary income by 50 per cent of their value. The capital gains tax on this item is a flat rate of 10 per cent but the taxpayer has the option to incorporate them into his normal taxable income and they are then taxed at the progressive income tax rates.

Capital gains are never subject to a withholding tax at source.

V. Investment grants generally available to the manufacturing sector

None.

VI. International aspects

6.1 International withholding taxes

6.1.1 Direct investment

The withholding tax rate on dividends for countries that have a tax treaty with Portugal is 15 per cent. For the non-treaty countries Australia, Canada, Greece, Ireland, Japan, Luxembourg, Netherlands, New Zealand, Sweden, Turkey and the United States, a rate of 25 per cent applies.

6.1.2 Portfolio investment

The withholding tax rate on interest for countries that have a tax treaty with Portugal is, in general, 15 per cent. However a rate of 10 per cent for Austria, Switzerland and the United Kingdom and 12 per cent for France.

6.2 Treatment of foreign source income

6.2.1 Non-treaty countries

No deduction for foreign tax paid.

6.2.2 Treaty countries

Income from foreign sources is segregated and the tax credit for foreign taxes paid is than only granted for a particular activity or investment in a particular country against the domestic tax due on that particular investment.

VII. Major changes

None.

Spain

I Corporation taxes

1.1 Relations with the personal income tax

Personal and corporation income tax are not fully integrated (see also table 3.1).

1.2 Definition of income subject to tax

Central government: the income for tax purposes for a resident company is the worldwide profit.

1.3 Rate structure

1.3.1 Central government

The national tax rate is 35 per cent.

1.3.2 Intermediate government

None.

1.3.3 Local government

None, but a surtax of 1.5 per cent on the corporate income is levied by the Chamber of Commerce (a public corporation but representing private businessmen and enterprises), although the base of this tax differs from that of the national tax. The tax is deductible.

1.3.4 Overall tax rate

The overall tax rate is: 35 per cent x 0.015 = 0.525 per cent;
0.525 per cent x (1 — 0.35) + 35 per cent = 35.34 per cent.

1.4 Treatment of intercorporate dividends

Companies receiving dividends from other resident companies are allowed to deduct the withholding tax plus 50 per cent of the tax payable on the receiving dividends (100 per cent if the recipient owns more than 25 per cent of the payer's capital).

1.5 Provisions applying to interest receipts and payments

1.5.1 Receipts

Interest receipts are treated as ordinary income.

1.5.2 Payments

Interest payments are deductible.

1.6 Treatment of trading losses

Normal domestic trading losses may be carried forward for five years. Trading losses cannot be carried backwards.

1.7 Capital gains and losses

1.7.1 Gains

Capital gains are taxed at the corporation income tax rates if not reinvested. Companies are liable for the municipal capital gains tax when the property is sold. Municipalities levy a tax rate on capital gains from the sale of urban land.

1.7.2 Losses

Capital losses can be carried forward for five years and offset against capital gains.

1.8 Depreciation

1.8.1 Machinery

Method of depreciation: straight line.
                           declining balance.
Rate of depreciation: based on estimated lives of assets.

Straight-Line Method:

	Rate (%)	Maximum years
Industrial buildings	3	50
Personal property	10	15
Tools and utensils	20	8
Machinery (in general)	8	18

Declining balance method:

Declining balance is allowed only if the useful life of the asset is three years or more.

Normal useful life	Rate
Up to 5 years	1.5 x straight line rate
5 to 8 years	2 x straight line rate
Over 8 years	2.5 x straight line rate

Two allowable variants are constant percentage method and the sum-of-the-years-digits method. A depreciation plan must be approved by the tax authorities.

1.8.2 Buildings

Method of depreciation: straight line.

Rate of depreciation: based on estimated lives of assets (see 1.8.1)

1.8.3 Switch-over

Not allowed.

1.9 Investment tax credits

A investment tax credit of 5 per cent can be taken in the first year on the acquisition of a new asset. For certain assets and expenses used in export activities the tax credit is 15 per cent.

1.10 Inventories

Trading stock is valued at cost price (market value at the acquisition date or cost of production). Cost price can be determined by the specific cost method FIFO. The LIFO method is not permitted.

1.11 Treatment of reserves

No investment or inventory reserve provisions.

1.12 Treatment of other business expenses

A tax credit of 15 per cent for intangibles and 30 per cent for investment in fixed assets is available for expenditure in R&D. Plant and machinery used for R&D can be depreciated in five years. Buildings used in R&D can be depreciated in seven years.

1.13 Tax period

1.13.1 Individuals

The fiscal year is the same as the calendar year.

1.13.2 Corporations

The fiscal year is the same as the accounting period, but may never exceed 12 months.

The corporate tax is paid in four instalments. The first three, of 20 per cent of the previous year's tax charge, must be paid on the twentieth of April, October and December. The balance on filing the tax return.

1.14 Life assurance/pension funds

Pension funds are exempt from the corporate tax.

II. Taxes on property and wealth
2.1 Taxes on net wealth
2.1.1 Individuals

Individuals are subject to a wealth tax:

Tax base (million)	Rate (%)
0 - 25	0.20
25 - 50	0.30
50 - 100	0.45
100 - 250	0.65
250 - 500	0.85
500 - 1 000	1.10
1 000 - 1 500	1.35
1 500 - 2 500	1.70
Over 2 500	2.00

2.1.2 Corporations

Companies are not subject to a net wealth tax.

2.2 Taxes on immovable property

There is a local tax upon this property, based upon "cadastral" values.
The tax on immovable property varies throughout the country.

III. Domestic withholding taxes
3.1 Withholding taxes on interest

The withholding tax is 25 per cent on interest.

3.2 Withholding taxes on dividends

The withholding tax is 25 per cent on dividends.

IV. Personal income taxes

4.1 Rate schedule

Taxable base	Medium rate	Tax liability	Rest taxable base	Rate
Ptas.	%	Ptas.	Ptas.	%
648 900	0	0	432 600	25
1 081 500	10	108 150	540 750	26
1 622 250	15.33	248 745	540 750	27
2 163 000	18.25	349 748	540 750	28
2 703 750	20.2	546 158	540 750	30
3 244 500	21.83	708 383	540 750	32
3 785 250	23.29	881 423	540 750	34
4 326 000	24.63	1 065 278	540 750	36
4 866 750	25.89	1 259 948	540 750	38
5 407 500	27.15	1 468 136	540 750	41
5 948 250	28.41	1 689 844	540 750	43.50
6 489 000	29.67	1 925 070	540 750	46
7 029 750	30.92	2 173 815	540 750	48.5
7 570 500	32.18	2 436 079	540 750	51
8 111 250	33.43	2 711 861	540 750	53.5
8 652 000	34.69	3 011 163	and more	56

4.2 Tax treatment of dividends

The tax payer can deduct 10 per cent of dividends received from his personal income tax.

4.3 Tax treatment of interest

Taxed as ordinary income.

4.4 Weighted average marginal taxes of personal income tax on dividends, interest and capital gains

Dividends:	28.4 per cent
Interest:	31.5 per cent

4.5 Taxes on capital gains

4.5.1 Gains

The gain is calculated as the difference between the selling price and the cost of the asset or the value for the wealth tax at 31 December 1978, whichever is higher. The capital gain is divided by the number of years it is held or five years if the holding period is unknown. The quotient is included into the normal taxable income. The remainder is taxed at the average rate for general income tax. Municipalities levy a capital gains tax on the sale of real property. The base for this tax is the cadastral value, which is in fact around 70 per cent of the market value.

V. Investment grants generally available to the manufacturing sector

None.

VI. International aspects

6.1 International withholding taxes

6.1.1 Direct investment

The withholding tax rate on dividends for countries that have a tax treaty with Spain is 15 per cent. In the case of subsidiary/parent relationships (usually the 25 per cent holding minimum participation is applied) rates for treaty partners are 10 or 5 per cent. For the non-treaty countries Australia, Greece, Ireland, New Zealand and Turkey, a rate of 25 per cent applies.

6.1.2 Portfolio investment

The withholding tax rate on dividends for countries that have a tax treaty with Portugal varies between 5 per cent and 15 per cent. The standard rate is 10 per cent, the rate for Belgium, Canada and Portugal is 15 per cent, for Italy a rate of 12 per cent applies and for Austria 5 per cent. For the non-treaty countries Australia, Canada, Greece, Ireland, New Zealand, and Turkey a rate of 25 per cent applies.

6.2 Treatment of foreign source income

6.2.1 Non-treaty countries

Income from foreign sources is segregated and the tax credit for foreign taxes paid is than only granted for a particular activity or investment in a particular country against the domestic tax due on that particular investment.

6.2.2 Treaty countries

Same as under 6.2.1.

In some cases different rules apply for dividend payments:

Switzerland:	If more than 25 per cent of the shares are held both companies are treated as if they were Spanish companies.
United Kingdom:	If more than 10 per cent of the shares are held a tax relief of 15/85 of the dividends received is given.

In some cases different rules apply for dividend payments:

Austria:	All interest on government bonds is tax exempt.
Portugal:	Interest on Portuguese securities is taxable in Portugal only.

VII. Major changes

None.

Sweden

I Corporation taxes

1.1 Relations with the personal income tax

Personal and corporation income tax are not fully integrated. However the tax rate on some distributed profits is lower (see also table 3.1).

Dividends are normally not deductible except for dividends on newly issued capital. Dividends on newly issued capital before 1 January 1979 can be deducted for up to 5 per cent of paid in capital during 10 years. The payments qualify for this deduction only if they are made within 15 years after the shares have been paid up. Dividends on new shares issued after January 1, 1979 qualify for a maximum deduction of 10 per cent of the paid in capital. The deduction is granted for a maximum of 20 years. The total deduction taken may never exceed the paid-in capital.

The deduction for dividends on newly issued capital is only available under the following conditions:

— Shares issued before 1 January 1980: no deduction is granted if 50 per cent or more of the qualifying shares are held by another Swedish company which is exempt from tax over the receiving dividends or a foreign company which is exempt from the coupon tax.

— Shares issued after 1 January 1980: no deduction is granted if 50 per cent of the voting power of the distributing company is owned by a holding company or 25 per cent or more of the voting power of such shares is owned by another Swedish company which is not liable for tax over the dividends received. In all other cases the deduction is granted if 50 per cent of the shares of the distributed company are held by recipients that are liable for the coupon tax on dividends received either at the full statutory rate or the reduced rate.

1.2 Definition of income subject to tax

Central government: the income for tax purposes of a resident company is the worldwide profit.

1.3 Rate structure

1.3.1 Central government

The national corporate income tax is 30 per cent.

1.3.2 Intermediate government

None.

1.3.3 Local government

None.

1.3.4 Overall tax rate

The overall tax rate is 30 per cent.

1.4 Treatment of intercorporate dividends

A company receiving dividends from another resident company in which it owns more than 25 per cent is not taxed on the received dividends. All other income is treated as normal business income.

1.5 Provisions applying to interest receipts and payments

1.5.1 Receipts

Interest receipts are treated as ordinary business income.

1.5.2 Payments

Interest payments are deductible.

1.6 Treatment of trading losses

Normal domestic trading losses may be carried forward without time limitation. Special rules apply when there is a change of ownership. Trading losses cannot be carried backwards.

1.7 Capital gains and losses.

1.7.1 Gains

A flat rate of 30 per cent is levied on nominal capital gains. Some alternative rules apply to real estate, owned by individuals

1.7.2 Losses

For corporations, capital losses can be offset against ordinary income, except for losses on shares, which can be offset only against capital gains on shares (in the income year or through saving in future years). For individuals, capital losses can only be offset against gains on shares (or with a reduction by 30 per cent against other capital income).

1.8 Depreciation

Assets with an useful life of less than three years can be depreciated in the year they are acquired. The same rule applies to assets with a low value.

1.8.1 Machinery

Method of depreciation: declining balance.

Rate of depreciation: 30 per cent

Declining balance (company must maintain adequate accounting records): the maximum rate for declining balance is 30 per cent, the taxpayer is allowed to depreciate less than 30 per cent in any year. The declining balance rate is taken over the total book value of all plant and machinery at the beginning of the year, increased by any new items and reduced by any sum received for sold items.

Declining balance (company not maintaining adequate accounting records): a maximum of 25 per cent of the total remaining value for tax purposes of plant and machinery at the end of the preceding year and increased by any new items and reduced by any sum received for sold items can be deducted.

Extra depreciation: regardless of the ceiling imposed by the 30 per cent declining balance method, the company may in any year depreciate whatever amount is necessary to reduce the book value of all its machinery and equipment to its total acquisition cost reduced by 20 per cent yearly depreciation on a straight line basis since acquisition.

In cases where the depreciation is not enough to reduce the value of plant and machinery to the actual value any depreciation may be taken to make up the difference.

1.8.2 Buildings

Method of depreciation : straight line

The rate of depreciation for industrial buildings is 3-5 per cent a year and for offices and commercial buildings 2 per cent.

1.8.3 Switch-over

Switch-over is allowed for machinery (see 1.8.1).

1.9 Investment tax credits

None.

1.10 Inventories

Cost price should be determined by FIFO. Alternatively valuation could be at 97 per cent of the total FIFO costs. According to the principle rule, each item of trading stock is valued at cost price or market value whichever is lower.

Unsaleable deduction: a deduction for unsaleable merchandise is allowed.

Raw materials: no special provisions.

1.11 Treatment of reserves

Tax equalisation reserve (SURV): corporations may allocate funds to a tax equalization reserve (SURV), to be based on the corporations' equity capital, to a maximum of 30 per cent. In principle the reserve will be based on the tax accounting values of various assets, less deductions for corporate liabilities in accordance with closing balance sheets. Shares in subsidiaries, resident in Sweden, are excluded from the reserve base. Shares in foreign subsidiaries are included for 65 per cent.

An alternative reserve option, normally preferable to corporations with a small equity capital, is a maximum of 15 per cent of the corporations' gross payroll minus social costs.

1.12 Treatment of other business expenses

1.13 Tax period

1.13.1 Individuals

The fiscal year is the same as the calendar year.

1.13.2 Corporations

The fiscal year is the same as the accounting period.

Corporate tax is paid in six equal instalments. They are based on last year's final tax assessment or on a preliminary tax return. The instalments must be paid every second month starting in March of the tax year. The balance must be paid in April the year after the tax assessment is made. Any balance to the taxpayer is normally refunded.

1.14 Life assurance/pension funds

A tax of 10 - 15 per cent is imposed on returns of investment.

II. Taxes on property and wealth
2.1 Taxes on net wealth
2.1.1 Individuals

Individuals are liable to a wealth tax according to the following rates:

Net wealth	Tax on lower amount	Percentage on excess
800 000 - 1 600 000		1.5
1 600 000 - 3 600 000	12 000	2.5
3 600 000	62 000	3

2.1.2 Corporations

For foreign corporations the rate is the same as for individuals.

2.2 Taxes on immovable property

No property tax on industrial buildings.

III. Domestic withholding taxes
3.1 Withholding taxes on interest

The withholding tax on interest is 30 per cent.

3.2 Withholding taxes on dividends

The withholding tax on dividends is 30 per cent.

IV. Personal income taxes
4.1 Rate schedule

The rate schedule is not applicable for capital income or capital gains (see 4.2, 4.3 and 4.5).

4.2 Tax treatment of dividends

All kinds of capital income, including interest, dividends and capital gains, are taxed separately from other income. A proportional flat rate of 30 per cent is applied (no basic allowance).

4.3 Tax treatment of interest

See above.

Most bonds held by individuals in Sweden are government premium bonds rather than ordinary interest bearing bonds. Winnings on such premium bonds are not subject to the ordinary income tax. Instead they are subject to a "lottery tax", imposed at a flat rate of 20 per cent.

4.4 Weighted average marginal rates of personal income tax on dividends, interest and capital gains

As a result of the proportional tax, all weighed average rates are 30 per cent.

4.5 Taxes on capital gains

See 4.2.

V. Investment grants generally available to the manufacturing sector

None.

VI. International aspects

6.1 International withholding taxes

6.1.1 Direct investment

The withholding tax rate on dividends for countries that have a tax treaty with Sweden varies between 0 per cent and 15 per cent. For the non-treaty countries (Portugal and Turkey) the withholding tax rate is 30 per cent.

6.1.2 Portfolio investment

The withholding tax rate on portfolio income is 0 per cent.

6.2 Treatment of foreign source income

6.2.1 Non-treaty countries

Income from foreign sources is segregated and the tax credit for foreign taxes paid is than only granted for a particular activity or investment in a particular country against the domestic tax due on that particular investment.

6.2.2 *Treaty countries*

Same as under 6.2.1.

Foreign dividends are tax exempt for the domestic tax unless:

— The recipient company is closely held and for purposes alien to exercise a business.

— The payer claims a deduction from tax for dividends paid.

— The shares are held as a portfolio investment (holding less than 25 per cent unless for sound business reasons)

— The shares are held by a bank or an other financial institution.

In some cases different rules apply for dividend payments:

For Australia, Austria, Canada, Denmark, Finland, France, Germany, Greece, Ireland, Italy, Japan, Netherlands, New Zealand, Norway, Spain, Switzerland, United Kingdom and United States, dividends are treated as if the dividends are received from another Swedish firm.

For Canada, Germany and Italy there is an additional condition that the holding must be at least 25 per cent.

In some cases different rules apply for interest payments:

Spain: All interest on government bonds is taxed by the debtor State.

VII. Major changes

None.

Switzerland

I. Corporation taxes

1.1 Relations with the personal income tax

Personal and corporation income tax are not integrated (see also table 3.1).

1.2 Definition of income subject to tax

Central government: the income for tax purposes for a resident company is the worldwide profit.

1.3 Rate structure

1.3.1 Central government

The rate for the federal corporate income tax depends on a progressive system of three rates, depending on the yield (the proportion of profits to capital and reserves).

Rate structure:

Corporation with capital and reserves less than SF 50 000:

Basic rate	3.63 per cent
Surtax	
Over a profit of more than SF 2000	3.63 per cent
Over a profit of more than SF 4000	4.84 per cent
The total tax rate can be no more than	9.80 per cent

Corporation with capital and reserves more than SF 50 000:

Basic rate	3.63 per cent
Surtax	
Over a profit with a yield of more than 4 per cent	3.63 per cent
Over a profit with a yield of more than 8 per cent	4.84 per cent
The total tax rate can be no more than	9.80 per cent

Cantonal, Municipal and Church tax rates: the cantonal, municipal and church tax are deductible from the federal corporate income tax. Rates are different for cantons as well as for municipalities and churches. A few cantons and municipalities do not use the yield (profits/net worth) as a base for the corporate income tax. Most cantons as well as municipalities and churches multiply the basic rate with a percentage. A minimum and maximum rate is laid down by law.

The rates for Zurich are given below as an example.

1.3.2 Intermediate government

Canton: Zurich.

The rate depends on progressive system of three rates, depending on the yield (the proportion of profits to capital and reserves)

Rate structure:

Basic rate	4 per cent
Surtax	
Over a profit with a yield of more than 4 per cent	5 per cent
Over a profit with a yield of more than 8 per cent	5 per cent
The total tax can be no more than	12 per cent

Cantonal multiplier: 1.08.

Example:

Net worth SF 1 000 000.

Taxable profit SF 50 000.[1]

Yield	=	50 000/1 000 000	=	5 per cent.
Tax rate	=	4 per cent on SF 50 000	=	SF 2 000.
		5 per cent on SF 10 000	=	SF 500.

SF 2.500 +
(5 per cent)

Effective income tax rate = 5 x 1.08 = 5.4 per cent

Example:

net worth SF 1 000 000.

taxable profit SF 350 000.[1]

Yield	=	3,500 000/1 000 000	=	35 per cent.
Tax rate	=	4 per cent on SF 350 000	=	SF 14 000
		5 per cent on SF 310 000	=	SF 15,500
		5 per cent on SF 270 000	=	SF 13,500

SF 43 000 +
(12.28 per cent)

Since the maximum rate is 12 per cent the effective income tax rate = 12 x 1.08 = 12.96 per cent.

1) After deduction of taxes.

1.3.3 Local government

City: Zurich.	
Base	: same as Canton
Rate	: same as Canton.
Municipal multiplier	: 1.18

Church tax rate:

Churches in the Canton of Zurich.
Base   : same as Canton
Rate   : same as Canton
Church multiplier   : 0.12.

1.3.4 *Overall tax rate*

The overall tax rate (Zurich) on income ranges between:

Federal income tax	3.63 per cent and	9.8 per cent
State income tax	1.08 x 4.0 per cent and	1.08 x 12 per cent
Local income tax	1.18 x 4.0 per cent and	1.18 x 12 per cent
Church income tax	0.12 x 4.0 per cent and	0.12 x 12 per cent
	13.15 per cent and	38.36 per cent

These rates relate to profits after deduction of taxes.

1.4 *Treatment of intercorporate dividends*

Corporations receiving dividends from other resident companies may claim for the federal tax as well as for the cantonal tax, a proportional tax reduction calculated according to the ratio existing between the adjusted gross yield and dividends received, or between net income and dividends received. The reduction is normally granted if the receiving company has at least 20 per cent of the paid-in capital of the distribution company or the market value of the share of the receiving company is at least two million Swiss francs.

1.5 *Provisions applying to interest receipts and payments*

1.5.1 *Receipts*

Interest receipts are treated as ordinary income.

1.5.2 *Payments*

Interest payments are deductible.

1.6 *Treatment of trading losses*

The Confederation (Central Government) levies the corporate income tax over the average income of the two preceding years (computation period). A loss from the computation period can be carried forward for three computation periods. In Zurich it can be carried forwards for four years.

1.7 *Capital gains and losses*

1.7.1 *Gains*

Capital gains are taxed at the corporation income tax rates. In some cantons the capital gains on real estate are taxed separately.

Zurich (companies): capital gains are included in taxable income. Capital gains on real estate are taxed differently. The difference between the actual book value and cost is regarded as recapture of depreciation and therefore is taxable income. The difference between the price of acquisition and the sales price is subject to a special tax (Grundstückgewinnsteuer), levied at progressive rates, but reduced for each year of ownership.

The maximum rate is 60 per cent for a holding period of less than one year and an annual capital gain of more than SF 50 000. The rate is reduced to 20 per cent for holding period of more than 20 years.

1.7.2 Losses

Capital losses can be offset against capital gains if capital gains are taxed. In some cantons a carry forward of such losses is allowed.

1.8 Depreciation

1.8.1 Machinery

Method of depreciation:	straight line, declining balance.
Rate of depreciation:	laid down by the tax authorities.

Normal federal rates (declining balance):

Office furniture and equipment:	25 per cent
Manufacturing machinery and other facilities:	30 per cent
Manufacturing machinery used under heavy conditions:	40 per cent
Motor vehicles of all type:	40 per cent
Intangible assets (patents, trademarks):	40 per cent

In case the straight line method is applied, one-half of the declining balance rate is allowed.

1.8.2 Buildings

Method of depreciation:	straight line. declining balance.
Rate of depreciation:	laid down by the tax authorities.

Normal federal rates (declining balance):
Buildings and land:

—	Rental dwellings for employees' housing:	1.5 — 2 per cent
—	Commercial and office buildings:	3 — 4 per cent
—	Industrial buildings, warehouses, workshops:	7 — 8 per cent

In case the straight line method is applied, one-half of the declining balance rate is allowed.

Cantonal depreciation rates:

Method of depreciation:	straight line. declining balance.

The cantonal depreciation rates generally do not differ from the federal rates.

The general rate structure can be summarized as follows:

Type of asset	Declining balance rates (%)
Buildings (dependent on type):	1 - 8
Heavy machinery and other fixed assets:	20
Intangibles	40
Light machinery and other smaller equipment	30 - 35

In case the straight line method is applied, one-half of the declining balance rate is allowed.

Assets (machinery and buildings) for environment protection and energy saving may be granted a 50 per cent declining balance depreciation for the first two years following completion.

1.8.3 Switch-over

Not allowed.

1.9 Investment tax credits

None.

1.10 Inventories

Trading stock is valued at the purchase price, or if lower, the market price. The LIFO or the FIFO method is allowed. A reserve may be set up in order to offset any later decrease in value. This reserve must not exceed one-third of the value of the stock concerned.

1.11 Treatment of reserves

No investment or inventory reserve provisions.

1.12 Treatment of other business expenses
1.13 Tax period

Individuals and Corporations: the federal and most cantonal taxes are assessed over a period of two years (assessment period) but collected annually. The tax is assessed on the average income derived by the taxpayer during the two years (computation period) immediately preceding the assessment or tax period.

The corporate tax is usually paid in two or three instalments and based on last year's assessment or the latest tax return. If the entire amount is paid in advance a discount is usually granted.

Example:

Computation Period	Assessment Period
Year 1987 and 1988	Year 1989 and 1990
Year 1989 and 1990	Year 1991 and 1992

A new taxpayer is taxed on the income attributable to the first tax year. Companies may select another period of 12 month than the calendar year.

1.14 Life assurance/pension funds

Pension funds are tax exempt.

II. Taxes on property and wealth

2.1 Taxes on net wealth

2.1.1 Individuals

The cantons and municipalities levy a tax on capital at graduated rates.

The annual tax burden for five Swiss cities for a married couple without children an a net wealth of SF 500 000 is as follows (as a percentage of net wealth) 1991:

City	Rate (%)
Basel	0.400
Bern	0.377
Geneva	0.387
Lausanne	0.612
Zurich	0.143

2.1.2 Corporations

Federal tax on capital: companies pay a flat rate of 0.0825 per cent on their capital (paid in capital plus reserves). Foreign permanent establishments and foreign-sites immovable property are excluded.

Cantonal, municipal and church taxes on capital: usually also at flat rates but in some cases graduated rates are applied. Each canton, municipality and church multiplies a basic rate with a fixed annual percentage to arrive at the effective tax on capital.

In case of Zurich the basic rate is 0.15 per cent on taxable net worth (capital plus reserves). Permanent establishments and the value of immovable property outside the canton are excluded. The basic rate of 0.15 per cent is multiplied with a coefficient. (See 1.3)

III. Domestic withholding tax

3.1 Withholding taxes on interest

Bank interest and bonds 35 per cent.

3.2 Withholding taxes on dividends

The withholding tax on dividends is 35 per cent.

IV. Personal income taxes

4.1 Rate schedule

Federal tax.
Married Couples:

Taxable income	Amount of tax	Plus for each 100 Frs	Over
0 - 18 800	0	0	
18 800 - 33 800	0	1.00	18 800
33 800 - 38 800	150.00	2.00	33 800
38 800 - 50 000	250.00	3.00	38 800
50 000 - 60 000	586.00	4.00	50 000
60 000 - 68 700	986.00	5.00	60 000
68 700 - 76 200	1 421.00	6.00	68 700
76 200 - 82 500	1 871.00	7.00	76 200
82 500 - 87 500	2 312.00	8.00	82 500
87 500 - 91 200	2 712.00	9.00	87 500
91 200 - 93 800	3 045.00	10.00	91 200
93 800 - 95 100	3 305.00	11.00	93 800
95 100 - 96 400	3 448.00	12.00	95 100
96 400 - 595 200	3 604.00	13.00	96 400
Over 595 200	68 448.00	11.50	595 200

Single persons:

Taxable income		Amount of tax	Plus for each 100 Frs	Over
0 -	9 600	0	0	
9 600 -	21 000	0	0.77	9 600
21 000 -	27 500	87.75	0.88	21 000
27 500 -	36 700	144.95	2.64	27 500
36 700 -	48 200	387.80	2.97	36 700
48 200 -	51 900	729.35	5.94	48 200
51 900 -	68 800	949.10	6.60	51 900
68 800 -	89 400	2 064.50	8.00	68 800
89 400 -	116 900	3 877.30	11.00	89 400
116 900 -	501 600	6 902.30	13.20	116 900
Over	501 700	57 695.50	11.50	501 700

Tax-rate schedule for the canton of Zurich:

Married Couples:

2 per cent	on the first SF.	4 500
3 per cent	on the next SF.	5 700
4 per cent	on the next SF.	6 800
5 per cent	on the next SF.	8 000
6 per cent	on the next SF.	10 200
7 per cent	on the next SF.	22 700
8 per cent	on the next SF.	22 700
9 per cent	on the next SF.	34 000
10 per cent	on the next SF.	40 900
11 per cent	on the next SF.	44 300
12 per cent	on the next SF.	51 000
13 per cent	over SF.	250 800

All other taxpayers:

2 per cent	on the first SF.	3 400
3 per cent	on the next SF.	3 400
4 per cent	on the next SF.	5 700
5 per cent	on the next SF.	6 800
6 per cent	on the next SF.	7 900
7 per cent	on the next SF.	9 100
8 per cent	on the next SF.	12 500
9 per cent	on the next SF.	23 800
10 per cent	on the next SF.	23 900
11 per cent	on the next SF.	37 400

| 12 per cent | on the next SF. | 48 800 |
| 13 per cent | over SF. | 182 700 |

The calculated tax is multiplied by 237 per cent.

The canton of Zurich	: 108.
City of Zurich	: 118
Church	: 11

4.2 Tax treatment of dividends

Taxed as ordinary income.

4.3 Tax treatment of interest

Taxed as ordinary income.

4.4 Weighted average marginal rates of personal income tax on dividends, interest and capital gains

| Dividends: | 30.8 per cent |
| Interest: | 30.8 per cent |

4.5 Taxes on capital gains

Capital gains on real estate are taxed by all cantons. The overall tax rate depends on the holding period. In most of the cantons a special immovable property gains tax (Grundstückgewinnsteuer) applies.

Capital gains on movable assets are not taxed provided they are not realised as a part of a business. In that case they are taxed at the normal income tax rate.

V. Investment grants generally available to the manufacturing sector.

None.

VI. International aspects

6.1 International withholding taxes

6.1.1 Direct investment

The withholding tax rate on dividends for countries that have a tax treaty with Switzerland varies between 0 per cent and 15 per cent. For the non-treaty countries Luxembourg and Turkey the withholding tax rate is 35 per cent.

6.1.2 Portfolio investment

The withholding tax rate on portfolio investment for countries that have a tax treaty with Switzerland varies between 0 per cent and 15 per cent. For the non-treaty countries Luxembourg and Turkey the withholding tax rate is 35 per cent.

6.2 Treatment of foreign source income

6.2.1 Non treaty countries

For non-treaty countries the general rule is deduction for foreign tax paid.

6.2.2 Treaty countries

Income from foreign sources is segregated and the tax credit for foreign taxes paid is only granted for a particular activity or investment in a particular country against the domestic tax due on that particular investment.

If more than 20 per cent of the shares of another company are held or the value of the total shares is in excess of SF 2 000 000 the company is entitled to a reduction of the federal corporate tax. The reduction is calculated as follows:

Total dividends received are added together and then divided by gross income. This ratio is taken as a percentage of the federal income tax and then deducted from federal income tax. Most cantons have similar reliefs.

VII. Major changes

No major changes.

Turkey

I. Corporation taxes

1.1 Relations with the personal income tax

Personal and corporation income taxes are integrated in the sense that no personal tax is charged on dividends distributed out of profits which have borne corporation tax. A withholding tax of 10 per cent is applied to profits exempt from corporation tax (see also table 3.1).

1.2 Definition of income subject to tax

Central government: the income for tax purposes for a resident company is the worldwide profit.

1.3 Rate structure

1.3.1 Central government

The national corporate income tax rate is 46 per cent. In addition there are supplementary levies up to 7 per cent of the basic tax.

1.3.2 Intermediate government

None.

1.3.3 Local government

None.

1.3.4 Overall tax rate

The overall tax rate is 46 per cent x 1.07 = 49.2 per cent.

1.4 Tax rate for intercorporate dividends

Dividends received from other resident companies are not included in taxable income.

1.5 Provisions applying to interest receipts and payments

1.5.1 Receipts

Interest receipts are treated as ordinary income.

1.5.2 Payments

Interest payments are deductible.

1.6 Treatment of trading losses

Normal domestic trading losses may be carried forward for five years. Trading losses can not be carried backwards.

1.7 Capital gains and losses.

1.7.1 Gains

Capital gains are taxed at the corporation income tax rate. The tax can be deferred for three years, if the capital gain is reinvested in new fixed assets. The capital gain on real estate and security are always taxed at the corporate income tax unless they are new shares and registered and listed on the stock exchange. These gains must be added to the company's capital in the year of sale.

1.7.2 Losses

Capital losses can be offset against capital gains if taxable.

1.8 Depreciation

Assets with a value of TL 100 000 or less can be depreciated 100 per cent in the year of acquisition (this amount for the year 1991 is TL 200 000.)

Taxpayers are free to select rates of depreciation for assets purchased after January 1 1983, subject to maximums of 25 per cent for straight-line depreciation and 50 per cent for the declining-balance method. In other cases the rates are subject to approval by the Ministry of Finance and Customs. Once the rate is chosen the taxpayer is not allowed to change the rate.

1.8.1 Machinery

Method of depreciation: straight line.
declining balance.

Rate of depreciation: set by the tax authorities.

Asset	Rate of depreciation straight line (%)
Machinery	6
Immovable property	2
Factory buildings	4
Cars, buses	15
Trucks	20
Office equipment	6 - 20
Industrial equipment	5 - 50

The declining balance rate is twice the straight line rate with a maximum of 50 per cent. If the taxpayer elects the declining method the number of years over which the asset must be depreciated remains the same as it would be under the straight line method. In the last year of depreciation the residual will be totally deducted and depreciated.

Example: if the taxpayer elects to depreciate an asset of 100 units in five years, the declining balance rate will be 2 x 20 per cent = 40 per cent.

The taxpayer depreciates:

Year 1 : 100 — 40   = 60
Year 2 : 60 — 24   = 36
Year 3 : 36 — 14.40   = 21.60
Year 4 : 21.60 — 8.64   = 12.96
Year 5 : the residual   = 12.96 is deducted.

1.8.2 Buildings

See 1.8.1.

1.8.3 Switch-over

A changeover from declining balance to straight line is allowed. A changeover from straight line to declining balance is not allowed. If the taxpayer switches from declining balance to straight line the remaining value of the asset is equally divided over the remaining years.

Revaluation of depreciable assets

Only corporate taxpayers have the right to depreciate on revaluation. The coefficient of revaluation is based on the rate of increase in wholesale prices during the previous year. This coefficient is 55.5 for the year 1990.

1.9 Investment tax credits

Turkey has three major investment incentives:

— Investment allowance
— Export incentive
— Free zones

Investment allowance: this allowance is available for investments over TL 1 billion (TL 250 million in priority areas). To qualify for the investment incentive the company must receive an "incentives certificate" from the State Planning Organisation; and these investments must be within the framework of the Five-Year Development Plans and should also expand production, increase productivity, stimulate exports, improve quality, provide energy savings, improve scientific and technical research and promote working safety requirements, and aim to attract foreign tourists to Turkey. Investment incentives include:

— Exemption from import duties and taxes on imported machinery and equipment;
— Investment allowance:

30 per cent generally;

40 per cent in special areas and agriculture;

60 per cent in less developed regions, importance of second degree;

100 per cent in less developed regions, importance of first degree; investment of water product; investment in sectors that are of special importance scientific research and improvements.

The above allowances are given as a deduction from taxable profits.

— Low-interest loans;
— Exemption from the construction tax;
— An investment allowance of up to 20 per cent for the cost of certain assets;
— During the operation of the company, imports are free of custom duties;
— 18 per cent of certain export profits are exempt from the corporate profit tax;

1.10 Inventories

Trading stock is valued at cost price. If the cost price exceeds the market price by approximately 10 per cent, the stock may be valued at market price. Cost price can be determined by FIFO. The LIFO method is not permitted.

1.11 Treatment of reserves

Investment fund: this reserve can only be set up for investments qualifying for the investment allowance (see above). The corporation can deposit 25 per cent of its profits in an account at the Central Bank, if invested in government securities an interest rate of 20 per cent is paid. The company must apply to the State Planning Organisation to obtain a "certificate" in order to withdraw the reserve. The amount placed in the investment fund may not exceed the total sum of qualified investments. The tax-exempt amounts withdrawn from the investment reserve must be added back to the profits in the year following the year in which they were placed into the reserve.

1.12 Treatment of other business expenses

None.

1.13 Tax period

1.13.1 individuals

The fiscal year is the same as the calendar year.

1.13.2 Corporations

The fiscal year is the same as the calendar year. Any other time period of 12 months may be chosen on approval of the Ministry of Finance and Customs.

1.14 Life assurance/pension funds

These institutions are not taxed.

II. Taxes on property and wealth

2.1 Taxes on net wealth

2.1.1 Individuals

2.1.2 Corporations

There are no net wealth taxes in the Turkish tax system.

2.3 Taxes on immovable property

The tax on immovable property varies throughout the country.

III. Domestic withholding taxes

3.1 Withholding taxes on interest

The withholding tax on interest is 10 per cent.

3.2 Withholding taxes on dividends

In the Turkish tax system corporation tax rate is 49.2 per cent. Profits exempted from corporation tax are taxed at a rate of 10 per cent (including some funds) withholding tax (see 1.1 above).

IV. Personal income taxes

4.1 Rate schedule

4.2 Tax treatment of dividends

Dividends received are not included in taxable income, (see 1.1 and 3.2 above).

4.3 Tax treatment of interest

The withholding tax on interest is the final tax paid.

4.4 Weighted average marginal rates of personal income tax on dividends, interest and capital gains

The weighted average rate of income tax on dividends is 10 per cent. The weighted average rate of tax on capital gains is 27 per cent (1988).

4.5 Taxes on capital gains

Profits derived from the sales of movable and immovable assets related to the commercial enterprises are subjected to the normal income tax rate. The profits derived from the sales of movable and immovable assets which are not included in commercial enterprises, are taxed as follows:

Movable assets

The profits obtained from the sales of movable assets which are registered on the stock market and the profits obtained without any compensation are not subjected to income tax.

If movable assets are sold within the first year, after purchase, the first TL 200 00 of the derived income is exempted from the tax. Beyond this income is taxed according to the normal income tax rate. The income derived from the sale of movable assets that are sold one year after the purchase date is not subjected to tax.

If movable assets are sold through banks or other intermediary financial institutions that are authorised to buy and sell movable assets, the profits derived the sale are not subjected to income tax (this will be valid by the end of 1993).

The part of profits that non-residents (limited liability) individuals obtain through the exchange rates from the sales of movable or market shares bought with foreign capital legislations, are not taxed.

Immovable assets

If immovable assets obtained by purchase are sold within the first year the profit is taxed according to the normal income tax rate. The profit derived from the sale of immovable assets that are sold one year after the purchase date is not subjected to tax.

V. Investment grants generally available to the manufacturing sector

None.

VI. International aspects

6.1 International withholding taxes

6.1.1 Direct investment

The rate of source taxation on dividends arising from direct investment and paid to the residents of Germany, United Kingdom, the Netherlands, Finland, France, Belgium and Sweden is maximum 15 per cent according to tax treaties with these countries. This rate is 25 per cent for the residents of Austria and Norway.

6.1.2 Portfolio investment

The rate of source taxation on dividends arising from portfolio investment and paid to the residents of Germany, United Kingdom, the Netherlands, Finland, France, Belgium and Sweden is maximum 20 per cent. This rate is 30 per cent for the residents of Norway and 35 per cent for the residents of Austria.

6.2 Treatment of foreign source income

6.2.1 Non-treaty countries

According to domestic tax laws, Turkey allows as a deduction from the tax on income of residents, an amount equal to the tax on income paid abroad. Such deduction can not, however, exceed that part of the income tax computed in Turkey before the deduction is given, which is appropriate to the income which may be taxed abroad.

6.2.1 Treaty countries

Same as under 6.2.1.

VII. Major changes

None.

United Kingdom

I. Corporation taxes

1.1 Relations with the personal income tax

The United Kingdom has a "partial imputation" system of corporate tax, under which the corporate tax paid by the company is deemed to cover the personal income tax liability (at the basic rate of income tax only) of shareholders on dividends received. The effect is that the resident shareholder can credit part of the corporation tax imposed on distributed profits against his personal income tax liability.

When paying out dividends the company is liable for ACT (advance corporation tax) equal to 25/75 of the net dividend or other qualifying distribution paid to the shareholder. The ACT can be credited against the corporation tax (CT) liability. However the maximum ACT that can be offset in any fiscal year is 25 per cent of taxable profits. If the company cannot offset all the ACT, the "surplus ACT" can be offset against CT in the ten preceding years (again subject to a limit in relation to the taxable profits of the preceding years). If the company has insufficient profits in the preceding years to offset the ACT, the ACT can be carried forward indefinitely (see also tables 3.1 and 3.2).

1.2 Definition of income subject to tax

Central government: the income for tax purposes for a resident company is the worldwide income.

1.3 Rate structure

1.3.1 Central government

The national corporate tax rate is 34 per cent. This rate applies to all companies earning more than £1 million.

Small company tax rates:

Taxable profits	marginal tax rate (%)
0 — £ 200 000	25
£ 200 000 — £ 1 million	36.25

1.3.2 Intermediate government

None.

1.3.3 Local government

None.

441

1.3.4 Overall tax rate

The overall tax rate is 34 per cent.

1.4 Treatment of intercorporate dividends

Dividends received by a resident company from another resident company are exempt from corporation tax. The receiving company is only liable to pay ACT (Advance Corporation Tax) on its own distributions to the extent that they exceed the amount of dividends (plus the tax credit attached thereto) received in the same accounting period.

1.5 Provisions applying to interest receipts and payments

1.5.1 Receipts

Interest receipts are treated as ordinary income.

1.5.2 Payments

Interest payments are generally deductible.

1.6 Treatment of trading losses

Normal domestic trading losses may be carried forward indefinitely and offset against future profits (excluding capital gains). Trading losses can normally be carried back and set against profits (including capital gains) of the preceding year.

1.7 Capital gains and losses

1.7.1 Gains

Capital gains are taxed at corporation tax rates. Gains are subject to indexation and those arising prior to April 1982 are ignored in the computation. However, capital gains tax on business assets can be deferred if a new asset is acquired or unconditionally ordered within 12 months before or three years after the disposal of an asset. Business assets which qualify for this relief are: land, buildings, fixed plant and machinery, ships, aircraft, goodwill, satellites, spacecraft and milk quotas.

1.7.2 Losses

Capital losses are computed in the same way as capital gains, and can be set against gains arising in the year. Unused capital losses can be carried forward and set against capital gains in subsequent years.

1.8 Depreciation

1.8.1 Machinery

Method of depreciation: declining balance (motor cars qualify for the same rate and method subject to a limit on the annual depreciation). Rate of depreciation: 25 per cent.

1.8.2 Buildings

Method of depreciation: straight line.

Rate of depreciation:

— industrial buildings: 4 per cent
— hotels and agriculture buildings: 4 per cent
— commercial buildings: 0 per cent

1.8.3 Switch-over

Not applicable.

1.9 Investment tax credits

There are no investment tax credits available in the United Kingdom.

1.10 Inventories

Trading stock is valued at the lower of cost price or market value. Cost price can be determined by FIFO. The LIFO method is not permitted.

1.11 Treatment of reserves

No investment or inventory reserve provisions.

1.12 Treatment of other business expenses

Accelerated depreciation can be used for plant and buildings employed in scientific research, the taxpayer is allowed to depreciate any expenditure at 100 per cent in the year they occur.

Expenditures for patents: patents can be depreciated at 25 per cent a year, using the declining balance method.

1.13 Tax period

1.13.1 Individuals

The fiscal year runs from 6 April to 5 April.

1.13.2 Corporations

The tax period is normally a company's own accounting period. Corporate tax is paid on annual basis, nine months after the end of the accounting period to which it relates.

1.14 Life assurance/pension funds

Pension funds are tax exempt and they are entitled to the repayment of tax credits accompanying dividends. Life assurance companies are essentially taxed at the basic rate of income tax on their investment income and capital gains (net of certain expenses).

II. Taxes on property and wealth

2.1 Taxes on net wealth

2.1.1 Individuals

None.

2.1.2 Corporations

None.

2.3 Taxes on immovable property

The UK has a system of uniform business rates which are levied on the base of estimated rental values. Present rateable values, effective from April 1990, reflect rental values as at 1 April 1988, and national non domestic rating multipliers are applied to these rateable values: for 1990-91, these were 34.8 per cent for England and 36.8 per cent for Wales. Transitional arrangement following the revaluation and switch from a locally varying business rate apply each year from 1990-91 to 1994-1995. These will limit the increases and decreases faced by individual properties in a single year. Somewhat different arrangements apply in Scotland and Northern Ireland.

III. Domestic withholding tax

3.1 Withholding taxes on interest

None.

3.2 Withholding taxes on dividends

None.

IV. Personal income taxes

4.1 Rate schedule

Taxable Income	tax rate (%)
0 - £20 700	25
Over £20 700	40

4.2 Tax treatment of dividends

The dividend which the shareholder receives must be grossed up with the tax credit accompanying it to form the taxable amount on which income tax is liable. The taxpayer receives a tax credit equal to the ACT paid by the company (equal to the basic rate of income tax). The effect is that the shareholder liable at the basic rate of income tax has no further liability on the dividends he receives. The taxpayer liable at the higher rate of income tax pays the additional tax due. If the tax liability of the taxpayer is not enough to offset the credit received on his dividends, the amount is refunded in cash.

4.3 Tax treatment of interest

Taxed as ordinary income.

4.4 Weighted average marginal rates of personal income tax on dividends, interest and capital gains

An estimated average marginal tax rate on:

—	interest	24 per cent
—	dividends	32 per cent
—	capital gains	33 per cent *)

*) The estimated effective rate on accrued capital gains is much lower than the weighted average of the marginal rates of tax.

4.5 Taxes on capital gains

Capital gains over £ 5 000, after allowing for indexation and ignoring gains accruing prior to April 1982, are treated as the top slice of taxable income and taxed at the appropriate rates.

V. Investment grants generally available to the manufacturing sector

None.

VI. International aspects

6.1 International withholding taxes

6.1.1 Direct investment

The UK does not have a withholding tax on dividends paid to non-resident investors. The tax credit is available only to UK residents but has been extended in part to non-resident individuals and corporate portfolio investors by tax treaties. The table below shows the amounts of tax credit not extended by the UK (expressed as a percentage of total dividends plus full tax credit) as at 1 January 1991.

6.1.2 Portfolio investment

As above, there is no withholding tax on dividends paid to non-resident direct or portfolio investors, although the tax credit may not be granted in full. The table below shows the amounts of tax credit not extended by the UK (expressed as a percentage of total dividend plus full tax credit) as at 1 January 1991.

Tax credit not extended to overseas investors
(% of total dividend plus full 25 per cent tax credit)

	Direct[1]	Portfolio
Australia	25	15
Austria	25	15
Belgium	16.875	20
Canada	21.25	15
Denmark	16.875	15
Finland	16.875	15
France	25	15
Germany	25	25
Greece	25	25
Ireland	25	15
Italy[2]	16.875	15
Japan	25	15
Luxembourg	16.875	15
Netherlands	16.875	15
New Zealand	25	15
Norway	21.25	15
Portugal	25	25
Spain	25	15
Sweden	16.875	15
Switzerland	16.875	15
Turkey	25	25
United States	16.875	15
Non-treaty countries	25	25

1. 10 per cent minimum shareholding required.
2. New treaty effective from 1 January 1991 (in Italy) and 6 April in the United Kingdom.

6.2 Treatment of foreign source income

6.2.1 Non-treaty countries

Income from foreign sources is segregated. Credit is available for direct foreign taxes which have been charged on the distribution, but only against the domestic tax which is due on that particular investment or source.

If more than 10 per cent of the voting shares of another company are held, credit is also available for the underlying taxes on the profits out of which the dividend was paid, but as above, only against the domestic tax which is due on that particular investment or source.

6.2.2 Treaty countries

Same as under 6.2.1.

Where the terms of a double taxation agreement so provide, credit may be also given against the relevant United Kingdom tax for tax "spared" in the overseas territory.

VII. Major changes

The national corporation tax rate in 1991/92 is 33 per cent, and applies to all profits of companies earning more than £1.25 million. The small company tax rates for 1991/92 are:

Taxable profits	Marginal tax rate (%)
0 - £250 000	25
£250 000 - £1 250 000	35

The personal tax rate schedule for 1991/92 is :

Taxable income	Tax rate (%)
0 - £23 700	25
Over £23 700	40

United States

I. Corporation taxes

1.1 Relations with the personal income tax

Personal and corporation income taxes are not integrated (see also table 3.1).

1.2 Definition of income subject to tax

Central government: the income for tax purposes for a resident company is the worldwide profit.

1.3 Rate structure

1.3.1 Central government

The federal tax rate structure is:

Taxable income	Rates 1991 (%)
0 - 25 000	15
25 000 - 50 000	15
50 000 - 75 000	25
75 000 - 100 000	34
over 100 000	34

An additional tax of 5 per cent is levied over profits between $ 100 000 and $ 335 000. The effect of this additional tax is that the tax rate on income within that range is 39 per cent.

Minimum tax: the minimum tax must be paid if it is higher than the corporate income tax. This tax ensures that a company with a commercial profit but a fiscal loss is taxed on its income. The Alternative Minimum Tax (AMT) rate is 20 per cent. The tax is levied over AMT income in excess of $40 000. The exemption is phased out for AMT income of over $ 150 000.

AMT income = taxable income plus tax preference items such as:

— Accelerated depreciation;

— Certain accounting methods for instalment sales and long-term contracts;

— The excess of financial accounting income over taxable income plus certain other adjustments.

State and Local taxes on corporations: State and local taxes are deductible from the federal corporate income tax. Rates vary mostly between 4 per cent and 12 per cent but can be higher in some cases. State and local taxes average between 6 and 7 per cent. State and local tax bases vary widely, but in many cases they are derived from the taxable income for the federal income tax.

1.3.2 Intermediate government

See above.

1.3.3 Local government

See above.

1.3.4 Overall tax rate

As an example the overall average tax rate is: 6.5 x (1 — 0.34) + 34 = 38.3 per cent.

1.4 Treatment of intercorporate dividends

A company receiving dividends from another resident company may deduct from gross income 70 per cent or 80 per cent of the receiving dividends, depending upon the recipient's ownership of the payer. Affiliated corporations may elect to deduct 100 per cent of the dividends received from gross income.

1.5 Provisions applying to interest receipts and payments

1.5.1 Receipts

Interest receipts are treated as ordinary income.

1.5.2 Payments

Interest payments are deductible.

1.6 Treatment of trading losses

Normal domestic trading losses may be carried forward for fifteen years. Trading losses can be carried backwards for three years. The corporation may waive the carry back of trading losses.

1.7 Capital gains and losses

1.7.1 Gains

Capital gains are taxed as ordinary income, when the property is sold or exchanged.

1.7.2 Losses

Capital losses can only be offset against capital gains. They can be carried back three years and forward five years. All losses carried back or forward are treated as short term capital losses.

1.8 Depreciation

The tax code's modified "Accelerated Cost Recovery System" (ACRS) of 1986 classifies tangible property into eight categories:

property that can be written off over

3 years: Assets with an useful life of no more than 4 years;

5 years:	Assets with an useful life of more than 4 years and no more than 10 years. Trucks, cars, assets used in Research and Experimentation, energy saving investments;
7 years:	Assets with an useful life of more than 10 years but no more than 16 years, including agriculture investments;
10 years:	Assets with an useful life of more than 10 years but no more than 16 years;
15 years:	Assets used in the service industry with an useful life of more than 20 years but no more than 25 years;
20 years:	Assets with an useful life of more than 25 years. Excluded are buildings with an useful life of more than 27.5 years;
27.5 years:	Residential structures;
30 years:	Non residential structures, including commercial and industrial buildings.

Taxpayers may elect a longer, but not a shorter, recovery period.

1.8.1 Machinery

Method of depreciation:

— For the three, five, seven, ten -years category: declining balance at 200 per cent of the straight line rate;

— For the 15-, 20 -years category: declining balance at 150 per cent of the straight line rate;

Rate of depreciation: based on ACRS.

1.8.2 Buildings

Method of depreciation: straight line, declining balance;

— Declining balance: for the 15-, 20 -years category: declining balance at 150 per cent of the straight line rate;

— Straight line: for the 27.5- and 30-years categories: straight line.

Rate of depreciation: based on ACRS.

1.8.3 Switch-over

The taxpayer may switch over from declining balance to straight line.

1.9 Investment tax credits

None.

1.10 Inventories

Trading stock is valued at cost price, selling value or replacement value. Cost price can be determined by FIFO. The LIFO method is permitted, cost must be used as the base.

1.11 Treatment of reserves

No investment or inventory reserve provisions.

1.12 Treatment of other business expenses

Expenses for research and experimentation may be deducted in the year they occur or ratably over five years beginning in the year benefits are first realized.

1.13 Tax period
1.13.1 Individuals

The fiscal year is the same as the calendar year. However taxpayers may elect (under certain conditions) a different period. If a different period is chosen the taxpayer must keep proper records.

1.13.2 Corporations

The fiscal period is the same as the accounting period.

Corporate tax must be paid in full by the filing of the return or the fifteenth of third month following the close of the tax year, whichever comes first. Failure to pay at least 90 per cent of the liability on dates mentioned earlier can result in a penalty.

1.14 Life assurance/pension funds

These funds are tax deferred or tax exempt. Life assurance companies are generally taxed like other corporations.

II. Taxes on property and wealth
2.1 Taxes on net wealth
2.1.1 Individuals

None at the federal level.

2.1.2 Corporations

None at the federal level.

2.2 Taxes on immovable property

The tax on immovable property varies throughout the country.

III. Domestic withholding tax
3.1 Withholding taxes on interest

None.

3.2 Withholding taxes on dividends

None.

IV. Personal income taxes

4.1 Rate schedule

The federal tax rate schedules for single taxpayers and married couples filing jointly are:*

Taxable income ($)		1989 Rates (%)
Single	Married	
0 — 20 350	0 — 34 000	15
20 350 — 49 300	34 000 — 82 150	28
49 300 and over	82 150 and over	31

*)   Other tax rate schedules apply for single heads of households and married couples filing separately.

The minimum tax must be paid if it exceeds the regular income tax. The minimum tax rate is 24 per cent. The tax rate is applied to a broad measure of income (that includes tax preferences) in excess of an exemption amount of $ 40 000 for taxpayers filling a joint return and $ 30 000 for single taxpayers. The exemption amount phases out when income exceeds $ 150 000 for joint returns and $ 112 500 for single taxpayers.

State and local income taxes vary, but add approximately 5 percentage points. Thus for example, the highest overall marginal tax rate could be 36 per cent.

4.2 Tax treatment of dividends

Taxed as ordinary income.

4.3 Tax treatment of interest

Interest receipts are generally taxed as ordinary income. Interest on investment indebtness and home mortgage interest are deductible, but subject to some limitations. Interest on consumer debt is not deductible.

4.4 Weighted average marginal rates of personal income tax on dividends, interest and capital gains

Dividends	31 per cent
Interest	28 per cent
Capital gains	7 per cent

4.5 Taxes on capital gains

4.5.1 Gains

Capital gains are taxed as ordinary income. Taxpayers who are 55 years or older may elect to exclude $ 125 000 of the gain realized on the sale of a principal residence when a property is sold or exchanged.

452

4.5.2. Losses

Capital losses are deductible against capital gains plus ordinary income up to $ 3 000. Net capital losses may be carried over for an unlimited time unless the losses are exhausted.

V. Investment grants generally available to the manufacturing sector

None.

VI. International aspects

6.1 International withholding taxes

6.1.1 Direct investment

The withholding tax rate on dividends for countries that have a tax treaty with United States ranges between 5 per cent and 30 per cent. For the non-treaty countries Portugal and Turkey the rate is 30 per cent.

6.1.2 Portfolio investment

The withholding tax rate on portfolio investment for countries that have a tax treaty with United States varies between 5 per cent and 30 per cent. For the non-treaty countries Portugal and Turkey the rate is 30 per cent.

6.2 Treatment of foreign source income

6.2.1 Non-treaty countries

Income from foreign sources is included in the taxable income of the US-taxpayer. The tax on the foreign income is calculated and a tax credit for the foreign income taxes paid is then granted against the domestic tax up to the amount of US tax on that income and subject to a variety of special limitations.

6.2.2 Treaty countries

Same as under 6.2.1.

VII. Major changes

None.

Weights, inflation and investement flows.

A. Introduction

This annex presents economic background information which is either necessary for the computation of effective tax rates or which may prove useful as supplementary information to the tax rates presented in the main body of the report. Section B presents the assets and financing weights used in the calculations of effective tax rates and section C describes in more detail the problems associated with the provision of internationally comparable data on cross-border investment flows. Section D presents the inflation data used in the calculations and a number of additional economic background variables.

B. Asset and finance weights

In order to weight the relevant tax wedges for each of the nine asset/ finance combinations to give an overall average tax wedge, weights are needed. Table A.5.1 below gives the proportion of investment in each type of asset and the proportion of company finance from each source of funds for those countries within the OECD where data are available. The weights shown reflect in principle an equiproportional increase in the capital stock and the way it is financed. The weights shown have been calculated in various different ways in the different countries depending on the statistical sources available. The problems associated with the use of this kind of weights are discussed in more detail in Chapter 4, Section C.

C. Direct investment flows
Purpose and scope

The aim of this section is primarily to indicate the substantial conceptual and practical statistical problems associated with the construction of comparable data on international direct investment. In the context of this report the data are used as a basis for the weights used to calculate effective corporate tax rates.

Capital flows may roughly be divided into direct investment and portfolio investment. Portfolio investments are the more volatile, whereas direct investments are generally believed to respond, to long term economic fundamentals (e.g. labour availability and real wage differentials). The focus of this report is on potential obstacles created by tax systems to direct investment, and the remainder of this section is therefore confined to foreign direct investment.

Table A.5.1 **Proportion of total investment in each type of asset and proportion of total finance by each source of capital[1].**

	Buildings	Machinery	Inventories	Retained earnings	New equity	Debt
Australia	0.26	0.49	0.25	0.38	0.21	0.42
Austria[2]	0.33	0.50	0.17	0.23		0.67
Belgium	0.35	0.30	0.35	0.23	0.21	0.56
Canada	0.28	0.51	0.21	0.56	0.09	0.35
Denmark	0.29	0.33	0.38	0.20	0.15	0.65
Finland	0.30	0.50	0.20	0.47	0.03	0.50
France	0.23	0.55	0.22	0.30	0.11	0.59
Germany	0.34	0.38	0.28	0.42	0.08	0.50
Greece	—	—	—	—	—	—
Iceland	0.60	0.18	0.22	0.61	0.00	0.39
Ireland	0.32	0.53	0.15	0.79	0.08	0.13
Italy	—	—	—	—	—	—
Japan	—	—	—	—	—	—
Luxembourg	—	—	—	—	—	—
Netherlands	0.35	0.53	0.12	0.55	0.06	0.39
New Zealand	—	—	—	0.56	0.10	0.34
Norway	0.50	0.38	0.12	0.15	0.07	0.78
Portugal	0.14	0.73	0.13	0.47	0.03	0.50
Spain	—	—	—	—	—	—
Sweden	0.35	0.37	0.28	0.59	0.05	0.37
Switzerland	0.26	0.40	0.34	0.40	0.00	0.60
Turkey[2]	—	—	—	0.58		0.42
United Kingdom	0.24	0.53	0.23	0.73	0.10	0.17
United States	0.23	0.48	0.29	0.59	0.00	0.41

1. For countries where figures are not available, the average is used.
2. No split between new equity and retained earnings available.

Because of different data sources, classifications and definitions and differences in data availability and accounting methods, national data on foreign direct investment are not fully comparable. Work has, however, been carried out in international organisations (e.g. UN, IMF, OECD) to set up general guidelines in the form of an operational or benchmark definition of direct investment which individual countries endeavour to move towards as they develop and change their statistical systems[1].

In the guidelines the definitional problem has been approached from different angles, i.e. what characterises the foreign direct investor, the investment firm, the stock of invested capital and earnings from investment and what are the main components of direct foreign investment.

a) A **foreign direct investor** is defined as an individual, an incorporated or unincorporated public or private enterprise, a government, a group of related individuals, or a group of incorporated and/or unincorporated enterprises which has a direct investment enterprise — that is, a subsidiary, associate or branch — operating in a country other than the country or countries of residence of the direct investment investor or investors.

b) A **direct investment enterprise** is defined as an incorporated or unincorporated enterprise in which a single foreign investor (as defined above) either: — controls 10 per cent or more of the ordinary shares or voting power of an incorporated enterprise or the equivalent of an unincorporated enterprise, unless it can be established that this does not allow theinvestor an effective voice in the management of the enterprise; or — controls less than 10 per cent (or none) of the ordinary shares or voting power of the enterprise but has an effective voice in the management of the enterprise.

An "effective voice" implies that the direct investor is able to influence or participate in the management of an enterprise. The legal structures of groups of related enterprises may be very complex and may bear no relationship to the management responsibilities. The "benchmark definition" recommends that inward and outward direct investment statistics should cover all directly and indirectly owned subsidiaries, associates, and branches, and provides detailed guidelines in that respect.

c) The **stock of direct investment** is measured as:

   (1) For subsidiary and associate companies:

      (i) The written-down book value of their share capital and reserves attributable to the direct investor (reserves include retained profits)

      (ii) Plus long- and short-term loans, trade credit and any other indebtedness due from the subsidiaries and associates to the direct investor, including dividends declared but not yet paid to the direct investor

      (iii) Less long- and short-term loans, trade credits and other indebtedness due to the subsidiaries and associates from the direct investor.

   (2) For branches, the net worth of these concerns to the direct investor is measured as:

      (i) The written-down book value of the concern's fixed assets, and the book value of its investments and current assets, excluding amounts due from the direct investor

(ii)   Less their liabilities to third parties, any provisions and the share of net assets due to other investors in the branch.

d)   Components of **direct investment earnings** are:

(1) For subsidiary and associate companies:

(i)   Dividends due for payment in the period to the direct investor gross of any withholding taxes

(ii)   Plus the direct investor's share of the company's reinvested or retained earnings

(2) Plus for branches:

(i)   Earnings remitted by the branch to the direct investor gross of any withholding taxes

(ii)   Plus the direct investor's share of the branch's reinvested or retained earnings

(3) Plus for all direct investment enterprises:

(i)   Interest due for payment in the period by the enterprise to the direct investor gross of any withholding taxes

(ii)   Less interest due for payment in the period by the direct investor to the enterprise gross of any withholding taxes.

e)   Finally, **direct investment flows** are defined as:

(1) For subsidiary and associated companies:

(i)   The direct investor's share of the company's reinvested earnings
(ii)   Plus the direct investor's purchases less sales of the company's shares and loans

(iii)   Plus the net increase in trade and other short-term credit given by the direct investor to the company

(2)   For branches, the increase in unremitted profits plus the net increase in funds received from the direct investor (i.e. increase in net worth less increases due to revaluations and exchange rate movements).

It could be added that company surveys are recommended as the main data source, that capital gains and losses are excluded from earnings and that direct investments are measured gross of depreciation.

Investment and Trade Weights for International Flows

For the purpose of this study, the ideal would be to create a matrix showing inward and outward direct investment flows between all 24 member countries for 1989, but this is not possible with the data currently available.

As also noted in Chapter 5 there are no available data which are obviously suitable to use as a set of weights for the transnational required rates of return. Even the data for the G7 group of countries reported in the chapter are not ideal. The data were taken from the Table 5 of the OECD Economic Outlook No. 48,

December 1990. This in turn was calculated from national sources of the G7 countries. The data are net of disinvestment. The Table 5 gives the percentage of investment flows going to each country, so not requiring a consolidation of estimates of outward flows to each country with the recipient countries' estimates of inflows. The average destination of investment flows over the period of 1985-1989 (1988 for the UK) was used to weight the outward flows for each country. Data were not available for flows from Canada to Germany, France and Italy, from Germany to Italy, and from the UK to Italy.

The weights used for inward investment are less reliable than those for outward investment. The aggregate investment flow between 1988 and 1989 (taken from the national data used to construct the OECD estimates of outward investment) was used to weight the importance of outward investment flows, and so to translate the outward flows into inward flows. In other words, the estimates of inward flows are not based on national estimates of inward flows, because they cannot be reconciled with the outward flows, but on the national estimates of the aggregate outward flow, and the destination of the outward flows. The resultant weights used in Table 5.15 in chapter 5 are shown in tables A.5.2 and A.5.3 below.

Selected **time series data** for outward and inward investment, are shown in tables A.5.5. Its major advantage is that it is up to date, i.e. data exist for almost all countries for 1988 or 1989 while the major disadvantage is that they are not broken down according to investor/investee country.

D. Selected economic variables

This section presents statistical information mainly in the form of time series data which shall be seen primarily as general background information to the descriptions and calculations provided in this study (though in the case of the inflation rate, the data have also been used directly in the calculation of effective tax rates).

Tables A.5.2 and A.5.3 provide information on direct investment flow weights within the G7 countries whereas tables A.5.4 and A.5.5 show weighs calculated on the basis of merchandise trade flows between all OECD countries. Table A.5.6 shows amounts of inward and outward direct investment in selected years.

Table A.5.7 provides information on the recent development in the inflation rate measured on the basis of consumer prices in OECD countries. The table also provides information on the development in exchange rates, long term interest rates and calculated rates of return on capital in the business sector.

Table A.5.8 gives general economic background information on private savings, investment (private and total) and real GDP per capita over the last decade.

Table A.5.2. **Outward flow weights within the G7 -**
percentage of flows going from each country.

To From	United States	Canada	Japan	Germany	France	Italy	United Kingdom
United States	-	26.9	10.7	1.2	10.2	5.3	45.7
Canada	89.9	-	0.2	-	-	-	9.9
Japan	81.4	2.5	-	1.9	1.9	0.6	11.8
Germany	69.8	3.8	1.9	-	9.4	-	15.1
France	57.1	5.0	0.5	6.7	-	7.7	22.9
Italy	33.0	3.1	2.5	19.1	24.7	-	17.6
United Kingdom	84.7	6.3	0.6	2.9	5.6	-	-

Table A.5.3. **Inward flow weights within the G7 - percentage source of flows**
into each country.

Into From	United States	Canada	Japan	Germany	France	Italy	United Kingdom
United States	-	75.8	87.9	16.5	48.1	79.3	74.7
Canada	6.2	-	0.2	-	-	-	1.6
Japan	20.9	2.6	-	9.8	3.4	3.4	7.2
Germany	15.5	3.5	5.1	-	14.4	-	8.0
France	5.9	2.1	0.6	13.8	-	17.3	5.6
Italy	2.3	0.9	2.1	26.2	11.7	-	2.3
United Kingdom	49.3	15.1	4.2	33.8	22.5	-	-

Table A.5.4 Percentage of imports from other OECD countries accounted for by each exporting country[1]

Importer \ Exporter	Australia	Austria	Belgium[2]	Canada	Denmark	Finland	France	Germany	Greece	Iceland	Ireland	Italy
Australia	—	*	1.2	3.2	0.6	1.0	3.3	8.6	0.1	*	0.5	4.3
Austria	*	—	3.0	0.3	0.8	0.8	4.4	54.6	0.3	*	0.3	10.1
Belgium[2]	0.3	0.8	—	1.2	0.6	0.5	16.9	26.9	0.2	*	1.0	5.4
Canada	0.5	0.3	0.5	—	0.2	0.3	1.6	2.6	*	*	0.1	1.6
Denmark	0.3	1.3	3.9	0.6	—	3.3	5.8	28.3	0.3	0.2	0.8	4.9
Finland	0.5	1.5	3.6	0.7	4.3	—	5.3	23.1	0.3	0.1	0.7	6.0
France	0.5	0.9	12.4	0.7	1.0	0.8	—	27.3	0.4	*	1.3	14.8
Germany	0.5	5.6	8.9	0.8	2.4	1.3	13.6	—	0.8	0.1	1.1	12.3
Greece	0.4	1.6	4.3	0.4	1.8	1.1	9.7	25.9	—	0.1	0.6	20.6
Iceland	*	0.9	*	0.9	11.8	2.2	3.3	13.6	*	—	0.5	5.1
Ireland	0.1	0.4	0.2	0.9	1.0	0.8	7.0	12.2	0.1	*	—	4.6
Italy	0.8	3.2	6.0	0.9	1.3	0.7	19.7	30.1	1.4	*	0.9	—
Japan	10.7	0.5	1.4	8.1	1.3	0.5	3.6	8.9	0.1	0.1	0.5	3.7
Netherlands	0.6	1.0	13.7	1.3	1.2	0.9	9.8	28.9	0.2	*	1.5	4.6
New Zealand	34.8	0.4	1.1	2.7	0.5	0.5	1.9	5.3	0.1	*	0.3	2.6
Norway	0.1	1.2	3.2	3.2	9.4	4.0	3.8	16.2	0.2	0.2	1.3	3.4
Portugal	0.2	0.9	4.1	0.8	1.2	0.7	14.7	18.6	0.2	0.7	0.5	11.6
Spain	0.4	1.3	4.5	0.6	1.0	0.8	18.4	21.9	0.2	0.8	0.8	13.4
Sweden	0.2	1.4	8.3	0.6	7.4	7.2	5.0	21.2	0.2	7.2	0.8	4.4
Switzerland	0.8	4.1	4.0	1.1	1.1	0.7	12.6	35.4	0.2	0.7	0.5	11.6
Turkey	0.5	1.7	3.7	1.4	0.5	0.8	8.0	24.7	0.9	0.8	0.1	11.0
United Kingdom	0.8	0.9	5.9	1.9	2.1	1.7	10.4	19.8	0.4	1.7	4.4	7.4
United States	1.4	0.3	1.7	29.8	0.6	0.5	3.9	8.6	0.1	0.5	0.6	4.5

Note:
* Indicates less than 0.05 per cent.
1. Based on total merchandise exports, 1989 excluding services.
2. Including Luxembourg

461

Table A.5.4 (Cont) Percentage of imports from other OECD countries accounted for by each exporting country[1]

Exporter:	Japan	Netherlands	N. Zealand	Norway	Portugal	Spain	Sweden	Switzerland	Turkey	UK	US
Importer:											
Australia	26.7	1.5	5.7	0.4	0.2	0.6	2.3	1.4	0.1	9.6	28.6
Austria	3.9	3.5	*	0.2	0.4	0.8	2.0	5.3	3.8	3.0	2.5
Belgium[2]	3.9	17.3	0.1	0.7	0.4	1.6	2.1	1.3	0.3	8.8	9.5
Canada	6.5	0.7	0.1	0.5	0.1	0.4	0.8	4.5	0.1	3.4	75.1
Denmark	3.3	7.9	0.1	5.5	1.1	1.1	15.0	2.5	0.3	8.7	4.6
Finland	6.9	4.7	*	3.3	1.0	1.0	20.4	2.3	0.2	8.6	5.5
France	3.2	7.1	0.1	1.5	1.2	5.3	1.7	3.1	0.4	9.4	7.1
Germany	7.7	13.5	0.1	1.5	1.0	2.6	3.2	5.2	1.1	8.8	8.2
Greece	4.4	8.1	0.3	0.6	0.4	2.4	1.8	2.2	0.9	7.1	5.3
Iceland	3.3	10.5	*	8.2	0.7	0.7	10.4	1.6	0.1	10.3	16.1
Ireland	2.9	0.3	0.1	0.4	0.4	1.4	0.4	0.7	0.1	49.3	16.7
Italy	2.6	6.6	0.1	0.6	0.5	4.1	2.2	4.1	0.1	7.2	6.8
Japan	—	1.2	1.7	0.5	0.2	0.7	1.1	2.4	0.3	4.0	48.7
Netherlands	5.1	—	0.1	1.8	0.7	2.0	2.6	1.4	0.4	10.7	11.4
New Zealand	24.8	1.8	—	0.2	0.2	0.4	1.5	1.3	0.1	1.0	18.4
Norway	3.5	5.1	*	—	1.3	1.2	24.7	1.6	0.2	10.1	6.0
Portugal	3.1	4.8	0.1	0.9	—	17.4	1.9	2.4	0.2	9.4	5.8
Spain	4.1	4.9	0.1	0.5	3.0	—	2.5	2.0	0.2	9.7	8.8
Sweden	4.7	4.6	*	7.3	1.1	0.9	—	1.9	0.2	8.3	6.8
Switzerland	4.6	3.3	*	0.4	0.4	1.2	2.0	—	0.3	6.4	8.6
Turkey	3.8	4.2	0.2	0.5	0.2	2.9	1.8	4.9	—	7.3	20.3
United Kingdom	6.7	7.5	0.4	4.5	1.0	2.8	3.6	2.6	0.4	—	13.1
United States	32.6	2.1	0.4	0.6	0.3	1.1	1.7	1.6	0.3	6.9	—

Note:
*   Indicates less than 0.05 per cent.
1.   Based on total merchandise exports, 1989 excluding services.
2.   Including Luxembourg

Table A.5.5   Percentage of exports from other OECD countries accounted for by each importing country[1]

Importer: Exporter:	Australia	Austria	Belgium	Canada	Denmark	Finland	France	Germany	Greece	Iceland	Ireland	Italy
Australia	—	0.1	1.4	2.2	0.3	0.4	3.4	4.3	0.2	*	*	3.7
Austria	*	—	2.8	1.2	1.1	1.0	5.7	43.9	0.8	*	0.2	12.9
Belgium[2]	0.4	1.2	—	0.5	1.0	0.7	23.0	20.8	0.6	*	*	7.2
Canada	0.9	0.1	1.0	—	0.1	0.1	1.0	1.6	*	*	0.1	0.9
Denmark	0.8	1.1	2.3	0.8	—	3.1	6.9	20.6	1.0	0.5	0.6	5.5
Finland	1.6	1.5	2.6	1.8	4.3	—	7.3	14.9	0.8	0.1	0.7	3.9
France	0.7	1.1	11.1	1.2	1.0	0.7	—	20.5	0.9	*	0.8	15.2
Germany	0.9	6.6	8.6	1.0	2.3	1.4	15.8	—	1.2	0.1	0.6	11.2
Greece	0.6	1.7	2.6	0.8	1.1	0.8	10.9	26.7	—	*	0.2	25.2
Iceland	*	*	0.1	*	0.5	0.2	0.9	1.7	0.2	—	*	0.5
Ireland	0.7	0.6	4.9	0.7	1.0	0.6	10.9	12.1	0.4	*	—	4.8
Italy	1.1	2.9	4.1	1.4	0.9	0.9	20.3	21.5	2.3	*	0.6	—
Japan	4.7	0.8	2.1	4.1	0.5	0.7	3.2	9.6	0.3	*	0.3	1.7
Netherlands	0.5	1.3	16.3	0.7	1.9	0.9	12.1	29.1	1.1	0.1	*	7.3
New Zealand	27.7	*	1.7	2.5	0.2	*	1.9	3.1	0.6	*	0.3	2.6
Norway	0.5	0.3	2.7	2.2	5.1	2.3	9.8	12.1	0.3	0.4	0.2	2.6
Portugal	0.4	1.2	3.4	1.1	2.2	1.5	16.6	17.4	0.5	0.1	0.5	4.7
Spain	0.5	0.7	4.0	1.0	0.7	0.5	23.9	14.8	0.9	*	0.6	11.8
Sweden	1.5	1.6	4.3	1.9	7.6	8.0	6.1	15.1	0.5	0.3	0.1	5.1
Switzerland	0.9	4.0	2.6	10.4	1.3	0.9	11.2	23.7	0.7	*	0.2	9.7
Turkey	0.5	17.4	3.5	0.9	1.0	0.4	7.9	29.1	1.7	*	0.3	1.8
United Kingdom	2.3	0.9	6.7	3.0	1.7	1.3	12.9	15.4	0.8	0.1	6.2	6.3
United States	3.6	0.4	3.7	33.7	0.5	0.4	5.0	7.3	0.3	0.1	1.1	3.1

Note:
*   Indicates less than 0.05 per cent.
1.   Based on total merchandise exports, 1989 excluding services.
2.   Including Luxembourg

463

Table A.5.5 (cont)   Percentage of exports from other OECD countries accounted for by each importing country[1]

Importer: Exporter:	Japan	Netherlands	N.Zealand	Norway	Portugal	Spain	Sweden	Switzerland	Turkey	UK	US
Australia	44.6	2.9	8.6	0.1	0.2	0.9	0.5	2.0	0.2	6.0	18.0
Austria	1.8	3.6	0.1	0.8	0.5	2.7	2.4	8.9	0.6	5.5	3.4
Belgium[2]	1.5	15.5	0.1	0.6	0.7	2.7	4.3	2.6	0.4	10.6	5.4
Canada	7.0	1.3	0.1	0.5	0.1	0.3	0.3	0.6	0.1	2.8	80.9
Denmark	5.0	4.8	0.1	6.6	0.8	2.2	14.0	2.5	0.2	13.9	6.6
Finland	2.7	5.2	0.1	3.8	0.7	2.4	18.8	2.2	0.4	15.7	8.4
France	2.4	7.1	0.1	0.5	1.7	7.3	1.7	5.3	0.6	12.0	8.2
Germany	2.9	10.2	0.1	1.0	1.0	4.2	3.4	7.1	0.8	11.1	8.7
Greece	1.5	4.0	0.1	0.6	0.4	1.7	1.9	1.6	1.4	9.2	7.1
Iceland	1.1	0.3	*	0.3	1.3	4.7	36.4	4.3	0.8	30.4	16.3
Ireland	2.4	7.7	0.1	1.2	0.4	2.3	2.0	1.6	0.1	36.6	8.6
Italy	2.9	3.9	0.1	0.5	1.5	6.1	1.7	5.6	0.9	9.9	10.8
Japan	—	3.1	0.8	0.4	0.3	1.3	1.3	1.6	0.2	6.5	56.5
Netherlands	1.1	—	0.1	0.9	0.8	2.8	2.2	1.9	0.4	12.4	6.2
New Zealand	25.4	1.8	—	0.1	0.2	1.0	0.3	0.3	0.3	10.5	19.3
Norway	1.8	7.3	*	—	0.6	1.0	13.4	1.0	0.2	28.6	7.3
Portugal	1.2	6.3	0.1	1.9	—	14.0	4.3	2.2	0.2	13.6	6.6
Spain	1.7	5.6	0.1	0.6	7.6	—	1.1	1.9	0.8	12.2	9.0
Sweden	2.2	5.8	0.2	9.4	0.7	3.0	—	2.6	0.4	12.9	10.8
Switzerland	4.8	3.1	0.2	0.6	0.8	2.5	2.0	—	1.1	9.3	10.1
Turkey	3.1	5.4	0.1	0.4	0.3	1.8	1.1	2.3	—	8.2	12.9
United Kingdom	3.0	8.9	*	1.4	1.3	4.4	3.2	3.1	0.6	—	16.6
United States	19.2	4.9	0.4	0.4	0.4	2.1	1.4	2.1	0.9	9.0	—

Note:
*   Indicates less than 0.05 per cent.
1.   Based on total merchandise exports, 1989 excluding services.
2.   Including Luxembourg

464

Table A. 5.6 **Inward and outward direct investment**

	Outward direct investment (US$ Billion)			Inward direct investment (US$ Billion)		
	1980	1985	1989	1980	1985	1989
Australia	0.46	4.44	3.91	1.84	2.09	7.38
Austria	0.10	0.05	*	0.24	0.17	*
Belgium¹	0.06	0.23	*	1.45	0.96	*
Canada	2.69	2.86	4.41	0.68	-2.05	2.87
Denmark	0.20	*	*	0.11	*	*
Finland	0.14	0.35	2.91	0.03	0.06	0.32
France	3.14	2.23	13.45	3.33	2.21	9.55
Germany	4.01	4.80	13.45	0.42	0.59	5.93
Greece	0	0	0	0.67	0.45	0.75
Ireland	0	0	0	0.29	0.16	0.09
Italy	0.75	1.82	2.00	0.59	1.00	2.53
Japan	2.38	6.45	44.13	0.28	0.64	-1.05
Netherlands	3.91	3.47	10.08	1.99	0.62	5.84
New Zealand	0.11	0.09	0.86	0.19	0.40	0.86
Norway	0.25	1.23	1.36	0.06	-0.41	1.37
Portugal	0.02	0.02	0.08	0.16	0.25	1.62
Spain	0.31	0.25	*	1.49	1.95	*
Sweden	0.62	1.27	*	0.25	0.27	*
Switzerland	*	4.57	*	*	1.05	*
United Kingdom	11.31	11.29	31.55	10.12	4.86	32.13
United States	19.22	13.16	31.72	16.92	19.02	72.24

1. Including Luxemburg.

Table A.5.7 **Selected economic variables**

Country	Inflation (1)			Exchange rates(2)		
	1980	1985	1991	1980	1985	1990
Australia	10.5	7.1	4.2	0.877	1.432	1.282
Austria	6.4	3.3	3.8	12.94	20.69	11.37
Belgium	6.2	6.0	3.3	29.25	59.43	33.42
Canada	10.0	3.7	5.8	1.169	1.366	1.167
Denmark	10.7	4.3	2.8	5.64	10.59	6.19
Finland	11.6	5.9	5.2	3.720	6.196	3.822
France	13.3	5.8	3.1	4.226	8.984	5.446
Germany	5.8	2.0	3.3	1.817	2.944	1.616
Greece	21.8	18.3	17.8	42.6	138.1	158.2
Iceland	55.4	32.6	6.1	4.80	41.54	58.36
Ireland	18.6	5.0	3.0	0.487	0.946	0.605
Italy	20.5	9.0	6.4	856	1909	1198
Japan	7.5	2.2	2.5	226.7	238.6	144.8
Luxembourg	7.5	4.3	3.4	(3)	(3)	(3)
Netherlands	7.0	2.3	2.7	1.988	3.322	1.821
New Zealand	17.8	16.4	4.0	1.027	2.026	1.678
Norway	10.0	5.9	3.8	4.937	8.594	6.258
Portugal	21.4	19.6	11.7	50.0	169.9	142.3
Spain	16.6	8.2	6.1	71.7	170.1	101.9
Sweden	14.4	7.0	9.5	4.229	8.602	5.918
Switzerland	4.5	3.7	4.8	1.676	2.457	1.389
Turkey	118.2	45.3	64.0	76	520	2606
United Kingdom	16.3	5.4	6.0	0.430	0.779	0.563
United States	10.8	3.3	4.3	1.000	1.000	1.000

1. Private consumption deflator percentage changes from previous year.
2. National currencies against the United States dollar.
3. See Belgium

Table A.5.7 (cont) **Selected economic variables**

Country	Interest rates (3)			Rates of return (4)		
	1980	1985	1991	1980	1985	1991
Australia	11.6	14.1	13.2	11.4	11.3	12.3
Austria	9.3	7.8	8.7	10.4	11.4	11.5
Belgium	12.2	10.6	10.1	11.0	12.1	14.5
Canada	12.5	11.1	10.8	17.1	17.9	16.3
Denmark	19.1	11.6	11.0	8.1	10.4	10.8
Finland	10.4	10.7	13.3	10.4	10.1	8.9
France	13.8	11.9	10.4	10.4	11.1	13.8
Germany	8.5	7.0	8.8	12.2	13.0	14.5
Greece	16.8	18.0	25.2	14.6	9.7	9.7
Iceland	39.9	32.5	n.a.	n.a.	n.a.	n.a.
Ireland	15.4	12.6	10.1	4.7	7.1	11.3
Italy	15.3	13.7	11.9	13.2	13.8	14.2
Japan	8.9	6.5	7.4	13.6	14.2	15.8
Netherlands	10.2	7.3	9.0	12.7	16.8	17.2
New Zealand	13.3	17.9	12.5	8.5	12.3	14.1
Norway	10.3	12.6	10.7	10.3	8.8	7.6
Portugal	20.5	30.1	n.a.	n.a.	n.a.	n.a.
Spain	16.0	13.4	14.6	14.2	13.9	17.7
Sweden	11.7	13.0	13.6	9.3	11.0	8.9
Switzerland	4.8	4.7	6.4	7.4	7.8	8.6
Turkey	36.0	55.0	58.0	n.a.	n.a.	n.a.
United Kingdom	13.9	11.1	11.8	8.4	10.3	8.0
United States	11.9	11.4	9.3	16.0	17.9	20.2

3   Long term, percentage per year.
4   On capital in the business sector.

Table A.5.8 Selected economic variables (billion US dollars)*

Country	Net private savings			Private investment		
	1980	1985	1990	1980	1985	1990
Australia	10.68	6.09	3.61	32.2	34.8	60.1
Austria	8.05	5.48	19.71	16.5	12.5	n.a.
Belgium	15.53	9.07	n.a.	20.6	10.7	n.a.
Canada	33.27	44.00	37.68	54.8	59.5	106.5
Denmark	3.90	3.48	10.65	10.2	9.6	n.a.
Finland	3.92	3.11	5.66	11.6	11.3	32.7
France	60.65	40.24	104.24	132.3	85.2	214.2
Germany	66.99	47.77	195.20	155.6	108.7	284.5
Greece	n.a.	n.a.	n.a.	8.7	4.9	n.a.
Iceland	0.15	-0.04	n.a.	0.5	0.4	n.a.
Ireland	2.16	2.55	4.66	4.5	2.8	n.a.
Italy	80.53	69.72	152.23	95.5	72.4	n.a.
Japan	167.08	181.50	320.60	234.1	279.4	765.6
Luxembourg	n.a.	n.a.	n.a.	n.a.	n.a.	n.a.
Netherlands	16.32	17.73	38.21	30.1	21.0	n.a.
New Zealand	n.a.	n.a.	n.a.	3.1	3.8	n.a.
Norway	3.56	2.44	20.17	12.0	11.3	n.a.
Portugal	6.27	4.19	n.a.	6.1	4.0	n.a.
Spain	21.76	17.13	43.96	43.2	25.2	n.a.
Sweden	8.12	7.18	-9.63	20.4	16.6	n.a.
Switzerland	n.a.	n.a.	n.a.	20.3	19.2	n.a.
Turkey	n.a.	n.a.	n.a.	5.0	4.5	12.7
United Kingdom	43.98	32.79	26.16	68.4	62.1	155.5
United States	174.60	228.00	214.40	n.a.	n.a.	n.a.

* Except for real GDP per capita.

468

Table A.5.8 (cont)   Selected economic variables   (billion US dollars)*

Country	Total investment			Real GDP per capita (1985 US dollars and prices)		
	1980	1985	1990	1980	1985	1989
Australia	36.5	39.4	67.1	9 304	10 070	10 941
Austria	19.7	14.8	39.1	8 088	8 623	9 532
Belgium	24.9	12.5	n.a.	7 800	8 095	9 050
Canada	61.8	69.0	120.9	12 508	13 795	15 285
Denmark	12.5	10.9	n.a.	9 939	11 350	11 955
Finland	13.2	13.0	37.1	9 799	11 026	12 829
France	152.8	101.4	252.9	9 005	9 482	10 442
Germany	184.8	123.3	319.5	9 535	10 189	11 178
Greece	9.7	6.4	n.a.	3 245	3 366	3 599
Iceland	0.8	0.6	n.a.	11 501	11 905	12 768
Ireland	5.6	3.6	n.a.	4 878	5 285	6 088
Italy	109.9	88.3	n.a.	6 968	7 451	8 400
Japan	335.3	370.5	959.9	9 370	10 981	12 778
Luxembourg	1.2	0.6	n.a.	n.a.	n.a.	n.a.
Netherlands	35.6	24.3	n.a.	8 470	8 688	9 308
New Zealand	4.5	5.5	n.a.	6 175	6 739	6 788
Norway	14.3	12.9	n.a.	12 075	14 009	14 816
Portugal	7.2	4.5	n.a.	2 130	2 144	2 535
Spain	47.0	31.1	n.a.	4 144	4 307	5 099
Sweden	24.6	19.1	46.2	11 062	12 051	13 033
Switzerland	24.2	22.2	62.3	13 562	14 201	15 425
Turkey	11.4	10.7	23.4	934	1 042	1 167
United Kingdom	96.7	78.0	185.0	7 348	8 047	9 259
United States	445.3	631.8	746.1	15 113	16 559	18 280

*   Except for real GDP per capita.

Notes and references

1. This work and the definition set up as described in *Detailed Benchmark Definition of Foreign Direct Investment*, OECD 1983. A summary of the definition is provided in *Recent Trends in International Direct Investment*, OECD 1987.

WHERE TO OBTAIN OECD PUBLICATIONS – OÙ OBTENIR LES PUBLICATIONS DE L'OCDE

Argentina – Argentine
CARLOS HIRSCH S.R.L.
Galería Güemes, Florida 165, 4° Piso
1333 Buenos Aires   Tel. 30.7122, 331.1787 y 331.2391
Telegram: Hirsch-Baires
Telex: 21112 UAPE-AR. Ref. s/2901
Telefax:(1)331-1787

Australia – Australie
D.A. Book (Aust.) Pty. Ltd.
648 Whitehorse Road, P.O.B 163
Mitcham, Victoria 3132   Tel. (03)873.4411
Telefax: (03)873.5679

Austria – Autriche
OECD Publications and Information Centre
Schedestrasse 7
D-W 5300 Bonn 1 (Germany)   Tel. (49.228)21.60.45
Telefax: (49.228)26.11.04
Gerold & Co.
Graben 31
Wien I   Tel. (0222)533.50.14

Belgium – Belgique
Jean De Lannoy
Avenue du Roi 202
B-1060 Bruxelles   Tel. (02)538.51.69/538.08.41
Telex: 63220   Telefax: (02) 538.08.41

Canada
Renouf Publishing Company Ltd.
1294 Algoma Road
Ottawa, ON K1B 3W8   Tel. (613)741.4333
Telex: 053-4783   Telefax: (613)741.5439
Stores:
61 Sparks Street
Ottawa, ON K1P 5R1   Tel. (613)238.8985
211 Yonge Street
Toronto, ON M5B 1M4   Tel. (416)363.3171
Federal Publications
165 University Avenue
Toronto, ON M5H 3B8   Tel. (416)581.1552
Telefax: (416)581.1743
Les Publications Fédérales
1185 rue de l'Université
Montréal, PQ H3B 3A7   Tel.(514)954-1633
Les Éditions La Liberté Inc.
3020 Chemin Sainte-Foy
Sainte-Foy, PQ G1X 3V6   Tel. (418)658.3763
Telefax: (418)658.3763

Denmark – Danemark
Munksgaard Export and Subscription Service
35, Nørre Søgade, P.O. Box 2148
DK-1016 København K   Tel. (45 33)12.85.70
Telex: 19431 MUNKS DK   Telefax: (45 33)12.93.87

Finland – Finlande
Akateeminen Kirjakauppa
Keskuskatu 1, P.O. Box 128
00100 Helsinki   Tel. (358 0)12141
Telex: 125080   Telefax: (358 0)121.4441

France
OECD/OCDE
Mail Orders/Commandes par correspondance:
2, rue André-Pascal
75775 Paris Cédex 16   Tel. (33-1)45.24.82.00
Bookshop/Librairie:
33, rue Octave-Feuillet
75016 Paris   Tel. (33-1)45.24.81.67
    (33-1)45.24.81.81
Telex: 620 160 OCDE
Telefax: (33-1)45.24.85.00 (33-1)45.24.81.76
Librairie de l'Université
12a, rue Nazareth
13100 Aix-en-Provence   Tel. 42.26.18.08
Telefax : 42.26.63.26

Germany – Allemagne
OECD Publications and Information Centre
Schedestrasse 7
D-W 5300 Bonn 1   Tel. (0228)21.60.45
Telefax: (0228)26.11.04

Greece – Grèce
Librairie Kauffmann
28 rue du Stade
105 64 Athens   Tel. 322.21.60
Telex: 218187 LIKA Gr

Hong Kong
Swindon Book Co. Ltd.
13 - 15 Lock Road
Kowloon, Hong Kong   Tel. 366.80.31
Telex: 50 441 SWIN HX   Telefax: 739.49.75

Iceland – Islande
Mál Mog Menning
Laugavegi 18, Pósthólf 392
121 Reykjavik   Tel. 15199/24240

India – Inde
Oxford Book and Stationery Co.
Scindia House
New Delhi 110001   Tel. 331.5896/5308
Telex: 31 61990 AM IN
Telefax: (11)332.5993
17 Park Street
Calcutta 700016   Tel. 240832

Indonesia – Indonésie
Pdii-Lipi
P.O. Box 269/JKSMG/88
Jakarta 12790   Tel. 583467
Telex: 62 875

Ireland – Irlande
TDC Publishers – Library Suppliers
12 North Frederick Street
Dublin 1   Tel. 744835/749677
Telex: 33530 TDCP EI   Telefax: 748416

Italy – Italie
Libreria Commissionaria Sansoni
Via Benedetto Fortini, 120/10
Casella Post. 552
50125 Firenze   Tel. (055)64.54.15
Telex: 570466   Telefax: (055)64.12.57
Via Bartolini 29
20155 Milano   Tel. 36.50.83
La diffusione delle pubblicazioni OCSE viene assicurata
dalle principali librerie ed anche da:
Editrice e Libreria Herder
Piazza Montecitorio 120
00186 Roma   Tel. 679.46.28
Telex: NATEL I 621427
Libreria Hoepli
Via Hoepli 5
20121 Milano   Tel. 86.54.46
Telex: 31.33.95   Telefax: (02)805.28.86
Libreria Scientifica
Dott. Lucio de Biasio 'Aeiou'
Via Meravigli 16
20123 Milano   Tel. 805.68.98
Telefax: 800175

Japan – Japon
OECD Publications and Information Centre
Landic Akasaka Building
2-3-4 Akasaka, Minato-ku
Tokyo 107   Tel. (81.3)3586.2016
Telefax: (81.3)3584.7929

Korea – Corée
Kyobo Book Centre Co. Ltd.
P.O. Box 1658, Kwang Hwa Moon
Seoul   Tel. (REP)730.78.91
Telefax: 735.0030

Malaysia/Singapore – Malaisie/Singapour
Co-operative Bookshop Ltd.
University of Malaya
P.O. Box 1127, Jalan Pantai Baru
59700 Kuala Lumpur
Malaysia   Tel. 756.5000/756.5425
Telefax: 757.3661
Information Publications Pte. Ltd.
Pei-Fu Industrial Building
24 New Industrial Road No. 02-06
Singapore 1953   Tel. 283.1786/283.1798
Telefax: 284.8875

Netherlands – Pays-Bas
SDU Uitgeverij
Christoffel Plantijnstraat 2
Postbus 20014
2500 EA's-Gravenhage   Tel. (070 3)78.99.11
Voor bestellingen: Tel. (070 3)78.98.80
Telex: 32486 stdru   Telefax: (070 3)47.63.51

New Zealand – Nouvelle-Zélande
GP Publications Ltd.
Customer Services
33 The Esplanade - P.O. Box 38-900
Petone, Wellington
Tel. (04)685-555   Telefax: (04)685-333

Norway – Norvège
Narvesen Info Center - NIC
Bertrand Narvesens vei 2
P.O. Box 6125 Etterstad
0602 Oslo 6   Tel. (02)57.33.00
Telex: 79668 NIC N   Telefax: (02)68.19.01

Pakistan
Mirza Book Agency
65 Shahrah Quaid-E-Azam
Lahore 3   Tel. 66839
Telex: 44886 UBL PK. Attn: MIRZA BK

Portugal
Livraria Portugal
Rua do Carmo 70-74, Apart. 2681
1117 Lisboa Codex   Tel.: 347.49.82/3/4/5
Telefax: (01) 347.02.64

Singapore/Malaysia – Singapour/Malaisie
See Malaysia/Singapore" – Voir «Malaisie/Singapour»

Spain – Espagne
Mundi-Prensa Libros S.A.
Castelló 37, Apartado 1223
Madrid 28001   Tel. (91) 431.33.99
Telex: 49370 MPLI   Telefax: 575.39.98
Libreria Internacional AEDOS
Consejo de Ciento 391
08009 - Barcelona   Tel. (93) 301-86-15
    Telefax: (93) 317-01-41
Llibreria de la Generalitat
Palau Moja, Rambla dels Estudis, 118
08002 - Barcelona   Telefax: (93) 412.18.54
Tel. (93) 318.80.12 (Subscripcions)
(93) 302.67.23 (Publicacions)

Sri Lanka
Centre for Policy Research
c/o Mercantile Credit Ltd.
55, Janadhipathi Mawatha
Colombo 1   Tel. 438471-9, 440346
Telex: 21138 VAVALEX CE   Telefax: 94.1.448900

Sweden – Suède
Fritzes Fackboksföretaget
Box 16356, Regeringsgatan 12
103 27 Stockholm   Tel. (08)23.89.00
Telex: 12387   Telefax: (08)20.50.21
Subscription Agency/Abonnements:
Wennergren-Williams AB
Nordenflychtsvägen 74, Box 30004
104 25 Stockholm   Tel. (08)13.67.00
Telex: 19937   Telefax: (08)618.62.32

Switzerland – Suisse
OECD Publications and Information Centre
Schedestrasse 7
D-W 5300 Bonn 1 (Germany)   Tel. (49.228)21.60.45
Telefax: (49.228)26.11.04
Librairie Payot
6 rue Grenus
1211 Genève 11   Tel. (022)731.89.50
Telex: 28356
Subscription Agency – Service des Abonnements
Naville S.A.
7, rue Lévrier
1201 Genève   Tél.: (022) 732.24.00
Telefax: (022) 738.48.03
Maditec S.A.
Chemin des Palettes 4
1020 Renens/Lausanne   Tel. (021)635.08.65
Telefax: (021)635.07.80
United Nations Bookshop/Librairie des Nations-Unies
Palais des Nations
1211 Genève 10   Tel. (022)734.14.73
Telex: 412962   Telefax: (022)740.09.31

Taiwan – Formose
Good Faith Worldwide Int'l. Co. Ltd.
9th Floor, No. 118, Sec. 2
Chung Hsiao E. Road
Taipei   Tel. 391.7396/391.7397
Telefax: (02) 394.9176

Thailand – Thaïlande
Suksit Siam Co. Ltd.
1715 Rama IV Road, Samyan
Bangkok 5   Tel. 251.1630

Turkey – Turquie
Kültur Yayinlari Is-Türk Ltd. Sti.
Atatürk Bulvari No. 191/Kat. 21
Kavaklidere/Ankara   Tel. 25.07.60
Dolmabahce Cad. No. 29
Besiktas/Istanbul   Tel. 160.71.88
Telex: 43482B

United Kingdom – Royaume-Uni
HMSO
Gen. enquiries   Tel. (071) 873 0011
Postal orders only:
P.O. Box 276, London SW8 5DT
Personal Callers HMSO Bookshop
49 High Holborn, London WC1V 6HB
Telex: 297138   Telefax: 071 873 2000
Branches at: Belfast, Birmingham, Bristol, Edinburgh,
Manchester

United States – États-Unis
OECD Publications and Information Centre
2001 L Street N.W., Suite 700
Washington, D.C. 20036-4910   Tel. (202)785.6323
Telefax: (202)785.0350

Venezuela
Libreria del Este
Avda F. Miranda 52, Aptdo. 60337, Edificio Galipán
Caracas 106   Tel. 951.1705/951.2307/951.1297
Telegram: Libreste Caracas

Yugoslavia – Yougoslavie
Jugoslovenska Knjiga
Knez Mihajlova 2, P.O. Box 36
Beograd   Tel.: (011)621.992
Telex: 12466 jk bgd   Telefax: (011)625.970

Orders and inquiries from countries where Distributors
have not yet been appointed should be sent to: OECD
Publications Service, 2 rue André-Pascal, 75775 Paris
Cedex 16, France.
Les commandes provenant de pays où l'OCDE n'a pas
encore désigné de distributeur devraient être adressées à :
OCDE, Service des Publications, 2, rue André-Pascal,
75775 Paris Cédex 16, France.

OECD PUBLICATIONS, 2 rue André-Pascal, 75775 PARIS CEDEX 16
PRINTED IN FRANCE
(23 91 02 1) ISBN 92-64-13596-0 - No. 45699 1991